WWW Plug-Ins Companion

WWW Plug-Ins Companion

Written by Mark R. Brown with

Simeon M. Greene • Galen Grimes • John Jung
Bernie Roehl • David Wall • Joe Weber

WWW Plug-Ins Companion

Copyright© 1996 by Que® Corporation.

All rights reserved. Printed in the United States of America. No part of this book may be used or reproduced in any form or by any means, or stored in a database or retrieval system, without prior written permission of the publisher except in the case of brief quotations embodied in critical articles and reviews. Making copies of any part of this book for any purpose other than your own personal use is a violation of United States copyright laws. For information, address Que Corporation, 201 W. 103rd Street, Indianapolis, IN, 46290. You may reach Que's direct sales line by calling 1-800-428-5331.

Library of Congress Catalog No.: 96-69599

ISBN: 0-7897-0845-0

This book is sold *as is*, without warranty of any kind, either express or implied, respecting the contents of this book, including but not limited to implied warranties for the book's quality, performance, merchantability, or fitness for any particular purpose. Neither Que Corporation nor its dealers or distributors shall be liable to the purchaser or any other person or entity with respect to any liability, loss, or damage caused or alleged to have been caused directly or indirectly by this book.

99 98 97 96   4 3 2 1

Interpretation of the printing code: the rightmost double-digit number is the year of the book's printing; the rightmost single-digit number, the number of the book's printing. For example, a printing code of 96-1 shows that the first printing of the book occurred in 1996.

Credits

PRESIDENT
Roland Elgey

PUBLISHER
Joseph B. Wikert

EDITORIAL SERVICES DIRECTOR
Elizabeth Keaffaber

MANAGING EDITOR
Sandy Doell

DIRECTOR OF MARKETING
Lynn E. Zingraf

PUBLISHING MANAGER
Jim Minatel

ACQUISITIONS MANAGER
Cheryl Willoughby

ACQUISITIONS EDITORS
Stephanie Gould
Philip Wescott

PRODUCT DIRECTOR
Mark Cierzniak

PRODUCTION EDITOR
Andy Saff

COPY EDITOR
Faithe Wempen

PRODUCT MARKETING MANAGER
Kim Margolious

ASSISTANT PRODUCT MARKETING MANAGER
Christy Miller

TECHNICAL EDITOR
Simeon M. Greene

TECHNICAL SPECIALIST
Nadeem Muhammed

BOOK DESIGNER
Ruth Harvey

COVER DESIGNER
Barb Kordesh

GRAPHIC IMAGE SPECIALISTS
Steve Adams
Debi Bolhuis
Kevin Cliburn
Tammy Graham
Dan Harris

PRODUCTION TEAM
Marcia Brizendine
Jennifer Earhart
Bryan Flores
DiMonique Ford
Jessica Ford

INDEXER
Chris Wilcox

ACQUISITIONS COORDINATOR
Carmen Krikorian

OPERATIONS COORDINATOR
Patricia J. Brooks

Composed in *Century Old Style* and *Franklin Gothic* by Que Corporation.

My "newspaper" is electronic and my "railroad" is a computer network, but I dedicate this book to the memory of my grandfathers: Conrad Rod the newspaper publisher, and Virgil Brown the railroad man. I wouldn't be who I am if you hadn't been who you were.

About the Authors

Mark R. Brown has been writing computer books, magazine articles, and software manuals for over 13 years. He was managing editor of *.info* magazine when it was named one of the best computer magazines of 1991 by the Computer Press Association, and was nominated by the Software Publisher's Association for the Software Reviewer of the Year award in 1988. Now a full-time freelance writer who has contributed to over a half a dozen Que books, Mark is the author of Que's *Special Edition Using Netscape 2* and *Special Edition Using HTML* (with John Jung). He is Webmaster of a Web site devoted to the topic of airships at **http://www2.giant.net/people/mbrown**. You can reach Mark by e-mail at **mbrown@avalon.net**.

Simeon M. Greene is the Internet Project Coordinator for Data-Core Systems (**http://www.dclgroup.com**) in Philadelphia. He contributed to Que's *Special Edition Using Java*. You can reach Simeon at **smgree@dclgroup.com** or **http://www.well.com/~smgree**.

Galen Grimes and his wife Joanne live in a quiet, heavily wooded section of Monroeville, Pennsylvania, a suburb of Pittsburgh, with an assortment of deer, raccoons, squirrels, possums, and birds, which are all fed from the Grimes' backdoor. Galen is also the author of several other Macmillan Computer Publishing books, including Sams' *First Book of DR DOS 6*, Alpha's *10 Minute Guide to NetWare, 10 Minute Guide to Lotus Improv*, and *Windows 3.1 HyperGuide,* and Que's *10 Minute Guide to Netscape for Windows 95* and *10 Minute Guide to the Internet With Windows 95*. Galen has a masters degree in information science from the University of Pittsburgh. By trade, he is a project manager and NetWare local area network (LAN) administrator for a large international bank and financial institution headquartered in Pittsburgh.

John Jung has been a contributing author for almost half a dozen books. When not working on books, he has a day job that he thoroughly enjoys. As a professional systems administrator for a worldwide information services company, he's around computers all day. He takes a break from writing and working by watching TV, surfing the Internet, and generally goofing off. You can reach John at his e-mail address, **jjung@netcom.com**.

Bernie Roehl is a software developer based at the University of Waterloo in Ontario, Canada. He is probably best known in virtual reality (VR) circles for REND386 and AVRIL, free software packages that are still in widespread use by hobbyists. REND386 recently won the 1995 Meckler award for outstanding software achievement. He is also the author of two books on VR, *Virtual Reality Creations* and *Playing God: Creating Virtual Worlds*. He is currently the product reviewer for *VR Special Report* and a regular columnist for *VR News*. In addition, Bernie has contributed articles to *Real Time Graphics* and *CyberEdge Journal*. He is also very active on the **www-vrml** e-mail list. When not writing, speaking, or developing software, Bernie is involved with an improvisational comedy troupe. He also performs regularly with a theater group that performs murder mysteries at dinner theaters.

David Wall works as a freelance writer in Charlottesville, Virginia, where he writes mainly about Internet and World Wide Web issues. He's written for the *Wall Street Journal*, the Washington *Post*, the Bloomberg Business News global information service, and several book publishers. David now focuses his attention on the personalities of the people behind the Web's great publishing ventures. David also spends time bicycling and playing with hypertextual literary analysis.

Joe Weber is the vice president of research and development for MagnaStar, Inc., the world's oldest Java consulting and development company. Joe has taught and mentored dozens of the world's best Java programmers. In addition, he has served on many Java advisory and expert panels. Joe's work has been published in several Java magazines, and he has written for three previous Que books. An Eagle Scout, Joe has 15 years of programming experience and is a founding member of TeamJava, a judge for the Java Application Review System, the moderator for the national Java-SIG, and the cofounder of *Javology* magazine.

Acknowledgments

First of all, a big "Whew! What a workout!" to the hundreds of plug-in developers out there who are churning out new plug-ins so fast that they made this book almost impossible to write! Keep up the good work, and a second edition will be a shoo-in.

Writing is generally a pretty thankless game (except for the occasional paycheck), but an extra special pat on the back goes to the writers associated with this project. They put forth a tremendous effort to keep up with the incredible pace of current plug-ins development, and the fact that they were able to persevere and produce a coherent, up-to-date volume is not much short of a miracle.

The editors and staff at Que certainly earned their kudos as well; special thanks go to Cheryl Willoughby, Stephanie Gould, Philip Wescott, and Mark Cierzniak for their invaluable assistance and infallible guidance. For battlefield heroism and keeping cool under fire, medals and honors go (in alphabetical order) to Jane Brownlow, Simeon M. Greene, Mike LaBonne, Caroline Roop, Andy Saff, "Scotty" J. Walter, and Faithe Wempen. Thanks, guys.

Of course, we wouldn't have a book at all if it weren't for the excellent product produced by the programmers, planners, and management of Netscape Corporation. Thanks for a great Web browser!

Then there "are all those wonderful people out there in the dark" who make up the World Wide Web. Certainly, to the people at CERN in Switzerland who first conceived and implemented the Web, our thanks. But the Web is made up of the efforts of literally millions of people, many of whom selflessly contribute, gratis, the thoughts, ideas, articles, stories, graphics, movies, sound clips, and all of the other elements that make up the multinational, multilingual, multimedia stew that is the World Wide Web. To all of them, our thanks for making Web surfing such an entertaining, enlightening, and engaging activity!

Writing's tough, but being a writer's spouse means spending lots of lonely nights near deadline. That's why this last line is always reserved for saying, "Thanks, Carol."

—Mark R. Brown

Trademark Acknowledgments

All terms mentioned in this book that are known to be trademarks or service marks have been appropriately capitalized. Que cannot attest to the accuracy of this information. Use of a term in this book should not be regarded as affecting the validity of any trademark or service mark.

We'd Like to Hear from You!

As part of our continuing effort to produce books of the highest possible quality, Que would like to hear your comments. To stay competitive, we *really* want you, as a computer book reader and user, to let us know what you like or dislike most about this book or other Que products.

You can mail comments, ideas, or suggestions for improving future editions to the address below, or send us a fax at (317) 581-4663. For the online inclined, Macmillan Computer Publishing now has a forum on CompuServe (type **GO QUEBOOKS** at any prompt) through which our staff and authors are available for questions and comments. The address of our Internet site is **http//:www.mcp.com** (World Wide Web).

In addition to exploring our forum, please feel free to contact me personally to discuss your opinions of this book: You can find me on the Internet at **mcierzniak@que.mcp.com**.

Thanks in advance—your comments will help us to continue publishing the best books available on computer topics in today's market.

Mark Cierzniak
Product Director
Que Corporation
201 W. 103rd Street
Indianapolis, Indiana 46290
USA

Contents at a Glance

I | Plug-Ins Explained

1. How Plug-Ins Work
2. Browser Plug-Ins
3. Creating Plug-In Content for the World Wide Web
4. Creating Plug-In Content for Intranets

II | Plug-Ins for Multimedia

5. RealAudio
6. LiveAudio and Other Audio Plug-Ins
7. Plug-Ins for Graphics Display and Compression
8. CorelDRAW!, AutoCAD, and Other Graphics Plug-Ins
9. Video and Animation Plug-Ins
10. Shockwave for Macromedia Director
11. ASAP WebShow and Other Multimedia Plug-Ins

III | Plug-Ins for VRML

12. Creating VRML Worlds
13. Moving Worlds and Live3D
14. VRML Plug-Ins

IV | Plug-Ins for Business Applications

15. Microsoft Office Online
16. Portable Documents
17. Communications Tools
18. Information and Navigational Tools
19. Programming Tools

V | Advanced Plug-Ins Development

20. Java Applets and JavaScript
21. Creating Your Own Plug-Ins

Appendix

A. What's on the CD-ROM

Index

Table of Contents

Introduction   1
    Who Should Use This Book?   3
    How Is This Book Organized?   3
    The Book's Companion CD-ROM   4
    Conventions Used in This Book   4

I | Plug-Ins Explained

1   How Plug-Ins Work   9
    Plug-Ins versus Helper Applications   10
    A Brief Course in MIME Types   13
    How Plug-Ins "Plug In"   15
    The Three Kinds of Plug-Ins   19
    What Plug-Ins Can (and Can't) Do   21
    The Future of Plug-Ins   22

2   Browser Plug-Ins   27
    Downloading, Installing, and Using Plug-Ins with Netscape   28
        Determining Which Plug-Ins You Have Installed   29
        Running a Plug-In   31
    Installing Plug-Ins for Internet Explorer   31
    Multimedia Plug-Ins   35
        Sound   35
        Graphics   40
        Video   48
        Animation   51
        Multimedia   52
    VRML Plug-Ins   57
        Live3D   57
        VR Scout   58
        WIRL   58
        Other VRML Browser Plug-Ins   58

Productivity Plug-Ins   60
    Acrobat Amber Reader   60
    Envoy   61
    Formula One/NET   62
    Word Viewer   63
    KEYview   63
    Other Document Viewers   63
    Navigational Aids   64
    Remote PC Access   65
    Miscellaneous Tools   66
    Groupware Applications   69
    ActiveX   69
    OpenScape   71
    QuickServer   71
    WinFrame   72
    WebBASIC   72

3 Creating Plug-In Content for the World Wide Web   73

Creating Web Page Content   74

Page Design versus Content   74

The *<IMG>* Tag   76

The *<EMBED>* Tag   76
    Embedding ActiveX Objects   77
    Embedding Inline Content   78

Linking Content   79

The *<OBJECT>* Tag   80

Server Issues   81
    Setting MIME Types   81
    Installing Content Servers   83

Limitations on Plug-In Content   84
    File Size and Dial-Up Connections   85
    Browser Compatibility   86
    Good Content versus Good Looks   89
    What Are the Best Uses for Plug-Ins?   90
    Plug-In Content-Creation Programs   91
    Keep Your Files Small   92

4 Creating Plug-In Content for Intranets 93

What Is an Intranet? 94

Who Needs an Intranet? 95
    The Case of Updating the Employee Handbook 95
    The Case of the Sales Training Program 97

Intranet Content versus Internet Content 98
    Internet Content 98
    Intranet Content 99

Plug-Ins and Intranets 100
    File Standardization 100
    Bandwidth and Multimedia 101
    Application Files—Word Processing, Presentations, and Spreadsheets 103
    Custom Applications 104

II Plug-Ins for Multimedia

5 RealAudio 109

Audio Hardware—What You Need 110

How RealAudio Works 110

The RealAudio Player 113
    Installation and Setup 115
    Controls and Menus 116

The RealAudio Encoder 118
    Installing the RealAudio Encoder 119
    Encoding 119

Using RealAudio Content on Your Web Pages 122

The RealAudio Servers 126
    The RealAudio Personal Server 126
    Setting MIME Types 128
    The RealAudio Server 2.0 128
    Synchronized Multimedia 130

6 LiveAudio and Other Audio Plug-Ins 133

Sound File Formats 134

Digitized Audio for the Web 134

Digitizing Your Own Sounds   135
    Sound Gadget Pro   137
        Waveform Hold and Modify   137
The LiveAudio Plug-In   138
ToolVox   142
Other Audio Plug-Ins for Digitized Audio   145
MIDI Music: Crescendo and Crescendo Plus   146
Other Music Plug-Ins   147
Talker and Other Macintosh Speech Plug-Ins   148

7 Plug-Ins for Graphics Display and Compression   151

Hardware Requirements for Netscape Graphics   152
How Computer Graphics Work   152
How Netscape Displays Graphics   154
Graphics File Formats   155
Creating Bitmap Images   158
    Borrowing Bitmaps   158
    Paint Programs   159
    Scanning Images   163
    Digitizing Video Images   163
Bitmap Graphics Display Plug-Ins   166
    FIGleaf Inline   166
    ViewDirector   170
Plug-Ins for Graphics Compression   171
    Lightning Strike   172
    Other Compression Plug-Ins   174

8 CorelDRAW!, AutoCAD, and Other Graphics Plug-Ins   175

Why Use Proprietary Graphics Formats?   176
AutoCAD Files   177
    Autodesk's WHIP!   177
    DWG/DXF Viewer   180
Vector Graphics   181
    Corel CMX   182
    Shockwave for Freehand   183
    SoftSource's SVF Plug-In   187

FutureSplash and Other Animated Graphics Plug-Ins 188
Miscellaneous Proprietary Graphics Formats 193
    Chemscape Chime 193
    ART Press 197
    QuickSilver 198
    WebXpresso 199

9 Video and Animation Plug-Ins 201

When To Use Video Content 202
    Speed 202
    Content 203

Creating Video Content 204

Video for Windows Plug-Ins 206
    LiveVideo 207
    VDOLive 208
    CoolFusion 211
    Other .AVI Video Plug-Ins 213

QuickTime Plug-Ins 213
    The Apple QuickTime Plug-In 213
    Other QuickTime Plug-Ins 216

MPEG Plug-Ins 217
    InterVU 217
    Action 219

Animation Plug-Ins 221
    Enliven 221
    Emblaze 222
    Sizzler 224
    Play3d 225

10 Shockwave for Macromedia Director 227

Director versus Java and JavaScript 228

What You Can Do with Shockwave for Director 229
    Animation 230
    Games 231
    Entertainment 233
    Training 233
    Education 234
    Presentations 236
    Applications 238

Creating Director Movies for Shockwave   239
　　Lingo Network Extensions   241
　　Director Limitations on the Internet   242
　　Web Page Design Considerations   242
　　Optimizing Director Movies for the Web   242
More Information   243

11   ASAP WebShow and Other Multimedia Plug-Ins   245

ASAP WebShow   246

Shockwave for Authorware   250

Astound Web Player   253

mBED   256

Neuron   257

Other Multimedia Plug-Ins   258

III   Plug-Ins for VRML

12   Creating VRML Worlds   263

What Is VRML?   264
　　The History of VRML   264
　　The Evolution of VRML   264

How VRML Works   265

The VRML Language   266
　　Basic VRML Syntax   266
　　The *DEF* and *USE* Statements   268
　　Shapes   268
　　Materials and Textures   268
　　Lights   269
　　Cameras   269
　　The *Group* and *Separator* Nodes   270
　　The *LOD* Node   270
　　The *Transform* Node   270
　　The *WWWInline* and *WWWAnchor* Nodes   271

A Sample VRML World   271

Creating VRML Content   274
　　The WCVT2POV Conversion Program   274

        The InterChange Conversion Program   275
        Object Libraries   276
        Home Space Builder   277
        The Virtus VRML Toolkit   278
        Caligari Fountain   278

Building Your Own VRML Worlds   279
        Plan Your Design   279
        Let the Real World Be Your Guide   280
        Keep Your Scenes Simple   280
        Use Textures Wisely   281

13 Moving Worlds and Live3D   283

The Need for Change   284

The Politics of VRML   284

Basic Concepts of VRML 2.0   285
        The New Scene Graph   285
        VRML 2.0 Syntax   287

Leaf Nodes   288
        The *Shape* Node   288
        The Geometry Nodes   289
        The *Appearance* Node   290
        Lights   290
        The *Sound* Node   290
        Viewpoints   291

Grouping Nodes   291
        The *Transform* Node   291
        The *Group* Node   292
        The *Switch* Node   292
        The *Anchor* and *Inline* Nodes   293
        The *LOD* Node   293
        Collision Detection   293

Miscellaneous Nodes   294
        The *Background* and *Fog* Nodes   294
        The *WorldInfo* and *NavigationInfo* Nodes   294

Sensors   295
        The *ProximitySensor* and *VisibilitySensor* Nodes   295
        The *TimeSensor* Node   295
        Geometric Sensor Nodes   295

Interpolators 296
Routes 296
The *Script* Node 297
Prototypes 297
Live3D 299
    Navigation in Live3D 299
    Menus in Live3D 301
    Live3D Extensions 301
Applications 302
    Education 302
    The Arts 302
    Entertainment 303
The Future 303

14 VRML Plug-Ins 305

WebSpace 306
CyberGate 307
VRweb 308
WIRL 309
VR Scout and Pueblo 310
Traveler 311
Liquid Reality 312
CyberPassage 313
V-Realm 314
Virtus Voyager 315
TerraForm 316
Microsoft's VRML Add-In for Internet Explorer 317
Which Browser Should You Choose? 318

IV | Plug-Ins for Business Applications

15 Microsoft Office Online 321

What WordViewer Can Do For You 322

Formula One/NET and Spreadsheets 323
    What Version of Formula One? 323
    Embedding Spreadsheets in Web Pages 324

Presentations with PointPlus 325

Using PowerPoint Files in Your Web Pages 326
    Creating PowerPoint Animation Files 326
    Viewing PowerPoint Animation Files 327

Using Quick View Plus 328
    Activating Quick View Plus 330
    Exploring the Features of Quick View Plus 330
    Configuring Quick View Plus 332

16 Portable Documents 337

Adobe Acrobat 338
    Navigating around Acrobat Reader 338
    Using Acrobat Files 341
    Creating Acrobat Files 342

Envoy 342
    Using the Envoy Plug-In 343
    Envoy and Web Pages 345
    Creating Envoy Documents 347

Techexplorer 347
    What Is TeX? 348
    Using Techexplorer To View TeX Files 348
    Creating TeX Files 349

17 Communications Tools 351

ichat 352
    Why Use ichat? 352
    Installing ichat 353
    Using ichat 354
    Connecting to IRC Servers 360
    Chat-Enabling Web Sites 362

Look@Me 362
    Installing Look@Me 362
    Running Look@Me 364

Exploring Possible Uses for Look@Me   366
Carbon Copy/Net   366
    Why Should You Use Carbon Copy/Net?   367
    Carbon Copy/Net Security Concerns   367
    Installing Carbon Copy/Net   368
    Running Carbon Copy/Net as a Guest   370
    Running Carbon Copy/Net as a Host   372

18 Information and Navigational Tools   375

Keeping Track of Time Zones with EarthTime   376
    Why Use EarthTime?   376
    Getting the Exact Time   378
Viewing the World with Argus MapGuide Viewer   379
    Obtaining Maps   380
    Navigating through Maps   380
Finding Old Web Pages with ISYS HindSite   382
    Getting and Installing HindSite   382
    Finding Old Pages   383
Organizing Web Pages with HotPage   385
    The Look and Feel of HotPage   385
    Navigating around HotPage   387
    What's Not in the Discovery Edition?   387
Managing the Influx of Information with the PointCast Network   387
    PointCast Network Channels   388
    Using the PointCast Network   389
    Configuring the PointCast Network   391
    Updating the PointCast Network   394
    PointCast Advertisements   395
    Downsides to the PointCast Network   395

19 Programming Tools   397

ActiveX Controls in Netscape with the NCompass Plug-In   398
    What Is the NCompass ActiveX Plug-In?   398
    What Are ActiveX Controls?   398
    Creating Custom Controls with Visual C++   399
    What Makes the .OCX File an ActiveX Control?   401
    Using the Microsoft ActiveX Development Kit   402

Embedding Your Control in an HTML File   402
Handling Dependencies with the NCompass Plug-In   403

Wayfarer Communications' QuickServer   404
Using QuickServer on the Internet or an Intranet   404
Supported SDKs   404
The Stock Watcher Application   405

V | Advanced Plug-Ins Development

20 Java Applets and JavaScript   409

Java and JavaScript Defined   410
Java Defined   410
JavaScript Defined   411

Java versus JavaScript   412
JavaScript Is Contained in the HTML File   412
JavaScript Is a Scripting Language   412
JavaScript Is Interpreted   412
Java Is Not as Easy To Steal   413

How Java and JavaScript Can Help You   414
Form Verification   414

Java versus Plug-Ins   417
You Don't Have To Download Programs   417
Many Browsers Support Java   417

The Downside of Java   418

Including a Java Applet in an HTML Page   418
Including Alternative Information for Non-Java Browsers   420
Using the <PARAM> Tag   420

Developing a JavaScript Page   422
Including a Script in Your Web Page   422
Testing the Script   422
Hiding the Script from Other Browsers   423
JavaScript outside of <SCRIPT> Tags   424
Mixing <SCRIPT> Tags and Event Handlers   426
Validating a Form before Submission   428

Beginning To Develop a Java Applet   435
The HelloWorld Applet   435

The Java Animator Applet   437
Interacting between JavaScript, Java, and Plug-Ins   441
Support with Browsers Other Than Netscape Navigator   442
Java and JavaScript Resources   442
    Finding Example Applets and JavaScript Pages   442
    Finding a Java Consultant   443

21 Creating Your Own Plug-Ins   445

Why Create Your Own Plug-Ins?   446
    Because You Have a Special Need   446
    Because You Can Build a Better Mousetrap   447
    Because You Enjoy Programming   447

A Brief Technical Introduction   448
    What Is a Plug-In, Technically Speaking?   448
    What Does a Browser Do with a Plug-In?   449

What You'll Need To Build a Plug-In   450
    Microsoft Foundation Class Programming   450
    C++ Programming Tools   450
    The Plug-In Software Development Kit   451

Exploring the Plug-In Software Development Kit   452
    HTML Documentation   452
    Samples   452
    Templates   454

How To Create Your Own Plug-Ins   454
    Getting Started and Using the AppWizard   454
    Inserting the Netscape Boilerplate   455
    Compiling Your Plug-In   456
    Testing Your Plug-In   456

Creative Advice   457
    Make Sure You're Filling a Need   457
    Test Your Code Extensively   458
    Document Everything   459
    Make Your Source Code Available   459

A What's on the CD-ROM   461
    VRML Plug-Ins   462
    Multimedia/Sound Plug-Ins   462
    Multimedia/Graphics Plug-Ins   463
    Multimedia/Video Plug-Ins   463
    Productivity Plug-Ins   464
    Navigational Aids Plug-Ins   465
    Miscellaneous Plug-Ins   465
    Helpers/Audio   465
    Helpers/Multimedia   466
    Helpers/Video and Image   466
    HTML Editors   466
    Java   467
    Web Servers   467

Index   469

INTRODUCTION

Introduction

The World Wide Web is expanding at an alarming rate. It has interjected itself into every aspect of human endeavor, expanding from its original role in academia and scientific research into the fields of business, commerce, government, international relations, and even entertainment.

Today the Web is truly world-wide in scope. You can find just about anything on the Web—scientific papers, library card catalogs, virtual tours of museums, galleries of art (both static and moving), live radio broadcasts, electronic-mail order catalogs, and even interactive chat rooms.

The original HTML (HyperText Markup Language) and HTTP (HyperText Transfer Protocol) specifications that were developed to deliver all this content have just not kept up with the demands of users and Web site developers for more—more content, more speed, and more capabilities. Although the HTML and HTTP specifications are being expanded and improved, the wheels of change are often mired in bureaucracy and tempered with caution. The Web is quite simply moving faster than the pace of these specifications' improvements. ■

Plug-ins offer one answer to this problem. Netscape—and, to a lesser extent, Microsoft—have developed plug-ins as a way of expanding the Web's capabilities without requiring immediate changes in the standards or endless iterations of ever-larger new browser software releases. Plug-ins put most of the burden on the browser program—not the server or the Internet connection—for properly interpreting new kinds of content, like live audio and video, integral spreadsheets, or custom applications.

Plug-ins are code modules that literally plug in to a browser program, adding capabilities that previously did not exist. Best of all, they plug in temporarily, only while they are needed, and then unplug themselves to free up system resources.

For example, if you install a Netscape plug-in for playing live audio files, Netscape detects the presence of a compatible file on a Web page, loads the plug-in into memory, downloads and plays the audio file, then unloads the plug-in and frees up memory. The plug-in would be loaded and used again only if Netscape later encountered another compatible file on the Web.

Plug-ins enable Web content providers to add an exciting array of new content types to their Web pages without having to wait for the standards to support them. Audio, video, graphics, multimedia, business, and custom applications are all now valid content for HTML pages. Content providers are no longer stuck with pages that contain only text and graphics augmented by a few static tables and forms.

Thanks to plug-ins, the Web is coming alive with animation, interactive applications, audio, and video. Using plug-ins, Web browsers can display live content of unlimited variety, including proprietary formats like Macromedia Director, Adobe Acrobat, and Apple QuickTime.

The term *live content* describes a key attribute of plug-in technology. Where browser helper applications require that a file be downloaded first, displayed in a separate window, and then closed, plug-ins enable content to be delivered live, in place, in real time. For example, a Web page can play a QuickTime movie as the page is downloading from the Internet. No separate window opens, and there is no long wait for the file to download completely before it begins playing. The video integrates seamlessly into the rest of the Web page's content. The effect is that of a consolidated package of information, not a disjunct series of unrelated, mistimed events.

Of course, all is not a bed of roses. This wide variety of content is available only if the following conditions are true:

- The user has installed the proper plug-ins required to view a page's custom content.
- The Web content provider has the tools, skills, and knowledge to create and deliver the required files.

The first problem is relatively easy to solve. The CD-ROM inside this book's back cover contains many of the current plug-ins, and Netscape provides links to all the latest versions at **http://home.netscape.com/comprod/products/navigator/version_2.0/plugins/index.html**. Savvy content providers also provide on their own Web pages links to the download sites for necessary plug-ins.

This book also addresses the second problem. In these pages, you'll find out what kinds of content go with which plug-ins, and how to create and deliver that content on your site.

Who Should Use This Book?

This book is intended for anyone and everyone who wants to learn to install and use plug-ins with Netscape Navigator, or who wants to develop pages for the World Wide Web (or for a corporate intranet) that take advantage of the features provided by the many plug-ins for Netscape Navigator and Microsoft Internet Explorer.

Novices will find overviews of which plug-ins are available and what they are capable of, as well as information on how to obtain, install, and configure Netscape and Internet Explorer plug-ins.

Intermediate users will discover how to create multimedia presentations, VRML three-dimensional worlds, custom spreadsheets, portable documents, and other live Web page content that takes advantage of the capabilities that plug-ins add to Web browsers.

Advanced users will learn tips, tricks, and techniques to squeeze the most out of plug-ins using proprietary content development programs, Object Linking and Embedding (OLE) controls, Java, and JavaScript. You'll even find out how to create your *own* browser plug-in applications!

How Is This Book Organized?

WWW Plug-Ins Companion is organized into five logical sections.

Part I, "Plug-Ins Explained," explains how plug-ins work and how they plug in, and tells you about the three different kinds of plug-ins. This part also provides a brief overview of all the currently available browser plug-ins, and briefly explains what they can do. Part I finishes with two chapters explaining the steps involved in creating plug-in-compatible content for the World Wide Web and for corporate intranets.

Part II, "Plug-Ins for Multimedia," is the heart of this book. This part takes you step-by-step through the processes of downloading, installing, using, and developing content for dozens of different plug-ins that display live audio, graphics, video, and multimedia presentations. Part II focuses on key plug-ins like RealAudio, Shockwave for Macromedia Director, and VDOLive.

Part III, "Plug-Ins for VRML," explains how to create 3-D worlds using the Virtual Reality Markup Language, and how to incorporate special features using the individual capabilities built in to the various VRML plug-ins. This part includes an in-depth look at Netscape's own Live3D plug-in, which adheres to the Moving Worlds standard.

Part IV, "Plug-Ins for Business Applications," explains the Adobe Acrobat and Envoy portable document formats and how to use them on your Web site or corporate intranet. It also takes you step-by-step through the many business applications available as browser plug-ins, from the Formula One/Net spreadsheet to automatic indexers to Word Viewer. The final two chapters in Part IV explain how to develop your own OLE-compliant applications that integrate smoothly into Web browser programs using applications development and integration plug-ins like OLE Control.

Part V, "Advanced Plug-Ins Development," helps you extend the utility of plug-ins by adding Java and JavaScript applications that take advantage of the Java capabilities that are built in to Netscape Navigator and Microsoft Internet Explorer. The final chapter in this part gets you started creating your *own* browser plug-ins for highly customized applications.

An appendix, "What's on the CD," finishes the book with information on what you'll find on the book's companion CD-ROM.

The Book's Companion CD-ROM

Inside the back cover of this book, you'll find a CD-ROM containing multimegabytes of plug-ins, links, tips, and programs that will help you get the most out of browser plug-ins.

Conventions Used in This Book

This book uses various stylistic and typographic conventions to make it easier to use.

Keyboard shortcut key combinations are joined by plus signs; for example, Ctrl+X means to hold down the Ctrl key, press the X key, then release both.

Menu items and dialog box selections often have a mnemonic key associated with them. This key is indicated by an underline on the item on screen. To use these mnemonic keys, you press the Alt key, then the shortcut key. In this book, mnemonic keys are underscored, as in the following example: File.

This book uses the following typeface conventions:

Typeface	Meaning
Italics	Terms used for the first time.
Bold	Text that you type in, as well as addresses of Internet sites, newsgroups, mailing lists, and Web sites.
Bold italics	Variables in addresses.
`Monospace computer type`	Commands and other keywords, as well as various messages displayed onscreen.
`Monospace italics`	Variables in commands.

 NOTE Notes provide additional information related to the topic at hand.

 TIP Tips provide quick and helpful information to assist you along the way.

CAUTION
Cautions alert you to potential pitfalls or dangers in the operations discussed.

TROUBLESHOOTING

Troubleshooting boxes address problems that you might encounter while following the procedures described in this book.

PART I

Plug-Ins Explained

1 How Plug-Ins Work   9

2 Browser Plug-Ins   27

3 Creating Plug-In Content for the World Wide Web   73

4 Creating Plug-In Content for Intranets   93

CHAPTER 1

How Plug-Ins Work

Although Netscape is a pretty versatile Web browser, you'll still encounter many files on the Web that Netscape can't display—video files, audio files, odd graphics files, strange document formats, and even compressed files. To display or play these files inline, you need to install the proper plug-ins or helper applications.

Plug-ins extend and complement Netscape's native capabilities, expanding and enhancing the type of content that can be delivered over the World Wide Web and corporate intranets. Using plug-ins, your Web browser can display animation, multimedia, audio, interactive applications, and video inline, right on the page, without launching external helper application programs.

Unlike a browser's built-in display capabilities, which are limited to generic file formats like GIF and JPEG images, plug-ins offer open-ended expansion that can include just about any content type.

How plug-ins differ from helper applications

In almost every application, you'll find that plug-ins are better.

How plug-ins "plug in" to a browser program

The whole process is completely automatic.

What the three kinds of plug-ins are

Versatility is the key.

How plug-ins extend browser functionality

Without upgrading your browser, you can view almost any file over the Web.

Numerous formatting tips for special situations

What the future holds for plug-ins development

You'll see your browser jumping through multimedia hoops.

http://www.mcp.com/que

Dozens of companies have released plug-ins capable of displaying their own proprietary multimedia, application, animation, and other data format files in Netscape Navigator and Microsoft Internet Explorer. Therefore, Web page developers can include on their Web pages multimedia files, for example, rather than just static images.

Netscape plug-ins now support most widely accepted cross-platform media formats; those that aren't currently supported soon will be. Currently supported formats include Macromedia Director multimedia presentations, Adobe Acrobat portable documents, Video for Windows and QuickTime movies, and RealAudio and ToolVOX audio files. But Netscape plug-ins aren't limited to media support; there are also plug-ins for applications like spreadsheets, word processor files, and even custom Object Linking and Embedding (OLE) application development.

Plug-Ins versus Helper Applications

Early in the history of the Web, it became obvious that Web site developers and Web surfers wanted and needed more variety in Web page content than Web browser programs could provide. Text, graphics, and elementary forms just weren't enough.

Helper applications filled the gap. Almost all Web browser programs enable you to set up external stand-alone programs as helper applications. Once properly installed and configured, a Web browser launches the helper application when it encounters a file of the defined type.

For example, here's how the process works with Netscape 3.0 and a helper application for .TIFF images (which Netscape can't normally display).

You start by finding a program capable of displaying .TIFF images. Suppose that you choose Paint Shop Pro for Windows 95, because it can display not only .TIFFs, but a wide variety of other graphics file formats.

1. First, download and install a copy of Paint Shop Pro normally, so that it works as a stand-alone application. (Paint Shop Pro is available for Windows 3.1 and Windows 95 at **http://www.jasc.com/products.html**.)
2. Launch Netscape and choose Options, General Preferences from the menu. You then see the Preferences dialog box as shown in figure 1.1.
3. Select the Helpers tab to display the Helpers page.
4. Scroll down through the list of file types until you find `image/tiff`. Select this type by clicking it. (If no .TIFF file type were defined, you would click the Create New Type button to create it.)

Plug-Ins versus Helper Applications 11

FIG. 1.1
Netscape's Helpers page enables you to define the Multipurpose Internet Multimedia Extensions (MIME) type and file name extension, and associate a helper application for just about any file type.

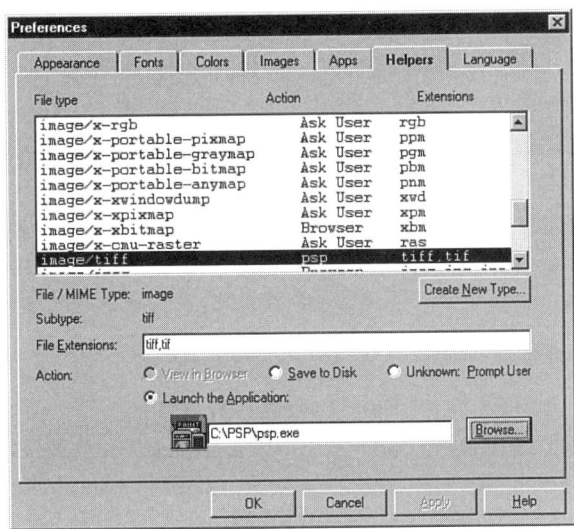

> **N O T E** If you choose to create a new MIME type by selecting the Create New Type button, you get the dialog box shown in figure 1.2. Enter a MIME type in the MimeType field; official MIME types must be one of the following: application, video, audio, image, text, multipart, or message. If you make up your own MIME type, prefix it with x- to indicate that it's nonstandard. Each MIME type has its own list of official subtypes as well. (These subtypes are all specified in the official MIME type definition document, RFC1521.TXT, available from **ftp:// ds.internic.net**.) If your subtype is a new one, use the x- prefix, as shown in figure 1.2, for the unofficial subtype x-blotto.

> **CAUTION**
> After creating a new MIME type in Netscape, there is no way to get rid of it, so make sure that you're sincere before you click OK.

5. Note that the File Extensions text box now says tiff,tif. This tells you that when you finish, any files that Netscape encounters with these file name extensions will use the helper application that you are configuring.

6. Click the Browse button to display a file requester dialog box that you can use to find Paint Shop Pro. After you select the program and return to the Helpers page, the Action button Launch the Application is autoselected and the file name PSP.EXE (with full path name) appears in the file name field. These indicators show you that you have properly configured your helper application.

7. Choose OK and you're done.

FIG. 1.2
In this Netscape dialog box, you can define a new MIME type and subtype for a helper application.

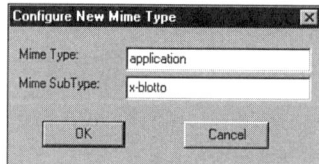

Now if you browse a Web page that contains an embedded .TIFF file, Netscape launches Paint Shop Pro and displays the file. You'll have to close Paint Shop Pro manually when you finish viewing the .TIFF image so that you can continue with your session.

Helper applications have many of the same uses and advantages as plug-ins:

- They extend your Web browser's capability to deal with additional file types.
- They load into memory only when needed, then unload to free up system resources when they are no longer useful (although you might have to close them manually).
- You need to install only the helper applications that you want.

However, helper applications have several disadvantages, too:

- They are external programs, so they're obtrusive; they don't display files inline, but in a separate program window.
- Most helper applications are overkill—they can do lots of things, not just what you want done—so they tend to be big and unwieldy.
- Because helper applications aren't integrated into your Web browser, you have to learn how to use each one separately. The learning curve can be steep.
- Because helper applications aren't standardized, Web page developers can't count on them being available to their audience; therefore, helper applications are not as likely to inspire the development of compatible Web page content.

Fortunately, the weaknesses of helper applications happen to be the strengths of plug-ins—plug-ins *are* integrated, focused, easy to use, and standardized. That's why plug-ins were developed to take the place of helper applications.

Installing a plug-in is much easier than setting up a helper application—you don't have to worry about defining MIME types or file name extensions. Many plug-ins are self-installing; an installation program handles everything for you automatically. Some plug-ins are distributed as archive files that you must first uncompress before you run the installation program. For a few plug-ins, you must move some files to the proper directories manually.

Netscape can also automatically assist you in the installation of plug-ins. If you run into a content type for which you haven't already installed a plug-in, Netscape opens the dialog box shown in figure 1.3.

FIG. 1.3
This Netscape dialog box enables you to download and install a needed plug-in on the fly automatically.

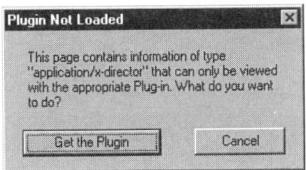

If the Web content provider provides a link to the appropriate plug-in, Netscape can automatically retrieve and install it for you. If not, Netscape jumps to its own directory of plug-ins, from which you can manually download and install the plug-in that you want.

Chapter 2, "Browser Plug-Ins," presents the steps for downloading and installing all the most useful Netscape plug-ins.

A Brief Course in MIME Types

Before Netscape can tell whether it can display a file internally or whether it needs a helper application or plug-in, it must determine the kind of data with which it's dealing.

If you've been using a personal computer for very long, you can probably identify many file types by their file name extensions. You know that a file named FOO.EXE is an executable program, because the file name ends with the extension .EXE, and that a file named BOO.DOC is a Microsoft Word document because it ends with the extension .DOC.

Netscape identifies files on the Web by *MIME type*. *MIME* is an acronym for *Multipurpose Internet Mail Extensions*, but this is a little misleading. MIME type definitions are not just for Internet mail; they are used to identify any file that can be transmitted over the Internet.

Web pages usually consist of not just a single file, but a collection of several files. For example, the text portion is usually a single HyperText Markup Language (HTML) text file, and each graphic is a separate .GIF or JPEG format file. When your browser reads a Web page, the server sends all this data as a stream, identifying each section with a preceding MIME type definition header.

A MIME type definition consists of two parts:

type/subtype

Here's a real-world example:

image/jpeg

As you can see, this MIME type definition describes an *image* file in *JPEG* format.

Before sending a file to Netscape, a Web server invisibly sends the MIME type definition for that file. Netscape reads this definition and looks it up to see whether it can handle the file internally, or whether a helper application or plug-in is defined for the file. In the case of the preceding example, Netscape knows that the file it is about to receive is an image in JPEG format, which, of course, it can display internally.

You can see a complete list of the MIME types that Netscape recognizes natively by choosing Options, General Preferences from the Netscape menu, then selecting the Helpers tab. You then see the Preference dialog box's Helpers page as shown in figure 1.1. However, Netscape isn't limited to only these file types; you can add a plug-in for *any* file type.

There are only seven sanctioned MIME types: text, audio, image, video, multipart, message, and application. Any new program or data file type must fit into one of these seven MIME types before a MIME-enabled application like Netscape can recognize it.

However, there are both "official" and "unofficial" MIME subtypes. Official subtypes appear on the file type list without an *x-* prefix. This prefix is the official way to label an unofficial MIME subtype. A MIME subtype being "unofficial" doesn't in any way make it a second-class citizen, however. It just means that the Internet Working Group, the organization that oversees the MIME standard, hasn't defined an official subtype for that kind of content—yet.

Fortunately, all this MIME stuff is totally transparent to the user. You don't usually have to worry about it at all, because MIME type registration for plug-ins is taken care of automatically during installation.

You can see which MIME types are registered and which plug-ins handle them by choosing Help, About Plug-Ins from the Netscape 3.0 menu. You'll get an internally generated page like that shown in figure 1.4.

TROUBLESHOOTING

I selected Help, About Plug-ins from the Netscape 3.0 menu, but I didn't get the About Plug-Ins screen shown in figure 1.4. What's wrong? A JavaScript application within Netscape Navigator generates the About Plug-Ins page, so you don't see the page if you have Java and JavaScript turned off. To enable Java and JavaScript, select Options, Network Preferences from the Netscape menu and click the Languages tab. Make sure that both the Enable Java and Enable JavaScript check boxes are selected, then click the OK button to end.

FIG. 1.4
The internally generated About Plug-Ins Netscape page lists the MIME types for which you have plug-ins installed.

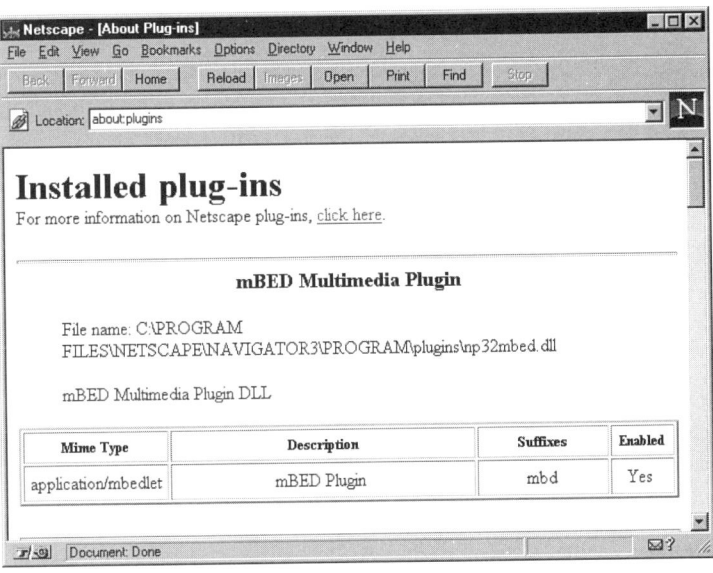

N O T E You can find out more about MIME types by obtaining the Internet Working Group's Request for Comments (RFC) document on the topic. You can download this document by pointing Netscape to the following address:

ftp://ds.internic.net

Look for the directory /RFC and the file name RFC1521.TXT.

You can also enter into discussions about MIME on UseNet. Just point Netscape's newsreader to the group **comp.mail.mime**.

How Plug-Ins "Plug In"

Plug-ins are simply feature add-ons that can understand and interpret files that Netscape can't handle itself. They extend the capabilities of Netscape in much the way that plug-in software modules are used to extend the capabilities of other products such as Adobe PhotoShop. They are essentially transparent, appearing as enhancements and supplements to the Netscape browser itself. The Netscape user interface remains relatively constant no matter what plug-ins are installed—if you're displaying an inline QuickTime movie, for example, the parts of the display that handle page navigation, scrolling, and so on aren't affected by the plug-in's presence.

In more technical terms, plug-ins are dynamic code modules that are a part of Netscape's application programming interface (API) for integrating third-party software into Netscape. It's a part of Netscape Corporation's "open systems" philosophy regarding Netscape Navigator; this approach allows third-party developers to use Netscape to integrate their products into the Web seamlessly.

N O T E Although this book often refers specifically to Netscape, Microsoft's Internet Explorer can also use plug-ins. Over time, you can expect to see many more plug-ins released specifically for Internet Explorer. Almost everything that this book says about Netscape plug-ins also applies directly to Internet Explorer plug-ins.

In fact, the latest version of Internet Explorer can even use Netscape plug-ins directly, so that you can add your favorite Netscape plug-ins to either browser.

Plug-ins enable you to customize Netscape to interact with third-party products and industry media standards. They are meant to supplement and complement, not supplant, other interapplication architectures such as Windows OLE (Object Linking and Embedding) and Java. Plug-ins can accomplish the following tasks:

- Create a window in Netscape for displaying information, as in a Video for Windows movie player.
- Execute an application such as a Musical Instrument Digital Interface (MIDI) player.
- Generate data for Netscape or other plug-ins. For example, a plug-in might create an index on the fly.
- Provide interapplication communication. For example, a plug-in might transfer data to a stand-alone spreadsheet program.
- Override a native Netscape capability and supply its own implementation. For example, a plug-in might provide an improved .GIF viewer
- Link to and receive data from Uniform Resource Locators (URLs). For example, some plug-ins can download stock quotes.

Because plug-ins are platform-specific, you must have a different version of each plug-in for every operating system that you use, such as Windows, Windows 95, UNIX, or the Macintosh operating system. Regardless of your platform, however, Netscape plug-ins should be functionally equivalent across all platforms.

 Many plug-ins ship with the copy of Netscape that you purchased or downloaded. These plug-ins are already designed for your platform. However, if you find other plug-ins that you want either to purchase or download from the Internet, make sure that they are for your specific platform.

For most users, the use of plug-ins is totally transparent. When Netscape starts up, it checks to see which plug-ins have been installed; if it encounters a data MIME type for which a plug-in is registered, Netscape launches the plug-in to handle that data. When you leave the page that contains that data, the plug-in unloads, freeing up system resources.

You activate a plug-in only by opening a Web page that initiates it; usually, you don't even see the plug-in at work. For example, after you install the Shockwave for Director plug-in, you notice no difference in the way that Netscape functions until you come across a Web page that features Shockwave content (see fig. 1.5).

FIG. 1.5
The Shockwave for Director plug-in in action, letting you blast Space Aliens inline on a Web page.

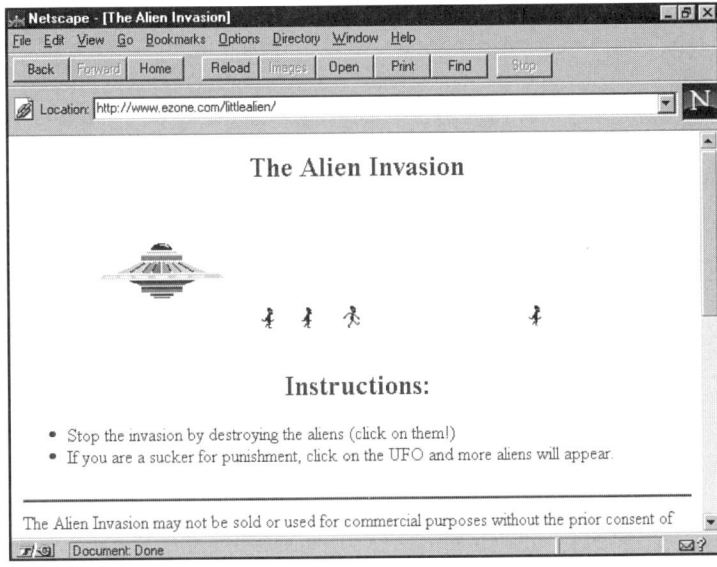

When the Netscape client launches, it notes any available plug-ins, but does not load any into random access memory (RAM). This way, a plug-in resides in memory only when needed; however, you still need to be aware of memory allocation, because many plug-ins can be in use at any one time. Plug-ins simply reside on disk until you need them. As soon as you move to another HTML page that doesn't require a plug-in, it is deleted from RAM.

At its most fundamental level, a plug-in can access a URL and retrieve MIME data just like a standard Netscape client. This data is streamed to the plug-in as it arrives from the network, making it possible to implement viewers and other interfaces that can display information progressively as it arrives from the server.

If a plug-in requires more data than a single data stream can supply, the plug-in can request multiple, simultaneous data streams, so long as the user's system supports such data streams.

Plug-ins can also handle data in the "old-fashioned" way: caching data for display only when it has all been downloaded. For instance, a plug-in can draw a simple frame and introductory graphic while the bulk of the data is streaming off the network into the Netscape cache.

If Netscape or another plug-in needs data while a plug-in is active, the plug-in can generate the needed data. Therefore, plug-ins not only process data, but also generate it. For example, a plug-in can be a data translator or filter.

The integration of plug-ins with Netscape is quite elegant and flexible, making the most of asynchronous processes and multithreaded data. All plug-ins are associated with a MIME type not native to the Netscape client, and can be associated with multiple MIME types. Netscape can concurrently run multiple instances of the same plug-in if the page contains several plug-in-compatible data files of the same type.

Netscape's plug-in API also attempts to address the concerns of programmers, providing a high degree of flexibility and cross-platform support to plug-in developers.

Plug-ins are a godsend for applications developers, who can extend the utility of existing products into the burgeoning Internet market by developing a quick and easy Netscape plug-in that reads existing data files, instead of developing a whole new product. Not only does this save developers time and effort, it lets them ride into a huge market on the coattails of Netscape, the Internet's most popular browser. Applications developers are happy, because their market expands quickly and almost for free; Web content developers are happy, because they have new formats that they can provide; Web users are happy, because they have new ways in which to use the Web; and even Netscape is happy, because its Web browser becomes more powerful and useful without any additional effort on its part. Everybody wins!

> **CAUTION**
>
> You should be keenly aware of the potential system security problems that plug-ins present. *Plug-ins have full access to all the data on your computer system.* They are written by third parties whom you may or may not know. Plug-ins are delivered by servers over whom you have no control. Each of these factors poses a potential security risk. Make sure that you trust the plug-in developer and the plug-in server before you install a plug-in on a system in which a security breach could cause serious problems.
>
> For example, a plug-in could easily be developed that scans through the Windows 95 registry looking for passwords, then passes them back to the plug-in developer through the Internet. Although you're unlikely to encounter such an insidious plug-in at a major developer's site, you might want to exercise more caution when downloading a plug-in from an individual's Web site.
>
> Almost worse is the case of a poorly written plug-in that means no harm, but through sloppy programming manages to reformat your hard drive or trash your system registry. *Be careful.*

The Three Kinds of Plug-Ins

After you install a plug-in on your machine and a Web page initiates the plug-in, it manifests itself in three potential ways:

- Embedded
- Full-screen
- Hidden

An *embedded* plug-in appears as a visible, rectangular window integrated into a Web page. This window might not look any different than a window created by a graphic, such as an embedded .GIF or JPEG picture. The main difference between the previous windows supported by Netscape and those created by plug-ins is that plug-in windows can support a much wider range of interactivity and movement, and thereby remain dynamic rather than static.

Embedded plug-ins can read and note mouse clicks, mouse location, mouse movement, keyboard input, and input from virtually any other input device. In this way, a plug-in can support the full range of user events required to produce sophisticated applications.

Examples of embedded plug-ins include a Moving Picture Expert Group (MPEG) movie player, the QuickTime movie player, the Shockwave for Macromedia Director player, or Video for Windows player like VDOLive (see fig. 1.6).

FIG. 1.6
VDOLive is an example of an embedded plug-in that can seamlessly integrate a window within an HTML document.

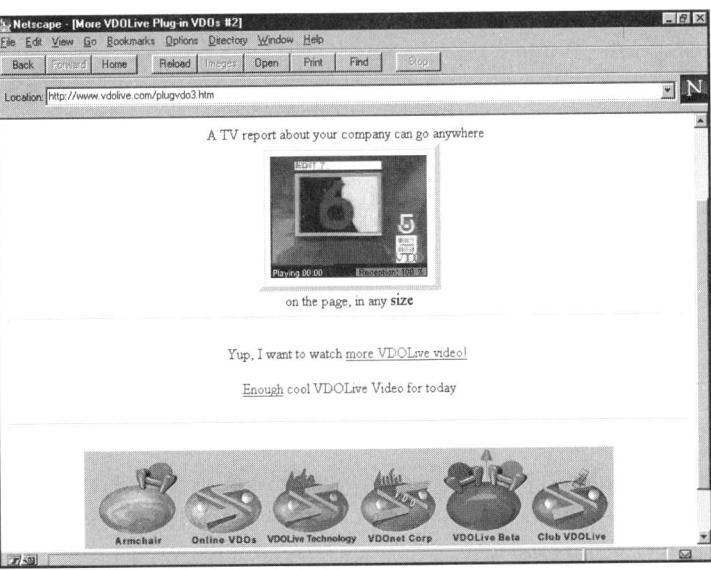

A *full-screen* plug-in takes over the entire current Netscape window to display its own content. This is necessary when a Web page is designed to display data that HTML does not support. An example of this type of plug-in is the Adobe Acrobat viewer (see fig. 1.7).

FIG. 1.7
The Adobe Acrobat viewer is a full-screen plug-in that even incorporates its own control bar.

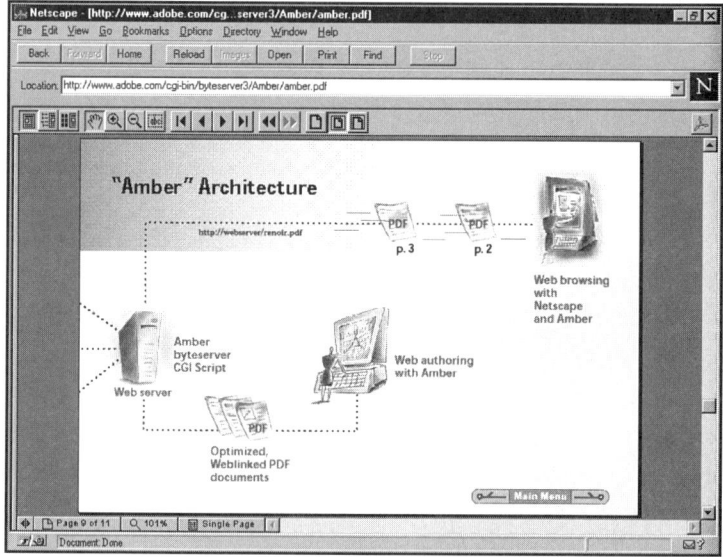

If you view an Acrobat page using the Netscape plug-in, the page displays just like any other Web page, but retains the look and functionality of an Acrobat document viewed in Adobe's stand-alone viewer. For instance, if a Web site uses Acrobat to display an online manual for a product, the site might enable you to scroll, print, and interact with the page just as if the stand-alone Acrobat Reader program were displaying it.

You can invoke some plug-ins in either embedded or full-screen mode. For example, you can launch Netscape's Video for Windows sample plug-in as either an inline window or a full-screen player, depending on the display mode specified in the page that you access.

A *hidden* plug-in doesn't have any visible elements, but works strictly behind the scenes to add some feature to Netscape that is otherwise not available. Examples of possible hidden plug-ins include MIDI music players or file decompression engines. A MIDI player plug-in could read MIDI data from a Web page whenever it's encountered, and automatically play the data through your local hardware without so much as even displaying a control panel. Similarly, a decompression engine might function much the way that it does on commercial online services—decompressing data in real time in the background—or delaying decompression until the user logs off the Internet.

Regardless of the plug-ins that you use, and whether they are embedded, full-screen, or hidden, the rest of Netscape's user interface remains relatively constant and available. Therefore, even if Netscape's main window is displaying an Acrobat page, you still can access Netscape's menus and navigational controls.

What Plug-Ins Can (and Can't) Do

The current version of the Netscape plug-in API supports four broad areas of functionality. Plug-ins can do the following:

- Draw into and receive events from a native window element that is a part of the Netscape window hierarchy
- Obtain MIME data from the network through URLs
- Generate data for consumption by Netscape or other plug-ins
- Override and implement protocol handlers

Netscape plug-ins are ideally suited to take advantage of platform-independent protocols, architectures, languages, and media types such as Java, Virtual Reality Modeling Language (VRML), and MPEG. Although plug-ins should be functionally equivalent across platforms, they should also complement platform-specific protocols and architectures such as OLE 2.

This book loosely groups plug-ins into three major categories: multimedia, VRML, and business applications. Multimedia plug-ins are the heart and soul of plug-ins development. This category includes inline players for audio, video, animations, and multimedia presentations. VRML plug-ins display three-dimensional, online "worlds" created using the Virtual Reality Modeling Language. These "worlds" are filled with 3-D objects that you can move around and through and with which you can (occasionally) interact. Quite a few VRML plug-ins are available, each having its own strengths, weaknesses, and additions to the VRML standard. Business plug-ins are a hot area of development, with plug-ins now available for the Adobe Acrobat portable document format, inline Excel-compatible spreadsheets, Word documents, and more. Some plug-ins even enable you to develop your own applications for use with Netscape; early examples include indexing programs, stock quote grabbers, and even a graphic world clock.

You can even write your own plug-ins. Netscape offers software developer's kits (SDKs) for Windows, Macintosh, and UNIX system plug-ins development. These kits are available for free downloading from Netscape's Web site. Chapter 21, "Creating Your Own Plug-Ins," provides details on how to download, install, and use these SDKs.

The Future of Plug-Ins

The Internet is hot, and the World Wide Web is the hottest place on the Internet. Literally thousands of new sites are coming online every month. Add in the huge number of corporate intranets that are being created at an even faster rate, and you have an almost incomprehensible amount of HTML content being created on a daily basis.

Much of that content isn't in the form of simple text and graphics that Netscape or other Web browsers can display natively. Much of the content consists of live audio and video, specialized graphics like AutoCAD drawings, heavily formatted brochures that can be properly represented only in a portable document format like Adobe Acrobat, or preexisting sales and marketing presentations in Macromedia Director or other proprietary formats.

The companies that publish the programs that create these proprietary file formats are quite interested in helping their customers deliver that content on the Web and on intranets. For this reason, most of these publishers are creating plug-ins that can display that content inline in Netscape and Internet Explorer.

In the first three months of 1996, a new plug-in was released for Netscape about every three days. This pace probably won't decrease until plug-ins are available to display most popular proprietary file types inline. Hundreds of new plug-ins are likely to be created and released in the next couple of years.

So, how can you keep up with this pace? Probably nobody can. Even Netscape is falling behind. Of the three dozen or so plug-ins currently available, only about two-thirds are listed on Netscape's plug-ins tracking site at **http://home.netscape.com/comprod/ products/navigator/version_2.0/plugins/index.html**. Because the Netscape Plug-Ins SDK has been released for free on the Web, many companies are developing and releasing plug-ins without Netscape's direct assistance or knowledge.

There are other resources, however. One of the best is the BrowserWatch Plug-Ins Plaza site at **http://www.browserwatch.com/plug-in.html** (see fig. 1.8). Yahoo! also maintains an index at **http://www.yahoo.com/Computers_and_Internet/Internet/ World_Wide_Web/Browsers/Netscape_Navigator/Plug_Ins/**. Sager Bell's Web page at **http://sager-bell.com/techdemo/** is dedicated to providing online demos of all the latest Netscape goodies, including new plug-ins. This page is not only a great place to go to find out about new plug-ins, but to test them after you install them. Finally, TUCOWS (The Ultimate Collection Of Winsock Software) has a very good index of Windows 95 plug-ins with ratings at **http://tucows.niia.net/plug95.html**.

FIG. 1.8
Plug-Ins Plaza is the best site on the Internet for up-to-date information on and links to the latest Netscape plug-ins.

Fortunately, you don't really have to go to all the work of finding plug-ins yourself. Most sites that contain content that you must use a plug-in to display are kind enough to include a link for downloading the required plug-in (see fig. 1.9). As plug-ins proliferate, let's hope that all Web page developers remember to remain as polite.

FIG. 1.9
Novell's Web site (**http://corp.novell.com/present/novell/**) features an online presentation using RealAudio, but just in case you don't already have the RealAudio plug-in, Novell has been thoughtful enough to include a link to the RealAudio site so you can download the plug-in immediately.

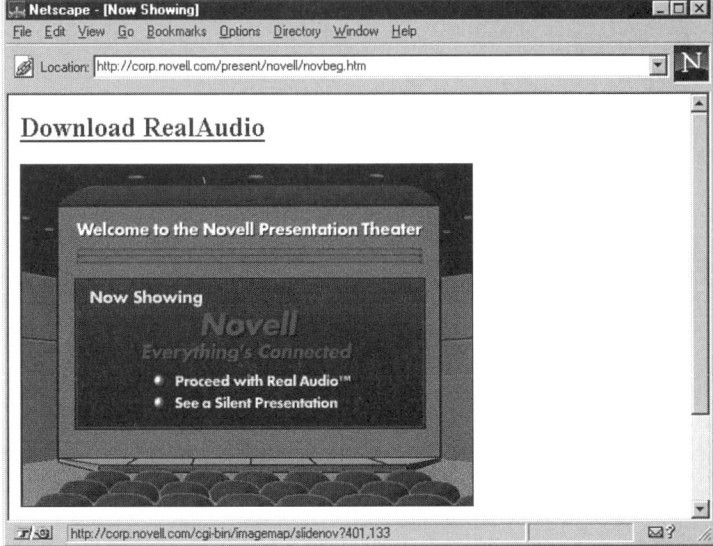

Several future changes have been proposed for HyperText Transfer Protocol (HTTP), the operating procedures that servers and browsers use to communicate with each other. These changes will affect future plug-ins development.

The proposed Byte Range extension to HTTP would enable plug-ins to access data from a server randomly. Database-style plug-in applications could load data selectively, not just as a linear stream. Although stream-based data is great for linear applications like listening to audio or viewing videos, a database-style random-access protocol would enable you to skip to different pages in an Adobe Acrobat document, do a fast-forward jump to interesting parts of a multimedia presentation, and more, all without having to wait for the whole data stream to download.

Another new HTTP concept, Content Negotiation, would enable your browser to determine the kinds of content that a page could potentially present, check its stock of plug-ins to see the kinds of content that the page can actually handle, and then request only the content that the page is set up to view. For example, if you're paying for download time and don't want to pay for viewing real-time videos, you could set up Netscape without a video viewer, letting it negotiate with a server to view a static graphic instead.

Some Web browsers have already implemented one innovative HTTP enhancement (albeit in nonstandardized ways): persistent HTTP connections. HTTP connections are inherently stateless and transient, requiring a separate Transmission Control Protocol (TCP) connection for each data transfer. For this reason, the status line at the bottom of the Netscape screen always seems to say `Contacting www.wherever.com`. Persistent connections maintain the connection for the duration of a data stream transfer. Although they hog Internet resources, such connections provide faster and smoother data stream reception. For applications like video conferencing, persistent HTTP connections are a virtual necessity.

HTTP is also likely to incorporate some form of state management. Currently, HTTP is stateless—that is, neither the server nor the browser really know or care what data has been previously transferred or what actions have been taken. Cookie files are a current attempt to handle this situation. If, for example, you add an item to your online shopping basket at an online store, your browser (not the server) is likely to store your order in a "cookie file" that includes a textual description of your user information and the item that you added to your basket. When you get ready to check out, the server queries Netscape, which in turn hands the cookie file to the server so that it can process your order (see fig. 1.10). State management would extend and formalize the cookie file concept to make it more versatile and standard.

FIG. 1.10
The **Amazon.com** bookstore uses Netscape's cookie file to keep track of online book orders. You can exit the **Amazon.com** Web site and come back days later, and your shopping cart (shown here) will still hold the books that you've selected, ready for purchase.

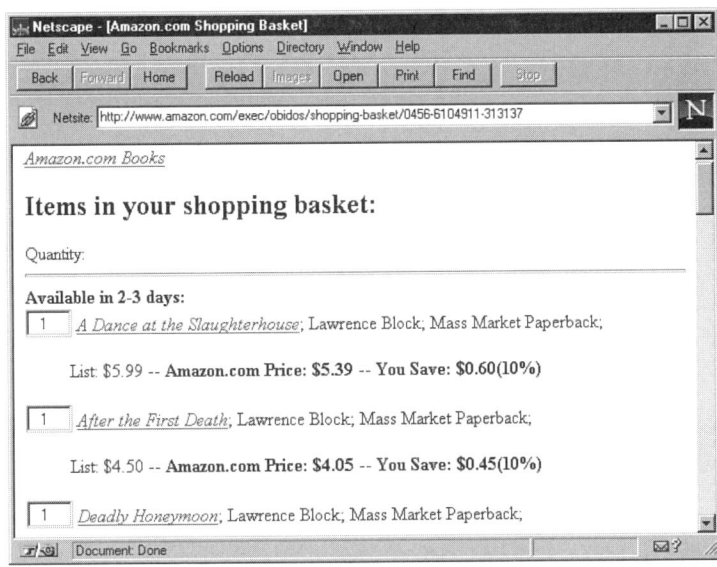

User authentication for server groups would enable them to establish protection spaces across multiple servers. Developers could then enhance plug-ins to handle groupware applications like whiteboards, secure video conferencing, and collaboration. With secure groups that span the Internet, the Web would become more like a local area network (LAN) and less like a communications service.

All these changes to HTTP would result in a richer environment for plug-ins development. Other advances in video and audio technology, data compression, communications, and even central processing unit (CPU) power, will open doors for new and better plug-ins for your favorite browser programs. One example is the recent announcement by Netscape and Pointcast (**http://www.pointcast.com**) to develop a multicasting plug-in for Netscape. This development, which will provide multimedia conferencing inline, is an outgrowth of a combination of advancements in data compression, high-speed communications, CPU power, and multicasting backbone (MBONE) technology. ●

CHAPTER 2

Browser Plug-Ins

Although a wide variety of plug-in modules is now available for Netscape (this book describes over 100) and more are under development, they fall roughly into three categories. In this chapter, you will learn about all three types: multimedia, VRML, and productivity or business applications.

This chapter is an overview of the plug-ins available for Netscape. Each plug-in type is covered in much more detail in its own part—Part II covers multimedia plug-ins, Part III covers plug-ins for VRML, and Part IV covers plug-ins for business applications. Each part fully covers the specific functions of each plug-in, along with instructions on developing Web page and intranet content that takes advantage of the capabilities of individual plug-ins.

This book doesn't list every plug-in ever created for Netscape or Internet Explorer—some (such as Animated Widgets) have been merely testbed projects or fun demos. However, you should find all the most useful plug-ins released so far. Of course, plug-in development proceeds apace, so keeping up-to-date is almost

- Multimedia, including viewers for video (.AVI, .MOV, and MPEG movies), audio (speech, music, and digitized sound), and graphics (including vector objects and supercompressed images), as well as multimedia presentation formats like Macromedia Director and Astound

- VRML (Virtual Reality Modeling Language) three-dimensional world display plug-ins (sometimes with extra features)

- Productivity or business applications, including viewers for application files such as Excel spreadsheets and Word documents, Web navigation tools, and plug-ins that link to ActiveX objects to call other programs, embed applications, or provide custom controls, as well as some interesting miscellaneous applications

http://www.mcp.com/que

impossible, even if you're checking online every day. Over 50 significant plug-ins were released in the three months that immediately preceded the writing of this book! ■

Downloading, Installing, and Using Plug-Ins with Netscape

Downloading Netscape plug-ins couldn't be much easier. Netscape maintains a page that lists many of the currently available plug-ins, with links to the pages from which you can download them. You can find the page at the following address:

http://home.netscape.com/comprod/products/navigator/version_2.0/plugins/index.html

(Adjust the version number as necessary to suit your version of Netscape, or simply follow the appropriate links from **http://home.netscape.com/comprod/products/navigator**.)

The Plug-Ins Plaza site seems to be even more consistently up-to-date than Netscape's own site. You can find the Plug-Ins Plaza at the following address:

http://www.browserwatch.com

For your convenience, this chapter provides the URL of the download site for each of the plug-ins described.

Before installing a plug-in, you should download the plug-in file into its own temporary directory. You might keep a directory called C:\INSTALL on your hard drive just for this purpose. Then you can download a single plug-in to the INSTALL directory, install the plug-in, then delete the files in C:\INSTALL so that the directory is empty and available for your next installation. (You might make sure that the plug-in is actually installed correctly and working properly before you delete the installation files.)

Each plug-in downloads as a single file. Installation involves one of two procedures:

- ■ If the file is called SETUP.EXE, all you have to do is run it. It will automatically install itself as a Netscape plug-in. The installation program might let you specify the directory into which to install the plug-in. Don't change the default unless you already have a directory by that name that contains something else.

- If the file has some obscure name like XX32B4.EXE, it is almost certainly a self-extracting archive. In this case, double-clicking the file in Windows 95 (or opening a DOS shell in Windows 3.1, cDing to the INSTALL directory, and typing the file name) extracts the archive into a whole bunch of files in your INSTALL directory. You then close the DOS window and run the program SETUP.EXE, using the same process described in the preceding prodedure.

In any event, the download page for a plug-in always contains complete instructions on downloading and installation. Read and follow these instructions carefully. Different plug-ins might require different instructions, and you don't want to be caught by surprise. (For example, you can optionally download a bare-bones version of the Crescendo MIDI player plug-in without a setup program, but if you do, you have to unpack and copy the file into the Netscape plug-ins directory yourself.)

> **CAUTION**
> Before you install any Netscape plug-in, make sure that you have the latest version of Netscape Navigator properly installed. The plug-ins discussed in this chapter do not work at all with versions of Netscape earlier than 2.0, and some require 3.0.

Determining Which Plug-Ins You Have Installed

Suppose that you have installed several plug-ins and now cannot remember which ones you have and which ones you don't. You installed a nice plug-in for playing an audio, video, or multimedia plug-in, but one plug-in that you installed later seems to have taken over this function, and you don't like that plug-in nearly as much. How can you figure out which plug-ins you have installed, and which ones you still need? Is there any way to get your old plug-in back?

In Netscape 3.0, you need only open the Navigator's Help menu and choose About Plug-Ins. Netscape then displays a nicely formatted table of all the plug-ins that you have installed (see fig. 2.1).

Navigator 2.0 had no easy menu selection or popup dialog box that told you exactly which plug-ins you had installed. However, if you are still using Navigator 2.0, you can check out three sources to find some good clues.

FIG. 2.1
Netscape 3.0 tells you the MIME type, application, and other important information associated with an installed plug-in.

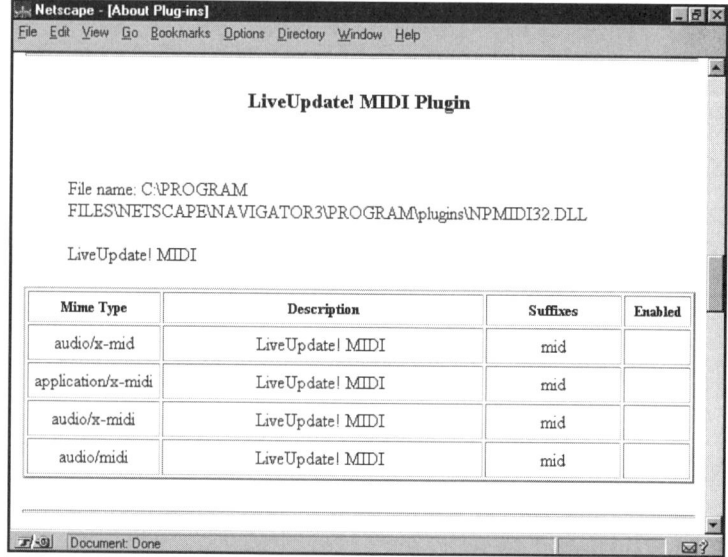

One is the Navigator <u>H</u>elp menu's About <u>P</u>lug-Ins command. This command generates a list formatted as follows:

```
File name:
Types:
Description: data
MIME Type: x-world/x-vrml
Suffixes: wrl
etc
```

This output lists the MIME types registered to launch plug-ins. Netscape enters each entry on this list whenever you install a plug-in. Although this list is a good indicator of the file types that launch plug-ins when encountered, the output doesn't tell you exactly which plug-ins the file types will launch.

If the list includes two or more entries documenting the same MIME type or suffix, you've installed one plug-in over another, and the more recent one is handling that type of file display.

You can also open the <u>O</u>ptions menu, choose <u>G</u>eneral Preferences, and select the Helpers tab from the dialog box that appears. The Helpers page includes a scrolling list of registered MIME types. Under the Action column is either the word *Browser* (indicating that Netscape itself handles the file type), *Ask User* (indicating that a dialog box displays to ask the user what to do), or the name of a helper application set up to handle that type of file for Netscape. If the Action field is blank, a plug-in is configured for the MIME type. Although you still don't know *which* plug-in is associated with the file type, at least you know that some kind of plug-in is handling the file type.

Finally, you can use Explorer to search the folder C:\PROGRAM FILES\NETSCAPE\ NAVIGATOR\PROGRAM\PLUGINS. (This folder is the default; if you installed Netscape in another path, you have to find the path to the plug-ins folder yourself.) The folder contains the Dynamic Link Libraries (DLLs) and other files used by the plug-ins that you've installed. Unfortunately, most of these libraries have obscure names like NPSKWAV.DLL or MICRDATE.DLL. Right-click a .DLL file name under Windows 95 and select Properties from the popup menu to get a variety of information about the file, including the name of the company that created the file and any developer's notes associated with the file. You can usually find enough information to determine the type of plug-in.

By combining this information with your memory of the plug-ins that you *think* you remember installing, you should be able to figure out which plug-ins you actually have installed and enabled.

If you can determine which plug-ins you have installed, you can easily reenable a plug-in superseded by another. To do so, you simply delete the newer plug-in. After you delete that plug-in, the older one takes over again, if it is still in the plug-ins directory. Otherwise, you have to reinstall the older plug-in.

Running a Plug-In

Running a plug-in is simple; in fact, you don't have to run a plug-in at all. Plug-ins run themselves whenever a Web page or link contains the proper kind of embedded file. You don't have to decide when to run them, and you don't have to figure out how to load the data file.

However, you do have to learn how the controls work. Many of these programs provide on the screen a set of specialized controls for zooming, printing, panning, scrolling, and so on. Each plug-in comes with detailed documentation explaining its specific controls and how they work. (In some cases, you might have to download a separate manual file, or the plug-in's documentation is online in the form of Web pages. Make sure that you get your plug-in's documentation.) Read the documentation so that you know all about a plug-in *before* you encounter any files that it will display. Then you won't have to spend valuable online time trying to figure out your plug-in's behavior.

Installing Plug-Ins for Internet Explorer

The most recent incarnations of Microsoft Internet Explorer can also use most Netscape plug-ins without modification.

If you've been using plug-ins with Netscape and you install Internet Explorer, it automatically notes the presence of the Netscape plug-ins that you have installed. Internet Explorer then loads and uses these plug-ins whenever it encounters a Web page that requires a plug-in to display embedded content.

Netscape plug-ins are installed in a folder, PLUGINS, which is located inside the Netscape PROGRAM folder. For example, under Windows 95, this folder's full path name is typically C:\PROGRAM FILES\NETSCAPE\ NAVIGATOR\ PROGRAM\PLUGINS. If you plan to keep both Netscape and Internet Explorer active on your system, you should continue to install future plug-ins in this directory. That way, they are always available to both browsers.

However, if you are switching permanently from Netscape to Internet Explorer and want to keep using the plug-ins that you have installed, you'll have to move them to a new directory under Internet Explorer. Under Windows 95, the full path name for this folder is typically something like C:\PROGRAM FILES\MICROSOFT INTERNET\PLUGINS.

If you want to move only a few plug-ins, you first have to identify which ones you want to move. To do so, load Netscape and select Help, About Plug-Ins. Netscape then displays the screen shown in figure 2.2.

FIG. 2.2
The Netscape About Plug-Ins screen helps you specify which files to move to your Internet Explorer folder.

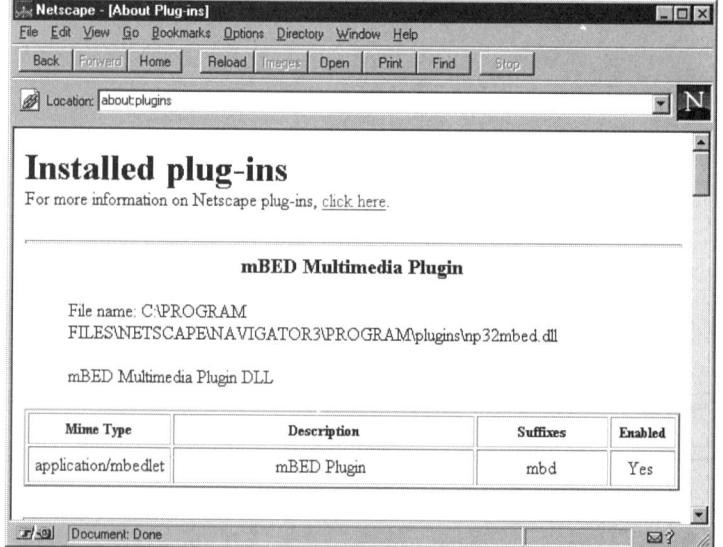

Note the full path name and file name for each plug-in that you want to keep. For example, in figure 2.2, the screen shows that the mBed plug-in is actually the file called NP32MBED.DLL. After identifying the plug-ins that you want to move, open Windows Explorer and drag the associated DLL files into the PLUGINS folder under the Microsoft Internet folder (see fig. 2.3). (If the PLUGINS folder doesn't exist, right-click the Microsoft Internet folder and select New, Folder to create it first.)

FIG. 2.3
If you're switching from Netscape to Internet Explorer for good, first drag and drop to move or copy your plug-ins from the Netscape PLUGINS folder to the Microsoft Internet PLUGINS folder.

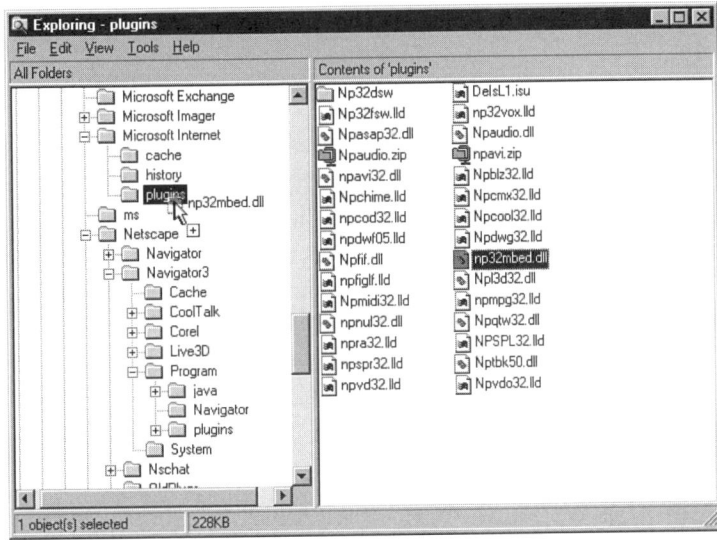

Of course, if you want to move all the plug-ins, you can skip the identification step and just drag all the DLL files from the Netscape PLUGINS folder to the Microsoft Internet PLUGINS folder.

But what if you're *not* migrating from Netscape Navigator? What if you're installing Internet Explorer as your first and only browser? No problem. Just install any plug-ins that you want to use directly into the Microsoft Internet PLUGINS folder.

Such an installation usually means that, somewhere in the process of running the setup program for your plug-in, you have to use the program's Browse option to select the Microsoft Internet PLUGINS folder—the default folder is almost always the Netscape PLUGINS folder. Sometimes this works, and sometimes it doesn't. For example, figure 2.4 shows the setup program for the Fractal Viewer plug-in. Although the program enables you to browse for a new folder in which to install the plug-in, the setup program won't actually install the plug-in unless it finds the Netscape executable.

FIG. 2.4
Sometimes you can install a plug-in to work with Internet Explorer, but sometimes you can't. Although this setup program's screen makes it looks as though the installation will work, the next step aborts it.

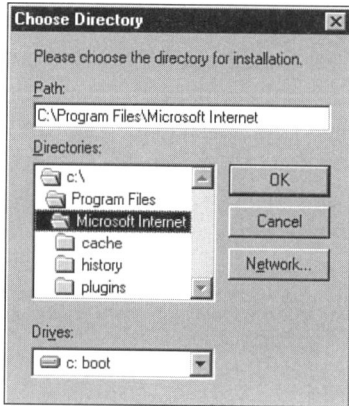

However, even if you can't install a plug-in for Internet Explorer, all is not lost. Remember, plug-in support is more or less a competitive afterthought for Internet Explorer—a way to ease the path for people to move from Netscape to Internet Explorer. Internet Explorer's preferred way of handling innovative Web page content is through ActiveX controls, not plug-ins. The odds are good that, for just about every plug-in, there is an equivalent ActiveX control (see fig. 2.5). In fact, if you are using Internet Explorer exclusively, you probably should stick with ActiveX controls rather than plug-ins where possible. Plug-ins are usually preferable only if you don't want to enable ActiveX controls for security reasons, or if you are planning on using both Netscape and Internet Explorer on your computer simultaneously.

FIG. 2.5
This page on Microsoft's Web site (**http://www.microsoft.com/activex/controls**) provides links that enable you to download the ActiveX control versions of many popular Netscape plug-ins, such as Shockwave.

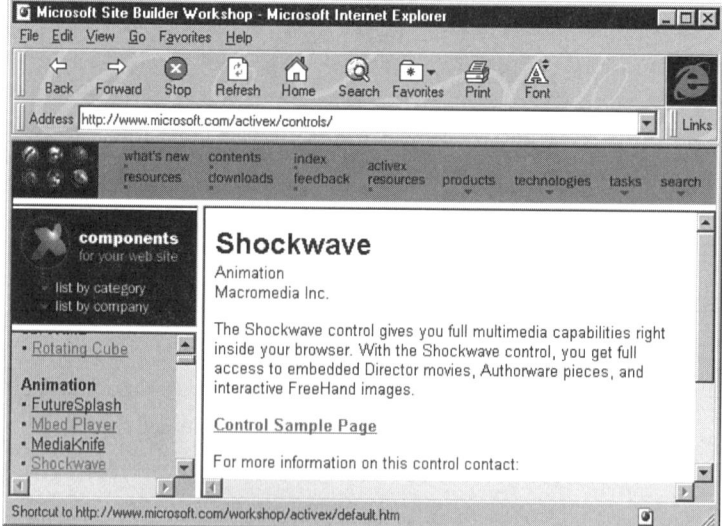

> **CAUTION**
> Don't try to install the NCompass ActiveX plug-in for Internet Explorer. ActiveX support is already built in to Internet Explorer.

Multimedia Plug-Ins

Interest in delivering multimedia content on the Web and on corporate intranets is driving plug-in development. Although plug-ins are available for purposes other than playing audio, video, and multimedia content, plug-ins that handle these tasks are by far the most pervasive.

This section lists and describes the sound, graphics, video, animation, and multimedia plug-ins currently being distributed for Netscape Navigator.

Sound

Internet audio is growing like gangbusters. More live audio programs, digitized sound files, and MIDI music files seem to be appearing on the Web each day. With the explosion of plug-ins development in this area, the use of Internet audio is sure to grow even faster in the near future.

In the beginning, the Web was mute. Eventually, some sites began to add a few digitized sounds. To download and play these sounds, you had to use helper applications. Now, several sound plug-ins enable Netscape to play live audio data streams in real time. Audio plug-ins are available for several varieties of digitized sound as well as MIDI music and speech.

LiveAudio Because it ships with Netscape 3.0, the LiveAudio plug-in is essentially the "official" Netscape audio player. Unlike the other audio plug-ins discussed in this chapter, LiveAudio doesn't use a proprietary sound file format, but instead plays standard AIFF, .AU, MIDI, and .WAV files. You can either embed or link sound files in or to a Web page. LiveAudio features an easy-to-use console with play, pause, stop, and volume controls.

RealAudio Progressive Networks' RealAudio plug-in provides live, on-demand, real-time audio over 14.4 kilobytes per second (kbps) or faster Internet connections. Users with 28.8kbps or better connections can now hear true FM-quality broadcasting. RealAudio's controls are like those of a CD player—you can pause, rewind, fast-forward, stop, and start play with onscreen buttons.

RealAudio is getting much support on the Internet from diverse sources—from big companies such as the ABC broadcasting network, to small, independent radio stations, to individual users. The plug-in is almost a necessity for browsing the Web. The latest version even has synchronized multimedia playback capabilities.

You create RealAudio format sound files by using the RealAudio Encoder 2.0 program. This program is available as part of the RealAudio Player 2.0 Standard Edition CD-ROM, which costs $29. To deliver RealAudio content, you have to set up your Web server with the RealAudio Server software.

Available for Windows 3.1, Windows 95, Windows NT, UNIX, and Macintosh, the RealAudio Version 2.0 player plug-in is included on Netscape's Power Pack 2.0 CD-ROM. You also can download the plug-in directly from the RealAudio Web site at the following address:

http://www.realaudio.com/products/ra2.0/

TrueSpeech   If nothing else, TrueSpeech is convenient. If you're using Windows 3.1 or Windows 95, the supplied Sound Recorder program can digitize sound files and convert them to TrueSpeech format. You can then use the TrueSpeech player to listen to them on the Web in real time. Despite its name, TrueSpeech can be used for any type of audio file. You don't need a special server. You can download TrueSpeech players for Windows 3.1, Windows 95, Windows NT, Macintosh, and PowerMac from the DSP Group's home page:

http://www.dspg.com

Crescendo and Crescendo Plus   Most sound cards go a step beyond merely digitizing and playing back sounds. They also can generate their own sounds. If your sound card is MIDI-compatible (as most are), you have more than a passive record-and-playback system—you have a full-fledged music synthesizer. With a MIDI plug-in, you can experience Web sites with a full music soundtrack.

LiveUpdate's Crescendo plug-in enables Navigator to play inline MIDI music embedded in Web pages. With a MIDI-capable browser, you can create Web pages that have their own background music soundtracks. Because MIDI instruments can be sampled sounds, you can also create sound-effects tracks.

Crescendo requires an MPC (MIDI-capable) sound card and Netscape Navigator version 2.0 or above. The plug-in launches automatically and invisibly and is a fun addition to Web browsing.

Crescendo is just a 10K self-extracting archive file for Windows 95 and Windows NT, or a 50K file for Windows 3.1. The Windows 95 and Windows NT version is very tiny—you might have to check twice to make sure that you have downloaded it! A Macintosh version is now also available.

You can download Crescendo from the following site:

http://www.liveupdate.com/midi.html

An enhanced version, Crescendo Plus, adds onscreen controls and live streaming (see fig. 2.6). With the live streaming feature, you don't have to wait for a MIDI file to download completely before it starts playing. You can purchase Crescendo Plus also from LiveUpdate's Web site.

FIG. 2.6
Crescendo Plus features a CD-player style control panel and a convenient popup menu.

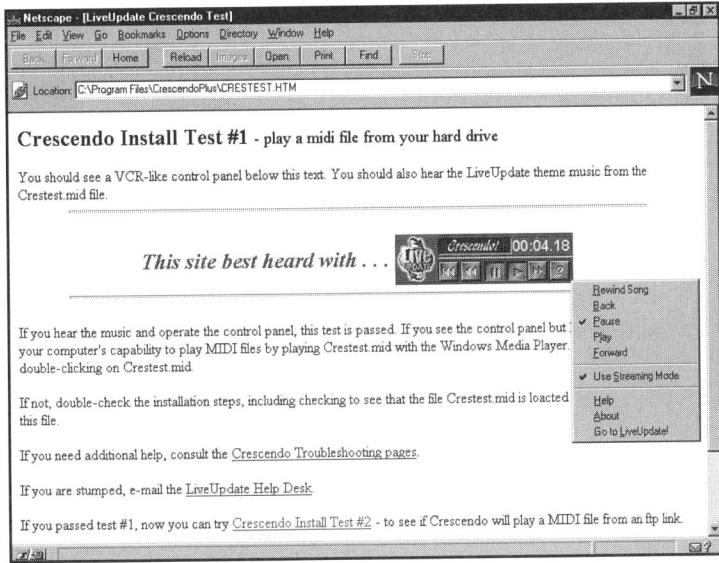

More Music Plug-Ins If you can't get enough music on the Web, this section describes a few more Netscape music plug-ins.

RapidTransit decompresses and plays music that has been compressed by a ratio of up to 40 to 1. The plug-in can provide full 16-bit, 44.1kHz. RapidTransit is available for Windows 95, Windows NT, and Macintosh from the following site:

http://monsterbit.com/rapidtransit/

Arnaud Masson's MIDI plug-in is for the Macintosh and PowerMac only. You can get it from the following site:

http://www.planete.net/~amasson/

Another Macintosh-only plug-in for MIDI files is GRAME's MidiShare. You can find this plug-in at the following address:

http://www.grame.fr/english/MidiShare.html

Do you prefer the sound of the orient? Then Sseyo's Koan might better suit your taste. It plays real-time, computer-generated Japanese Koan music on Windows 3.1 and Windows 95 versions of Netscape. You can find Koan at the following site:

http://www.sseyo.com/

ToolVox If all you need is speech, three kinds of speech plug-ins are available for Netscape:

- Players for digitized audio that is of less-than-music quality
- Text-to-speech converters, currently available only for the Macintosh
- A speech recognition plug-in, which is also for the Macintosh only

ToolVox provides audio compression ratios of up to 53:1, which creates very small files that transfer quickly over the Internet. Speech can be delivered in real time even over 9,600-baud modems. One unique feature is that you can slow down playback to improve comprehension, or speed it up to shorten listening times without changing voice pitch.

Like the higher-fidelity RealAudio, ToolVox streams audio in real time, so you don't have to wait for a file to download before you can listen to it.

ToolVox doesn't need special server software to deliver audio content from your Web server. The player, in the form of a Netscape Navigator 2.0 add-in, controls buffering and playback. As a result, any standard HTML server can act as a streaming media server. Even the encoder is free. It compresses a speech file from .WAV format to an 8kHz, 2,400 bits per second (bps) VOX file.

Netscape Communications Corporation has become part owner of Voxware, the maker of ToolVox, so you can expect to hear much more about the plug-in. Netscape has also licensed key elements of Voxware's digital voice technology, including the Voxware RT24 compressor/decompressor (codec) and ToolVox, for incorporation into the Netscape LiveMedia multimedia standard.

Voxware has also announced plans to release ToolVox Gold, an enhanced version of ToolVox.

ToolVox Navigator plug-ins are available for Windows 3.1 and Windows 95. Voxware also promises Macintosh and PowerMac versions. You can download these plug-ins from the Voxware site:

http://www.voxware.com/download.htm

EchoSpeech EchoSpeech compresses speech at a ratio of 18.5:1. Therefore, 16-bit speech sampled at 11,025Hz is compressed to 9,600bps. Even users with 14.4kbps modems can listen to real-time EchoSpeech audio streams. Because EchoSpeech is designed to code speech sampled at 1,1025Hz rather than 8,000Hz, EchoSpeech files sound better than ToolVox.

Real-time decoding of 11kHz speech requires only 30 percent of a 486SX-33 CPU's time. EchoSpeech plug-ins are also small—40–50K when decompressed.

No server software is required to deliver EchoSpeech content; your Internet service provider (ISP) or server administrator need only declare a new MIME type and pay a one-time $99 license fee. To add EchoSpeech files to your Web pages, you compress them with the EchoSpeech Speech Coder (available for evaluation with free downloading) and then use the HTML <EMBED> tag to include the files in your documents.

EchoSpeech is available for Windows 3.1 and Windows 95, and a Macintosh version is promised. You can get EchoSpeech from the following address:

http://www.echospeech.com

Talker and Other Macintosh Speech Plug-ins   MVP Solutions' Talker plug-in is just for the Macintosh. The plug-in uses the Macintosh's built-in PlainTalk speech-synthesis technology to create text-to-speech voice messages—in other words, Talker reads text files to you out loud. This plug-in uses much less bandwidth than recorded audio, and you can change the words that your Web page speaks by editing a text file.

Speech capability is one area in which Macintosh owners can claim a considerable edge over Windows and Windows 95 Netscape users—this plug-in simply will never work on those platforms because they lack the speech-synthesis technology of the Macintosh. You can find Talker at the following address:

http://www.mvpsolutions.com/PlugInSite/Talker.html

If you haven't yet installed Apple's English Text-to-Speech software on your Macintosh, you can download a copy of the software's installer from Apple's site:

ftp://ftp.info.apple.com/Apple.Support.Area/Apple.Software.Updates/US/Macintosh/System/PlainTalk_1.4.1/English_Text-to-Speech.sea.hqx

William H. Tudor's Speech Plug-In for the Macintosh and PowerMac does essentially the same thing as Talker. You can get Tudor's plug-in at the following address:

http://www.albany.net/~wtudor/

Macintosh plug-ins aren't limited only to talking to you—they can also listen to you and understand what you say!

Bill Noon's ListenUp is for the Power Macintosh running System 7.5 or above. The plug-in also requires the PlainTalk Speech Recognition v1.5 program. You can find out all the details and download the plug-in from the following address:

http://snow.cit.cornell.edu/noon/ListenUp.html

Digital Dream's ShockTalk speech recognition plug-in isn't a Netscape plug-in at all; it's a plug-in for the Shockwave for Director plug-in. ShockTalk is available for Macintosh and PowerMac. You can find the plug-in at the following address:

http://emf.net:80/~dreams/Hi-Res/shocktalk/

Graphics

Although Netscape Navigator displays inline GIF and JPEG images just fine, there's more to graphics than those two file formats. Besides knowing nothing about other bitmap formats such as TIFF and PNG, Navigator is completely ignorant of vector graphics formats like Computer Graphics Metafiles (CGM) and Corel's CMX. Graphics plug-ins fill that void. The real-time demands of the Internet are also pushing graphics compression to the limit, with new high-tech encoders coming out all the time. Netscape plug-ins can handle some of the latest compression techniques.

FIGleaf Inline   Bitmaps are the canvas of computer graphics. Every image that you see on your screen is a bitmap, a collection of colorful, lit pixels in a grid. Computers usually also store screen images in bitmap format. This format is, after all, the easiest way to store images, because of the one-to-one relationship between the pixels in the picture and the pixels on the screen. Netscape can handle GIF and JPEG bitmap images all by itself, but they are far from the full range of bitmap formats. Dozens—perhaps hundreds—of different bitmap formats are available on the Web. To view them, you must install the appropriate Netscape plug-ins.

Carberry Technology's FIGleaf Inline plug-in enables you to zoom, pan, and scroll both vector (CGM format) and bitmap graphics, including GIF, JPEG, TIFF, CCITT GP4, .BMP, WMF, Sun Raster, PNG, and other graphics file formats. The plug-in even handles Encapsulated PostScript (EPS) files, as well as the new proposed standard PGM and PBM file types. FIGleaf Inline can even improve the display of your GIFs and JPEGs.

The plug-in can rotate all images to 0, 90, 180, or 270 degrees, and can display multipage files. Scrollbars are available when you zoom in on an image or when the image is too large to display within the default window.

Figure 2.7 shows the FIGleaf Inline version for Windows 95. Carberry also plans to release Macintosh and Windows 3.1 versions. The self-extracting archive is big—1.5M including sample files—but in one fell swoop the plug-in practically eliminates the need for other Netscape graphics plug-ins or helper applications. If the file size disturbs you, a smaller version, FIGleaf Inline Lite, is also available.

FIG. 2.7
This tight zoom on two graphics being displayed inline by the FIGleaf plug-in demonstrates the superiority of CGM vector graphics (left) versus GIF bitmap graphics (right). Note that, because FIGleaf is now handling the display of Netscape's inline GIFs, they are zoomable as well. FIGleaf Inline is an excellent example of how plug-ins can improve even Netscape's built-in capabilities.

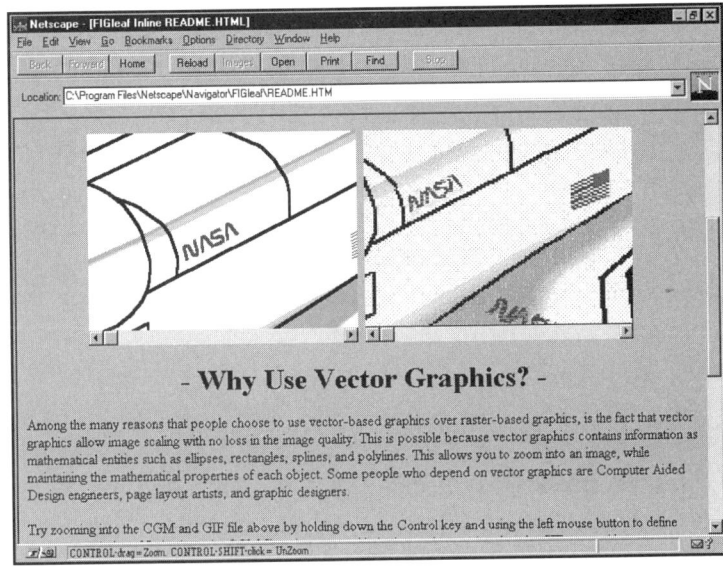

FIGleaf Inline is available for free evaluation at the following site:

http://www.ct.ebt.com/figinline/download.html

You can buy this plug-in for $19.95.

ViewDirector   The ViewDirector Imaging plug-in from TMS displays black-and-white, grayscale, and color raster images in TIFF (uncompressed, modified Huffman, G3 1&2D, and G4), CALS Type 1, JPEG, .PCX/.DCX, .BMP, and other image formats. With ViewDirector, you can zoom, pan, and rotate images embedded in Web pages. ViewDirector even enables you to enhance image quality by turning on scale-to-gray and color-smoothing functions. A professional version adds the capability to view multipage images, magnify them, and more. You can download ViewDirector, which is available for Windows 95 and Windows NT, from the following address:

http://www.tmsinc.com

AutoDesk's WHIP!   Most architects, engineers, and designers create their masterworks in AutoCAD, the *de facto* standard computer-aided drafting (CAD) program. Just about every modern manufactured object or constructed edifice that you encounter started out somewhere as an AutoCAD drawing. With the rise of the corporate intranet, there is increased interest in making these drawings available for viewing in Web browsers. Thanks to a handful of Netscape plug-ins, achieving this objective is now possible.

Although AutoDesk, the publisher of AutoCAD, was not the first developer to produce a Netscape plug-in for viewing two-dimensional (2-D) AutoCAD drawings on the Web,

AutoDesk's plug-in is almost certain to end up being the most popular. AutoDesk based its WHIP! plug-in on the same rendering technology as the WHIP! driver in AutoCAD Release 13. This technology allows for panning, zooming, and embedding URLs in AutoCAD drawings.

WHIP! uses a new DWF (Drawing Web Format) file type, which future versions of AutoCAD will support. Although WHIP! doesn't view current DXF AutoCAD files, the new file type is highly compressed and optimized for fast transfer over the Internet. Although it will take time for existing AutoCAD files to be converted to the new format, AutoDesk's promotion of WHIP! should make the plug-in very popular very quickly.

You can download WHIP! from AutoDesk's Web site:

>http://www.autodesk.com/

DWG/DXF Viewer   SoftSource's DWG/DXF plug-in is the first Netscape plug-in to enable users to view AutoCAD and DXF drawings on the Web (see fig. 2.8). Zoom, pan, and layer visibility controls make it simple to explore complex CAD drawings online. DWG/DXF Viewer's advantage over WHIP! is that it can view standard AutoCAD DXF or DWG format drawing files. Therefore, you don't have to translate existing libraries of AutoCAD drawings before you can view them.

FIG. 2.8
SoftSource's DWG/DXF plug-in makes viewing AutoCAD format drawings an online activity.

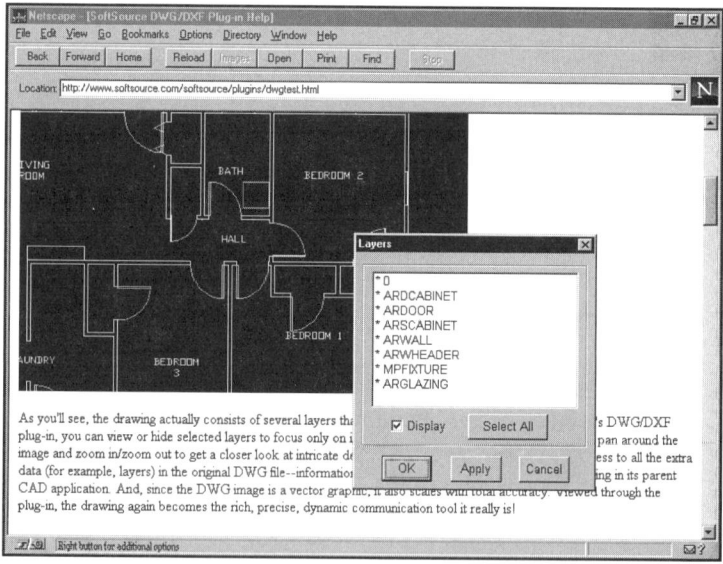

You can download DWG/DXF, which is available for Windows 95 and Windows NT, from the following site:

>http://www.softsource.com/softsource/plugins/plugins.html

N O T E European users might particularly want to check out NetSlide 95 by Alessandro Oddera, an AutoCAD file plug-in for Windows 95. NetSlide 95 is available at the following site:

http://www.prog.arch.unige.it/~aoddera/Homeao.htm

Corel CMX The problem with bitmaps is that they're chunky. Because they consist of square pixels arranged in a grid, bitmaps aren't really scalable. Where a bitmap is an actual map of a picture, a vector graphics file is more of a description of how to draw a picture. A vector graphics file tells a drawing program how to use lines, curves, fill patterns, rectangles, and other elements to re-create an image. The size at which the program draws the image is an entirely different question. For this reason, vector graphics can be rescaled to any size and retain their good looks, without losing detail.

Many vector graphics formats are available, and with the following plug-ins, Netscape can display quite a few of the formats.

CorelDRAW! is perhaps the most popular vector-graphics creation program for both the PC and the Macintosh. Corel's CMX Viewer plug-in for Navigator 2.0 enables you to view Corel CMX vector graphics in Web pages inline (see fig. 2.9). The CMX viewer currently is available only for Windows 95 and Windows NT, although Corel promises a Macintosh version.

FIG. 2.9
Corel's CMX vector graphics viewer enables you to view smooth Corel format vector graphics images inline in Navigator.

There are no special controls or considerations with the CMX Viewer—when installed, the plug-in simply displays CMX images when they are encountered. You'll enjoy watching CMX Viewer draw the pieces of the image onscreen in real time, instead of opening like a window shade as bitmap graphics do.

You can download the Corel CMX Viewer from the following site:

> http://www.corel.com/corelcmx/

Other Vector Graphics Viewers SoftSource, the creator of the DWG/DXF AutoCAD plug-in, also has its own vector graphics drawing program. The Simple Vector Format (SVF) plug-in for Netscape Navigator enables you to view vector graphics on the Web. SVF uses an officially registered MIME type and features single-download navigational capabilities and scalable vector graphics. You can pan and zoom an SVF image, and hide and display layers. SVF works similarly to SoftSource's DWG/DXF plug-in. The SVF plug-in also enables you to include HTML hyperlinks (either URLs or textual annotations) in an SVF file. The plug-in is part of SoftSource's Vdraft (Virtual Drafter) suite of Internet CAD tools. You can download both Windows 3.1 and Windows 95 versions of the SVF plug-in from the following address:

> http://www.softsource.com

You can create CGMs for use by a wide variety of programs; they're an industry standard. InterCAP Graphics Systems' InterCAP InLine plug-in is an online adaptation of the company's MetaLink RunTime CGM viewer. With InterCAP InLine, you can view, zoom, pan, and magnify an image. Animation of intelligent, hyperlinked CGM graphics is also possible. A Windows 95 and Windows NT version is available at the following site:

> http://www.intergraph.com/icap/

FutureSplash's CelAnimator is software for creating vector-based drawings and animations for multimedia and Web pages. You can use CelAnimator to create static or fully animated cartoons, logos, technical drawings, and interactive buttons. You can export these animations as FutureSplash, animated GIF, Windows .AVI, or QuickTime files. From FutureSplash's Web site you can download a free trial version of CelAnimator for Macintosh or Windows 95 and Windows NT. Although not a plug-in, CelAnimator enables you to use animated GIF, .AVI, and QuickTime files with other plug-ins.

The FutureSplash plug-in for Netscape (available for Macintosh and Windows 3.1, Windows 95, and Windows NT) enables you to view FutureSplash format animations as well. These animations are vector-based, and thus zoomable and scalable.

This plug-in is a truly unique product. With the plug-in, you can even display FutureSplash animations as they download, which enables you to begin playing long animation sequences immediately. The plug-in even supports scalable outline fonts and antialiasing to eliminate jagged edges. Interactive buttons enable you to get URLs and play animations. The plug-in is small (90–150K uncompressed). FutureSplash plans to release UNIX and Java versions.

All versions of the plug-in and CelAnimator are available from the following site:

> http://www.futurewave.com/

Lightning Strike   Graphics files can take up multimegabytes of hard disk space in no time, and seem to take an eternity to load over the Web. JPEG images are better than most graphics files, compressing some images dozens of times smaller than they started. But JPEG has its limitations, and the bandwidth demands of Web browsing have people searching for even better solutions. At least three Netscape plug-ins improve transfer times for graphics considerably.

Infinet Op's Lightning Strike plug-in competes directly with JPEG image compression. Images compressed with Lightning Strike have higher compression ratios, smaller image files, faster transmissions, and improved image quality.

JPEG uses a method based on Fourier analysis, such as discrete cosine transform (DCT). Infinet Op, however, uses a form of the wavelet transform. Lightning Strike images look as good as JPEG images and transfer quickly. It's difficult to predict whether Lightning Strike will gain a following. However, if you are into graphics, you'll definitely want to install Lightning Strike and take a look at some of the sample compressed images on Infinet Op's site. They're awesome.

Infinet Op's plug-ins for Macintosh, Windows 3.1, Windows 95, and Windows NT are available at the following site:

> http://www.infinop.com/html/extvwr_pick.html

FIF Viewer   Iterated Systems' FIF (Fractal Image Format) viewer plug-in for Navigator displays fractally compressed images inline in the Netscape window. FIF images are smaller and load faster than JPEGs, and you can scale and zoom FIF images on the page. One typical 768-by-512 image in the Iterated Systems gallery compressed from 1.15M to only 47K with remarkable fidelity.

The FIF plug-in is available for Windows 3.1, Windows 95, Windows NT, and Macintosh platforms. You can download the FIF Viewer plug-in from the following address:

> http://www.iterated.com/cnplugin.htm

Summus Wavelet Viewer   Summus' Wavelet Viewer is another plug-in for decompressing images inline that were compressed with Summus' proprietary wavelet technology.

Versions of this plug-in are currently available for Windows 3.1, Windows 95, and Windows NT at the following site:

ftp://ftp.scsn.net/software/summus/

Special Graphics Formats   Sometimes a "standard" graphics format is just not good enough. When you need a graphic to do something special, you turn to proprietary formats.

For example, Freehand is the major competitor to CorelDRAW! as the top illustration program. If your studio or company uses Freehand, you'll be glad to know that Macromedia's Shockwave for Freehand plug-in enables you to put your Freehand drawings on the Web or on your company intranet. (Don't let the name confuse you; Macromedia has given *all* its plug-ins the name Shockwave. The first plug-in was for Macromedia Director; this one is for Freehand.)

The Shockwave for Freehand plug-in enables users to view compact 24-bit vector graphics with panning and zooming up to 25,600 percent. These graphics can contain irregularly shaped hot objects that link to other Web pages.

Delivering Freehand content on the Web actually involves three modules: the Shockwave for Freehand plug-in for Netscape; the Shockwave Afterburner Xtra module, which is installed into the Freehand drawing program to compress Freehand images up to 50 percent for distribution on the Web; and the Shockwave URL Managers, which enable the designer to add URL references to hot spots on drawings. Windows 3.1, Windows 95, Windows NT, and Macintosh versions are available at the following site:

http://www.macromedia.com/Tools/Shockwave/Info/index.html

Although its end result is a graphic image, the Chemscape Chime plug-in from MDL Information Systems is more of a scientific and chemical engineering tool than a graphics plug-in. MDL Information Systems supplies chemical information-management solutions to the pharmaceutical, agrochemical, and chemical industries. The plug-in enables scientists and engineers to display "chemically significant" (that is, scientifically accurate) 2-D and 3-D structures within an HTML page or table. You can download Windows 3.1, Windows 95, Windows NT, Macintosh, and PowerMac versions from the following site:

http://www.mdli.com/chemscape/chime/download.html

Micrografx's QuickSilver is a highly popular business graphics tool. Micrografx now offers the ABC QuickSilver plug-in for Netscape. This plug-in makes QuickSilver files usable over the Web or corporate intranets. You create these vector images with ABC Graphics Suite, which can move drawings, display messages, or link to URLs. The plug-in uses a

32-bit vector graphics rendering engine for fast display. You can download the Windows 95 and Windows NT version of the plug-in at the following address:

http://www.micrografx.com/download/qsdl.html

Johnson-Grace's ART Press program creates ART image format files, which you can view online using Johnson-Grace's ART Press plug-in. The plug-in is available from the following site:

http://www.jgc.com/aip/artpub.html

America Online's TurboWeb browser already uses ART compression. Johnson-Grace claims that ART Press images download and display three times faster than GIF and JPEG images.

Lari Software's Vertigo displays pictures in GX format, which you can create by using LightningDraw GX or any other application that saves files in GX format. This plug-in performs automatic smoothing (antialiasing) and enables you to animate pictures using HTML tag spin, stretch, move, loop, and time attributes. You can download PowerPC and Macintosh versions from the following address:

http://www.larisoftware.com/Products/WebPlugin.html

WebXpresso displays 2-D and 3-D drawings, graphs, and controls. It supports real-time interaction and continuous or periodic updating from a server data stream. In addition, WebXpresso controls objects that can return data to the server. The WebXpresso Drawing Editor creates arbitrary 2-D and 3-D object hierarchies. Java Native Methods enable the client-side to manipulate graphics. Download WebXpresso and view the sample pages. For Windows 95, Windows NT, and UNIX, WebXpresso is available from the following site:

http://www.dvcorp.com

Plastic Thought's Web-Active displays dynamic 3-D images that you can rotate and tumble onscreen. You can download sample Web virtual reality (VR) files and plug-ins for Macintosh and PowerMac from the following site:

http://www.3d-active.com

Two Macintosh-only plug-ins are now available for viewing Apple QD3D (QuickTime VR) files in Netscape. John Louch's WurlPlug is available from the Apple site:

ftp://ftp.info.apple.com/Apple.Support.Area/QuickDraw3D/Test_Drive/Viewers/

You can get WebActive 3D (which promises a Windows version) at the following address:

http://www.3d-Active.com/pages/WebUtilities.html

You can create QuickTime VR scenes from photographs, video stills, or computer renderings. Most scenes consist of a series of photographs taken at 30-degree increments while turning the camera in a full circle. These photos are organized into a panorama and combined with multiframe photos of real objects taken at a variety of angles. This technology creates scenes that are quite realistic. You can find out more about the technology from Apple's Web site:

http://qtvr.quicktime.apple.com/

Video

Video plug-ins enable Netscape Navigator to play inline videos in real time. With the right plug-in, you can play Video for Windows, QuickTime, and MPEG movies.

Video for Windows Plug-Ins   Video for Windows is the standard for PC platforms. Several programs and video boards can create .AVI format animations or digitized scenes. With the following plug-ins, you can deliver such video as Web page content in Netscape.

LiveVideo   Netscape's official plug-in for .AVI video is LiveVideo, which is included with the Netscape distribution. LiveVideo automatically installs and configures as your Video for Windows player of choice. You click a movie image to play the plug-in, and click again to stop it. Right-clicking an image pops up a complete menu of controls, including Play, Pause, Rewind, Fast Forward, Frame Back, and Frame Forward. If you failed to receive this plug-in with Netscape, you can download it by following the links from Netscape's home page:

http://www.netscape.com

VDOLive   The VDOLive plug-in for Netscape enables you to include specially compressed inline Video for Windows (.AVI) clips in HTML pages, and play back the clip in real time (see fig. 2.10).

If you are operating over a slow connection, VDOLive intelligently downloads a video file and skips over enough information to retain real-time playback. In cases of severe bandwidth shortage (such as 14.4kbps PPP connections), you get a low frame rate (approximately one frame every one to three seconds) but can still view videos. In other cases, the VDOLive Player and the VDOLive Server try to converge at the best possible bandwidth, which sometimes might result in blurry display or low frame rate. Although this technique can also result in jerky playback (especially over a slow modem SLIP or PPP connection), it sure speeds up video over the Web!

Autostart, Stretch, Width, and Height options enable HTML designers to customize inline Web page video for just about any purpose.

FIG. 2.10
VDOLive displays video files inline and can deliver reasonable performance over even a very slow Internet connection.

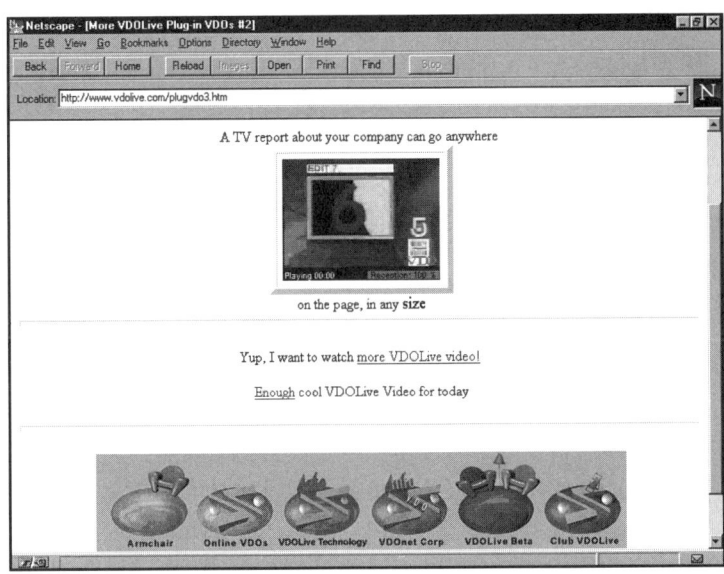

To deliver motion video from your Web server, you need the VDOLive Personal Server. The VDOLive Personal Server and Tools 1.0 enable you to deliver as many as two streams of video, to capture, compress, and serve as much as one minute of video and audio, and to scale connections as long as 256kbps.

VDOLive is available for Windows 3.1, Windows 95, and Windows NT from VDONet's site:

http://www.vdolive.com/download/

CoolFusion   Iterated Systems' CoolFusion is a plug-in for Navigator that plays inline Video for Windows (.AVI) movies. Using the plug-in, you can view videos of any size, including full screen. CoolFusion offers a full set of controls for stopping, replaying, and saving the videos.

One self-extracting archive, CF_B6_32.EXE, is for Windows 95 or Windows NT. This archive requires only a 256-color graphics card, although a 24-bit or high-color graphics adapter is recommended. You also need at least 8M of RAM.

You can download CoolFusion from the following site:

http://webber.iterated.com/coolfusn/download/cf-set32.htm

Other .AVI Video Plug-Ins   Developed as a joint venture between the University of Illinois and Digital Video Communications, Vosaic, or Video Mosaic, is another inline video plug-in. Versions are available for both Netscape and Spyglass Mosaic. Features include the capability to embed hyperlinks within the video stream, and to access other documents by clicking moving objects in the video stream. You can download Macintosh PowerPC and Windows versions from the following address:

http://vosaic.com/html/video.html

The VivoActive Player is a streaming .AVI video plug-in that uses Video for Windows .AVI files compressed up to 250:1 into a new .VIV file format. You can transmit .VIV files using the standard HTTP protocol, and thus don't need special server software to use them on your Web pages. The VivoActive Player plug-in is available for Windows 95 and Windows NT from the following site:

http://www.vivo.com

QuickTime Plug-Ins   Where Microsoft's standard video format is Video for Windows (.AVI files), Apple's video standard is QuickTime. Because many creative people use the Macintosh, many QuickTime movies are available on the Web.

Apple (**http://www.apple.com**) has had a QuickTime movie player plug-in for Netscape in the works for some time, although the plug-in still wasn't available as this book was being written. However, quite a few third-party plug-ins are available that can play QuickTime movies in Netscape.

Knowledge Engineering's MacZilla is a Macintosh-only Navigator plug-in. MacZilla is a sort of Swiss Army knife of plug-ins. Besides QuickTime movies, MacZilla plays or displays MIDI background music; .WAV, .AU, and AIFF audio; and MPEG and .AVI movies. Using its own plug-in component architecture, MacZilla can extend and update itself over the Internet with the click of a button. You even get a built-in MacZilla game! You can download MacZilla from Knowledge Engineering's site:

http://maczilla.com

MovieStar by Intelligence at Large is less ambitious—it's only for QuickTime movie playback. Using MovieStar Maker, a multimedia editing application also available for downloading, Webmasters can optimize QuickTime movies so that Navigator users can view them as they download. You can also use autoplay, looping, and many other settings. This plug-in is available for Windows 3.1, Windows 95, and Macintosh from the following site:

http://www.beingthere.com/

Three other QuickTime player plug-ins are available for Netscape: Ivan Cavero Belaunde's ViewMovie for Windows 95 and Macintosh at **http://www.well.com/~ivanski/**; TEC Solutions' TEC Player, also for Windows 95 and Macintosh, at **http://www.tecs.com/ TECPlayer_docs**; and Kevin McMurtrie's Macintosh-only Multimedia Plugin at **ftp:// ftp.wco.com/users/mcmurtri/MySoftware/**.

MPEG Plug-Ins MPEG is currently the bright and shining star of multimedia. The MPEG2 movie compression standard is destined to provide full-screen, full-motion movies on a highly compressed CD-ROM, among other things. Because of its high compression ratios, MPEG is also a good choice for delivering movies over the Internet.

MPEG works best with a video board capable of doing hardware decompression. But even running in software on fast Pentium systems, MPEG shows promise.

At least four Netscape plug-ins are available for playing inline MPEG videos.

Open2U's Action MPEG player plug-in can also play included synchronized soundtracks, or sound-only files compressed with MPEG. Action doesn't require special hardware or even a special Web server. You can download Windows 95 and Windows NT versions for trial from the following site:

http://www.open2u.com/action/action.html

InterVU's PreVU plug-in also plays streaming MPEG video without specialized MPEG hardware or a proprietary video server. This plug-in gives you a first-frame view inline, streaming viewing while downloading, and full-speed cached playback from your hard drive. PreVU requires a 486 or Pentium processor. Windows 95, Windows NT, and Macintosh versions are available. You can download PreVU from the following site:

http://www.intervu.com/download.html

Xing, well known for its MPEG applications, will be providing a Navigator plug-in to support live-streaming MPEG and low bit rate (LBR) audio and full-motion MPEG video from Xing StreamWorks Web servers. Check out Xing's Web site for availability information:

http://www.xingtech.com

Animation

Pictures that move—that wonderful concept has brought millions of children (and adults who hold onto their childlike wonder) untold hours of entertainment and enjoyment. When computers got powerful enough, animation made the move to the computer. With the advent of powerful animation-player plug-ins for Netscape, animation is making the transition to the World Wide Web and even to corporate intranets.

Sizzler Totally Hip Software's Sizzler plug-in and companion converter program enable you to create and display Web animation. The Sizzler converter (currently available only in a version for the Macintosh) converts .PIC files or QuickTime movies into sprite files that Navigator can play in real time.

Totally Hip's core technology (Object Scenario) allows for streamed delivery of several media types, including text, animation, video, sound, and interactivity. The company plans to add all these features to Sizzler soon.

The Sizzler plug-in is available as a free download for Windows 3.1, Windows 95, Windows NT, and the Macintosh, from the Totally Hip site:

> http://www.totallyhip.com/tools/Win/2f_tools.html

Emblaze   GEO Interactive Media Group's Emblaze plug-in is a real-time animation player. It plays a proprietary animation format that GEO says requires only 3M to 4M of disk space for approximately 30 minutes of play time. The animations can display at a rate of 12 to 24 frames per second in 256 colors in real time over a 14.4kbps connection. You must create the animations with the commercial Emblaze Creator program.

You can obtain Windows 3.1, Windows 95, Macintosh, and PowerMac versions at the following address:

> http://www.Geo.Inter.net/technology/emblaze/index.html

Other Animation Plug-Ins   Two more animation plug-ins for Netscape are noteworthy: Web Animator and Play3D.

Deltapoint's Web Animator is for the Macintosh only (although Deltapoint plans to release a Windows version). This plug-in combines animation, sound, and live interaction. The authoring tool for creating animations to add to your own site is also available from Deltapoint's Web site:

> http://www.deltapoint.com/animate/index.htm

Heads Off's Play3D plug-in supports real-time, interactive 3-D and 2-D sprites, and .WAV and MIDI sound playback. With this plug-in, you can link objects to URLs, media files, or Play3D "scene" files. The free demo version enables you to author and play back files without leaving Netscape. You can download Play3D, which is for Windows 95 only, from the following site:

> http://www.headsoff.com

Multimedia

Multimedia is a good buzzword, but what does it really mean? The term literally translates as *more than one medium,* but when most people use the term to refer to a presentation that includes some combination of sound, graphics, animation, video, and even interactivity. Interactivity is an important part of multimedia. It's the part that puts the flow of the whole presentation under the user's control. Although this control can be as simple as an onscreen button that the user clicks to move to the next slide, more often the user has to make selections from multiple choices.

Multimedia currently is the hottest topic on the Web, so it's not surprising that a dozen or more multimedia player plug-ins are already available for Netscape.

Shockwave for Macromedia Director   Perhaps one of the most significant and awe-inspiring plug-ins that Netscape supports directly is Macromedia Shockwave for Director (see fig. 2.11). With this plug-in, you can view Director movies directly on a Web page. (Don't confuse Director "movies" with other file types of the same name, such as QuickTime movies.) To create Director movies, you use Macromedia's Director, a cross-platform multimedia authoring program that enables multimedia developers to create fully interactive multimedia applications, or titles. Because of its interactive integration of animation, bitmap, video, and sound media, and its playback compatibility with a variety of computer platforms including Windows, Macintosh, OS/2, and SGI, Director is now the most widely used professional multimedia authoring tool.

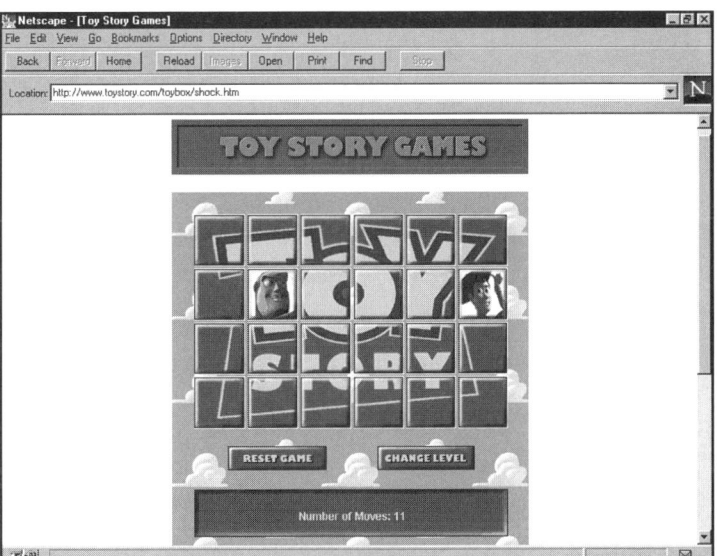

FIG. 2.11
The Shockwave for Director plug-in for Netscape plays interactive multimedia Director files inline in the Netscape window. These can range from simple animations to complex interactive games, like this "concentration" game from the *Toy Story* Web site.

A Director movie running over the Internet can support the same sort of features as a Director movie running off a CD-ROM, including animated sequences, sophisticated scripting of interactivity, user input of text right into the Director window (or "stage"), sound playback, and much more. Developers can even include hot links through URLs.

Shockwave for Director consists of two main components: the Shockwave plug-in itself, and Shockwave Afterburner, a compressor program that squeezes a Director file by 40 to

50 percent for faster access over the Internet. You can download the plug-in from Macromedia's site:

> **Shockwave http://www-1.macromedia.com/Tools/Shockwave/Plugin/plugin.cgi**

Shockwave for Authorware   Another in Macromedia's series of Shockwave plug-ins, the Shockwave for Authorware plug-in enables users to interact with Authorware interactive multimedia "courses" and "pieces" within the Netscape Navigator window. With Shockwave for Authorware, you can integrate animation, clickable buttons, links to other Web pages, hybrid layout and delivery, streaming .PICs, movies, sound, and more into a piece to deliver an interactive multimedia experience.

Intended for the delivery of large, content-rich multimedia presentations such as courseware and training materials, Authorware can also write viewer data back to a Web server using the File Transfer Protocol (FTP), so the plug-in is useful for creating market surveys, tests and quizzes, and customer service applications.

Like all Shockwave plug-ins, Authorware includes an Afterburner module. You can use this module to compress files for delivery on the Web. Authorware developers package their multimedia pieces without Runtime Project (which Macromedia usually includes with its Shockware products), then drag and drop this file onto the Authorware Afterburner program. Afterburner compresses the Authorware file by 50 to 70 percent and creates one map file and multiple segment files. Developers can optimize the number and size of segment files to the bandwidth of the network. You can also create a single map file referencing both Macintosh and Windows segment files for display in the same Web page, making platform-specific segments transparent to the viewer.

You can download Windows 3.1, Windows 95, Windows NT, and Macintosh versions of Shockwave for Authorware from the Macromedia Web site:

> **http://www.macromedia.com/Tools/Shockwave/Info/index.html**

ASAP WebShow   Software Publishing Corporation's ASAP WebShow is a Netscape Navigator 2.0 plug-in presentation viewer for viewing, downloading, and printing presentations created with ASAP WordPower. Similar to PowerPoint presentations, WordPower presentations can contain tables, organization charts, bulleted lists, and other graphics and text elements, in a slide show format. Because the files are compressed, you can transmit them quite quickly over the Internet.

You can embed presentations and reports as icons, as live thumbnails, or in a window on a Web page. Users can view each slide in a small, live window, enlarged to fill the current Web page or zoomed to full screen. You can select one slide at a time or watch a continuously running show.

A Windows 95 and Windows NT version is available, and Software Publishing Corporation also plans to offer a Windows 3.1 version. For a free 30-day trial for creating your own WebShow-compatible presentations, you can download a fully functional copy of ASAP 1.0 or ASAP WordPower 1.95 from the following site:

> http://www.spco.com/asap/asapwebs.htm

Astound Web Player   Gold Disk's Astound Web Player displays multimedia "greeting cards" and other interactive documents created with Gold Disk's Astound or Studio M programs. These presentations can include sound, animation, graphics, video, and even interactive elements.

Version 1.0 of the Astound Web Player is for Windows 95 and Navigator 2.0. Versions are also available for Windows 3.1 and for Navigator 1.1. You can even get a stand-alone version for use with browsers other than Netscape.

If you already own Studio M or Astound, you can download a "slim" version of the player that omits the chart, texture, and animation libraries. If you plan to include movies in your presentations, you need QuickTime for Windows, which is also available from the Gold Disk site.

With the Astound Web Player, you can actively view one multimedia slide while the plug-in downloads the next slide in the background. However, the main appeal of Studio M and Astound is that they enable nonprogrammers to create multimedia presentations by using predesigned templates that integrate animation, graphics, sound, and interactive elements. If you think that multimedia might be too difficult to integrate into your site, you might want to check the specifications for Studio M and Astound on Gold Disk's site:

> http://www.golddisk.com/awp/index.html

Other Multimedia Plug-Ins   Although the preceding four plug-ins are arguably the hottest multimedia plug-ins for Netscape, this section describes a few more to keep you busy.

The mBED plug-in for Netscape plays multimedia "mbedlets." The .MBD file format and the built-in mBED players are open and license-free. mBED is available for Windows 3.1, Windows 95, Windows NT, Macintosh, and PowerMac. You can download mBED and find more information about the plug-in from the following site:

> http://www.mbed.com

RAD Technologies offers RAD PowerMedia, a plug-in that plays back multimedia applications. Designed for corporate communicators and Web designers, the RAD PowerMedia plug-in provides authoring and viewing of interactive content, presentations, training, kiosks, and demos. This plug-in is available for Windows 95 and Windows NT at the following address:

http://www.rad.com

Asymetrix's ToolBook is one of the top multimedia authoring tools. With Asymetrix's new Neuron plug-in for Netscape, you can deliver ToolBook multimedia titles over the Internet. The Neuron plug-in supports external multimedia files so that you can access, in real time, either complete courseware or multimedia titles, or just the relevant portions of titles. Content does not download unless you request it, saving you download time and making the application more responsive. Check the following site for more information and the download files:

http://www.asymetrix.com/

The mFactory Netscape plug-in promises streamed playback of and communication between fully interactive multimedia worlds embedded in Web pages. mFactory supports the following file formats: for video, QuickTime, QTVR, and Video for Windows (.AVI); for graphics, PICT; for text, dynamic and editable text; for audio and sound, AIFF, SND, and MIDI; for animation, PICT, .PIC, and QuickTime. Their cel-based proprietary mToon animation format enables you to define and play ranges of cels. To find out information about downloading and more, check the following site:

http://www.mfactory.com/

7th Level offers Top Gun, a multimedia and animation authoring and playback engine for Windows 95. A Macintosh version is planned. You can read all about the plug-in at 7th Level's site:

http://www.7thlevel.com

This site is 7th Level's prototype for an Internet-based educational cartoon network.

Powersoft's media.splash plug-in for Windows 3.1 and Windows 95 resides at the following address:

http://www.powersoft.com/media.splash/product/index.html

The SCREAM inline multimedia player is for Windows 3.1, Windows 95, and Macintosh. You can find it at the following site:

http://www.savedbytech.com/sbt/Plug_In.html

Kaleida Labs also plans to offer a multimedia player plug-in for Navigator. The developer of ScriptX, an object-oriented programming language for multimedia, Kaleida currently offers a free, platform-independent Kaleida Media Player (KMP) for playback of ScriptX applications. You can configure the player as a helper application. To find out when you can get Kaleida's plug-in, check the following site:

http://www.kaleida.com

VRML Plug-Ins

VRML (Virtual Reality Modeling Language) promises to deliver real-time virtual 3-D worlds over the Web. Although it's arguable whether this objective has actually been accomplished yet, VRML's promise looms great. VRML plug-ins bring 3-D worlds right into the Navigator window.

Live3D

Silicon Graphics and Sony have developed Moving Worlds as a proposed extension to the VRML specification. Netscape and many other online developers, including heavy-hitters like Adobe and IBM, are hoping that Moving Worlds will become the VRML 2.0 standard.

Moving Worlds goes beyond the current VRML standard to include Java and JavaScript integration and support for third-party plug-ins. This integration and support enables developers to incorporate live content, such as video and RealAudio, into 3-D VRML worlds. A key new element is the ability to link to databases.

The Moving Worlds specification allows 3-D data sets to be scaleable for viewing on a variety of computer systems ranging from low-cost Internet PCs to powerful 3-D graphics workstations. You can use integrated Java applets to create motion and enable interactivity.

Advocates claim that the Moving Worlds version of VRML will finally make possible the development of real "cyberspace" applications, such as 3-D shopping malls, collaborative 3-D design, 3-D visual database and spreadsheet display, 3-D interactive real-time online games, and photorealistic geographic landscapes.

Silicon Graphics will make the source code for Moving Worlds application development available to all developers.

Netscape's Live3D Navigator plug-in is a VRML viewer that implements the proposed Moving Worlds VRML extensions. The plug-in is feature-packed, fun, and—best of all— Netscape's official VRML browser. Live3D comes bundled with Navigator 3.0 and installs automatically when you install Netscape 3.0. If you missed installing Live3D somehow, you can download it from the following site:

http://www.netscape.com/comprod/products/navigator/live3d/index.html

VR Scout

Chaco Communications' VR Scout VRML plug-in displays VRML worlds inline. Chaco's viewer implements the full VRML 1.0 standard.

VR Scout uses Microsoft Reality Lab for fast software rendering and hardware acceleration. The plug-in is multithreading, so different aspects of a scene download simultaneously. Toys include a headlight with a brightness control, and Walk/Fly/Examiner viewing modes with a heads-up toolbar. VR Scout also supports textures (GIF, JPEG, .BMP, and SFImage).

The VR Scout 1.22 plug-in is for Windows 95 and Windows NT, and its size is 2.96M. Windows 3.1 users can download a stand-alone viewer to use as a Netscape helper application. You can download VR Scout from the following site:

http://www.chaco.com/vrscout/plugin.html

WIRL

WIRL, VReam's Windows 95 VRML plug-in for Navigator, supports object behaviors (motion, rotation, gravity, weight, elasticity, throwability, and sound), logical cause-and-effect relationships, multimedia capabilities, and links to Windows applications.

WIRL's full object interactivity enables you to pick up objects and throw them around in 3-D space. This feature goes far beyond mere passive VRML viewing. Of course, a VRML world has to include the code to enable all these behaviors—you won't get to handle things in a "normal" VRML world without behavior extensions. In a nutshell, WIRL supports VRML worlds with VREAMScript interactive extensions. The plug-in uses Microsoft's Reality Lab for very fast performance—100,000 polygons per second on a 90mHz Pentium. If you're into computer graphics and programming, you might be impressed that WIRL uses real-time Gouraud and Phong Shading, real-time Z-buffering, real-time perspective corrected texture wrapping, and multiple light sources and lighting models. Under Windows, you get full Dynamic Data Exchange (DDE), ActiveX, and Media Control Interface (MCI) support. VReam promises support for multiple interface devices (mouse, head-mounted displays, gloves, and so on) for an ultrarealistic virtual reality experience.

WIRL is currently available only for Windows 95 from the current site:

http://www.vream.com/3dl1.html

Other VRML Browser Plug-Ins

Although there are more VRML plug-ins than any other type, most VRML plug-ins are fairly similar. Still, some offer a few special features. Choosing the best VRML browser (like choosing the best Web browser) is pretty much a matter of personal preference. This section lists some other VRML browser plug-ins that you might want to check out.

With SuperScape's Viscape, you can grab objects, do walkthroughs, and hear sounds in VRML worlds. Viscape is available for Windows 95 and Windows NT at the following site:

http://www.superscape.com

Integrated Data Systems' VRealm VRML plug-in also adds some features to VRML worlds, like object behaviors, gravity, collision detection, autopilot, and multimedia support. You can download VRealm, which is available for Windows 95 and Windows NT, from the following site:

http://www.ids-net.com/ids/downldpi.html

Topper supports VRML extensions for dynamic 3-D interactive worlds with keyframe animations and proximity triggers. The plug-in also supports the 3DS and DXF file formats. Windows 95 and Windows NT users can download Topper from the following site:

http://www.ktx.com/products/hyperwire/download.htm

Template Graphics Software adapted its WebSpace/VRML plug-in from Silicon Graphics' VRML browser. WebSpace supports the complete Open Inventor 2.x feature set plus the VRML 1.0 subset. You can download WebSpace, which is available for the Windows platform, from the following site:

http://www.sd.tgs.com/~template

Express VR for the Macintosh resides at the following address:

http://www.cis.upenn.edu/~brada/VRML/ExpressVR.html

You can find Liquid Reality for Windows 3.1, Windows 95, and Macintosh at the following site:

http://www.dimensionx.com/products/lr/index.html

Cybergate for Windows 95 supports multiuser interaction, chat, and avatars in VRML worlds delivered by servers equipped with Cybergate's Cyberhub server. You can find Cybergate at the following address:

http://www2.blacksun.com/beta/c-gate/download.html

Paragraph 3D for Windows 95 enables users to view ParaGraph Virtual Home Space Builder Files, which are VRML worlds that can include animations, sounds, and behaviors. You can find Paragraph 3D at the following site:

http://russia.paragraph.com/vr/d96html/download.htm

Virtus Voyager is currently a stand-alone VRML viewer, but a plug-in is promised for Netscape. You can find Virtus Voyager at the following address:

http://www.virtus.com/voyager.html

TerraForm Free is a VRML browser plug-in for Internet Explorer, although the plug-in should work with Netscape, too. For more information, check out the Brilliance Labs home page:

http://www.brlabs.com/files/terraform.zip

Productivity Plug-Ins

Productivity is a nebulous category that includes real-world tools such as word processors and spreadsheets, development systems that enable you to create your own integrated controls and programs, and miscellaneous tools such as clocks and calculators. Most of these tools are already available as Netscape plug-ins and the rest should eventually follow.

Acrobat Amber Reader

If you're like most Web users, you have many files that you would like to put on the Web. Unfortunately, the files are in a wide variety of formats, and the task of translating that much content into HTML files seems intimidating if not impossible.

Never fear. A broad spectrum of document viewer plug-ins are becoming available for Netscape. Whether your information is in the form of Word documents, Excel worksheets, Adobe Acrobat portable documents, or most any other format, the odds are good that a Netscape plug-in capable of displaying it is available—or soon will be.

Adobe's Amber version of the Acrobat Reader enables you to view and print Acrobat Portable Document Format (PDF) files. In a nutshell, PDF files are viewable documents that have the visual integrity of a desktop-published document that has been printed on paper. PDF viewers are available for UNIX, Macintosh, and Windows platforms, and each displays PDF documents identically. If the integrity of your documents is important to you (as it is, for example, to the Internal Revenue Service, which uses Acrobat to distribute accurate tax forms over the Web), PDF files are for you.

When activated, the Amber plug-in creates a dockable toolbar in the Netscape window (see fig. 2.12). The toolbar provides controls for zooming, printing, and navigating the Acrobat document.

FIG. 2.12
The Adobe Acrobat Amber PDF reader plug-in in action in Netscape Navigator 2.0. Amber provides a full set of Acrobat navigational and viewing controls.

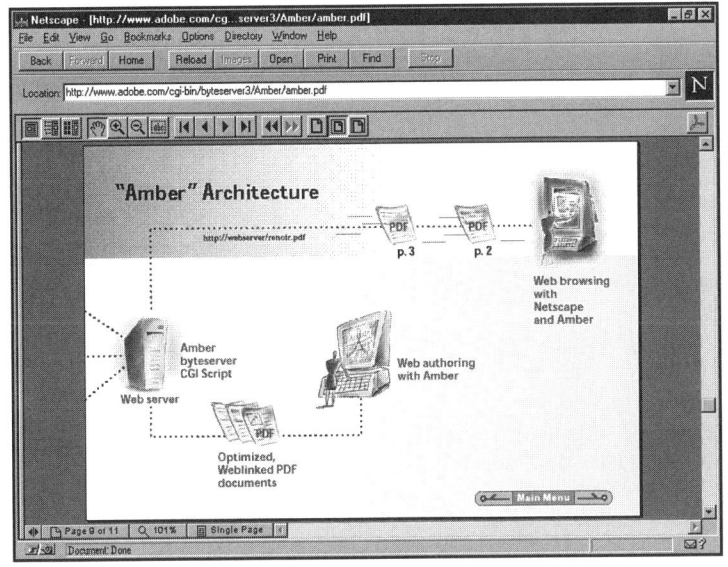

The Amber plug-in is available for Windows 3.1, Windows 95, and Macintosh; a UNIX version is in the wings. You can download Amber from the Adobe Web site:

   http://www.adobe.com/Amber/Download.html

Envoy

With Tumbleweed Software's Envoy plug-in, you can view Envoy portable documents in Navigator inline. Envoy documents, like Acrobat PDF files, maintain their look and feel no matter where or how you display them. An Envoy document is usually much smaller than the original document.

Envoy's live hypertext links enable you to jump to other URLs. Zoom features let you fit your document to the width or height of the browser and move in and out of the document from 3 percent to 2,000 percent magnification. Using buttons or the scrollbar, you can scroll or pan the display and jump to different areas of the document. Envoy even enables you to search for text strings within a document. You can use any application to create your document; you publish it in Envoy format using a custom printer driver that translates the content into an Envoy format file.

You can download the Envoy plug-in from the following address:

   http://www.twcorp.com/plugin.htm

Formula One/NET

Visual Components' Formula One/NET is an Excel-compatible spreadsheet plug-in for Navigator. The plug-in enables you to display fully functional worksheets that can include live charts, links to URLs, formatted text and numbers, calculations, and clickable buttons and controls (see fig. 2.13).

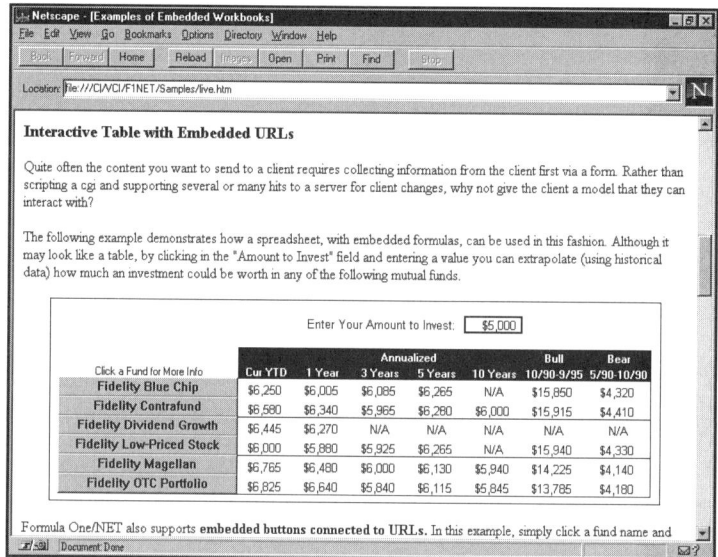

FIG. 2.13
This embedded spreadsheet displayed by the Formula One/NET plug-in looks and acts just like an Excel spreadsheet. Unlike a form, the embedded spreadsheet doesn't require that data be transmitted back and forth to a server if you make changes and want to update your calculations.

The plug-in is absolutely amazing; you can actually place the functionality of a full spreadsheet program inline in Navigator. Formula One/NET has all the fancy formulas, formatting options, and even the charts and graphs that you need to do everything from simple forms to the quarterly taxes for General Motors.

Formula One/NET is the plug-in for viewing spreadsheets, and Formula One/NET Pro adds a popup inline designer for creating them. The Pro package also comes with a stand-alone version of the program that adds the capability to read, write, and work with Excel workbook files, all for $39. An even more "professional" version of the whole works with ActiveX controls is available for $249.

Formula One/NET is available for Windows 3.1, Windows 95, or Windows NT. You can download the plug-in from the following site:

http://www.visualcomp.com/f1net/download.htm

Word Viewer

Inso's Word Viewer plug-in displays Microsoft Word for Windows 6.0 or 7.0 documents in Netscape Navigator 2.0 inline. Based on Inso's Quick View Plus viewer, this plug-in enables you to copy and print Word documents with all original formatting intact.

You can find versions for Windows 3.1, Windows 95, Windows NT, and Macintosh at the following site:

http://www.inso.com/plug.htm

KEYview

With FTP Software's KEYview Netscape plug-in, you can view, print, and convert nearly 200 different file formats. Therefore, you can use just about any file format, including Microsoft Word, WordPerfect, Microsoft Excel, EPS, .PCX, and compressed files. You can download Windows 3.1, Windows 95, and Windows NT evaluation versions from the following site:

http://www.ftp.com

The upcoming KEYviews version 5.0 promises to display even more file types, including popular multimedia formats.

Other Document Viewers

This section rounds up some of the other document viewers available as Netscape plug-ins.

PointPlus displays Microsoft PowerPoint presentations within the Netscape browser window. You can view each slide manually or display presentations automatically with the autoplay feature. For more information, check out the PointPlus home page:

http://www.net-scene.com

Not to be outdone by a third party, Microsoft has its own PowerPoint plug-in for Windows 95. This special viewer is for compressed PowerPoint files that can include audio. Microsoft has also made the publisher for these files available, so if you have PowerPoint 95, you can save slides in this new format. Even though this plug-in is from Microsoft and intended for Internet Explorer, it seems to work great with Netscape. You can download this plug-in from the following site:

http://www.microsoft.com/mspowerpoint/internet/player/default.htm

Texture Viewer plays interactive files created with the Texture program. You can find Texture Viewer, which is available for Windows 95, at the following site:

http://www.futuretense.com/viewdown.htm

Techexplorer is an exciting new Netscape plug-in from IBM. Techexplorer processes and displays a large subset of TeX/LaTeX, the professional markup language used for typesetting and publishing in education, mathematics, and many of the sciences. Tuned for onscreen readability, Techexplorer provides many options for formatting and customization. Because it formats on the fly, Techexplorer source documents are small, often just one-fourth the size of documents in Acrobat format. Techexplorer can help authors and publishers rapidly. If you publish in TeX, this plug-in enables you to put your files right on the Web. You can find Techexplorer at the following site:

http://www.ics.raleigh.ibm.com/ics/techexp.htm

Navigational Aids

The Web is huge, and it's easy to get lost. What was that site you visited early this morning that was so funny? Where did you find that info on the new model Ford cars? You read a great inside scoop on your competitor's new product, but where?

You need a plug-in to help you track, organize, and recall sites that you've visited—the more automatic the plug-in, the better. If you have this need, you'll love the plug-ins described in this section.

ISYS/Odyssey Development's ISYS HindSite remembers everywhere you've been and everything that you've seen. You can perform full-text, plain English searches on the contents of all the Web pages that you've visited. For example, to find previously accessed Web documents related to bananas, you enter **Where did I see bananas?**. HindSite indexes and saves the text content of all Web pages visited within a time frame that you set—a week, a month, or six months, for example. Menu-assisted queries enable you to build accurate queries quickly with push-button operators. ISYS HindSite can also display a structured tree outline of every previously accessed URL. HindSite is available for Windows 3.1, Windows 95, and Windows NT from the following site:

http://www.isysdev.com

Iconovex plans to release an AnchorPage client plug-in that automatically indexes and abstracts all HTML documents read by Navigator. AnchorPage is built from Iconovex's Syntactica engine, which incorporates the semantic and syntactic rules of the English language to analyze HTML documents. AnchorPage extracts the significant phrases and concepts and automatically creates the HTML links from those phrases and concepts to their occurrences within the source document. Finally, AnchorPage generates four content-driven navigation views of the documents (Table of Contents, Abstract, Phrase, and Concept). Check Iconovex's Web site for availability:

http://www.iconovex.com

HistoryTree for Windows 3.1 and Windows 95 records your Web explorations in a tree, not just a list. You can find HistoryTree at the following address:

http://www.smartbrowser.com/

DocuMagix's HotPage captures, organizes, and manages World Wide Web and intranet information and content. With DocuMagix HotPage, you can view saved Web pages offline, link back to the original sites without having to remember the exact URL, organize Web pages, and merge them with other Windows documents. You can search for a particular Web page that contains references to a particular topic, forward a Web page document by fax or e-mail within your company, mark annotations on a Web document, or even add URL links to any Windows documents. HotPage is available for Windows 3.1 and Windows 95 at the following site:

http://www.documagix.com/

Remote PC Access

Many companies use Carbon Copy, Timbuktu, or other remote access programs to enable their field service personnel to log in to remote computers for troubleshooting or control. These programs require a modem on each end and dial-up access. Now Netscape plug-in versions of both Carbon Copy and Timbuktu are available that work with any computers connected to the Internet. These programs can make your life much easier, freeing you from long-distance dial-up charges, dedicated modem lines, and dialing hassles.

Carbon Copy/Net is Microcom's plug-in version of its extremely popular Carbon Copy remote access program. In brief, Carbon Copy/Net enables you to control another PC over the Internet remotely. You can run applications, access files, and view or edit documents on a remote PC as though they were on the PC in front of you. Your screen looks like the remote PC's screen, and what you type goes to the remote computer. Carbon Copy/Net is an ideal tool for remote access to Windows applications, collaboration, remote software demonstrations, remote support, and remote file transfer access to CD-ROMs and other data. The only requirement is that both machines must be running a copy of Carbon Copy/Net, and (for security reasons) the machine that you are accessing must be set up to allow remote access. Carbon Copy/Net is currently available for Windows 3.1 and Windows 95 at the following site:

http://www.microcom.com/cc/ccdnload.htm

Not to be outdone, Farallon has released a plug-in based on its equally useful Timbuktu Pro remote access package. The plug-in, Look@Me, enables you to view another Look@Me user's screen anywhere in the world in real time. From within Navigator, you can view a remote computer screen and watch the activity taking place. You can edit documents, go over presentations, review graphics, or provide just-in-time training and support via Netscape Navigator and the World Wide Web. Look@Me is also available as a stand-alone application for use outside a browser in Windows 3.1, Windows 95, or Macintosh machines. The plug-in is available for Windows 95 only at the following site:

http://collaborate.farallon.com/www/look/download.html

Miscellaneous Tools

There's no end of things that can be implemented as Netscape plug-ins. This section describes a few miscellaneous plug-ins available for Netscape.

Starfish Software's EarthTime plug-in is a world clock that displays the local time and date in eight cities of your choice (see fig. 2.14). The plug-in features a dynamic world map that shows the day and night regions and automatically adjusts for daylight savings time. EarthTime also includes a conversion calculator that translates distances, weights, volumes, power, and other measurements between U.S. and metric measurement systems. This plug-in is handy for determining just what time of day it is at a faraway place.

FIG. 2.14
EarthTime is a world time clock plug-in for Navigator 2.0 from Starfish Software.

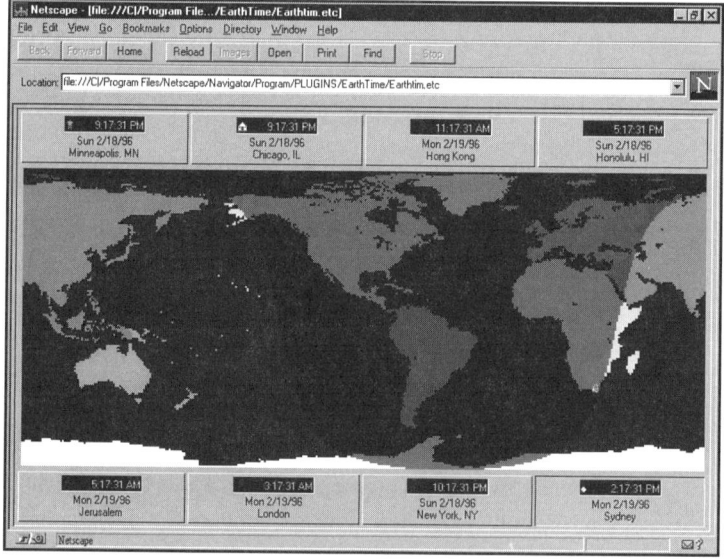

To invoke EarthTime from Navigator, you open the File menu, choose Open File (or press Ctrl+O), select the new file type EARTHTIME, .ETC from the Files of Type field, and load the file ///C|/PROGRAM FILES/NETSCAPE/NAVIGATOR/PROGRAM/PLUGINS/EARTHTIME/EARTHTIM.ETC. This invocation displays the world map shown in figure 2.14. Although a more intuitive interface (perhaps a toolbar button) would have been preferable, the world clock is still just a few keystrokes away. After you set up EarthTime once, you should bookmark it. Then you can invoke it quickly and easily just by selecting EarthTime from the Bookmark menu.

EarthTime is for the Windows 95 and Windows NT version of Netscape only. The plug-in is a self-installing file. You can get EarthTime at the following site:

http://www.starfishsoftware.com/getearth.html

The PointCast Network is a free online service that broadcasts up-to-the-minute news and other information through the Internet. The PointCast Network plug-in delivers this content inline in Netscape. The service provides headline news stories, sports, financial news (including stock indices), lifestyle stories, weather forecasts for 250 cities, and business news covering both individual companies and entire industries. The PointCast Network also includes Time-Warner's Pathfinder channel, which presents daily news from *Time, People,* and *Money* magazines. New Englanders can also find stories from the Boston *Globe* newspaper, and southern Californians have access to the Los Angeles *Times.* The PointCast Network supports live URL links in all news stories, so you can jump right to relevant Web sites. The plug-in is available for Windows 3.1 and Windows 95, with a Macintosh version under development. You can download the PointCast Network plug-in from the following site:

http://www.pointcast.com

The Argus Map Viewer displays vector-based maps composed of multiple layers of information. These dynamic, interactive, vector-based scaleable maps change based on your inquiries. With Argus Map Viewer, you can zoom in on items of interest; the plug-in then automatically redraws the map to display new and more detailed information matching the scale of view. Each item on the map is a selectable, dynamic object. Information on selected objects is viewable in reports. You also can activate URL links attached to map objects. These links take you directly to other maps, documents, images, and Web sites. Versions for Windows 3.1 and Windows 95 are available from the following site:

http://www.argusmap.com/mbr_main.htm

Globalink provides translation services and software, and has now added a truly impressive set of Web Translator Netscape plug-ins. These plug-ins perform bidirectional translation that converts between English and French, Italian, German, or Spanish. Therefore, you can translate a German-language site into English on your screen. This plug-in is a tremendous step toward making the World Wide Web truly world-wide. When you encounter a foreign site, you can simply click a button to translate the page. Translated pages maintain all graphics, hotlinks, and formatting. You can generate these translations online while surfing; alternatively, you can download and save pages and then translate and view them offline. The dictionaries for the Web Translator plug-ins have been specially prepared for use on the Web and include Internet terminology that helps ensure the translation's accuracy. Globalink's Web Translator plug-ins come on a single CD-ROM that includes both domestic and localized versions. Although Web Translator is not available as a downloadable demo, the price is only $49.95. You can get further information from Globalink's Web site:

http://www.globalink.com

With the JetForm Filler plug-in, you can fill in online forms that have been designed using JetForm Design, a commercial product from JetForm. Windows 3.1, Windows 95, and Macintosh versions are planned. Check out the following site for more information on this product:

http://www.jetform.com/

Alpha Software's Concerto plug-in also adds form data-entry capabilities to Netscape Navigator. You can use Concerto to connect to any existing CGI script that processes a Web-based form. A Concerto-enabled Web site operates faster than a traditional forms-based site, because the client browser, not the server, validates all data locally. Concerto includes validation rules that can apply to all its data-entry controls to require users to enter data into certain fields, to show or hide fields, to validate credit card numbers, and to use masks and templates. Concerto is available for Windows 95 only. You can download Concerto and check out some samples at the following address:

http://www.alphasoftware.com

To enable users to download, decompress, and install software from your site simply by clicking a link, try 20/20 Software's NET-Install plug-in. 20/20 designed this installation plug-in specifically for distributing software from Web pages. Versions are available for Windows 3.1, Windows 95, and Windows NT at the following site:

http://www.twenty.com

Interestingly, Netscape Communications Corporation's official Internet relay chat (IRC) solution is a helper application rather than a plug-in. Although the Netscape Chat application autoconfigures, it's a separate program. If you want to do your IRC chatting inline in the Netscape window, you need the ichat IRC Plug-In for Windows. After you install ichat, Web pages can become chat rooms. When you visit a chat-enabled Web page, the plug-in opens a frame in the lower part of the browser window. Within that frame, ichat displays a real-time, ongoing chat session among all visitors to that page. Users can enter the conversation and communicate with each other simply by typing. ichat is a hot product; you can expect to see Netscape trying to catch up soon. You can find ichat at the following site:

http://www.ichat.com/

Groupware Applications

Groupware is software that enables people in groups (usually on corporate intranets) to exchange information and to collaborate on projects. It currently is one of the hottest areas of software development. Already a couple of Netscape plug-ins are available that can be classified as legitimate, powerful groupware applications.

Lotus Notes is the best-established groupware solution for corporations. Brainstorm Technology's Groupscape is a visual, object-oriented development tool for building and extending Lotus Notes workgroup applications to the Web. With this plug-in, an organization can standardize on Netscape as the front-end to both the World Wide Web and the organization's existing Lotus Notes infrastructure. For corporate users, Groupscape is as easy to use as Netscape clients and offers the security and replication strengths of Lotus Notes.

To demonstrate Groupscape's capabilities, Brainstorm has released the free Groupscape Notes Browser, an interactive Netscape and Groupscape application that enables corporate users to view, browse, and surf internal Lotus Notes networks. This plug-in provides a sample of the types of applications that you can build with Groupscape. The Groupscape standard development system costs $995 per developer with no run-time fees, but the Notes Browser is free for downloading. You can find it at the following site:

>   http://www.braintech.com/gscape.htm

Galacticomm Worldgroup, for Windows 3.1 and Windows 95, is a Netscape plug-in that supports dozens of off-the-shelf groupware applications. These applications range from real-time video conferencing to online fax-back services, questionnaires with graphed results, and more. Worldgroup's focus is on information, commerce, multimedia databases, and other real-world, corporate-level solutions. The plug-in supports secure buying and selling through the Web, forms management, powerful document searching, and more.

Galacticomm has an impressive list of high-profile clients in business, industry, and government. If you're looking to bring your big business onto the Web in a big way, with more than just a set of Web pages for the public to peruse, you should look into Worldgroup. You can find more information and download the plug-in from the following site:

>   http://www.gcomm.com/show/plugin.html

ActiveX

If you can't find a plug-in that does what you need, you can always write your own from scratch. You can find online information about the Netscape plug-ins software developer's kit (SDK) at the Netscape site:

http://www.netscape.com

However, other solutions are available. If you're mainly concerned about delivering to all types of Windows platforms, several plug-ins enable you to launch ActiveX applications inline in Netscape.

ExCITE's NCompass division has created a Navigator plug-in for Windows 95 with which you can embed ActiveX controls as applets created with standard programming languages and development tools, such as Visual C++, Visual Basic, and the Microsoft Windows Game SDK.

With the ActiveX Control plug-in, a software developer can create a version of any Windows ActiveX-compliant program customized for use with Netscape and the Web. For example, you can create games, investment programs, multimedia players, and just about anything else for Windows, and then compile the programs in a version for the Web.

Because ActiveX plug-ins use compiled native Windows code, Internet applications can run just as quickly as stand-alone Windows 95 applications while also supporting data exchange and data updating over the Web.

NCompass provides several examples on its Web site, including a multiplayer DirectX game, a real-time OpenGL rendering of a robot arm, inline .AVI movie player control, and more (see fig. 2.15).

FIG. 2.15
A Windows 95 program running in the Netscape window, courtesy of NCompass's ActiveX plug-in.

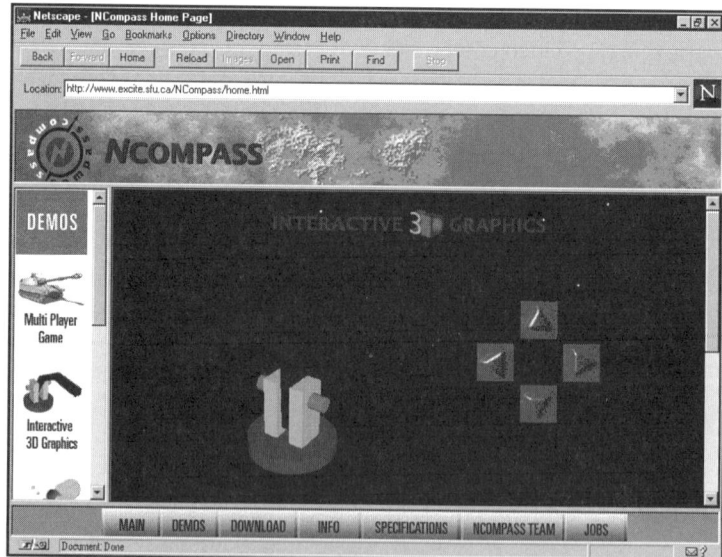

The ActiveX plug-in requires a 486 DX33 with 8M RAM, 14.4K Internet connection, and Windows 95 or Windows NT. You can download the plug-in from the following site:

http://www.excite.sfu.ca/NCompass/nchome.html

OpenScape

Business@Web's OpenScape plug-in is similar to NCompass's ActiveX plug-in in that it enables developers to create ActiveX-compatible applications that run inline in Netscape over the Web. However, to create OpenScape applications, you must use the OpenScape development system rather than Visual Basic or C++.

Four versions of the OpenScape product are available for actually creating the applications that the OpenScape plug-in runs. Use OpenScape if you want to build Web pages using Visual Basic-style tools. Then you can create reusable and customizable OCXs with a Visual Basic-compatible scripting language. You can also use OpenScape to create stand-alone desktop applications with embedded OCXs, ActiveX servers, and DLLs. With OpenScape Professional, you can actually create OCXs and ActiveX servers. OpenScape Workgroup is for creating applications that you can distribute securely across a network. Finally, OpenScape Enterprise is for large, corporate development work.

The OpenScape Navigator plug-in is currently downloadable for Windows 3.1, Windows 95, and Windows NT from the following site:

http://www.busweb.com/download/f_down.html

QuickServer

Wayfarer Communications' QuickServer is for high-performance intranet and Internet client/server applications developed with Visual Basic, PowerBuilder, C++, and Java. Using this plug-in, applications developers can build the client component of Internet applications using the leading development tools and run them inside Netscape Navigator. QuickServer reduces development time by leveraging leading client/server development tools, such as Visual Basic, PowerBuilder, Visual C++, Delphi, and Java, and by simplifying communications programming.

You can download the 30-day evaluation version of the QuickServer SDK. Also available for downloading is StockWatcher, a demo application written in Visual Basic that uses Wayfarer's plug-in. StockWatcher displays live, dynamic stock quotes inside Netscape Navigator. The QuickServer SDK and StockWatcher are both for Windows 95 and Windows NT, and are available at the following site:

http://www.wayfarer.com/

WinFrame

Citrix Systems' WinFrame plug-in for Windows 3.1 and Windows 95 enables you to execute Windows programs over the Internet. With the WinFrame client, you can publish applications as easily as you publish Web documents. Just download this plug-in, run the setup program, and try WinFrame for yourself on such standard Windows applications as Microsoft Access, Lotus Notes, and Adobe Acrobat. WinFrame is available at the following site:

> http://www.citrix.com

WebBASIC

You can also create Internet applets with Visual Basic for Applications (VBA) and Amara's WebBASIC API. WebBASIC is a simple, low-bandwidth, and low-end applet development system. The plug-in is available for Windows 3.1, Windows 95, and Windows NT. You can find WebBASIC, along with several demos created in WebBASIC, at the following site:

> http://www.inetnow.net/~webbasic/webbasic.html

CHAPTER 3

Creating Plug-In Content for the World Wide Web

- **How to physically put plug-in-compatible content on your Web pages**

  This process involves more than just using the <EMBED> tag.

- **What kinds of information are most suitable for presentation through plug-ins rather than straight HTML**

  More types of information are appropriate than just multimedia.

- **How to create and present that content**

  The tools vary depending on content type.

Video, audio, multimedia, and interactive applications can liven up your Web pages. They attract and involve your audience in a way that simple text and static graphics can't. Of course, to present inline interactive multimedia elements, you must create and deliver a whole new kind of page content that browser programs cannot display if they understand only HTML. Only plug-in-capable browsers can display such a wide variety of multimedia content.

Although plug-in-compatible content integrates almost seamlessly into your Web pages, developing and delivering that content involves steps that are quite different than those involved in creating straight HTML pages. To create each type of content—audio, video, animation, MIDI music, and so on—you must use a different program specifically designed to create that type of content. Likewise, to display each type of content, you have to use a different browser plug-in.

http://www.mcp.com/que

Throughout this chapter, you learn how plug-in content compares and contrasts with "normal" Web page content and how presentation style and format relate to information. ■

Creating Web Page Content

You don't actually "create" headings, tables, forms, and other standard Web page HTML elements. Instead, a browser program creates them on the fly. You merely mark up elements in a text file, which the browser uses as a guideline for picking the fonts, colors, lines, and other elements that it then assembles into a viewable document. Although you should put some thought and effort into how various browser programs present your page, your role in creating HTML content is mostly that of supplying and prioritizing information, not defining look and feel.

Page Design versus Content

In recent versions of Netscape Navigator, Microsoft Internet Explorer, and other Web browser programs, HTML extensions give Web page creators a degree of control over the look and feel of their Web pages that goes well beyond the intentions of the original definers of HTML.

Originally, HTML was intended, as its name implies, to be a HyperText Markup Language—that is, a language with which you can mark up text so that it can be properly interpreted and displayed by a wide variety of different user platforms, from text-only terminals to 16-million color, high-resolution graphics displays.

HTML elements, or tags, were intended only to indicate which parts of a file are headings, which are body text, and so on, so that individual browser programs can format and display that information properly on the machine on which they are running. For this reason, logical formatting tags like <STRONG> are traditionally preferred over physical formatting tags like <B> (bold) or <I> (italics).

Unfortunately, HTML has evolved into what might more accurately be called a page description language rather than a markup language. Like a desktop publishing (DTP) program, new extensions to HTML enable Web page designers to define everything from background graphics and colors to font sizes and typefaces. Although these capabilities enable designers to create more attractive Web pages, they "break" HTML by making pages browser-specific. For example, someone running the all-text browser Lynx on a monochrome UNIX workstation has difficulty reading Web pages that use many Netscape-specific markup tags to present a full-color display.

The HTML v3.0 standard, now being defined by the World Wide Web Consortium (W3C), makes a concerted effort to return HTML to its roots. To do so, W3C is divorcing browser-specific design elements from the HTML core by incorporating *style sheets*. Style sheets pull out color, font, and other DTP-type layout information from the core HTML document and then place that information in a separate file. Browsers that can handle the styles that the style sheet defines can use that information to paint a page that contains all the fancy elements that the sheet defines. Even if a browser doesn't support such elements, it still can display the core page content more easily.

The proposed style sheet definition is available online at the following site:

http://www.w3.org/pub/WWW/TR/WD-style

Figure 3.1 shows the WWW Consortium's specification for style sheets.

FIG. 3.1
The World Wide Web Consortium's new style sheet specification is available online.

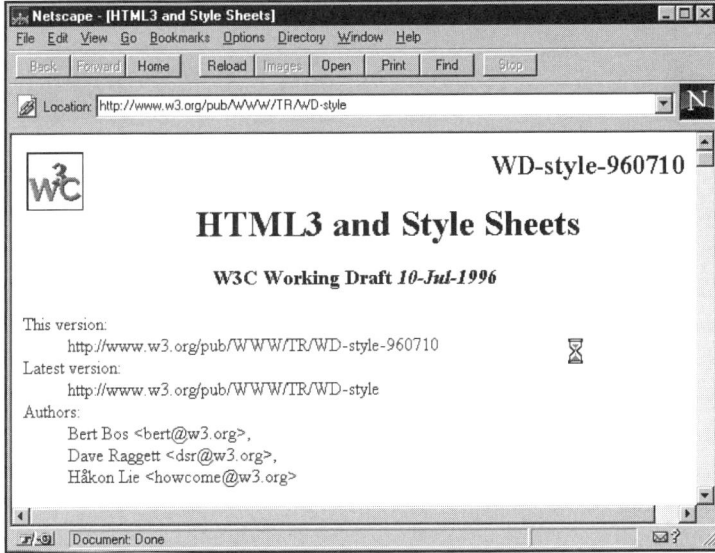

Let's hope the Web community will fully support this effort to make the Web accessible to everyone, not just those with specific browser programs.

The <IMG> Tag

One type of standard Web page element *is* created and delivered just like plug-in content: inline GIF and JPEG graphics. When you include a graphic on a Web page, you first create it in a separate, stand-alone paint program, and then use the <IMG> tag to incorporate the graphic into your HTML code (see fig. 3.2).

FIG. 3.2
Inline graphics are an integral part of almost every page on the Web. To insert them inline, you use the HTML <IMG> tag.

For example, if you want to include a title graphic on your site, you load up a paint program, create the graphic, and then save it as a GIF or JPEG file. To display on your Web page the image TITLE.GIF, for example, you include the following line of HTML code:

```
<IMG SRC="title.gif">
```

Plug-in-compatible content works the same way—you first create your content file in a separate, stand-alone development program, then incorporate it into your HTML code. However, plug-ins use the <EMBED> tag rather than <IMG>.

The <EMBED> Tag

To present live objects inline on a Web page, you use the <EMBED> tag. Netscape Navigator, Microsoft Internet Explorer, and several other popular Web browser programs support this relatively new, nonofficial HTML extension.

Here is a typical use of `<EMBED>`:

```
<EMBED SRC="video.avi" WIDTH=100 HEIGHT=200 AUTOSTART=TRUE LOOP=TRUE>
```

This line of HTML code embeds a Video for Windows movie, VIDEO.AVI, in the Web page. When the page displays, the plug-in configured for playing .AVI files launches invisibly in the background. The `WIDTH` and `HEIGHT` attributes create a playback area 100 pixels wide and 200 pixels high in the browser window. The `AUTOSTART=TRUE` command starts the video playing automatically, and the `LOOP=TRUE` attribute indicates that the video should play in a loop until stopped. In this example, the `<EMBED>` tag's `AUTOSTART` and `LOOP` attributes are defined for this specific plug-in. (This generic sample plug-in is available on the Netscape site at **http://www.netscape.com/comprod/development_partners/plugin_api/win_avi_sample.html**.) Each real-world plug-in has its own attribute syntax for the `<EMBED>` tag, which the plug-in's publisher defines.

Embedding ActiveX Objects

Since Netscape 1.1, the `<EMBED>` tag has been in use for another purpose—embedding Windows ActiveX objects. Here's an example:

```
<EMBED SRC="sample.txt">
```

When viewed with a Windows browser, this example places a text file icon on the displayed Web page (see fig. 3.1). When double-clicked, the icon launches the defined ActiveX program for the file type .TXT, which is usually Notepad.

FIG. 3.3
Using the `<EMBED>` tag to incorporate OLE objects, rather than plug-in content, on a Web page.

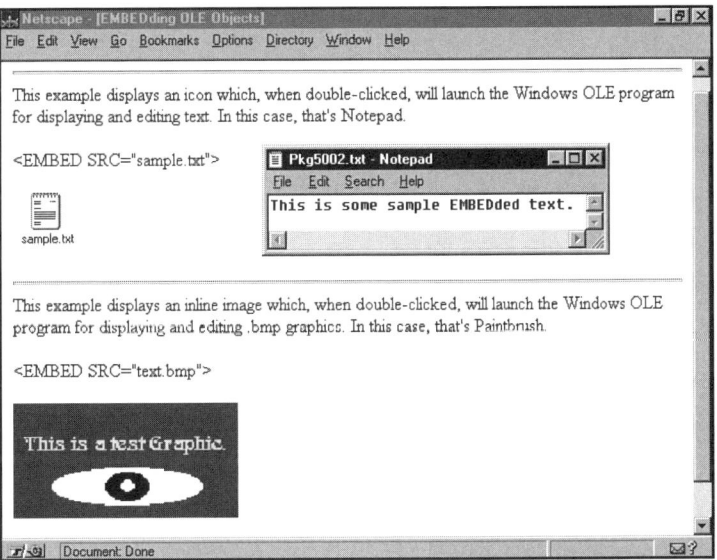

ActiveX drivers—or Object Linking and Embedding (OLE)drivers—are automatically installed when you install Windows, Windows 95, or Windows NT. You can configure these drivers as a part of your Windows setup.

You can also use the WIDTH and HEIGHT tags when displaying images with the <EMBED> tag. The following is an example of embedding a .BMP file that is an embedded object:

```
<EMBED SRC="test.bmp" WIDTH=200 HEIGHT=100>
```

If no plug-in or helper application has been defined for handling .BMP files, this .BMP image displays inline on the page just as though you included the image by using the <IMG> tag. However, when double-clicked, the image launches the OLE editor for .BMP images, which by default is Paintbrush.

In this type of usage, the <EMBED> tag acts more like an automatic helper application launcher than a plug-in launcher. The ActiveX applications launched by this use of <EMBED> are external applications, like helper applications; the only difference is that Windows itself—not the Netscape Helper setup dialog box—defines the applications.

Embedding Inline Content

An <EMBED> tag line in an HTML document must include the SRC attribute, which specifies the URL of the file to load, as well as the WIDTH and HEIGHT of the window that is to display the plug-in. You can also optionally specify PALETTE and PLUGINSPAGE values, as well as additional attributes specific to individual plug-ins. Here's the syntax for a generic <EMBED> tag call:

```
<EMBED SRC="URL" WIDTH=n HEIGHT=n [PALETTE=FOREGROUND¦BACKGROUND]
[PLUGINSPAGE="URL"]>
```

SRC="URL" specifies the URL of the data file to include when the HTML document is viewed. This attribute is required.

WIDTH=n and HEIGHT=n determines the width and height of the plug-in display window, where n is a value in pixels. This attribute is also required.

PALETTE=FOREGROUND¦BACKGROUND is optional. You should specify *either* FOREGROUND or BACKGROUND as the value for PALETTE. When more than one plug-in is on a page that uses a palette, you should use the PALETTE attribute to indicate which plug-in takes palette precedence—that is, which plug-in sets the page's palette. The <EMBED> tag call for this plug-in should have the attribute PALETTE=FOREGROUND. All other plug-in <EMBED> calls on the page should define PALETTE=BACKGROUND. If you don't specify the PALETTE attribute, PALETTE=BACKGROUND is assumed.

`PLUGINSPAGE="URL"` defines the URL of the page from which a plug-in can be downloaded for the current file type. If a user accesses your Web page but hasn't installed a plug-in for the file type that you specify in your `<EMBED>` tag, the `PLUGINSPAGE` attribute enables Netscape to jump right to the page from which the appropriate plug-in can be downloaded and installed. Although optional, the `PLUGINSPAGE` attribute is a godsend for users, enabling them always to view your plug-in content with relatively few hassles.

Each individual plug-in almost always also includes some optional attributes designed specifically for that plug-in. The preceding example includes `AUTOSTART` and `LOOP` attributes, which are appropriate for a Video for Windows movie player. Other plug-ins include their own optional attributes. The only way to know what these attributes are and how you should use them is to check each plug-in's documentation or section in this book.

Linking Content

You can also call plug-ins through normal HTML links. For example, the following HTML line links to a stand-alone .AVI video file:

```
<A HREF="birdfly.avi">Click here to see flying birds!</A>
```

This simple link provides a linked line of text that, when clicked, jumps to a new browser page that contains only the Video for Windows file BIRDFLY.AVI. Although not as elegant as embedded content, placing plug-in content on its own page is perfectly acceptable, and can be the preferred method if the required display window or the content file is large. The technique is especially appropriate for linking to .WRL VRML "world" files, which often require the whole browser window to display properly.

If you have installed the NCompass ActiveX plug-in in Netscape, or if you're using Internet Explorer (which has built-in ActiveX support), you can even use links to Excel, PowerPoint, Word, and other documents to display them in your browser window, complete with full editing toolbars (see fig. 3.4).

Although figure 3.4 shows Internet Explorer, you could also invoke Word in Netscape. If you did so, Netscape would call the NCompass ActiveX plug-in and then display the Word document in a manner identical to Internet Explorer. Here's the line of HTML that brought this Word document into the browser:

```
<A HREF="chap11.doc">Click here to display Chapter 11</A>
```

FIG. 3.4
Linking to a Word document from an HTML page results in this display, with Word embedded in Internet Explorer.

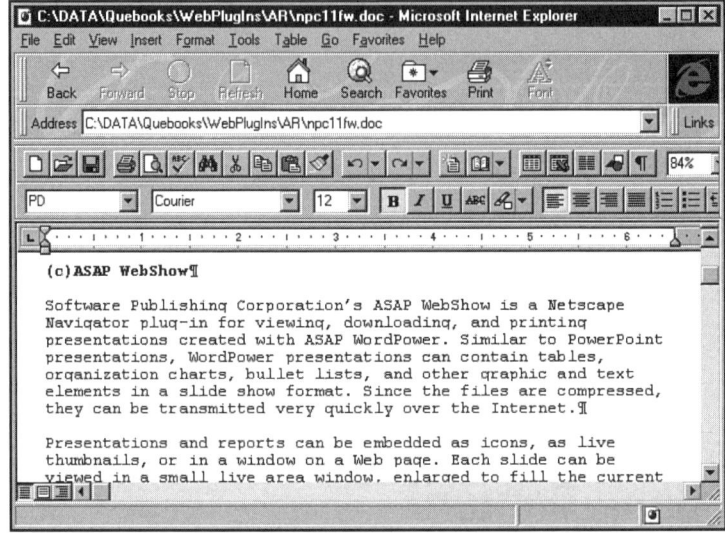

The <*OBJECT*> Tag

The W3 Consortium is working with IBM, Microsoft, Netscape, Spyglass, and Sun Microsystems to establish a standard way to insert live objects into Web pages for the coming HTML 3.0 standard.

The new standard will allow multiple implementations of the same object as, for example, a Java applet, an .AVI movie, and an OLE object. The browser will be able to pick content that matches its capabilities. This standard will go a long way toward making every Web site accessible to every browser program, instead of requiring developers to set up pages to suit a particular brand of browser.

To implement this standard for live content, you use the new HTML 3.0 <OBJECT> tag. (The newer <OBJECT> tag supersedes the previously proposed HTML 3.0 tag <INSERT>.) <OBJECT>, which will replace the <IMG> or <EMBED> tag, enables the Web designer to insert a variety of objects. A full set of attributes provides a wide range of flexibility for presenting multimedia content:

```
<OBJECT DATA=TheEarth.avi TYPE="application/avi">
<IMG SRC=TheEarth.gif ALT="The Earth">
</OBJECT>
```

Note that the TYPE parameter indicates the MIME type of the content file whose URL is defined in the DATA parameter. <OBJECT> is a container, so it also has a closing </OBJECT> tag. In between the <OBJECT> container tags, you place alternate content—in this example, a GIF image with an ALT parameter defining alternate text of its own.

The result is that this example displays the text *The Earth* on a text-only browser such as Lynx, the image THEEARTH.GIF on a graphics browser, and the Video for Windows movie THEEARTH.AVI on a browser enabled with an .AVI movie player plug-in.

The <OBJECT> tag will be versatile enough to define client-side image maps, present overlapping objects, and include multimedia content.

Microsoft Internet Explorer already supports the <OBJECT> tag, and Netscape Navigator will surely add it in the future if it becomes a part of the official HTML standard.

You can find the full specification for the <OBJECT> tag at the following site:

http://www.w3.org/pub/WWW/TR/WD-object.html

Server Issues

Before you can use your Web server to deliver plug-in-compatible content, you must configure your server to deliver the proper MIME data type. Depending on the type of content that you're delivering, you might even have to install a custom server program.

Setting MIME Types

The HyperText Transfer Protocol (HTTP) is the defined protocol for delivering Web page content over the Internet. Web server computers use HTTP to send packets of Web page data over the Internet to a user's Web browser program, which then interprets and displays that data as Web pages.

Under HTTP, each separate block of data is invisibly preceded by its MIME type. The browser program uses this MIME type definition to determine how to interpret the subsequent block of data. If a plug-in has been defined to handle the data type indicated in the MIME type definition, the browser launches the appropriate plug-in before trying to display the data.

Therefore, you must configure a server to know and send the proper MIME type before it can send plug-in-compatible data. For example, if your Web site is going to include MIDI music files, you must set up your Web server to send the proper MIME type header before delivering the actual MIDI file. Otherwise, your viewers' browser programs don't know when to launch their MIDI plug-in.

Here's a typical Web server setting for delivering MIDI content files:

```
MIME type = audio/midi or audio/x-midi or application/x-midi or
audio/x-mid
action = binary
suffix = .mid
type = midi
```

This particular example defines four different MIME types: `audio/midi`, `audio/x-midi`, `application/x-midi`, and `audio/x-mid`. The file name extension that the example defines for MIDI files is .MID. Whenever a Web page that this server delivers embeds a file type with the file name extension .MID, the Web server sends a MIME type header that contains the four MIME types defined for MIDI files. The browser on the other end must use this MIME type header to determine which plug-in that it must use to play the data that the associated .MID file contains.

You have to include this information in your Web server software's setup file for MIME type information. How you do so depends on the specific server software that you are using.

> **NOTE** When the user installs a plug-in, the browser program automatically determines which plug-in is associated with which MIME type. If you choose Help, About Plug-Ins from the Netscape menu, you see a page that shows you which MIME types are set up to launch which plug-ins.

If you set up your Web site through an Internet service provider (ISP), you must inform it that you want to deliver content of a certain type or types. You also must provide the MIME configuration information that the ISP needs to set up its Web server files properly, if it hasn't already done so.

If your company or institution runs its own server, you must contact your system administrator to set up the MIME types for you. If you run your own Web server, you must set them up yourself. Netscape Corporation offers extensive online documentation to assist you in setting MIME types for its servers. You can find this documentation at the following site:

> **http://home.netscape.com/comprod/server_central/support/index.html**

Figure 3.5 shows this site's initial page.

Consider the real-world example of setting up the MIME type in the Netscape Communications Server to deliver RealAudio files. First, you would edit Netscape Communications Server's MIME.TYPES file by adding the following line:

```
type=audio/x-pn-realaudio    exts=ra,ram
```

To the Communications Server's main configuration file (MAGNUS.CONF in the examples provided in the Netscape Communication Server's documentation), you add the following line:

```
Init fn=load-types mime-types=mime.types
```

FIG. 3.5
For help with all aspects of configuring Netscape servers, check out the extensive technical documentation on Netscape's Web site.

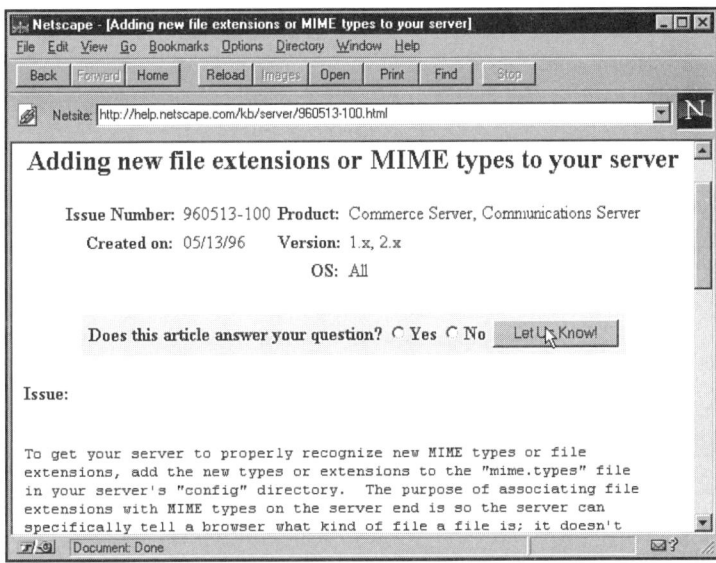

After changing both files, you reinitialize the Web server to activate the changes.

In any case, each plug-in that this book discusses includes documentation that specifies the MIME type definition for the type of content with which it deals. You must define that MIME type for your Web server software. The procedure for defining MIME types for any particular Web server is explained in the server's documentation; including specific information on the steps involved in setting up MIME types for every available server is beyond this book's scope. While discussing each plug-in, this book provides information on the plug-in's MIME type definition. But refer to your Web server documentation for an explanation of how to set up specific MIME types for your particular brand of Web server software.

Installing Content Servers

After you set up the MIME type, a Web server program can deliver most plug-in-compatible content just as though it were text, GIF graphics, or other standard Web page content.

However, some plug-in content—particularly files that must be sent as continuously streamed data—might require a custom content server program.

Your Web server already uses several custom content server programs. The Web server itself is a HyperText Transfer Protocol Daemon (HTTPD)—a program designed to deliver content that conforms to the HTTP standard (in other words, Web pages). However, most Web server computers cede control to other server programs for other types of content. For example, if a Netscape user calls up the Netscape mail client, the Web server switches control to a mail server program that can handle mail data. If the user invokes Netscape's built-in newsreader, the Web server switches in a news server.

> **CAUTION**
>
> Remember that special content server programs use up disk space, memory, CPU time, and other resources on your server computer. Don't overload your server with too many special content server programs.

Although these processes are invisible to the user, you must set up a Web server computer properly to make the switch to a news, mail, or other content server program smoothly and automatically when necessary.

Some plug-ins also require that you install and configure special data servers on your Web server computer. RealAudio is a prime example. Because RealAudio files must be delivered in real-time, without breaks or interruptions, a Web server must use a special server program to deliver RealAudio content. When a Web page includes a RealAudio file, the Web server program simply switches control to the RealAudio server. When the RealAudio file finishes downloading, control returns to the Web server program.

RealAudio files must be delivered in real time, so for a site to deliver RealAudio content, you or your system administrator must install and configure a RealAudio server program on your Web server computer.

So far, perhaps a half dozen plug-in-compatible data types require their own specialized server software program. When discussing a plug-in that requires installation of special server software, this book tells you how to install the software.

Limitations on Plug-In Content

Many real-world factors place a practical limit on what kinds of plug-in-compatible content that you can use on your site. File size (mainly a concern in regard to throughput over dial-up connections) and browser compatibility are certainly two primary considerations. Another issue is good content versus good appearance, and how that issue helps determine which plug-ins are best for your site. There's the issue of the sheer number of plug-ins that are available, and how you quickly run into the practical problem of how many plug-ins you can install. Finally, some plug-ins are simply not available for some operating systems—most plug-ins are available for Windows or Windows 95, for example, but many do not come in Macintosh or UNIX versions. This section discusses all these issues.

File Size and Dial-Up Connections

When developing plug-in-compatible content for delivery over the World Wide Web, a prime consideration is *bandwidth*, or how much data you can deliver to your audience in a given amount of time.

Under ideal conditions, users with fast, direct, dedicated T1 or T3 landline connections have no problem viewing real-time videos or listening to real-time audio broadcasts. Systems with such connections can even display interactive multimedia presentations within a reasonable amount of time.

However, conditions on the Internet are often less than ideal. Lockups and delays over the Internet backbone can affect all users, no matter how fast their personal connections. You can't do anything to address such conditions. However, these conditions affect standard HTML text and GIF graphics just as much as plug-in-compatible multimedia content. For this reason, you shouldn't bother trying to make special adjustments to handle "backbone trouble" simply because your site is content-rich. Even text-only sites are in the same boat if the performance of the entire Internet is pulled down.

About all you can do is lobby for more and faster connections on the Internet backbone, which are becoming increasingly available anyway. The problem is that the demand for Internet data—particularly the World Wide Web—has far outstripped the Internet's physical structure. It will probably be playing catch-up for years.

However, you can do something about one other cause of slow content delivery: Web server overload. If your site is so popular that your server can't keep up, you can add (or lobby your ISP to add) more lines, faster computers, more computers, and so on, to try to keep up with demand.

Users connecting to your site through dial-up connections will have problems viewing huge files of any type. Over a standard 14.4kbps (kilobit per second) or 28.8kbps dial-up connection, even large GIF and JPEG graphics can take several minutes to load. Pages that are extremely graphics-rich can take 15 minutes or more to download over such slow connections.

Multiply the problem by a factor of 10 or even 100 for video and multimedia content, and you begin to see that plug-in-compatible content is not usually a realistic option for users connecting to the Web through a dial-up connection.

However, remember that the real issue is file size, not content. If a MIDI music file consists of only a couple of kilobytes, it is a good candidate for delivery even over dial-up lines. Even slow dial-up connections can receive RealAudio files with low sampling rates in real time. Videos and even multimedia presentations are not totally out of the question, either, as long as your viewers are willing to wait for them to download first—you can't stream such content for viewing in real time. The issue is whether the content is worth the wait.

 TIP Think small! If you're thinking of using a video, try a still graphic or small animation in combination with a small sound file instead. The result might be almost as impressive as a video and will run smoother over slow connections.

If you consider your audience, you can easily determine the types of content that you can provide. If your viewers are likely to be connecting from university, corporate, or government sites with direct Internet links, bandwidth usually isn't an issue, and your Web pages can incorporate almost any type of content. On the other hand, if most of your viewers are likely to be connecting to the Internet through dial-up lines from home or through online services, your Web pages should be sparser, with smaller files that can be viewed in a reasonable amount of time over a slow dial-up connection.

A good rule of thumb is that a 14.4kbps dial-up can read a maximum of about 1.7K (kilobytes) of data per second from the Internet. Therefore, a 25K file takes about 15 seconds to download (if all goes well). A 250K file takes two-and-a-half minutes. If that 250K file is a 10-second animation, your viewers probably will feel cheated after waiting so long for such a short display. If you keep this wait/reward ratio in mind when developing any plug-in-compatible content for your Web pages, you should keep your site under control and your audience happy.

Some plug-ins address this problem by using specially compressed files. The plug-in decompresses the data before displaying it. The savings in download time more than make up for the time required to decompress the data before it is displayed.

Browser Compatibility

Many companies are promoting their own proprietary formats on the Web for everything from video to audio to compressed graphics to animation to…well, you get the picture.

The problem with proprietary formats on the World Wide Web, however, is that they can quickly keep the Web from being worldwide at all. Each new proprietary format leads to further Balkanization of the Web, as it divides into ever smaller, ever more proprietary pieces.

Not that innovation is bad. It has become painfully obvious that older technologies—.WAV audio and GIF graphics, for example—just aren't robust enough for future use on the Web. The files are too big for the information that they hold. Compression is the key to the future expansion of the Web, and certainly the key to emerging multimedia and three-dimensional technology.

How can you address this issue? You need to continue experimenting with new formats, but without scattering them throughout the Web willy-nilly. You should initially localize your experiments, trying them out on your own system before using them on your Web sites. Discussion should be encouraged in the appropriate UseNet groups. Then, new standards should be proposed for adoption Web-wide. W3C (the World Wide Web Consortium) is the governing body that supervises most changes on the Web.

The HTML 3.0 standard will incorporate many of Netscape's innovative extensions. The Virtual Reality Modeling Language (VRML), as shown in figure 3.6, will certainly be following the standardization path as the "Moving Worlds" extensions are considered for inclusion in the VRML 2.0 standard (see Chapter 14, "Moving Worlds and Live3D"). Graphics, audio, video, and multimedia standards should be pursued as well.

FIG. 3.6
VRML plug-ins such as WebFX incorporate many custom extensions that some advocates hope to make a part of the upcoming VRML 2.0 standard.

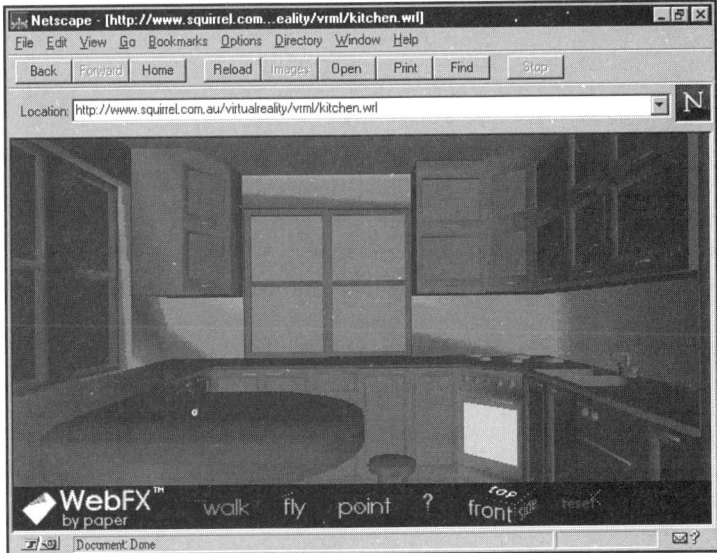

In the meantime, plug-ins provide an excellent way to experiment with new and different types of Web page content, hopefully without dividing Web users into drastically opposing camps. If you keep your content *optional*, you'll go a long way toward promoting feelings of cooperation and good will among all Web users.

How can you do this? Keep your home page generic. Use only HTML-formatted text and standard GIF and JPEG graphics on your home page, then use links to jump to pages that contain your plug-in-compatible content files. For example, your home page might use a GIF image of a still from a video as a link to a separate page that includes the entire video.

It's also good form to include text-only versions, or at least text-and-GIF-graphics versions, of your pages; then users who aren't using plug-ins can view your pages and experience their full impact. After all, the Web is about communication, and you can't communicate with users who can't view your Web pages.

Here's the HTML code for a courteous Web page that provides only text and graphics up front, but provides a link to both enhanced and unenhanced pages:

```
<HTML>
<HEAD>
<TITLE>The Wonderful World of Weebles</TITLE>
</HEAD>
<BODY>
<H1>The Wonderful World of Weebles</H1>
<HR>
Weebles are cool! I've been into those rockin', sockin'
little Playschool Weebles since I was a kid, and think
there must be a lot of people out there on the Web who
share my interest. That's why I've created the Wonderful
World of Weebles!<P>
<A HREF="Animated.htm"><IMG SRC="weebles2.gif" ALT="[LINK]"></A>
Click here for Multimedia...
<A HREF="Standard.htm"><IMG SRC="weebles3.gif" ALT="[LINK]"></A>
or here for standard Weebles.<P>
</BODY>
</HTML>
```

This page loads quickly over even slow dial-up lines, and displays well in any graphical Web browser program (see fig. 3.7). It then provides links to pages both with and without multimedia content. The fancy stuff can come on page two. Then, viewers can choose to bookmark your fancy page rather than your home page.

FIG. 3.7
This example does everything that a home page should—it's courteous, presents its case right up front, loads quickly, and provides links to more user-friendly pages.

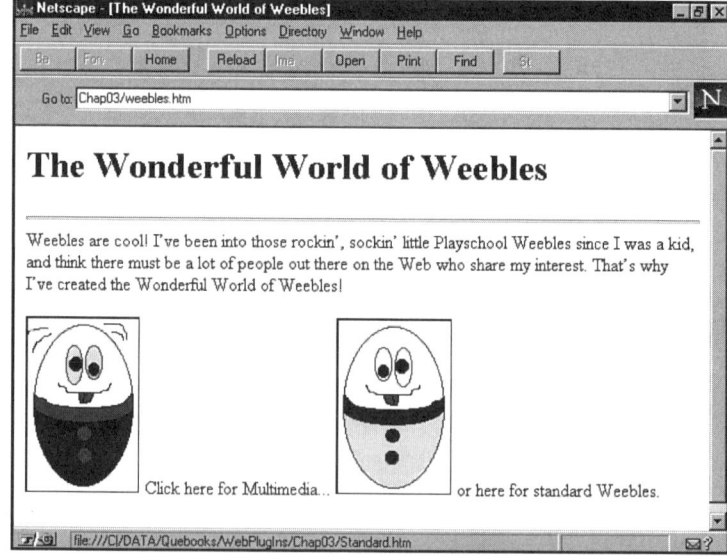

The key is courtesy—your home page should be generic, keeping fancy multimedia content optional. Then everyone can view your site.

Good Content versus Good Looks

Good looks might draw people to your site, but good content will keep them coming back. If your site uses all the latest and greatest Web design techniques, but lacks solid content to keep users' attention, they'll just move on.

The flip side of this maxim, of course, is that if your site has excellent content but isn't visually appealing, people aren't likely to examine it long enough to find out just how good it is. People have a tendency to judge a book by its cover, and with so many well-done, visually attractive sites available on the Web, your site is up against some stiff competition.

It's important to have a *reason* for the plug-in content—indeed, for *all* content—that you add to your site. Define first the site's purpose. Are you selling a product or service? Are you trying to encourage investment in your company? Do you just want to entertain your audience? Is user support the main issue? Or are you trying to build name recognition? You can do all these things at once, but it's best to create clearly delineated areas on your Web site for each purpose.

Every audio, video, multimedia, or other fancy plug-in-compatible file on your Web site should have a purpose. Does the file help you tell your story? Does the element illustrate a point? Does the file involve your viewer in your message? You should ask all these questions before adding anything (including simple text and graphics elements) to your Web page.

Simply asking yourself whether your page is "cool" is not enough. Users might decide that a multimedia game is cool, and then move on. You want to engage users so that they feel compelled to learn more about your page's content (see fig. 3.8). Like any good Web page content, your plug-in content should deliver your message in spades. The content's purpose shouldn't be simply to entertain, but to help you accomplish your site's goals. (You do *have* goals for your site, don't you? If not, you need to ask yourself why you are on the Web at all.)

FIG. 3.8
This Shockwave multimedia game on the movie *Toy Story*'s Web site is more than just cool—it involves viewers with the story's characters, and thus entices viewers to see the movie.

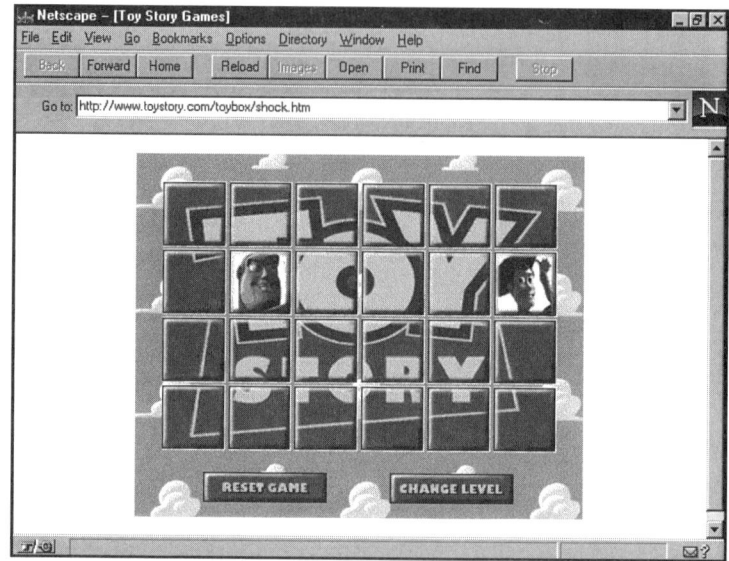

What Are the Best Uses for Plug-Ins?

Plug-ins can deliver content that is more vibrant, interactive, and involving than straight HTML text or GIF graphics. The best use for plug-ins is to deliver content that goes beyond what text and graphics can do.

For example, figure 3.4 shows an interactive concentration-style game that the *Toy Story* site presents. The game's purpose is to involve the viewer with the story's characters and make them familiar, but in a fun way. By making the experience interactive and hands-on, the creators of the *Toy Story* site have achieved at least three positive things:

- Because the page is unique (presenting a game rather than just static text and images), the experience is memorable.
- The game requires the player to memorize images of the movie's characters. In the process, the player becomes more familiar and comfortable with the characters, and more likely to want to see more of the characters.
- Because the game is interactive, the player has to hang around long enough to finish the game—and for the page to imprint the message, "*Toy Story* is fun!"

All these things help the creators of the *Toy Story* site achieve their primary goal: to increase interest in the movie *Toy Story,* and thus sell more tickets and licensed merchandise.

Expressed in these terms, the site's goal sounds rather mercenary, but of course the relationship between sites and viewers isn't all that bad. A Web surfer exploring the *Toy Story* site is looking for entertainment, and this game certainly provides it. Both the site and the viewer win.

If your plug-in content provides the same kind of experience on *your* Web site, you've done things the right way. Your site should leave the viewer with a positive impression, a sense of having experienced something good, and a clear idea of what you are trying to communicate.

Before you include any plug-in-compatible content on your Web pages, ask yourself these questions:

- What is my message?
- How does this content help me deliver my message?
- Will viewing this content be a pleasing experience to my viewers?
- Will viewers get my message better by interacting with this content than they would without it?

If you can answer these questions in the positive, you can justify using plug-in-compatible content on your Web pages.

Plug-In Content-Creation Programs

Every plug-in requires content created by its own unique content-creation program. Just as you must use a paint program to create GIF graphics, you must use the proper audio digitizing, video grabbing, spreadsheet creating, or other type of program to create each type of plug-in content.

Each content-creation program is unique, with its own user interface, controls, quirks, and capabilities. Unfortunately, you have to install and learn to use a whole new program for each type of content that you want to create.

This imposes a practical limit on the amount and types of content that your Web pages can provide. Although it might sound appealing to have a site include audio, video, multimedia, interactive games, spreadsheets, and so on, you simply don't have time to learn how to create and deliver every single kind of plug-in content in existence. You have to be selective.

> **NOTE** The types of plug-in content that you use also affects your audience. Visitors have to install a plug-in for every type of plug-in content that you use. If they have to download and install a half dozen plug-ins before viewing your page, viewers most likely will simply move on to a more user-friendly site!

Being selective means sifting through the chaff to find the kernels of wheat. And, of course, what's chaff to some is wheat to others. Although you want to display animation on your "Looney Toons" site, an investment analyst might be more interested in displaying spreadsheets.

Chapter 2, "Browser Plug-Ins," should help you become familiar with the plug-ins that are currently available. Choose those plug-ins that are most suitable to the types of information that you think will work best on your site.

Keep Your Files Small

For delivery on the World Wide Web, bandwidth is the primary consideration. Therefore, non-real-time plug-ins are most appropriate for Web pages. Video in real time is impractical or impossible on Web connections, especially on dial-up connections. Your Web pages should not use real-time video; however, non-real-time files (those files that you download before you view) are acceptable if you warn your audience that long download times are involved.

Real-time audio isn't out of the question, especially if most of your viewers will be accessing your site through direct (not dial-up) lines. RealAudio in particular claims to faithfully deliver real-time FM-quality mono audio over 28.8 dial-ups.

You should usually keep your files as small as possible. Multimedia games are fine if they download quickly. Remember that much of a plug-in-compatible file's capabilities derive from the plug-in itself. Data files might be relatively small while incorporating a lot of flashy content. Watch your file sizes, and don't worry about how much the file is doing. The key to successful use of plug-ins over the Internet is to ensure that your file does a lot, but does it efficiently. ●

CHAPTER 4

Creating Plug-In Content for Intranets

- What an intranet is, and how it differs from the Internet
- Who needs an intranet, and why
- How intranet and Internet content contrast
- What kinds of plug-in compatible content are appropriate for use on an intranet

The technical details involved in creating plug-in compatible content for intranets are much the same as for creating pages for the World Wide Web. The <EMBED> tag works the same, the same plug-ins are available, and the server must be set up to deliver the proper MIME type information (and, in some cases, must have special data servers installed and configured).

However, the types of information normally delivered on an intranet are quite different than the types of data delivered over the Internet, and that information includes plug-in content. ■

http://www.mcp.com/que

What Is an Intranet?

An intranet is, quite simply, an internal computer network—one that is accessed only by people within a corporation, institution, or organization. Unlike the Internet, an intranet's purpose is not to give people around the world access to information on your computer network, but to give organization insiders access to the information.

So far, an intranet sounds much like a standard computer network. However, an intranet goes one step further: It makes your organization's data more accessible by organizing it in much the same way that you might organize it if you were setting up a Web site. In other words, instead of just supplying users with a network file structure through a network server and shared printing through networked printers, an intranet uses an organization's internal computer networks as the backbone for an Internet-style information system that might include e-mail, news, Web, and other services. Specifically, it is set up using Internet Protocol (IP), the same data transmission standard used on the Internet.

NOTE Intranets are not necessarily limited to a single physical location. You can connect multiple locations through the Internet while still limiting access to the resulting network to people within your organization. The whole works still comprise an intranet; you are using the Internet just as a means to tie different locations together.

The resulting system is still an intranet because access is limited to insiders and not open to the world. In this case, you can think of the Internet as simply being an extension to your internal computer network system, not as a means to open up access to outsiders.

For example, a corporate intranet might include company-wide e-mail, an internal news server organized by departments, and a set of Web pages containing sales information, the company employee handbook, current price lists, and even the company newsletter.

Think of an intranet as groupware that makes use of technology from the Internet—e-mail and news servers, and Web browsers such as Netscape—rather than dedicated groupware applications such as Lotus Notes.

Three major advantages that you get from establishing an intranet are data standardization, low cost, and ease of use (see fig. 4.1). You can use the same data file types on your intranet that you use on your Web site, and the same tools to browse and display that data.

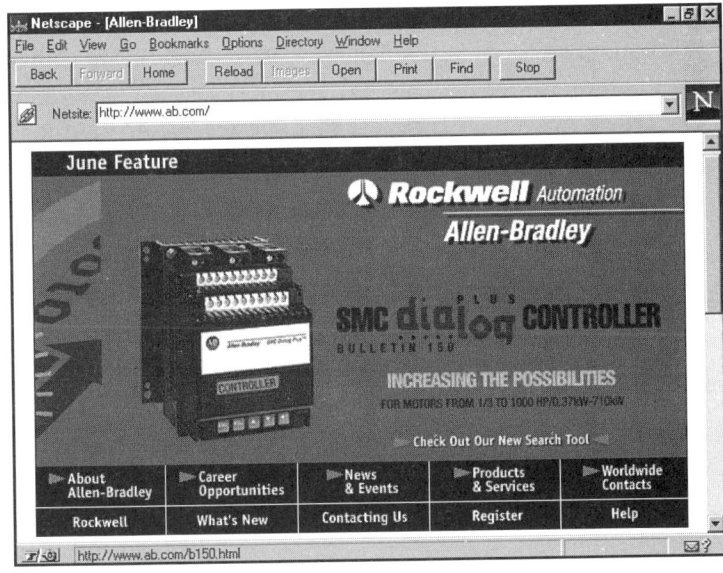

FIG. 4.1
Rockwell's Allen-Bradley factory automation system division uses a corporate intranet to share ideas and information, track competitive products, and implement forms-based applications for business automation.

Who Needs an Intranet?

Recent studies show that intranet installations are likely to outpace Internet installations in the near future by as much as two to one. Over 50 percent of businesses have installed, are planning to install, or are studying the option of installing a corporate intranet, and annual investment in intranets is likely to top a billion dollars in 1996.

What's all the fuss? How could something so new become so indispensable to so many businesses so suddenly?

The key is that intranets save the two things that are most valuable to a company: time and money. Intranets save time by enabling employees to control their own access to corporate data in real time without having to go through layers of corporate red tape. They save money by making data immediately available throughout an organization without expensive printing and distribution costs.

The Case of Updating the Employee Handbook

Suppose that Company A has 10,000 employees. Each employee has an employee handbook that contains the company's mileage reimbursement rate (25 cents per mile), vacation schedule (one week after one year, two weeks after five years, and three weeks after 10 years), and a list of employee grades with pay scales.

Six months after the manual's initial printing, Company A raises the mileage rate to 30 cents per mile. This nickel increase isn't significant enough to warrant the reprinting of 10,000 employee manuals, so the company issues 10,000 memos instead. However, 5,000 of these memos are mislaid, and in subsequent months the company has to redo many travel vouchers because they contain the wrong mileage rate.

A couple of months later, Company A revamps its vacation schedule. To keep up with its competitor, Company B, Company A decides to give employees two weeks of vacation after only three years, and three weeks after seven years of service. Again, Company A issues 10,000 memos and confusion reigns over how much vacation everyone gets. Any employee who mistakenly refers to the now-outdated employee handbook (which is supposed to be the "official" employment contract) gets the wrong answer.

In addition, all new-hire employees are still getting the outdated manual, with a handful of "update" memos shoved into the binding—when the human resources department remembers to stick them in there.

Finally, the human resources department decides to change the employee grade and pay scale chart, and determines that the old manual is just too far out-of-date. After only a year, Company A has to reprint and distribute 10,000 new employee manuals.

Contrast Company A's situation with that of Company B, which has put its employee handbook on its corporate intranet.

Company B simply gives its new employees the URL (intranet address) of the employee handbook. Using Netscape, any employee can access this handbook at any time from his or her desktop. Because the employee handbook pages have a built-in search feature, any employee can answer any question quickly and easily. If mileage rates change, the online employee handbook reflects the change immediately and each employee receives an e-mail memo announcing the change. Anyone who subsequently checks the mileage rate in the online handbook gets the correct rate. Likewise, the human resources department can update vacation schedules, grades, rates, and other information as soon as they change, and can notify employees by e-mail where to look in the online handbook for updated information.

Company B projects that its intranet-based employee handbook will save tens of thousands of dollars each year simply by avoiding hundreds of refiled mileage claims, eliminating dozens of calls to the human resources department every day about vacation and pay issues, and saving reprint costs for 10,000 employee manuals annually.

Thousands of companies are currently using corporate intranets to keep employees up-to-date on company information (see fig. 4.2).

FIG. 4.2
Genentech's internal Web, or intranet, provides employees with access to information on company announcements, building facilities, the employee directory, commuting options, benefits, child care, and more.

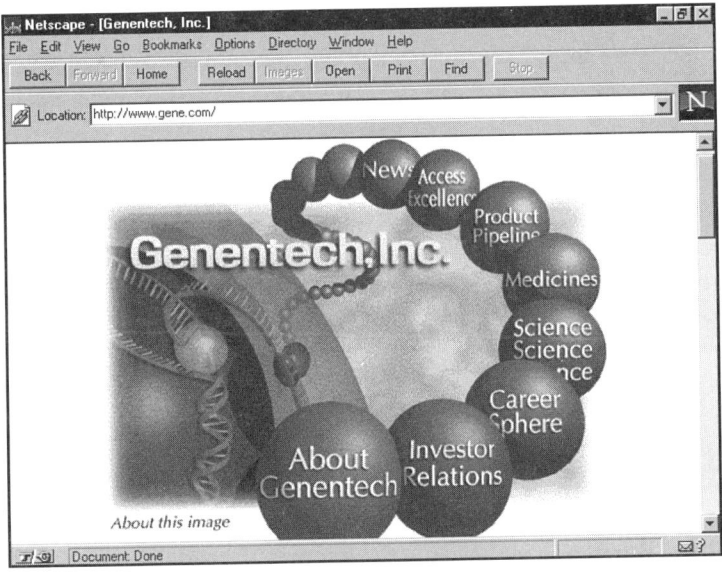

The Case of the Sales Training Program

But how do plug-ins fit into this scenario?

Consider Company C's dilemma. Joe Crackerjack, Company C's top salesperson, is sharp. Joe was Company C's most successful saleperson, accounting for over 15 percent of the company's total sales. The second most successful salesperson didn't sell half as much product as Joe. Therefore, the company asked Joe to organize and hold a day-long seminar for the other salespeople, to pass along what he knows about sales. However, with all the salespeople on the road 90 percent of the time, it is impossible to get them all in one place at one time so that Joe can present his seminar. Company C can't afford to pull its top salesperson off the road for several weeks just to train its other salespeople.

To address this problem, Company C hired a Web multimedia production consultant. After videotaping Joe's seminar, she digitized key sequences of the presentation as video clips. She turned his printed handouts into HyperText Markup Language (HTML) Web pages, and Joe's PowerPoint slides into an online presentation. Finally, she put the whole works up on Company C's corporate intranet. Now, when they make it back to the office, Company C's salespeople can take in Joe's presentation at their leisure. They can print the Web pages containing his notes, view key parts of his speech, and go backward and forward through his slide presentation. They can even e-mail their questions to Joe, so that he can respond when he has time.

Best of all, new salespeople can also access Joe's seminar when they join the company. Even though his presentation has become a permanent part of Company C's training program, Joe still can spend his time on the road doing what he does best—selling.

To display both the video clips and the PowerPoint slides, the consultant used Netscape plug-ins. The sales department is planning to add some Excel spreadsheets showing corporate sales trends, and these also will be displayed using a plug-in.

 You can find an excellent online resource for intranet information at the following site:

http://www.lochnet.com/client/smart/intranet.htm

Intranet Content versus Internet Content

The preceding two scenarios set the stage for examining the most important difference between an intranet and the Internet: the audience.

Where a World Wide Web site is geared to a world-wide audience, an intranet site is targeted to an internal audience.

Internet Content

Content on World Wide Web sites on the Internet is typically geared toward *selling* or *informing*.

Selling a product or service is usually the primary goal of a corporate Web site. There are, of course, direct and indirect ways to sell your product to the public. You can do so subtly by building brand awareness through contests, games, and fan clubs, or overtly by offering your catalog directly on the Web. Your goal might even involve a different kind of salesmanship—perhaps you're more interested in stimulating investment in your company than in selling your product. In any case, you're practicing Web salesmanship. Even if you just want to do a public relations job—showing the public how involved you are in the environment, for example—your ultimate goal is still to promote interest and trust in your company, and thus to promote sales.

Institutions and organizations are more often interested in informing the public about their cause than in selling a product. However, the overall goal might be similar to sales—to stimulate a donation, offers to volunteer, or even just letters of support. Even educational institutions often regard their Web presence as an extension to their catalog and a recruiting tool.

A good place to begin looking for intranet-related information on the Web is the Intranet Links page:

http://www.infoweb.com.au/intralnk.htm

Intranet Content

Neither selling nor informing is a central goal of an intranet. In fact, either would tantamount to "preaching to the choir." You don't need to sell your products to your employees, and you don't need to convince your organization's members of the validity of your goals. They're already convinced. They're already on the team.

N O T E In this context, the term *informing* means to pass along information about the company's products or services, which might also be called *promoting*. Of course, informing in its general sense is also a primary duty of an intranet, although the type of information passed along is much different.

So what is an intranet good for? The earlier examples touched on two possibilities: employee manuals and training. But there are many other uses for an internal Web. Consider these possibilities:

- Company newsletters
- Sales figures, charts, and forecasts
- Product specifications
- Product service information
- Product demos
- Software and system tutorials
- Employee handbooks
- Corporate directories
- Software distribution and updates
- Project white papers and schedules
- Meeting schedules and minutes

In short, you can probably use an intranet to perform almost any task that requires dissemination of information to employees or organization members. For more ideas about the possible uses of intranets, visit Netscape Corporation's Full Service Intranet Applications page (see fig. 4.3). You can find this page at the following address:

http://home.netscape.com/comprod/at_work/white_paper/intranet/vision.html

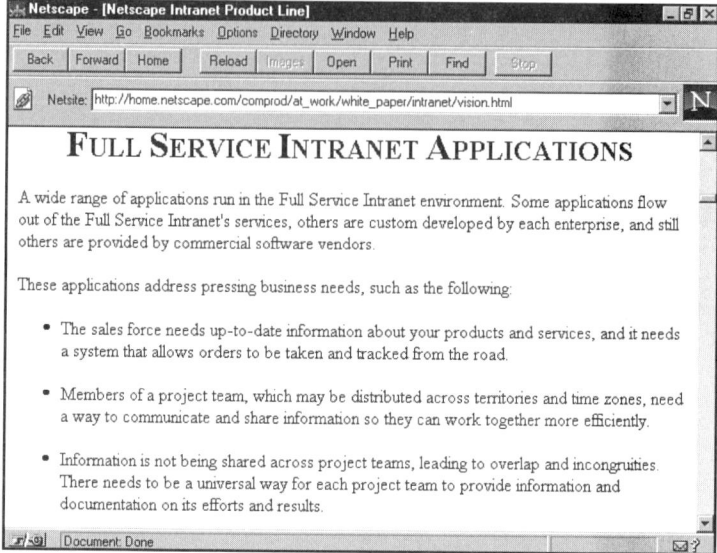

FIG. 4.3
Netscape Corporation's Full Service Intranet Applications page describes Netscape's vision of the future of intranets.

Plug-Ins and Intranets

Although plug-ins open up many new possibilities when browsing the World Wide Web, they really shine on intranets. Organizations can benefit greatly from the file standardization that intranets impose. Also, intranets don't suffer from the bandwidth problems that can hound sites on the Internet.

File Standardization

As a corporation grows, it inevitably Balkanizes—that is, departments and groups drift apart in the way they work, and even in the tools that they use to do that work. For example, your company's accounting department might use Lotus 1-2-3 as its spreadsheet, while engineering uses Microsoft Excel. The secretarial pool might use WordPerfect, while research and development uses Word. Worse, the secretaries might all be on Macintoshes, while engineering uses UNIX workstations. If this sort of situation prevails at your organization, communication among departments might be spotty at best.

However, a corporate intranet can help smooth over these communications problems. Macintosh, Windows, and UNIX computers running Web browser programs can all read HTML Web documents. If the accounting department creates a report in HTML on a Windows 95 machine, that report can easily be read by engineering on a UNIX workstation or by the human resources department on its Macintoshes. As plug-ins become more widely available across platforms, they'll also be capable of viewing MPEG movies, listening to RealAudio sound clips, and viewing Word documents included in intranet pages. If nothing else, HTML makes it easy to include alternative content for machines that cannot read proprietary formats, so that everyone can access the same information, regardless of the format.

 TIP   A great online source of up-to-date information on intranets is the online Intranet Journal:
   http://www.brill.com/intranet/

Bandwidth and Multimedia

Bandwidth is the major factor in limiting the kinds of content that you can put on Web pages. With most of the Web's audience dialing up through 14.4kbps or 28.8kbps modem connections, real-time live streaming video and other data-intensive applications are often not realistic features to include in Web pages.

However, because corporate intranets run over fast computer networks, intranet sites can easily include streaming video, real-time audio, and other bandwidth-intensive data. For this reason, video-based in-house training, interactive multimedia, and other data-intensive applications are a natural for inclusion on an intranet (see fig. 4.4). Because many Netscape plug-ins are geared toward displaying multimedia, they are likely to see much more use on corporate intranets than on the Web.

FIG. 4.4
By publishing multimedia files on the intranet, HBO is saving thousands of dollars previously incurred for printing, duplication of videocassettes, and distribution of marketing campaign materials among 200 to 300 sales representatives.

Here is a sampling of the plug-ins that you might want to consider using for viewing intranet audio, video, and multimedia presentations:

- Netscape's own LiveAudio plug-in ships with Netscape 3.0. It plays digitized .AIFF, .AU, and .WAV files, as well as MIDI music files.
- DSP Group's TrueSpeech player plays compressed TrueSpeech sound files.
- LiveUpdate's Crescendo and Crescendo Plus plug-ins enable Navigator to play inline MIDI music embedded in Web pages.
- The ToolVox plug-in plays speech files that have been compressed at ratios of up to 53:1. Echospeech provides higher-quality compressed speech at compressions of 18.5 to 1.
- Macintosh-only plug-ins like Talker and ShockTalk enable Macintosh applications to speak using text files or to respond to spoken commands.
- FutureSplash's CelAnimator creates vector-based drawings and animations that you can view with the FutureSplash Netscape plug-in.
- WebXpresso displays 2-D and 3-D drawings, graphs, and controls.
- Plastic Thought's Web-Active displays dynamic 3-D images that you can rotate, turn, and tumble onscreen.
- Two Macintosh-only plug-ins (WurlPlug and WebActive 3D) are available for viewing Apple QD3D (QuickTime VR) files in Netscape.
- Netscape's official plug-in for .AVI video, LiveVideo, ships with Netscape Navigator 3.0. The VDOLive, CoolFusion, Vosaic, and VivoActive plug-ins also play inline Video for Windows (.AVI) clips.
- The Apple QuickTime plug-in—as well as Maczilla, MovieStar, ViewMovie, and TEC Player—all play back QuickTime format movies in Netscape.
- Action, PreVU, and Xing are all plug-ins for playing MPEG movies inline.
- Totally Hip Software's Sizzler plug-in and companion converter program enable you to create and display Web animation.
- GEO Interactive Media Group's Emblaze plug-in is a real-time animation player.
- Deltapoint's Web Animator combines animation, sound, and live interaction.
- Heads Off's Play3D plug-in supports real-time interactive 3-D and 2-D sprites, and .WAV and MIDI sound playback.
- Top Gun, media.splash, SCREAM, mFactory, and MBED are all multimedia playback plug-ins.
- Netscape's own Live3D is a VRML (Virtual Reality Modeling Language) plug-in. Many other VRML plug-ins are available.

Application Files—Word Processing, Presentations, and Spreadsheets

Many Netscape plug-ins are available for viewing proprietary data formats like Microsoft Word documents, PowerPoint presentations, and Excel spreadsheets. Although these plug-ins have limited value on the World Wide Web, an intranet is the perfect place for sharing such data. In fact, much of a company's or organization's current data is likely to already be available in one of these formats. Using Netscape plug-ins, you can make this data available on a corporate intranet without first having to go through a time-consuming (and potentially error-prone) conversion process. Moreover, you can easily update these documents using current applications, and make the files available instantly on the intranet.

The following are just a few of the plug-ins that can help you present existing data on your intranet:

- AutoDesk's WHIP! and SoftSource's DWG/DXF plug-in both display AutoCAD drawings.
- Corel's CMX Viewer displays CorelDRAW! vector graphic files.
- The InterCAP InLine plug-in enables you to view CGM (Computer Graphic Metafile) vector images.
- Macromedia's ShockWave plug-ins can display Freehand graphics as well as Director and Authorware multimedia files.
- The ABC QuickSilver plug-in can display inline ABC Micrografx QuickSilver business graphics.
- Software Publishing Corporation's ASAP WebShow plug-in displays WebShow presentations.
- The Astound Web Player displays multimedia documents created with Gold Disk's Astound or Studio M programs.
- Rad Technologies' Netscape plug-in can play back presentations created with RAD PowerMedia.
- Asymetrix's Neuron plug-in plays multimedia presentations created using ToolBook.
- The Kaleida Media Player can play back, in an intranet page, multimedia applications developed with ScriptX, an object-oriented programming language for multimedia.

- Adobe's Acrobat Amber Reader displays Adobe Acrobat documents inline in Netscape.
- Tumbleweed Software's Envoy plug-in displays Novell's Envoy documents.
- Visual Components' Formula One/NET is an Excel-compatible spreadsheet plug-in for Netscape Navigator.
- Inso's Word Viewer plug-in displays Microsoft Word 6.0 or 7.0 documents in Netscape Navigator 2.0 inline.
- The KEYview Netscape plug-in from FTP Software enables you to view, print, and convert nearly 200 different file formats, including Microsoft Word, WordPerfect, Microsoft Excel, Encapsulated PostScript (EPS), .PCX, and compressed files.
- The PointPlus plug-in displays Microsoft PowerPoint presentations (Microsoft also has its own PowerPoint plug-in).
- IBM's Techexplorer processes and displays a large subset of the TeX/LaTeX typesetting language.
- Brainstorm Technology's Groupscape is an object-oriented development tool for extending Lotus Notes workgroup applications to the Web or the intranet.

You can find the download site for each of these plug-ins in Chapter 2, "Browser Plug-Ins," or in the appropriate chapters later in this book.

NOTE If you're using Carbon Copy or Timbuktu Pro to enable people to log in to your network remotely, you'll also be interested in these two Netscape plug-ins:

- Carbon Copy/Net is Microcom's plug-in version of Carbon Copy.
- Farallon's Look@Me is a plug-in based on Timbuktu Pro.

This section has listed only those plug-ins designed to enable you to use preexisting content on your intranet. Many other plug-ins let you create entirely new content types, from multimedia to animations to customized applications.

Custom Applications

What if you can't find a plug-in to do what you want on your intranet? No problem. Just make your own. A multitude of tools is available to help you create custom applications that work with Netscape. If you have a programmer or two on your staff, creating custom intranet applications is often much easier than creating custom stand-alone programs to do the same job (see fig. 4.5).

FIG. 4.5
Mobil Corporation's customized intranet distributes timely data to its North American distributors.

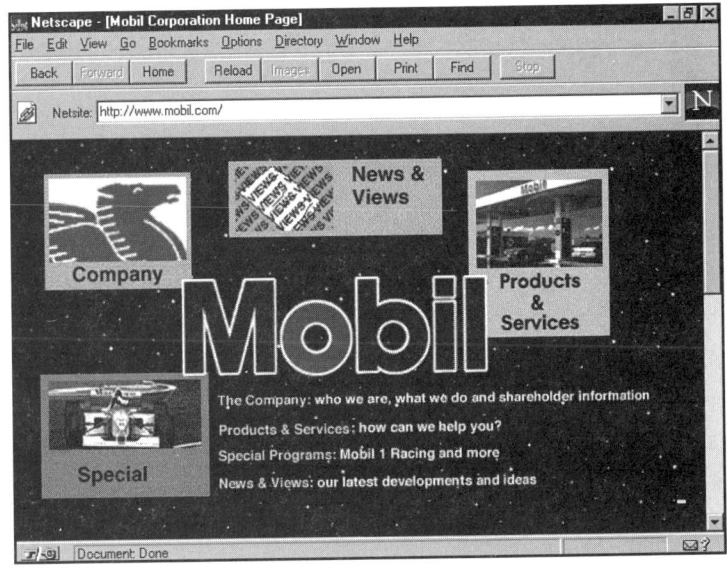

N O T E You can also write your own plug-ins from scratch using the Netscape Plug-In SDK (Software Developer's Kit), available online from the Netscape site:

http://www.netscape.com

Here are a few of the Netscape customization plug-ins currently available:

- ExCITE's NCompass plug-in enables you to embed ActiveX controls as applets. You create the controls using standard programming languages and development tools such as Visual C++, Visual Basic, and the Microsoft Windows Game SDK.
- Business@Web's OpenScape plug-in also lets developers create ActiveX-compatible applications. However, to create OpenScape applications, you have to use the OpenScape development system.
- The QuickServer plug-in from Wayfarer Communications is for applications developed with Visual Basic, PowerBuilder, C++, and Java.
- Visual Basic for Applications (VBA) and Amara's WebBASIC API (applications programming interface) also enable you to create intranet applets.
- The Galacticomm Worldgroup plug-in supports dozens of off-the-shelf groupware applications.
- Citrix Systems' WinFrame plug-in for Windows 3.1 and Windows 95 enables you to execute Windows programs over the Internet.

Chapter 4 Creating Plug-In Content for Intranets

 TIP Remember that you can also use Java and JavaScript to create custom Netscape applets.

 TIP Netscape's Web pages profile its suite of intranet software:

> http://home.netscape.com/comprod/at_work/index.html

> **NOTE** For the full scoop on setting up your own organization's intranet, check out the following Que books:
>
> - *Introducing Intranets*
> - *10 Minute Guide to Intranets*
> - *Intranet Publishing*
> - *Special Edition Using Intranet HTML*
> - *Building an Intranet with BackOffice*

PART II

Plug-Ins for Multimedia

- **5** RealAudio 109
- **6** LiveAudio and Other Audio Plug-Ins 133
- **7** Plug-Ins for Graphics Display and Compression 151
- **8** CorelDRAW!, AutoCAD, and Other Graphics Plug-Ins 175
- **9** Video and Animation Plug-Ins 201
- **10** Shockwave for Macromedia Director 227
- **11** ASAP WebShow and Other Multimedia Plug-Ins 245

CHAPTER 5

RealAudio

- What hardware you need to play online audio files
- What RealAudio does and how it does it
- How to download, install, and use the RealAudio plug-in
- How to create RealAudio content using the RealAudio Encoder
- How to set up a Web server to deliver RealAudio content

With any emerging technology, being first is a tremendous advantage. RealAudio was the first program to deliver real-time streaming audio over the World Wide Web.

After starting as a stand-alone program that could also serve as a Netscape helper application, RealAudio quickly transformed into a Netscape plug-in. Since its introduction, thousands of Web sites have begun to deliver RealAudio content over the Internet. Today, RealAudio is undoubtedly the most popular streaming audio application on the Internet, with more than four million RealAudio players downloaded from the Progressive Networks Web site. ■

Audio Hardware—What You Need

Back in the "good old days" of personal computing—when *PC* was always followed by *XT*, processor numbers were only four digits long, and software ran directly off of floppy disks—every PC shipped with a tinny little AM-radio-quality speaker that beeped nastily at you each time that you did something wrong. Some masochists (the kind who like to scrape their fingernails on blackboards) even wrote a few annoying DOS programs that played what they claimed to be digitized sounds on that little speaker. But no normal human being ever heard a single recognizable sound in the cacophonous din that emanated from a PC when those programs ran.

Now, in the high-tech age of multimedia computers—complete with 24-bit TrueColor animations, 16-bit stereo music soundtracks, and digitized CD-ROM voice-overs by the likes of *Star Trek: The Next Generation*'s Patrick Stewart—all PCs still ship with that same nasty, tinny little speaker.

Microsoft has a Windows driver that purportedly plays music and audio using only the internal PC speaker, but the driver freezes up your system when running, and all audio still sounds as though it were being fed through a weather-beaten drive-in movie speaker with a shorted connection.

To get real audio from your PC, you need a sound card. If you bought your computer recently, or if you've spent a few bucks upgrading, the odds are good that you already have a sound card. But if you don't, you can buy one for anywhere between $30 and $800, depending on what you want it to do.

A good 16-bit stereo Sound Blaster Pro (or compatible) sound card does just about everything the average user needs to do with audio, and does it for under $100. If you haven't invested in a sound card yet, drop this book right now, scan a few computer magazine reviews and ads, run to your local computer store, buy a sound card, and plug it in. You'll need one for RealAudio or any other sound player plug-in that you might choose to use with Netscape.

How RealAudio Works

Computers can play three different kinds of audio files: digitized audio, music files, and text-to-speech. Text-to-speech is a technique for converting text files into somewhat recognizable speech by replacing the letters with phonemes (the individual sounds of spoken speech). Music files are like sheet music—they specify a sequence of notes and the "instruments" to play them. Digitized audio is sound that has been run through an analog-to-digital converter to turn it into data. RealAudio files are digitized audio.

RealAudio is actually a suite of three programs that work together. The RealAudio Encoder encodes preexisting sound files or live audio streams into the RealAudio format. The RealAudio Server delivers these encoded RealAudio streams over the Internet or your company intranet. (A RealAudio Server and a Web server usually run simultaneously on the same server computer.) Finally, the RealAudio Player plays these streams when your computer receives them. Versions of each program in the suite are available from the Progressive Networks Web site:

http://www.realaudio.com

Figure 5.1 shows the Progressive Networks Web page.

FIG. 5.1
The Progressive Networks RealAudio site is a treasure trove of downloadable software, technical information, and audio streams.

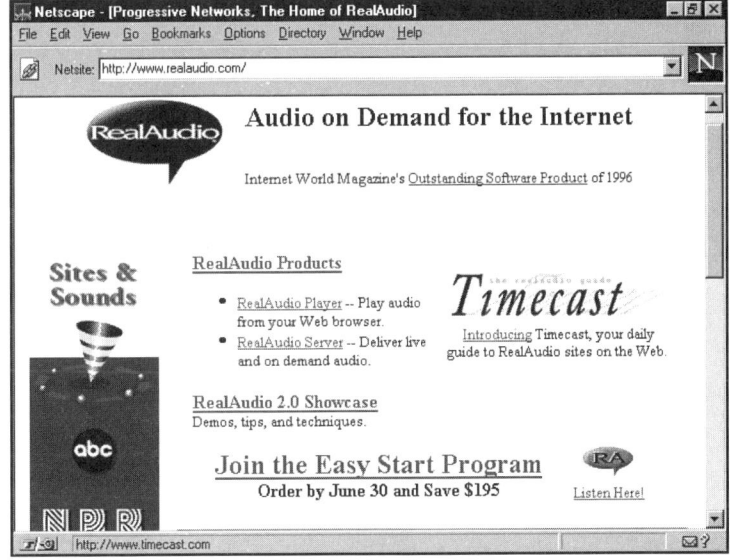

If you're planning only to listen to RealAudio on the Web or on your company's intranet, all you need is the RealAudio Player. If you want to create RealAudio content for your Web server to deliver, you also need the RealAudio Encoder. If you run your own Web server, you need the RealAudio Server as well.

N O T E In all its RealAudio products, Progressive Networks supports the LiveMedia Real-Time Transport Protocol (RTP) and Microsoft's ActiveMovie Streaming Format (ASF). ■

RealAudio streams are compressed and encoded from either a preexisting sound file or live audio. The RealAudio Encoder can create files that are optimized for either 14.4kbps or 28.8kbps modem delivery. (If a file is intended for delivery over a fast, direct Internet or intranet connection, the higher-quality 28.8kbps encoder is used.) The resulting file is always much smaller than the original. For example, a one-minute .WAV file (sampled at 22kHz) takes up about 2.6M; the 14.4kbps RealAudio encoded version is only 60K, and the 28.8kbps version is about twice that size. Those file sizes represent compression ratios of about 40:1 and 20:1, respectively. The resulting 14.4kbps encoded RealAudio file has a quality comparable to an AM radio broadcast and is best for speech only; the 28.8kbps file sounds like monophonic FM and is adequate for most music.

The compression routines in the RealAudio Encoder omit some sound file information—such is the nature of compression. You give up a little quality to achieve much faster transmission. In the resulting audio stream, these omissions manifest themselves as a sort of "graininess" or loss of depth and tone quality.

The RealAudio Server delivers audio streams in a unique manner. The Internet can send data in one of two ways. The Transmission Control Protocol (TCP), on which the Web is based, emphasizes reliability. TCP ensures that accurate data packets are always received, even if some must be retransmitted to overcome errors. On the other hand, the UDP (User Datagram Protocol) emphasizes speed, sometimes at the cost of accuracy. For text or graphics, sacrificing accuracy can be too great a cost. However, if you hear inaccurate or incomplete audio transmissions, you perceive the inaccuracy only as a little noise, like a skip or static in a radio station signal. Much more important to audio is the uninterrupted transmission of the signal, so that large blocks of audio aren't skipped and transmission continues in real time. For this reason, RealAudio uses a special server program to deliver RealAudio data packets using the UDP protocol. Although this use of this server program might result in an occasional skipped "sound byte," the data stream continues uninterrupted in real time.

> **NOTE** To get around the problem of occasional packet loss, the RealAudio server incorporates a loss correction system that minimizes the impact of lost packets. This system works well when packet loss is in the 2 to 5 percent range, and even works acceptably when packet loss is as high as 8 to 10 percent. ■

A RealAudio Server connection is actually a two-channel, two-way communication system—UDP transmits sound data, and TCP negotiates the proper bandwidth (14.4 or 28.8) and also communicates pause, fast-forward, play, and rewind commands. Because of this two-channel communication, you can listen to a RealAudio stream just as you would an audio tape. Because the stream is delivered to your computer on demand, in real time, the RealAudio Player's commands to the RealAudio Server can jump you back and forth to different spots in the audio stream. (These commands work only when you are listening to prerecorded audio. Listening to live audio broadcasts is much like listening to the radio.)

> **RealAudio Developer Support**
>
> Progressive Networks developed RealAudio as an open architecture application and encourages RealAudio development by third parties.
>
> The Playback Engine application programming interface (API) provides software developers with direct access to the RealAudio Player's functionality. Because of this access, commercial Web authoring tools and other applications can incorporate RealAudio streams.
>
> The Encoder API enables developers to use a variety of audio compression algorithms with RealAudio. For example, using RealAudio Encoder 2.0 Xtra for Macintosh, you can use Macromedia's SoundEdit 16 to save sound files directly into the RealAudio format.
>
> The RealAudio APIs are available as part of the RealAudio Software Development Kit, available from the Progressive Networks Web site at **http://www.realaudio.com**.

The RealAudio Player

You can download the RealAudio Player for Windows 3.1, Windows 95, Windows NT, Macintosh, or UNIX, in either 14.4 or 28.8 versions. (You should obtain the 14.4 version only if you have a 14.4kbps dial-up connection; otherwise, get the 28.8 version.) You get two RealAudio Players: a stand-alone program that you can also use as a browser helper application, and a Netscape-compatible plug-in.

The RealAudio stand-alone application is a fully functional program that you can use to play RealAudio files from any source, including your own hard drive, a corporate intranet, or the World Wide Web. It's one of a growing number of applications that can access the Web independently of a browser program. Figure 5.2 shows the stand-alone application's interface.

Whether you listen to a prerecorded or live audio stream, and whether the audio comes from your own system, network, or the Web, a RealAudio stream begins playing as soon as the Player latches onto a few packets. You don't have to wait for the whole stream to load before it starts playing. Because you are using a stand-alone application, you can browse other Web pages while the RealAudio file continues to play in the background.

The Netscape plug-in also installs automatically when you install RealAudio. The plug-in automatically plays inline RealAudio files included on Web pages with the <EMBED> tag. The Netscape plug-in manifests itself as controls that appear inline on the Web page. The number of controls that display depends on how the RealAudio file has been embedded. (The <EMBED> tag attributes that determine which controls are displayed are covered in detail later in this chapter.) Figure 5.3 shows this plug-in's interface.

FIG. 5.2
You can use the stand-alone RealAudio Player as a browser helper application or use it to play sound files from any source.

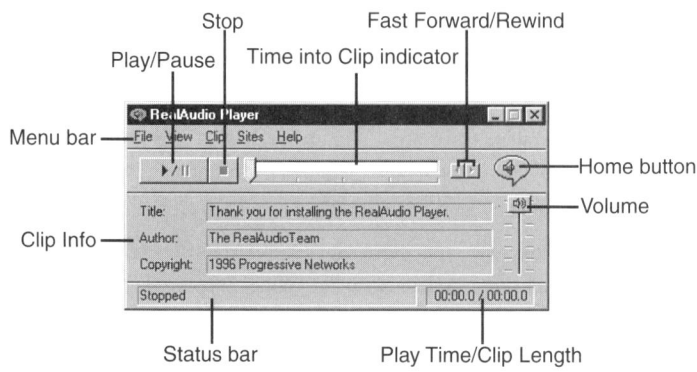

FIG. 5.3
You can verify the installation of the RealAudio plug-in by opening Netscape's Help menu and choosing About Plug-Ins.

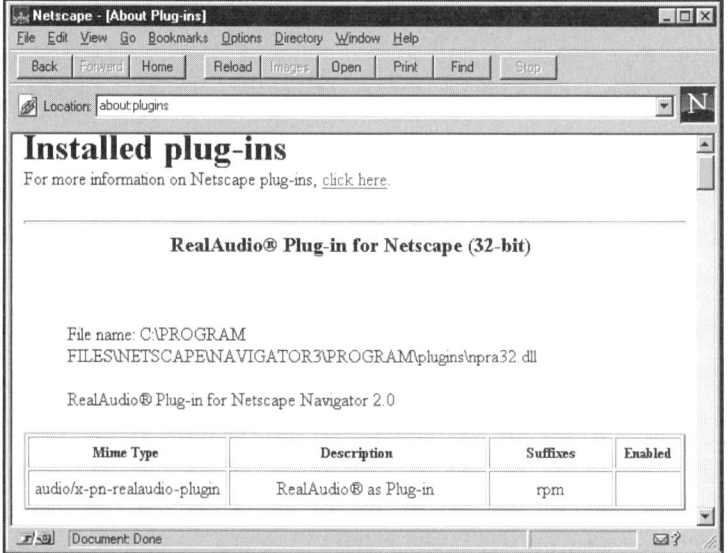

> **N O T E** If a Web page includes RealAudio content using a standard link, you must click the link to hear the audio stream. Your browser then launches the stand-alone RealAudio Player as a helper application. You must close the Player when the clip finishes playing.
>
> However, if the <EMBED> tag was used to include the RealAudio content, your browser automatically uses the RealAudio plug-in, and any activated controls appear inline on the Web page. Depending on the page design, the clip might even begin playing automatically. The plug-in remains in place until you leave the associated Web page.

Installation and Setup

You can download the latest version of the RealAudio Player setup program from the Progressive Networks Web page at **http://www.realaudio.com/products/player2.0.html**. In the online form, select the proper version and connection speed for your computer.

> **NOTE** The RealAudio Player 2.0 Standard Edition CD-ROM (for Windows 95 only) includes the RealAudio Player 2.0, technical support by e-mail, a manual, the RealAudio Encoder 2.0, and the American Recordings Jukebox. Progressive Networks describes the latter as "today's hottest music groups in a RealAudio synchronized multimedia presentation." You can order this CD-ROM, which retails for $29, by calling 1-800-632-8920.

After copying the RealAudio Player setup program to your hard drive, you install the Player for Windows as follows (Macintosh installation is similar):

1. Find the .EXE file that you downloaded to your hard drive. Double-click the file to run the setup program.
2. Accept the license.
3. Enter your name and, if applicable, company.
4. Select your Internet connection speed: 14.4, 28.8, ISDN, or T1.
5. Choose Express Setup (unless you want a custom setup).

The RealAudio Player files copy to your system. A success message then appears. The Player application automatically launches and plays a welcome message.

You can get full instructions for setting up the UNIX version of RealAudio from the Progressive Networks site:

> **NOTE** http://www.realaudio.com/help/player/unix2.0/quick.html.

If you choose Custom Setup rather than Express Setup in step 5, you can change the default directory (usually C:\RAPLAYER in all Windows versions) so that the stand-alone RealAudio Player installs. You can also choose whether to install the plug-in version of the RealAudio playcr into any browsers installed on your system.

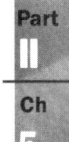

NOTE In most cases, the default RealAudio Player preferences settings should work just fine. If you have problems, you can find help on setting the preferences. This help is available at Progressive Network's Web site:

http://www.realaudio.com/help/player/win2.0/prefs.html

If you're having trouble playing RealAudio streams through your local area network's firewalls, check out the instructions at the following site:

http://www.realaudio.com/firewall.html

Controls and Menus

The RealAudio Player controls are elementary (refer to fig. 5.2).

The toolbar includes Play/Pause and Stop buttons and a Time into Clip indicator. You can also find Fast Forward/Rewind buttons, which work in 10-second increments, and a Home button. The Home button displays a spinning speaker while the Player is receiving a file, and displays a lightning bolt when encountering a high data loss. Clicking the Home button takes you to the RealAudio home page at **http://www.realaudio.com**.

The Volume slider is at the right side of the Player window. To the left of the Volume slider, the Clip Info window displays title, author, and copyright information. The status bar at the bottom of the Player window displays the Player's current state. The right side of the status bar indicates the play time and clip length.

When listening to a Web page with embedded RealAudio content, you might find inline versions of any or all these controls inside the Web page, depending on the Web page's setup.

TROUBLESHOOTING

Why don't I hear any sound from very short sound clips? The file might be too short. Current versions of the RealAudio 2.0 Player do not play files shorter than one second.

The Play, Pause, and Stop commands are also available from the context-sensitive popup menu that appears when you right-click.

The RealAudio Player menus are also pretty simple. The RealAudio File menu enables you to open a RealAudio file from a drive on your system or network, or from a server on an intranet or the World Wide Web. Open File (Ctrl+O) loads an .RA or .RAM file from a disk or network; Open Location (Ctrl+L) enables you to specify the URL of a file located on an intranet or Web site; Open Recent displays a list of recently played RealAudio files.

RealAudio URLs

A RealAudio URL has the following format:

pnm://*Server:Port#***/***pathname*

pnm:// indicates that the file is located on a RealAudio Server system. ***Server:Port#*** is the address of the RealAudio server. ***pathname*** is the complete directory path and file name. Here's a real-world example:

pnm://audio.realaudio.com/welcome.ra

From the View menu, you can choose Player Info & Volume to turn on or off the display of the Clip Info window and the Volume control, or you can choose Status Bar to control the display of the status bar. Choosing Preferences (or pressing Ctrl+P) displays the Preferences dialog box, in which you can set Network, Proxy, and other advanced options. The Statistics command displays a dialog box that contains information about the current connection. (The Preferences and Statistics dialog boxes are also available from the context-sensitive popup menu that displays when you right-click.) Finally, you can choose Always on Top to keep the RealAudio Player window on top of all other open windows.

From the Clip menu (or the context-sensitive popup menu), you can choose Previous (or press Page Up) or Next (or press Page Down) to navigate through the clip. The Sites menu takes you directly to some helpful pages; you can choose RealAudio Home Page, RealAudio Guide, or RealAudio Help Page. Finally, the Help menu offers two choices: Contents (which is the same as pressing F1) or About.

> **N O T E** If you want to find some cool RealAudio sound sites, check out Timecast (see fig. 5.4). You can find this site at **http://www.timecast.com**. Continually up-to-date, Timecast is the definitive guide to live RealAudio broadcasts and the best prerecorded RealAudio content on the Web. It's all here, from ABC news to PBS specials, from live FM radio to real-time sports broadcasts. You can even customize your own daily news broadcast with time-sensitive audio content delivered live.

FIG. 5.4
Timecast is the ultimate Web guide to RealAudio sites.

The RealAudio Encoder

To translate audio format files into RealAudio files, you use the RealAudio Encoder (see fig. 5.5). You can then play this encoded RealAudio material over an intranet or the Internet in real time, using the RealAudio Server to send and the RealAudio Player to receive.

FIG. 5.5
With the RealAudio Encoder, you can specify a source file and a destination file, and set description elements. You can also choose the compression type in the Options window.

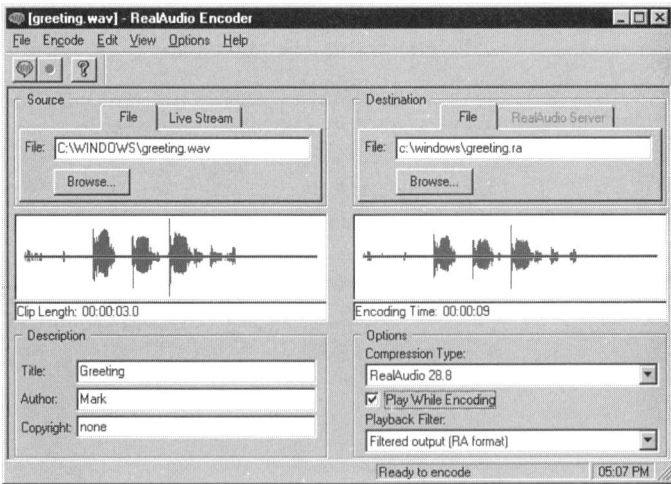

The RealAudio Encoder 2.0 is available for Windows 3.1, Windows 95, Windows NT, Macintosh, and UNIX.

Table 5.1 lists the input file formats that the RealAudio Encoder supports. Note that the RealAudio Encoder does not support stereo or compressed files.

Table 5.1 Supported File Formats for the RealAudio Encoder

Type	Sampling Rate (kHz)	Resolution
.WAV audio	8,11,22,44	8- or 16-bit, monophonic
.AU audio	8,22,44	Monophonic
Raw .PCM data	8,11,22,44	8- or 16-bit, monophonic

Installing the RealAudio Encoder

You can download the RealAudio Encoder from the Progressive Networks site:

http://www.realaudio.com/products/encoder2.0.html

Installation and setup are almost identical to that of the RealAudio Player. See the section "Installation and Setup" to review that process.

Audio encoding is more demanding than simply playing back encoded files. Progressive Networks recommends a minimum of a 486/66 CPU with 8M of RAM and 1M of hard drive space for installation of the Encoder program, plus an additional 1–2K of hard drive space per second of audio that you plan to encode and store. You also need a 16-bit sound card capable of recording an 8kHz signal, like Sound Blaster Pro or a compatible sound card.

Encoding

To start encoding, you need a sound file in .WAV, .AU, or .PCM format. The Web is a great source for a wide variety of sound files. You can find many at the following site:

http://www.yahoo.com/Computers_and_Internet/Multimedia/Sound/Archives

If you want to record your own sound files, you need an audio digitizing program. Most sound cards come with such a program. You can record audio from tape or other external audio sources using your sound card's line input, or you can record live audio using the sound card's microphone input. For the specifics of how to record sound with your particular sound card, check your sound card manual.

Adjusting Your Audio Files

The RealAudio Encoder does not support stereo or compressed files, or files of a format other than .WAV, .AU, or .PCM. If your file is in a different format, you can use a shareware program for editing audio files to convert the file to a compatible format. Pick your platform and search for *sound edit* at the following site:

> http://www.shareware.com/

When encoding a sound file, you can sometimes achieve better results if you make some adjustments to the file before you encode it. Almost any adjustment that makes the file sound cleaner and clearer will also make the final encoded version sound better. Most audio digitizing programs enable you to make at least a few basic adjustments, such as equalization or noise gating. (Along the way, you can also add cool effects like echo.) For specific audio editing tips, check out the following site:

> http://www.realaudio.com/help/content/audiohints.html

To encode audio files for RealAudio, follow these steps (refer to fig. 5.5):

1. In the RealAudio Encoder Source panel, select the File tab, click Browse, and choose the source file.
2. A default file name automatically appears in the Destination panel. Either use the default file name or select a different destination.
3. In the Options panel, select the desired compression type. RealAudio 28.8 provides higher fidelity and requires a 28.8kbps modem or faster Internet connection. RealAudio 14.4 compression is optimized for 14.4kbps modem connections, and also works with RealAudio Player 1.0.
4. In the Description panel, enter the clip's title, author, and copyright information. You can choose to leave these fields blank.
5. If you want to listen to the audio file as it is being encoded, select the Play While Encoding check box in the Options panel. Then choose to play the original audio file or the .RA file that the Encoder is creating.
6. Choose Start Encoding from the Encode menu or click the leftmost toolbar button.

Live Audio Cybercasting

The RealAudio Encoder 2.0 can encode live audio input directly from your PC's sound card. However, only the RealAudio Live Encoder provided with the RealAudio Server 2.0 can send the RealAudio output directly to the RealAudio Server for live broadcast on the Internet. A special server utility, the Live Transfer Agent (LTA), acts as a bridge between the RealAudio Live Encoder and the Server. The LTA transfers encoded RealAudio from the Live Encoder to the Server in real-time to allow for live cybercasting.

> You can encode any sound data delivered to your sound card, including CD audio. Encoder's downloadable trial version disables this feature by default.

By choosing the Options menu's Show Audio Signal command, you display amplitude graphs of the source and destination files.

The Encoder menus offer a minimal set of controls. To learn more about these intuitive controls, open the Help menu and choose Contents.

Drag and Drop and Command-Line Encoding

The RealAudio Encoder automatically encodes a .WAV or .AU file when you drag an icon of the file to the RealAudio Encoder shortcut on your Windows 95 desktop.

You can also run the Encoder from the command line. By doing so, you can have the Encoder automatically encode multiple audio files with options from a setting file. To find complete instructions for this process, see Progressive Network's Web site:

```
http://www.realaudio.com/help/encoder/win2.0/settings.html
```

Once you have an .RA format file, you need to create an associated .RAM metafile. This metafile is simply a single-line text file that contains the .RA file's full URL. The following is a typical .RAM file:

```
pnm://audio.realaudio.com/welcome.ra
```

The .RAM file containing this line would probably be called WELCOME.RAM, to clarify its association with WELCOME.RA, the encoded RealAudio file that it calls. Why do you use an intermediary .RAM file to play an .RA file? .RAM files can contain a list of URLs for .RA files that will play in sequence. (Just make sure that the .RAM files that contain lists of .RA file URLs don't contain any blank lines!) Also, .RAM metafiles can contain timing instructions that start an .RA file playing at some point within the file rather than at the beginning.

To use timing instructions, enter a dollar sign and then append the starting time to the end of the URL, as in the following example:

```
pnm://audio.realaudio.com/welcome.ra$0:30
```

This file would begin playing 30 seconds into the .RA file. The following is the complete format:

```
$dd:hh:mm:ss.t
```

where *dd* signifies days, *hh* hours, *mm* minutes, *ss* seconds, and *t* 10ths of a second (note the decimal point before the *t*).

Using RealAudio Content on Your Web Pages

If you are content with having your site's visitors launching the stand-alone RealAudio Player as a browser helper application, you can use a standard HTML link to play RealAudio files on your Web page, as in this example:

```
<A HREF="pnm://audio.realaudio.com/duck.ram">Duck Quacking</A>
```

This line of HTML code produces a text link labeled Duck Quacking that, when clicked, launches the stand-alone RealAudio Player. The visitor must then click the Play button to hear the DUCK.RAM file, then exit the RealAudio Player program.

> **CAUTION**
> You must have the RealAudio Server software installed and properly configured on your Web server computer before you can use RealAudio content on your Web pages.

A more elegant solution is to use the <EMBED> tag to incorporate an inline RealAudio file, as in the following example:

```
<EMBED SRC=" pnm://audio.realaudio.com/duck.rpm" WIDTH=300 HEIGHT=134>
```

The SRC attribute specifies the URL of the RealAudio file to play. Note that, to avoid backward-compatibility conflicts with the stand-alone RealAudio Player, URLs for use with the <EMBED> tag (which invokes the RealAudio plug-in) use an .RPM extension rather than the .RAM extension. In all other ways, however, files with an .RPM extension are identical to .RAM files—they differ only in the file name extension.

The WIDTH and HEIGHT attributes specify the size of the embedded component. Unlike images, plug-ins do not size automatically. You can specify the WIDTH and HEIGHT in pixels (the default) or percentages of screen width (as in WIDTH=100%).

The following is the generic syntax for using the <EMBED> tag with RealAudio files:

```
<EMBED SRC=source_URL WIDTH=width_value HEIGHT=height_value
    [CONTROLS=option] [AUTOSTART=True] [CONSOLE=value] [NOLABELS=True]>
```

The CONTROLS, AUTOSTART, CONSOLE, and NOLABELS attributes are all optional and unique to RealAudio.

The CONTROLS attribute defines which RealAudio Player controls appear embedded on the Web page. Table 5.2 lists all the valid values for the CONTROLS attribute.

Table 5.2 Values for the CONTROLS Attribute

Value	Meaning
All	Embeds a full Player view that includes the control panel, info volume panel, and status bar. (This setting is CONTROLS' default if you do not specify another value.)
ControlPanel	Embeds the Play/Pause button, the Stop button, and the Position slider. (The result is the same as the stand-alone Player application with none of the options on the View menu selected.)
InfoVolumePanel	Embeds the information area showing the title, author, and copyright with a Volume slider on the right side. (The result is the same as the panel that the stand-alone Player application displays when you choose the Info & Volume command from the the View menu.)
InfoPanel	Similar to InfoVolumePanel, but embeds the information area showing the title, author, and copyright without the Volume slider.
StatusBar	Embeds a status bar showing informational messages, current time-into-clip position, and clip length. (The result is the same as the panel that the stand-alone Player application displays when you choose the Status Bar command from the View menu.)
PlayButton	Embeds the Play/Pause button only.
StopButton	Embeds the Stop button only.
VolumeSlider	Embeds the Volume slider only.
PositionSlider	Embeds the Position slider (scrollbar) only.
PositionField	Embeds the field of the status bar that shows time-into-clip and clip length.
StatusField	Embeds the field of the status bar that displays message text and progress indicators.

AUTOSTART-TRUE automatically begins playing the RealAudio file when the page is visited. Use this feature to automatically begin a narration or play background music. Only one RealAudio clip can play at a time, so if you specify AUTOSTART for more than one <EMBED> tag, only the last one to load plays automatically. (The order in which the source files arrive depends on the Web server and Netscape's cache.)

The CONSOLE attribute enables you to relate any number of clips that appear on the same Web page. Normally, each clip is independent; however, those clips that are related by the CONSOLE attribute are controlled by the same controls. To relate two RealAudio clips on the same page, you simply give each clip a CONSOLE attribute with the same name. Here's an example:

```
<EMBED SRC="sample1.rpm" WIDTH=30 HEIGHT=33 CONTROLS="PlayButton"
    CONSOLE="Clip1">
<EMBED SRC="empty1.rpm" WIDTH=300 HEIGHT=33 CONTROLS="PositionSlider"
    CONSOLE="Clip1">
```

Normally, the first clip would have an associated Play button, and the second would have a Position slider. However, because these clips both have the attribute CONSOLE="Clip1", the Play button and Position slider work for both clips.

You can specify a CONSOLE value of master to link one clip to all the others on a Web page. Use this value when you want a control such as a status bar to display information for all your audio clips.

If your clip includes controls (such as InfoPanel or InfoVolumePanel) that display the title, author, and copyright information, you can suppress this information by using the attribute NOLABELS=TRUE.

Don't be concerned about those visitors who are using browsers that lack support for the <EMBED> tag. Simply use the <NOEMBED> tag to include alternate content. Follow your <EMBED> line with a line such as the this one:

```
<NOEMBED> Content for noncapable browsers </NOEMBED>
```

For example, a convenient feature is to launch the RealAudio helper application automatically if a browser doesn't support plug-ins. The following code provides this feature:

```
<EMBED SRC="sample1.rpm" WIDTH=300 HEIGHT=134>
<NOEMBED><A SRC="sample1.ram"> Use the RealAudio helper app! </A></NOEMBED>
```

> **CAUTION**
>
> Don't make the mistake of accidentally using an .RPM file rather than a .RAM file to launch the standalone RealAudio Player as a helper application. If you do so, you get a full-screen version of the RealAudio plug-in instead.
>
> The following is an example of what *not* to do:
>
> ```
> <A HREF="sample1.rpm">Play sample clip full-screen!</A>
> ```

The following HTML code implements three instances of RealAudio clips on the same Web page. Figure 5.6 shows the results.

```
<HTML>
<HEAD>
</HEAD>
<TITLE>RealAudio EMBED Examples</TITLE>
<BODY>
Here are three examples of the RealAudio plug-in.<P>
These examples require the RealAudio Player 2.0 and Netscape Navigator 2.0
    or greater.<P>
<H3>(1) Play and Stop buttons only</H3>
<EMBED SRC="audio/jazz.rpm" ALIGN=BASELINE WIDTH=40 HEIGHT=20
    CONTROLS=PlayButton CONSOLE="jazz2">
<EMBED SRC="audio/jazzs.rpm" ALIGN=BASELINE WIDTH=40 HEIGHT=20
    CONTROLS=StopButton CONSOLE="jazz2">
The "CONTROL" command specifies which attributes of the plug-in you
    want displayed.<P>
The "CONSOLE" command allows the two elements to affect the same music clip.
<H3>(2) Control Panel only</H3>
<EMBED SRC="audio/tchai.rpm" WIDTH=200 HEIGHT=35 CONTROLS=ControlPanel>
<H3>(3) Entire Plugin</H3>
<EMBED SRC="audio/pace.rpm" WIDTH=300 HEIGHT=135 CONTROLS=All>
</BODY>
</HTML>
```

FIG. 5.6
This page uses the RealAudio plug-in in three different ways.

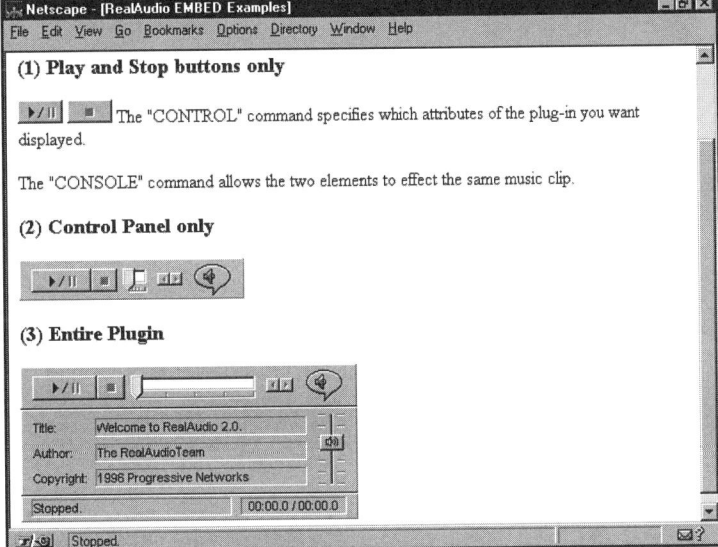

The RealAudio Servers

Two versions of the RealAudio Server are available: the RealAudio Personal Server and the RealAudio Server 2.0. Both incarnations send RealAudio audio streams over a TCP/IP network (intranet or Internet) to users of the RealAudio Player. The versions differ mostly in the number of simultaneous audio streams that they support—the Personal Server can handle two, whereas the 2.0 version can deliver from 5 to over 100 simultaneous audio streams, depending on its configuration.

The RealAudio Personal Server

The RealAudio Personal Server runs on a 486 or Pentium system running Windows 95, Windows NT, or Macintosh OS 7.5.x. To start, stop, and configure the Personal Server, you use a user-friendly graphical Windows interface. The RealAudio Personal Server can deliver two simultaneous audio streams. Each stream requires 10kbps of network bandwidth; therefore, you need a 56Kbaud or T1 leased line to use Personal Server effectively. It supports full random access for each stream and generates a log file containing usage statistics and error information.

The RealAudio Personal Server has been tested with the following Web server software:

- Netscape Netsite
- EMWAC HTTPS 0.96
- NCSA HTTPD (versions 1.3 and 1.4)
- CERN HTTPD (version 3.0)
- O'Reilly Website NT

You can set up the Personal Server to work with any Web server that supports configurable MIME types.

The suggested retail price for the RealAudio Personal Server is $99. However, as this book is being written, Personal Server is available for free downloading for evaluation purposes from the following site:

http://www.realaudio.com/persserv/apply.html

You probably want to install the RealAudio Personal Server on the same computer running your Web server. You can run Personal Server on a separate machine, but you shouldn't need to, because the server consumes so few resources. To install the Personal Server, you need only double-click the server setup file icon. When installation is complete, the RealAudio Personal Server Control Panel opens and the Personal Server is activated. However, before setting up your RealAudio Web site, you must identify the location of the file in which you want to store your audio and log files. To do so, you use the Personal Server Control Panel Setup dialog box (see fig. 5.7).

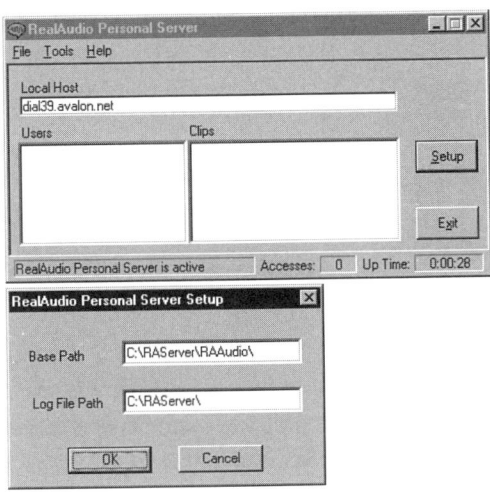

FIG. 5.7
The RealAudio Personal Server incorporates a simple Setup dialog box for defining server directory paths.

To open the Personal Server Setup dialog box, click the Setup button located on the right side of the Personal Server Control Panel. The Control Panel Setup dialog box shows two configurable paths: the base path and the log file path. All RealAudio files must reside in or beneath the directory that the Base Path control specifies. This directory contains the RealAudio Personal Server executable file. All files associated with the Personal Server, such as audio clips and Server logs, should reside in this directory's subdirectories.

To enter the base directory's full path name, you should use the following format:

   C:*path**to**rafiles*

If you specify a directory name that does not currently exist, Personal Server automatically creates one when you click the OK button to exit the Setup dialog box.

The log file path points to the location of the Personal Server log. The Personal Server log records information about clients who have connected to the Personal Server and about errors that the Personal Server has generated. To enter this directory's full path name, use the following format:

   C:*path**to**ralogfiles*

When you have entered all relevant information in the Setup dialog box, click OK. You then need to restart your system to activate the Personal Server.

Setting MIME Types

Before either version of the RealAudio Server can deliver RealAudio content, you must configure your Web server to recognize the MIME types listed in table 5.3.

Table 5.3 RealAudio MIME Types

Extension	MIME Type Definition
.RA, .RAM	Audio/x-pn-realaudio
.RPM	Audio/x-pn-realaudio/plugin

The process for setting MIME types varies from Web server to Web server—check your server documentation for details on how to set MIME types for your particular server. If you fail to set them up correctly, your site might display a screen full of indecipherable text instead of emitting any RealAudio sound.

The RealAudio Server 2.0

Progressive Networks sells the RealAudio Server 2.0 in packages that can deliver 5, 20, or 100 streams, and you can create larger custom servers. Version 2.0 also handles live audio streams as well as prerecorded ones. RealAudio Server 2.0 is available for the following Windows NT and UNIX platforms:

- DEC Alpha Digital UNIX version 3.2
- DEC Alpha Windows NT 3.51
- Hewlett-Packard PA/RISC HP/UX 10.01
- 486/Pentium Microsoft Windows NT 3.51
- 486/Pentium BSDI 2.0
- 486/Pentium LINUX 1.x, including ELF
- 486/Pentium FreeBSD 2.x
- IBM PowerPC AIX 4.0
- Sun SPARC SunOS 4.1x
- Sun SPARC Solaris 2.x
- Silicon Graphics IRIX version 5.2

Progressive Networks also plans to release a Macintosh version soon.

The RealAudio Server 2.0 requires a network bandwidth of at least 10kbps for 14.4 format and 22kbps for 28.8 format for each client connected to the Internet backbone. Therefore, a 56kbps leased line can accommodate only approximately five simultaneous 14.4kbps connections. A T1 line can accommodate over 100 simultaneous 14.4 connections and is recommended for commercial RealAudio Server applications.

Bandwidth Negotiation

Only RealAudio Server 2.0 supports the Bandwidth Negotiation feature. It allows a RealAudio Player to select automatically whether to receive a 14.4 or 28.8 encoded audio stream.

To use this feature, you must use the RealAudio Encoder to create both 14.4 and 28.8 stream files. In the directory that you have set up as your source for .RA files, you create a subdirectory for each sound that you want to deliver. Each subdirectory should contain both encoded files, and the subdirectory's name should include the .RA extension. You should call the 14.4 encoded file 14_4.18, and the 28.8 file 28_8.36. The URL listed in the associated .RAM or .RPM file should reference the subdirectory rather than a specific file. The RealAudio Server 2.0 includes the utility raconv, which automates the process of creating .RAM and .PRM files. See the Server documentation for full details.

The RealAudio Server 2.0 has been tested with the following Web servers:

- Webstar and Webstar PS
- Macintosh HTTP
- HTTPD4Mac
- Netscape Netsite
- EMWAC HTTPS 0.96
- NCSA HTTPD (versions 1.3 and 1.4)
- CERN HTTPD (version 3.0)
- O'Reilly Website NT
- Microsoft Internet Information Server

You can configure the RealAudio Server to work with any Web server that supports configurable MIME types.

> **NOTE** Installation and configuration of the RealAudio Server 2.0 can vary depending on the platform and operating system. Providing detailed instructions for this process is beyond this book's scope. Complete documentation comes with the RealAudio Server 2.0 CD-ROM, which currently costs $495 to $11,490, depending on configuration. You can purchase the Server online at the following address:
>
> http://www.realaudio.com/products/server.html

Synchronized Multimedia

Perhaps the most advanced feature of the RealAudio Server 2.0 is its capability to synchronize RealAudio clips to serve as elements in a multimedia presentation. The process is straightforward, but involves several distinct steps.

First, synchronized multimedia presentations should take place only on pages that include frames. One frame is reserved for the RealAudio plug-in with its associated controls, so you need at least one other frame to display the multimedia content. This other frame is necessary because loading a new page would otherwise replace the page containing the plug-in, and thus stop the plug-in from playing. By using frames, you keep the plug-in active.

> You can find information on creating frames on Netscape's Web site:
>
> http://home.netscape.com/assist/net_sites/frames.html

Second, you create a text file listing the times that the frame content should change, and the URLs that should load at those times. The format is as follows:

```
u starttime endtime   &&framename&&URL
```

Each line requires the starting u. The *starttime* and *endtime* elements have the format *dd:hh:mm:ss.t*, where *dd* is days, *hh* is hours, *mm* is minutes, *ss* is seconds, and *t* is 10ths of a second. (You use the same format for delayed play in .RAM files.) These times refer to the time in the clip at which the frame should begin and end playing. &&*framename*&& is the ampersand-delimited name of the target frame for the intended content change. URL is the URL of the frame to display at the indicated time. The list should include no blank lines. However, the input file can contain comment lines that begin with the pound sign (#).

The following is a real-world example:

```
u 00:00:10.0 00:00:59.9 http://www.RealAudio.com/
u 00:01:00.0 00:02:00.0 http://www.mysite.com/page2/
```

This input file tells the Player to send the Web browser to the RealAudio home page 10 seconds into the audio clip. At one minute into the audio clip, the Web browser displays a page from **www.my_site.com**.

After creating this text file, you must compile it into binary using the cevents command-line tool supplied with the RealAudio Server 2.0. The syntax is as follows:

```
cevents source.txt audiofilename.rae
```

You then place the resulting .RAE file (which should have the same base name as the associated .RA audio file) in the same directory as the .RA audio file. The RealAudio Server automatically locates this file when the visitor opens the associated .RA file. The Server streams audio and event information to the Player. As the event information streams to the RealAudio Player, it sends requests to the Web browser telling it when to update the page's content.

> **NOTE** You can find detailed information on creating RealAudio Synchronized Multimedia files at the following site:
>
> http://www.realaudio.com/products/ra2.0/features/synchmm.html

CHAPTER 6

LiveAudio and Other Audio Plug-Ins

- The hardware requirements for playing sound files in Netscape
- The kinds of audio file formats that you're likely to encounter on the World Wide Web
- The plug-ins available for playing sounds from Web pages

Netscape is mute; by itself, it can't play sound or music files. But by setting it up with the right plug-ins, you can turn Netscape into a veritable Caruso. Netscape comes with one audio plug-in, LiveAudio, but many others are available.

You need not only the right sound software, but the right hardware. Then you'll be ready to find some noisy places to visit on the Web. Fortunately, such sites are in ample supply.

http://www.mcp.com/que

Sound File Formats

On the Web, you encounter basically three kinds of sounds: digitized audio, MIDI music, and speech.

Digitized audio begins as analog audio, such as a tape, radio, or microphone signal. This audio is then digitized by the analog-to-digital converter chip in your computer's sound card.

MIDI (Musical Instrument Digital Interface) music files are actually similar to sheet music. They consist of "scoring" information that contains the notes, durations, and instrument information required to create a musical piece. Besides encountering MIDI, you might also occasionally run into other, less common, proprietary music file types, such as Sseyo's Koan music (**http://www.sseyo.com/**).

Speech comes in three formats on the Web. The first is a sort of low-quality digitized audio, similar to the digitized audio files discussed earlier, but generally with lower fidelity; they almost always are also highly compressed. The second is text that is converted to speech by breaking it into phonemes that are then delivered as sound. The last is speech recognition, which involves breaking up an audio input file into its component parts, which are then interpreted as commands. These last two forms of Web-based speech are currently the exclusive domain of the Macintosh, thanks to special Apple system files created just for those purposes.

> **NOTE** You can find out all about audio file formats by checking out the Audio FAQ (frequently asked questions) list on UseNet. You can retrieve the latest version by pointing Netscape to **ftp://ftp.cwi.nl/pub/audio**. Look for the files AUDIOFORMATS.PART1 and AUDIOFORMATS.PART2.
>
> You also can obtain more information by reading the UseNet newsgroup **alt.binaries.sounds**.

Digitized Audio for the Web

Most of the sounds from your PC are *digitized*—that is, the waves that make up the sound were fed through some kind of analog-to-digital converter, which converted the waves into a stream of digital bits and bytes. You can perform this conversion yourself on any audio source, such as a microphone or tape player, by using the software that came with your sound board. After digitizing the sound data, you save it as a file on disk.

Digitized sound files vary in at least three important ways. First is the sampling rate, or the number of times each second that the audio wave form is sampled as it is converted to digital data. PC sound file sampling rates usually range from 8,000 to 44,100 samples per second. (More samples equal higher-quality sound.)

Second is the way that the file organizes the data. For example, a digitized sound file might include header information that describes the file; might interleave the data from multiple sound tracks (such as two tracks for stereo); or might consist of a library of different instrument sound samples followed by a "play list" for using the samples to play a song.

Finally, the data in a sound file might be compressed in some way to save disk space and transfer time. For example, MPEG audio files are compressed at a 6:1 ratio.

There are a dozen or more relatively popular sound file types, each of which varies in the way that it stores sound data.

Digitizing Your Own Sounds

If you want to deliver digitized audio on the Web using any of the plug-ins discussed in this chapter, you must start with a digitized sound file. You can download many from the Web itself, but you have to ensure that any files that you intend to use were not copyrighted. For example, you cannot use sound clips from cartoons or movies without the copyright owners' permission. You can begin your search for digitized sounds on the Web at the following site:

> http://www.yahoo.com/Computers_and_Internet/Multimedia/Sound/Archives

To digitize your own sounds, you need the sound-digitizing program that came with your sound card. Just check your documentation and follow the steps. As an example, this section describes a typical session with Creative Wave, the sound-digitizing program bundled with the Sound Blaster Pro audio card.

First, you need to determine whether you want to record live or prerecorded audio. If you choose to use prerecorded audio, you must plug your tape player or other sound source into the Line In jack on the back of your audio card. If you want to record live audio, you need to use a microphone plugged into the Mike jack. Suppose that you plug in a mike and record live.

Figure 6.1 shows the Creative Wave program's interface. Creative Wave is a typical sound-digitizing program in that it has a common control window (at the top of the screen). You use this window to select functions ranging from setting up "jukebox" playback sessions, to playing MIDI music files, to the current task at hand, digitizing audio.

FIG. 6.1
A sound-digitizing program ships with just about every sound card sold. This one, Creative Wave, is bundled with the Sound Blaster Pro.

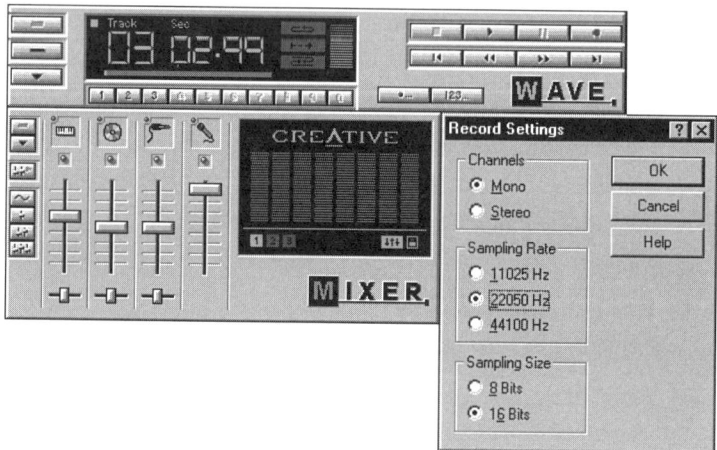

The leftmost window is the audio source selection window, which you can find by experimenting with the menus. It shows level controls for MIDI, audio CD, line, and microphone inputs. Because you're recording a mike input, you slide all these controls to zero except the mike input, which you run about three-fourths full. You adjust this setting later, after experimenting with recording some audio.

The rightmost window enables you to set some basic file options. These options vary depending on the type of file that you want to create. For voice, you might choose mono output, at a low sampling rate like 11kHz, with only eight bits of resolution. For music, you might want stereo at the highest sampling rate and 16-bit resolution. The requirements of the plug-in that you intend to use usually determine these factors.

After you set up everything to record with this program, you simply click the record button on the main console window. A file requester dialog box displays in which you can specify a file name for your recording. After clicking OK, you speak into the microphone, then click the Stop button to end the recording session. You can then play back your recorded message by clicking the Play button.

The whole process is fairly straightforward—as similar to using a tape recorder as the programmers could make it.

Some sound-recording programs are more complex, and include sound editing and special effects that can make your recordings sound more professional. If these features aren't built in to your digitizing program, a couple of shareware programs for Windows 95 and Windows 3.1 enable you to spice up your digitized sounds. Similar programs exist for the Macintosh, PowerPC, and UNIX systems.

Sound Gadget Pro

Using Sound Gadget Pro, you can dissect sounds and then reassemble them in new and different ways. The plug-in can handle digitized sounds in .AU, .SND, .WAV, and .VOC (Sound Blaster) formats, as well as raw sound files. Figure 6.2 shows Sound Gadget Pro's interface.

FIG. 6.2
Sound Gadget Pro enables you to view, edit, and listen to digitized sound files.

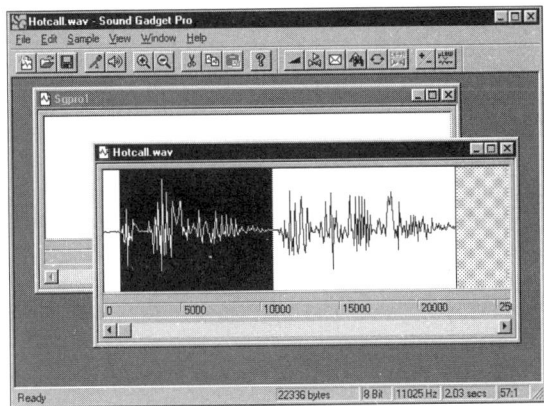

Even though shareware author Nigel Magnay has chosen to inconvenience you a bit when this program launches (you have to click three randomly selected buttons before it runs), this program is such a nice sound editor that you won't mind these minor inconveniences. You'll probably even figure out how much 10 British pounds is in American dollars and send Nigel his shareware fee.

Sound Gadget Pro enables you to view a sound's waveform and manipulate it in a seemingly infinite number of ways. You can reverse it, convert it to another format, change it from 8 to 16 bits or vice versa, and likewise from mono to stereo. You can fade, cross-fade, cut, paste, and even apply a dynamic envelope. After only a few minutes of playing around with SGPro's highly intuitive Windows 95 interface, you'll be turning staid voice-overs into Hollywood-style sound-effect extravaganzas.

Waveform Hold and Modify

Waveform Hold and Modify (WHAM) not only plays .VOC, .IFF, .AU/.SND, .WAV, and raw sound files, but also enables you to edit those files in dozens of different ways. Figure 6.3 shows WHAM's interface.

FIG. 6.3
WHAM is a great sound-editing program for Windows 3.1.

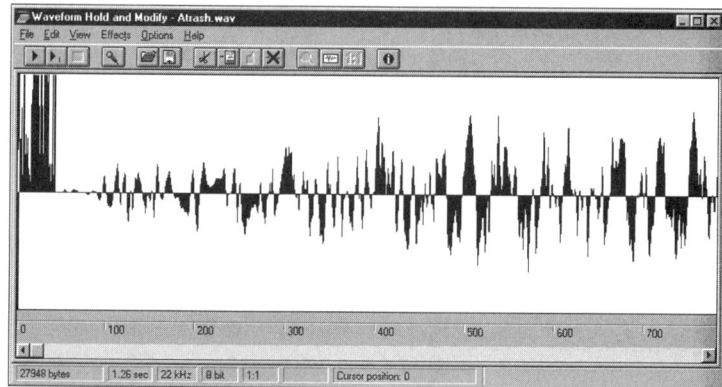

Like Sound Gadget Pro for Windows 95, WHAM lets you reverse, cut, paste, convert, and do just about anything you want to sound files.

If you like WHAM and continue to use it, Australian author Andrew Bulhak requests a shareware fee of $25–30.

The LiveAudio Plug-In

After producing a satisfactory a sound file, you choose a plug-in for listening to your sound over the Web.

The Windows 3.1, Windows 95, Macintosh, and PowerPC versions of Netscape 3.0 include the LiveAudio plug-in. The Windows 3.1 and Windows 95 versions require a minimum of a 386 processor and a compatible sound card. The Macintosh version requires at least a Macintosh 68030 with System 7.1. The PowerPC version needs a PPC 601 (66mHz) with System 7.1.2. Both Macintosh versions also require QuickTime 2.1 with Musical Instrument Plug-In and Sound Manager 3.1. When you install Netscape 3.0, you automatically install the LiveAudio plug-in.

As long as your system is equipped with a sound card, LiveAudio enables you to listen to audio tracks, sound effects, music, and voice files embedded in Web pages. You can also use LiveAudio to listen to stand-alone sound files both on the Web and on your own computer system.

LiveAudio is a huge improvement over the NAPlayer audio helper application that Netscape shipped with previous versions of Netscape Navigator. Where NAPlayer played only Sun/NeXT (.AU and .SND) and Mac/SGI (.AIF and .AIFF) sound files, LiveAudio automatically identifies and plays four of the most popular standard sound formats:

The LiveAudio Plug-In   139

- .AIFF, the Mac/SGI sound format
- .AU, the Sun/NeXT sound format
- MIDI, the Musical Instrument Digital Interface music format
- .WAV, the Microsoft Windows sound format

.AU files were once the Internet standard file format, .AIFF files are the Macintosh standard, and .WAV files are the Windows standard file, so LiveAudio can play a good percentage of the nonproprietary sound files that you're likely to encounter on the Web. Add in its capability to play MIDI music, and LiveAudio proves itself a very good "Swiss Army Knife" plug-in for Web audio.

When you encounter a LiveAudio-compatible sound file embedded or linked into a Web page, LiveAudio creates the onscreen control console shown in figure 6.4.

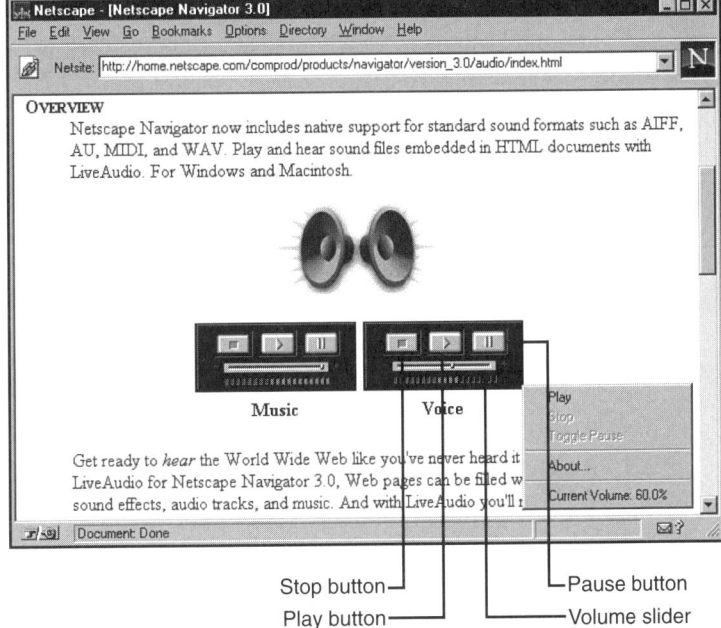

FIG. 6.4
The LiveAudio plug-in appears as a minimalist inline audio-player control console, shown here on a Netscape Web site demo page. The LiveAudio audio player control box features four manual controls and a simple drop-down menu.

The LiveAudio plug-in works with both embedded sound files, like the two that it encountered in figure 6.4, and with stand-alone sound files. In the case of stand-alone files, a blank Netscape window displays that contains only a LiveAudio console.

The LiveAudio console controls are intuitive and easy to use (refer to fig. 6.4). The Stop, Play, and Pause buttons work just as they do on a tape or CD player. You click the Play button to play the sound, the Stop button to stop it, and the Pause button to pause audio playback. If you click the Pause button a second time, play resumes from the point at which you paused the sound.

Click to the right or left of the Volume slider knob to increase or decrease volume. The volume can be jumped only in increments of 20 percent—you can't slide the volume smoothly from 0 percent to 100 percent. The light-emitting diode (LED) bar graph below the Volume slider indicates the current volume level. The dark green LEDs are for the 0–40 percent range; light green LEDs take over for 40–100 percent.

Clicking the LiveAudio console displays the popup menu shown in figure 6.4. This menu includes selections that duplicate the Play, Stop, and Pause buttons. The menu also provides a selection to display the program's About dialog box and a final nonselectable menu item that tells you the volume level as a percentage of the maximum.

The LiveAudio player has a single keyboard hot key: the spacebar. Pressing the spacebar reactivates whichever button you pressed last (Stop, Play, or Pause). Restopping an already stopped playback is of limited use, but if you last pressed Pause, the spacebar becomes an unpause/repause toggle. If you last pressed Play, the spacebar becomes a handy replay key.

The way in which you use the <EMBED> tag determines how the LiveAudio console actually appears. In fact, <EMBED> tag's attributes control several different aspects of the LiveAudio plug-in's functionality. Here's a typical example:

```
<EMBED SRC="audio.aif" WIDTH=144 HEIGHT=60 AUTOSTART=false VOLUME=100
    CONTROLS=Console>
```

This example plays the Macintosh sound file AUDIO.AIF (SRC="audio.aif") only when the user presses the Play button (AUTOSTART=false). The LiveAudio control window is 144 pixels wide (WIDTH=144) and 60 pixels high (HEIGHT=60) and contains a complete control console (CONTROLS=Console).

Table 6.1 lists all the attributes associated with the <EMBED> tag for the LiveAudio plug-in, as well as their legal values. All attributes are optional except for SRC, WIDTH, and HEIGHT.

Table 6.1 <EMBED> Tag Attributes for the LiveAudio Plug-In

Attribute	Values
SRC="*filename*"	A file name with an extension associated with a MIME type assigned to be played by LiveAudio (.AU, .AIFF, .AIF, .WAV, .MIDI, or .MID). Required.
WIDTH=*integer*	The control console width in pixels. Required.
HEIGHT=*integer*	The control console height in pixels. Required.

Attribute	Values
AUTOSTART=TRUE¦FALSE	If True, the sound clip plays automatically. The default is False.
AUTOLOAD=TRUE¦FALSE	If False, the sound clip does not automatically load. The default is True.
STARTTIME="mm:ss"	The start time in minutes and seconds from the start of the clip. The default is 00:00.
ENDTIME="mm:ss"	The end time in minutes and seconds from the start of the clip. The default is the end of the clip.
VOLUME=percentage	Playback volume expressed as a percentage of the maximum. The default is the last previously set volume.
ALIGN="value"	The point at which to align the control panel with respect to adjoining text. The possible values are CENTER, BASELINE, TOP, LEFT, and RIGHT. BASELINE is the default.
CONTROLS="value"	The controls to include on the control panel. The values can be CONSOLE, SMALLCONSOLE, PLAYBUTTON, PAUSEBUTTON, STOPBUTTON, or VOLUMELEVER. The remainder of this table describes the sets of controls associated with each of these values. The default is CONSOLE.
CONSOLE	A full set of controls: Play, Pause, Stop, and Volume.
SMALLCONSOLE	A reduced set of controls consisting of Play, Stop, and Volume. AUTOSTART defaults to True.
PLAYBUTTON	The Play button only.
PAUSEBUTTON	The Pause button only.
STOPBUTTON	The Stop button. Also, the sound file unloads.
VOLUMELEVER	The Volume control only.
CONSOLE="name"	A combination of controls that enables you to include multiple sound clips on a page. For example, you could specify CONSOLE="MySetup" as an attribute on two <EMBED> lines on a single HTML page; then each line would use the controls defined by the other as well as its own.

N O T E If you specify the settings CONTROLS="VolumeLever" and CONSOLE="_MASTERVOLUME", the user changes the system's master volume (not just the sound clip's volume) by manipulating the volume slider.

To enable your Web server to deliver LiveAudio-compatible content, you first must set up the proper MIME types. How you do so varies with the specific server software; check your server documentation or ask your system administrator to set up the following MIME types with associated file name extensions:

MIME Type	Extensions
audio/basic	.AU
audio/x-aiff	.AIF, .AIFF
audio/aiff	.AIF, .AIFF
audio/x-wav	.WAV
audio/wav	.WAV
audio/x-midi	.MID, .MIDI
audio/midi	.MID, .MIDI

ToolVox

Optimized for delivery of digitized speech, the ToolVox plug-in provides audio compression ratios of up to 53:1, so that you can transfer very small files over the Internet. Digitized speech can be delivered in real time even over 9,600-baud modems. You can slow down playback by two times to improve comprehension, or speed it up to reduce listening times in half without changing voice pitch. Like the higher-fidelity RealAudio (see Chapter 5, "RealAudio"), ToolVox streams audio in real time so that you don't have to wait for a file to download before you can listen to it.

Netscape Communications Corporation has become a part-owner of Voxware, the makers of ToolVox, so you can expect to hear a lot more about it in the future. Netscape has also licensed key elements of Voxware's digital voice technology, including the Voxware RT24 compressor/decompressor (codec) and ToolVox, for incorporation into the Netscape LiveMedia multimedia standard.

Unlike RealAudio, ToolVox transfers audio data through a standard TCP connection, not UDP, so the plug-in doesn't need special server software to deliver audio content from any Web server. All you need to do is add to your Web server the MIME type audio/voxware with the associated file name extension .VOX.

ToolVox consists of two elements: the ToolVox Player plug-in and the ToolVox Encoder.

ToolVox Player plug-ins are available for Windows 95 and Windows 3.1, and Voxware plans to release Macintosh and PowerMac versions. You can download them from the Voxware site:

http://www.voxware.com/download.htm

All versions are self-installing executables, so installation is simply a matter of running the file that you download. If you use a browser that can't implement plug-ins, you can configure the ToolVox Player as a helper application.

As you can see in figure 6.5, the ToolVox Player implements itself by default as a small control box consisting of an LED-style sound level bar graph, an elapsed time counter, a rewind button, a Play/Stop button, and a playback speed control.

FIG. 6.5
The ToolVox Player is utilitarian but effective. You can also display the ToolVox Player as a simple click-to-play icon by using the <EMBED> tag attribute VisualMode=ICON.

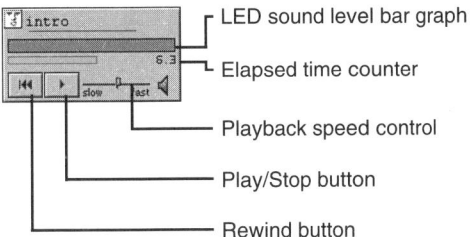

- LED sound level bar graph
- Elapsed time counter
- Playback speed control
- Play/Stop button
- Rewind button

N O T E Voxware has announced plans to release an enhanced version of ToolVox called ToolVox Gold. For the latest information on this incarnation of ToolVox, check the Voxware site:

http://www.voxware.com

The ToolVox Encoder compresses speech files from .WAV format to an 8kHz, 2,400bps .VOX file, using Voxware's RT24 codec. The self-installing Encoder is available for the same platforms and from the same Web page as the Player. Encoder outputs compressed .VOX format files that you can add to Web pages by using the <EMBED> tag.

To create .VOX files using the ToolVox Encoder, you start with a .WAV or .AIF audio file containing clear, simple speech. The simpler the audio content, the more successful the conversion process will be. Source files should be at least two seconds long; otherwise, you should pad them with enough silence to make the file at least that long.

You use the <EMBED> tag to add a .VOX file to your Web page. For example, to play the file WELCOME.VOX when a page first loads and displays the Player, you would enter the following:

```
<EMBED SRC="welcome.vox" PLAYMODE=auto VISUALMODE=player HEIGHT=82
WIDTH=160>
```

Table 6.2 describes the attributes that you can associate with the `<EMBED>` tag for ToolVox.

Table 6.2 *<EMBED>* Tag Attributes for Use with the ToolVox Plug-In

Attribute	Values	
SRC="*filename*"	A file name with an extension (.VOX) associated with the MIME type assigned to be played by ToolVox. Required.	
WIDTH=*integer*	The control console's width in pixels. Required.	
HEIGHT=*integer*	The control console's height in pixels. Required.	
PLAYMODE=*value*	How and when the .VOX file is played. The values can be USER, AUTO, or CACHE. Default is AUTO.	
	USER	To begin playing sound, the user must click either the Voxware icon or the Play button in the Player.
	AUTO	The sound begins to play automatically when the browser displays the Web page.
	CACHE	After the .VOX file first downloads, the user must click either the Voxware icon or the Play button in the Player to hear the file.
VISUALMODE=*value*	The Player's display. Values can be ICON, PLAYER (or EMBED), BACKGROUND, or FLOAT. The default is PLAYER.	
	ICON	The Voxware icon appears on the Web page. Users click the icon to start or stop playback. You *must* use the exact parameters HEIGHT=50 and WIDTH=50 to display a large icon, or HEIGHT=27 and WIDTH=27 for the small icon.
	PLAYER	You can use `<EMBED>` rather than PLAYER but this is too easily confused with the `<EMBED>` command. The full Player interface appears on the Web page. You *must* use the exact parameters HEIGHT=82 and WIDTH=160.
	BACKGROUND	The page has no user interface—and provides no way for the user to stop the sound from playing. You *must* also specify the setting PLAYMODE=AUTO.
	FLOAT	The Player appears in a separate window. (Only Windows ToolVox Players recognize this value. The Macintosh OS Player substitutes the setting VISUALMODE=PLAYER.)

> **NOTE** To add a .VOX file to your Web page for delivery using ToolVox as a helper application, use the HTML tag HREF. For example, the following line plays the file WELCOME.VOX:
>
> ```
> <A HREF=welcome.vox>Click here to play VOX file.</A>
> ```
>
> Use both the `<EMBED>` plug-in version and the HREF helper application version if you want to enable all browsers to play ToolVox sounds as gracefully as possible.

Other Audio Plug-Ins for Digitized Audio

As ToolVox is to highly compressed digitized speech, RapidTransit is to highly compressed digitized music. RapidTransit decompresses and plays music that has been compressed up to 40:1. It can provide full 16-bit, 44.1kHz sound quality. RapidTransit is available for Windows 95, Windows NT, and Macintosh. You can find out all about it at the following site:

http://monsterbit.com/rapidtransit/

If nothing else, developing content for the TrueSpeech plug-in is convenient. If you're using Windows 3.1 or Windows 95, the system-supplied Sound Recorder program can digitize sound files and convert them to TrueSpeech format. You can then use the TrueSpeech Player to listen to them on the Web in real time. Despite its name, TrueSpeech can be used for any type of audio file. No special server is needed. You can download TrueSpeech players for Windows 3.1, Windows 95, Windows NT, Macintosh, and PowerMac from the DSP Group's home page:

http://www.dspg.com

Echospeech compresses speech at a ratio of 18.5:1. Therefore, 16-bit speech sampled at 11,025Hz compresses to 9,600bps. Even users with 14.4kbps modems can listen to real-time Echospeech audio streams. Echospeech was designed to code speech sampled at 11,025Hz rather than 8,000Hz, so the plug-in sounds better than ToolVox. No server software is required to deliver Echospeech content; your Internet service provider (ISP) or server administrator only needs to declare a new MIME type and pay a one-time $99 license fee. To add Echospeech files to your Web pages, you compress the files with the Echospeech Speech Coder (which you download and evaluate for free) and then use the HTML `<EMBED>` tag to include them in your documents. Echospeech is available for Windows 95 and Windows 3.1, and a Macintosh version is promised. You can get Echospeed from the following site:

http://www.echospeech.com

The Bamba audio plug-in is of interest mostly because of its pedigree—it is apparently the only Netscape plug-in from IBM. For Windows 95 and Windows NT only, the Bamba plug-in is delivering the audio content on the official 1996 Olympics Web site. You can download the player from the following site:

http://www.ibm.com/Technology/adtech/ibmbamba.exe

You can then test Bamba at the Olympic site:

http://www.atlanta.olympic.org/

MIDI Music: Crescendo and Crescendo Plus

Most sound cards go a step beyond merely digitizing and playing back sounds. They can also generate their own sounds. If your sound card is MIDI-compatible (and most are), you have more than a passive record-and-playback system—you have a full-fledged music synthesizer.

MIDI music files (.MID and .MIDI) are completely different than other sound file formats. Originally developed to control electronic musical instruments, the MIDI file format has become extremely popular on PCs since the advent of MIDI-capable sound cards.

MIDI files combine sound definitions called *instruments* with MIDI sequence control commands that tell a MIDI device (such as your PC's sound board) which instruments to play, when to play them, how long to play them, and with what settings. In a way, a MIDI file is more like a printed sheet-music score than a digitized sound file. In fact, MIDI files don't contain digitized sounds at all, unless the file uses custom instrument definitions.

With a MIDI plug-in, you can experience Web sites with a full music soundtrack. LiveUpdate's Crescendo plug-in enables Navigator to play inline MIDI music embedded in Web pages. With a MIDI-capable browser, you can create Web pages that have their own background music soundtracks. MIDI instruments can be sampled sounds, so you can also create sound-effects tracks.

Crescendo requires a Multimedia Personal Computer (MPC), MIDI-capable sound card, and Netscape Navigator version 2.0 or above. It launches automatically and invisibly and is a fun addition to Web browsing.

You can download Windows 3.1, Windows 95, and Macintosh versions of Crescendo from the following site:

http://www.liveupdate.com/midi.html

An enhanced version called Crescendo Plus adds onscreen controls and live streaming (you don't have to wait for a MIDI file to download completely before it starts playing). You can purchase Crescendo Plus from LiveUpdate's Web site. Figure 6.6 shows the plug-in's interface.

FIG. 6.6
Crescendo Plus features a convenient popup menu and a control panel that resembles a CD player.

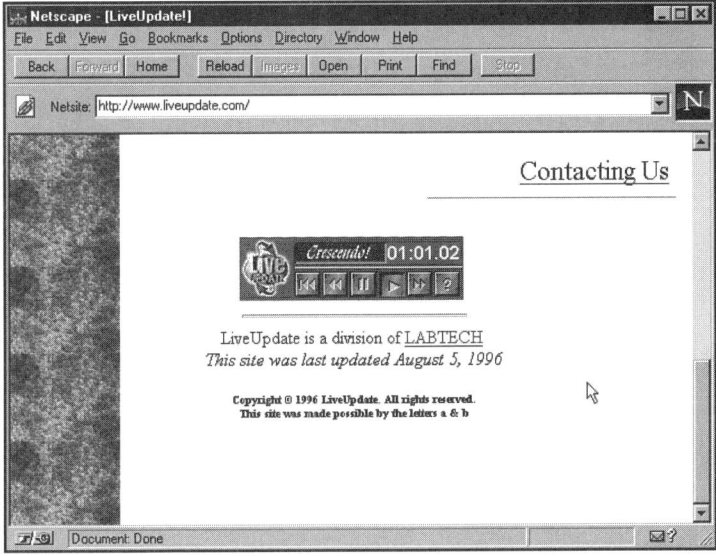

To deliver Crescendo-compatible MIDI music from your Web server, you need only set the proper MIME types—`audio/midi`, `audio/x-midi`, `application/x-midi`, or `audio/x-mid`—with the extension .MID.

The `<EMBED>` tag uses the `SRC`, `WIDTH`, and `HEIGHT` attributes that are ubiquitous with embedded content, as well as one other: `AUTOSTART`. If you specify the setting `AUTOSTART=TRUE`, a MIDI file begins playing automatically. Here's a typical example:

```
<EMBED SRC="song.mid" WIDTH=200 HEIGHT=55 AUTOSTART=TRUE>
```

Note that, if you set the value of `WIDTH` and `HEIGHT` too low, you cannot view the Crescendo Plus control panel, and even the Crescendo icon could be too small to read.

Other Music Plug-Ins

Yamaha's MIDPlug is available for Windows 3.1, Windows 95, and PowerPC. This plug-in features a built-in Yamaha "Soft Synthesizer." You can find MIDPlug at the following site:

http://www.yamaha.co.jp/english/xg/html/midhm.html

Arnaud Masson's MIDI plug-in is for the Macintosh and PowerMac only. This plug-in is available at the following site:

http://www.planete.net/~amasson/

Another Macintosh-only plug-in for MIDI files is GRAME's MidiShare. You can find MidiShare at the following address:

http://www.grame.fr/english/MidiShare.html

If you prefer the sound of the Orient, Sseyo's Koan might suit you. Koan plays real-time computer-generated Japanese Koan music on Windows 95 and Windows 3.1 versions of Netscape. You can find Koan at the following site:

http://www.sseyo.com/

Talker and Other Macintosh Speech Plug-Ins

MVP Solutions' Talker plug-in is just for the Macintosh. Talker uses the Macintosh's built-in PlainTalk speech synthesis technology to create text-to-speech voice messages—in other words, it "reads" text files to you out loud. This technology uses much less bandwidth than recorded audio, and you can change the words that your Web page speaks by editing a text file.

Talker gives Macintosh owners an advantage over Windows and Windows 95 Netscape users—this plug-in will never work on those platforms because they lack the speech-synthesis technology of the Macintosh. You can find Talker at the following site:

http://www.mvpsolutions.com/PlugInSite/Talker.html

Talker text files usually contain many inflection commands, as in the following example:

```
[[pmod +1; pbas +1]]Hello! [[pmod -1; pbas -1]] This World Wide Web page
     [[emph -; emph -]] can [[emph + ; emph +]] talk. You can make it
     [[emph + ]] stop talking by pressing [[emph -]] thee
     [[emph + ; emph +]] escape key.
```

You can find out all about the Talker text-to-speech process—and the commands used to create Talker speech files—at the following site:

http://www.mvpsolutions.com/PlugInSite/TalkerTutor.html

William H. Tudor's Speech plug-in for the Macintosh and PowerMac does essentially the same thing as Talker. You can get it from the following site:

http://www.albany.net/~wtudor/

NOTE Talker and the Speech plug-in rely on Apple's English Text-to-Speech software. If you haven't yet installed this software on your Macintosh, you can download a copy of the English Text-to-Speech installer from Apple's site:

> ftp://ftp.info.apple.com/Apple.Support.Area/Apple.Software.Updates/US/Macintosh/System/PlainTalk_1.4.1/English_Text-to-Speech.sea.hqx

Macintosh plug-ins aren't limited only to talking to you—they can also listen to you and understand what you say!

Bill Noon's ListenUp is for the Power Macintosh running System 7.5 or above. This plug-in also requires the PlainTalk Speech Recognition version 1.5 program. Essentially, when you speak a keyword or two, this plug-in then takes you to a corresponding URL. You can find out all the details and download the plug-in from the following site:

> http://snow.cit.cornell.edu/noon/ListenUp.html

Digital Dream's ShockTalk speech-recognition plug-in isn't a Netscape plug-in at all; it's a plug-in for the Shockwave for Director plug-in! ShockTalk is available for Macintosh and PowerMac, and you can get it from the following site:

> http://www.surftalk.com/

CHAPTER 7

Plug-Ins for Graphics Display and Compression

- How Netscape works with graphics
- The graphics file formats that you're likely to encounter on the World Wide Web
- Plug-ins for displaying bitmap images in a variety of formats
- Plug-ins for graphic compression

If the World Wide Web were a box of Raisin Bran, the text would be the bran flakes and the graphics would be the raisins. Although most of the Web's "nutritional content" may be in the text, the graphics are what make the Web tastier and just plain more fun than the rest of the Internet.

Netscape can display GIF and JPEG graphics just fine, but there are many, many more graphic formats out there. Graphics files can be large, and some of the newer formats compress images so that they transfer across the Internet more quickly. This chapter discusses plug-ins that display a greater variety of the "standard" graphics formats than Netscape itself is capable of handling. You also look at some graphics compression plug-ins. Chapter 8, "CorelDRAW!, AutoCAD, and Other Graphics Plug-Ins," discusses plug-ins that display proprietary graphic formats for special purposes, such as engineering, business, and 3-D. ■

http://www.mcp.com/que

Hardware Requirements for Netscape Graphics

Many older desktop PCs and notebook computers are limited in their graphics capabilities. If your machine can't display any more than 16 colors, this chapter isn't for you. (And face it, it's time to upgrade that antique!)

The minimum for cruising the Web these days is a 640×480 screen capable of displaying 256 colors. If your computer can do at least this well, you'll be able to view 85 percent or more of the graphics you find on the Web with no problem.

Of course, the *real* cutting-edge sites have pages that look good only on an 800×600 (or more) screen, with 16-bit (65,536 colors) or 24-bit (16,777,216 colors) palettes. Personally, I try to avoid such sites. They are a real killer on a 28.8kbps dial-up connection because the more colors a graphic uses, the longer it takes to transfer.

Trying to view a big page on a small screen? No problem! Just use the scrollbar at the bottom of the Netscape window to move horizontally. Most people don't pay any attention to it on "normal" size screens, so they forget it's there when viewing pages that are a little wider than normal.

Still, some of those images are well worth waiting for. And once you've got them, you've got to have *some* way to display them.

Check the manual for your PC's display card to see what it's capable of. If your display card is more than a couple of years old, you may want to upgrade so you can handle those big, beautiful images. If your pocketbook says "no," don't despair. You can still look at them…if you're willing to compromise a bit.

Read your display card manual carefully! Even if your display isn't what you'd like it to be, it may be possible for you to plug in more *video RAM* and bring it up to speed. This is a much cheaper solution than buying a whole new graphics card!

How Computer Graphics Work

Most computer graphics are bitmapped images; that is, they consist of a grid of dots called pixels that are mapped to a color palette. For example, the minimum Windows 95 display screen is 640 pixels wide by 480 pixels high (640×480), with a palette of 16 colors.

Many of the graphics images you'll encounter on the Web come in one of four "standard" sizes, which happen to match the screen sizes of common computer displays: 320×200,

640×480, 800×600, and 1,024×768. However, you'll find bitmaps on the Web in sizes ranging from tiny "thumbnails" with dimensions of only a few pixels to images so huge your computer can't even load them, much less display them.

The number of colors in an image is dependent on how many bits are used to define the color for each pixel. Table 7.1 shows how many bits are required for the four most common color palette depths.

Table 7.1 Number of Bits Needed To Define Different Image Color Palettes

Number of Bits	Colors in Palette
4	16
8	256
16	65,536
24	16,777,216

Don't forget that black, white, and gray are colors, too! A two-color image (one bit) is always monochrome (black-and-white). But four- and eight- bit images are sometimes grayscale images, with each pixel's value indicating brightness, not color.

An image's color palette is generally defined in one of two ways.

For images with 16, 256, or 65,536 colors, the number that defines each pixel's color is usually a pointer into a table of predefined or user-definable colors. For example, a bit with the color "233" would point to the 233rd color defined in the color palette table. A color palette table defines colors using more bits than are used to indicate the color for each pixel. In this way, you can have images that, for example, use 256 colors out of a possible 24-bit color palette of 16 million.

But images with 24-bit color definitions usually indicate color values directly. This is done on a pixel-by-pixel basis using the same scheme that defines color palettes for entire low-color images—by splitting the number of bits for each color value into RGB (Red, Green, Blue) values. (This is because a video monitor builds up an image from red, green, and blue dots.) For example, a 24-bit image splits the palette into eight bits each for red, green, and blue values. That is, each color is made up of 256 different shades each of the three colors, for a total of 16,777,216 possible colors in a single image.

How Netscape Displays Graphics

Most computer graphic images do not share the same set of colors. This can result in color "thrashing" if, for example, your computer tries to display two 256-color images with different color palettes on the same 256-color screen. Your computer picks the palette for one of the images and uses that palette to display both images. The image whose palette was picked ends up looking good, but the other can look like an op-art or impressionist painting, depending on how close the colors happen to match.

You can also run into problems trying to display an image with more colors than your display can handle, like a 16 million color JPEG on a 256-color screen.

Fortunately, Netscape is very clever about how it displays inline graphics. It handles these problems by using a process called "dithering."

Dithering uses a pattern of available colors to create a visual illusion of displaying more. For example, if the Netscape screen palette had no orange available to it, it might try to "fake" orange by displaying a grid of yellow and red pixels. Your eye interprets the area as orange if you don't look at it too closely.

NOTE Netscape actually does a very good job of dithering images. Dithering selection is automatic in Netscape 2.0 and above, although you can change it manually.

To change Netscape's setting for dithering images, follow these steps:

1. Select Options, General Preferences from the Netscape menu.
2. Select the Images tab.
3. You can then choose one of the three dithering methods by selecting the proper radio button:
   - Automatic is checked by default. If you leave it checked, Netscape continues to decide when it does and doesn't need to dither an image.
   - Dither causes Netscape always to dither images to its internal "Color Cube" of reference colors.
   - Substitute Colors turns off dithering altogether; Netscape then always picks the closest solid color available.
4. Click OK to end.

Graphics File Formats

There are three ways that images can be stored in files: bitmaps, vector images, or metafiles.

Most computer graphics file formats store image information as bitmaps. All three of the image types that Netscape can display natively—GIFs, JPEGs, and XBMs—are bitmapped images.

> **NOTE** GIFs and JPEGs aren't really bitmapped image files; they're *compressed* bitmapped image files.

GIFs are 256-color (or less) images that are compressed using LZW compression, a technique similar to the file-compression algorithms used in various archive file formats.

A JPEG image begins life as a 24-bit bitmapped image; then a very sophisticated image-compression algorithm takes over. This analyzes the picture and compresses it greatly. JPEG compression is actually "lossy"—that is, it usually doesn't care if it throws away some picture detail in order to make the image a whole lot smaller.

XBMs are monochrome bitmapped images, but XBM files aren't binary bitmaps—they are C language source files that represent images as numeric (hexadecimal) arrays; they can be read by C compilers, as well as Netscape and a few image-display programs.

It just goes to show you that, when it comes to graphics-image file formats, there are a *lot* of extremely different ways to store an image! ■

Vector image files take a different approach—they actually describe how an image is drawn. For example, when a vector image calls for a circle, it uses a mathematical formula that describes the circle's size and location on the page. When a computer displays a vector image file, it follows the instructions in the file to redraw the image. While it sounds tedious, vector images are much easier to rescale to different sizes, because the image doesn't have a hard-and-fast correlation between its definition in the file and the pixel-by-pixel image on the screen.

Metafiles use a combination of bitmapped and vector image definition—essentially, a single metafile contains both a full bitmap and full vector description of the image. When the image displays "normally," the bitmap image information is used; when scaled, the vector image data comes into play. Windows Metafile (.WMF) format images are used quite often under Windows for clipart images that need to be resized frequently.

Graphics File Formats

You can find out more about graphics file formats by checking out the four-part Graphics FAQ (Frequently Asked Questions) list on UseNet. You can retrieve the latest version by pointing Netscape to either of the following sites:

> ftp://rtfm.mit.edu/pub/usenet/news.answers/graphics/fileformats-faq
>
> http://www.smartpages.com/faqs/graphics/fileformats-faq/part[1-4]/faq.html

This FAQ is also distributed monthly on the UseNet newsgroups **comp.graphics, comp.answers**, and **news.answers** as four separate files.

More information on graphics files can also be obtained by reading the UseNet newsgroup **comp.graphics.misc**.

Netscape can display inline GIF, JPEG, and XBM images. These three formats account for probably 80–90 percent of the inline images on the Web. But other formats are making some inroads. If you encounter a file in a format that Netscape can't handle, you'll have to install a plug-in for it.

The graphics file MIME types and file name extensions that Netscape knows about are listed in table 7.2. (You can see this list by selecting Options, General Preferences from Netscape's menu and clicking on the Helpers tab.)

Table 7.2   Graphics File Types Recognized by Netscape

Type/Subtype	Extensions	Description
image/ief	.IEF	Image Exchange Format
image/x-png	.PNG	Portable Network Graphics
image/x-photo-cd	.PCD	Photo CD
image/x-MS-bmp	.BMP	Windows Bitmap
image/x-rgb	.RGB	RGB Image
image/x-portable-pixmap	.PPM	PPM Image
image/x-portable-graymap	.PGM	PGM Image
image/x-portable-bitmap	.PBM	PBM Image
image/x-portable-anymap	.PNM	PBM Image
image/x-xwindowdump	.XWD	X Window Dump Image
image/x-xpixmap	.XPM	X Pixmap
*image/x-xbitmap	.XBM	X Bitmap
image/x-cmu-raster	.RAS	CMU Raster Image

Type/Subtype	Extensions	Description
image/tiff	.TIFF, .TIF	TIFF Image
*image/jpeg	.JPEG, .JPG	JPEG Image
*image/gif	.GIF	CompuServe Image Format

Image formats that Netscape can display internally

NOTE The Portable Network Graphics (PNG) format was created mostly as a response to the Unisys/CompuServe GIF graphics copyright controversy. According to the first drafts of the PNG specification, "The PNG format is intended to provide a portable, legally unencumbered, simple, lossless, streaming-capable, well-compressed, well-specified standard for bitmapped image files which gives new features to the end user at minimal cost to the developer." Many hope that PNG graphics will carve a major niche for themselves on the Web in the months to come.

Just because Netscape knows about a graphics file type doesn't mean it knows what to do with it, however. It can display only the three file types marked with asterisks in table 7.2. The rest are configured to "Ask User" what to do.

Of course, there are also dozens more graphics image file formats in use on the World Wide Web. Table 7.3 lists some of these, though it is by no means an exhaustive list.

Table 7.3 Other Graphics File Types on the Web

Extension	Description
.CGM	Computer Graphics Metafile
.DEM	Digital Elevation Model
.DXF	Autodesk Drawing Exchange Format
.IFF	Interchange File Format
.NAPLPS	North American Presentation Layer Protocol Syntax
.PCX	ZSoft PC Paintbrush
.PIC	Pegasus Imaging Corporation Format
.PSD	Adobe Photoshop
.RIFF	Microsoft Resource Interchange File Format
.SGI	Silicon Graphics Image File Format
.SPIFF	Still Picture Interchange File Format

continues

Table 7.3 Continued

Extension	Description
.TGA	Truevision (Targa) File Format
.WMF	Windows Metafile
.WPG	WordPerfect Graphics Metafile

> **CAUTION**
> There are several very different image file formats that share the file extensions .PIC ("picture") and .IMG ("image"). The only way to properly identify what kinds of images these really are is to use a program that actually reads and interprets the file's header information, or to rely on the MIME type that precedes the file transmission, if any. Don't assume that either of these (or any other) file extensions can be used to accurately identify an image's real file type.

TROUBLESHOOTING

I downloaded an image that looks just fine in [*insert the name of your favorite generic graphics display program here*], but Netscape doesn't display it properly, even though I think I have the right plug-in installed. You're probably running into an older (or newer) version of that particular image file format. Though most image display and manipulation programs can handle older versions of various file formats just fine, some will "choke" on unknown variations. And standards groups are always updating file format definitions, sometimes coming up with variations that "break" older viewers. Because of the real-time nature of the Internet, these changes will often show up first on the Web. Make sure your Netscape graphics plug-ins can always handle the latest versions of a graphics file format.

Creating Bitmap Images

To deliver Web page graphics using any of the plug-ins discussed in this chapter, you need to first create a bitmap image. There are four time-honored ways of coming up with a bitmap image: "borrowing," painting, scanning, and digitizing.

Borrowing Bitmaps

The first method of getting your own bitmaps is to "borrow" them. But in these litigious days, you must be careful about where you get images for use on your Web site. Copyright issues are becoming hot. If you decide to "borrow" an image, you must be sure first that you have the express written permission of the copyright holder. "Hey, there's no copyright on *this* image," you say. Wrong! Current copyright law says that whoever creates an image is the copyright holder, no matter whether the creator labels it with a copyright notice or not. If there's ever a dispute, whoever establishes the most legitimate claim to a piece of artwork can demand royalties from others who use it without permission.

Stick to downloading images for your use from sites that specifically give permission to reuse their images. You can find graphic resource sites for Webmasters listed at the Web Developers' Virtual Library at **http://WWW.Stars.com/**, the Icons and Images page at **http://www.uncg.edu:80/~bucknall/uncg/icons/**, the HTML Writers' Guild at **http://www.hwg.org/**, the Yahoo! list at **http://www.yahoo.com/Computers_and_Internet/Internet/World_Wide_Web/Page_Design_and_Layout/**, and other Web development resource sites on the Web.

Generally, though, if you're no artist, it might be better to buy your artwork. Clipart collections abound. You can sometimes pick up a bargain collection on CD-ROM for under $10 with literally thousands of licensed images in dozens of categories. Be sure you check the license carefully, though. The collection's manufacturer may limit online use, or might limit you to personal use only (not business use).

There are also stock photo services that charge you a one-time license fee to use their library images on your Web site. One of the best-known is Publisher's Depot at **http://www.publishersdepot.com/**. It has a collection of tens of thousands of digitized images, and the fee for one-year use on your site can be as low as $40 per image. While probably prohibitive for your personal site, this is an excellent choice for small and medium-size businesses.

Paint Programs

Solution number two is to paint or draw your own bitmap images. Even if you're not much of an artist, there are paint programs out there that can do much of the work for you.

There are a great many tools for the creation of bitmaps, starting with those supplied with your computer. All versions of Windows from 3.1 to 95 to NT include some version of Paintbrush (or Paint), which can be used to draw Windows .BMP bitmap images. There are also a good many shareware image-creation tools available out there on the Web for a variety of platforms and a variety of image types. You'll find everything from tools for drawing simple images to software that lets you generate realistic-looking 3-D shaded images.

A good place to start looking for graphics utilities for all platforms is Brian Stark's Graphics Utilities Site and Version FAQ at **http://www.public.iastate.edu/~stark/gutil_sv.html**. Just for an example, take a quick look at one of my favorites, Paint Shop Pro for Windows.

You know how you feel when you get nostalgic about an old friend? Well, I feel that way when I talk about JASC's Paint Shop Pro (see fig. 7.1). I have used it every day for a couple of years now, both at work and at home. I use it for creating graphics for software manuals and magazine articles. I used it to snapshot the screens in this chapter. Here's just how serious I am about Paint Shop Pro: I paid JASC the $69 registration fee. I just wouldn't have been able to live with my conscience otherwise.

FIG. 7.1
Paint Shop Pro is the Cadillac of Windows image-manipulation programs.

PSP directly supports 35 file formats, and can handle more through the use of external filters, including the ones shipped with Microsoft Office. PSP's native file types are listed in table 7.4.

Table 7.4 File Types Supported by Paint Shop Pro

Extension	File Type
.BMP	RGB-encoded Microsoft Windows
.BMP	RGB-encoded OS/2
.BMP	RLE-encoded Microsoft Windows
.CDR	CorelDRAW!
.CGM	Computer Graphics Metafile
.CLP	Bitmap Windows Clipboard
.CLP	Device-Independent Bitmap Windows Clipboard

Extension	File Type
.CUT	Dr. Halo
.DIB	RGB-encoded Microsoft Windows
.DIB	RGB-encoded OS/2
.DIB	RLE-encoded Microsoft Windows
.DRW	Micrografx Draw
.DXF	Autodesk
.GEM	Ventura/GEM
.GIF	Ver. 87a (interlaced) CompuServe
.GIF	Ver. 87a (noninterlaced) CompuServe
.GIF	Ver. 89a (interlaced) CompuServe
.GIF	Ver. 89a (noninterlaced) CompuServe
.HPGL	Hewlett-Packard Graphics Language
.IFF	Compressed Electronic Arts
.IFF	Uncompressed Electronic Arts
.IMG	New Style GEM Paint
.IMG	Old Style GEM Paint
.JIF	Huffman-compressed Joint Photo. Expert Group
.JPG	Huffman-compressed Joint Photo. Expert Group
.LBM	Compressed Deluxe Paint
.LBM	Uncompressed Deluxe Paint
.MAC	With header MacPaint
.MAC	Without header MacPaint
.MSP	New version Microsoft Paint
.MSP	Old version Microsoft Paint
.PBM	Portable Bitmap UNIX
.PCD	Kodak Photo CD
.PCX	Version 0 ZSoft PC Paintbrush
.PCX	Ver. 2 (with palette info.) ZSoft Paintbrush
.PCX	Ver. 3 (without palette info.) ZSoft Paintbrush
.PCX	Version 5 ZSoft Paintbrush

continues

Table 7.4 Continued

Extension	File Type
.PGM	Portable Graymap UNIX
.PIC	Lotus Development Corp.
.PIC	Pictor/PC Paint
.PNG	Portable Network Graphics
.PPM	Portable Pixelmap UNIX
.PSD	RGB or indexed Photoshop
.RAS	Type 1 (Modern Style) Sun Microsystems
.RAW	Unencoded pixel data
.RLE	CompuServe
.RLE	Microsoft Windows
.TGA	Compressed Truevision
.TGA	No compression Truevision
.TIFF	Fax Group 3 compressed Aldus Corporation
.TIFF	Fax Group 4 compressed Aldus Corporation
.TIFF	Huffman-compressed Aldus Corporation
.TIFF	LZW-compressed Aldus Corporation
.TIFF	Noncompressed Aldus Corporation
.TIFF	Pack bits compressed Aldus Corporation
.WMF	Microsoft Windows Metafile
.WPG	Version 5.0 WordPerfect
.WPG	Version 5.1 WordPerfect
.WPG	Version 6.0 WordPerfect

PSP can create and convert to/from all of these formats. It can also tweak graphics images in a plethora of useful ways, with features like edge detection, histogram functions, gamma correction, deformations, and even user-defined functions. You can use it as a versatile screen image capturing program, and its file browser acts as a handy thumbnail graphic cataloger. PSP also includes built-in scanner support and a full set of paint tools.

You can download the latest evaluation version of Paint Shop Pro from JASC's Web site at **http://www.jasc.com/**.

Scanning Images

A third way to get your hands on bitmap images is to scan them. Scanners come in all shapes and sizes, from small hand-held units that digitize images in black and white at a miserly 100 dots per inch to large, automatic sheet-fed scanners that can scan 16 million colors or more at resolutions up to 2,400 dots per inch. Prices range from under $100 to tens of thousands of dollars.

My setup at home includes a Logitech ScanMan 256, a hand-held scanner that digitizes in 256 gray levels at a maximum resolution of 400 dots per inch. It cost less than $150, and it came with its own interface card, FotoTouch image-retouching software, and OmniPage Direct OCR (Optical Character Recognition) software for scanning in text. This scanner is TWAIN-compliant, which means that it can be used directly from within many software packages, including Paint Shop Pro. The bundled scanning software can save images in many formats supported by Netscape plug-ins, from TIFF to BMP to JPEG. Although the software supports only grayscale images, you can add touches of color if you want to use a graphics editing program. You can purchase a color version of the scanner for about $250.

The first and most difficult step in scanning images is to find a copyright-free picture. The best choice is a photo you've taken yourself. The worst is a picture printed in a magazine, since these are *always* copyrighted by somebody. Getting permission to use such an image on your Web site is probably next to impossible. Not only that, but pictures printed in magazines and newspapers are composed of tiny dots of ink, and scanning them can produce unwanted interference patterns.

Digitizing Video Images

The final choice for obtaining bitmap images for your Web site is to digitize a video image. There are two ways to do this.

The first is to use a standard video source such as a VCR or video camera, and feed its output through a video digitizer. Like the audio digitizer built in to your computer's sound card, a video digitizer takes a video signal and converts it to digital data. This data is then stored on disk in the image file format of your choice.

There are a great many video digitizers available. Most are boards that plug into a slot in your computer, and many are quite expensive. However, there is one that is not only inexpensive, but external, so you can easily switch it from computer to computer—including laptops! And, because you don't have to open up your computer to use it, it's easy for anyone to use. It's called the Snappy, and it's from Play Incorporated.

Chapter 7 Plug-Ins for Graphics Display and Compression

The Snappy is a self-contained, palm-sized unit that plugs into your computer's printer port. You run a cable from the video out port of your VCR or other video source into a jack on the Snappy, install the software, and start digitizing.

As you play a video, you preview it onscreen in the Snappy window (see fig. 7.2). Clicking a button instantly freezes and captures a digital image up to 1500×1,125 in 16.8 million colors, which can then be enhanced or saved in one of several common file formats. The Snappy software is even TWAIN-compliant, so you can digitize images from within many software programs that support scanners.

FIG. 7.2
The Snappy video-digitizing software lets you adjust brightness, contrast, and other image characteristics.

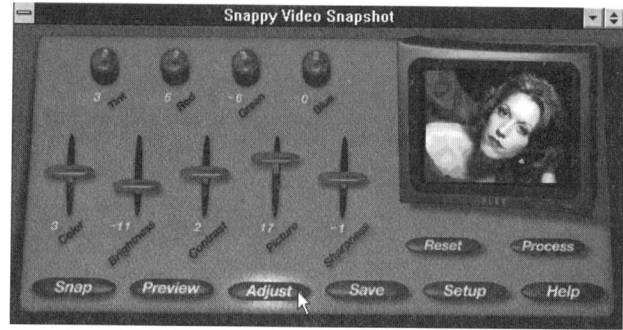

Fauve Matisse, an image creation and editing program, and *Gryphon Morph*, a morphing system, are both included in the package, so you can modify images for use on your Web site to your heart's content.

For more information on the Snappy, check out Play Incorporated's site at **http://www.play.com**.

The second way to digitize video images is to use a video camera that is designed to interface directly with a computer. The most famous inexpensive computer-interfaced digital video camera is the Connectix QuickCam (see fig. 7.3). A tiny ball-shaped video camera that connects to your computer's serial and keyboard ports, the $99 fixed-focus QuickCam can digitize gray scale video clips and still images up to 340×240 resolution. It's a great way to get bitmap pictures into your computer, if you can live with digitizing images of things that are close by. A new $299 version can do the same thing in color, and has a focusable lens. You can get more information at the Connectix site at **http://www.connectix.com**.

FIG. 7.3
The Connectix QuickCam is tiny and easy to hook up and use.

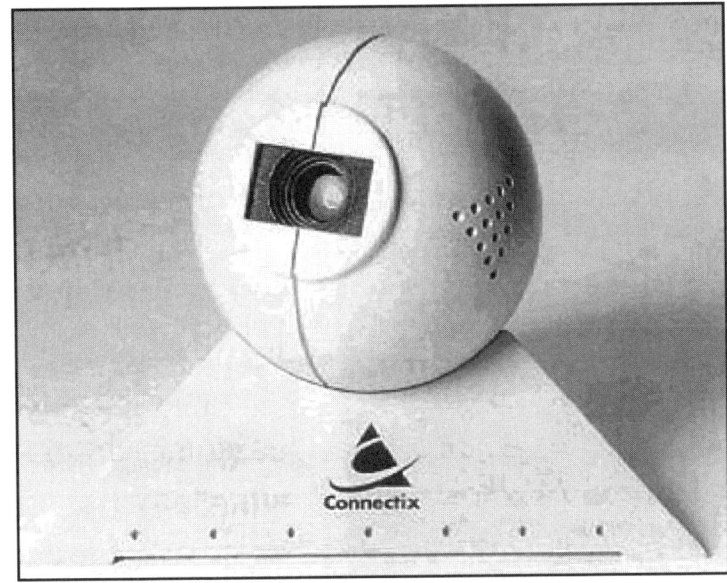

But my personal experience is with a similar (if slightly larger) $199 video still camera called WinCam.One. Like the Color QuickCam, WinCam.One uses an inexpensive CCD (Charge Coupled Device) array and a focusable plastic lens in a combination that is the video camera equivalent of an inexpensive film camera. The included digitizing software gives you a great deal of control over brightness and color, but it's mostly an easy-to-use point-and-shoot setup (see fig. 7.4).

FIG. 7.4
The WinCam.One digitizing software features a control panel that allows minute control over image quality.

WinCam.One digitizes in high-quality, 24-bit color images at 640×480 resolution. However, it doesn't do video streams—just single image still capture. (A stop-motion video stream version is under development.) It is perfect for single-image capture, however, which is the topic at hand. Not only that, but its serial interface cable can be up to 250 feet, and WinCam.One can even be run from a remote site using only a modem and a telephone line! More information can be had online at **http://www.wincam.com**.

Both QuickCam and WinCam.One are totally digital—they deliver their images to the computer without ever using an analog signal. Both do most of the work in the computer software, not in the camera circuitry, so they are ridiculously cheap. Each is targeted to a slightly different audience, but either can be used to create digital images for use on your Web site.

NOTE Several models of digital still frame cameras are also now available from Epson, Canon, and other manufacturers. These look and act like normal film cameras but store their images digitally. After taking 20 to 60 pictures (depending on the model), you download the images directly to your computer. Although digital still frame cameras currently cost $500 or more, prices should come down as such cameras become more common.

Bitmap Graphics Display Plug-Ins

Although Netscape Navigator displays inline GIF and JPEG images just fine, there's more to graphics than those two file formats. As you saw in tables 7.1 and 7.2, there are dozens of other popular bitmap formats, like TIFF and PNG. Graphics plug-ins like the ones described in the following sections can fill the gap.

FIGleaf Inline

Carberry Technology's FIGleaf Inline plug-in lets you display both bitmap and vector (CGM format) graphics inline in the Netscape window. It can display all of the graphics file formats listed in table 7.5.

Table 7.5 Graphics File Formats Displayed by the FIGleaf Plug-in for Netscape

File Type	File Name Extension
Computer Graphics Metafile	CGM
Tagged Image File Format	TIFF
Encapsulated PostScript	EPSI, EPSF

File Type	File Name Extension
CCITT Group 4 Type I	G4
CCITT Group 4 Type II	TG4
Microsoft Windows Bitmap	BMP
Microsoft Windows Metafile	WMF
Portable Network Graphics	PNG
Portable Pixmap	PPM
Portable Greymap	PGM
Portable Bitmap	PBM
Sun Raster files	SUN
Graphics Interchange Format	GIF
Joint Photographic Experts Group	JPEG
Silicon Graphics RGB	RGB

Note that, on installation, FIGleaf takes over the inline display of GIF and JPEG graphic images from the default Netscape display routines. If for some reason you ever decide you want to switch back to using Netscape to display GIFs and/or JPEGs again, follow these steps:

1. Select Options, General Preferences from the Netscape menu.
2. Choose the Helpers tab.
3. Scroll down to the image/jpeg MIME type. Note that the Action field in the list is empty. This indicates that a plug-in is active for displaying this MIME type.
4. Click the MIME type to highlight it in the list. The File Extensions field should now list the file name extensions associated with JPEG images.
5. By default, the Unknown: Prompt User button is selected. Select View in Browser instead.
6. Repeat steps 3–5 for the image/gif MIME type.
7. Click OK to end.

FIGleaf Inline is a subset of Carberry's commercial product CADleaf Plus, which provides additional features like the ability to export various file formats, image rotation, flipping, cropping, and image markup. The plug-in, shown in figure 7.5, is currently available only for Windows 95, though Macintosh and Windows 3.1 versions are planned. The self-extracting archive is 1.5M in size, including sample files, but in one fell swoop it practically eliminates the need for other Netscape graphics plug-ins or helper applications.

FIG. 7.5
A tight zoom on two graphics being displayed inline by the FIGleaf plug-in.

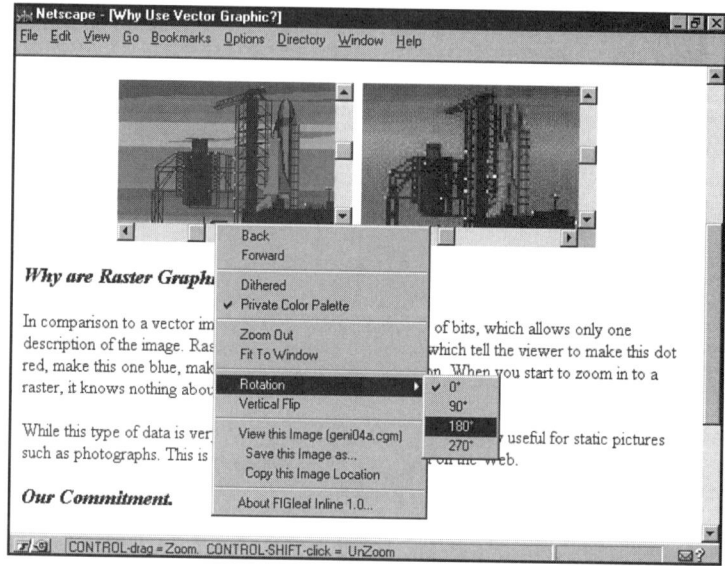

Figure 7.5 demonstrates the superiority of CGM vector graphics (left) versus GIF bitmap graphics (right). Because FIGleaf now handles the display of Netscape's inline GIFs, they are zoomable as well. FIGleaf is an excellent example of how plug-ins can even improve Netscape's built-in capabilities.

To zoom in on an image being displayed by FIGleaf Inline, hold down the Ctrl key while dragging a rectangle on the displayed image. To zoom back out, hold down the Shift and Ctrl keys simultaneously and click the image once.

FIGleaf Inline gives you control over many aspects of image display via a popup menu shown in figure 7.5, which is invoked by right-clicking the mouse while the cursor is over a FIGleaf-displayed image. The following are the menu items and their functions:

Command	Description
Dithered	Dithers the colors in your image from a palette of 16 colors.
Private Color Palette	Displays an image using a custom palette.
Zoom Out	Zooms out a level.
Fit to Window	Scales the image to fit in the window.
Rotation	Displays a submenu that enables you to rotate the image in 90 degree increments.
Vertical Flip	Flips image vertically.

View This Image	Views an image FULL mode.
Save This Image As	Enables you to save the image locally.
Copy This Image Location	Copies the URL of the image to the Windows Clipboard.
Actual Size	Enables you to display the image at actual size.
Scaled	Enables you to zoom the image or fit it to the window.

The last two choices are available only if the image is a raster image. Only one of the two will ever be checked at any one time.

As with all plug-ins, you use the <EMBED> tag to embed an image into your HTML document. Remember that if you are going to include in your own Web pages any of the graphics file types that FIGleaf supports, your system administrator must first configure your Web server to associate the proper MIME types with the proper file name extensions.

Here's an example of using the <EMBED> tag to deliver a FIGleaf-compatible CGM file:

```
<EMBED SRC="gcanyon.cgm" HEIGHT=150 WIDTH=200 COLORMAP=DITHERED BORDER=2>
```

This example displays an image called GCANYON.CGM in a format 200 pixels wide and 150 pixels high. The image will use a dithered color map, and will have a border around it that is two pixels wide. As with all <EMBED> tag uses, you *must* set the SRC, HEIGHT, and WIDTH attributes; otherwise, your browser will crash. Additional attributes are optional. Table 7.6 lists the attributes that FIGleaf Inline supports.

Table 7.6 <EMBED> Tag Attributes for Use with FIGleaf Inline

Attribute	Effect
SRC=*value*	Specifies the URL of the image to be displayed. Required.
WIDTH=*value* HEIGHT=*value*	Determines the width and height of the display area in pixels or a percentage of the screen size (if followed by a % sign). Required.
COLORMAP=PRIVATE¦DITHERED	A value of DITHERED builds up image colors by dithering a set palette of 16 colors. A value of PRIVATE uses a custom palette of the best colors for the individual image. The default is PRIVATE.
ACTUALSIZE=TRUE¦FALSE	If True, displays the image in its original size. If False, scales the image to fit the specified display area size. Valid for raster images. The default is False.

continues

Table 7.6 Continued

Attribute	Effect
BORDER=value	Sets the thickness (in pixels) of the border around the embedded image.
PICTNUM=value	If the source file specified in the SRC attribute is a multipage TIFF or CGM, then the value following PICTNUM indicates which picture should appear in the <EMBED> frame. Picture numbering starts at 1. Placing a value greater than the number of pictures in the file will display the first image. The default is to display the first image in the file.
ROTATION=0¦90¦180¦270	This rotates the image 0, 90, 180 or 270 degrees. The default is 0 degrees.
VFLIP=TRUE¦FALSE	If True, the image is flipped vertically. The default is False.
ZOOMAREA=left,top,right,bottom	Zooms the image to the specified coordinates. The coordinates must be separated by commas with no spaces. All values must be less than the HEIGHT and WIDTH attributes and greater than 0. Rotation is applied before zooming, so you must adjust zoom coordinates appropriately.

Figleaf Inline is available for free evaluation at **http://www.ct.ebt.com/figinline/ download.html**, and you can buy it for $19.95. To install FIGleaf Inline, quit Netscape Navigator, and then run the self-installing file. You will be prompted where to place the sample files that are included, which can go anywhere.

A helper application version of FIGleaf is also available for separate download, and a smaller version of the FIGleaf plug-in called FIGleaf Inline Lite is available. It supports only CGM, JPEG, and TIFF file formats, and can't rotate or flip images from the popup menu. However, FIGleaf Inline Lite is entirely free.

ViewDirector

With the ViewDirector Imaging plug-in from TMS, you can display images in a variety of raster formats. You can even zoom and scroll images embedded in Web pages. A professional version ($59.95) adds the ability to rotate images, magnify them, copy them to the Clipboard, and view multipage TIFF images, among others. You can download ViewDirector, which is available for Windows 3.1, Windows 95, and Windows NT, from the following site:

  http://www.tmsinc.com/solution/plugin/pluginap/pluginap.htm

The file is a self-installing executable.

ViewDirector is similar in many ways to FIGleaf Inline (though it displays a different set of image formats) and many of its advanced features are available only in the registered and paid-for "Professional Version." The image MIME types that ViewDirector handles are:

- `image/TIFF`   *.TIF
- `image/jpeg`   *.JPG
- `image/x-MS-bmp` *.BMP
- `image/x-pcx`   *.PCX
- `image/x-dcx`   *.DCX
- `image/x-cals`   *.MIL;*.CAL
- `image/x-pda`   *.PDA

When invoked, the ViewDirector plug-in implements its features as a popup menu, which you call by right-clicking the mouse on the displayed image (see fig. 7.6). The menu functions are largely self-explanatory.

FIG. 7.6
The ViewDirector popup menu controls zooming and other special features, many of which are ghosted in this freely distributable version. The Professional Version has all functions enabled.

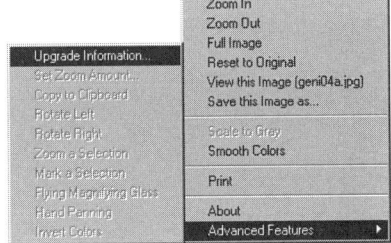

Plug-Ins for Graphics Compression

Graphics are big. Huge, in fact. Graphics files can take up multimegabytes of hard disk space in no time, and can seemingly take an eternity to load over the Web. JPEG images were developed to meet the need of compressing photographic-quality digitized images with a controllable amount of lost detail. JPEGs can compress some images dozens of times smaller than they started out. But JPEG has its limitations, including an inherent "lossiness," and the bandwidth demands of Web browsing have people searching for even better solutions. There are at least three Netscape plug-ins that can improve graphics transfer times considerably—Lightning Strike, Iterated Systems' FIF Viewer, and Summus' Wavelet Viewer.

Lightning Strike

Infinet Op's Lightning Strike plug-in is meant to compete directly with JPEG image compression. Images compressed with Lightning Strike have higher compression ratios, smaller image file size, faster transmissions, and improved image quality. In my tests, it was relatively easy to create a Lightning Strike compressed image half the size of a comparable-quality JPEG version of the same image.

Infinet Op says that JPEG uses a Fourier analysis based method, such as discrete cosine transform (DCT), while Lightning Strike uses a form of the wavelet transform. Okay. All I know is that Lightning Strike images look every bit as good as JPEG and come down the line faster. It's hard to say whether they will gain a following. But if you are into graphics, you'll definitely want to install Lightning Strike and take a look at some of the sample compressed images on Infinet Op's site.

The Lightning Strike plug-in is a simple decompressor with no user interface to speak of. When you load an inline .COD file, the Lightning Strike plug-in displays it. Although you can invoke a popup menu by right-clicking, the menu offers only two options: Image Info and Save Image. Selecting Image Info brings up the dialog box shown in figure 7.7, which displays image compression and size information.

FIG. 7.7
The Lightning Strike plug-in can provide you with detailed information about the displayed .COD format compressed image when you select Image Info from the popup menu.

Versions of the Lightning Strike plug-in are available for Digital and Solaris UNIX systems, as well as Macintosh 040 and PowerPC, Windows 3.1, Windows 95, and Windows NT. You can find InfinOp's download site at the following address:

> http://www.infinop.com/html/extvwr_pick.html

All are available for free evaluation and use by private individuals, non-profit, or educational organizations. Registering costs $99.95, and entitles you to technical support and future software upgrades.

To deliver Lightning Strike's compressed .COD format files on your Web site, you'll first have to set your Web server to associate the MIME type `image/cis-cod` with the .COD file name extension.

To create compressed .COD files, you use the Lightning Strike Image Compressor, currently available as a Windows program (see fig. 7.8).

FIG. 7.8
The Lightning Strike Image Compressor is a sophisticated image-compression tool that can reduce image size by a factor of as much as 130:1 or more.

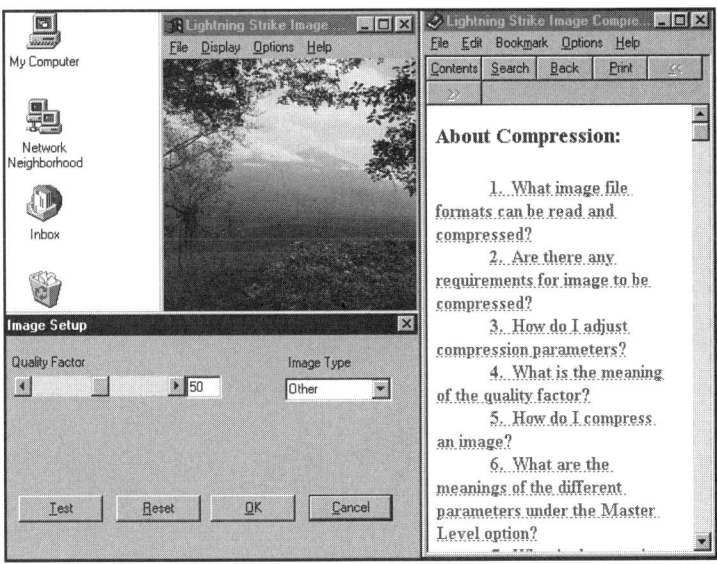

Compression is best used on digitized photographic-quality images. The Compressor can import its own native .COD files, Windows .BMPs, or uncompressed Targa format .TGA files. If you have JPEG images you'd like to convert, you'll first have to convert them to Targa format using an image file format conversion program like Paint Shop Pro.

To compress a file, you load it in and select File, Compress from the menu. You can also set compression options from the Options menu, but the defaults work pretty well and you'll want to get lots of information from the built-in Help before you start diddling with the settings. Even complex images will compress in just a few seconds. Selecting File, Save will then enable you to save the resulting .COD format Lightning Strike compressed image file.

Here's a sample line of HTML code which embeds a Lightning Strike compressed .COD file in a Web page:

```
<EMBED SRC="butterfly.cod" WIDTH=320 HEIGHT=240>
```

SRC, WIDTH, and HEIGHT are always required. In addition, the Lightning Strike plug-in supports three proprietary attributes, each of which has only True and False logical states:

Attributes	Description
COLORMAP=TRUE¦FALSE	A fixed colormap is used by default for displaying 24-bit images on monitors capable of only 256 colors. This makes all images look as good as possible without degrading other images. If you have images that have the same colors throughout, then you may want to use a custom colormap by setting COLORMAP=FALSE.
DITHER=TRUE¦FALSE	This attribute enables or disables color dithering.
INCREMENTAL=TRUE¦FALSE	The INCREMENTAL attribute determines whether or not an image displays incrementally as it loads or waits until the image is completely loaded before displaying.

Other Compression Plug-Ins

Summus' Wavelet Viewer is another plug-in for decompressing images inline that have been compressed using their own proprietary wavelet technology. Versions of this plug-in are currently available for Windows 3.1, Windows 95, and Windows NT at the following site:

ftp://ftp.scsn.net/software/summus/

Unlike Lightning Strike and the Summus Wavelet Viewer, Iterated Systems' FIF (Fractal Image Format) viewer plug-in for Navigator displays fractally compressed—not wavelet-compressed—inline images. FIF images are also smaller and load faster than JPEGs, and can be scaled and zoomed on the page. One typical 768×512 image in the Iterated Systems gallery compressed from 1.15M to only 47K with excellent fidelity. The FIF plug-in is available for Windows 3.1, Windows 95, Windows NT, and Macintosh. You can download the FIF Viewer plug-in from the following address:

http://www.iterated.com/cnplugin.htm

CHAPTER 8

CorelDRAW!, AutoCAD, and Other Graphics Plug-Ins

- Why you might want to use special-purpose graphics plug-ins
- What plug-ins are available for viewing proprietary graphics formats on the Web and on intranets
- How to create content for viewing with specialized graphics plug-ins

You learned in the preceding chapter that there is much more to graphics on the Web than just GIFs and JPEGs. Although Netscape itself is limited to viewing just these types of graphics, by using plug-ins there is no limit to the variety of graphic formats that you can view inline in Web pages.

Chapter 7 discussed general-purpose, multiformat viewer plug-ins, as well as plug-ins that can deliver highly compressed images. This chapter focuses on plug-ins for viewing specialized graphics format images such as CAD drawings, scientific images, and even animated graphics images. ∎

http://www.mcp.com/que

Why Use Proprietary Graphics Formats?

Suppose that you're in charge of the intranet for a large engineering or architectural firm. The CEO has a vision of enabling the members of the engineering team, marketing, and management to view and comment on works in progress, and to give them access to the company's huge archive of past projects. Converting all that legacy data to GIF or JPEG format would be an almost impossible task. And keeping up with new data would require additional Herculean effort. Not only that, but you'd lose important information in the translation from CAD format to bitmap images.

All of your company's blueprints are in AutoCAD format, and Netscape can't display AutoCAD files. However, there are at least three plug-ins that can display them inline. To make all your company's blueprints available to everyone, all you have to do is install an AutoCAD display plug-in on everyone's workstation, and make the archives available on your intranet. The work involved is minimal when compared to converting that many files, and is much more satisfying, as the files retain all their original functionality and detail.

This is a good example of why you might want to use a proprietary graphics file format plug-in with Netscape. Intranet applications in which you have a lot of legacy data in a specific format are especially good candidates for using specialized graphics plug-ins.

Does this mean you would never use them on the Internet? Not necessarily. Imagine a university's Engineering department making technical drawings available not only to its students on campus, but to other students at other colleges around the world. It could quickly build an impressive library of drawings by building a network of engineering drawing Web sites worldwide. Chemistry departments at major universities are already building an impressive collection of (so far) independent sites showcasing chemical structures using the Chemscape Chime chemical modeling plug-in.

Specialized plug-ins also enable people who use a common software tool to share ideas and templates. For example, the Shockwave for Freehand plug-in provides an excellent opportunity for Freehand artists and illustrators to share their work in a collaborative, cooperative atmosphere via the Web.

Will you want to use proprietary graphics formats on most Web sites? The answer is probably no. If a standard format like GIF or JPEG serves your purpose, and you need to reach a wide audience, you are better off using a standard format that all can view without using a special plug-in. However, if the main purpose of your pages is to provide a forum for exchanging data or templates for a specific application, a special-purpose graphics plug-in is not only appropriate but necessary.

AutoCAD Files

Most of the buildings that we occupy, the vehicles in which we travel, and the objects that we use every day are designed in AutoCAD. It is the most popular drafting and design software package on the market. Even those who use other CAD programs usually have the option to save in or convert their files to AutoCAD format. This means that architects, engineers, and designers from a wide variety of disciplines can share design drawings—provided they can get access to one another's files.

Fortunately, there are three (maybe more) plug-ins that enable Netscape to view AutoCAD drawings inline, opening up the Web as an unprecedented design collaboration network.

In addition, there is an increasing need in corporations to open up access to designs to different departments—engineering, marketing, and management—that may often be located miles or even continents apart. Plug-ins enable them to place the designs on a secure corporate intranet, where those with the proper security clearance can access the latest versions of the plans for multimillion dollar design projects.

Autodesk's WHIP!

Autodesk is the publisher of AutoCAD in all its various incarnations. Though Autodesk was not the first to come out with a Netscape plug-in for viewing 2-D AutoCAD drawings on the Web (3-D images are not supported), its plug-in is almost certain to end up being the most popular. Autodesk's WHIP! plug-in is based on the same rendering technology as the WHIP driver in AutoCAD Release 13. It allows for panning, zooming, and embedding URLs in AutoCAD drawings. DWF files are displayed incrementally as they stream into a browser, so the reader doesn't have to wait until they've completely downloaded before viewing them.

WHIP! uses a new DWF (Drawing Web Format) file type that is supported in AutoCAD through a downloadable upgrade file. Though WHIP! won't view standard DWG or DXF AutoCAD files, the new file type is said to be highly compressed and optimized for fast transfer over the Internet. WHIP! uses 32-bit precision and is vector-based. The WHIP! plug-in and DWF files maintain the same precision and detail as AutoCAD. Autodesk is publishing the new DWF file format as an open standard, and other software vendors are being encouraged to adopt the DWF file format as well.

The older DWG file format is the actual editable AutoCAD drawing, so DWF files offer a form of security in that the audience cannot edit them. However, if you want, you can bundle the DWG data in a DWF file (for use over a secure corporate intranet, for example) so that the end user can drag-and-drop the file into a copy of AutoCAD for modification. Autodesk says to think of a DWF file as an electronic plot—the DWF file format presents the drawing, but it does not contain the actual data behind the geometry. The DWG file format component contains all the data components that make up the image, such as arcs, vectors, splines, annotations, and extended entity data.

Although there will be a time lag as existing AutoCAD files are converted to the new format, the new format is bound to become very popular very soon with Autodesk pushing it.

The compressed WHIP! plug-in is less than 1.4M, so it will fit on a single floppy, and requires Windows NT 3.51 or Windows 95. A stand-alone file-conversion utility is promised soon. Also available will be a free WHIP! Development Kit for other software vendors who plan to support the DWF file format. You can download WHIP! from Autodesk's Web site:

> **http://www.autodesk.com/**

It's a self-installing executable file.

The WHIP! plug-in is based on the same rendering technology as the WHIP driver in AutoCAD Release 13 (see fig. 8.1). In addition to viewing, the WHIP! plug-in offers pan, zoom, and embedded URL capabilities.

FIG. 8.1
The WHIP! plug-in from Autodesk features a popup menu with a full set of display and control options.

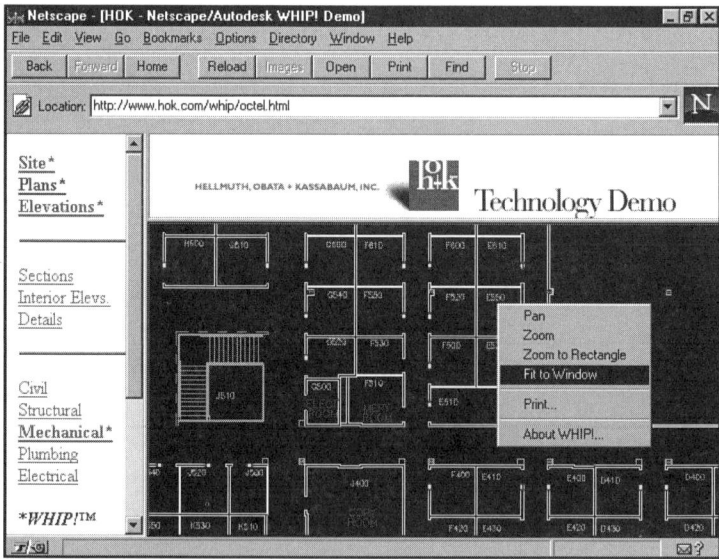

To jump to a URL embedded in a drawing, point to the link (a hand icon will appear) and click. The Netscape status bar at the bottom of the page shows the hyperlink location.

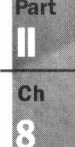

Right-clicking the mouse invokes the WHIP! popup menu, which contains the following options:

Option	Description
Pan	The default mode. Your mouse pointer is a cross with arrowheads. Click and drag to scroll.
Zoom	The cursor is a magnifying glass. Click and drag to zoom in and out.
Zoom to Rectangle	The cursor is a cross. Click and drag a rectangle to zoom to the defined area.
Fit to Window	The drawing is automatically zoomed to fill the view window.
Print	Prints the DWF file in the current view.

The Autodesk Internet Utilities are also available from the same download Web site. These add the capability to save DWF files to AutoCAD Release 13c4. If you plan to use the WHIP! plug-in on your site, you'll need these utilities to convert your current AutoCAD drawings to DWF format. The Internet Utilities contain the following files:

- An updated WHIP ADI driver that implements the DWF file format.
- The ARX (AutoCAD Runtime Extension) application, which adds commands to AutoCAD Release 13c4 for saving DWF files and embedding URLs within drawings.
- A README file containing detailed user information.

Once you have installed the Internet Utilities and activated the new driver, you can begin using the features. Three new commands are available:

Command	Description
DWFOUT	Saves the open DWG drawing file in the DWF file format.
URLATTACH	Associates a URL with one or more selected objects.
URLLIST	Displays the URLs that are associated with one or more selected objects.

To save a DWG file in DWF file format, follow these steps from within AutoCAD after you have successfully installed the Autodesk Internet Utilities:

1. Start AutoCAD and open a drawing file.
2. On the command line, enter **DWFOUT**. The DWF File Name dialog box appears.
3. Enter the name you want for the DWF file. The DWG file's name is used as a default.

4. Select Compressed (the default) to create a compressed DWF file.
5. Choose OK.

To add DWF files to your HTML pages, you need to use the `<EMBED>` tag. Here's a minimal example:

```
<EMBED SRC="example.dwf" WIDTH=300 HEIGHT=300>
```

As with all `<EMBED>` statements, `SRC`, `WIDTH`, and `HEIGHT` are required.

You also need to add the MIME type `drawing/x-dwf` to your Web server, and associate it with the .DWF extension.

NOTE If you need to present 3-D models over the Internet, open your 3-D model and save a 2-D projection of that model as a DWF file. Although the model will appear to be three-dimensional, user controls like pan and zoom are strictly two-dimensional.

DWG/DXF Viewer

SoftSource's DWG/DXF plug-in was the first Netscape plug-in to make it possible to view AutoCAD and DXF drawings on the Web (see fig. 8.2). Zoom, pan, and layer visibility controls make it simple to explore complex CAD drawings online. Its advantage over WHIP! is that it can view standard AutoCAD DXF files (both the display-only and the editable types) and editable DWG format drawing files. Therefore, existing libraries of AutoCAD drawings don't have to be translated before they can be viewed. (However, remember that the new DWF format is compressed for faster transfer, and offers a level of security, since it isn't editable unless you want it to be.)

The DWG/DXF plug-in supports AutoCAD versions 2.5 through Release 12. (There is no target date for Release 13 support.) You can download this plug-in from the following site:

http://www.softsource.com

You embed DWG and DXF files for use with the SoftSource plug-in in almost exactly the same way you embed SoftSource's proprietary format SVF vector image files. For information related to this process, see the section "SoftSource's SVF Plug-In," later in this chapter.

NOTE European users especially might want to check out NetSlide 95 by Alessandro Oddera, an AutoCAD file plug-in for Windows 95 available in Italy from the following site:

http://www.archserver.unige.it/caadge/ao/first.htm

FIG. 8.2
SoftSource's DWG/DXF plug-in makes viewing AutoCAD format drawings an online activity.

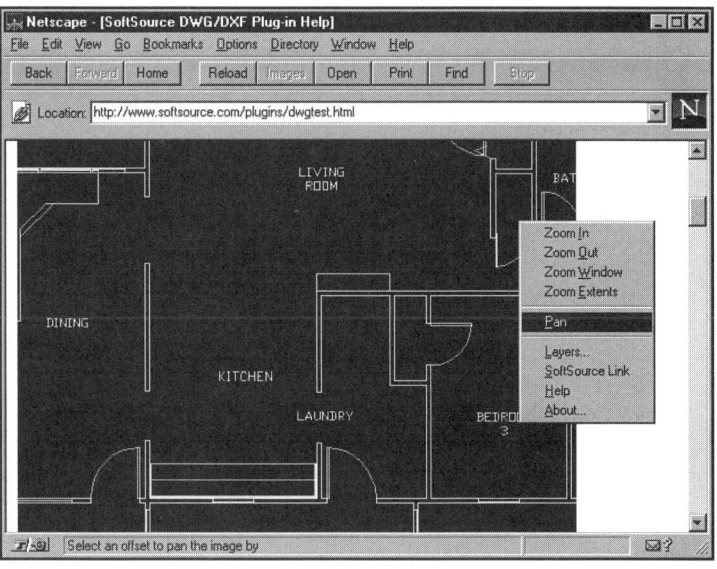

> **N O T E** If you use Corel Visual CADD rather than AutoCAD, there's good news for you! Corel has a free, downloadable Corel Visual CADD Netscape plug-in. It can also load AutoCAD DWG and DXF files. This plug-in isn't just a simple viewer. You can use it to edit and save CAD files inline in Netscape. The plug-in is available for Windows 95 and Windows NT from the following site:
>
> http://www.corel.com/products/CAD/visualCADD/plug-ins.htm

Vector Graphics

Bitmaps like GIF and JPEG images are fine for static pictures, but if you want graphics that you can scale in size, you need vector graphics. Vector graphic images don't contain a bit-for-bit map of a picture, but rather a set of instructions for how to re-create it the way the artist did—a curve here, a line there, a fill pattern in this area, a solid color in another, all connected together. A display program can then take that information, along with a separate set of instructions concerning reproduction size, and create a version of the image in any size, to any scale.

You can use a vector graphics image to reproduce the same image as small as a postage stamp or as big as a billboard. Vector graphics are very popular in the print graphics trade, in which they are used for just those kinds of reasons.

Onscreen, there are less compelling reasons to make graphics scaleable. After all, a 25 percent screen size image isn't that much different than a full-screen size version of the same image. Not only that, but you usually have a very clear, single-size use in mind when you create a graphic.

There is another reason that scaleable vector graphics are awkward to use on Web pages. When you move or resize them, they have to be redrawn. Depending on the complexity of the image, that can take a considerable amount of time, because each picture element—each rectangle, irregular blob, circle, and line—must be redrawn, colored, and layered properly.

Still, if you are part of a community of artists interested in sharing your work—a group of desktop publishers intent on exchanging clipart, for example—you might welcome a way to use your existing CorelDRAW! or Freehand art on the Web. Fortunately, there are Netscape plug-ins that let you do just that.

Corel CMX

CorelDRAW! is perhaps the most popular vector graphics creation program for both the PC and the Mac. Corel's CMX Viewer plug-in for Navigator 2.0 enables you to view Corel CMX vector graphics in Web pages inline (see fig. 8.3). The CMX viewer plug-in is, so far, available only for Windows 95 and Windows NT, although a Macintosh version is promised; you can find the download site at the following address:

> http://www.corel.com/corelcmx/

FIG. 8.3
Corel's CMX vector graphics viewer lets you view smooth Corel format vector graphic images inline in Navigator.

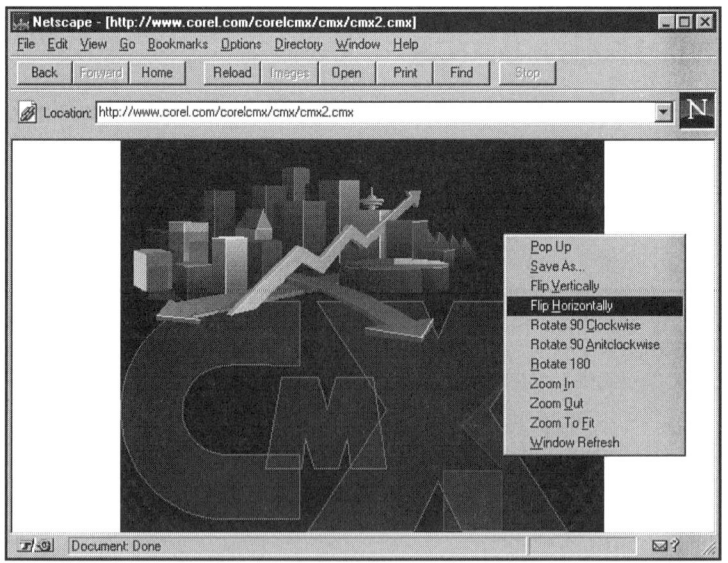

There are no special controls or considerations with the CMX Viewer—when installed, it simply displays CMX images when they are encountered. It's a kick to see them "draw" in pieces onscreen in real time, rather than coming in like a window shade, as bitmap graphics do.

Corel CMX images must be created using some incarnation of CorelDRAW! (see fig. 8.4). Information on the latest versions is available from the Web address. CMX images are inserted in a Web page using the <EMBED> tag using the following syntax:

```
<EMBED SRC="path/filename.cmx" WIDTH=xxx HEIGHT=yyy>
```

SRC, WIDTH, and HEIGHT are, as always, required. You can also include additional attributes such as ALIGN and BORDER with the <EMBED> tag. Full documentation is available on the Corel Web site:

http://www.corel.com

FIG. 8.4
CorelDRAW! comes in several different versions, but all offer a wide assortment of tools for creating highly detailed vector graphics images.

To deliver CMX images, you must associate the MIME type image/x-cmx with the CMX file name extension on your Web server.

Shockwave for Freehand

Freehand is the major competitor to CorelDRAW! as the top-of-the-heap illustration program. If your studio or company uses Freehand, you'll be glad to know that the Shockwave for Freehand plug-in from Macromedia will let you put your Freehand drawings on the Web or on your company intranet.

Don't be confused by the name—Macromedia calls *all* of its plug-ins Shockwave. The first was for Macromedia Director; this one is for Freehand. The Shockwave for Freehand plug-in lets users view compact 24-bit vector graphics with panning and zooming up to 25,600 percent. These can contain irregularly shaped hot objects that link to other Web pages.

There are actually three modules involved here: the Shockwave for Freehand plug-in for Netscape; the Shockwave Afterburner Xtra module, which is installed into the Freehand drawing program to compress Freehand images by up to 50 percent for distribution on the Web; and the Shockwave URL Managers, which enable the designer to add URL references to hot spots on drawings. Windows 3.1, Windows 95, Windows NT, and Macintosh versions are available from the following site:

http://www.macromedia.com/Tools/Shockwave/Info/index.html

You can use Macromedia's Freehand drawing program to create the graphics you view with Shockwave for Freehand. It includes complete text-handling features, unlimited object layering, editable blends, 100 levels of undo and redo, edit in preview, and TIFF and EPS support, and is available in both Windows and Macintosh versions. It offers extensive file format compatibility—you can import RTF, ASCII, CDR, DXF, CGM, TIFF, WMF, EPS, and .BMP files, and you can export RTF, ASCII, EPS, .BMP, TIFF, and WMF files.

Figure 8.5 shows the Shockwave for Freehand plug-in in action.

FIG. 8.5
The Shockwave for Freehand plug-in may include the toolbar shown here, depending on the attributes used when the Freehand drawing was embedded in the Web page viewed.

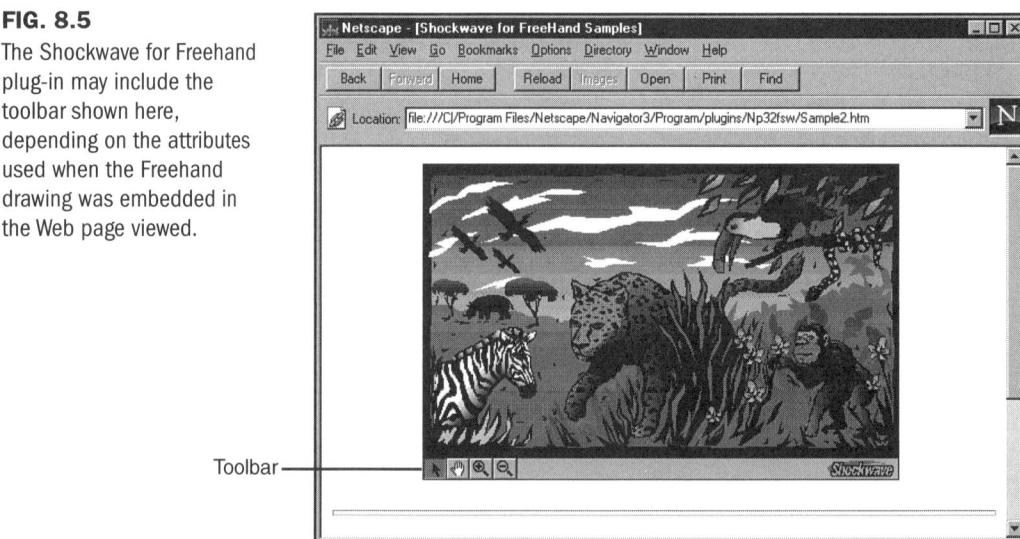

Freehand objects can have URLs attached to them. When one does, the pointer changes to a pointing finger cursor when it is moved over that object. To go to that URL, simply click on the object while the pointing finger cursor is visible.

Shockwave for Freehand uses Zoom tools similar to those found in Freehand itself. You can zoom in and out or zoom to a defined area. When active, the cursor looks like a small magnifying glass with a + or - in it, showing whether you are about to zoom in or zoom out. If the toolbar is enabled, you can click on the appropriate magnifying glass on the toolbar to activate the corresponding zoom mode. Otherwise, to activate the Zoom tool on the Macintosh, hold down the Command key and click your mouse button to zoom in on the desired area. Holding down Command+Option while clicking zooms out. If you press Command+Shift+click, the view returns to its original magnification.

To activate the Zoom tool with the Windows version, right-click the portion of the document you want to zoom in on. (To zoom out, hold down the Alt key as you right-click.) You can also use the left mouse button: Ctrl+left-click to zoom in or Ctrl+Alt+left-click to zoom out. Shift+Ctrl+left-click or Shift+right-click returns the view to its original magnification.

You can also magnify a specific area by clicking and dragging. With the zoom tool active, just click and drag the mouse (with the left mouse button) to draw a dotted rectangle (marquee) around the area that you want to magnify. The area you selected enlarges to the width of the original Freehand window.

The Shockwave toolbar can appear at the top or bottom of an image, depending on the <EMBED> tag attributes. The toolbar displays Arrow, Grabber Hand, Zoom In, and Zoom Out tools, and the Shockwave logo. Clicking on these tools provides access to the same linking, zooming, and panning features available through keyboard commands. Clicking on the Shockwave logo button on the toolbar returns an image to its original state. (You can also use the keyboard command—Command+Shift+click for Macintosh or Ctrl+Shift+click for Windows—or reload the page to return to the image's normal view.) By accessing a feature using the toolbar, you can remain in that mode until you click another tool to change to another mode.

Images must be at least 85 pixels wide in order to display a graphics toolbar. If there is no graphics toolbar displayed with an image, use the keyboard commands.

You can pan or move around within the Freehand document by dragging it with the Grabber Hand tool, which you can select from the active toolbar. To use the Grabber Hand without resorting to the toolbar, hold down the Control key (Macintosh) or the spacebar (Windows) as you click and drag with your mouse.

You can click on the Arrow tool to return to normal cursor mode. Hotlinks are available only in cursor mode. You will not be able to see any embedded links when in pan or zoom modes.

If you are designing Web pages, you'll need the Shockwave Xtras package, which is also provided on the Macromedia Web site. This package includes the URLs and Afterburner Freehand Xtras. These Xtras will work in Freehand 5.0 or later. The URL Manager Xtra allows users to add URL hot spots to Freehand graphics of any shape, and the Afterburner Xtra allows for the import and export of compressed Freehand files.

To use Freehand images on your Web site, have your system administrator create a MIME type entry that associates `image/x-Freehand` with the file name extensions FH4, FH5, and FHC. Then use `<EMBED>` to include your Freehand graphic in HTML documents.

Here's a minimalist example:

```
<EMBED SRC="image.fhc" WIDTH=500 HEIGHT=400>
```

As always, `SRC`, `WIDTH`, and `HEIGHT` are required attributes.

To add a toolbar to the Freehand graphic displayed in an HTML document, you use the `TOOLBAR` attribute, which can have a value of either `TOP` or `BOTTOM`, like this:

```
<EMBED SRC="image.fhc" WIDTH=500 HEIGHT=420 TOOLBAR=TOP>
```

An image must be at least 85 pixels wide in order to display the graphics toolbar. The toolbar will expand to fit the width of your image. The graphics toolbar itself is 20 pixels high. To display the toolbar, as in the previous example, you must add 20 pixels to the height portion of your HTML code, as follows:

```
<embed SRC="filename.ext" width=171 height=150 toolbar=bottom>
```

Images between 85 and 149 pixels wide can display the Shockwave toolbar, but the Shockwave logo will not be visible. Clicking the Shockwave logo in the toolbar returns an image to its original view, so you have to use a keystroke command (Command+Shift+Click for Macintosh or Ctrl+Shift+Click for Windows) if the image is too narrow for the toolbar to display the Shockwave logo.

> **CAUTION**
> Remember that many of the people viewing your site will not have the same fonts installed in their systems as you. Keep the use of custom fonts to a minimum, or convert them to paths if you want to preserve the look of your graphics.

SoftSource's SVF Plug-In

SoftSource, the creator of the DWG/DXF AutoCAD plug-in discussed in this chapter's "DWG/DXF Viewer" section, also has its own vector graphics drawing program. The SVF plug-in for Netscape Navigator lets you view those images on the Web. SVF (Simple Vector Format) uses an officially registered MIME type and features single-download navigational capabilities and scaleable vector graphics. You can pan and zoom an SVF image, and hide and display layers. It is unsurprisingly similar to their DWG/DXF plug-in in the way it works. The SVF plug-in also lets you include HTML hyperlinks (either URLs or textual annotations) in an SVF file. The SVF plug-in, one of Softsource's Vdraft (Virtual Drafter) suite of Internet CAD Tools, is available for Windows 95 or Windows 3.1. You can download the plug-in from the following site:

http://www.softsource.com

The SVF file format includes a full array of vector graphics objects: points, lines, polylines, rectangles, circles, arcs, cubic beziér curves, and text. Color, layer, pen width, and fills can be specified. Hyperlink regions can be defined from all the basic types of objects.

Using the SVF plug-in, you can magnify portions of the drawing or toggle layer visibility without requiring multiple downloads. The SVF plug-in also features navigation via HTML hyperlinks. In action, it looks almost exactly like the SoftSource AutoCAD viewer plug-in shown in figure 8.2.

The way the two plug-ins embed content is almost identical as well. The only major difference is in the file type, which is DXF or DWG for the AutoCAD plug-in and SVF for the vector drawing plug-in.

To embed SVF files in your Web pages, you have to associate the following MIME type in your server setup:

SVF .SVF or .svf   `image/x-svf`

For the AutoCAD plug-in, you need these associations:

.DWG or .dwg   `image/x-dwg`
.DXF or .dxf   `image/x-dxf`

The minimum `<EMBED>` tag example is typical for all plug-ins, and uses only the `SRC`, `WIDTH`, and `HEIGHT` attributes:

```
<EMBED SRC="image.svf" WIDTH=100 HEIGHT=50>
```

Optional attributes include the ability to specify a list of layer names that can be turned on or off:

```
layeron=name1,name2,name3

layeroff=name3,name2
```

With the AutoCAD plug-in, you can specify a named view that has been saved in the drawing:

```
namedview=viewname
```

If you need to simply display a short text message to the user, you can use the status tag to show the message on the status bar. Put quotes around the message if it contains spaces.

```
STATUS="This is a short message."
```

Various user interface features can be turned on or off. Zoom, Pan, and the layer list are normally available through the popup menu that appears when you right-click. You can disable these by using the following tags:

```
ZOOM=false
PAN=false
LAYERS=false
```

With SVF, the left mouse button usually activates a hyperlink or zooms to the cursor. To disable link activation, use the following tag:

```
LINKS=false
```

When the left mouse button is moved over a hyperlink, most browsers display the associated URL on the status bar. An SVF hyperlink can also contain text that appears on the status bar in place of the URL. This can aid in understanding what the link does, since URLs can look cryptic. To have the URL always displayed, you can turn off this feature with the following tag:

```
SHOWURL=true
```

NOTE SVF notifications are hyperlinks that get activated when the user passes a certain magnification level, and require a CGI-BIN script to operate. Detailed information on implementing SVF notifications can be found on the SoftSource Web site:

http://www.softsource.com

FutureSplash and Other Animated Graphics Plug-Ins

FutureSplash's CelAnimator is software for creating vector-based drawings and animations for multimedia and Web pages. CelAnimator can be used for creating static or fully animated cartoons, logos, technical drawings, and interactive buttons. You can export these animations as FutureSplash, animated GIF, Windows AVI, or QuickTime files. You can download a free trial version of CelAnimator for Macintosh, Windows 95, and Windows NT from FutureSplash's Web site:

http://www.futurewave.com/

CelAnimator isn't a plug-in, so you might wonder why you should be interested in it. Besides the fact that you can use .AVI, animated GIF, and QuickTime files with other plug-ins, the FutureSplash plug-in for Netscape —available for Macintosh, PowerPC, Windows 3.1, Windows 95, and Windows NT—enables you to view CelAnimator format animations as well (see fig. 8.6). "Wait," you ask, "what's an animation plug-in doing in this section?" Read those last few lines again, and you'll see that these animations are vector graphics based, which means they're zoomable and scaleable. This is a truly unique product. The plug-in is small (90-150K uncompressed), and UNIX and a Java versions are planned. All are available from the following site:

http://www.futurewave.com/

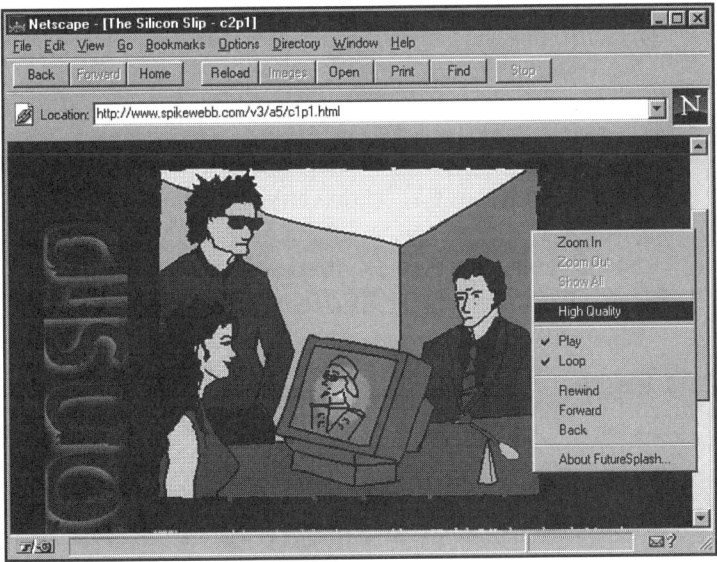

FIG. 8.6
The online animated comic book Spike Webb (**http://www.spikewebb.com**) uses FutureSplash animation to make comic panels move.

FutureSplash files are relatively small for what they do, and provide streaming content, so they can be displayed as they are downloaded. They even offer nice graphic touches such as antialiasing, which means no jagged edges on vector graphics, and outline fonts, which enable the creation of large headlines with very small files. Animations can also include interactive buttons, which means you can do those fancy "multimedia" things that Java programmers and Director mavens do, but without programming. (Each button has three images—up, mouse-over, and pressed—to provide the user with feedback on the button's action.)

In the future, FutureWave plans to add synchronized MIDI and digitized sound, transparency, shape morphing, LiveConnect and ActiveX compatibility, and more.

To use a FutureSplash button, you just click the button. The designer of the FutureSplash graphic controls the actual button action, which can include starting or stopping an animation or loading a new page into the browser. The designer of a button also controls the feedback that a button provides. The cursor changes to a hand when the mouse is over a button, and buttons that open a new page display the name of the page in the Netscape status bar at the bottom of the window.

FutureSplash displays a popup menu when you click the right mouse button. It includes Zoom, Play, Forward, Back, and About functions.

You zoom an image by choosing the Zoom In or Zoom Out commands from the popup menu. Show All resets the view to show the entire graphic. When you are zoomed in, the cursor changes to a hand that can be used for scrolling—click and drag to scroll the image. The view redraws when you release the mouse or pause. (Note that buttons are still active, so click in the space between buttons to move around.)

You create FutureSplash animations using FutureWave's CelAnimator program, which is also available for free evaluation from the FutureWave Web site in versions for Macintosh, PowerMac, Windows 95, and Windows NT. Animation sequences created with CelAnimator are streamed onto the Web pages, which means the animations play as they are downloaded. Sequences using the new FutureSplash vector-based format can be played at any color depth, and are scaleable to any size.

CelAnimator supports a variety of Import/Export file formats for drawings and animations. CelAnimator includes a full set of tools, like erase, brush, and lasso, as well as beziér curves. There's even support for digitizing tablets. Its extensive font support is particularly impressive. Make no mistake—just because you can download CelAnimator for a free trial from the Web doesn't mean it's a low-class product. It's a very powerful vector graphics animation system.

Table 8.1 shows some of the files formats that CelAnimator supports.

Table 8.1 Supported CelAnimator File Formats

Macintosh Animation Formats

FutureSplash SPL

Animated GIF

Quicktime Movie

EPS 3.0 Sequence

Adobe Illustrator Sequence

DXF Sequence

JPEG Sequence

PICT Sequence

GIF Sequence

Windows Animation Formats

Animated GIF

FutureSplash

Windows AVI

EMF Sequence

WMF Sequence

EPS 3.0 Sequence

Adobe Illustrator Sequence

DXF Sequence

Bitmap Sequence

JPEG Sequence

GIF Sequence

Macintosh Image Import/Export Formats (No Animation)

Adobe Illustrator EPS

PICT (bitmap & vector-based)

AutoCad DXF

JPEG image

GIF image

FutureSplash SPL (Export)

continues

Table 8.1 Continued
Windows Image Import/Export Formats (No Animation)
Adobe Illustrator EPS
Enhanced Metafile EMF
Windows Metafile WMF
AutoCad DXF
Bitmap BMP
JPEG image
GIF image
FutureSplash SPL (Export)

To incorporate FutureSplash content on your Web pages, you'll need to set your server's MIME types to support application/FutureSplash with the file name extension .SPL. CelAnimator files are incorporated into Web pages using the <EMBED> tag. Full instructions for using the <EMBED> tag with FutureSplash, as well as documentation for creating CelAnimator files, are available on FutureWave's Web site.

> **NOTE** CGM (Computer Graphics Metafiles) can be created and used by a wide variety of programs; they're an industry standard. The InterCAP InLine plug-in from Intercap Graphics Systems is an online adaptation of its MetaLink RunTime CGM viewer. With this plug-in, you can view, zoom, pan, and magnify an image. Animation of intelligent, hyperlinked CGM graphics is also possible. A Windows 95 and Windows NT version is available from the following site:
>
> http://www.intergraph.com/icap/

Macintosh Animated Graphics

Vertigo from Lari Software displays pictures in GX format, which can be created using LightningDraw GX or any other application that saves in GX format. This plug-in performs automatic smoothing (antialiasing), and enables pictures to be animated using HTML tag spin, stretch, move, loop, and time attributes. PowerPC and Mac versions can be downloaded from the following site:

http://www.larisoftware.com/Products/WebPlugin.html

Web-Active by Plastic Thought displays dynamic 3-D images that can be rotated, turned, and tumbled onscreen. You can download sample Web VR files and plug-ins for Macintosh and PowerMac from the following site:

http://www.3d-active.com

Two Macintosh-only plug-ins are now available for viewing Apple QD3D (QuickTime VR) files in Netscape. WurlPlug by John Louch is available from the Apple site:

ftp://ftp.info.apple.com/Apple.Support.Area/QuickDraw3D/Test_Drive/Viewers/

You can obtain WebActive 3D (which promises a Windows version) from the following site:

http://www.3d-Active.com/pages/WebUtilities.html

QuickTime VR scenes can be made from photographs, video stills, or computer renderings. Most scenes are made from photographs using a series of photos taken at 30 degree increments while turning the camera in a full circle. These are organized into a panorama and combined with multiframe photos of real objects taken at a variety of angles. The experience of viewing these scenes is said to be very realistic. You can find out more about the technology from Apple at the following site:

http://qtvr.quicktime.apple.com/

Miscellaneous Proprietary Graphics Formats

There are dozens of other special-purpose graphics formats that don't fit neatly into a specific category. This section takes a quick look at some of the most interesting of these formats.

Chemscape Chime

Though its end result is a graphics image, the Chemscape Chime plug-in from MDL Information Systems is more of a scientific and chemical engineering tool than a graphics plug-in (see fig. 8.7). The Chemscape Chime plug-in lets scientists and engineers display "chemically significant" (that is to say, scientifically accurate) 2-D and 3-D structures within an HTML page or table. MDL Information Systems supplies chemical information-management solutions to the pharmaceutical, agrochemical, and chemical industries.

You can download Windows 3.1, Windows 95, Windows NT, Macintosh, and PowerMac versions from the following site:

http://www.mdli.com/chemscape/chime/download.html

The .DLL file must be manually installed in the PLUGINS directory, though an automatic installation file is promised soon.

FIG. 8.7
The Chemscape Chime plug-in can generate live 3-D molecular models from a wide variety of standard chemical definition file types, and incorporates a popup menu with dozens of display options.

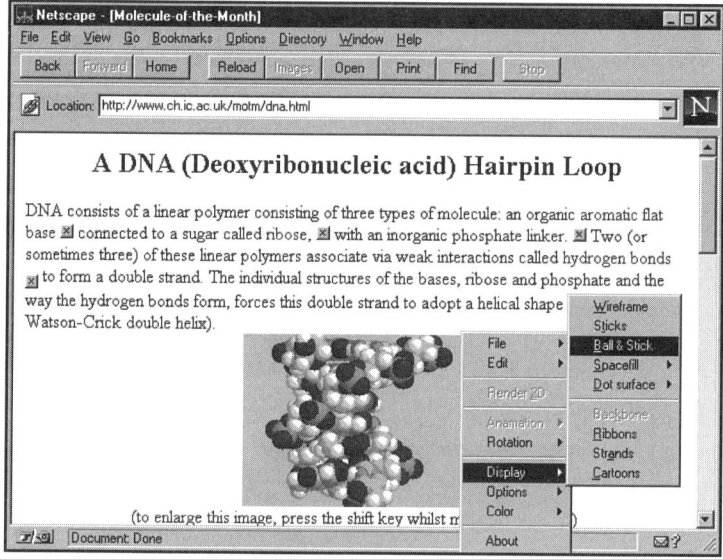

The Chime plug-in creates 3-D molecular models that can be displayed in stick, ball-and-stick, and full 3-D formats. These images can be zoomed, rotated, and spun using a combination of mouse movements and popup menu selections.

Right-clicking over a plug-in displays a popup menu that enables you to change the display type, many display options, and the display color. You can also turn on and off molecule rotation, turn on and off animation, and perform other more esoteric functions.

By clicking and holding down the left mouse button while over a plug-in, you manually rotate the molecule. Clicking and holding down the left mouse button while pressing the Shift key enables you to resize the displayed molecule.

To use Chemscape Chime on your own Web pages, you need to have molecular data available in one of the formats shown in table 8.2. This table also shows the associated MIME type that must be set in your Web server.

Table 8.2 Chemscape Chime Supported File Formats

Format	MIME Type	File Name Extension
MDL Molfile	chemical/x-mdl-molfile	.MOL
Brookhaven Protein Databank	chemical/x-pdb	.PDB
IEMBL Nucleotide Format	chemical/x-embl-dl-nucleotide	.EMB, .EMBL

Miscellaneous Proprietary Graphics Formats | 195

Format	MIME Type	File Name Extension
Minnesota Supercomputer Center's XMol XYZ	chemical/x-xyz	.XYZ
Gaussian Input	chemical/x-gaussian-input	.GAU
Rasmol Script	application/x-spt	.SPT
Mopac Input	chemical/x-mopac-input	.MOP
Chemical Structure Markup Language	chemical/x-csml	.CSM, .CSML
MDL Transportable Graphics	chemical/x-mdl-tgf	.TGF
MDL RxnFile	chemical/x-mdl-rxnfile	.RXN

By using the <EMBED> tag in an HTML document, you can insert a plug-in into a Web browser page. The generic format of the <EMBED> statement is as follows:

```
<EMBED SRC="file.ext" HEIGHT={hvalue} WIDTH={wvalue}>
```

SRC, HEIGHT, and WIDTH are, of course, required. But the <EMBED> tag has a plethora of attributes associated with the Chime plug-in. Table 8.3 lists these attributes.

Table 8.3 <EMBED> Tag Attributes for Use with Chemscape Chime

Attribute=Values	Notes
startspin={True¦Yes¦False¦No}	Flags whether you want to spin the structure displayed in the selected plug-in.
spinX={degrees per second}	Specifies the rotation speed along the X-axis in degrees per second.
spinY={degrees per second}	Specifies the rotation speed along the Y-axis in degrees per second.
spinZ={degrees per second}	Specifies the rotation speed along the Z-axis in degrees per second.
spinfps={spin frame rate/second}	Specifies the frame rate per second for spinning.
startanim={True¦Yes¦False¦No}	Flags whether you want to start an animation of a concatenated XYZ file.
animfps={animation events per second}	Specifies the animation events per second.

continues

Table 8.3 Continued

Attribute=Values	Notes
`display3D={wireframe¦backbone¦sticks¦spacefill¦ball&stick¦ribbons¦strands¦cartoons}`	Specifies the type of display.
`color3d={monochrome¦cpk¦shapely¦group¦chain¦temperature¦structure¦user}`	Specifies the color scheme.
`options3d={slab¦hydrogen¦hetero¦specular¦shadows¦stereo¦labels¦dots}`	Specifies 3-D display options. If more than one 3-D option is specified for the `<EMBED>` tag, the options are combined.
`name={name}`	Specifies the name of the plug-in.
`target={target}`	Specifies the target of the plug-in's actions.
`button={push}`	Indicates that the plug-in is a button. Currently, it only accepts the "push" value.
`palette={foreground¦background}`	"Foreground" allows Chime to use the colors it needs outside of the current color palette to smoothly display space-filling structures.
`hbonds={on¦off¦number}`	Turns on and off the display of hydrogen bonds, or specifies the diameter of cylinders used to represent the hydrogen bonds. "On" displays the hydrogen bonds as dashed lines.
`ssbonds={on¦off¦number}`	Turns on and off the display for disulphide bonds, or specifies the diameter of cylinders used to represent the disulphide bonds. "On" displays the disulphide bonds as dashed lines.
`script={valid RasMol script commands}`	Specifies any valid `RasMol` script commands to apply to the plug-in. Multiple commands can be separated with a ¦ or ;.
`csml={valid CSML script commands}`	Specifies any valid CSML script commands to apply to the plug-in. Multiple commands can be separated with a ¦ or ;.

Many of these attributes mirror popup menu commands.

Chemscape ChimePro and Chemscape Server

MDL Information Systems also offers a professional version of Chemscape Chime, as well as a Chime server-side program.

Chime Pro is a Netscape Navigator plug-in with all of the features of the basic version of Chime plus the ability to accept a structure query and inline data.

Chemscape Server is a server system which directly integrates Netscape Server with ISIS/Host to provide full structure and textual searching from within a Web browser.

Chime Pro and Chemscape Server provide full access to ISIS/Host databases including molecule, reaction and Oracle databases. They offer the same structure searching capabilities found in ISIS including substructure, similarity, and exact match for molecules and reactions within the easy-to-use motif of the Web browser.

ART Press

Johnson-Grace's ART Press program creates ART image format files, which can be viewed online using Johnson-Grace's ART Press plug-in, which was not yet available as this book went to press. However, it should be available soon from the following site:

http://www.jgc.com/aip/artpub.html

For now, you can use a stand-alone program as a helper application (see fig. 8.8).

FIG. 8.8
ART Press, seen here in its stand-alone ART creation incarnation, will soon be available as a Navigator plug-in.

Because ART compression is already being used in America Online's TurboWeb browser, and because it has been licensed for use on over 5,000 Web sites, it is of more than passing interest, even though the Netscape plug-in is not yet ready.

Johnson-Grace says ART Press images download and display three times faster than GIF and JPEG images. Johnson-Grace is adding sound, animation, and scaleable video capabilities to ART Press.

The heart of the ART format is a "fuzzy logic" classifier that automatically detects the type and color depth of any image and draws from a toolbox of ART compression techniques to optimally compress each type of image. This means that publishers using ART do not have to toggle between JPEG and GIF depending on whether the image is a low-resolution graphic or a 24-bit photo.

The current stand-alone version of ART Press includes an image editor which allows importing images from Photo CDs, scanners, or other sources, and provides tools for scaling, cropping, filtering, and compressing images into the ART format. It also features playback simulation for previewing ART images as they would appear if played back at 2,400, 9,600, 14,400, or 28,800 bits per second.

To encode your Web pages for ART image/sound files, you will use the <EMBED> tag with the standard SRC, WIDTH, and HEIGHT attributes:

```
<EMBED SRC=xxx.art WIDTH=200 HEIGHT=100>
```

In addition, the ART Press plug-in supports these attributes:

Attribute	Description
AUTO = on¦off	Controls the automatic playing of sound with an image
COLORDEPTH = 8¦24	Displays at 8-bit or 24-bit color
DITHER = on¦off	Turns dithering on or off
SPLASH = on¦off	Controls the splash rendering feature for ART images

ART sound functions activate when you right-click anywhere within the ART image.

QuickSilver

Micrografx's QuickSilver is a popular business graphics tool, and now its ABC QuickSilver plug-in for Netscape makes QuickSilver files usable over the Web or corporate intranets. You create these vector images with ABC Graphics Suite, which can make drawings move, display messages, or link to URLs. The plug-in uses a 32-bit vector graphics rendering engine for fast display.

You can download QuickSilver, which is available for Windows 95 and Windows NT, from the following site:

http://www.micrografx.com/download/qsdl.html

WebXpresso

WebXpresso displays 2-D and 3-D drawings, graphs, and controls. It supports real-time interaction and continuous or periodic updating from a server data stream. In addition, WebXpresso controls objects that can send data back to the server. The WebXpresso Drawing Editor allows creation of arbitrary 2-D and 3-D object hierarchies. Java Native Methods allow client-side manipulations of graphics. Download WebXpresso and view sample pages. Available for Windows 95, Windows NT, and UNIX, you can get WebXpresso from the following site:

http://www.dvcorp.com

CHAPTER 9

Video and Animation Plug-Ins

- When video and animation content can help your Web pages—and when it can be deadly
- What video and animation plug-ins are available for Netscape
- How to create video and animated content for your own Web pages

Pictures that move—that's the magic of video and animation. With only sound and graphics, Web pages are static. But with video and animation, Web pages come alive with television-like action.

Of course, all this motion comes at a price—even a few seconds of video or animation can come in a package several megabytes large, and with the transmission times involved in transmitting data over the Internet, that can mean sluggish response and jerky images. ■

http://www.mcp.com/que

When To Use Video Content

You've got a stunningly cute VHS video recording of your little niece Gloria spitting up her first mouthful of strained peas, and you have a hunch it would make a wonderful addition to your Web page.

Probably not. Unless you have a million relatives out there browsing the Web, the odds are good that nobody will be willing to wait the dozens of minutes it will take his or her dial-up connection to download that 15 seconds of video that shows dear little Gloria at her worst. Not only that, but it's probably going to take you a few hours—or at least a couple of hundred dollars—to get that short video clip onto your Web site.

Speed

As with all Web page content, when considering when to use video or animation content, it's important to keep in mind the effort/payoff ratio. And with video and animation, that ratio is often very low.

If your audience mostly connects to the Internet via dial-up connections, your use of video should be sparse. Not only that, but you should give your viewers ample warning. Don't put a video on your home page. Instead, put a link to your video content, and include a warning next to the link that tells them how long they can expect the download to take, and how long a video clip they're going to be able to view for their trouble. Figure 9.1 shows a site that uses this solution.

A 14.4kbps connection can deliver, at best, 1,800 bytes of information per second; a 28.8kbps dial-up delivers twice as much (3,600). Divide the size of your file (in bytes) by these numbers, and put those figures in the warning on your Web page, like this:

> Click here to see the .AVI video of Lindbergh Landing.
>
> This video is 1M in size. On a 14.4 connection, it will take approximately 9 3/4 minutes to download. On a 28.8 connection, it will download in approximately 4 1/2 minutes.

If you are delivering information mostly to those who connect directly to the Internet via commercial, university, or government sites, then you can be more generous in your use of video. Users on a 56kbps direct line can download a 1M video in just a little over two minutes. Still, two minutes is a good chunk of time. If you are using a video plug-in capable of streaming its content, so that the video can be viewed as it's coming down the line, you'll have a lot better chance of keeping your viewers with you. However, you also stand a chance, even on a fast direct line, of having your video content not keep up with real time. In other words, your viewers may experience skips and jumps.

FIG. 9.1
A site promoting the blockbuster film *Independence Day* places each video clip on its own page and links to each page from a menu that warns of large file sizes.

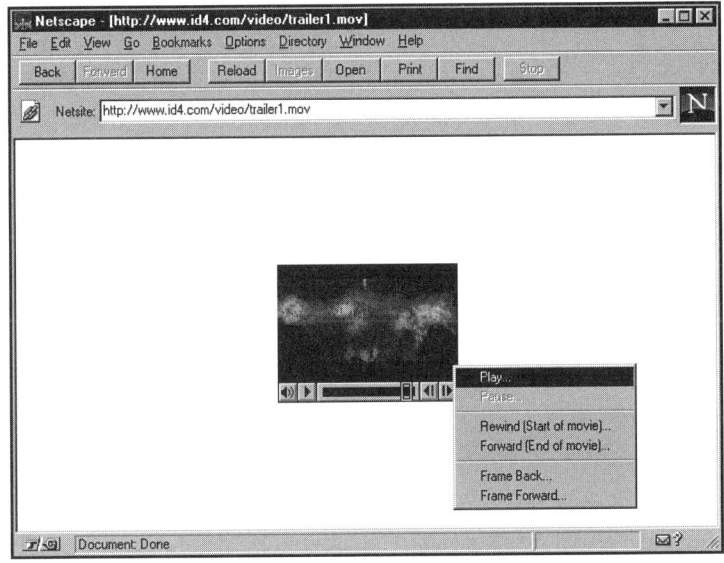

On a corporate intranet, all such worries vanish. You should be able to deliver video content at will. However, if your corporate intranet includes remote sites connected via the Internet, remember their special needs when planning your offerings.

Content

As always, once the technical details are worked out, your major consideration should be this: Does the content add to the value of your site? Is it relevant? Does it fit your theme and topic? If the answer to any of these questions is *"no,"* you should probably ask yourself whether something else would do the job better.

Videos and animations are especially suited to the following tasks:

- Training—There's nothing like being able to watch someone else do something "hands on."
- Education—Historical film clips, entertaining animations, and other visual aids can be extremely useful in helping to emphasize and illustrate important concepts.
- Entertainment—If your site is mostly devoted to entertaining your viewer, video clips and fun animations are some of the best entertainment around.
- News—If you are in the business of delivering news to your viewers, clips of important events connote an immediacy and sense of involvement you just can't get from text and still images.

Pages where video and animation should be used sparingly or not at all include:

- **Lengthy Presentations**—If your presentation goes on for many pages, using too many video or animation clips will slow down your presentation to the point that only the most dogged viewer will ever get through it all.
- **Index Pages**—Pages of links are used as reference points, not as sources of entertainment. If your links pages include videos, it's a sure bet that people won't be willing to suffer through their long load times again and again just to use your links. They'll go elsewhere.
- **Reference Material**—If the main purpose of your site is to serve as a reference source, at least have the courtesy to link to any videos or animations—or big graphics, as far as that goes. If people are going to come back to your site on a regular basis, they are not going to want to have to load in video data every time.

Not only do you need to consider the time your viewers will be putting into downloading and watching your videos and animations, but you also need to consider the time you'll be investing in creating them.

Creating Video Content

When you get down to it, videos and animations are the same thing—a series of still images presented one after the other to give the illusion of motion. The only real difference is the source. Videos are generally a series of digitized, real-world images, while animations are usually hand-drawn (or at least hand-assembled).

Using a PC to digitize video from a live source is surprisingly complex and expensive. Just as you need a sound card to digitize audio, you need a video digitizer card to digitize video. These cards aren't cheap. You can buy a card (or external box) to digitize a single image for a couple of hundred dollars. But to capture live video streams requires a superfast card that will set you back in excess of a thousand dollars. Not only that, but you also need a fast computer system with a lot of memory and a huge amount of online storage, too. A computer system set up to do real-time video digitizing will set you back a minimum of $6,000–$10,000, and that figure doesn't even count VCRs, video mixers, and other esoteric add-ons.

For example, the Salient Video Capture Subsystem model VCS89 **(http://www.salientsys.com/)** offers real-time video digitization, image processing, data compression, high resolution graphics display, and mass storage of captured images. It comes with 8M of video buffer memory and up to 128M of program memory. It can capture images at up to 1,280 × 1,024 resolution and 16 million colors using its onboard Texas Instruments DSP (Digital Signal Processor) chip, the TMS320C80-40. This is a PCI card that includes a fast wide SCSI-2 interface. The VCS board with no program RAM and 8M display RAM retails for $5,000.00. Of course, you'll also need a fast Pentium PCI bus computer with lots of RAM of its own, as well as several gigabytes of available hard drive storage space, to use this card.

Other video capture cards include the Targa 1000, DPS Perception, Quadrant Q-Motion 250, and MiroVideo DC-20. Popular video capture software programs you can use with these cards include Adobe Premiere 4.0, Ulead Media Studio Pro 2.5, and Asymetrix Digital Video Studio.

If you've got the budget to investigate this avenue further, you can find more information by checking out the Yahoo! index for video frame grabbers at **http://www.yahoo.com/Business_and_Economy/Companies/Computers/Peripherals/Graphics_Cards/Frame_Grabbers/**. But there are cheaper solutions. Unfortunately, they involve that annoying equation you seem to run into everywhere in life:

Time = Money

There are always people looking for ways to turn a quick buck with their computers, and the odds are good that living close to you is someone who has already shelled out for one of the mondo-expensive frame-grabbing systems. The odds are also good that he's dying to recoup some of his investment by digitizing video clips for people like you. Check your local phone book for Video Digitizing Services. Prices vary greatly, but you can probably get a rate of something like $40/minute. (That's per minute of video time, not per minute of conversion time.) There are, of course, companies that offer these services over the Web, too. You'll find some listed at **http://www.yahoo.com/Computers_and_Internet/Multimedia/Video/**.

A less expensive (although more time-consuming) method of creating video clips is to employ an animation technique: Digitize individual frames using an inexpensive frame capture device like the Snappy (mentioned in the previous chapter), save them to disk, and then assemble them using an animation program.

You can, of course, also draw an animation frame-by-frame. Even at a slow playback rate such as 11 frames per second (considered the absolute minimum, even by today's cheap Saturday morning cartoon production houses), this will take you a bit of time. It's another great argument for using video and animation sparingly.

Figure 9.2 shows one Web site that displays animation consisting of hundreds of individual drawings.

FIG. 9.2
Even a short animated cartoon like this one at the official "Pinky & the Brain" Web site can be composed of hundreds of individual drawings.

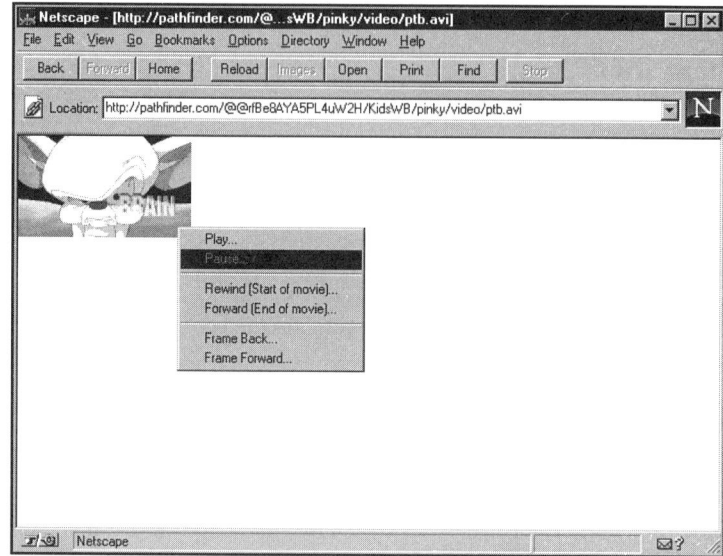

For more information on the topic, including links to many publishers of animation programs, check the Yahoo! links at **http://www.yahoo.com/Computers_and_Internet/ Graphics/Computer_Animation/**.

Video for Windows Plug-Ins

There are three standard video formats: Video for Windows, QuickTime, and MPEG. Video for Windows is the standard for PC platforms; QuickTime is used extensively on the Macintosh; and MPEG is the standard for high-end video. Plug-ins for each platform are discussed later in this chapter.

A Video for Windows driver is built in to the Windows 3.1, Windows 95, and Windows NT operating systems. Windows' Media Player is the system-supplied stand-alone application for playing Video for Windows movies, which are identified by the file name extension .AVI. Not surprisingly, .AVI format movies have also become popular on the Web. With the right Netscape plug-in, you'll have no problem viewing them inline in Web pages.

TROUBLESHOOTING

When I try to play an online .AVI files using a plug-in, I get a message saying "Cannot find vids:msvc decompressor." What's wrong? Your Windows 95 MS Video 1 video compressor may not be loaded. It's required for playing any .AVI file. In the Windows 95 Control Panel, select Add/

Remove Programs, click the Windows Setup tab, and then double-click Multimedia. Scroll down to Video Compression and make sure there is a check mark in the box. If there isn't, click to put one there, and you will be prompted to insert your Windows 95 system CD or diskettes.

LiveVideo

Netscape's official plug-in for .AVI video is LiveVideo, which is included with the Netscape Navigator distribution. It automatically installs and configures as your Video for Windows player of choice. You click a movie image to play it and click again to stop. Right-clicking an image displays a complete popup menu of controls, including Play, Pause, Rewind, Fast Forward, Frame Back, and Frame Forward. If you didn't get LiveVideo with Netscape, you can download it by following the links from Netscape's home page at **http://www.netscape.com**.

LiveVideo installs automatically side-by-side with Netscape 3.0. You don't have to do anything to install, set up, or configure it. Since it's a plug-in, you don't have to do anything to launch it, either. It sits there blithely waiting until you encounter a Web page with an embedded .AVI format video, at which time it plugs its video player into the Netscape window, as shown in figure 9.3.

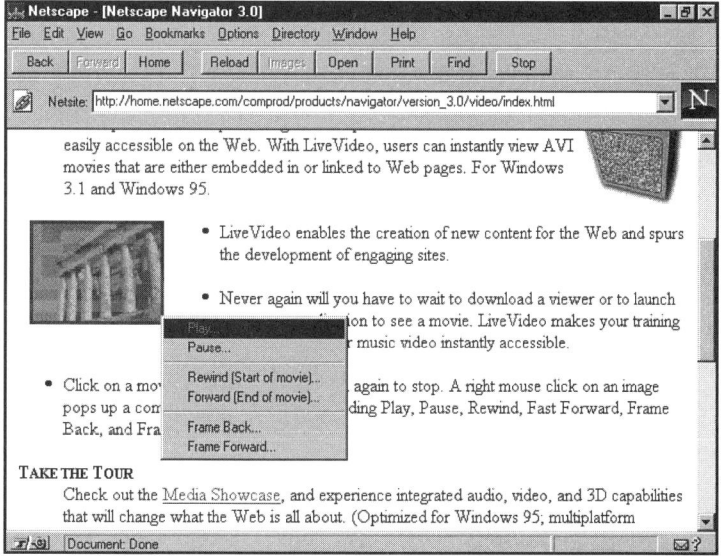

FIG. 9.3
LiveVideo plays .AVI videos inline in the Netscape window. To display this popup menu, right-click.

You simply click on the embedded video frame to start it playing. Click again to pause the video, if needed, and then click to resume.

TIP You can also use LiveVideo to play stand-alone .AVI videos, either from the Web, your corporate intranet, or your hard drive. Just select File, Open File (Ctrl+O) and pick a file of type .AVI.

To access the LiveVideo player controls, you right-click the displayed video frame. You'll get the popup menu shown in figure 9.3.

There are six basic controls available from the LiveVideo popup menu. You can Play, Pause, Rewind to the start of the movie, and Fast Forward to the end. As on a VCR, once you've played a video through to the end, you have to rewind it before you can play it again. You can also select Frame Back or Frame Forward to step backward or forward through the movie a frame at a time.

LiveVideo is included in the Windows 3.1 and Windows 95 versions of Netscape 3.0. Both require a system with at least a 386 CPU and a compatible sound card. Windows 3.1 also requires the Video for Windows driver. (Video for Windows is automatically installed in Windows 95.)

To embed an .AVI format Video for Windows movie in a page, use the <EMBED> tag, using this generic format:

```
<EMBED SRC=[URL] WIDTH=integer HEIGHT=integer AUTOSTART=[TRUE|FALSE]
       LOOP=[TRUE|FALSE] CONTROLS=[TRUE|FALSE]>
```

SRC, WIDTH, and HEIGHT are required attributes. There are three optional attributes:

AUTOSTART=TRUE|FALSE	If True, the video starts playing automatically.
LOOP=TRUE|FALSE	If True, the video plays repeatedly until stopped.
CONTROLS=TRUE|FALSE	If True, the video appears with a set of player controls.

Remember to set your Web server's MIME type to associate video/x-msvideo with the file name extension .AVI.

VDOLive

Before Netscape came up with its own video plug-in, VDOLive enabled inline Video for Windows clips to be included in HTML pages and played back in real time (see fig. 9.4).

Unlike the other .AVI video plug-ins discussed in this chapter, VDOLive requires a separate VDOLive Personal Server program to deliver video from your Web server. The VDOLive Personal Server and Tools 1.0 software package enables you to deliver up to two streams of video; to capture, compress, and serve up to one minute of video and audio; and to scale up to 256kbps connections. The server and plug-in work as a team. You need the server and your viewers need the plug-in.

FIG. 9.4
VDOLive displays video files inline, and can deliver reasonable performance over even slow Internet connections.

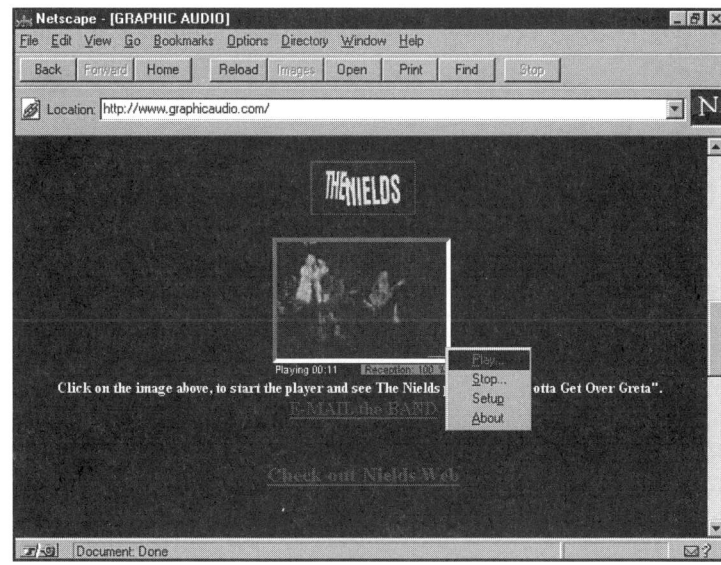

What's the advantage? Well, if a viewer has a slow connection, VDOLive intelligently downloads a video file to that viewer, skipping over enough information to retain real-time playback. The percentage of actual reception appears in the lower right corner of the VDOLive display window (see fig. 9.4). In cases of severe bandwidth shortage, such as 14.4kbps connections, you'll get a low frame rate (approximately one frame each 1–3 seconds) but you'll still be able to view videos. In other cases, the VDOLive Player and the VDOLive Server will try to converge at the best possible bandwidth, which may sometimes result in blurry display or low frame rate. While this can result in jerky playback, especially over a slow modem connection, it makes for adequate viewing rather than intolerable viewing.

VDOLive is available for Power Macintosh, Windows 3.1, Windows 95, and Windows NT from VDONet's site at **http://www.vdolive.com/download/**.

VDOLive actually consists of three components. The VDOLive Video Player plug-in provides real-time VDO playback. The VDOLive Video Server provides the dynamic bandwidth scaling needed to maximize video quality throughout each connection, and can handle clips ranging from a couple of seconds to a couple of hours. The third component, VDOLive Tools, provides the basic capture and compression utilities to create VDO content. (You can also use other multimedia development tools, such as Adobe Premiere 4.2 for Windows.)

The VDOLive Server is available for the following platforms:

- Windows NT
- Sun Solaris
- SunOS
- SGI Irix
- IBM AIX
- Linux
- FreeBSD
- BSDI
- DEC Alpha NT and UNIX

Using the VDOLive tools, you can create videos in 16- or 24-bit-per-pixel color at resolutions from 64×64 to 240×176. Associated audio is 8kHz, 16-bit, and mono.

Embedding a VDOLive video in an HTML page is done using the Netscape <EMBED> tag. SRC, HEIGHT, and WIDTH attributes are required. There are two optional attributes:

STRETCH=TRUE/FALSE	If True, stretches the video content to fit the specified size of the plug-in window.
AUTOSTART=TRUE/FALSE	If True, the video starts playing immediately.

Example:

```
<EMBED SRC="sample.vdo" WIDTH=160 HEIGHT=128 STRETCH=TRUE AUTOSTART=TRUE>
```

Rather than play an .AVI file directly, VDOLive actually references a .VDO file, a text file that contains the URL for the actual .AVI video file. The .VDO file includes the following information:

- Resource type—vdo:// for VDOLive videos
- Server address—the name or IP address of the server where the .AVI file is located
- Port number—the TCP port used by the server (default is 7000)
- Full path to an .AVI file

The URL syntax is vdo://server_address:port/path. You can create .VDO files using any text editor. Here's an example of a .VDO file's content:

vdo://vdo1.vdo.net:7000/pub/movies/example.avi

To deliver VDOLive content, your Web server must also be configured to associate the .VDO file name extension with the proper MIME type.

CoolFusion

Iterated Systems' CoolFusion is another plug-in for Navigator that plays inline Video for Windows (.AVI) movies. It lets you view videos at any size all the way up to full-screen, and you can stop, replay, and save them using a full set of controls. Using optional <EMBED> tag attributes, CoolFusion can even play video when the user drags the mouse pointer over it, or provide an alternate audio track (perhaps another language) that plays with a double-click. Like LiveVideo, CoolFusion needs no special server software. A future version will support playback of QuickTime movies (which have an .MOV extension) as well as .AVI files.

For Windows 95 or Windows NT, CoolFusion requires only a 256-color graphics card, although a 24-bit or high-color graphics adapter is recommended. You can download CoolFusion at **http://webber.iterated.com/coolfusn/download/cf-set32.htm**.

Right-clicking the playback window displays the popup menu shown in figure 9.5.

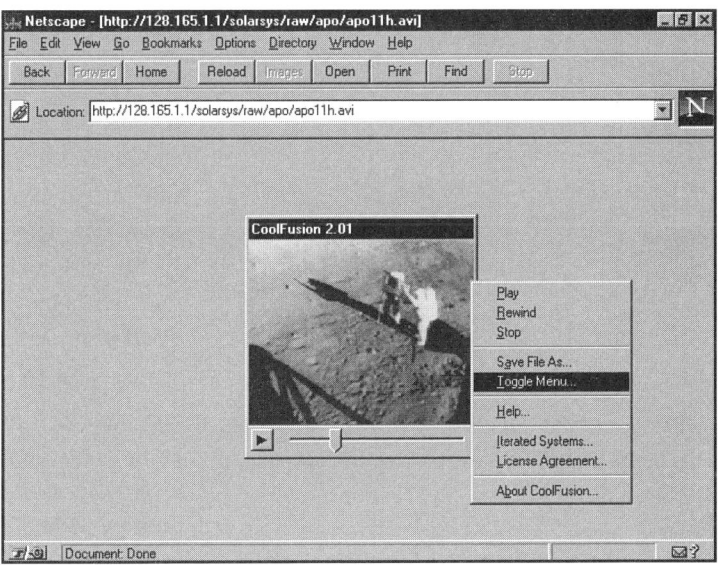

FIG. 9.5
CoolFusion features a playback control toolbar, as well as a popup menu.

The popup menu provides the following choices:

Play   Plays the clip from its current position in the queue.

Rewind   Rewinds the clip to the beginning. (You can Rewind and Play a video clip while streaming is in progress.)

Stop   Stops the clip.

Save File As	Displays the Save As dialog box, which lets you choose a location to save your .AVI video clip. (You can save a clip at any time during the clip streaming session.)
About CoolFusion	Displays the About dialog box.
Iterated Systems	Moves you directly to the Iterated Systems home page at **http://www.iterated.com**.

To embed .AVI videos on your Web pages for use with CoolFusion, you must associate the MIME type `video/x-msvideo` with the file name extension .AVI on your Web server. Then you use the <EMBED> statement, including the standard required SRC, WIDTH, and HEIGHT attributes.

But CoolFusion also supports an incredible array of optional <EMBED> tag attributes. Here are a few:

`SHOWCONTROLS=TRUE¦FALSE`	If True, the playback controls are displayed. Defaults to False.
`NOMENU=TRUE¦FALSE`	If True, the playback menu is not displayed. Defaults to False.
`NOERROR=TRUE¦FALSE`	If True, the streaming error message is not displayed. Defaults to False, which causes CoolFusion to display the streaming error dialog box. This directive is designed to give HTML authors the ability to allow .AVI content use that is not fully compatible with CoolFusion.
`STREAMONLDOUBLECLK=TRUE¦FALSE`	If True, the content streams to the first frame and waits for a left button double-click to resume streaming. Defaults to False, which directs the plug-in to stream the content in its entirety without user intervention. This feature is very useful when an HTML page design requires multiple video clips while providing the best streaming performance of the individual clips.

There are many other useful attributes, which are fully documented on the CoolFusion Web site.

Other .AVI Video Plug-Ins

There are at least two other Netscape plug-ins for displaying .AVI video.

Vosaic, or "Video Mosaic," has been developed as a joint venture between the University of Illinois and Digital Video Communications. Plug-ins are available for both Netscape and Spyglass Mosaic. Vosaic allows embedded hyperlinks within the video stream, and moving objects in the video stream are clickable and can lead to other documents. PowerPC and Windows versions can be downloaded from **http://vosaic.com/html/video.html**.

The VivoActive Player is a streaming .AVI video plug-in. It uses Video for Windows .AVI files that have been compressed up to 250:1 into a new .VIV file format. These files can be transmitted using standard HTTP protocol, so you don't need special server software to use them on your Web pages. The VivoActive Player plug-in is available for Windows 95 and Windows NT from **http://www.vivo.com**.

QuickTime Plug-Ins

QuickTime is the video format used on the Apple Macintosh. However, because it was one of the first movie formats, and because it is so widely used by the "artsy" community that favors the Mac, QuickTime .MOV movie files are in ample supply on the Web. Whether you own a Mac or a Windows computer, you owe it to yourself to make sure you have a Netscape QuickTime plug-in up and running.

The Apple QuickTime Plug-In

Long-promised and finally shipping as a part of the Navigator 3.0 distribution, Apple's QuickTime plug-in lets you view QuickTime content directly in the browser window (see fig. 9.6). The QuickTime plug-in works with existing QuickTime movies, as well as with movies prepared to take advantage of the plug-in's "fast-start" feature. The fast-start feature presents the first frame of the movie almost immediately, and can begin playing even before the movie has been completely downloaded.

You can download the latest versions of the QuickTime plug-in for the Mac, PowerMac, Windows 3.1, Windows 95, and Windows NT from **http://quicktime.apple.com/qt/sw/sw.html**. After you have it up and running, check out Apple's QuickTime Plug-in Sample Site at **http://www.mediacity.com/~erweb**.

Chapter 9 Video and Animation Plug-Ins

FIG. 9.6
The Apple QuickTime plug-in features an integrated control toolbar and a popup menu that displays when you right-click.

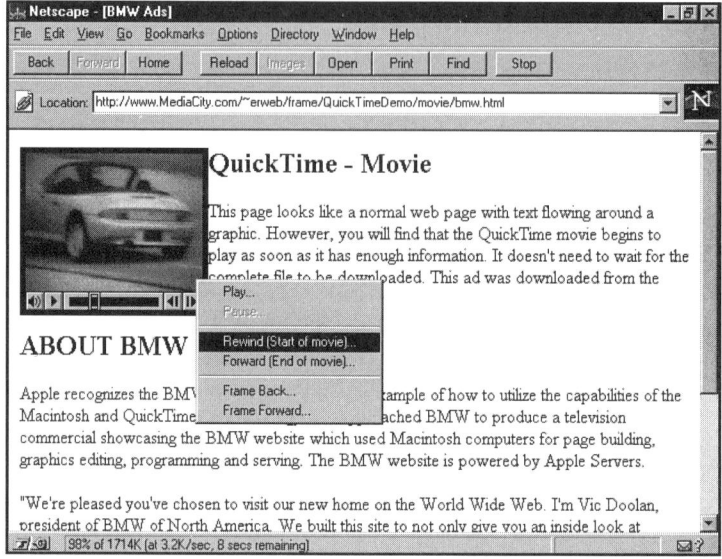

All flavors of the Apple Macintosh ship QuickTime-enabled, but if you want to play QuickTime movies on your Windows computer, you'll need the proper version of QuickTime for Windows, in addition to the QuickTime plug-in. You can download versions for Windows 3.1, Windows 95, and Windows NT from **http://quicktime.apple.com**.

The plug-in can play many kinds of QuickTime movies (.MOV files), including movies with text, MIDI, and other kinds of data. The QuickTime plug-in supports a varied set of embedded commands, allowing changes in user interface and background content (for example, music). If you have downloaded and installed the QuickTime VR component, you can also interact with QuickTime VR Panoramas and Objects.

QuickTime VR stitches together a series of images into a panorama or scene (see fig. 9.7). To view VR scenes, you'll need to get the QuickTime VR Component from the QuickTime Software page and drop it into your Netscape plug-in folder. It's available at **http://quicktime.apple.com/qt/sw/sw.html**.

If you're interested in creating QuickTime movies to play back on your site, you'll find tools for Webmasters (like the Internet Movie Tool for the Mac) at **http://quicktime.apple.com/qt/sw/sw.html#tool**. You can also check into **http://quicktime.apple.com/qt/dev/devweb.html** for more information on how to use QuickTime on the Web.

FIG. 9.7
To view a QuickTime VR panorama, you just click and drag the mouse.

To use QuickTime movies on your Web site, you'll have to associate the MIME type video/quicktime with the file name extension .MOV on your Web server. Then use the <EMBED> tag, complete with the required SRC, HEIGHT, and WIDTH attributes. (If you want to display the movie's controller, you will need to add 24 pixels to the HEIGHT.)

In addition, you can use the following optional attributes:

HIDDEN	Hides the movie. Appropriate only for sound-only QuickTime files.
AUTOPLAY=TRUE¦FALSE	If True, plays the movie automatically. Default is False.

`CONTROLLER=TRUE｜FALSE`	If True, displays the control toolbar. Default is True. If you display the toolbar, the `HEIGHT` parameter should be 24 pixels greater than the actual height of the movie, to make room for the toolbar. (Do not use `CONTROLLER=TRUE` with QuickTime VR files.)
`LOOP=TRUE｜FALSE｜PALINDROME`	Defaults to False. If True, plays the video over and over. `PALINDROME` is an overly cute value that really means *"ping-pong";* in other words, it plays the movie forward, then backward, then repeats in an infinite loop. (Not used with VR files.)
`PLAYEVERYFRAME=TRUE｜FALSE`	If True, plays every frame as it is received, even if this means playing at a slow rate. Defaults to False. (Automatically turns off audio.)
`HREF="URL"`	Provides a link for the movie object.
`TARGET="FRAME"`	Provides a targeted link for the movie.
`PAN=integer`	For VR movies only. Specifies initial pan angle, from 0.0 to 360.0 degrees.
`TILT=integer`	For VR movies only. Specifies initial tilt angle, from –42.5 to 42.5 degrees.
`FOV=integer`	For VR movies only. Specifies initial field of view angle, from 5.0 to 85.0 degrees.
`NODE=integer`	For VR movies only. Specifies initial node for a multinode VR movie.
`CORRECTION=NONE｜PARTIAL｜FULL`	Optional VR movie parameter.

Other QuickTime Plug-Ins

There are a lot of QuickTime movie plug-ins out there on the Web. Here are a few more you might want to try out.

Knowledge Engineering's MacZilla is a Mac-only Navigator plug-in that's a sort of Swiss Army knife of plug-ins. Besides QuickTime movies, it plays or displays MIDI background music; .WAV, .AU, and .AIFF audio; and MPEG and .AVI movies. Using its own plug-in component architecture, MacZilla can extend and update itself over the Internet with the click of a button. You even get a built-in MacZilla game! Download it from Knowledge Engineering, **http://maczilla.com**.

MovieStar by Intelligence at Large is less ambitious—it's only for QuickTime movie playback. A multimedia editing application, MovieStar Maker, is also available for download. Using it, Webmasters can optimize QuickTime movies so that Navigator users can view them while they download. You can also use autoplay, looping, and many other settings. This one is available for Windows 3.1, Windows 95, and Macintosh at **http://www.beingthere.com/**.

Need more choices? There are at least three more QuickTime player plug-ins for Netscape: Iván Cavero Belaúnde's ViewMovie for Windows 95 and Macintosh at **http://www.well.com/~ivanski/**; TEC Solutions' TEC Player, also for Windows 95 and Macintosh, at **http://www.tecs.com/TECPlayer_docs**; and Kevin McMurtrie's Mac-only Multimedia Plugin at **ftp://ftp.wco.com/users/mcmurtri/MySoftware/**.

MPEG Plug-Ins

MPEG is the standard video compression method developed by the Motion Picture Experts Group. MPEG video delivers excellent quality with better compression than other methods. The MPEG-1 standard is used for computer-based video on the Internet and CD-ROMs, while MPEG-2 is designed for commercial broadcast applications.

MPEG works best with a video board capable of hardware decompression. But even running in software on fast Pentium systems, MPEG works pretty well. There are two Netscape plug-ins currently available for playing inline MPEG videos: InterVU and Action.

> **NOTE** Xing (**http://www.xingtech.com**), well-known for its MPEG applications, will be providing a Navigator plug-in to support live streaming MPEG and LBR (low bit-rate) audio and full-motion MPEG video from Xing StreamWorks Web servers. Check out Xing's Web site for availability information.

InterVU

InterVU's MPEG plug-in (sometimes called PreVU) plays streaming MPEG video without specialized MPEG hardware or a proprietary video server. It gives you a first-frame view inline, streams viewing while downloading, and supports full-speed cached playback off your hard drive. InterVU is available for PowerMac, Windows 95, and Windows NT. It can be downloaded from **http://www.intervu.com/download.html**.

InterVU has no popup menu, but it does have an integrated control toolbar (see fig. 9.8).

218 Chapter 9 Video and Animation Plug-Ins

FIG. 9.8
The InterVU MPEG player plug-in has minimalist controls, but offers full streaming playback.

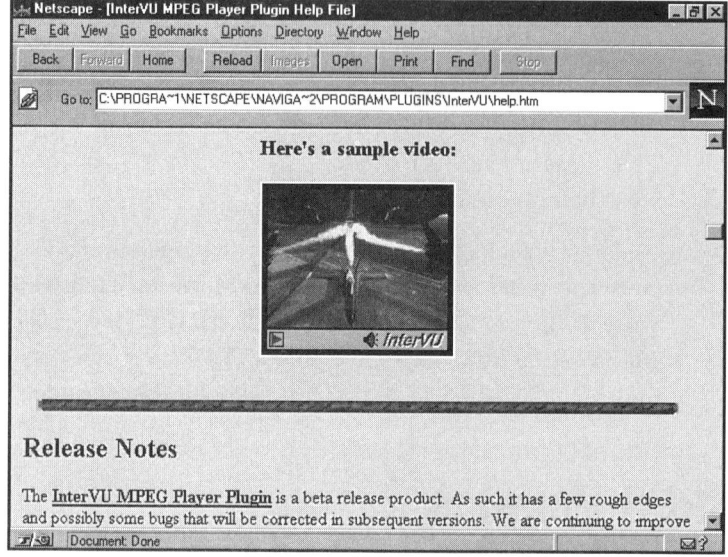

You click the Play button to start a video playing. While a video is playing, the Play button is replaced by a Stop button. Left-clicking anywhere on the video will also start and stop the video. As you download the file, a speaker symbol appears if the file has sound, and a crossed out speaker symbol appears if the file is silent.

After the MPEG file has played to completion, a disk button appears on the control bar next to the Play button. If you would like to save the file, click this disk button to open a Save As dialog box. To replay an MPEG video, click the Play button again.

> **N O T E** If you want to play back a video from your Netscape cache later, you must allow the video to play to completion the first time. Otherwise, Netscape will not save the video in its cache. ■

Clicking on the InterVU logo in the lower-right corner connects you to the InterVU Web site.

To embed MPEG videos into your Web pages for viewing with InterVU, you first need to make the following MIME type associations in your Web server software:

```
video/mpeg         mpg;*.mpe;*.mpv;*.mpeg;*.mp1;*.mp2
video/x-mpeg       mpg;*.mpe;*.mpv;*.mpeg;*.mp1;*.mp2
```

Then you use the `<EMBED>` tag, including the standard SRC, WIDTH, and HEIGHT attributes, as well as these optional attributes:

AUTOPLAY=NO¦YES	If Yes, the clip is automatically played. No is the default. (It's unfortunate that this plug-in doesn't use True and False with AUTOSTART, which is the standard usage.)
FRAMERATE=*integer*	Legitimate values are from 1 to 25, representing frames per second. (This attribute automatically disables sound.)
LOOP=*integer*	Enter the number of times you want the video to play. Each time the start button is pressed, the video will play the specified number of times.
DOUBLESIZE=YES¦NO	Default is No. If Yes, the video is shown at double the encoded size.
HALFSIZE=YES¦NO	Like DOUBLESIZE, but half the size.
CONBAR=YES¦NO	If No, the control toolbar is not displayed. Default is Yes.
FRAMES=YES¦NO	If Yes, autoplays the video on a Macintosh when Netscape Framesets are used.
PALETTE=FOREGROUND¦BACKGROUND	If FOREGROUND, specifies that the video's palette be used as the standard palette on a 256-color screen.

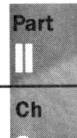

Action

Open2U's Action MPEG player plug-in can also play included synchronized soundtracks or sound-only files that have been compressed using MPEG. Action doesn't require special hardware or a special Web server. Action is available for Windows 95 and Windows NT; you can download it for trial at **http://www.open2u.com/action/action.html**.

ActionStudio is Open2U's companion MPEG movie creation program. It can take a standard Microsoft .AVI movie clip and convert it to MPEG. You can also convert a sequence of images into an MPEG movie, and can add a sound sequence (.WAV and other formats) from files. Action Studio is $250.

The Action plug-in can achieve approximately 24 frames a second for an image the size of 240-by-160 pixels on a T1 Internet connection or LAN. Lower frame rate is observed over an ISDN or a regular telephone line. However, Action enables you to capture the movie and replay it at a later time. Other features include dynamic color/mono selection, display size enlargement (viewing area is increased fourfold), and video and audio synchronization.

By right-clicking in Action, you display a popup menu that enables you to play, pause, capture, or replay an MPEG video (see fig. 9.9). A submenu lets you alter attribute-controlled features, like Color, Sizex2, Sync (audio), and Debug.

FIG. 9.9
The Action MPEG movie viewer plug-in has no onscreen controls, but displays a popup menu when you right-click.

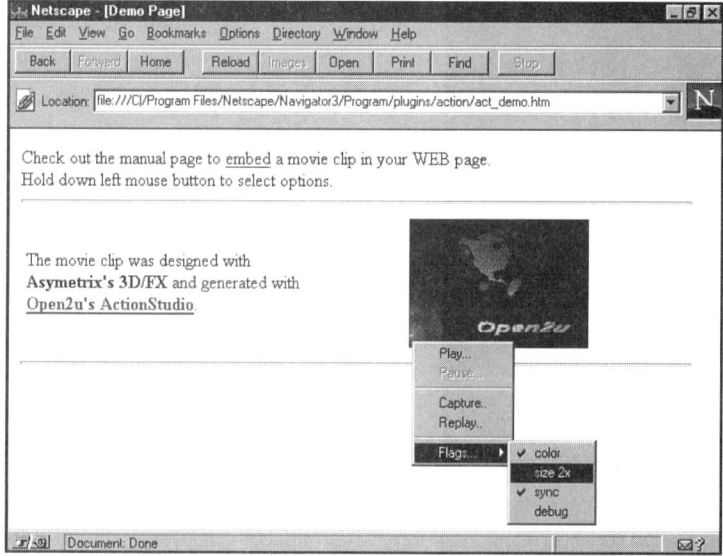

To embed Action-compatible MPEG movies, you set the same MIME types on your Web server as for InterVU:

video/mpeg	mpg;*.mpe;*.mpv;*.mpeg;*.mp1;*.mp2
video/x-mpeg	mpg;*.mpe;*.mpv;*.mpeg;*.mp1;*.mp2

The <EMBED> tag works the same, as far as the standard required attributes SRC, WIDTH, and HEIGHT are concerned. Even the PALETTE attribute works the same. After that, there is a different set of optional attributes, though:

AUTOSTART=TRUE	Starts a movie as soon as the page is loaded.
LOOP=TRUE	Continuously replays the movie.
SYNC=ON	Enables video and audio synchronization.

SIZE=DOUBLE	Doubles the display image size.
COLOR=MONO	Plays the movie in grayscale.
DEBUG=ON	Enables Debug mode.

Note that these last four attributes are also changeable from the popup submenu under Flags.

Animation Plug-Ins

Everybody loves a good cartoon. A simple animation can add a lot to your Web page. Though animations are essentially the same things as videos, there can be a great difference in scale.

Videos take up a lot of memory, storage space, and transfer bandwidth, because video images are usually complex, real-world images composed of a lot of pixels in a wide variety of colors.

Animations, on the other hand, are often simple images consisting of only a few colors. Because of this, they compress extremely well in comparison to video. If they are put into a proprietary format that is optimized for the delivery of simple animation, they can be even smaller. That's one good reason to consider animation when livening up your Web pages. If you pick a good format, you can deliver animations hundreds of times faster than you can deliver video clips.

This section is intentionally sparse on information about how to embed animations, for a very good reason. Animation always requires at least two proprietary programs—one to create animations and save them in a special format, and a second to play back those special format files. Since you can't create animations unless you use these companies' animation-creation products, you won't have any material to embed unless you download or buy their programs anyway. These animation creation programs all contain extensive information on how to include the final result in your pages.

This section looks at four Netscape animation player plug-ins: Enliven, Emblaze, Sizzler, and Play3D.

Enliven

The Enliven suite consists of three distinct software components: Enliven Viewer, a plug-in for Netscape Navigator; Enliven Server, software for Windows NT Web servers to feed multiple streams of animation to Web browsers; and Enliven Producer, a post-production environment to prepare content for online delivery.

The Enliven product family features patent-pending streaming technologies, including a new multimedia object format and a time-based scene description language specifically designed for Internet use. Called Narrative MediaElements and the Narrative Screen Description Language (NSDL) respectively, these technologies stream animation components over the Web by separating media-specific components—such as audio, graphics and animation—and then applying optimized media-specific compression solutions to each media class. The individual codecs used to perform the element compression and decompression are individually upgradable into the various Narrative products, which means they can easily take advantage of any compression technology breakthroughs.

Enliven Producer is a scene-based, drag-and-drop, post-production environment for importing existing digital content from sources such as Macromedia Director or the Microsoft WinToon .AVI, and then optimizing that content for delivery via the Enliven Server. This makes it easy to convert animated content you may have already produced, and you can continue to use familiar tools to create future content as well. Enliven animations can even include interactive hot spots for full interactivity. Enliven Producer runs on Windows 95 and Windows NT and a future version is promised for the Macintosh.

The Enliven Server works in conjunction with your standard Web server to deliver multiple simultaneous animation streams. The Enliven Server manages real-time streaming of animation sequences with accompanying sound and graphics, while transferring data for subsequent portions of an animation in the background. The Enliven Server currently runs on Windows NT and can reside on the same server as an existing HTTP Web server or, optionally, on its own server. A UNIX Enliven server is also planned.

The Enliven Viewer plug-in (fig 9.10) can also be used as a helper application for a Mosaic browser, or as a stand-alone application for displaying content in the Enliven format. A beta version of the Enliven Viewer plug-in for Windows 95 and Windows NT can be downloaded from **http://www.narrative.com**.

Emblaze

GEO Interactive Media Group's Emblaze plug-in is a real-time animation player that plays a proprietary animation format that GEO says needs only 3M to 4M of disk space for approximately 30 minutes of play time (see fig. 9.11). The animations can be displayed at a rate of 12 to 24 frames per second in 256 colors in real time over a 14.4kbps connection.

Animations are created using the commercial Emblaze Creator program, which can integrate animation with sound. The end result is an animated cartoon that plays quickly over the Web, even over slow 14.4kbps dial-up connections.

Animation Plug-Ins | 223

FIG. 9.10
Broderbund Software converted this sample Enliven animation from a CD-ROM storybook originally produced in Macromedia Director.

FIG. 9.11
The Emblaze plug-in displays highly compressed animations like this, with audio, in Netscape-viewed Web pages.

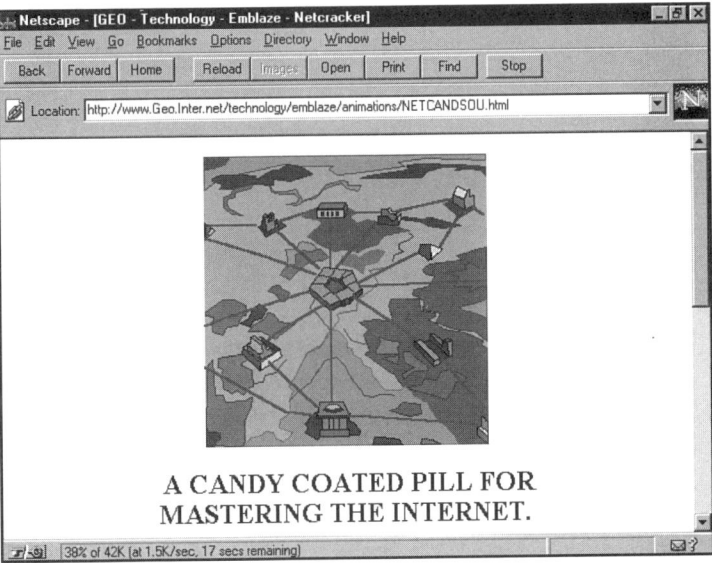

Windows 3.1, Macintosh, PowerMac, and Windows 95 versions of both the player plug-in and the Creator program can be had at **http://www.Geo.Inter.net/technology/ emblaze/index.html**.

Sizzler

Totally Hip Software's Sizzler plug-in (fig 9.12) and companion converter program let you create and display small, efficient Web animations that are among the best on the Web. These animations display like an interlaced GIF or progressive JPEG still image, only *moving*. That is, they start out blocky but animated, and fill in with detail as the data streams in. Sizzler animations are perfect for spot animation attention-getters, as well as motion illustrations. It's a perfect replacement for those GIF 89a animations that don't always work right.

FIG. 9.12
Sizzler animations—like the TV set in the upper-left corner of this screen—integrate unobtrusively into almost any Web page.

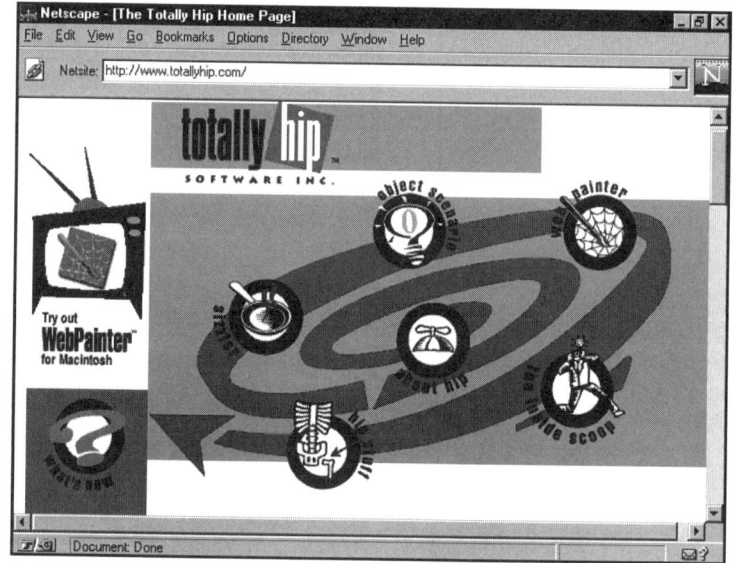

The Sizzler converter (currently available only in a version for the Macintosh) takes Macintosh .PIC files, QuickTime movies, .BMP files, .AVI videos, or DIB lists for Windows, and converts them into sprite files that can be played in real-time in Navigator. Totally Hip's core technology (called Object Scenario) allows for streamed delivery of several media types, including text, animation, video, sound, and interactivity. Totally Hip plans to add all of these to Sizzler in the near future.

The Sizzler plug-in and Converter are available as free downloads for Windows 95, Windows NT, Macintosh, and PowerPC (only the plug-in is available for Windows 3.1) from **http://www.totallyhip.com/**.

Animation Plug-Ins | 225

N O T E Coming soon from Totally Hip will be the WebPainter animation creation system for Macintosh, which will include advanced features like a cel strip window, onion skinning, multiple cel editing, foreground/background drawing cels, increased file format support, and hot keys. It will also save animations as animated GIFs that can be played back in the Netscape window without the need for a plug-in player.

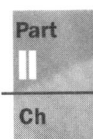

Play3d

Heads Off's Play3D plug-in supports real-time interactive 3-D and 2-D sprites as well as .WAV and MIDI sound playback (see fig. 9.13). Objects can be linked to URLs, media files, or Play3D *"scene"* files. The free demo version allows for authoring and playback without leaving Netscape. For Windows 95 only, Play3D is downloadable from **http://www.headsoff.com**.

FIG. 9.13
Play3D is weird, wonderful, and fun to play with. It lets you manipulate 3-D worlds in real time over the Web.

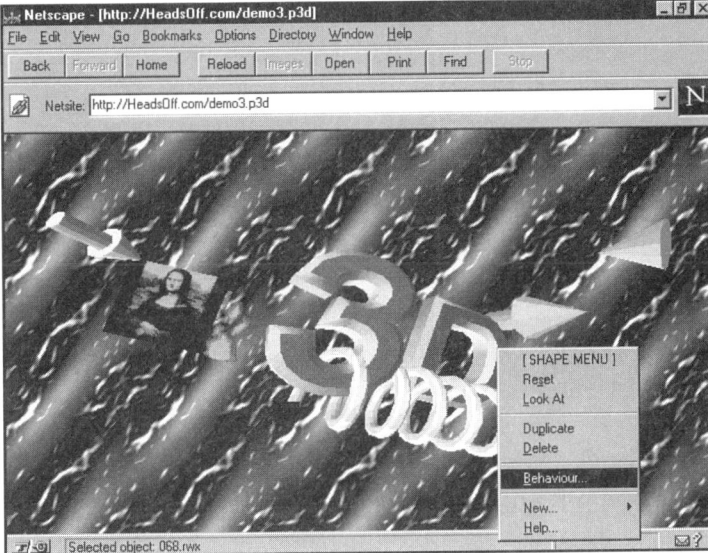

Play3D produces animations that are reminiscent of VRML worlds, and is probably more interesting to study than to use in a real-world setting. Objects can have behavior attached, so, for example, you can set an object to play a MIDI file, link to another URL or another 3-D scene file, and so on. It uses vector-based 3-D shape files that can be created with most 3-D design programs. This plug-in is unusual in that it can be used to create, view, and manipulate its animation files in real time. Licensed custom versions of the Play3D module are available from Heads Off.

> **NOTE** Deltapoint's Web Animator, for the Macintosh only (a Windows version is promised), combines animation, sound, and live interaction. The authoring tool for creating animations to add to your own site is also available from Deltapoint's Web site at **http://www.deltapoint.com/animate/index.htm**.

CHAPTER 10

Shockwave for Macromedia Director

- How Director compares to Java and JavaScript
- How Shockwave for Director can liven up your Web site
- How to create Director multimedia movies for delivery over the Internet

Multimedia is a good buzzword, but what does it really mean? Literally translated as *more than one medium*, when most people use the term they mean a presentation that includes some combination of sound, graphics, animation, video, and even interactivity.

Interactivity is an important part of multimedia. It's the part that puts the flow of the whole thing under the user's control. Though this can be as simple as an onscreen button that you have to click to move to the next slide, more often it involves making selections from multiple choices.

Shockwave for Director is a Netscape plug-in that lets you play multimedia "movies" created with the most popular multimedia creation tool available today—Macromedia Director. ■

http://www.mcp.com/que

Director versus Java and JavaScript

The Director plug-in came first, introduced at about the same time as Netscape Navigator 2.0, the first version of Netscape to have plug-in capability. Hundreds of developers began using Macromedia Director—literally overnight—to add animation and interactive multimedia content to their Web sites. Many of them already had Director movies on hand that they had created for other applications. All they had to do was run them through the new Afterburner Xtra module and place their converted movies on their Web pages using the new <EMBED> tag. Suddenly, Web pages included inline animations, games, and button-rich interactive multimedia presentations. It was clear that the Web would never be the same again.

But then Netscape added support for Java and JavaScript. Shockwave didn't go away, but suddenly Java became the new darling of Web site developers. Animations, presentations, and even interactive multimedia sites multiplied by the thousands. Nowadays, it seems like all you hear about are Java and JavaScript.

Did Java and JavaScript kill Shockwave? Did they completely take over the multimedia/animation niche that the Shockwave for Director plug-in had created? Hardly. With a quarter of a million copies of Director in use, Macromedia is still doing quite well, thank you. What happened is that Java and JavaScript jumped into a niche that was expanding so rapidly that there was plenty of room for Shockwave to not only hold its own, but keep expanding its influence on the Web. In the meantime, Java and JavaScript also carved out their own territories.

In truth, Java and Director appeal to two inherently different types of people. You develop content with Macromedia Director in a friendly, point-and-click environment that uses a "stage" metaphor. You bring in "casts" composed of "actors," who strut their stuff on a "stage." The end result is even referred to as a "movie." Director includes painting and animation tools with menus, dialogs, and buttons. People who are used to creating content with end-user applications like Word and Paint are those who are most comfortable developing Web page multimedia content using Director.

> **NOTE** Don't confuse Director "movies" with digitized video "movies" like Video for Windows or QuickTime files. Although they share a common name, Director movies are much more than a simple sequence of images—they also include interactive elements.

On the other hand, Java and JavaScript are programming languages. They resemble the C programming language, which is the most popular language for developing applications, so they appeal mostly to programmers. People who think in terms of code and programs are more likely to develop their multimedia Web page content with Java and JavaScript.

What You Can Do with Shockwave for Director

The Shockwave for Macromedia Director plug-in can integrate animation, bitmap, video, and sound, and can bundle all of them up with an interactive interface, complete with control buttons and graphic "hot spots" (see fig. 10.1). Its playback compatibility with a variety of computer platforms including Windows, Mac OS, OS/2, and SGI has helped to make Director the most widely used professional multimedia authoring tool.

FIG. 10.1
The Shockwave for Director plug-in features no playback controls or menus of its own. Any such controls must be provided as part of the Director movie being played, like the Replay button shown below this "Netman" animation.

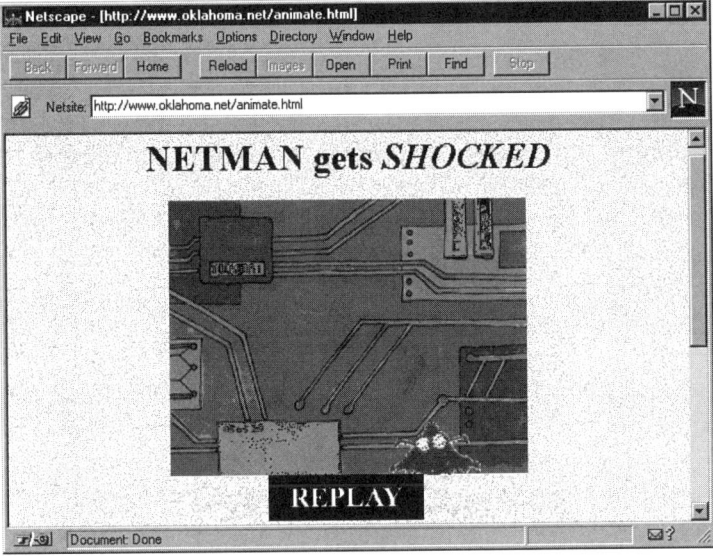

Using Shockwave for Director, a Director movie run over the Internet can support the same sort of features as a Director movie run from a CD-ROM, including animated sequences, sophisticated scripted interactivity, user text input, sound playback, and much more. You can even add hot links to URL addresses.

Shockwave for Director consists of two main components: the Shockwave plug-in itself and Shockwave Afterburner, a compressor Xtra program that runs from within Macromedia Director to squeeze a Director movie file by 40-50 percent for faster access over the Internet. You can download the Shockwave for Director plug-in and Afterburner from Macromedia's Web site at **Shockwave http://www-1.macromedia.com/Tools/Shockwave/Plugin/plugin.cgi.**

> **N O T E** Don't be confused by the abundance of "Shockwave" plug-ins at the Macromedia site. Besides Shockwave for Director, you'll also find a Shockwave plug-in for playing Authorware files, as well as one for viewing Freehand drawings.

But before getting too deeply into the mechanics of Director, consider what you can do on your Web site with the Shockwave plug-in for Director.

Though you are really only limited by your imagination (and network download times), there are several categories that lend themselves well to Director solutions:

- Animation—You can use Director to create frame animations (including audio, if you want) that are second to none.
- Games—Director games can be as fast and as much fun as those written in high-level programming languages.
- Entertainment—You can tie together video and audio content and deliver it as a unified package.
- Training—Interactivity through onscreen buttons and graphic "hot spots" means student-guided training is a snap.
- Education—The ability to tie together myriad components means you can compose impressive educational materials.
- Presentations—With a variety of built-in transitions and the ability to link text and graphics with voice-overs, Director presentations are a step above conventional "slide shows."
- Applications—Everything from user navigational interfaces to out-and-out application programs are candidates for creation with Director.

This section takes a look at some examples of each.

Animation

Macromedia Director animations range from simple silent cartoons of only a few frames to lengthy branching multimedia stories incorporating sound and interactivity.

Animation isn't just for cartoons; it can be useful in more serious situations, too, as shown on the Accuweather five-day forecast site at **http://www.accuwx.com/travelers/5day?LAX** (see fig. 10.2).

The simple 56K animated graphics on this page emulate the weather prediction animations featured on most TV news show weather forecasts. In the frames shown in figure 10.2, the clouds move and the sun shines. That makes this Web site look more "professional" because it conforms to the same standard as a TV weather slide.

There are hundreds of other "Shocked" sites (as Macromedia calls them) that feature animations from the simple to the sublime. You'll find links to many of them at **http://www.macromedia.com/shockwave/epicenter/guide/animation.html**.

FIG. 10.2
Although the animations on this page are simple, they add a splash of much-needed color and motion to an otherwise static page.

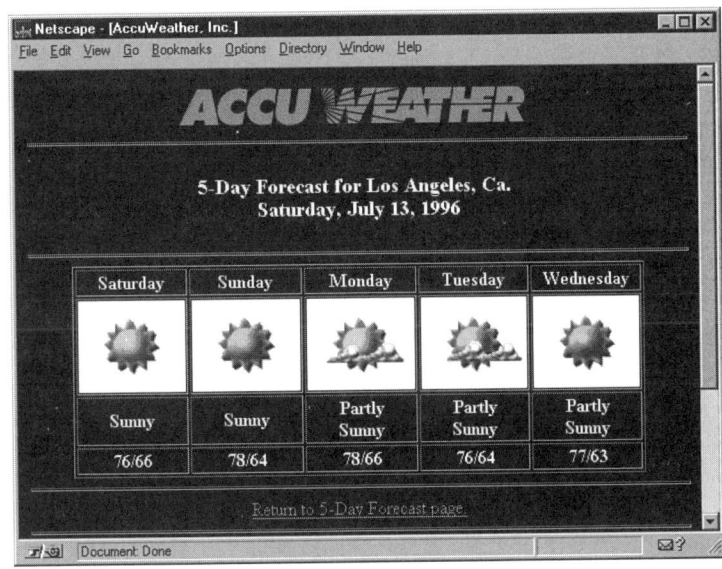

Games

Director can also be used to create Web page games that can be every bit as fast and entertaining as those created by high-level programming languages. The secret is to keep the files small so that they download quickly. Of course, they also have to be attractive, fast, and play well!

One of my favorite all-time Web games is the "Shocked" *Toy Story* Concentration Game at **http://www.disney.com/ToyStory/toybox/shock.htm?GL=H** (see fig. 10.3).

This 150K game is a masterpiece of both Web page design and Director implementation. It works well as a promotional piece for the Disney movie because it involves you with the *Toy Story* characters in a unique and fun way. The game is easy for kids to play, but features two advanced skill levels for cocky adults who think it's going to be "just too easy." If you think you might want to put a game or two on your site, it wouldn't hurt to meditate awhile on what Disney's Web designers have accomplished on this site.

Another excellent example of great Web page game design comes, not surprisingly, from a company that specializes in designing Shockwave games for Web sites—AfterShock. Their Web Invaders game (45K) shown in figure 10.4 is tiny, quick, and a perfect knock-off of the old Space Invaders arcade classic.

FIG. 10.3
The *Toy Story* Concentration Game is intuitive, fast, colorful, and a whole lot of fun to play!

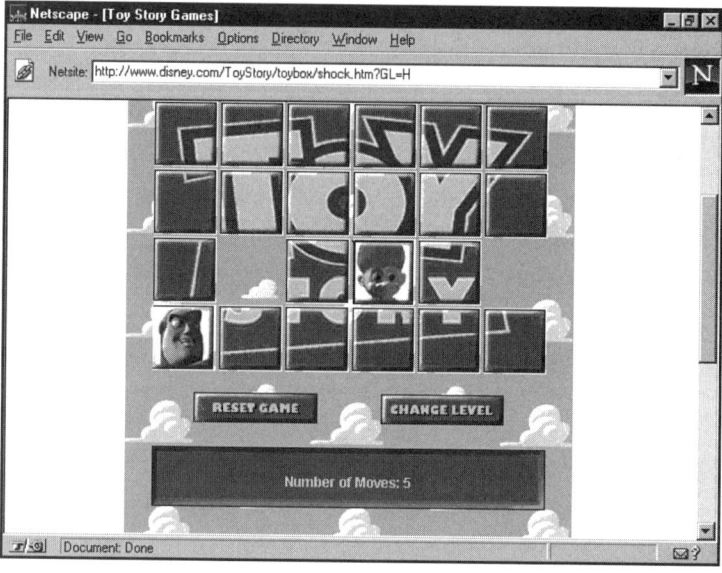

FIG. 10.4
AfterShock's Web Invaders squeezes onscreen instructions, controls, and playfield into a tight space on the screen, but the gameplay is big, big, big!

This game's genius is not in its originality, but in its cozy familiarity, achieved through adherence to the original. The fact that it downloads super-fast and plays quickly and smoothly doesn't hurt a bit, either. You can find Web Invaders (and WebFrog, another arcade classic) at AfterShock's Arcade Alley, **http://www.ashock.com/html/arcadealley.html**.

Entertainment

You'd expect entertainment sites to make good use of the Shockwave for Director plug-in, and they do. You'll find lots of slick animations and interactive presentations on Web sites devoted to entertaining you.

Sportsline USA's site at **http://ps1.sportsline.com/u/multimedia/shockwave/mlb/index.html** (see fig. 10.5) provides a unique combination of sports news and information with an entertaining way of showing you the game.

FIG. 10.5
This Sportsline USA site uses up-to-the-minute baseball game data to re-create a ballgame for your viewing pleasure.

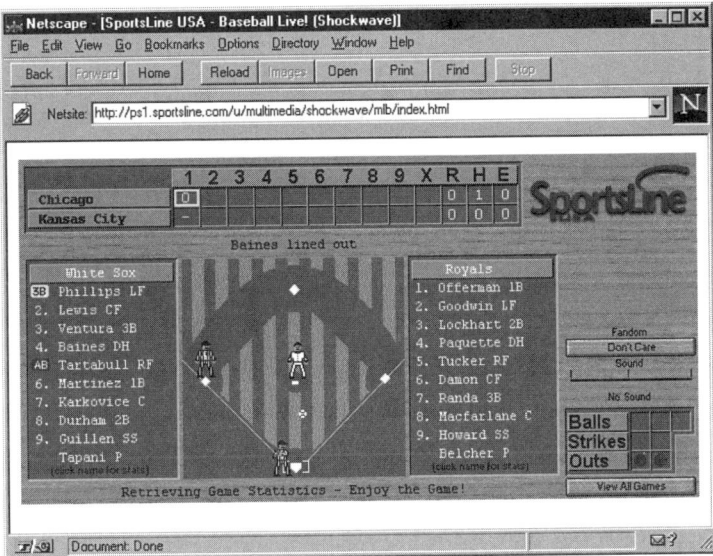

At this site, you are first presented with a screenful of scores from today's baseball games. (You can also pick past games this season.) Clicking a score loads a 150K (without sound) or 300K (with sound) Director movie. This movie loads in a statistics file that replays the game play-by-play as a little animated cartoon. You can click on players' names in the rosters to retrieve player stats, too. Although probably only the most die-hard ball fan will sit through this site's cartoonish replay of a whole nine-inning game, the concept is mind-blowing, and shows just how much can be done with Director and some ingenuity.

Training

From the lofty heights of the glamorous entertainment world, you now drop back down to Earth. How far down, you ask? Just about as low as you can go. Basement level, in fact. You are going to learn all about the High-Lift Grouting of Masonry Walls (see fig. 10.6).

FIG. 10.6
They may not be glamorous, but multimedia training sessions like this can be a valuable part of your Web site. It's solid content like this that keeps your audience coming back, and makes them recommend your site to others.

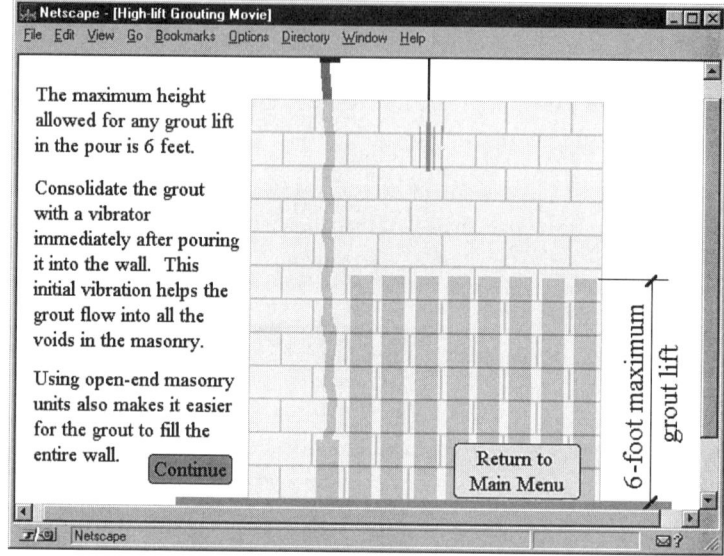

This site, at **http://ourworld.compuserve.com/homepages/thor_matteson/ brikintr.htm**, is a solid example of using the Shockwave plug-in to deliver real-world training over the Web. This site presents the know-how required to build a masonry wall using a button-controlled animated slide show created in Macromedia Director.

Not all Shockwave training movies have to be as serious as this, however. Hobbies also provide ample opportunities for training sequences. Take Kite Paradise at **http:// www.hermes.de/KITE/Tip1.html** (see fig. 10.7), for example.

This German site uses a series of interactive slides with voice-overs (in English) to show you how to "tune" your kite. This particular sequence, which demonstrates how to adjust kite string clips, is 179K in size, and downloads relatively quickly over a 28.8kbps dial-up connection even from overseas.

Education

Separating education from training probably isn't valid, although people do tend to look on the former as more related to real-world tasks, and the latter as more formal in structure.

However you cut it, sites such as the Passage to Vietnam (180K) presentation at **http:// www.nbn.com/home/adhoc/passage.htm** make good use of Shockwave to present information of an educational nature. This site is ad*hoc Interactive's on-the-Web promotional piece for the CD-ROM version of Rick Smolan's impressive photo book about Vietnam 20 years after the war (see fig. 10.8).

What You Can Do with Shockwave for Director | 235

FIG. 10.7
If you know something unique, such as how to tune a kite, consider using Shockwave to create training materials such as this for your Web site.

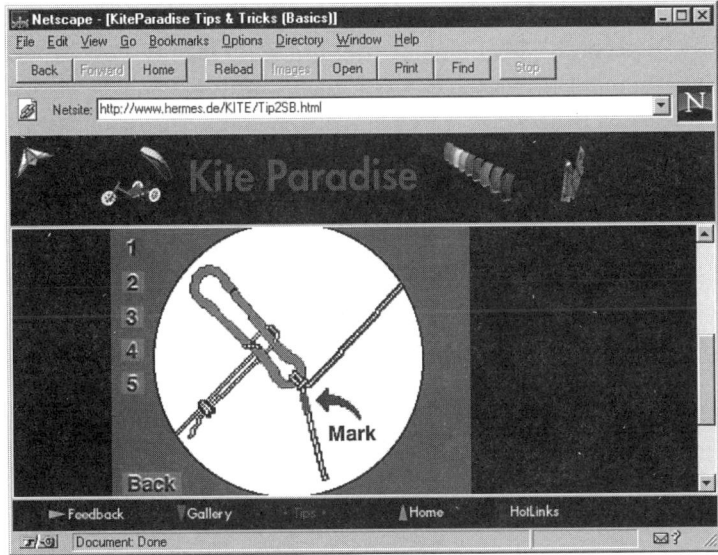

FIG. 10.8
The Passage to Vietnam presentation shown here is an excellent showpiece for the quality of the CD-ROM. The image is sharp, the audio is clear, and the user interface is minimalist.

Though the site shows only a still image with a single play button that you click to hear a voice-over, the understated simplicity of the presentation underscores the emotion conveyed in the voice-over. Sometimes it's best to just let the elements tell their own story, and not overwhelm them with flash. Though promoting a product, this site also manages to convey a feeling for history, geography, politics, and war.

Of course, there's no reason why the kids can't get involved in educational projects, too. Cyberkids' "My Computerized House" at **http://www.cyberkids.com/cyberkids/Multimedia/Shockwave/MCH/mch1.html** is an online presentation of an original story by Wulia Beakoi, age 9, who also provided the illustrations (see fig. 10.9).

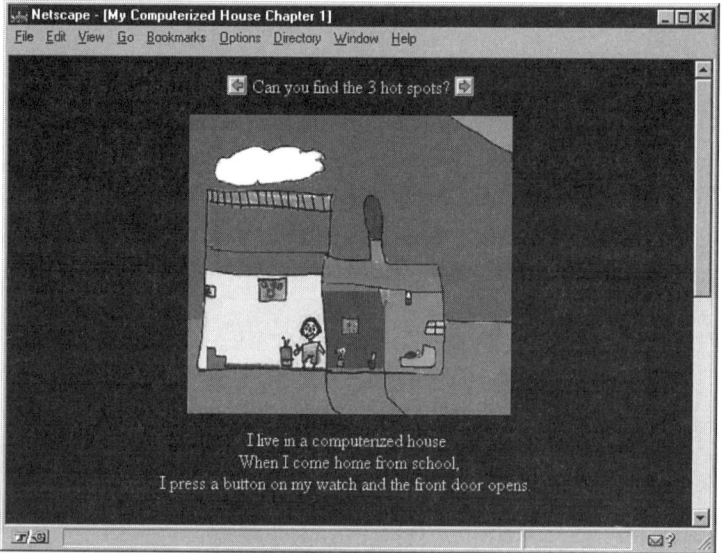

FIG. 10.9
My Computerized House is an entertaining story with great illustrations, nice bits of animation, and even hidden interactivity.

The clouds roll by in the background of this animated illustration, and when you move the mouse cursor over the three hidden hot spots, a word balloon, an animated cat, and a ticking watch pop up. It's cool, it's fun, and it shows what a kid with a great imagination, creativity, and cooperative adults can accomplish. With a little practice, maybe you can do as well on *your* Web site!

Presentations

Presentations are traditionally created using PowerPoint or Harvard Graphics or some other business graphics tool, but Macromedia Director can do just about anything they can do, and a lot more, too. The CNN Oklahoma Bombing Page at **http://cnn.com/US/OKC/shockwave/shock1.html** illustrates this point well (see fig. 10.10).

One of the largest Director files showcased here at 760K, the presentation at this site is well worth the download time. A look back at that infamous day in Oklahoma City, this file is essentially a simple slide show with a voice-over soundtrack and a single Play/Stop button. This site demonstrates how it's sometimes best to just let the pictures say it for you.

FIG. 10.10
CNN's Oklahoma City Bombing Page packs a lot of image and audio material into a simple but poignant presentation.

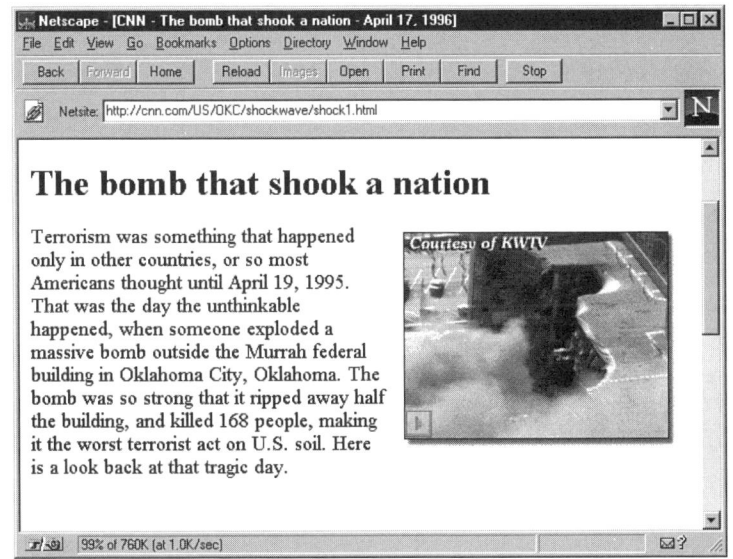

Another site that showcases simple slide shows with voice-overs (this time incorporating some of Director's slide transition special effects) is the *Time Magazine* Daily State of the Union Pages site. The Welcome video (740K, shown in fig. 10.11) provides a simple introduction. The site contains several such presentations, all centered around the theme of the State of the Union. You can view it at **http://www.macromedia.com/shockwave/epicenter/shockedsites/time/**.

FIG. 10.11
Time Magazine's Daily State of the Union pages are a sit-back-and-relax series of slides with voice-overs, but they're as slick and professional as it gets.

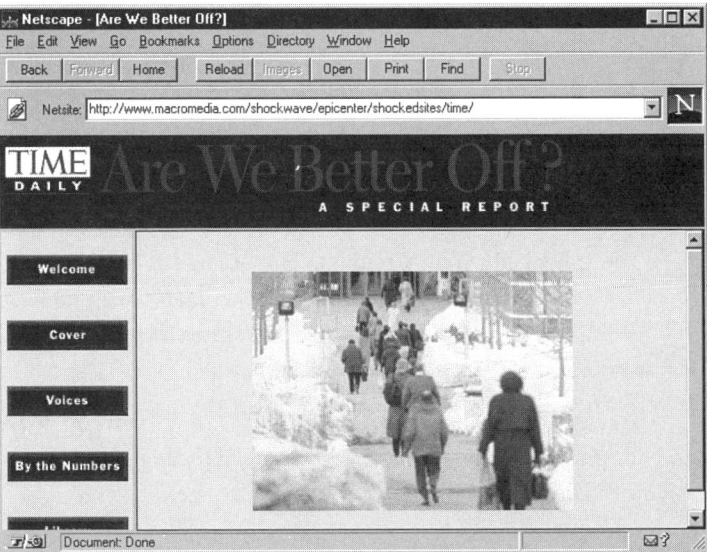

Applications

Now comes the real hard-core stuff—applications. On the Web, Director applications often manifest themselves as user navigation tools.

One excellent example comes from the Netscape site itself. The animated toolbar at **http://www.netscape.com/comprod/products/navigator/version_2.0/plugins/ director_examples/director_example1.html** is actually a 20K Director file. Though it looks like the standard Netscape site toolbar in this static image, the toolbar cels fly into place when you access this URL (see fig. 10.12). Not only that, but the individual selections highlight as you move the mouse cursor over them. When clicked, they act like a standard imagemap, but the associated URLs are defined in the Director movie, not by a CGI-BIN script, and they are consequently called by the browser (via the Shockwave plug-in), not the server.

FIG. 10.12
The toolbar on this Netscape page is actually a Director animation, though it functions much the same as the normal Netscape Web page toolbar.

The "Shocked" Apple Computer Home Page at **http://www2.apple.com/sw/** (fig. 10.13) is another example of a custom-animated user interface created using Director. This 256K Director application incorporates a QuickTime VR image (on the right) and clickable navigation buttons (on the left).

This is far from an exhaustive list of the things you can do with the Shockwave for Director plug-in, but it should give you a good many ideas of the types of content you can create with Director for use on your own Web pages.

FIG. 10.13
This user interface at the Apple Computer site "unfolds" in an animated sequence when the page is loaded.

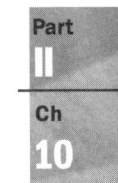

Creating Director Movies for Shockwave

But how do you actually create Director movies?

The simple answer is "with Macromedia Director." But that involves a great many steps, and a bit of a learning curve. Though Director is an excellent tool, multimedia files are very complex and content-rich. Even a relatively unambitious file can include still graphics, animation sequences, digitized audio or video, and interactive components. Creating all of that content and tying it all together is a significant challenge, even if you've got the right tools.

To start with, you'll need a copy of Macromedia Director. At $850 retail, it's not cheap, but it's worth every penny if you plan to create much in the way of multimedia.

Director 5.0 (the latest version) is available for the following platforms:

- Windows 95
- Windows NT
- Windows 3.1
- Power Macintosh
- Macintosh

Director is based on a theater metaphor (even though the end product is called a "movie"—go figure). With this metaphor, you have a Stage where you can view your Director movie. Behind the scene, you have a Cast window that stores all of your media objects. These media objects can be sounds, 2-D and 3-D graphics, animations, digital video, text, and even database objects. You use the Score to organize your media elements on the Stage. The Score window enables you to precisely sync your media elements and provide different layers of elements on the screen.

The main Director screen is shown in figure 10.14.

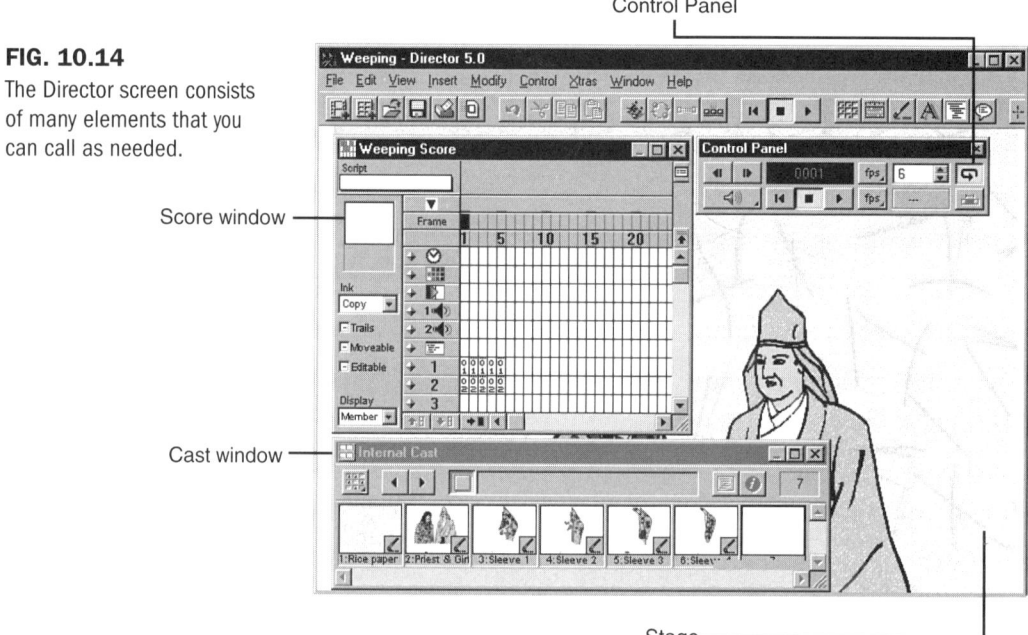

FIG. 10.14
The Director screen consists of many elements that you can call as needed.

Director movies are composed of Cast members, which are media elements like images or sounds. These are inserted into the Score window, which sequences all of the file's elements. (Director also includes a full set of Paint and other tools for creating media elements.) Once you've created and coordinated all of a movie's elements, you save the result as a Director movie file.

To use a Director movie on the Web, you first need to run it through Afterburner, a post-processor application that compresses and converts your Director movies for Internet playback. The Afterburner application doesn't alter the way a Director movie appears or behaves; it merely preps it for use on the Internet by compressing it and changing its file format. Afterburner is available for download from the Macromedia Web site at

Shockwave http://www-1.macromedia.com/Tools/Shockwave/Plugin/plugin.cgi.
Once you have downloaded and installed Afterburner, you can run it by selecting it from the Director Xtras menu. Compressed (or "shocked") Director movies have the file name extension .DXR rather than .DIR.

Before serving up "Shocked" Director movies, your Web server must be configured to recognize and handle them by associating the file name extensions .DIR, .DXR, and .DCR with the MIME type `application/x-director`.

The final step in the process is, of course, to `<EMBED>` your Director movie files on your Web pages. You use the ubiquitous `<EMBED>` tag and the required `SRC`, `WIDTH`, and `HEIGHT` parameters. You can also elect to use the `PALETTE` attribute. If `PALETTE=FOREGROUND`, this loads the Director movie's palette and uses it as the palette for the entire page. The default is `PALETTE=BACKGROUND`.

Of course, there are a few "gotchas," which the following sections explain.

Lingo Network Extensions

Macromedia Director ties together all of its elements with the Lingo scripting language. This is a rich language with a great many complex commands, and it's documented in the Director box with two thick manuals, plus comprehensive online Help.

There are many new extensions to the Lingo language that are specifically designed to work in the context of delivering multimedia content over the Web. For example, new Lingo commands can enable your Director movie to continue to display an animation while it's streaming the next segment of the movie from the network. Most of the new network Lingo commands enable you to set some sort of process in motion, check back later to see whether it's finished, and then act once the process is complete. This is different from most non-network Lingo commands, which execute a process and then immediately give you a result.

Even if you're an old Lingo wrangler, make sure you familiarize yourself with these new Lingo commands before you attempt to create content for the Web.

> **NOTE** Many online resources are available that teach the Lingo language, from Gary Rosenzweig's free-for-the-download, 32-page Lingo book at **http://www2.csn.net/~rosenz/director.html** to the for-credit (and for-money) online CyberEd course from the University of Massachusetts—Lowell, offered at **http://www.umassd.edu/cybered/lowell/LINGO.HTM**.

Director Limitations on the Internet

There are some special limitations for "Shocked" Director movies that do not apply to standard Director movies. Most of these limitations are due to the fact that the Director movie must be able to interact over a network (either an intranet or the Web).

For example, Shocked Director movies can't use "movie-in-a-window," nor can they use any of the "Wait for…" options in the tempo channel. The Director documentation covers all of these Internet limitations in detail.

> **NOTE** The latest version of the Shockwave for Director plug-in now supports streaming audio. Therefore, you can play audio files on demand, as they come down from the Web, without waiting for them to download completely first. This streaming audio requires no special server and can rival an audio CD in quality.

Web Page Design Considerations

The majority of Web users use relatively slow 14.4kbps or 28.8kbps dial-up connections. At these rates, the user can receive about 1K of information a second. At that rate, it takes one minute to transfer a 60K file. Remember this when creating the Director files for your Web pages. Don't torture your viewers with overly long download times.

Here are some other things to consider when designing Web pages with Shocked content:

- Although technically there's no limit to how many movies you can incorporate into a Web page, don't include more than three. Remember that when a user leaves a page containing Shocked Director movies, the Shockwave plug-in frees the RAM it was using to play them.

- You might encounter technical problems when Netscape tries to sort out the soundtracks of two movies playing simultaneously. Use automatically played sound in only one movie per page, and program the others so that the user can play the soundtracks by clicking the mouse.

- Movies programmed to loop indefinitely tie up the processor. It is strongly recommended that you program the movie to stop playing after a given number of loops, or program some way for the user to stop the movie.

Optimizing Director Movies for the Web

Here are some tips and techniques that will help you to create effective and efficient Director movies for your Web site:

- Keep each cast member as small as possible to keep down the file size.
- Use small graphics and resize them up to the size you need. Use the Sprite Info dialog box to reset a cast member back to its normal size, or any specific size.
- Use Lingo to add interactivity to your application. If possible, use Lingo loops and branches to sections of your movie.
- Use the Transform Bitmap dialog box to dither a graphic down to a lower bit depth.
- Set the background or foreground color of a black and white bitmap to another color with the Tools window to add spectral variety without adding size.
- Use scalable text in text fields instead of bitmapped text.
- Use objects from the Tools window whenever possible in place of bitmapped graphics.
- Use ink effects on graphics you already have before creating a new bitmap. Layering graphics with different ink effects can produce some interesting results.
- Use film loops to reuse cast members.
- Tile small bitmaps to produce backgrounds. Create tiles that have heights and widths of 16, 32, 64, or 128 pixels to maintain perfect tiling.
- Use small looping music clips instead of long soundtracks.
- Sample all sounds at 11.025 kHz to keep file sizes down.
- Try capturing and sequencing a few single frames from a video clip in lieu of playing a whole video.
- Render antialiased bitmaps to solid system colors, especially black or white, to reduce the number of colors.

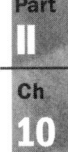

More Information

The Online Shockwave Developer's Guide at **http://www.macromedia.com/shockwave/director5/contents.html** contains a great deal of detailed information about building Web sites that use Shocked content. You might also want to check out the Director 5 Shockwave Movie Lab at **http://www.macromedia.com/shockwave/director5/movielab.html**. This page includes many samples of Shocked Director movies with source code for both Mac and Windows, such as the "Under Construction" animation with sound shown in figure 10.15.

FIG. 10.15
The source code for this little "Under Construction" animation is available from the Macromedia Web site.

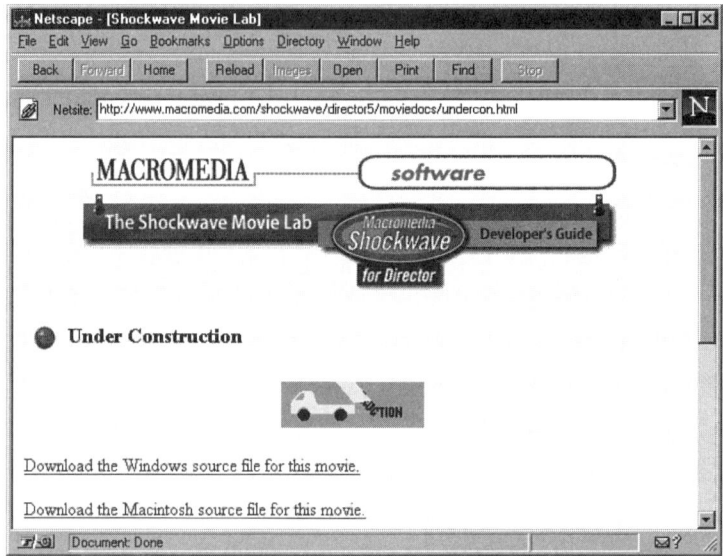

CHAPTER 11

ASAP WebShow and Other Multimedia Plug-Ins

- What multimedia plug-ins are available besides Shockwave for Director (covered in Chapter 10)
- How you can create multimedia content using the proprietary development systems and file formats that go with these plug-ins
- How you can incorporate that content into your own Web site or corporate intranet

There are dozens of multimedia authoring systems out there, and it seems like every one of them will soon have a plug-in for delivering its particular brand of multimedia file over the Web. Is all this really necessary?

Taken in the context of the "Big Picture," probably not. Java and JavaScript are turning out to be the new tools of choice for application, animation, and multimedia applications on the Web, mostly because the major browser programs—Netscape Navigator and Microsoft Internet Explorer—now both support embedded Java applets.

That means that, to develop multimedia content for Web pages, you would have to be a programmer—if not for multimedia plug-ins. If your users are willing to download and install a plug-in, you can use just about any of the multimedia programs discussed in this chapter to bring multimedia content to your Web site. You can pick the one that's most appropriate to your requirements.

http://www.mcp.com/que

Over corporate intranets, the solution is even simpler—if you've been using one of these programs to create presentations, training materials, or other multimedia content for your company, you can instantly make that content available to your entire organization by installing the right plug-in on all your desktop systems. You get another advantage from this: Anyone can develop multimedia for your intranet using end-user development programs. You don't have to rely on your programmers to do it for you. ■

ASAP WebShow

Software Publishing Corporation's ASAP WebShow is a Netscape Navigator plug-in for viewing, downloading, and printing presentations created with ASAP WordPower. Similar to PowerPoint presentations, WordPower presentations can contain tables, organization charts, bulleted lists, and other graphic and text elements in a slide show format. Since the files are compressed, they can be transmitted very quickly over the Internet.

Presentations and reports can be embedded as icons, as live thumbnails, or in a window on a Web page. Each slide can be viewed in a small live area window, enlarged to fill the current Web page, or zoomed to full screen. You can select one slide at a time or watch a continuously running show.

A Windows 95 and Windows NT version of the WebShow plug-in is now available (see fig. 11.1), and a version for Windows 3.1 is promised. You can even download a fully functional copy of ASAP WordPower for a free 30-day trial for creating your own WebShow-compatible presentations. All are available at the following site:

>   http://www.spco.com/asap/asapwebs.htm

WordPower helps you create slide shows for your Web pages. It can import PowerPoint 7.0 files and convert them to ASAP WordPower format. You can even drag and drop individual slides from the PowerPoint slide viewer into WordPower. ASAP WordPower also imports graphics files in .PCX, .BMP, .WMF, TIFF, and GIF formats. Built-in transition effects, dozens of border styles, and a set of startup templates simplify the creation of compelling slide shows. The suggested retail price for ASAP WordPower is $99

Slide show sound is handled through integration with RealAudio.

The ASAP WebShow Presentation Kit contains everything you need to create, view and hear a presentation on the World Wide Web. For $129, you get both Windows 95 and Windows 3.1 versions of the ASAP WordPower presentation creation program, the ASAP Viewer plug-in, the ASAP Image Compressor, the RealAudio Player program, a two-stream RealAudio Server (Windows 95 and Windows NT only), and the RealAudio Encoder.

ASAP WebShow 247

FIG. 11.1
The ASAP WebShow toolbar and context-sensitive popup menu give you complete control when viewing the plug-in's PowerPoint-style slide show presentations with Netscape.

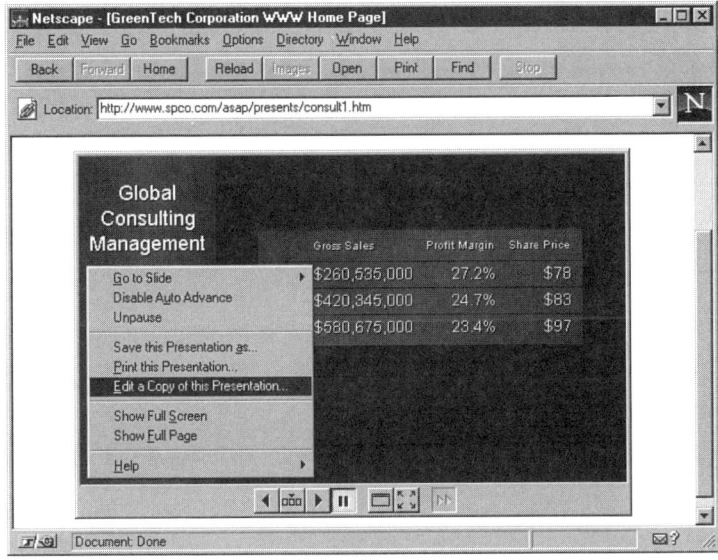

The ASAP Image Compressor is an add-on for ASAP WordPower that lets you save presentations in a compact format for delivery over the Web. The Compressor enables you to adjust the balance of image quality and file size in a compressed presentation. (Only the bitmap images in a presentation are compressed.) The ASAP Image Compressor is also available free for the downloading from the ASAP Web site.

For faster transmission time, don't include OLE objects in presentations that you embed in a Web page. OLE objects significantly increase the size of the .ASP file and aren't compressed.

To use ASAP WebShow presentations in your own Web pages, you'll first have to set the MIME type application/x-asap to the file name extension .ASP on your Web server.

ASAP WebShow content is embedded on Web pages using the <EMBED> tag, along with the required SRC, HEIGHT, and WIDTH parameters.

In addition, WebShow supports a wide range of additional <EMBED> tag parameters. If you don't use any of the optional parameters, default settings will result in a display that puts the presentation in an embedded window, includes a navigation bar, and provides the ability to save, print, and edit the presentation. Table 11.1 lists some of the most important WebShow optional parameters. For a full list, consult the WebShow documentation, or refer to the help pages on the ASAP Web site.

Table 11.1 *<EMBED>* Tag Parameters for the ASAP WebShow Plug-In

Parameter	Effect
AutoAdvance= ON|OFF	If on, automatically advances to each slide. To stop AutoAdvance temporarily, click the Pause button on the navigation bar or right-click the ASAP WebShow window and select Pause from the popup menu. To completely turn off AutoAdvance, right-click the ASAP WebShow window and then click Disable Auto Advance. To turn on AutoAdvance from the current slide, select Enable Auto Advance from the popup menu.
Border= RAISED|RECESSED|SLIDE|SHADOWED|SIMPLE|NONE	Changes the border type.
DelayTime= *integer*	In seconds, the delay before advancing to next slide when in AutoAdvance mode.
Dithering= EMBED|PAGE|SCREEN|NONE	For 256-color screen display only; specifies dithering method.
Effect= *effectname, direction*	Transition effect between slides. Transitions include the following: Blinds, left|right / Blinds, up|down / Close, horizontal|vertical / Fade / Default / Iris, in|out / None / Open, horizontal|vertical / Rain, up|down / Replace / Scroll, up|down / Scroll, right|left / Wipe, up|down / Wipe, right|left / Peel, upper-right|lower-left / Peel, upper-left|lower-right
LoopBack= ON|OFF	If on, presentation loops on playback.

Parameter	Effect
Menu= ON|OFF	If on, enables the context-sensitive popup menu.
NavBar= ON|OFF	If on, displays the navigation bar.
NavButtons= ON|OFF	If on, displays the Next Slide, Previous Slide, and Go to Slide buttons on the navigation bar.
Orientation= LANDSCAPE|PORTRAIT|N:M|FREEFORM	Specifies how the presentation slide page fits in the window.
	Landscape or portrait maintains the aspect ratio by displaying the slide show in letter-box format.
	N:M uses the custom aspect ratio specified, where *N* and *M* represent the proportion between width (*N*) and height (*M*).
	With freeform (the default), the slide fills the available window space.
Palette= FOREGROUND|BACKGROUND	If FOREGROUND, uses the embedded object's palette as the palette for the display window.
Pause= ON|OFF	If on, AutoAdvance slide shows pause before playing.
PauseButton= ON|OFF	If on, includes the Pause button on the navigation bar.
Printing= ENABLED|DISABLED	If enabled, the Print This Presentation menu item appears on the popup menu.
SaveAs= ENABLED|DISABLED	If enabled, the Save This Presentation As menu item appears on the popup menu.
Sound= *URL of a soundconfiguration file*	Specifies a sound configuration file to play.
ZoomButtons= ON|OFF	If on, Zoom buttons for full page and full screen appear on the navigation bar.

ASAP WebShow supports sound by invoking the RealAudio server (covered in Chapter 5). Because RealAudio uses a special server program, WebShow presentations can't embed RealAudio .RA files directly. Instead, you use the `<EMBED>` tag's Sound attribute to specify the URL of a Sound Configuration file, which is simply a text file that contains the URL of the actual RealAudio file.

You can create a Sound Configuration file using a text editor. Here's the syntax:

```
<slide#>=<URL of the RealAudio sound file on the RealAudio server>
```

Here's a real-world example:

```
1=pnm://audio20.prognet.com/test/jupiter/slide1.ra
2=pnm://audio20.prognet.com/test/jupiter/slide2.ra
3=pnm://audio20.prognet.com/test/jupiter/slide3.ra
```

You can include as many .RA files in a Sound Configuration file as you wish. However, the URL you put in the Sound attribute definition with the `<EMBED>` tag must be absolute, not relative. In other words, it must be a complete URL. Here's an example:

```
<EMBED SRC="DEMO2.ASP" Width="300" Height="170" sound=
➥ "http://www.spco.com/asap/presents/rasound.txt">
```

ASAP WebShow is a powerful tool for creating Web-based business slide show presentations, and its powerful `<EMBED>` tag attributes let you control most of the plug-in's behavior through HTML.

Shockwave for Authorware

Another in the series of "Shockwave" plug-ins from Macromedia, the Shockwave for Authorware plug-in enables users to interact with Authorware interactive multimedia "courses" and "pieces" right in the Netscape Navigator window (see fig. 11.2). Animation, clickable buttons, links to other Web pages, hybrid layout and delivery, streaming PICS movies and sound, and more can be integrated within a piece to deliver an interactive multimedia experience.

Intended for the delivery of large, content-rich multimedia presentations, such as courseware and training materials, Authorware can also write viewer data back to a Web server using FTP. This makes it useful for creating market surveys, tests and quizzes, and customer service applications. Because of the size of Authorware files, even when compressed, it is probably best used over corporate intranets or fast, direct Internet connections.

Like all Shockwave plug-ins, this one includes an Afterburner module for compressing files for delivery on the Web. Authorware developers package their multimedia pieces

FIG. 11.2
The Shockwave for Authorware plug-in delivers high-end, complex multimedia applications over the Web.

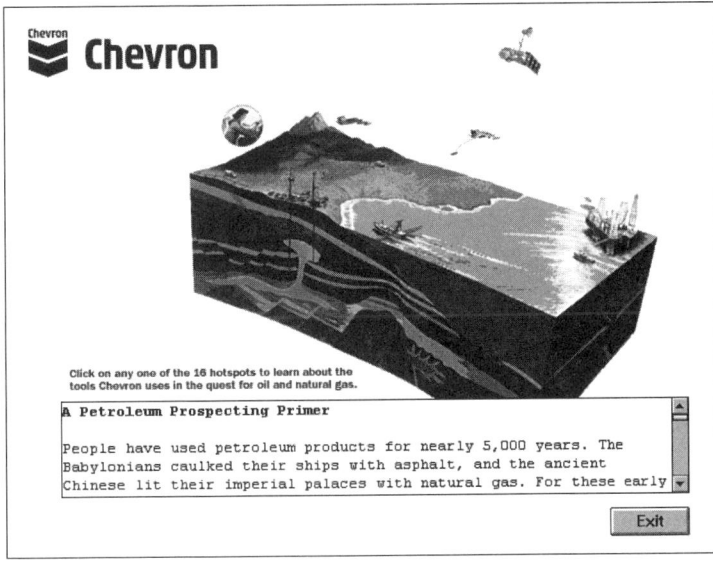

without the usually included Runtime Projector, and then drag and drop this file onto the Authorware Afterburner program. Afterburner compresses the Authorware file by 50 to 70 percent and creates one map file and multiple segment files. Developers can optimize the number and size of segment files to the bandwidth of the network. Developers also are able to create a single map file referencing both Macintosh and Windows segment files for display in the same Web page.

Windows 95, Windows NT, Windows 3.1, and Macintosh versions of Shockwave for Authorware and Authorware Aftershock can be downloaded from the Macromedia Web site:

> http://www.macromedia.com/Tools/Shockwave/Info/index.html

The Authorware development system runs natively on Windows 95, Windows NT, and Windows 3.1 and PowerMac and Macintosh. Authorware uses a flowchart model for creating multimedia applications, and sports an icon-based interface. Database management (through ODBC drivers for Windows) and hypertext functions are built in, and you can even integrate Director productions in your Authorware applications, sending Lingo language commands from Authorware to Director movies and receiving information back from Director. Authorware includes support for Macromedia Open Architecture (MOA) transition Xtras (add-on modules), which are available for both Authorware and Director. Over 50 transitions are built in to Authorware.

Authorware has the ability move text, graphics, and movies from one point to another over a given amount of time or at a specified speed. It can use a wide variety of special effects to erase text, graphics, animations, and digital movies from the screen. A Navigate icon provides 10 different hyperlinks for navigating among frameworks, including links to specific pages, dynamic text searching, previous and next links, first and last links, and custom links. Framework, Decision, Interaction, Calculation, and Map features allow the creation of highly interactive and intelligent applications.

There are three MIME types you need to set for your Web server if you plan to deliver Authorware content on your Web site: `application/x-authorware-map` (.AAM) for the map file, `application/x-authorware-seg` (.AAS) for the segment files, and `application/x-authorware-bin` for external files on the Macintosh that have been "flattened" for proper downloading.

In authoring an Authorware piece for intranet or Web distribution, you can use virtually all the features of Authorware 3.5. You can include text, graphics, audio, animations, and movies, as well as all response types, data tracking, and database management. You can embed your piece within a Web page or have it take over the full screen. Your piece can retrieve information from the intranet and send information back to the server. You can jump to other URLs from your piece.

The main limitation on just about everything you do is the data transmission speed of the network that carries your piece. The slower the transmission speed, the less ambitious you can be with multimedia.

You use the Afterburner application to turn a packaged Authorware 3.5 piece into a Shocked Authorware piece. Afterburner compresses and segments pieces so they can be delivered over an intranet as efficiently as possible, without requiring long waits for downloading. A Shocked Authorware piece looks and works exactly the same as it did before conversion.

On the Macintosh, Afterburner also has a second function. It "flattens" external files such as movies, reorganizing certain information in the files so they can download properly over intranets.

Afterburner produces two types of files from an Authorware piece: one or more segment files (extension .AAS), each of which contains a compressed section of the piece, and one map file (extension .AAM), which contains information that the Authorware plug-in needs to retrieve each segment and to retrieve external files used with your piece, such as movies.

The specific steps required to "shock" an Authorware piece and <EMBED> it in your Web page are detailed in full in the Authorware documentation, and on the Macromedia Authorware Web site.

Astound Web Player

Gold Disk's Astound Web Player plug-in displays multimedia "greeting cards" and other interactive documents created with Gold Disk's Astound or Studio M programs (see fig. 11.3). These presentations can include sound, animation, graphics, video, and even interactive elements.

FIG. 11.3
This Astound application features animated icons and integral hot links.

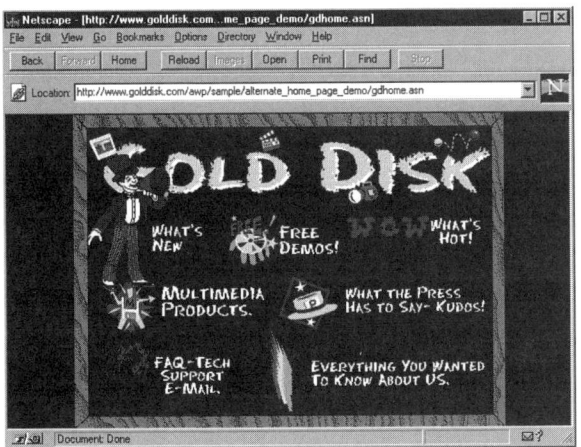

The Astound Web Player is available for Windows 95 and Windows 3.1. You can even get a stand-alone version for use with browsers other than Netscape. You can choose to download a "slim" version of the player without chart, texture, and animation libraries if you already own Studio M or Astound. If you plan on including movies in your presentations, you'll need QuickTime for Windows, which is also available from the Gold Disk site:

http://www.golddisk.com/awp

The Astound Web Player lets you actively view one multimedia slide while it downloads the next one in the background. But the main appeal of Studio M and Astound is that they let non-programmers create multimedia presentations by using predesigned templates that integrate animations, graphics, sound, and interactive elements. If you've thought that multimedia might be too difficult to integrate into your site, you might want to check the specs for Studio M and Astound on Gold Disk's Web site.

The Astound Web Player plug-in downloads an application's initial resources, and then plays the animation, sound, and graphics while the rest of the file downloads. This means, among other things, that animated elements display in blocky bitmap format like interlaced GIFs or progressive JPEGs, moving as they do so. It's a kick to watch.

You create content for this plug-in using Gold Disk's Astound, which can build overheads, slides, demos, handouts, kiosk presentations, and just about anything else. You can choose from over 70 predesigned templates or you can create one of your own. Every template has its own mix of multimedia effects built in, and you can add your own text charts, graphics, sound, video clips, and animated clip art. Interactive buttons and hot spots can make items jump, appear, disappear, and more. Text can be automatically formatted with up to four bullet levels, and data can be formatted using a variety of 2-D and 3-D chart styles.

You can edit your entire presentation graphically in slide view, or edit all of your text in the outliner. You can animate any object by drawing a line, or apply a variety of transitions like dissolves, wipes, rotations, and much more. A built-in texture generator enables you to fill an object with custom textures like fire, marble, or clouds. You can import graphic images in TIFF, EPS, GIF, PICT, JPEG, .BMP, .PCX, TGA and Photo CD formats, and load .WAV, .AIFF, or .SND sound files. Astound also supports Video for Windows and QuickTime movies.

Astound comes with Astound Studio, a set of six multimedia editing tools, and the Astound Media Manager, which allows you to catalog, organize, search, and preview your multimedia files. The suggested retail price is $249.95, and it's available for Windows 3.1, Windows 95, Macintosh, and PowerMac.

The Astound Web Player plug-in can also display files created with Gold Disk's Studio M, which is designed to let you create your own personalized multimedia greeting cards, invitations, and family albums. There are 50 predesigned Studio M templates to which you can add your own text, photos, and sounds. Studio M supports standard media formats, including:

- Graphics Formats: .BMP, GIF, CGM, TIFF, .PCX, .WMF, JPEG, TGA, and PhotoCD
- Sound Formats: .WAV and MIDI
- Video/Animation Formats: .AVI, FLI, FLC, and AWM

Gold Disk even has an "Installer" application that can automatically create a Web page for your Astound or Studio M file. The Web page is a customizable template that allows you to add your own text to direct visitors to your Web project. This page even contains a clickable JPEG image of the first slide of your project and a hyperlink that lets visitors download the Astound Web Player from the Gold Disk Web site if they don't already have it. This Installer is an especially nice touch for novice Web page designers who are still feeling their way around HTML.

Of course, you still need to make sure that your Web server is configured to deliver the proper MIME type, which in this case is `application/x-asn` (.ASN) for Astound files, and `application/x-smp` (.SMP) for Studio M files.

Make sure you save your project as "self-contained" before you try to install it on the Web. If you created your project in Astound, make sure you also purge any unused resources.

Of course, you use the <EMBED> tag to embed Astound or Studio M files in your Web pages, but the Astound Web Player plug-in makes use of only the default <EMBED> tag attributes SRC, WIDTH, and HEIGHT. It uses no optional attributes at all.

As with all multimedia files, you need to optimize your Astound presentations to make for the most efficient (fastest) viewing over the Web. Here are a few of Gold Disk's suggestions:

- If you are using charts and textures in a project, make sure your intended audience downloads the version of the Astound Web Player that includes the chart and texture library so they can view these components. If they don't have this library, charts will not animate and textures will not appear in the Web project. If they have already installed the Player without the library, they can download the library separately.
- Use only text on the first couple of slides in your presentation. Your presentation will begin playing sooner, and while your audience is reading the text, the following pages will download, minimizing how long the viewer waits.
- Use system or embedded fonts. Your audience may not have the same fonts installed on their computers as you have. By using standard Windows fonts, such as Arial and Times New Roman, or embedding your fonts when you save the project, you can be assured that your audience will be able to view your presentation just as you created it.
- Interactivity may slow down the playback of the project over the Web because the Astound Web Player may not have preloaded the files needed for the playback of the slide that a hyperlink jumps to.

N O T E If you have QuickTime for Windows installed (version 2.01 or later) and you want to view Astound presentations that contain QuickTime movies, you also need to download the QuickTime library from the Astound Web site. You need to extract the file and place it in your Astound Web Player directory.

- Using a large actor in a project will slow down the time it takes for the slide containing the actor to load. Reduce the number of large actors whenever possible.
- Avoid animating other objects when a video or animation is playing on a slide or page.
- AWM, SCM, AIM, and AWA files contained in a project will not play back over the Web.

- Using pictures for backgrounds greatly increases your file size. As an alternative, consider using solid colors, patterned backgrounds, or gradients.
- Use small images in your project instead of large ones that can slow down the playback.
- The Astound Web Installer uses JPEG compression algorithms to compress graphics files. You can manually adjust the amount of compression. The Installer creates an AII.INI file (located in your Windows directory). In the [AWP] section of the file, you can adjust the JPEG compression value by specifying a value between 0 and 100. The lower the value, the greater the compression. A value of 100 or 0 turns the compression off. A value of 1 is the highest amount of compression.
- Avoid adding gradient fills to objects that also have transitions or path animation.
- Adding transitions or path animation to two or more objects at the same time can be a distraction for your audience and can slow the slide playback.
- Animate small objects rather than large objects that tend to slow down the project playback.
- Adding path animation to large objects can slow the slide playback.
- If your objects have a jerky motion when they play back, lengthen their timelines.
- Use short sounds to reduce the file size. Sounds can also be sampled at a lower rate to create smaller files. You should not record sounds in stereo because it doubles the size of the file.
- Use compressed sounds in your project. There are many commonly supported compressed sounds available.

mBED

The mBED plug-in for Netscape plays multimedia *mbedlets,* small applets intended as interesting interactive on-the-page components (see fig. 11.4). mBED is not intended for those big, "killer" multimedia applications. It's intended to create interactive multimedia buttons and spot animations.

The .MDB file format and the built-in mBED players are open and license-free. They are available for Windows 95, Windows NT, Windows 3.1, Macintosh, and PowerMac. You can find out more and download these plug-ins from **http://www.mbed.com**.

mBED applets are scripted as text files. They can use standard graphics and sound formats. They understand server posts, and can be edited (like an HTML file) with any text editor. The mBED language, players, plug-in, and control for ActiveX are all free and can be used with no licensing fees.

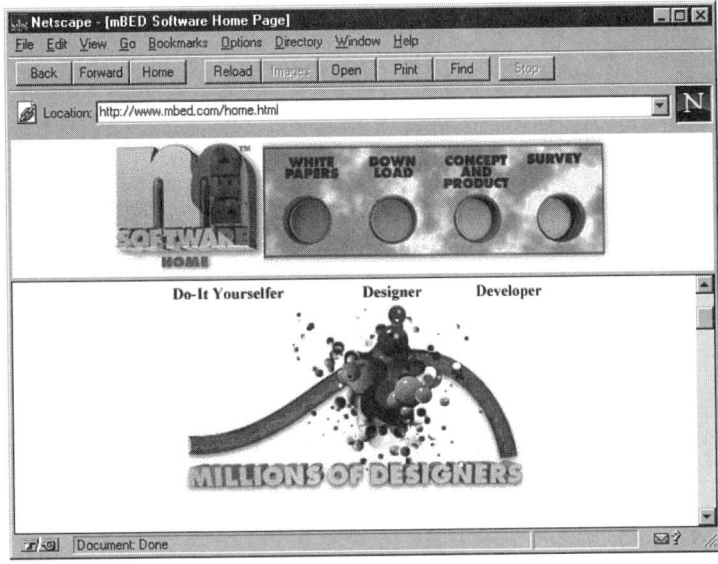

FIG. 11.4
When you pass your mouse over the "Millions of Designers" curve (an "mbedlet"), the colorful bubbles dissolve into view. mBED is designed to create these simple, quick multimedia Web elements.

New "Incredible Mbedable Machines" let you make mbedlets without even writing a script. The Logo Machine makes path animations with sound and mouse control using presets or your own resources. The Menu Machine makes navigation menus of variable size and orientation on tiled backgrounds with active, antialiased buttons and sound. All are online tools accessible from the mBED Web site. Once an mbedlet has been created, you can download the result and use it for navigation on your site or use it as a set of multimedia bookmarks. An authoring tool called the Mbedlet Designer should be available from the mBED site by the time this book hits the stands.

Data streaming and small run-time modules are characteristics of mBED applets. Antialiased text and graphics, Bézier curve animation, compressed sound, and mouse-aware objects are also in there. They can make use of GIF and JPEG, HTML, server posts, and Java. Multiplatform compatibility is ensured through the availability of Windows, Mac, and UNIX plug-ins.

Neuron

Asymetrix's ToolBook is one of the top multimedia authoring tools. Now, with the new Neuron plug-in for Netscape, you can deliver ToolBook multimedia titles over the Internet (see fig. 11.5). The Neuron plug-in supports external multimedia files, so you can access either complete courseware or multimedia titles, or just the relevant portions of titles in real time. Content that is not requested is not downloaded, saving you download time and making the application more responsive. The Neuron plug-in and a 30-day trial version of the ToolBook II program are both available for free download at Asymetix's Web site at **http://www.asymetrix.com/**.

FIG. 11.5
This ToolBook-created application is an example of an educational test—in this case, related to dentistry—delivered over the Web.

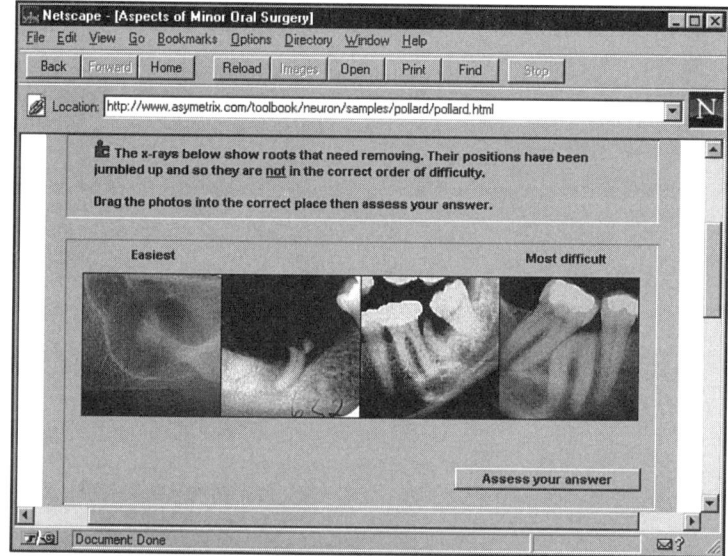

The Neuron plug-in includes a simple means to choose between nonsecure and secure modes. In nonsecure mode (the default), Neuron has access to virtually all of ToolBook's features. In secure mode, Neuron has access to a smaller subset of ToolBook's features, thus protecting your system against ToolBook applications that might carry out processes you didn't authorize, such as writing to your hard drive.

Other Multimedia Plug-Ins

There are at least a half dozen more multimedia plug-ins available for Netscape, with more coming all the time. You can keep up-to-date on multimedia plug-ins development by checking in at the Plug-Ins Plaza Web site:

http://browserwatch.iworld.com/plug-in-mm.shtml

RadMedia (**http://www.radmedia.com**) has a plug-in to play back multimedia applications built in RAD PowerMedia. Designed for corporate communicators and Web designers, PowerMedia provides authoring and viewing of interactive content, presentations, training, kiosks, and demos. It's available for Windows 95, Windows NT, and several UNIX platforms. The download file for this plug-in is over 9M, and the sample PowerMedia applications on the RadMedia site are also in the multimegabyte range.

If your multimedia needs are serious—especially if you are going to be running over a fast T1 or intranet connection—you should check out this solution. Free Demonstration CD-ROMs for PowerMedia are available for qualified users.

The mFactory Netscape plug-in promises streamed playback of and communication between fully interactive multimedia "worlds" embedded in Web pages. Here are the supported file formats:

- Video: QuickTime, QTVR, Video for Windows (.AVI)
- Graphic: PICT
- Text: Dynamic and editable text
- Audio/sound: .AIFF, SND, MIDI
- Animation: PICT, PICS, QuickTime

The cel-based proprietary mToon animation format enables ranges of cels to be defined and played. Check out **http://www.mfactory.com/** for info and download availability.

7th Level has Top Gun, a multimedia and animation authoring and playback engine for Windows 95, with a Macintosh version planned. You can read all about it at **http://www.7thlevel.com**. The site is 7th Level's prototype for an Internet-based educational cartoon network.

Powersoft's media.splash plug-in for Windows 3.1 and Windows 95 resides at the following site:

> http://www.powersoft.com/media.splash/product/index.html

The SCREAM inline multimedia player is for Windows 3.1, Windows 95, and Macintosh. You can find it at the following site:

> http://www.savedbytech.com/sbt/Plug_In.html

Kaleida will have a multimedia player plug-in for Navigator, too. Kaleida Labs is the developer of ScriptX, an object-oriented programming language for multimedia, and currently offers a free platform-independent Kaleida Media Player (KMP) for playback of ScriptX applications which can be configured as a helper application. To find out when you can get this plug-in, check out the following site:

> http://www.kaleida.com

PART III

Plug-Ins for VRML

- **12** Creating VRML Worlds   263
- **13** Moving Worlds and Live3-D   283
- **14** VRML Plug-Ins   305

CHAPTER 12

Creating VRML Worlds

This chapter examines VRML, the Virtual Reality Modeling Language. If you're already familiar with three-dimensional (3-D) modeling concepts, you should have no trouble picking up VRML. Even if you're approaching the language from scratch, it's easy to create simple, three-dimensional worlds that others can view with VRML browsers. ■

What VRML is
You'll see why it is important and what it brings to the World Wide Web.

Where VRML came from
You take a look back at the foundations of the language and its evolution.

How to access VRML files
You explore the MIME type that VRML uses, and how HTTP daemons serve VRML.

How to use VRML syntax
You examine how VRML files represent nodes and fields.

What tools are available for creating VRML worlds
You briefly survey some of the more popular tools and Web resources available to world builders.

How to use VRML to design and build worlds
You examine some basic guidelines that should get you started on building your first world.

http://www.mcp.com/que

What Is VRML?

VRML is the standard way to represent three-dimensional virtual environments on the World Wide Web. Just as you write text documents in HTML and store images in JPEG, you store worlds in VRML format. VRML files use the ASCII character set, which means that you can create, examine, and modify them using an ordinary text editor

Because VRML is a standard, Web browsers will have built-in support for it; Netscape already supports VRML, and other browsers are sure to follow soon. Many powerful tools will be available for authoring VRML documents ("worlds"), enabling even novice users to create effective three-dimensional content easily.

The History of VRML

VRML was first conceived by Mark Pesce, who anticipated in 1993 a need for some kind of standard for three-dimensional graphics on the Web. He and Tony Parisi wrote a program called Labyrinth, which served as a "proof of concept" that they could show to others. In May 1994, Pesce presented Labyrinth at the First International Conference on the World Wide Web in Geneva, Switzerland. The program attracted a lot of attention, and soon an electronic mailing list was created to foster discussion of a standard.

By October 1994, Pesce, Parisi, and Silicon Graphics, Inc. (SGI) engineer Gavin Bell completed a first draft of the specification and made it available over the Internet. The draft was based largely on the file format used by OpenInventor, a software toolkit from SGI. The early draft of VRML had some problems, and a revised version followed in April 1995. That VRML 1.0 specification served as the basis for over a dozen VRML browsers from a variety of developers.

The Evolution of VRML

The VRML 1.0 specification had several limitations, and several aspects of the design proved difficult or impossible to implement using standard graphics libraries. Other aspects made the specification inefficient, and early browsers were notoriously slow. Also, the specification was plagued by ambiguities, the result of which was that no two browsers displayed a world the same way.

The VRML 1.0C specification (with the *C* standing for *clarifications*) addressed some of these problems, but it was agreed that a complete reworking was needed. The result was the VRML 2.0 specification, the first draft of which was made available in April 1996. VRML 2.0 not only fixes several problems that developers encountered while trying to implement browsers, but also adds important new features such as behavior scripting and sound. Chapter 13, "Moving Worlds and Live3D," looks at VRML 2.0 in more detail.

This chapter examines those aspects of VRML common to both the 1.0 and 2.0 versions. Because it might take a while before the 2.0 standard stabilizes, this chapter's examples are all in VRML 1.0 format. When VRML 2.0 browsers hit the Web (starting in September 1996), there will also be converters that turn 1.0 files into 2.0 files.

How VRML Works

Ordinary Web servers store VRML worlds just as they do HTML files. VRML files have an extension of .WRL (which stands for *world*). By using GZIP, you can store and transmit worlds in compressed form. A VRML browser accesses the file in exactly the same way that a regular Web browser accesses HTML files: The browser opens a TCP connection to the server and uses the HTTP protocol to transfer the VRML file to the user's machine. The MIME type for a VRML file is `x-world/x-vrml` (although this type is expected to change eventually to `model/vrml`).

Once the file has been transferred (and unzipped, if necessary), the VRML browser parses it and builds a set of internal data structures that represent the virtual world. The browser then draws (or *renders*) the world. The user can navigate around in the world using the browser, without any further interaction with the network. This navigation is roughly analogous to scrolling through an HTML document in a Web browser.

You can designate individual objects within a virtual world as *anchors,* so that clicking such an object takes the user to another VRML world or to any other kind of Web document. Thus anchors are useful as "portals" between worlds.

Many VRML browsers provide a user interface similar to that of ordinary Web browsers. You can perform basic operations the same way as you do for documents in an HTML browser. Such operations include entering a world by specifying its URL or moving backward and forward through the list of worlds that you've already visited. Just as you can set bookmarks for HTML documents to which you want to return later, you can bookmark worlds in a VRML browser.

You can install most VRML browsers as stand-alone programs, as helper applications, or as plug-ins for Netscape or Internet Explorer. The latter approach makes the use of VRML completely seamless; simply by clicking a link in an ordinary HTML document, users can move to a VRML world. Similarly, by clicking an anchored object in a VRML world, users can go either to another VRML world or to an HTML document.

The bottom line is that VRML browsers work much like HTML browsers. This greatly reduces the learning curve for users; except for having to learn how to navigate within a three-dimensional world, users should find VRML browsers extremely easy to use.

The VRML Language

Browsing VRML worlds is easy; building them is considerably more complex. The average user can learn HTML easily, and create very sophisticated documents using nothing more than a text editor. Although VRML isn't much more complicated than HTML, several factors make it hard for the average user to cobble together VRML worlds using Windows Notepad (or vi on UNIX).

The first obstacle is simply the fact that VRML worlds are three-dimensional. Everyone knows how to create text, so learning HTML requires only that you become familiar with the tags and their meanings. In contrast, few users know how to model objects in three dimensions. The second obstacle is the fact that most objects in a virtual environment consist of vertices and polygons, and therefore much of the modeling task involves specifying precise numeric values.

This chapter examines some of the tools that make this modeling task easier. First, however, you take a look at VRML's actual syntax. Understanding what's going on at a low level will make it easier to use the tools, and will also enable you to examine existing VRML files to see how they work. As mentioned earlier, this chapter deals primarily with VRML 1.0 syntax; Chapter 13 examines VRML 2.0 in more detail.

The name Virtual Reality Modeling Language is, in some ways, a little misleading. Unlike most computer languages, such as C, Pascal, or BASIC, VRML doesn't specify instructions for the computer to follow; instead, VRML is a file format for describing worlds. Conceptually, VRML is more similar to earlier graphics file formats, such as DXF and 3DS, than it is to actual programming languages.

The following sections provide an overview of the basic syntax and features of VRML 1.0. This is not by any means a comprehensive look at the language; if you are planning to build VRML worlds, check out Que's *Special Edition Using VRML*.

Basic VRML Syntax

VRML files are ASCII, and mostly free format—that is, anywhere that a space can appear, you can have a tab or a newline. The one exception involves comments embedded in a VRML file; comments begin at the first pound sign (#) and continue to the end of that line. Note, however, that the # character can appear within a quoted string without marking the start of a comment.

The first line of a VRML file is a header. This header identifies the file as being VRML, gives the version number, and specifies the character set that the file uses. The header looks like this:

```
#VRML V1.0 ascii
```

Because the line begins with #, it's technically a comment line. V1.0 is the version number, and ascii indicates that the file consists of only ASCII characters (tab, newline, and hexidecimal 0x20 through 0x7F). The VRML 2.0 header is similar, but of course has V2.0 rather than V1.0. It also uses utf-8 rather than ascii, to allow for an international character set.

Following this header line is a single node, which can contain other nodes. A node, which is the basic syntactic element of VRML, looks like this:

```
DEF name nodetype { fields children }
```

DEF *name* is optional; it assigns a name to this particular instance of this node for future reference. The name must consist of alphanumeric characters, and it must begin with a letter.

nodetype identifies the type of node. Node types are case-sensitive. *fields* is a list of field name/value pairs that specify the node's parameters, and *children* are additional nodes (again, with optional node names). Starting with VRML 2.0, a field called *children* holds the children to make the syntax a little more consistent.

Here's a short VRML 1.0 file that demonstrates how this syntax works:

```
#VRML V1.0 ascii
Group {
        PointLight { position 0 15 0 }
                    # a single white point-source light, 15 meters overhead
        Material { diffuseColor 0 0 1 }    # a bright blue color
        Sphere { radius 2.0 }              # a sphere with a radius of 2 meters
}
```

Note the free format; the PointLight, Material, and Sphere nodes are each contained on a single line, whereas the Group node spans several lines. Also notice the three comments, each with a leading # character.

This file has four nodes. The Sphere node has a single field, which specifies that the radius has a value of 2.0 meters (meters being the standard unit of distance in VRML). The PointLight node also has a single field, but notice that the value has three numbers; the position field's value is a three-element vector that expresses an object's position in terms of X, Y, and Z.

The Material node also has a single field, which gives the color for subsequent shapes in terms of red, green, and blue components (each of which can range from 0.0 to 1.0 inclusive). VRML 2.0 will have a closer connection between Material and the shape to which it applies, so that Material will no longer affect subsequent shapes. Chapter 13 explains this change.

Finally, the enclosing Group node has no fields, but does have three children: the PointLight, Material, and Sphere nodes. The Group node is required, because the VRML 1.0 specification requires a single node at the file's top level.

This example is deceptively simple. Although VRML does have some high-level graphics primitives (such as Sphere) that you can use to build trivial worlds, most VRML files are much more involved than the preceding example indicates.

The *DEF* and *USE* Statements

The DEF statement enables you to assign a name to a node so that you can create instances of the node by using the USE statement. For example, if you create a complex shape, you can use DEF to name the shape and then use USE to duplicate the shape as many times as you want without respecifying the shape's details.

You can greatly reduce the size of your files by using these statements. For example, if you use DEF to specify one detailed streetlight, you can then use the USE statement to create identical streetlights repeatedly all the way down the street.

Shapes

VRML 1.0 has eight different types of shape primitives that you can use to create all the visible objects in a VRML world. The Sphere, Cube, Cone, and Cylinder nodes do exactly what you would expect: They create the corresponding primitive shapes. The AsciiText node, which creates thin, flat text that's positioned and oriented in three dimensions, is useful for creating objects like signs. The PointSet node enables you to specify a constellation of one-pixel points in three-dimensional space, and the IndexedLineSet enables you to create objects consisting of line segments.

Finally, the IndexedFaceSet node is by far the most common node in most VRML files. This node enables you to specify arbitrary geometric shapes by listing the faces (polygons) of which they consist.

The PointSet, IndexedLineSet, and IndexedFaceSet nodes use lists of vertex coordinates that the Coordinate3 node stores. Also useful are the Normal node, which lists an object's "normal vectors" (used to compute light intensities on the object), and the TextureCoordinate2 node, which specifies indices into texture maps.

Materials and Textures

In the previous example, the Material node specifies that the color of the subsequent sphere is bright blue. The diffuseColor field, like all fields that specify color, lists three values: the color's red, green, and blue components. By using some combination of these three values, you can create any color imaginable. The `Material` node can also specify the material's shininess (which can give it a metallic finish) and the material's transparency (to give the material a glasslike appearance). Each of the values in a `Material` node can consist of multiple values; for example, one `Material` node might specify six colors to apply to the faces of a cube.

In addition to specifying colors, you can also provide texture maps for your objects. A *texture map* is a two-dimensional image that you can apply to an object to make it appear more detailed than it actually is. For example, you might create a flat wall with a texture map that looks like wallpaper. Likewise, you might create a front lawn by using a single flat polygon with a "grass" texture map applied to it. To specify a texture, you use the `Texture2` node, which contains the URL of a texture map in JPEG or PNG format.

Lights

VRML features three types of lights: `DirectionalLight`, `PointLight`, and `SpotLight`. Directional lights work like the sun; their light travels in parallel lines, coming from infinitely far away in a specific direction. Point lights are like light bulbs; they originate from a specific location from which the light radiates outward in all directions. Spot lights are similar, but they have a specific "cone" of light that determines which objects are illuminated.

> **NOTE** In VRML 1.0, lights affect only those objects that appear after them in the "scene graph" (the data structure that represents the world). This limitation has proved to be peculiar and cumbersome, so VRML 2.0 has eliminated it. When building VRML 1.0 worlds, you should put all your light sources at the start of the file to avoid this problem. ■

Cameras

A camera defines the user's initial point of view in the virtual world. The `PerspectiveCamera` node specifies the camera's location and orientation, and indicates the field of view (the angle through which the user views the world). VRML 1.0 also has an `OrthographicCamera` node, but this node isn't widely implemented and has been dropped for VRML 2.0.

> **NOTE** Some VRML 1.0 browsers don't render scenes correctly unless you specify the camera before any of the shapes. If you're building VRML 1.0 worlds, you should put your `PerspectiveCamera` node near the start of the file. ■

The *Group* and *Separator* Nodes

VRML 1.0 has several "grouping" nodes that can contain other nodes as children. The previous example used the Group node, but the most commonly used grouping node is Separator. A Separator node works like a group, in that it gathers together several other nodes. However, Separator also limits the range of effect of Material, Texture2, Transform, and other nodes. By wrapping a set of nodes within a Separator node, you ensure that nothing "leaks" and affects other objects in the scene. For more details about Separator nodes, see Que's *Special Edition Using VRML*. VRML 2.0 has eliminated Separator in favor of a simpler and more sensible scene structure that Chapter 13 describes.

The *LOD* Node

The LOD node specifies multiple "levels of detail" for an object. Because the speed with which a user can navigate through a world relates to the scene's complexity, you should avoid having too many faces visible at once. The LOD node is a powerful tool for maintaining performance, because the node enables the VRML browser to switch to a less detailed version of a shape to reduce the scene's overall complexity.

You should give any object with more than a few dozen faces multiple levels of detail. For example, consider a mountain range; when it's far away, it might require only a few faces. As you move closer, you'll want to see more details, and as you actually start climbing the mountain, you'll want as much detail as possible.

Consider also a tree. When you're up close, you want to see each individual leaf; when you're a little farther away, you might want to see only a few branches; from a greater distance, you might see only a green sphere for the leaves and a brown cylinder for the trunk. From even farther away, the tree might not be visible at all.

The LOD node is a grouping node, whose children are the different versions of the object in order of decreasing level of detail.

The *Transform* Node

You use the Transform node to specify the location, orientation, and size of objects in the virtual environment. A typical Transform node might look like the following:

```
Transform {
     scaleFactor 21 34 45
     translation 12 14 27
     rotation 0 1 0 1.5708
}
```

This node specifies that the object should be scaled by a factor of 21 in the X direction (width), a factor of 34 in the Y direction (height), and 45 in the Z direction (depth). After scaling, the object is rotated 1.5708 radians (90 degrees) around the Y axis (0 1 0), and then *translated* (moved) to X=12, Y=14, Z=27. Note that the order of these operations is always the same—scale, rotate, then translate—regardless of the order in which you list the fields.

In VRML 1.0, the Transform node applies to everything that follows it in the scene graph, but its influence is confined to the nearest enclosing Separator node.

The *WWWInline* and *WWWAnchor* Nodes

Two nodes give VRML files access to other VRML files across the Web. The first is WWWInline, which retrieves a VRML file and loads it in as if you had specified it in place of the WWWInline node. This node is quite useful when used within an LOD node, because the browser might not have to load an object's most detailed version.

WWWAnchor is a grouping node that associates all its children with an anchor. This node works like an HTML <a>...</a> tag pair. When the user clicks any of the children objects (or any of their children, and so on down the levels of hierarchy), the URL specified in the WWWAnchor node loads in place of the current world.

A Sample VRML World

Listing 12.1 demonstrates many of the concepts discussed so far in this chapter. To use PLUG.WRL, just put it in a file and make it available as you would any HTML document (making sure to give it a .WRL extension). Also make sure that your Web server is configured to serve VRML. You should be able to access the document from within your browser simply by entering the URL as you would for any Web document.

Listing 12.1   PLUG.WRL—a Sample World

```
#VRML V1.0 ascii

# Sample world to illustrate various VRML 1.0 nodes

# Created by Bernie Roehl, April 1996

Group {  # outermost grouping node
        DEF cameras Switch {  # multiple cameras
            whichChild 0
            DEF First_camera PerspectiveCamera {
                position 1.5 1.5 7
            }
            DEF Second_camera PerspectiveCamera {
                position 1.5 7 1.5
```

continues

Listing 12.1 Continued

```
                orientation 1 0 0 -1.5873
            }
            DEF Third_camera PerspectiveCamera {
                position 7 1.5 1.5
                orientation 0 1 0 1.5873
            }
    }
    SpotLight {
        location 3 3 3
        direction 0 0 0
        cutOffAngle 0.3
    }
    Separator { # visible cone for the light
        Transform { rotation 1 0 -1 0.7854 translation 2.875 2.875 2.875 }
        Cone { bottomRadius 0.25 height 0.25 }
    }
    Separator { # floor
        Transform { translation 1.5 -0.25 1.5 }
        Material { diffuseColor 0.15 0.30 0.15 }
        Cube { height 0.5 width 3 depth 3 }
    }
    Separator {   # walls and wire framework
        Coordinate3 { point
            [
            0 0 0, 0 3 0, 3 3 0, 3 0 0,
            0 0 3, 0 3 3, 3 3 3, 3 0 3
            ]
        }
        Material { diffuseColor [ 0.25 0.75 0.725, 0.75 0.25 0.25 ] }
        MaterialBinding { value PER_FACE }
        IndexedFaceSet { coordIndex [ 3, 2, 1, 0, -1, 0, 1, 5, 4, -1 ] }
        Material { diffuseColor 0 0 0 }
        IndexedLineSet { coordIndex [ 5, 6, 7, -1, 6, 2, -1 ] }
    }
    Separator {   # a set of points just inside the room
        Coordinate3 { point
            [
            0.2 0.2 0.2, 0.2 2.8 0.2, 2.8 2.8 0.2, 2.8 0.2 0.2,
            0.2 0.2 2.8, 0.2 2.8 2.8, 2.8 2.8 2.8, 2.8 0.2 2.8
            ]
        }
        PointSet { }
    }
    DEF statue Separator {  # cylinder with sphere on top
        Transform { translation 2 0.5 1 }
        Separator {
            Texture2 { filename "mandrill.bmp" }
            Cylinder { radius 0.5 height 1 }
        }
        Separator {
```

A Sample VRML World

```
                Transform { translation 0 1 0 }
                Material {
                        diffuseColor 0.25 0.25 0
                        shininess 0.2
                        specularColor 0.2 0.2 0.2
                }
                WWWAnchor {
                        name
        "http://sunee.uwaterloo.ca/~broehl/using_vrml/worlds/main/main.wrl"
                        description "Sample link"
                        Sphere { radius 0.5 }
                }
            }
        }
        Separator {  # second copy of the cylinder and sphere
                Transform { translation -1 0 1 }
                USE statue
        }
        WWWInline { name "plugtext.wrl" }
}
```

Notice the use of a named `Switch` node around the cameras. Many VRML 1.0 browsers have adopted this convention to enable the user to select from several viewpoints into the virtual world. Also notice that the cameras and lights are specified at the start of the file.

You use the same `Coordinate3` node for both the walls and the wireframe edges of the world; the eight entries mark the corners of an imaginary cube. The statue is a sphere with a cylinder beneath it; the texture-map that you apply to the cylinder is one of the oldest images in the world of computer graphics, a mandrill (a type of baboon). You then define the statue, and employ USE to duplicate it a second time. The `Sphere` nodes have a `WWWAnchor` around them, so when users click them, they move to another world.

Using `WWWInline`, the "hello world" text loads from a separate file, shown in listing 12.2.

Listing 12.2 PLUGTEXT.WRL—the "Hello World" File That *WWWInline* Retrieves and Loads

```
#VRML V1.0 ascii

Group {
        Transform { scaleFactor 0.05 0.05 0.05 translation 0.5 0 3 }
        Material { diffuseColor 0.3 0.3 0.3 }
        AsciiText { string "Hello world" }
}
```

Figure 12.1 shows the resulting world.

FIG. 12.1
The sample world, displayed in Netscape/Live3D.

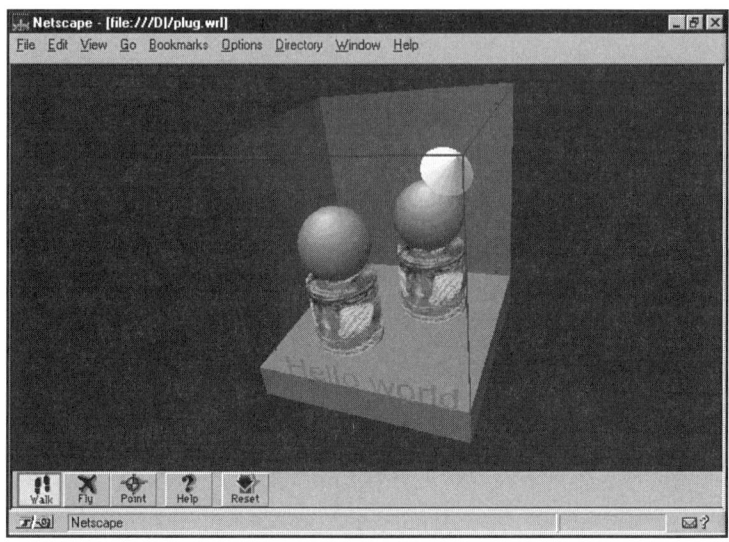

Creating VRML Content

There are three basic ways to provide VRML content: converting existing three-dimensional objects or scenes into VRML, using libraries of previously created objects, or creating VRML files from scratch.

Many existing packages (3D Studio, Caligari TrueSpace, and others) have built-in utilities for converting their data into VRML; if you're using one of those packages already, creating VRML is straightforward (for example, if you're using 3D Studio, AutoDesk offers an IPAS module that does the job). There are also stand-alone conversion programs that read objects in a wide variety of formats and write them out in VRML, so even if you aren't using one of the popular modeling packages, you can still use files created with them.

The WCVT2POV Conversion Program

One of the most popular 3-D file-format conversion programs is WCVT2POV, written by Keith Rule. This book's companion CD-ROM includes WCVT2POV, and you can find the latest version of the program on the Web at **http://www.europa.com/~keithr**. This freeware program is the product of a tremendous amount of time and effort. If you use it, you might want to drop Rule a note to tell him that you appreciate all his efforts.

The name WCVT2POV derives from the fact that Rule originally designed the program to convert various file formats into POV, the format used by the Persistence of Vision raytracing program. The current version of WCVT2POV is a Windows program that can read many file formats including 3D Studio, AutoCAD DXF, Sense8 NFF, RAW, OFF, and Wavefront OBJ. Currently, the program outputs VRML 1.0 files, so you might have to use a separate program to convert them to VRML 2.0, and possibly yet another program to convert them to a binary format. However, the process is pretty painless and you shouldn't have to do it more than once.

Figure 12.2 shows WCVT2POV, with the menus for loading various input file formats.

FIG. 12.2
WCVT2POV's File Open menu.

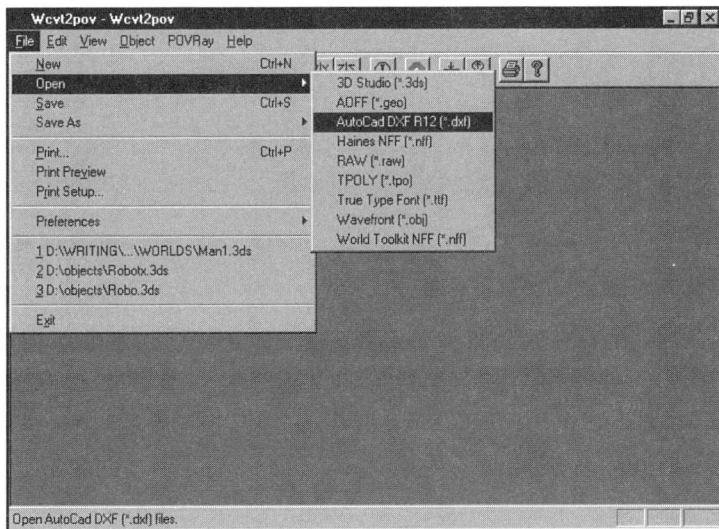

After loading a file into WCVT2POV, you can perform simple operations on the file such as flipping it around any of the X, Y, or Z axes or scaling the file. Figure 12.3 shows an object loaded into WCVT2POV from a 3D Studio file.

Figure 12.4 shows the same object flipped around the Z axis and scaled.

You can also change the colors and textures of individual segments of the object.

The InterChange Conversion Program

WCVT2POV supports several widely used formats, but it still cannot handle several others. InterChange, a file-conversion program from Syndesis, handles 40 different formats and can save any of them as VRML. However, this commercial package costs hundreds of dollars; unless you need its more sophisticated conversion capabilities, you might want to stick with WCVT2POV.

FIG. 12.3
A 3D Studio file loaded into WCVT2POV.

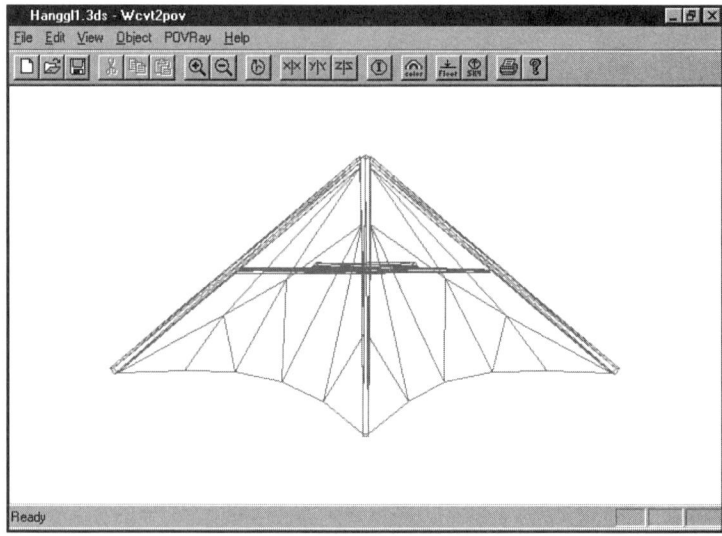

FIG. 12.4
The 3D Studio file's object, flipped and scaled by WCVT2POV.

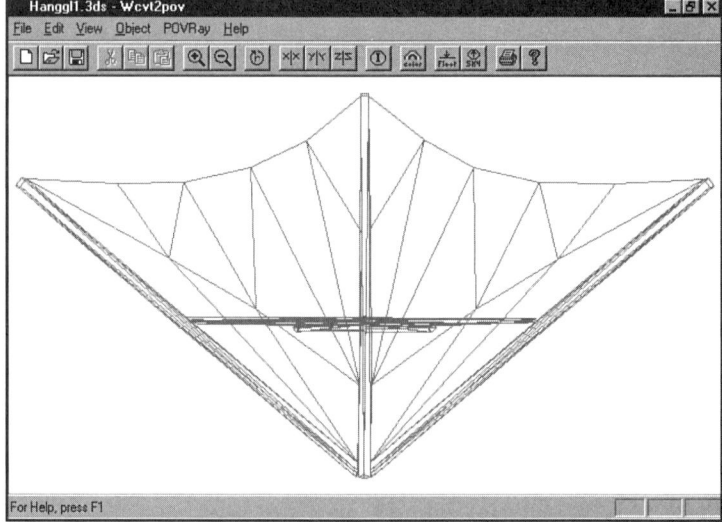

Object Libraries

The Internet offers several collections of 3-D clip art. Among the better-known collections is MeshMart (**http://cedar.cic.net/~rtilmann/mm/index.htm**). MeshMart is a good starting point; it has a nice collection of objects in VRML and other formats. Retrieving files from MeshMart and converting them using WCVT2POV is a quick and inexpensive way to populate your virtual world with interesting objects.

This book's companion CD-ROM includes a small collection of VRML objects. Feel free to use these when assembling your first few VRML worlds.

There are also commercial suppliers of 3-D objects; the best known is Viewpoint Datalabs. However, its models cost hundreds of dollars each, and you cannot use them in VRML worlds because the data is not secure. In effect, you are giving away the objects by making them accessible in your VRML worlds.

Home Space Builder

Several authoring tools are available that enable you to create VRML files directly, and you can expect more such tools to appear in the months to come as VRML becomes increasingly popular.

One of the first tools to appear was Paragraph's Home Space Builder. It enables you to create axis-aligned rectangular blocks, and to subtract other such blocks from them. Creating a room with a doorway and two windows is easy: Start with a cube, subtract a smaller cube from inside it to hollow it out, then subtract even smaller cubes to create the openings in the wall. Figure 12.5 shows a simple house being constructed with Home Space Builder.

FIG. 12.5
A simple house created with Home Space Builder.

The Virtus VRML Toolkit

The Virtus VRML Toolkit has an interface similar to Home Space Builder. You can create simple buildings, add doors and windows, fill them with prebuilt furniture, and save the result as a VRML file. Figure 12.6 shows a typical Virtus VRML Toolkit screen. Note how similar this interface is to that of Home Space Builder.

FIG. 12.6
The Virtus VRML Toolkit in action.

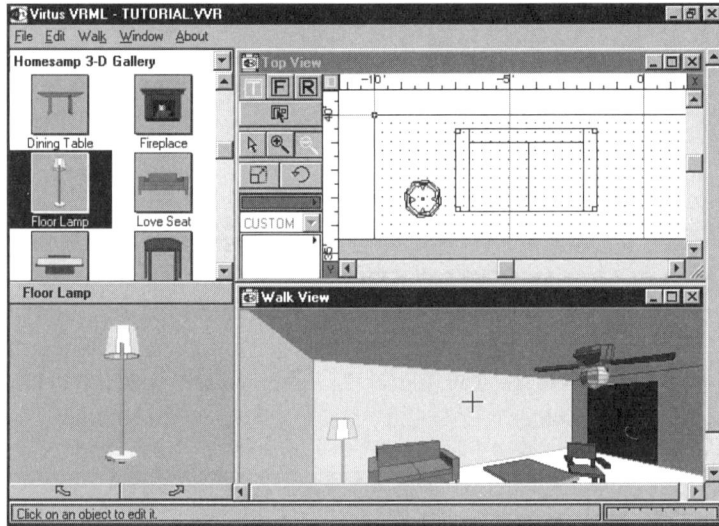

One of the Virtus VRML Toolkit's most important features is its clip-art library of objects. However, this feature also highlights one of the toolkit's principal disadvantages: It doesn't enable you to create such objects yourself. The Virtus VRML Toolkit might be more powerful than Home Space Builder, but is still not a general-purpose modeling tool for building VRML objects and worlds.

Caligari Fountain

Caligari Fountain is a 3-D modeling program that can both read and write VRML files. The program derives from a more powerful package called Caligari TrueSpace, which is competing in the 3D Studio market. TrueSpace and Fountain have similar interfaces that present a single three-dimensional view of the world that's much easier for the casual user to learn than the more complex, multiwindowed view that most computer-aided design (CAD) packages and 3-D modelers offer. Figure 12.7 shows Fountain being used to create a simple VRML scene.

FIG. 12.7
Caligari Fountain presents a single-perspective view.

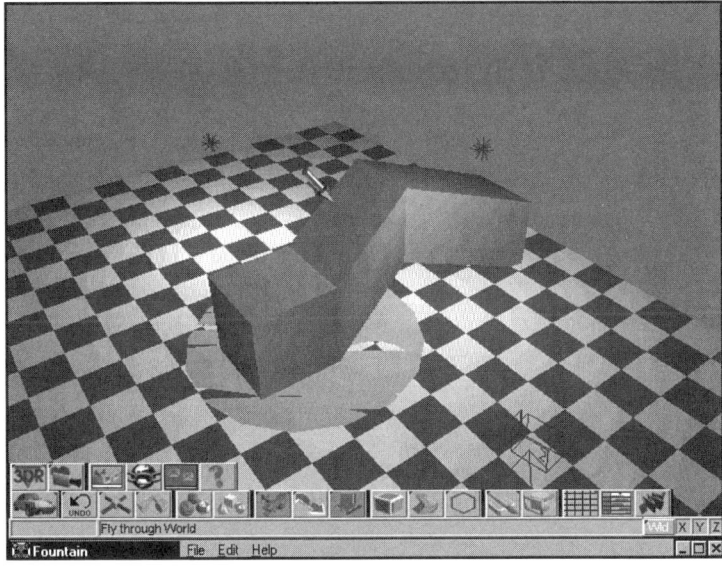

Building Your Own VRML Worlds

Only a poor craftsman blames his tools. Your ability to create interesting VRML worlds comes not from the software that you use, but from your imagination and your visual design sense. As powerful as packages such as Fountain are, they don't do the creative work for you. This section provides some guidelines to help you create effective VRML content.

Plan Your Design

You first need to plan your design. Far too many people just pop into an authoring package and start to build; the resulting world is often confusing to its visitors. You need to identify the purposes of your world, and then design with those purposes in mind. Also remember the kind of visitors who will be coming to your world, and what kinds of things they'll be doing there. Will they be looking for information? Playing with objects in the world? Admiring the design itself?

Also remember that you need to direct the visitor's attention to where you want it to go. Left on their own, visitors will wander through a world without necessarily encountering the things that you feel are important. If you want visitors to see a particular piece of artwork, for example, then make it the center of your world. Throw a spotlight on it. Make it spin. Put a red carpet on the floor that leads to that point.

Beta-test your world before announcing it. Have people wander through it. Don't talk with them as they explore your world; simply watch where they go, what they try to do, and so on. These observations will indicate any necessary changes or clarifications.

Let the Real World Be Your Guide

When in doubt, you should base your world on the kinds of things that you see around you in the real world. It takes a talented artist indeed to create something completely surreal and at the same time accessible to the average Internet surfer. For the most part, you should stick to fairly conventional architecture until you gain more experience.

However, sticking to conventional architecture doesn't have to be a big limitation. Try experimenting with winding staircases, arches, windows, and unusual lights. Put in a balcony, bridge, or turret. Choose a historical period and try to capture its essence.

The guideline of using the real world as a reference point extends to your choice of colors as well. Silver trees with bright orange leaves can create an interesting effect, but unless you have a specific reason for making that choice, you are better off with the more conventional brown and green. The same advice applies to light sources; the sun is basically a single directional source, but you will undoubtedly have other, smaller light sources as well. Place them wisely, and make sure that every `PointLight` or `SpotLight` has a visible source (so that you don't leave visitors wondering where the light is shining from).

Keep Your Scenes Simple

One of the most important considerations when building a virtual world is to ensure that visitors can navigate through it smoothly. Their ease of navigation is proportional to rendering speed; if the world renders (redraws) too slowly, navigation becomes difficult.

The way to keep rendering speeds fast is to simplify your world. The most important thing that you can do to simplify your world is to reduce the number of polygons (faces) that are visible at any one time. The `LOD` node that you examined earlier in this chapter is one technique for managing scene complexity. Avoiding curved surfaces is also important; a `Sphere` node is easy to use, but might ultimately produce dozens of polygons (depending on the browser that you use).

Another important thing that you can do is to reduce the number of lights. Lighting calculations take time; if possible, stick to just a couple of light sources. Directional lighting is much less computationally expensive than point lighting, which is less expensive than spot lighting.

You might consider splitting your world into several pieces and then linking them using WWWAnchor. For example, you might break a house into seven or eight rooms, setting up doors between them using anchors.

In the months ahead, 3-D graphics accelerators will become more popular. Although they can dramatically improve the performance of VRML browsers, it's still important to design with efficiency in mind.

Use Textures Wisely

Texture mapping is an expensive operation that can slow down most software-based VRML browsers. However, producing an equivalent amount of detail without using textures requires many more polygons. Therefore, you have to consider this trade-off when using texture mapping.

The biggest mistake that most designers make when using textures in VRML is to texture map *everything*. They're used to seeing games like Doom and Quake in which everything is texture-mapped, and assume that they need to do the same in their worlds. However, the purpose of a VRML browser is far more general than that of most computer games. As a result, VRML browsers can't perform certain types of optimizations that computer games can. For this reason, such browsers can never run as quickly as games do, and texture-mapping everything simply makes the browsers run more slowly.

For example, a Doom-type engine knows that all the walls are vertical and that the user cannot look up or down; this simplifies many aspects of the transformation and rasterization algorithms. Simpler algorithms run faster.

The key is to use texture maps selectively, and keep them small (because the computational burden is proportional to the amount of screen area that the texture covers). Pictures in a frame and small throw rugs are examples of good uses for texture mapping.

CHAPTER 13

Moving Worlds and Live3D

The previous chapter explored the Virtual Reality Modeling Language (VRML) version 1.0 as well as some of the basic concepts underlying VRML itself. This chapter examines the next generation of VRML 2.0. The chapter also examines Live 3D, the most powerful and popular of the VRML browsers.

The first draft of the VRML 2.0 specification was released in April 1996. Changes are possible along the road to the final version, so check the actual specification itself when it comes out; you might find that the final version differs somewhat from this chapter's descriptions. ■

- **Problems with VRML 1.0**
  You learn about why VRML 2.0 is needed.

- **The origins of VRML 2.0**
  You look at the process by which 2.0 was developed and some of the players involved.

- **The basic structure of worlds created with VRML 2.0**
  You explore the essential elements of 3-D world building using VRML 2.0.

- **New features in VRML 2.0**
  You examine some of the important capabilities that version 2.0 adds.

- **Behavior scripting**
  You discover how VRML 2.0 interfaces to programming languages that enable your worlds to move and change.

- **VRML 2.0 applications**
  You see how to use VRML 2.0 to solve real-world problems.

- **Netscape's Live3D plug-in**
  You get familiar with the VRML plug-in that's likely to have the largest following.

http://www.mcp.com/que

The Need for Change

The VRML 1.0 specification was a remarkable first step. It enabled designers to create beautiful three-dimensional worlds accessible over the Internet, and to create some powerful browsers.

However, the language itself had several serious problems. Because it was based on OpenInventor, VRML 1.0 inherited several "OpenInventorisms" that led to serious implementation problems. The result was slow browsers and inconsistent rendering. The OpenInventor scene graph was difficult to optimize, impossible to parallelize, and generally quite difficult to work with. The use of Separator nodes to limit the range of effect of lighting was kludgy, and was impossible to implement on many renderers. The meanings of the various fields of the Material node were ambiguous, so the fields were hard to implement.

The only browser to implement the entire VRML 1.0 specification fully was Silicon Graphics' WebSpace. Unfortunately, this browser is also one of the slowest available, partly because it is based on the OpenGL renderer. OpenGL is a general-purpose rendering library, but it's also painfully slow.

Users were thus left choosing between a very slow (but correct) browser, or higher-performance browsers that didn't implement all the language's problematic features. Not surprisingly, this limited choice led to a certain amount of frustration in the user community.

There were other problems to address. Because the VRML 1.0 specification doesn't allow objects to move, the resulting worlds were static. This flaw led some wits to dub VRML as the Virtual Reality Museum Language. VRML 1.0 also provided no support for sound, and no clean way to add support for multiuser environments.

Because VRML 1.0's deficiencies, inefficiencies, and ambiguities were so serious, work began almost immediately to correct them. An interim VRML 1.0C specification addressed some of these problems and proposed some extensions. However, this version was just a stopgap measure; what VRML really needed was a complete rewrite.

The Politics of VRML

Silicon Graphics Inc. (SGI), which had volunteered its OpenInventor file format for use as the basis for VRML 1.0, was eager to spearhead the development of the language's next generation. SGI began doing some work inhouse, and sought the support of other companies in the effort. However, many people felt that this approach was far too closed, and that more could be gained from an open process.

A call for proposals was issued, and half a dozen of them materialized. All the major players in the computer industry got involved, including Microsoft, IBM, Sun, Apple, and of course SGI. All the proposals had technical merit, but ultimately the bandwagon effect took over, and SGI's proposal (the "Moving Worlds" specification) was selected as the basis for VRML 2.0.

Fortunately, the slightly more open process did lead to several significant improvements in the SGI proposal. The resulting VRML 2.0 standard solves all the problems that were encountered in VRML 1.0, and introduces several important new features. VRML 2.0 should also ultimately become easier to implement and more efficient. Apple's binary file structure (based on the one that Apple uses for its 3DMF format) is likely to be adopted as the standard for the binary version of VRML, although 3DMF itself will have little influence on the language.

N O T E Microsoft might choose to continue developing its own proposal (Active VRML) as an alternative to mainstream VRML. How successful this specification will be remains to be seen. On the one hand, Microsoft is coming to the party late, and most of the support has already gone to VRML 2.0. On the other hand, Microsoft is Microsoft. Its deep pockets enabled it to wait almost a decade for people to start using Windows, and the same pockets may be deep enough to wear down VRML 2.0's early support.

Sun will likely proceed with the development of Java3D, although how much impact this specification will have remains to be seen.

Basic Concepts of VRML 2.0

VRML 1.0 and VRML 2.0 differ in several important and fundamental ways. The very structure of the scene graph has changed, and despite the syntactic similarities and some familiar nodes, the two are really quite different languages.

The New Scene Graph

The most basic change in the structure of VRML is the elimination of state-based scene graph traversal. Under VRML 1.0, the effects of such nodes as `Material` and `Texture2` would accumulate; in other words, a `Material` node affects every shape node that follows it in the scene graph until the next `Material` node or the end of the enclosing `Separator`. This accumulation was awkward for several reasons, not the least of which was that it made it impossible to take advantage of multiprocessing capabilities. Because you had to traverse the scene graph in sequence, there was no way to parallelize it. VRML 2.0 addresses these problems, by moving toward a simple attachment hierarchy.

The best way to visualize a VRML 2.0 world is as an inverted tree. This concept should be familiar to you if you have experience using the DOS or UNIX file systems. Nodes in a VRML 2.0 world are conceptually equivalent to DOS or UNIX files and directories.

Nodes fall into two general categories: leaf nodes and grouping nodes. Leaf nodes are like files, or like the leaves of a tree. Grouping nodes are like directories, or the branches of a tree. Just as a directory can contain files and other directories, a grouping node can contain leaf nodes and other grouping nodes. Figure 13.1 illustrates this structure.

FIG. 13.1
The basic VRML 2.0 scene structure.

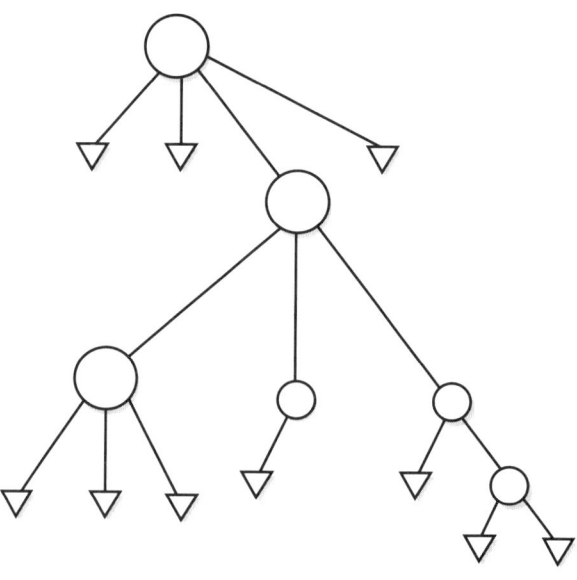

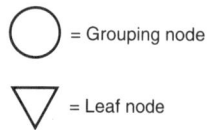

The leaf nodes correspond to the entities that you expect to find in the world—things like shapes, sounds, and lights. Other leaf nodes do not correspond to visible objects, but instead control aspects of the behavior of visible objects. There are also sensors that can detect user actions.

You use the grouping nodes to create an attachment hierarchy. For example, your hand is connected to your lower arm, which is connected to your upper arm, which is connected to your torso. You can move your hand by itself, but if you move your upper arm, your lower arm and hand "come along for the ride." This concept is called an attachment hierarchy.

The grouping nodes serve to join several leaf nodes together as a unit, and to keep track of the group's position and orientation relative to its parent node. You can also use grouping nodes for other purposes, such as automatic level-of-detail management.

DEF and USE work the same way as they do in VRML 1.0. If you're familiar with the UNIX file system, think of USE as a symlink. USE enables a single node (even a grouping node) to exist in multiple places within the world. Figure 13.2 shows an example of the scene graph structure resulting from a USE statement.

FIG. 13.2
Multiple instancing using USE.

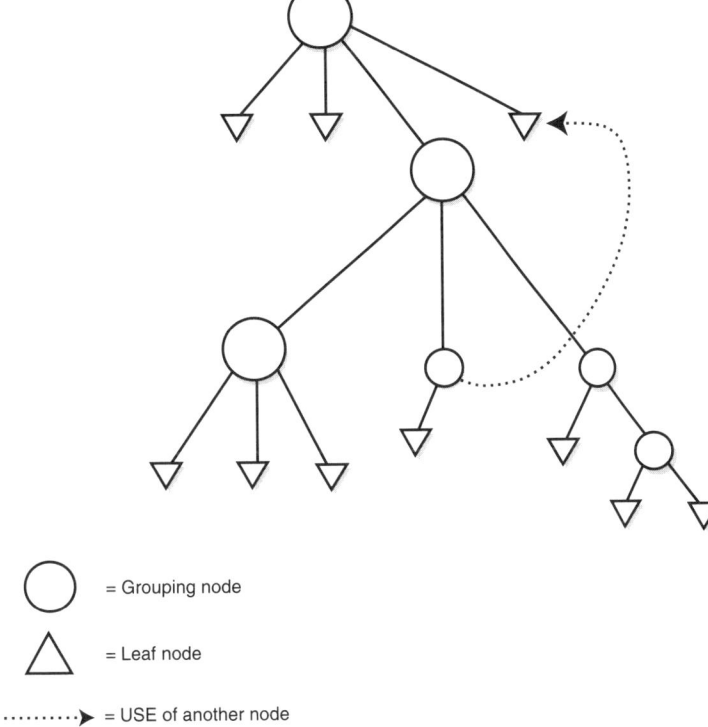

Using the USE statement makes the scene graph more complex, but can save you a lot of space both in memory and on disk. More importantly, USE can reduce the bandwidth requirements for downloading worlds.

VRML 2.0 Syntax

As Chapter 12 mentioned, all VRML 2.0 files start with the following header line:

```
#VRML V2.0 utf8
```

However, some early version 2.0 files have a "draft" number in the header that looks like the following:

```
#VRML Draft #n V2.0 utf8
```

where *n* is the draft number. Note the following example:

```
#VRML Draft #3 V2.0 utf8
```

This header is followed by a series of nodes, plus ROUTE statements and prototypes. Routes and prototypes are described later in this chapter.

The nodes are conceptually similar to those of VRML 1.0, but VRML 2.0 has introduced some changes. The structure of all nodes is now identical, and simpler than before. A VRML 2.0 node simply looks like the following:

```
NodeType { fields }
```

Unlike a VRML 1.0 node, the children of the VRML 2.0 node are not separate from the fields; instead, a children field contains them. For example, a Group node containing a sphere and a cone looks like the following in VRML 2.0:

```
Group {
  children [ Shape { geometry { Sphere { } }, Shape { geometry Cone { } } ]
}
```

This change makes VRML 2.0's syntax much more consistent.

Leaf Nodes

As mentioned previously, there are several different kinds of leaf nodes. Chief among these are shapes, sounds, lights, viewpoints, and sensors.

The *Shape* Node

Instead of accumulating materials, textures, and other properties during a sequential traversal of the scene graph, VRML 2.0 treats each shape as being independent of all other shapes. This allows the scene graph traversal process to be parallelized, and also makes it easier to design worlds using VRML.

A Shape node has two components: geometry and appearance. geometry describes the vertices and faces of an object, whereas appearance determines its surface properties. A Shape node looks like the following:

```
Shape {

   appearance Appearance node
```

```
        geometry any geometry node

}
```

The appearance field can contain only one kind of node: an Appearance node. This node itself can contain a Material node, a TextureTransform node, and one of the texture nodes. The geometry field can contain any of the ten basic geometric shape nodes.

For example, the following Shape node defines a greenish-blue, transparent cylinder:

```
Shape {
  appearance Appearance {
       material Material {
              diffuseColor 0 0.5 0.5 transparency 0.8
       }
  }
  geometry Cylinder { }
}
```

The sequences appearance Appearance and material Material might seem odd and redundant. They are. However, they make sense from a syntactic standpoint; appearance Appearance indicates that a field named appearance has a value that is an Appearance node.

The Geometry Nodes

VRML 2.0 has a total of 10 geometry nodes. The Sphere, Cylinder, and Cone nodes are identical to those in VRML 1.0, and Box is just a VRML 1.0 Cube node with a more accurate name. The Text node (which was called AsciiText in VRML 1.0) enables you to create flat text and position it in three dimensions. The node can use a variety of sizes, fonts (such as Serif or Typewriter), and type styles (such as bold or italic).

The PointSet, IndexedLineSet, and IndexedFaceSet are similar to those in VRML 1.0, but VRML 2.0 changes their syntax somewhat. The major difference is that the Coordinate, Normal, and TextureCoordinate nodes are now stored as fields inside the geometry node, along with a set of colors. For example, the following Shape node defines two triangles:

```
Shape {
  appearance Appearance {
   material Material { transparency 0.8 }
  }
  geometry IndexedFaceSet {
   coord Coordinate { point [ 0 0 0, 5 0 0, 5 7 0, 0 7 0 ] }
   coordIndex [ 0 1 2 -1 2 3 0 -1 ]
  }
}
```

VRML also introduces two new geometry nodes: ElevationGrid creates terrain, and Extrusion creates surfaces of extrusion or revolution.

The *Appearance* Node

The Appearance node has three fields:

```
Appearance {
  material <Material node>
  texture <one of the texture nodes>
  textureTransform <TextureTransform node>
}
```

The Material node is simpler in VRML 2.0, and describes only the overall surface properties for a shape. The node's fields (diffuseColor, transparency, and so on) are each a single value, not a list of values as they were in VRML 1.0. These single values apply to the entire Shape node. You can specify individual face and vertex colors in the geometry nodes; for example, an IndexedFaceSet can contain a list of colors for its faces.

You can use the textureTransform field to stretch, shift, and rotate textures on the faces of objects. You can specify the textures themselves with an ImageTexture (which loads static images from JPEG or PNG files), a MovieTexture (which places an MPEG movie on one face of an object), or a PixelTexture (which generates textures procedurally).

Lights

VRML 2.0's only significant change to lighting is that all lights are global; that is, they don't stop at Separator nodes (which no longer exist).

The *Sound* Node

One important new addition to VRML is the Sound node and the accompanying AudioClip node. AudioClip loads a sound file from the Internet. Several Sound nodes can reference that AudioClip and position the sound in three-dimensional space. The AudioClip node can play a sound once, or loop it indefinitely; the node can also shift the sound's pitch. The Sound node controls sound placement, orientation, intensity, and range of effect. The use of Sound nodes can greatly enhance a virtual environment's realism.

The sound sample that AudioClip loads can be in any format, but browsers must support at least the .WAV format using uncompressed pulse code modulation (PCM). Browsers are also expected to support MIDI file type 1 format, using the General MIDI patch set.

For example, the following example demonstrates how you might use a Sound and AudioClip:

```
Sound {
     location 15.5 23 0.2
     intensity 0.75
     source AudioClip {
```

```
                description "a bell ringing"
                loop TRUE
                url "http://somewhere.com/sounds/bell.wav"
            }
    }
```

Viewpoints

The concept of virtual cameras has changed slightly; VRML 2.0 calls them Viewpoints. They store a location, orientation, and field of view, and are in some respects similar to VRML 1.0's `PerspectiveCamera` node. You can place multiple Viewpoints in a scene, and attach them at any point in the hierarchy. You can use interpolators or scripts to animate a Viewpoint's behavior, producing simple, noninteractive "walkthroughs" of a virtual environment.

Grouping Nodes

VRML 2.0 offers several different grouping nodes. The only thing they have in common is that they have children associated with them; otherwise, each grouping node serves a unique purpose.

The *Transform* Node

VRML 1.0 featured several different transformation nodes that accumulate sequentially to affect subsequent shapes. In VRML 2.0, the `Transform` node has essentially replaced `Separator`, and defines a spatial relationship between nodes and their parent nodes.

The `Transform` node contains fields that describe how the group formed by its children should be oriented, scaled, and repositioned relative to the `Transform` node's parents. A `Transform` node looks like this:

```
Transform {
  translation X Y Z
  rotation AX AY AZ ANGLE
  scale SX SY SZ
  scaleOrientation OX OY OZ ANGLE
  center X Y Z
  children [ ... ]
}
```

The `translation` field consists of three numbers that give the location of the `Transform` node and its children on the X, Y, and Z axes. The `rotation` field consists of a three-element vector (pointing in some X, Y, Z direction) and an angle; children of the `Transform` node should rotate around that vector by the specified angle. The `center` field is the point around which the rotation should occur.

The scale field specifies three numbers to scale the size of the Transform node and its children. The scaleOrientation field controls the directions in which the stretch takes place. Figure 13.3 shows how Transform nodes fit into the hierarchy.

FIG. 13.3
The hierarchy, with Transform nodes and leaves.

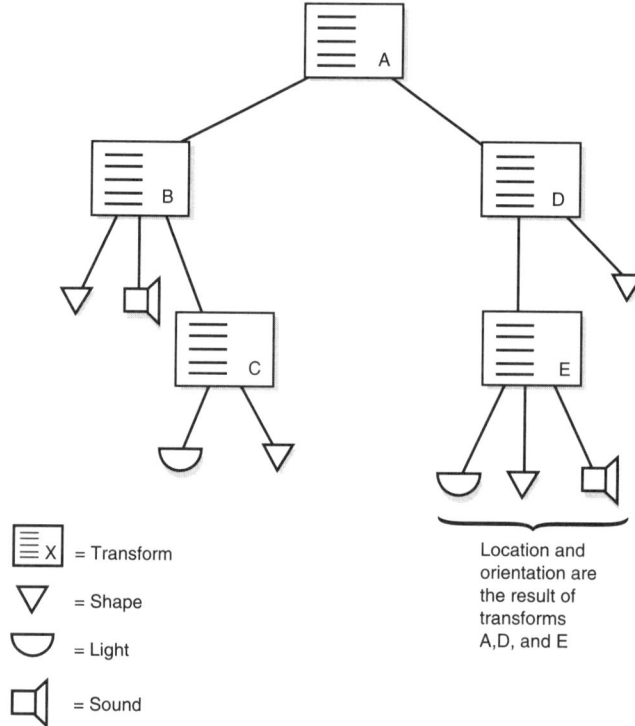

The *Group* Node

The simplest of the grouping nodes is Group, which does nothing more than gather together its children. In effect, Group is a Transform node with all the fields set to their default values.

The *Switch* Node

The Switch node causes just one of its children to be rendered, or none of them. The node has a field called whichChoice that specifies which child to traverse (starting from zero). If the whichChoice field is less than zero, none of the children is processed.

For example, the following code selects one of several different shapes depending on the whichChoice value:

```
Switch {
        whichChoice 2
        choices [
                Shape { geometry Sphere { } }
                Shape { geometry Box { } }
                Shape { geometry Cone { } }
        ]
}
```

The `whichChoice` field is set to 2, so the initial shape is the cone (because the children are counted starting from zero).

The `Switch` node is useful for turning off certain parts of the scene when they're not visible, and for creating simple animations consisting of multiple versions of the same object.

The *Anchor* and *Inline* Nodes

The `Anchor` and `Inline` nodes are just the `WWWAnchor` and `WWWInline` nodes from VRML 1.0. The following code loads the VRML file SOMEFILE.WRL and adds it to the world:

```
Inline { url "somefile.wrl" }
```

The *LOD* Node

The `LOD` node is basically the same as in VRML 1.0 and is described in Chapter 12. Instead of having a `children` field, the VRML 2.0 version has a levels field. The node looks like the following:

```
LOD {
        range [ 10, 27 ]
        level [
                Inline { url "roundThing.wrl" }
                Shape { geometry Sphere { } }
                Shape { geometry Box { } }
        ]
}
```

The detailed version of the object loads from ROUNDTHING.WRL and displays up to 10 meters away. Beyond 10 meters, the sphere would be used; beyond 27 meters, the box would be used.

Collision Detection

The `Collision` node prevents the user from passing through any of its children's geometry. This node is useful for creating solid walls, for example. You can also supply a simpler set of geometry that serves as the basis for collision detection, to make the collision calculations more efficient.

Miscellaneous Nodes

Several nodes are new to VRML 2.0 and add useful features, but are not exactly leaf or grouping nodes. You typically use these nodes to enhance your world in some way, by providing more information or controlling the world's appearance.

The *Background* and *Fog* Nodes

The Background node does two things: It creates a sky and ground, and enables you to create a panorama for such things as distant mountains and stars.

Background gives a range of colors for the sky, a range of colors for the ground, angles for the dividing plane between the sky and ground, and a set of six URLs that reference images to apply to an imaginary cube that surrounds the user. The sky and ground display farthest away, followed by the (possibly transparent) images; that way, you can place mountains between the user and the sky. You can, of course, animate the Background node, so you can effectively change the sky color during the course of the day and night cycle.

The Fog node enables you to define regions of fog and haze. The VRML 2.0 specification recommends making the fog color the same as the background sky color, so that the two blend together in the distance.

The *WorldInfo* and *NavigationInfo* Nodes

The WorldInfo node enables you to include information such as author, copyright information, creation date, and so on. Unlike information contained in comments, the contents of a WorldInfo node are not discarded. Instead, they are provided to the browser for display.

The NavigationInfo node contains a hodge-podge of viewer-related information, including such information as whether the user has a headlight on or not, what type of motion is allowed (walking or flying), how fast the user should move, and how large the user's avatar is (for collision detection, terrain following, and so forth). Currently, VRML 2.0 assumes that the avatar is a perfect sphere, which very few people are. A later revision of the specification should include a more detailed description of the avatar's geometry.

> **NOTE** An *avatar* is the user's representation in a virtual environment. In a multiuser world, you see the other users represented by their avatars.

Sensors

One important new addition to the VRML 2.0 specification is a set of sensor nodes. Sensors generate events based on user interaction; for example, a TouchSensor node can detect when the user clicks it. There are seven sensor nodes: TouchSensor, ProximitySensor, VisibilitySensor, CylinderSensor, PlaneSensor, SphereSensor, and TimeSensor.

The *ProximitySensor* and *VisibilitySensor* Nodes

The ProximitySensor node defines a box-shaped region of space that can detect when the user enters, exits, or moves around inside it. This sensor reports the user's location and orientation so long as the user remains inside the box. Script nodes can use this information for a variety of purposes.

The VisibilitySensor node is quite similar, but instead of reporting when the user enters or leaves the box, this node reports when the box is visible or invisible.

The *TimeSensor* Node

The TimeSensor node doesn't detect user interaction, but instead sends messages at regular intervals. This node is quite flexible as well as simple. It can generate a single event, or generate events at a regular rate. TimeSensor can run once or loop repeatedly. It can generate continuous or discrete time values. You can use the node to control various types of animation. The TimeSensor node is the basis for any kind of periodic or time-varying activity in VRML.

Geometric Sensor Nodes

VRML 2.0 has three different types of geometric sensors: CylinderSensor, PlaneSensor, and SphereSensor. The purpose of each type is to define and constrain the user's capability to manipulate some virtual control device.

The CylinderSensor node maps a dragging motion of the mouse (or other pointing device) into a rotation around the local vertical axis. The PlaneSensor node maps dragging into a sliding action in the X,Y plane, and SphereSensor gives you control similar to a trackball.

Interpolators

Interpolators are special nodes that generate a series of values for other nodes. You use interpolators to generate various types of simple animation. More complex animation requires the use of Script nodes.

There are half a dozen different types of interpolator, but all follow the same basic model. Each interpolator contains an array of values for its output, and a corresponding array of key values. Each key has a value, and the keys are sorted in increasing order with no duplication. In other words, the key values steadily increase through the list.

There is also a control input, called the *fraction*. Whenever you set the control input to a particular value, the browser locates the keys on either side of that value along with their corresponding output values. The output values are interpolated based on the value of the fractional input relative to the neighboring keys.

Routing a TimeSensor node to an interpolator causes the interpolator to generate a smooth series of values that you can then apply to other nodes by using ROUTE statements.

You can use interpolators to generate scalar values (floating-point numbers) for such effects as light intensity. You also can use them to generate a series of position vectors, or orientations, that are useful for making things move and spin. They can interpolate coordinates to generate a kind of three-dimensional morphing, or they can interpolate colors to make objects change their hue over time.

Even without using Script nodes, you can generate some remarkably complex animations using TimeSensor nodes, interpolators, and the ROUTE statement.

Routes

A *route* is a connection between an output field of one node and an input field of another. The previous example—of routing a TimeSensor's output to an interpolator node—is a typical use of ROUTE. You might also route a TouchSensor to trigger a TimeSensor node, which you can then hook to an interpolator whose output goes to an intensity setting on a light; when the user touches the TouchSensor, the light slowly begins to dim.

A ROUTE statement has four components: the node whose output you are reading, the field from which to read the value, the node to which to send the output, and the field to which to write the value.

The following example causes the light intensity to increase slowly when you touch the switch:

```
DEF Lightswitch TouchSensor { }
DEF Lamp SpotLight { intensity 0.0 }
DEF Interval TimeSensor { cycleInterval 5 }   # seconds
ROUTE Lightswitch.touchTime TO Interval.startTime
ROUTE Interval.fraction TO Lamp.intensity
```

NOTE Again, all the information in this chapter is based on a preliminary draft of the VRML 2.0 specification. The specification's final release might include some changes. Currently, no VRML 2.0 browsers are available, so none of this chapter's examples could be tested.

The *Script* Node

Interpolators are quite powerful, but sometimes you need to perform more complex tasks that involve decision making. In such situations, you would use the Script node.

Using the Script node, you can write a short program and interface it to a VRML world. You can route other nodes' output to a Script node, and route a Script node's output to other nodes. The script itself processes the input and generates the output. The script can do just about anything, including interacting with special input and output devices and communicating over the Internet.

The VRML specification doesn't explicitly state which languages it will support, but JavaScript is a good bet. Java itself might also be a contender, but that language is more complex for novice users to learn and can be overkill for many simple applications. Most likely, browsers eventually will support both Java and JavaScript, and quite possibly also allow access from external applications written in C, Visual Basic, Pascal, or other languages.

JavaScript is useful for simple applications, Java is useful when you need more power, and languages such as C are useful when you need high performance.

Prototypes

One of the serious concerns with VRML is the fact that it's not particularly object-oriented. Object-oriented programming (OOP) is a powerful technique for ensuring that projects are reliable and scaleable. One of the key concepts of OOP is *encapsulation*—

combining code and data into a single object. Clearly, using ROUTE statements to string together a loose collection of shapes, interpolators, sensors, and scripts is almost the exact opposite of OOP. VRML imposes this "telephone switchboard" structure by forcing separation of code (scripts and interpolators) and data (such as sensors and shapes). The structure can quickly lead to chaos, and to worlds that are difficult to manage and maintain.

Another concern is the difficulty of adding features to VRML. From the start, developers have been requesting such things as NURBS (Non-Uniform Rational B-Spline) surfaces as an efficient way to convey the geometry of curved shapes; however, the specification still doesn't include such features.

The solution to both of these problems is the use of prototypes. A *prototype* is a collection of nodes and ROUTE statements packaged into a kind of "black box" that you can use to define a new node. The following example defines a new type of node, Automobile:

```
PROTO Automobile [
  field SFColor body_color 0 0 1
  field SFString bumper_style "modern"
  field SFBool tinted_windshield FALSE
  eventIn SFTime engine_starttime
]
{
  <scene graph with geometry of car, referencing the fields above>
  <script that knows how to start the engine sound>
  <routes that link engine_start time to one of the scripts>
}
```

You could use Automobile as follows:

```
Automobile {
  body_color 1 0 0
  tinted_windshield TRUE
}
```

This usage creates an instance of Automobile, with a red body (1 0 0), a tinted windshield, and the default "modern" bumper styling. When you set the engine_starttime field (using a ROUTE statement elsewhere in the file), the script starts up the engine and perhaps makes a sound (by triggering a Sound node within Automobile).

You could use the Automobile node repeatedly, just like a regular node. You also could use DEF and USE statements with Automobile, just as you could with a regular node. In fact, Automobile *is* a regular node—it just happens not to be one that is built in to VRML itself.

Prototypes provide tremendous extensibility. Developers who want NURBS shapes need only write a NURBS generator in Java (or JavaScript, or any other language) and make their prototype available to anyone who wants to use it.

Prototypes also provide an encapsulation of code and data; only eventIn fields can receive values from outside the prototype, and only eventOut fields can be routed to other objects in the scene graph. The code in the scripts remains within the prototype.

Getting used to prototypes takes some time, but they're one of VRML 2.0's most powerful features. Eventually, you can expect to see libraries of commonly used prototypes for everything from materials to shapes to behaviors.

Live3D

Live3D didn't yet support the VRML 2.0 standard while this book was being written, but probably will by the time that you read this.

A tiny startup company in New York state, Paper Software, developed Live3D as a program called WebFX. Of all the VRML browsers that appeared during the first rush of excitement following the release of the VRML 1.0 specification, WebFX was clearly the best. It was fast and supported most of the language's features.

Netscape liked WebFX so much that it bought Paper Software. Renaming the WebFX plug-in Live3D (to be consistent with other Netscape *Live* features), Netscape made the program available almost immediately. The latest release of Netscape bundles Live3D, so in the months ahead you can expect full-featured VRML browsers on every desktop.

Although Live3D deserves its current success, nothing lasts forever. Eventually, you can expect to see the emergence of new VRML browsers that provide more features and offer faster rendering speeds than Live3D. In the short-term future, however, Live3D is the VRML browser of choice.

Navigation in Live3D

Navigating through a virtual environment using Live3D is straightforward. The main screen looks like figure 13.4.

Along the bottom of the screen is a toolbar that enables you to perform various simple operations. You can click the question-mark icon to display onscreen navigation help, as shown in figure 13.4. After you get a feel for moving around in three-dimensional space, you can turn off the help.

By holding down the left mouse button, you can walk through the world. Moving the mouse forward moves you forward, moving it backward moves you backward. Sideways motion of the mouse lets you turn left or right, and you can combine this motion with the forward or backward motion.

FIG. 13.4
The main screen of Live3D, a plug-in for Netscape.

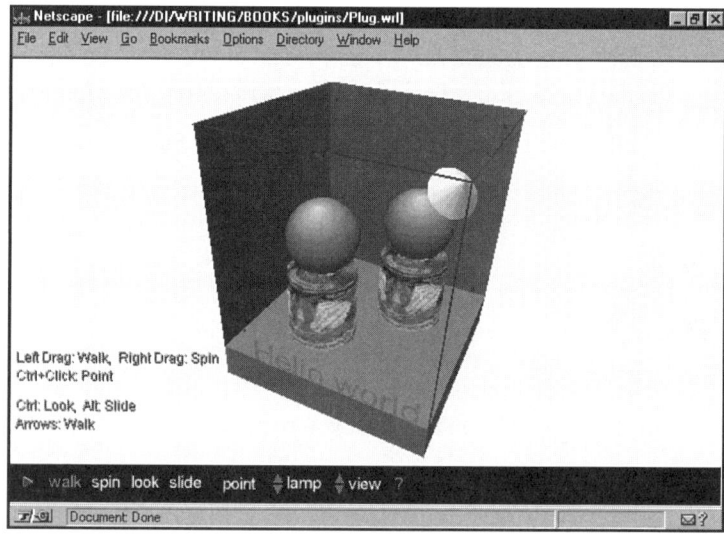

Holding down the Ctrl key with the left mouse button enables you to *look* in different directions without moving at all. Moving the mouse forward and backward enables you to look up and down, for example. Holding down the Alt key makes the left mouse button slide you around, both left/right and up/down.

Holding down the right mouse button spins the world around, so that you can look at it from different angles. Holding down the Ctrl key and clicking an object once moves your camera until it looks right at the object.

The toolbar enables you to modify the action that your left mouse button performs. If you click Spin, the left mouse button does the same as the right mouse button does: It spins the world. If you click Look, the left mouse button does the same as when you hold down the Ctrl key: It lets you look around. Clicking Slide makes the left mouse button behave the way that it does when you hold down the Alt key. When you click the Point button, left mouse clicks have the same effect as holding down Ctrl while left-clicking: You go to the object that you clicked.

The toolbar also enables you to turn your headlight (the light source attached to your viewpoint, like the lamp on a miner's helmet) on and off (which you can also do by pressing Ctrl+T) and adjust the overall scene brightness up or down (which you can also do by pressing Ctrl+1 and Ctrl+2). The toolbar also lets you cycle between several Viewpoints in the file, or return to the most recently selected Viewpoint (which you can also do by pressing Ctrl+V).

Menus in Live3D

The Live3D menus duplicate much of the toolbar's functionality, but also enable you to do such things as navigating to a particular Viewpoint by name, leveling yourself (by choosing the Navigation menu's Straighten command), staying on the ground, and so on. You can control display quality and the visibility of various controls.

To access the menus, right-click anywhere in the main window. Figure 13.5 shows a typical set of menus.

FIG. 13.5
Menus in Live3D.

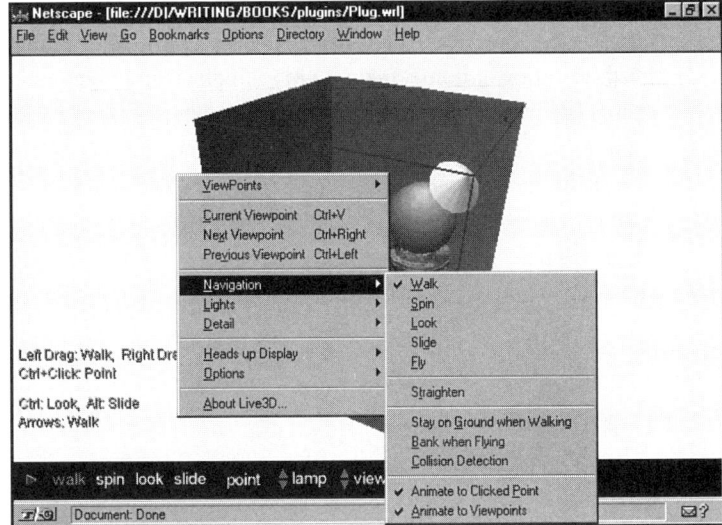

By using the menus and the toolbar, you have considerable control over the Live3D plug-in's features.

Live3D Extensions

Live3D supports several extensions to the VRML 1.0 standard. Many of the extensions are similar to features that VRML 2.0 provides, except that you implement them slightly differently. In particular, Live3D includes support for background colors and images, collision detection, sound, and animated texture maps.

Live3D also adds an `Animator` node that can use 3D Studio VUE files for keyframed animation, and a Spin group that makes its children spin around a particular axis.

Applications

People used to criticize virtual reality as being a solution in search of a problem. Eventually, application areas were found: medical work, high-end museum displays, location-based entertainment, training applications, and so forth. VRML will go through a similar process of finding its application areas. However, several obvious opportunities have been identified.

Education

Online education is an exciting area, and much work is being done to bring it to fruition. Imagine sitting at home, taking a kind of electronic "correspondence course" in a field such as cellular biology. The lecture notes are all online (in HTML, of course), along with some nice JPEGs of electron micrographs and MPEGs of things like mitosis. Also, online is a VRML model of the human cell. You can "shrink down" and enter the model, and watch the various parts of the cell at work. You can wander around, seeing protein synthesis taking place, watching viruses invade, and even experimenting to see what happens if you alter the cell's environment in some way.

Imagine going on a field trip to the surface of Mars, then traveling backward in time to watch the planet's formation. Imagine operating a virtual cyclotron to learn more about atomic structure, or fitting together molecules to understand how they bond.

The use of three-dimensional, fully interactive applications can greatly enhance the educational experience—and VRML is the specification that will make the experience possible.

The Arts

VRML gives creative people a whole new medium for self-expression. If you've always wanted to be an architect, now's your chance. If you've always wanted to try your hand at sculpture, or painting, or making wind chimes, you can do it in VRML.

If you've wanted to stage a play—complete with sets, props, costumes, lighting, and so forth—there's now nothing standing in your way. In fact, theater is an excellent metaphor for the experience of participating with others in a virtual environment. You're always "playing a part," through your avatar's interactions with other people in the world. Live performances in cyberspace are one of the many killer apps for VRML.

Entertainment

Of course, virtual reality offers great opportunities for entertainment—not just games, but also social interaction in a three-dimensional environment. Some interesting experiments have already been conducted in this area: WorldsChat, AlphaWorld, and others have broken important new ground. The work of such companies as Black Sun Interactive, Onlive, and Sony is leading the way to interactive role-playing environments that go far beyond games, MUDs (multiuser dungeons), MOOs (multiuser dungeons, object-oriented), and IRC (Internet relay chat), and into the area of complete alternative realities whose sole purpose is to mediate social interaction.

The Future

What does the future hold for VRML? Eventually, there will be a VRML 3.0—but don't hold your breath. The jump from 1.0 to 2.0 was so large and difficult (and political), it'll be a while before anyone wants to take a stab at yet another major revision.

However, one prediction can be made with confidence: Multiuser worlds are on their way. Multiuser worlds are the holy grail of virtual reality applications in general, and VRML in particular. So far, most virtual worlds are just ghost towns. What people really want to do in cyberspace is interact with other humans, and that requires protocols that enable them to share virtual worlds.

VRML 2.0 specifically avoids multiuser issues in the same way that 1.0 avoided behavior. Unfortunately, given the enormous pressure for multiuser worlds, the most likely outcome is a proliferation of incompatible standards for shared worlds.

The future will also bring improvements in performance, as a result of 3-D graphics accelerator boards. All VRML browsers are render-bound, and would benefit greatly from hardware assistance at the rendering level. Such boards are expected to proliferate in the months ahead.

Also on the hardware front, you can expect new input and output devices. Spaceballs (ball-shaped devices that you can push and twist with six degrees of freedom) will make navigation in virtual worlds easier than ever, and devices like 3-D shutter glasses and head-mounted displays (HMDs) will bring more immersive, three-dimensional display capabilities to standard VRML browsers.

And of course, the future will bring more interesting, exciting, and entertaining worlds to the Web. ●

CHAPTER 14

VRML Plug-Ins

The previous chapter explored Live3D, the most popular of the available Virtual Reality Modeling Language (VRML) browsers. Many other browsers are available, of course, and some offer special features that set them apart from the rest. This chapter surveys some of the more interesting ones.

Note that unless specified otherwise, all these are VRML 1.0 browsers. The only one that currently supports VRML 2.0 is Sony's CyberPassage, although Liquid Reality will be 2.0-compliant quite soon, and you can expect a 2.0 version of WebSpace to follow shortly thereafter. Also note that (unless stated otherwise) all these packages are designed for Windows 95 and Windows NT, although many of the developers have indicated that they plan to have Macintosh versions available eventually. ■

- WebSpace from Silicon Graphics and Template Graphics (TGS)
- CyberGate from Black Sun Interactive
- VRweb from IICM/NCSA/ University of Minnesota
- WIRL from VREAM
- VR Scout and Pueblo from Chaco Communications
- Traveler from Onlive Technologies
- Liquid Reality from Dimension X
- CyberPassage from Sony
- V-Realm from IDS
- Virtus Voyager
- TerraForm from Brilliance Labs
- VRML Add-In for Microsoft Internet Explorer

http://www.mcp.com/que

WebSpace

WebSpace is, in some ways, the grandfather of all VRML browsers. Built around OpenInventor from Silicon Graphics (SGI), WebSpace supports a superset of VRML's functionality. OpenInventor is a C-language toolkit for creating three-dimensional graphics, primarily on SGI machines. OpenInventor is built on top of OpenGL, a lower-level graphics application programming interface (API) that has been ported to a variety of platforms, including Windows NT and Windows 95.

After licensing the OpenInventor source code from Silicon Graphics, Template Graphics (TGS) ported the source code to Windows NT and Windows 95. TGS sells the library for application development, and also uses it inhouse to develop and maintain its port of WebSpace.

WebSpace is the most complete implementation of VRML, largely because VRML started as a subset of OpenInventor. Other developers often use WebSpace as a reference, because its implementation is considered "correct" even regarding those areas in which the VRML 1.0 specification is unclear or ambiguous.

As shown in figure 14.1, WebSpace features an onscreen "dashboard" that enables you to navigate through the virtual world in a fairly intuitive way. The central T-shaped joystick lets you move forward and backward, and turn left and right. The arrow pad to the joystick's right lets you move up and down and side to side. The seek tool to the joystick's left turns your cursor into a crosshair; when you click an object, you move smoothly through the environment until that object is centered in your view.

You can turn off the dashboard, because you can perform all its functions using the mouse and keyboard. In fact, there are keyboard shortcuts for many of the menu items as well; WebSpace enables you to turn off its toolbar and other onscreen user interface features to obtain a larger view of the virtual world that you're exploring.

WebSpace also has an *examiner* mode in which you can select and then rotate an object (and the entire world) so that you can view the object from different angles. To toggle between the two navigation modes (walk and examiner), you choose menu items. Other menu items enable you to select from multiple viewpoints in the world, toggle your "headlight" on and off, and set various rendering-quality parameters to enhance performance.

Performance enhancement is particularly important because WebSpace is one of the slowest of the VRML browsers. Neither OpenInventor nor OpenGL is known as a high-performance engine, and the combination can be slow as molasses. OpenGL was designed for systems that include a 3-D accelerator, and really bogs down on systems that don't have one.

FIG. 14.1
A world seen in WebSpace, with the dashboard displayed.

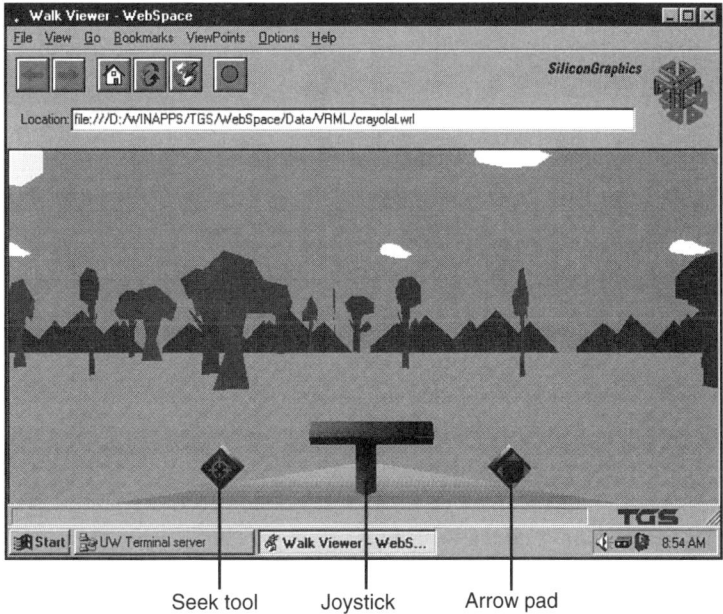

Seek tool   Joystick   Arrow pad

You can find WebSpace on the Web at **http://www.sd.tgs.com** (Template Graphics) and **http://www.sgi.com/Products/WebFORCE/WebSpace** (Silicon Graphics).

CyberGate

Black Sun Interactive has created a multiuser VRML browser called CyberGate. CyberGate is, in most respects, an ordinary VRML browser. What sets it apart is the fact that it enables you to connect to worlds that other users are visiting, and to interact with those users in an online "chat" type environment. Other users are represented by their *avatars*—three-dimensional models of their virtual bodies.

You can select your own avatar from a library or create a custom avatar. Figure 14.2 shows the main Black Sun host world, which is usually populated by several other avatars.

CyberGate is a "central hub" type system, which Black Sun administers. Currently, to enable a world for use with CyberGate, you must submit the world's URL to Black Sun so that it can verify that the world conforms to a simple set of guidelines (syntactically correct VRML, dimensions and lighting consistent with other worlds intended for use with CyberGate, and so on). Black Sun then e-mails you a small snippet of VRML code that you insert into your world to enable it to work in the multiuser CyberGate environment. Browsers other than CyberGate ignore this snippet.

FIG. 14.2
Exploring a multiuser world using CyberGate.

Constructing your own avatar is even more straightforward. You should keep the file size manageable (GZIP can help) and ensure that the file consists of syntactically correct VRML. The origin (0,0,0) is at the eye point of the avatar, so when you look at an avatar's head, you see the avatar and it sees you.

If the multiuser features of CyberGate appeal to you, you should also check out Onlive's Traveler (described later in this chapter), which has a similar set of features. One unfortunate aspect of the current VRML standard is that each multiuser environment requires the use of a different browser; at some point, standards will begin to emerge that enable various worlds and browsers to interoperate with each other.

You can find CyberGate at **http://www2.blacksun.com**.

VRweb

Developing VRML browsers, particularly for VRML 1.0, is something of a black art. Most groups that have succeeded in getting such a browser up and running have played their cards close to their chest, for fear of giving their competitors an advantage.

Therefore, finding a browser that comes with complete source code is refreshing. VRweb is available for more platforms than any other VRML browser, and is being ported to several more. So far, versions have been released for Windows 95, Windows NT, Windows 3.1, and a variety of different versions of UNIX (IRIX, Solaris, SunOS, Ultrix, HP-UX, AIX, and Linux). Versions for the Macintosh and the PowerPC are in the works. Although

VRweb doesn't support the entire VRML specification (few browsers do), the browser will continue to grow and develop.

VRweb is the result of a collaboration between the Institute for Information Processing and Computer-Supported New Media (IICM), the National Center for Supercomputer Applications (NCSA), and the University of Minnesota. IICM, based at the Graz University of Technology in Austria, has been doing work on Web-based 3-D worlds for several years, with Hyper-G, a package that IICM developed. Hyper-G has served as the basis for VRweb.

NCSA has a well-earned reputation for excellent free tools for use with the Web. Early work on the Mosaic Internet browser took place at NCSA, and that work led to the development of Netscape. NCSA has also developed the most popular Web server software.

Hyper-G (and therefore VRweb) is built on top of OpenGL, but is also designed to work with Mesa, a freeware implementation of OpenGL. Mesa in turn runs on top of Microsoft Windows 3.1 and X Window (a graphical environment for UNIX workstations). VRweb can take advantage of hardware acceleration, but only on OpenGL-based platforms that support it. Those platforms include SGI, DEC Alpha, Windows 95, and Windows NT.

VRweb is available from **http://hyperg.iicm.tu-graz.ac.at/Cvrweb**. From that site, you can access mirror sites all over the world.

WIRL

VREAM is one of the first software companies to embrace virtual reality in a big way. The original VREAM (Virtual Dream) software enabled users to create three-dimensional virtual worlds interactively, long before Mark Pesce envisioned VRML. This base of experience is likely to give VREAM an edge in the burgeoning VRML marketplace. VREAM's first VRML product is the WIRL browser.

WIRL, shown in figure 14.3, has several powerful features. Like many other browsers, VREAM has adopted the Microsoft RealityLab engine (now called Direct3D Retained Mode), which enables the browser to take advantage of hardware-based 3-D acceleration as it becomes available. Even using software-based rendering, WIRL gets 100,000 polygons per second on a 90mHz Pentium.

WIRL benefits from much of the work done on earlier VREAM products, including powerful interactivity features. Some of its features—such as gravity, elasticity, object paths, and animations—are not currently found in many other VRML browsers. VREAM provides this support through an extension to VRML that interacts with the VREAMScript language, which VREAM originally developed for use with its earlier products.

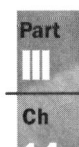

FIG. 14.3
WIRL is a powerful VRML browser from VREAM.

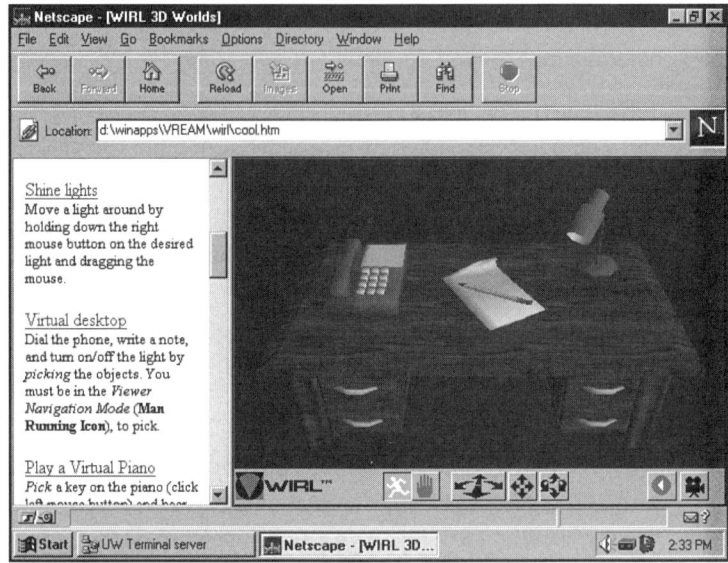

VREAM also did some early work on multiuser worlds, and you can expect VREAM to bring this capability to its VRML browsers soon. However, the lack of standards in this area creates interoperability problems. Another strength of VREAM is its support for such virtual reality peripherals as head-mounted displays and data gloves.

WIRL is available at **http://www.vream.com**.

VR Scout and Pueblo

Chaco Communications has produced two VRML-based products: VR Scout, a standard VRML browser; and Pueblo, a front-end for exploring multiuser dungeons or dimensions (MUDs), which supports special VRML-based MUDs.

VR Scout is one of the first browsers to support the complete VRML 1.0 specification. The initial version is based on Intel's 3DR graphics library, but Chaco has converted the newest version to the much faster RealityLab from Microsoft and RenderMorphics. One trade-off is that VR Scout runs somewhat more slowly on antique computers (such as a 386 or 486SX) because they lack floating-point acceleration.

VR Scout also supports some of the nodes found only in OpenInventor. This support is handy, because some poorly authored VRML worlds use these nodes. VR Scout offers good built-in help, and is fairly intuitive to use. The browser uses multiple threads for downloading `WWWInlined` objects and texture maps while you explore a world in progress.

Figure 14.4 shows VR Scout in action.

FIG. 14.4
VR Scout at work.

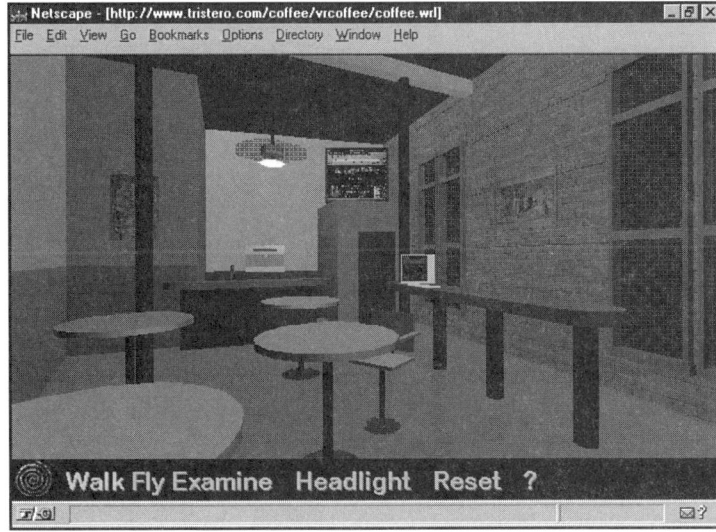

Pueblo is a client for use with MUDs. Traditionally, a MUD is an online multiuser environment that is entirely text-based. The use of VRML in Pueblo brings a graphical element to MUDs, and adds much to the experience. Pueblo borrows many of its features from TinTin, a popular MUD client that has macros and triggers that respond to incoming text. Pueblo is beginning to incorporate support for VRML 2.0.

VR Scout and Pueblo are both available from Chaco's Web site, **http://www.chaco.com**.

Traveler

One of the most exciting developments in shared online virtual worlds is the use of speech rather than text for communicating with other users. One of the pioneers in this area is Onlive Technologies, which offers a multiuser, three-dimensional environment in which you can wander and talk with other users. Figure 14.5 shows Onlive Traveler in operation.

Using Traveler, you not only can talk with other users in real time, but you see their avatars' lips moving as they speak. This impressive effect greatly enhances the world's realism. Avatars can also express emotions; the environment offers a menu of different feelings from which you can select the one most appropriate to your mood. Everyone else sees your avatar with a facial expression that matches your emotional state.

FIG. 14.5
The main demo world for Onlive Traveler.

To take advantage of the multiuser and speech aspects of Onlive's technology, you must be running Traveler. Here again, some sort of open standard for shared worlds would be nice, so that users don't have to keep changing VRML browsers when switching from one multiuser world to another. Fortunately, Onlive lets you license its technology to other VRML browser vendors. This solution will do until open standards are in place. With any luck, you'll soon see widespread use of speech and emotion in products from several companies.

Traveler is now in beta release. It will be available on Onlive's Web site, **http://www.onlive.com**. Traveler requires a Pentium, 16M of RAM, a sound card, and at least a 14.4K modem (28.8K is much better). If you plan to use Traveler regularly, it's worthwhile getting a headset that combines headphones and a microphone.

Liquid Reality

Liquid Reality is unique: it's a VRML browser written in Java. It consists of a set of Java classes that together provide VRML functionality.

Java has a well-earned reputation for being slow, so you certainly wouldn't want to write a rendering engine in it. Fortunately, Dimension X has created a native-code 3-D API, ICE, that does all the computationally intensive work of turning a set of data structures into an image on the screen.

One interesting feature of Liquid Reality is its dynamic extensibility. Whenever it encounters a node type that it doesn't recognize, Liquid Reality contacts the server from which the VRML file was loaded and requests a Java class that implements the node. Although VRML 2.0's prototypes provide a more general and powerful extension mechanism, Liquid Reality is the first company to actually implement dynamic extensibility.

The ICE engine is platform-independent, which has its advantages and disadvantages. One advantage is portability; it should be easy to port ICE to anything that has an accessible frame buffer. A disadvantage is that you can't easily take advantage of 3-D graphics accelerators. Another problem is that ICE assumes that it can access the frame buffer; in an X Window environment, where the buffer is actually on a different host, you have to send every single rendered frame over the network, which affects performance and perhaps other network users.

Liquid Reality is available from Dimension X's Web site at **http://www.dnx.com**.

CyberPassage

In the race to create a VRML 2.0 browser, Sony got an early lead. Sony's CyberPassage is a Moving-Worlds-compatible browser. At the moment, CyberPassage lacks *some* features (most sensors, texture transform, elevation grid, extrusion, point set, indexed line set, font style, pixel texture, billboard, and prototypes). After this lengthy list of missing features, you might well wonder what's left. Actually, Sony has done a pretty good job with the majority of the VRML nodes discussed in Chapter 13, "Moving Worlds and Live3D"; most of the preceding omissions are due to limitations in the rendering engine.

Sony is a big corporation, and one of the first to get behind the Moving Worlds specification; the corporation is likely to produce a fully compliant browser sometime soon. Figure 14.6 shows CyberPassage's main screen.

Sony is also proposing several extensions and modifications to the initial 2.0 draft of VRML, and the final design might very well incorporate many of the corporation's ideas. More importantly, Sony has done much important work on multiuser protocols. Sony is one of the few companies to share its work with the rest of the VRML community, and for that reason the corporation should be well positioned to shape future standards in this area.

CyberPassage is available on Sony's Web site at **http://vs.sony.co.jp/VS-E/vstop.html**.

FIG. 14.6
The main screen of Sony's CyberPassage.

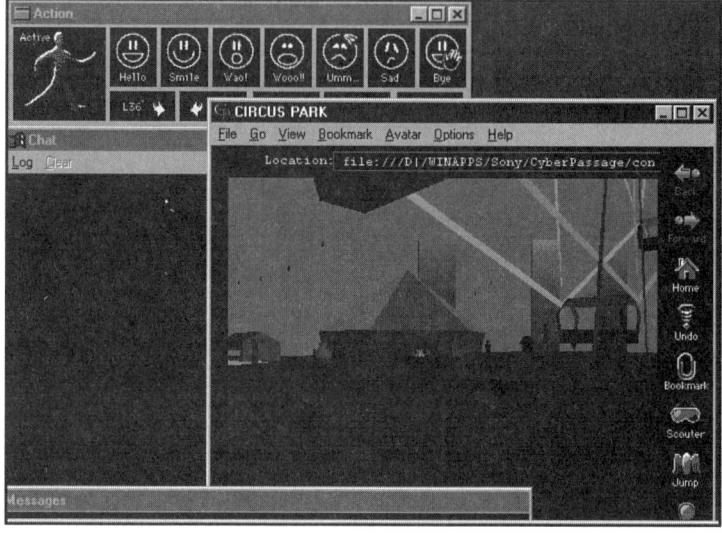

V-Realm

V-Realm (not to be confused with VREAM) is a VRML browser that was codeveloped by Integrated Data Systems (IDS) and Portable Graphics. The browser supports the entire VRML 1.0 specification and can read OpenInventor files as well. V-Realm has behavior engines, but they are incompatible with VRML 2.0's approach to behavior.

In some ways, V-Realm is the most ordinary of the VRML browsers. V-Realm has no multiuser features, no VRML 2.0 support—nothing much to set it apart from the rest of the pack. The browser offers reasonable performance and image quality, good compliance with the VRML 1.0 specification, and a fairly straightforward user interface. Figure 14.7 shows V-Realm.

V-Realm can run on its own or as a helper application from Netscape. Its only distinguishing features are gravity, behavior engines, and the capability to set 3-D bookmarks in a world.

V-Realm is available on **http://www.ids-net.com/ids/vrealm.html**.

FIG. 14.7
V-Realm is a nice, straight-forward VRML browser.

Virtus Voyager

Virtus started by designing a virtual reality product, called Walkthrough, for the Macintosh. Later, Virtus ported the package to Windows and finally adapted Walkthrough to create a VRML browser called Voyager.

Voyager has a good user interface and is reasonably fast. It also has the distinction of being one of the very few browsers available for the Macintosh platform; many developers have chosen to develop for Windows first and then create a Macintosh version only if there's sufficient demand. Because Virtus started as a Macintosh-oriented company, its strong support for that platform is not surprising. What is surprising is the fact that Voyager is available for the older 68K-based Macintosh computers as well as the Power Macintosh. Figure 14.8 shows Voyager running under Windows 95.

Unfortunately, Voyager is not an ideal VRML browser. It does not support many basic features of VRML (such as points and lines), which limits Voyager's usefulness as a general-purpose tool. Future versions of the product doubtlessly will eliminate some of these deficiencies.

Virtus Voyager is available at **http://www.virtus.com**.

FIG. 14.8
Voyager running on Windows 95.

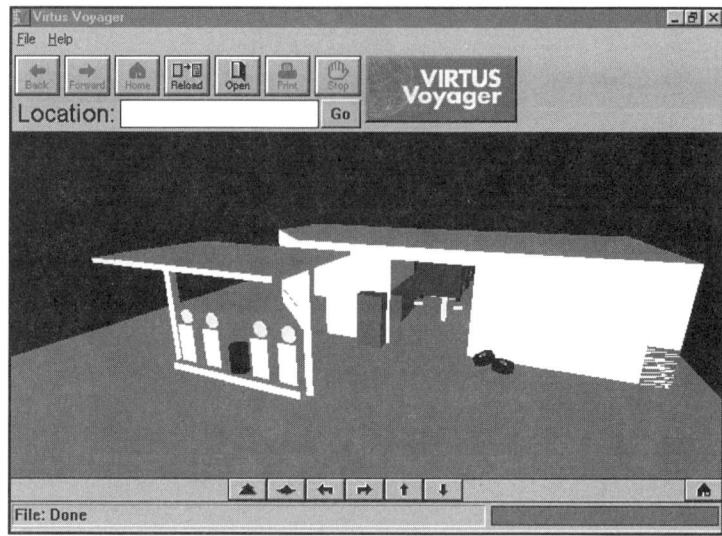

TerraForm

Like V-Realm, TerraForm is a standard VRML browser. Created by Brilliance Labs (whose slogan is "Holistic Wetware"), TerraForm runs either as a stand-alone application or as a Netscape 2.0 plug-in. The browser takes advantage of multithreading in Windows 95 and Windows NT, which improves responsiveness while loading. TerraForm is tightly integrated with OLE (Object Linking and Embedding), so browsing from within other applications is straightforward.

Figure 14.9 shows TerraForm's view of the world.

TerraForm uses Intel's 3DR rendering engine, the same one that early versions of VR Scout used. Although this engine produces excellent image quality, TerraForm's no speed demon.

One of TerraForm's useful features is its capability to display the VRML node hierarchy in a tree structure. This feature can help you to become familiar with how VRML really works.

TerraForm works properly only in HiColor (16-bit) or TrueColor (24-bit) graphics modes; the more common 8-bit paletted mode shows serious color problems. Whether Brilliance Labs continues to use 3DR remains to be seen; Intel has discontinued the library, and the same attractive licensing terms that applied to 3DR will soon apply to RealityLab (in other words, RealityLab will be free!).

TerraForm is available on the Brilliance Labs Web site, **http://www.brlabs.com**.

FIG. 14.9
TerraForm is a standard, straightforward browser.

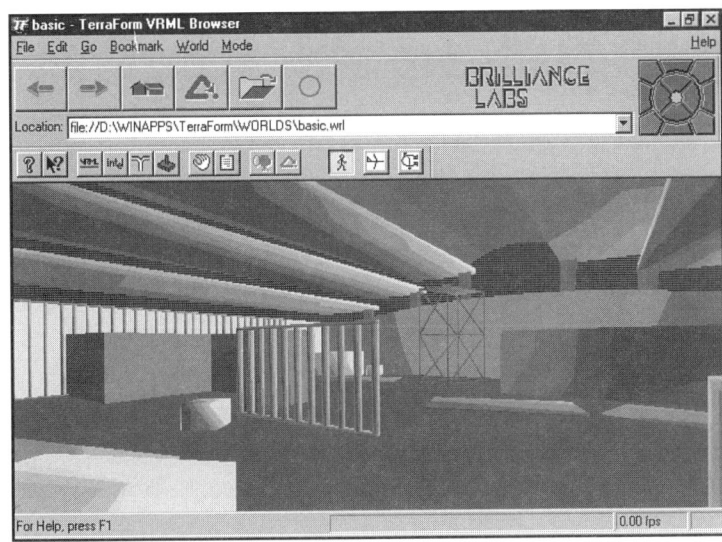

Microsoft's VRML Add-In for Internet Explorer

Despite its rather uninspiring name, Microsoft's VRML add-in is actually pretty good. The add-in uses RealityLab, originally developed by RenderMorphics in the United Kingdom. Microsoft bought RenderMorphics, and has released an updated RealityLab as Direct3D. Microsoft will eventually incorporate Direct3D into Windows itself.

Because it's an add-in for Internet Explorer, Microsoft's VRML software will not run with Netscape. This might be an obstacle for many users. Microsoft's future plans for the software are unclear; because its proposal for VRML 2.0 (which it calls ActiveVRML) lost out to Moving Worlds (see Chapter 13 for details), it remains to be seen whether Microsoft will fully embrace VRML 2.0 or shift support to its own proposal. Early indications are that Microsoft will do both; after all, the corporation isn't exactly short of development resources.

The VRML browser race will certainly be an interesting one in the next year or so. Netscape is certainly the most popular Web browser, so Live3D (Netscape's VRML browser) will make considerable inroads. However, Microsoft might bundle its Internet Explorer (and therefore its VRML browser) with future releases of Windows, which would put it on even more desktops. Perhaps by then it won't matter which VRML browser you run; in theory, all browsers should eventually interoperate perfectly.

Which Browser Should You Choose?

Each VRML browser has its own features and strengths, so no simple formula can help you make the best choice.

Live3D is the fastest VRML browser and, because it's integrated into Netscape, also the most widely used. WebSpace is the most "technically correct," but is also as slow as molasses. The multiuser browsers (CyberGate and Traveler) are necessary if you plan to explore worlds designed for them. VRweb includes complete source code, so you can learn how a browser works on the inside. VR Scout is a good compromise between thoroughness and speed.

If you need VRML 2.0 support immediately, CyberPassage currently is the only choice, although soon others will become available. WIRL has some neat animation features, Voyager runs on the Macintosh, and Liquid Reality is dynamically extensible. Ultimately, the choice is up to you.

Fortunately, all these browsers are available on the Web, so trying them all out doesn't cost you anything (aside from download time). Whatever decision you make, be sure to keep checking the Web sites occasionally to see whether there are any updates. VRML technology is moving very quickly, even compared to other Web software; by the time this book reaches the stores, a lot will have changed.

A good place to find links to VRML resources, software, and tools is the VRML Repository (**http://sdsc.edu/vrml**). If you're looking for a VRML browser, that site should be your first stop.

In any case, big changes are in the wings. Starting with VRML 2.0, new players might enter the market, and old ones might drop out. It will be a whole new ballgame, especially with the increasing availability of Microsoft RealityLab and 3-D graphics accelerators. The coming year will be an exciting one; now that you know who some of the major players are, you might want to dig in and start learning how to build worlds in VRML.

PART IV

Plug-Ins for Business Applications

- **15** Microsoft Office Online 321
- **16** Portable Documents 337
- **17** Communications Tools 351
- **18** Information and Navigational Tools 375
- **19** Programming Tools 397

CHAPTER 15

Microsoft Office Online

- What WordViewer can do for you
- Formula One/NET and spreadsheets
- Presentations with PointPlus
- Using PowerPoint files in your Web pages
- Quick View Plus for almost everything else

Despite the many advances of the Web, there are still many hurdles in front of it. One of them is that much of the legacy data—that is, preexisting data—isn't in HTML format. In many companies, the majority of the data is in Microsoft Office format instead.

Although there are a number of programs that will help you convert these files into HTML, they are still imperfect. Often mechanical, these converters simply convert existing data into predefined patterns. In complicated documents, this can result in subtle data loss, such as incorrect bullets or numbering. Fortunately, there are now plug-ins that enable you to view legacy data from within Netscape. While some of these plug-ins require you to convert to a new file format, the new format often has new features. ■

http://www.mcp.com/que

What WordViewer Can Do For You

Microsoft Word is one of the most popular word processing programs on the market. Word documents can contain anything from letters to press releases to term papers. Because Word is so widely used, a plug-in that views Word documents can be extremely handy.

Inso Corp. (**http://www.inso.com/**) fills this need with its WordViewer plug-in. This free plug-in enables you to view Microsoft Word 6.0 and Microsoft Word 7.0 documents directly in Netscape. Simply start up Netscape and click File, Open File, and you'll be presented with a file selection dialog box. Click the Files of Type drop-down list, and scroll down and find the new file type Microsoft Word 6 and 95. Locate the file you want to view, and WordViewer automatically displays it in the Netscape window. Figure 15.1 shows a Word file displayed in Netscape through the use of WordViewer.

FIG. 15.1
WordViewer enables Netscape to display Word documents in a Netscape window.

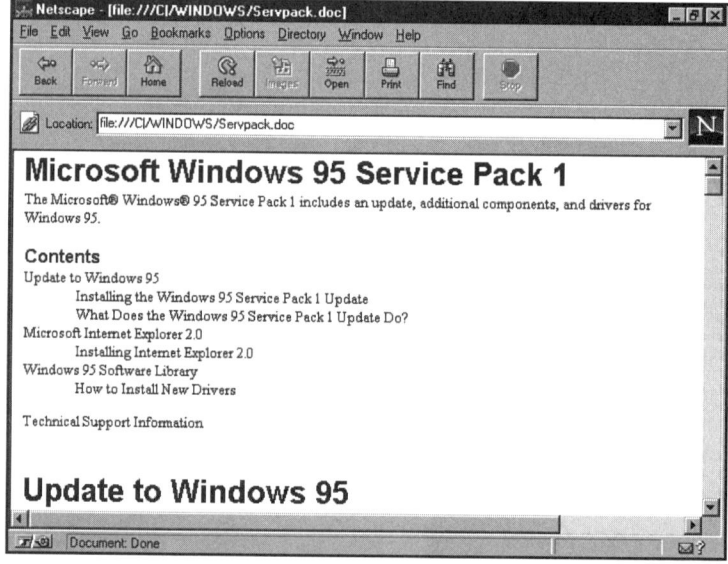

If your readers have the WordViewer plug-in, you should consider embedding Word documents in your Web pages with the proposed <EMBED> HTML tag. Simply use <EMBED>'s SRC attribute and specify the path to a Word document. The Word document will subsequently be displayed as part of the Web page itself, as shown in figure 15.2. You can also control the screen size to be used by the Word document by using the HEIGHT and WIDTH attributes for <EMBED>. These attributes use integer values to indicate the size in pixels for the corresponding direction.

FIG. 15.2
If your readers have WordViewer, you can embed existing Word documents into the Web pages they'll view.

Embedded Word document

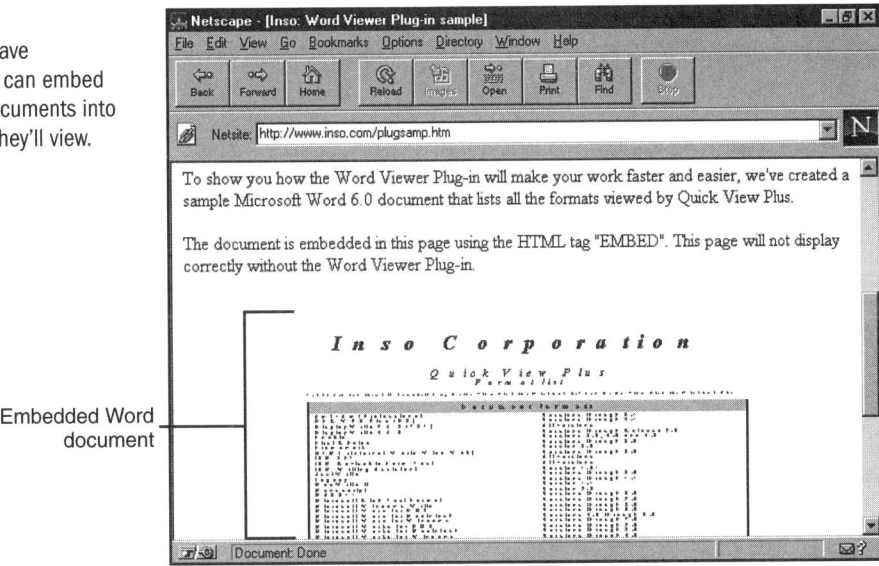

Formula One/NET and Spreadsheets

The Microsoft Excel spreadsheet is another widely used format. Spreadsheets enable you to manage large amounts of numbers easily. You can change the numbers, graph them, or move them around. Because of Microsoft Excel's popularity, its file format has become almost a standard format for spreadsheets. Visual Components (**http://www.visualcomp.com/**) has a Netscape plug-in, Formula One/NET, that enables you to view Excel-compatible spreadsheets, although you cannot view the spreadsheets directly. Many different versions of Formula One are available.

What Version of Formula One?

There are actually three different versions of Formula One, each with a different price tag.

The stand-alone program enables you to use complicated spreadsheet functionality in many programs. Because Formula One is significantly smaller than Microsoft Excel, this is an attractive alternative. In addition to all its features, Formula One enables you to import and export Excel spreadsheets directly. The full-fledged version of Formula One can be had for $249. For people interested in spreadsheet features, but not Excel's excessive size, this is a good option.

There is also a scaled down version of Formula One called Formula One/NET Pro. This Netscape plug-in offers the ability to create spreadsheets from within Netscape directly. It can be purchased for $79, and comes with a program that enables you to directly import and export Excel files. It also comes with complete online documentation, and the ability to add URLs to buttons. For those who only use a spreadsheet occasionally, this is a reasonably priced option.

The final version of Formula One is Formula One/NET, which is basically just a spreadsheet viewer. It can display only Visual Component's proprietary spreadsheet format. This file format is much more compact than Excel's, and allows for greater flexibility. This Netscape plug-in, while not able to create spreadsheets, is still a useful tool. It can be downloaded directly from Visual Components (**http://www.visualcomp.com/**) for free.

Embedding Spreadsheets in Web Pages

If you've used Formula One to create a custom Formula spreadsheet (VTS), it can be used in Web pages. (See the example in fig. 15.3.) This file can be embedded, like any other file format, by using the <EMBED> tag. Use this tag in exactly the same way as you'd use it to embed other types of file. You simply specify <EMBED>'s SRC attribute and assign it the path to the VTS file. Just like with any other embedded data, you can control the display size for the VTS file.

FIG. 15.3
Formula One/NET Pro enables you to easily embed Excel-compatible spreadsheets into Web pages.

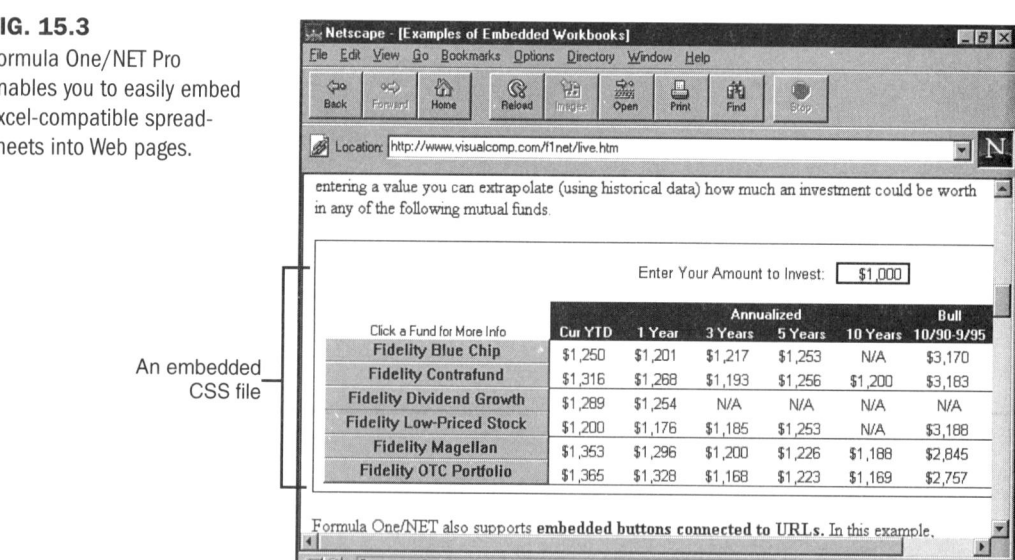

Formula One can embed URLs into buttons, making it possible to create "live" spreadsheets. You can create spreadsheets so that data entered can be relayed back to the Web server. This enables you to create Web pages with Formula One spreadsheets that can be dynamically changed. Not only can the data be updated automatically, but so can the associated buttons.

Presentations with PointPlus

PowerPoint is the business presentation component of Microsoft Office. It enables you to create slides and slide shows that you can use when making presentations, complete with transitions and sound effects. Although all this functionality is fine for corporate meetings, many developers need to incorporate PowerPoint presentations on the Internet. To fill this need, Net-Scene (**http://wwww.net-scene.com/**) offers PointPlus.

PointPlus, like Formula One, doesn't really make use of Microsoft Office file formats. Rather, it compresses an existing PowerPoint presentation, and corresponding support files, into a new file in a proprietary format. This new file format, the Compress Slide Show (CSS), creates files that are significantly smaller than the original PowerPoint files. The CSS format fully integrates sound and animation of slide show presentations into a Web page. Like other files, CSS files can be embedded into any Web page by using the <EMBED> tag. You can use PointPlus presentations for a variety of purposes, including animated advertisements on a Web page. PointPlus can be purchased for $299 directly from Net-Scene.

The PointPlug plug-in is completely free, and can display CSS files in a Netscape window (see fig. 15.4). When installed, it enables users to see automated slide shows in Netscape. The slides automatically cycle through their sequence; the reader does not have to press a button to advance them.

Microsoft provides a PowerPoint HTML converter, but PointPlug's capabilities are greater. Microsoft's converter simply converts each slide's graphic and generates an HTML file that will make use of it. It does not provide sound support, as PointPlug does. Companies that are assembling Web advertising, therefore, find PointPlug especially helpful. Instead of presenting a bland slide show of pretty pictures, they can create a live multimedia display.

FIG. 15.4
PointPlus enables you to embed animated slide shows into your Web page.

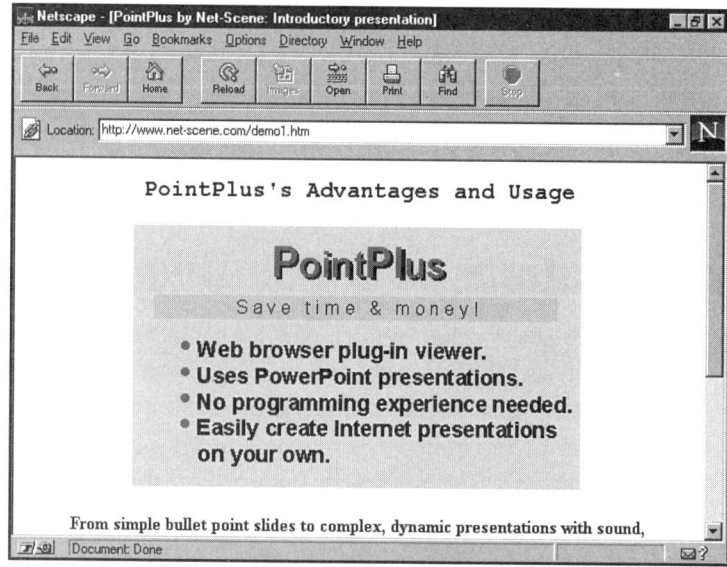

Using PowerPoint Files in Your Web Pages

If you want to use your original PowerPoint files in your Web pages, fear not. Microsoft has released a PowerPoint view plug-in. The plug-in displays only a new type of PowerPoint file, the PowerPoint Animation file (PPZ). Fortunately, you can easily create PowerPoint Animation files without any special programs. Although originally designed for Internet Explorer, the plug-in works fine with Netscape Navigator. You can get the plug-in directly from Microsoft by pointing your Web browser to the following address:

http://www.microsoft.com/mspowerpoint/internet/player/default.htm

Simply download the player and then install it on your system.

Creating PowerPoint Animation Files

The PowerPoint Animation Player, in addition to being a viewer plug-in, is also a file creator. When you install the plug-in, you also install a new PowerPoint function. PowerPoint 7.0 provides a new menu item under the File menu (see fig. 15.5). The new Export as PowerPoint Animation converts the currently loaded PowerPoint file into a new PPZ file.

FIG. 15.5
The PowerPoint Animation plug-in also adds functionality to PowerPoint 7.0.

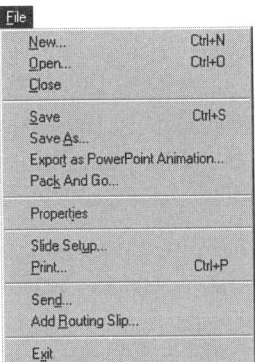

Viewing PowerPoint Animation Files

After creating a PowerPoint Animation file, you probably will want to incorporate it into your Web page. To include the PPZ file, you simply use the HTML <EMBED> tag, as you would any other special file format. When a user with Netscape and the plug-in encounters a page that includes such a file, the presentation's first slide is displayed (see fig. 15.6). To display the next slide, the user can right-click anywhere in the PowerPoint Animation file. To go to the previous slide, the user left-clicks the PPZ file and selects Previous from the popup menu.

FIG. 15.6
PowerPoint Animation files appear in the midst of other HTML elements.

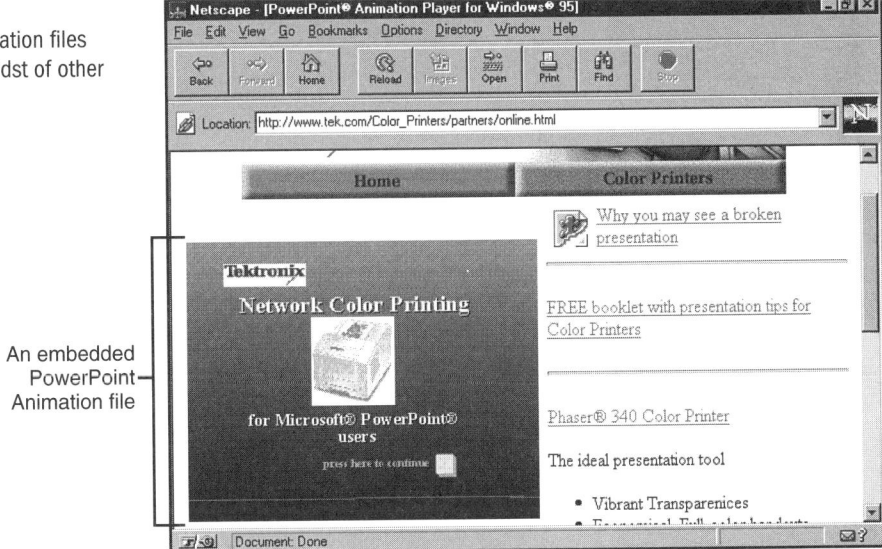

An embedded PowerPoint Animation file

Using Quick View Plus

Although there are plug-ins that target certain file formats, one plug-in aims for everything: Quick View Plus. This plug-in is available from Inso Corporation (**http://www.inso.com/**), the same people who brought you WordViewer, the Microsoft Word viewing plug-in discussed at the beginning of this chapter.

With all the different file formats out there, it's almost impossible to keep track of all of them. Quick View Plus tries to end all those problems by being a plug-in that will view over 200 different file formats. These formats range from graphics formats to spreadsheets to documents. It can read and display files in their native formats directly into the Netscape browser window (see fig. 15.7). This makes it incredibly useful for people who might be confused by all the different file formats around. This also makes it unnecessary to keep different programs that view different file formats. Perhaps the best feature of Quick View Plus is that it's absolutely free. Table 15.1 lists some of the more popular file formats that Quick View Plus supports.

FIG. 15.7
Quick View Plus enables you to view many file formats, such as this PowerPoint file, directly in Netscape.

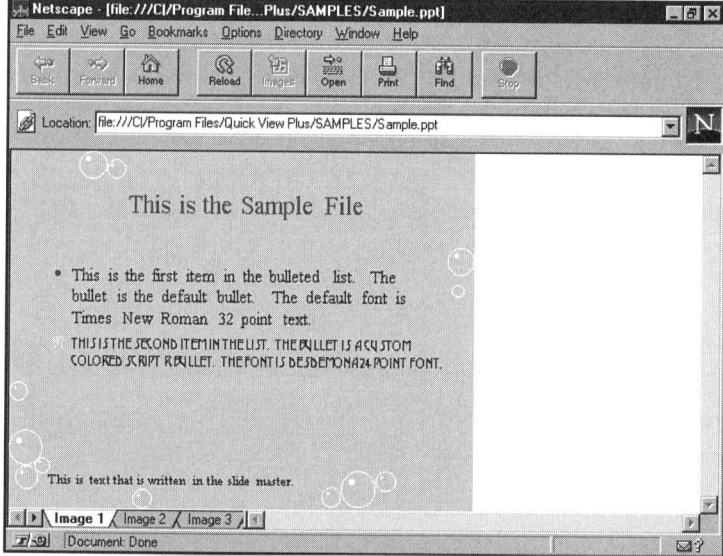

Table 15.1 Some File Formats That Quick View Plus Supports

File Type	Version Supported
Ami/Ami Pro	Up to 3.1
Computer Graphics Metafile	N/A
dBASE	Up to 5.0
Freelance for Windows	2.0
Harvard Graphics for DOS	2.0–3.0
HPGL (Hewlett-Packard Graphics Language)	2.0
Lotus 1-2-3 for DOS and Windows	Up to 5.0
MacPaint	N/A
Microsoft Access	Up to 2.0
Microsoft Excel for Macintosh	3.0–4.0
Microsoft Excel for Windows	2.2–7.0
Microsoft PowerPoint for Macintosh	Up to 4.0
Microsoft PowerPoint for Windows	Up to 7.0
Microsoft Word for Macintosh	4.0–6.0
Microsoft Word for Windows	Up to 7.0
Paradox for Windows	Up to 1.0
PCX (Paintbrush)	All
QuattroPro for Windows	Up to 6.0
TIFF	Up to 6
Truevision TGA (TARGA)	2.0
UNIX Compress	N/A
UNIX TAR	N/A
UNIX Uuencode	N/A
WordPerfect for Macintosh	1.02–3.0
WordPerfect for Windows	Up to 6.1
ZIP	Up to PKWARE 2.04g

NOTE When you load a UNIX-uuencoded file into Quick View Plus, the file is automatically decoded. That means that you will see only the decoded file.

Activating Quick View Plus

As with other plug-ins, the Quick View Plus plug-in can be activated in either of two methods. The most direct method is to simply have Netscape load in the file, and Quick View Plus will take care of the rest. It will display the desired file in a Netscape window. You can scroll through the file, and with some file formats, highlight portions of it. You can use this method by starting up Netscape and selecting File, Open File. You can find the file type you want in the Files of Type drop-down list. Next, locate the file you want to load, highlight it, and click the OK button. The Quick View Plus plug-in displays its banner while loading the file. After the plug-in finishes loading it, the file appears in the Netscape window.

 TIP By dragging and dropping files directly onto Netscape, you can make Quick View Plus load them automatically.

Another method of activating Quick View Plus occurs when Netscape encounters a file type that it supports embedded in an HTML document. Typically, as with other plug-in file formats, this embedding can be done with the proposed HTML <EMBED> tag. The SRC attribute must be specified and must point to an existing file. While the Web page is being loaded, if the embedded file is of a type that Quick View Plus knows, it'll be loaded. The embedded file won't be loaded in a separate window; instead, it'll be part of the current Web page (see fig. 15.8). As a result, with this plug-in, you can embed a much wider array of files directly into a Web page.

Exploring the Features of Quick View Plus

Quick View Plus would be a great plug-in even if all it did was provide more file format support. Fortunately, however, Inso Corp. has put in some extra features. One of the most important is that when viewing a file through Quick View Plus, you can right-click to open a menu of extra features. The features available change depending on the type of file loaded.

The simplest set of features comes when you load in spreadsheet files. All you can do with this format is copy highlighted cells onto the Clipboard and toggle the display of gridlines. If you load in a document file format, such as Windows Write or WordPerfect, you have a simple set of features available (see fig. 15.9) that enable you to print or copy the document. For example, suppose that you want to copy a portion of the document to the Clipboard. You would select the text with the left mouse button, right-click the text, and select Copy.

FIG. 15.8
With the Quick View Plus plug-in, your browser can view Web pages that embed files of any of its supported file formats, such as this Micrografix Draw file.

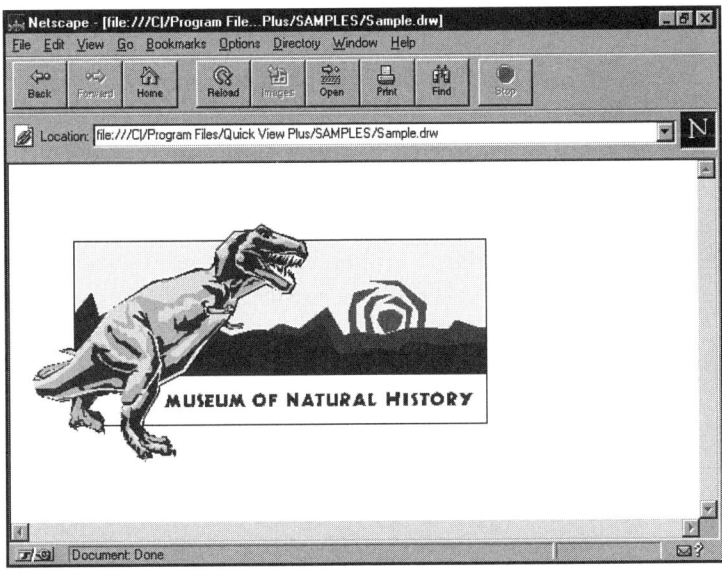

FIG. 15.9
When working with document files, you can right-click to open this menu.

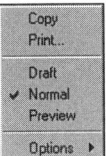

The same popup menu enables you to change the way that the document appears onscreen. The Draft mode displays the entire file in the default font (see the section "Configuring Quick View Plus"). The Default mode uses the formatting features specified in the file itself. The Preview mode indents the text and wraps lines at 50 characters.

Image file formats such as PCX and TIFF have many more features at your disposal. If the image loaded is larger than the Netscape window, you can use the scrollbars to view more of the picture. While an image is loaded, you can right-click to access some image manipulation tools (see fig. 15.10).

FIG. 15.10
A basic set of image manipulation tools is available for your use.

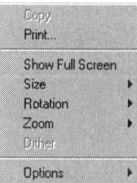

You can use the Show Full Screen option on the popup menu to show the image using the entire screen image. The Size menu heading lets you control how the image is displayed. You can also have it shown in its original size, fit to window, fit the window horizontally, or fit the window vertically. The Rotation menu options enable you to rotate the image by 90 degrees, 180 degrees, or 270 degrees. The Zoom menu options let you zoom in and out of the center of the displayed image. You can also reset the current zoom at any time. If the loaded image has allocated more colors than your display can support, the Dither menu option will be available.

N O T E Image rotation is done relative to the original image. That means that if you rotated the image by 90 degrees, you can't rotate it again by 90 degrees. ■

> **CAUTION**
> There is no limit to how much you can zoom into an image. Typically, however, after about zooming in 10 times, it becomes almost impossible to navigate. The Netscape scrollbars and sliders tend to move the display either too much or too little.

You can also move and copy portions of a graphic file displayed in Quick View Plus. Simply click and drag the left mouse button to specify a selection region. You can then right-click and select Copy to copy that portion to the Clipboard. Once on the Clipboard, the selected portion can be inserted into other programs. You can also have Quick View Plus zoom into the selected region.

N O T E Vector images and presentation files have a slightly different set of tools. You can't rotate the image, but you have a new image size option. This new option, the Stretch to Window option, forces the image to be as large as the window width. The difference between this option and the Fit to Window Width is that this option won't adjust the height of the image. ■

Configuring Quick View Plus

While Quick View Plus is a useful plug-in, there are times when you might not want it to activate. For example, if you have a preferred application to handle a certain file extension, you won't want Quick View Plus to get in its way. You can get a list of file extensions and their associations by going into the Quick View Plus directory. Next, go into the Support subdirectory and run Qvpmime to open the dialog box shown in figure 15.11. This dialog box enables you to easily add and remove MIME types, which programs use to discern a file type. When you highlight an existing MIME type, you can change Quick View Plus' behavior for that type.

FIG. 15.11
Quick View Plus comes with a utility to help you change the MIME types and their associated file.

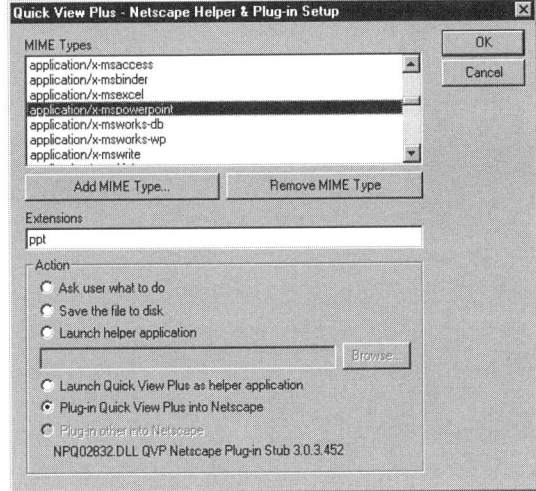

Another useful utility that comes with Quick View Plus is the Qvpsupp program, also in the Support folder. This program enables you to tweak its installation.

Its dialog box has three tabs. The Status tab gives you information on the current state of Quick View Plus. This is often blank, with errors appearing at the bottom of the dialog box. You can also have Quick View Plus verify its own installation by clicking the Verify tab. Clicking the Verify button starts a series of checks to see whether Quick View Plus is installed correctly. If there are any problems, they will be listed, and you can have the program fix the problem.

The final tab, Program, enables you to hook Quick View Plus into some other programs (see fig. 15.12). When you first install Quick View Plus, it scans your hard disk system for the four programs. If it finds any of them, it allows you to enable or disable a setup to Quick View Plus. If you install one of these programs after installing Quick View Plus, you can have it look for the new program. Simply highlight the program and click the Scan button. You can also remove Quick View Plus from any of the four programs simply by clicking the check box next to it.

FIG. 15.12
Quick View Plus can be made to look for one of the supported programs at any time.

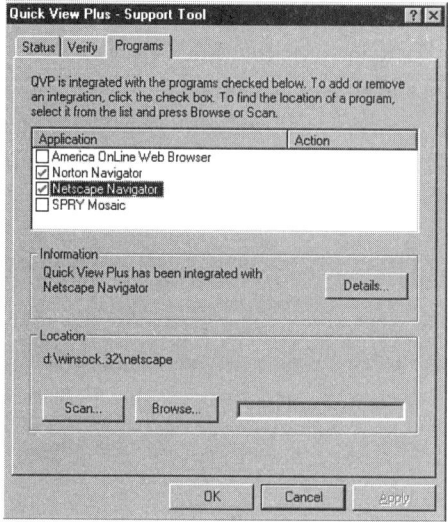

> **CAUTION**
> It's impossible to configure Quick View Plus so that it doesn't scan for two of the supported four programs: Norton Navigator and SPRY Mosaic. Similarly, you cannot get Quick View Plus to uninstall from the same two programs. Quick View Plus automatically looks for and hooks into Navigator and Mosaic.

Quick View Plus also enables you to easily configure how text is handled. When you load in any file that Quick View Plus supports, you can right-click to open a popup menu. This menu contains an Options menu item at the bottom. When you select Options, a submenu appears from which you can configure the properties for the display, printer, or the Clipboard.

The Display menu option lets you change the default font, which is used when you want the text displayed in "Draft" mode. You can also specify what type of font should be used for unknown files. The Print menu option allows you to configure how printouts appear. You can also specify the font the printer should use when printing out a loaded document file. The last configurable option is the Clipboard option (see fig. 15.13). This option lets you determine how supported file formats will be placed on the Clipboard. Simply click the check box next to the file format that you want to be able to put on the Clipboard.

FIG. 15.13
You can tell Quick View Plus the file formats for which it should provide Clipboard support.

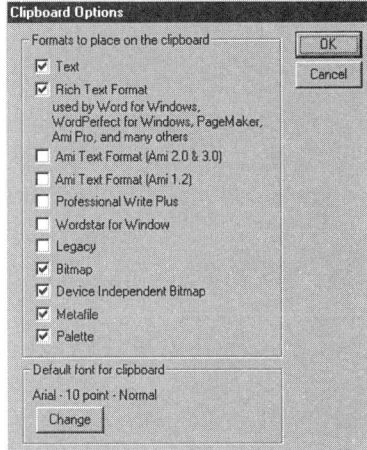

CHAPTER 16

Portable Documents

- Viewing Acrobat files
- Creating Acrobat files
- Viewing Envoy files
- Creating Envoy files
- Using Techexplorer to view TeX files
- Creating TeX files

Although many file formats will work on most machines, there are always exceptions to the rule. Some file formats simply cannot be read on all platforms. This is especially true on the Macintosh platform, for which there are different methods of storing data at the operating system (OS) level. Also, in HTML, the representation of data isn't necessarily consistent; depending on their HTML browser's configuration, one user could see the same information differently than another user. Consequently, it's possible to have data of a common file type that is nevertheless not readable on other computers. As a result, some companies have started creating "portable documents." These are documents, that by design, will work on any computer that has a corresponding viewer. This makes portable documents very similar in nature to Web pages. ■

http://www.mcp.com/que

Adobe Acrobat

Many years ago, Adobe Systems, Inc. (**http://www.adobe.com/**) created a printing language known as PostScript. This language has become the one of the most widely used languages that can be found in printers. The PostScript language defines a printed page layout. A PostScript file sent to any Postscript printer will come out the same regardless of computer platform or printer maker.

Acrobat is an attempt by Adobe to strike gold twice, by creating a graphical display format. Acrobat has met with limited success by becoming popular in some large businesses. Unfortunately, it's still largely unused and ignored by most end users. However, because of its strong corporate presence, it's still a useful format. While the actual programs available to create Acrobat files (PDF) are expensive, a program that reads Acrobat files (Acrobat Reader) is free.

Previous versions of Acrobat Reader were stand-alone programs that simply displayed a PDF file. The problem with it was that the end user had to download the actual PDF file to be read, and then open Acrobat Reader separately to read it. Nowadays, however, users can simply install an Acrobat plug-in and read Acrobat files directly in their Web browsers.

The Adobe Acrobat Reader plug-in enables you to view PDF files directly in a Netscape Window (see fig. 16.1). The plug-in offers many of the same features found in the full Acrobat Reader program. With the plug-in, you have access to the toolbar options but not the menu items. This enables you to navigate through a PDF file, but not fully utilize it. You can't view the PDF file in the full screen, configure the behavior of the plug-in, or utilize other minor features.

The full version of Acrobat Reader is actually a part of the plug-in installation, so it's already installed on your system if the plug-in is installed. You can preview an Acrobat file with the plug-in, and if you like it, you can have Netscape save it as a regular PDF file, and then load it into the full Acrobat Reader later.

Navigating around Acrobat Reader

The Acrobat Reader plug-in will activate only when you load in a PDF file into Netscape. If a Web author has integrated an Acrobat file into his Web page (with the <EMBED> HTML tag), the plug-in won't fully kick in. You see the first page of the Acrobat file in the Netscape window, but you cannot navigate through it (see fig. 16.2). You have to click the Acrobat object to load it into Netscape (as shown in fig. 16.1). This might seem a little awkward because the plug-in has its own toolbar.

Adobe Acrobat

FIG. 16.1
The Adobe Acrobat Reader plug-in lets you view Acrobat files from within Netscape.

FIG. 16.2
Acrobat files that are embedded into Web pages only show the first page.

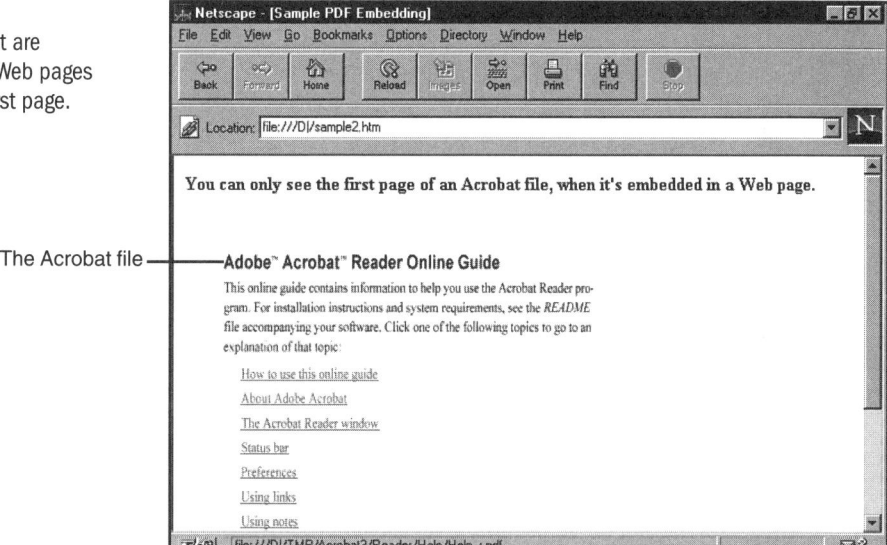

The top toolbar (see table 16.1) is pretty much the same toolbar that's in the regular Acrobat Reader program. The notable icon missing is the Search button. The Netscape searching facility won't work on an Acrobat file because it's not a text or HTML file. There is also a toolbar at the bottom of the plug-in, just like in the stand-alone Reader program. The plug-in bottom toolbar (see table 16.2) behaves just like the one in the Adobe Reader program. Because the plug-in is embedded within Netscape, none of the familiar Acrobat Reader keystrokes work in the plug-in.

Table 16.1 The Acrobat Reader Plug-In Toolbar Is Almost Identical to the Stand-Alone Program

Icon	Purpose
	Displays only the page, but not any Adobe bookmarks or thumbnails.
	Displays the page and the Adobe bookmarks.
	Displays the page and thumbnails for each page.
	Switches to the hand tool. When you're zoomed into a region of the page, you can scroll through the page with the hand. The hand is also useful when you're viewing more than just one page.
	Zooms into a specified region on the page.
	Enables you to highlight a region of text on the page. Currently, there is no facility to copy the region onto the Clipboard with the plug-in.
	Moves to the first page.
	Moves to the page immediately before this one.
	Moves to the page immediately after this one.
	Moves to the last page.
	Moves to the previously displayed page.
	Moves to the next displayed page.
	Displays the document at 100 percent of its size.
	Fits the current view into the size of the window.

Icon	Purpose
	Fits the current view into the width of the window.
	Jumps to the previous highlight.
	Jumps to the next highlight.
Page 2	Displays the current page that you're viewing. When you click it, you can specify the page you want to view.
76 %	Displays the current magnification. You can change the magnification by clicking this button. You can specify a custom value, or choose from a predefined list of values.
	Indicates the display method being used. You can click the button to change the display method. You can have the plug-in show you only the current page, all the pages in a single column, or all the pages in double-column format.

The general navigation of a PDF file is pretty intuitive—simply use the scrollbars to move around. Hypertext links are underlined in red. If you click one, you jump to another part of the PDF document. Part of the Acrobat Reader plug-in navigation is dependent on the current view settings. For example, if you're viewing only one page at a time, the vertical scrollbar will jump you by entire pages. If you're viewing all pages in a single column, the vertical scrollbar will enable you to view parts of adjoining pages.

Using Acrobat Files

As with any custom file type, you can make use of an Acrobat file either by embedding it into a Web page or by making a link to it.

As with most other file formats, you can easily use the <EMBED> tag to make a PDF file part of the Web page. However, it's usually best to avoid doing this. Whenever a PDF file is encountered—in a Web page or a separate file—the plug-in activates. But as you just saw, if the PDF file is embedded in the document, the reader can't read all of it immediately—he must click it to open it in its own window first. This is an annoying extra step.

A better use of PDF files is to create a link for them (see fig. 16.3). Simply use the standard A HREF convention to point to a PDF file. This enables the entire PDF file to be loaded, and the user activates the plug-in only when he really needs to. This is also useful because not everybody is running on the fastest system possible. When the Acrobat Reader plug-in first activates, a banner displays some details about the plug-in. By simply using a link, you know that the user will want to view the banner, your PDF file, and can navigate through it. If you were to embed the file to put an Acrobat file in your Web page, the introductory banner would display all the time. Regardless of whether the user is interested in that file, the Acrobat Reader would start up.

FIG. 16.3
If you want to use PDF files in your Web pages, make them available through hypertext links.

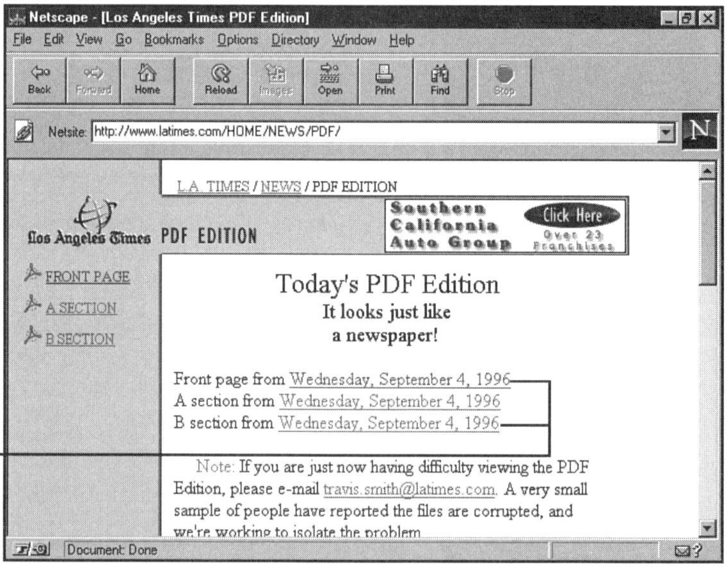

Hypertext links to Acrobat files

Creating Acrobat Files

If you purchase Acrobat from Adobe directly, you can create your own Acrobat files. Acrobat retails for $295 for a single-user license, or $1,595 for 10 user licenses. Acrobat enables you to create PDF files from popular word processors, business applications, or desktop publishing tools. Creating portable documents is as easy as printing a file in one of those programs.

Envoy

Envoy by Novell Corporation (**http://www.novell.com/**) is a file format similar to PDF. It was designed by Tumbleweed Software (**http://www.twcorp.com/**), the company that continues to develop it. Envoy offers the same capabilities as Acrobat, but its data files are smaller. Like Acrobat, Envoy is marketed toward the business community as an easy method of distributing documents. Also like Acrobat, Envoy's documents can be displayed on any platform that has an Envoy viewer.

The Envoy viewer plug-in enables you to view Envoy documents from within Netscape (see fig. 16.4). Unlike the Acrobat Reader, the plug-in comes with a sufficient number of features. The Envoy viewer plug-in transparently and automatically handles any Envoy documents (EVY). It doesn't matter whether the documents are embedded in a Web page or as separate files—the plug-in takes care of displaying them.

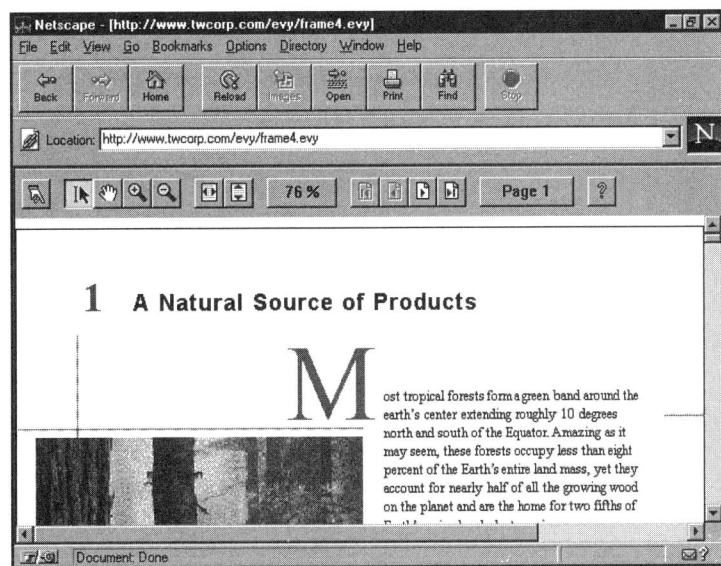

FIG. 16.4
The Envoy viewer plug-in enables you to view Envoy documents without a separate program.

Using the Envoy Plug-In

The Envoy plug-in is very easy and straightforward to use. When you load in an Envoy document through Netscape, you'll get the entire document in the Netscape window. There will also be an Envoy toolbar (see table 16.2) across the top of the document. The toolbar offers a basic set of image-manipulation tools.

Table 16.2 The Toolbar for the Envoy Viewer Plug-In

Icon	Purpose
	Finds a text string in the current Envoy document.
	Activates the selection tool. When you use this tool, you can either highlight some text or specify a region on an image. You can copy the selected portion directly onto the Windows 95 Clipboard.

continues

Table 16.2 Continued

Icon	Description
(hand)	Activates the hand tool. This tool enables you to scroll around an Envoy document that's larger than the current window.
(zoom in)	Zoom In. This button enables you to specify a region on the document, and zoom into it.
(zoom out)	Zoom Out. This button zooms you out of the current view.
(fit width)	Forces Envoy to fit the document within the width of the Netscape window.
(fit height)	Forces Envoy to fit the document within the height of the Netscape window.
76 %	Indicates a percentage describing the current zoom factor for the document. You can change the zoom factor by clicking this button and selecting from a predefined list of values.
(first page)	Moves to the first page in the document.
(previous page)	Moves to the previous page in the document.
(next page)	Moves to the next page in the document.
(last page)	Moves to the last page in the document.
Page 2	Identifies the page that you're currently viewing. You can go to a specific page by clicking this button and entering a value.
(help)	The help button. Tries to access Tumbleweed Software's online documentation.

When an Envoy document is embedded in a Web page, the Web author can control its interface. He can, for instance, disable the toolbar. Fortunately, if the toolbar is missing, you can access its functions with just a mouse. Simply right-click the Envoy document to open a popup menu that offers the same functions as the toolbar. The only new function on the popup menu is the ability to open the Envoy document in a full window.

Envoy and Web Pages

As previously mentioned, the Envoy viewer plug-in can take care of both stand-alone Envoy documents and embedded documents. Therefore, unlike with Acrobat, both are viable options, and there is no performance difference between the two.

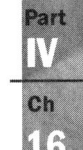

The most straightforward method of using the plug-in is to have Netscape simply load in an Envoy document. This method displays the document in the entire Netscape window. The Envoy toolbar appears at the top of the document window. You can navigate through the document by using the mouse and toolbar or popup menu.

Another method of using Envoy documents is to embed them directly in your Web page. This can easily be done by using the proposed <EMBED> tag. This tag, when used with the SRC attribute pointing to an Envoy document, puts the Envoy file directly in the Web page. It effectively becomes part of the Web page, seamlessly integrated. If you specify no other attributes, aside from the screen dimension for the Envoy file, the document appears as part of the Web page (see fig. 16.5). You can also specify custom attributes to be used by the Envoy file. Table 16.3 lists common HTML attributes for Envoy documents, what they do, and their acceptable values. These attributes *must* be used within the <EMBED> tag. Figure 16.6 shows you what an embedded Envoy document looks like with the entire interface enabled.

FIG. 16.5
When you embed an Envoy document as you would any other document, the document will look like everything else on the Web page.

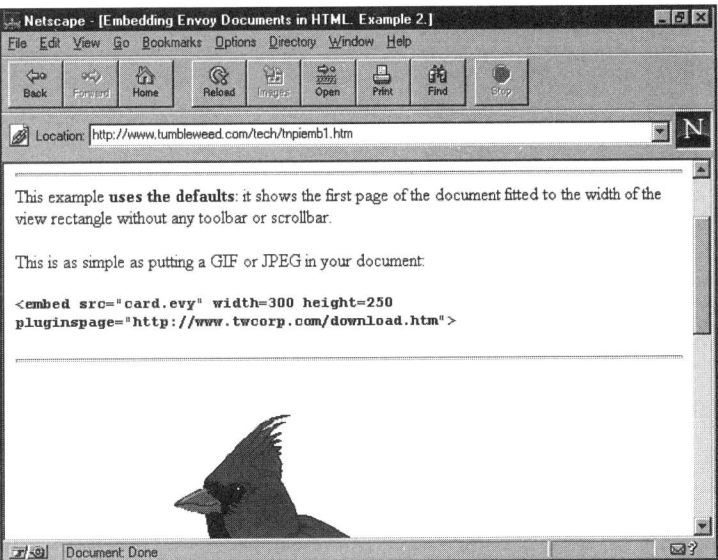

FIG. 16.6
You can add the viewer's interface to an Envoy document.

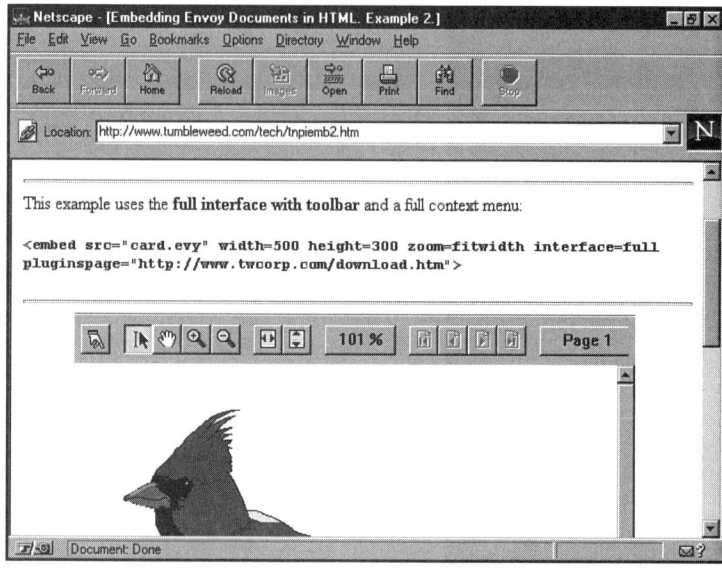

Table 16.3 HTML Attributes for Envoy Documents

Attribute	Function	Values
interface	Specifies the default interface to be used by Envoy.	Full (toolbar and scrollbar), Scroll (scrollbar only), Static (no toolbar or scrollbar, limited right mouse button menu).
page	Specifies which page number will be the first one displayed.	Any integer value for the page to be displayed.
bookmark	Specifies an Envoy bookmark to be used when the document is opened.	An Envoy bookmark name.

Attribute	Function	Values
zoom	Specifies how the display Envoy page should be fitted, or a specific zoom factor.	fitwidth (fits width of window), fitheight (fits height of window), fitpage fits entire page into (window), integer_value (starting zoom value)

Creating Envoy Documents

You can create Envoy documents by purchasing Envoy from Tumbleweed Software. For a limited time, the full-fledged Envoy creation program costs only $49. As with Acrobat, you can use whatever program you want to create the actual document. To make it into an Envoy document, you simply print the file to the Envoy print driver. This creates an Envoy document that you can embed in your Web pages or distribute.

Techexplorer

IBM's Techexplorer plug-in enables users to use a Web browser to view TeX documents. The plug-in interprets most TeX commands and macros automatically and displays them onscreen correctly. Techexplorer dynamically formats and displays documents coded in TeX and LaTeX. It provides support for a large subset of TeX and LaTeX. IBM has chosen a subset of TeX tags that it feels are essential for publishing documents electronically.

Before obtaining and installing techexplorer, you must create a temporary directory. To get a copy of Techexplorer, you first point Netscape to the following address:

    http://www.ics.raleigh.ibm.com/ics/techexp.htm

Then click Download Techexplorer Now Hypertext Link. A Web page registration form displays. Fill in your personal information and select the product to download. After you finish entering your information, click the button at the bottom of page. Simply select the Techexplorer plug-in and download it to the temporary directory. The Techexplorer plug-in is about 1M.

After downloading the entire file, exit Netscape. Then double-click the file that you just downloaded; this extracts the file's contents to the temporary directory. Next, double-click the SETUP.EXE file. The Techexplorer installation program displays. Simply specify the Netscape plug-ins directory to install Techexplorer in that directory. After the installation, you can restart Netscape. Now, whenever you access a TeX document, or access a Web page with a TeX document, Techexplorer interprets the contents.

What Is TeX?

Before Acrobat and Envoy, there was a file format called TeX. TeX actually predates many desktop publishing programs and popular operating systems. The file format was originally written by Donald Knuth, a computing legend and professor emeritus at Stanford University. TeX enables users to typeset documents accurately and consistently. Even if you print a TeX file on different computers and different printers, the output always looks the same.

Through the years, many extensions to TeX have been made. The most popular extension is LaTeX, a set of macros written in TeX. LaTeX was created to simplify TeX's typesetting aspects. Using LaTeX, you can focus more on the document's content rather than the layout.

TeX is especially well suited for presenting mathematical symbols in a document.

Using Techexplorer To View TeX Files

After installing Techexplorer, you can view TeX and LaTeX files with Netscape. Whenever you access a file with the .TEX extension, the Techexplorer plug-in kicks in (see fig. 16.7). You can thus use Netscape as a general-purpose TeX viewer program. The plug-in also activates if you access a Web page with an embedded TeX file.

Techexplorer also comes with a fair number of configurable options. When you are viewing a TeX document, simply right-click in some unoccupied region of the document. Then select Techexplorer Options. You can control the appearance of various components and TeX tags by clicking the tabs across the top of the dialog box. For example, to change the fonts used to render TeX tags, you can click the Fonts tab (see fig. 16.8).

FIG. 16.7
You can view TeX documents directly in Netscape with the Techexplorer plug-in.

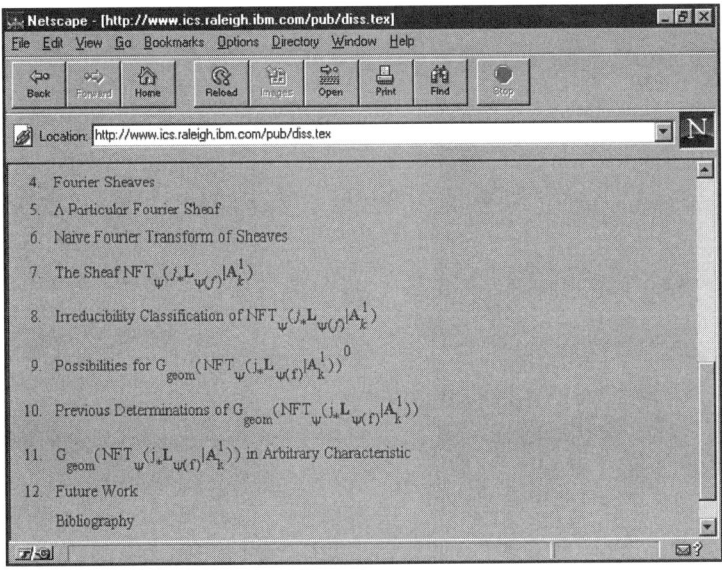

FIG. 16.8
You can configure the fonts that Techexplorer will use to render various TeX tags.

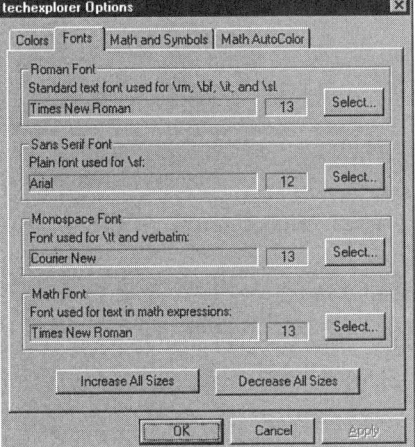

Creating TeX Files

A TeX file is quite similar to an HTML file—it's really just a plain text file. All that matters is the content of the text file and the tags used. Unfortunately, unlike HTML, TeX is rather complicated and cryptic. However, unlike many modern desktop publishing systems, TeX enables users to create impressive documents with a slow computer and a plain text display. Therefore, no matter how limited your computer system is, if you know TeX, you can create documents that match many desktop publishing products. ●

CHAPTER 17

Communications Tools

- Use ichat to communicate both over Ichat servers and standard IRC servers
- Use Look@Me to view presentations on another user's PC
- Run Carbon Copy/Net in guest mode to view and control another user's PC
- Run Carbon Copy/Net in host mode to enable other users to view and control your PC

Netscape is ripe with plug-in communications tools that extend your reach over the Internet. In real time, Netscape mostly offers only one-way communications—you use Netscape to view the contents of Web pages. Regardless of whether those pages contain text, graphics, animation, or sound, real-time communication still flows mostly one way—from the Web site to your PC.

The Netscape plug-ins described in this chapter—ichat, Look@Me, and Carbon Copy/Net—allow actual, real-time, two-way communications between you and another Internet user, albeit in three different methods. ■

http://www.mcp.com/que

ichat

The ichat plug-in makes connections possible to most of the Internet's chat resources, including ichat's Web-integrated servers and most standard IRC servers (see fig. 17.1). Although many non-plug-in chat solutions exist, ichat is unique in that it enables a Web site's visitors to chat in real time with other visitors. Other chat programs require users leave the Web to launch a text-only IRC chat client application. ichat's integrated approach is more user-friendly and more capable than previous chat applications.

FIG. 17.1
ichat's interface provides connections to most Internet chat resources.

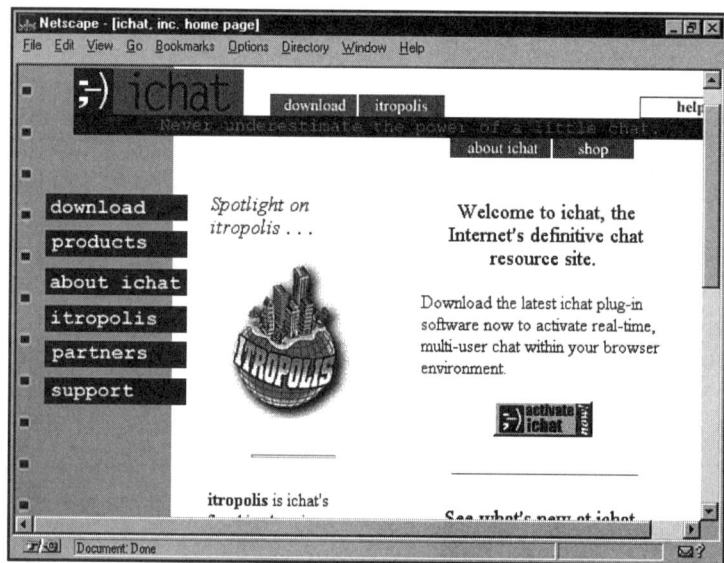

Why Use ichat?

By adding real-time, two-way communications to a Web site, ichat transforms the site from a static display of information and entertainment into an interactive chat-session site. With ichat, when users visit a chat-enabled Web site, they can communicate with each other, and possibly also discuss the contents of the site and exchange ideas about information found on the site. In short, the ichat plug-in enables users to become a part of a small community when visiting a chat-enabled Web site.

ichat also enables Web administrators and users to act as tour guides on the Web. With this feature, Web administrators can employ humans or automated robots to educate new users as to the value and location of services and products on a site. Individual users might also use this feature to show friends, family, and colleagues new points of interest on the Web—all while continuing to chat.

ichat also offers unique tools for business users. To save travel and time expenses, many people, both on- and offsite, can meet together on a company Web site in a specially arranged conference room. Within this room, conference participants can review and discuss materials ranging from weekly sales targets to human resources policies to technical design. Administrators can record and save these conversations for a variety of purposes.

ichat also provides a great technical support system. Users can surf a company Web site—with either a friend, fellow user, or company representative—to find the solution to a problem. By integrating chat into their Web site, manufacturers simplify life for these users by providing a single, easy-to-find place for toll-free technical support.

Installing ichat

To begin the installation, connect to ichat's home page:

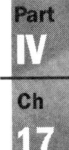

   http://www.ichat.com

Then click the *download* link to move to the download area. The download page contains several versions of ichat for various platforms, including Windows 95 and Macintosh. (These versions also operate under Windows NT and Macintosh PowerPC, respectively.) To download, simply click the link for the version of ichat appropriate to your machine.

From this point, installation varies depending on the platform.

> **CAUTION**
> When you install ichat or any Netscape plug-in, make sure that you exit Netscape before installing the plug-in, and don't restart Netscape until you have completed the installation. Netscape loads installed plug-ins at startup, so unless you restart Netscape after installing a plug-in, it will not operate.

Installing ichat on a Macintosh   If you are using a Macintosh, Netscape automatically downloads to your desktop a compressed version of the plug-in. Typically, Macintosh-downloaded files have the extension .HQX. If you are using a 28.8K modem, this process should last about five to six minutes.

After downloading the plug-in, Netscape automatically runs another program, StuffIt, to decode and decompress the plug-in. This process usually takes less than a minute. When StuffIt finishes, three files are present on your desktop: the original downloaded file with the .HQX extension, an intermediate self-extracting archive with the extension .SEA, and the actual plug-in, now ready for use with Netscape Navigator.

Because Netscape recognizes only those plug-ins present when the browser starts up, you need to exit Netscape and return to the desktop before working with these files. Locate the plug-in (it looks like a puzzle piece and might be in a folder with a README file), then click and drag it into the PLUGINS folder located inside the Netscape Navigator folder. Typically, the Navigator folder is within the Applications folder on your hard drive. After completing this step, delete the original downloaded and intermediate file to clean up your desktop. On restarting, Netscape automatically recognizes the newly available ichat plug-in.

Installing ichat for Windows 95 Windows 95 users install ichat a bit differently. You download the ichat plug-in into a temporary directory. The downloaded file, ICNP200.EXE, is a self-extracting archive file that automatically starts the install wizard to install ichat on your PC. To install ichat, follow the prompts. Make sure that you exit Netscape if you have it running. After the installation, you restart Netscape so that it can recognize the newly installed plug-in.

Using ichat

Whether you have installed ichat for Windows 95 or Macintosh, you are now ready to use your new plug-in.

ichat supports connections to both ichat and IRC servers. To connect to an ichat server, just visit a Web site running ichat; the plug-in connects automatically. The best source of these Web sites is ichat itself. A directory of these servers is available on ichat's Web site:

   http://www.ichat.com

If all else fails, connect to one of the most popular Web chat sites, Treasure Quest (see fig. 17.2). You can find this site at the following address:

   http://www.treasurequest.com

Treasure Quest is popular because it's not just a Web chat site. It is also a game with a $1 million prize to the first user who can solve the puzzle.

Creating a User As with all chat systems, ichat, for security purposes, requires that visitors log in. *Logging in* is the process of identifying yourself by name (or pseudonym) and password. By authenticating users who attempt to log in, administrators can prevent unauthorized visitors from participating in conversations.

First-time visitors must create a user. Typically, sites open to the public provide a link labeled, simply enough, Create User. Clicking this link displays a form that usually requires only that the visitor choose a username and password. Figure 17.3 shows a typical user-creation form.

FIG. 17.2
The Treasure Quest Web chat site is also a strategy/puzzle with a $1 million prize.

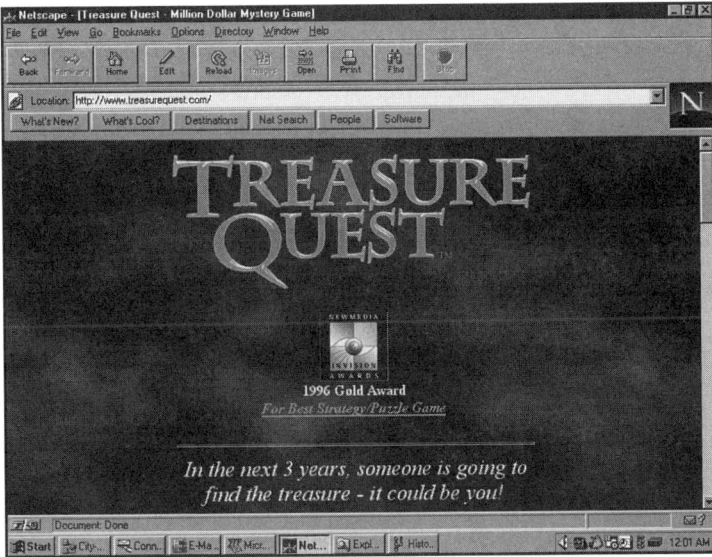

FIG. 17.3
A typical user-creation form.

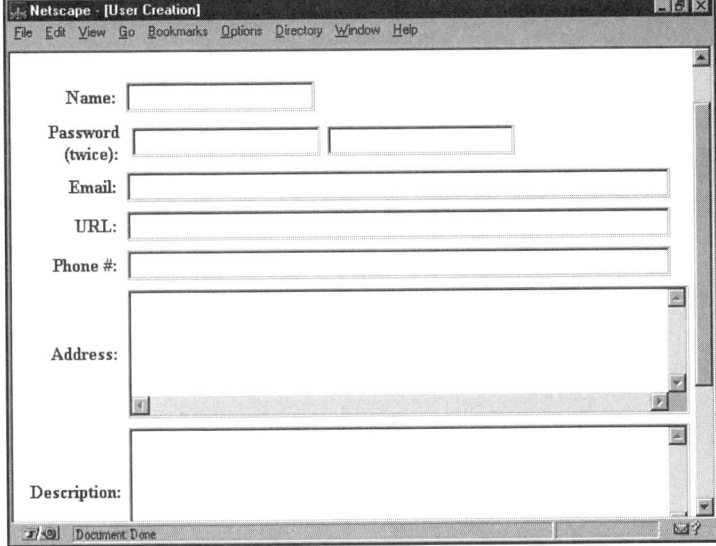

Depending on the site, some administrators might require additional information, such as an actual name, telephone number, or address. Although good netiquette admonishes administrators from publishing this information, the general rule in such matters is that you should not provide any information that you would not want to be known to the public. After creating a user, you can enter the site thereafter by clicking the Enter link and typing at the prompt the username and password that you just created.

Exploring ichat's User Interface   After logging in, the ichat plug-in opens a frame in the lower portion of the Netscape browser (see fig. 17.4). Within that frame, the plug-in displays a real-time conversation among visitors to the site. Above the frame, Netscape continues to display the Web site itself. ichat is the only plug-in that enables users to chat while surfing a Web site.

FIG. 17.4
Because ichat splits your screen with a frame, you can continue surfing a Web site as you chat.

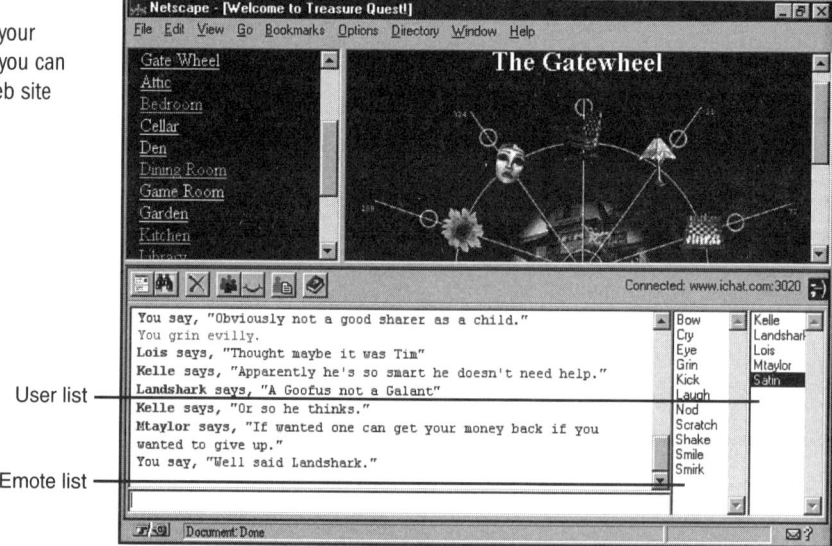

> **N O T E**   Many of the features described in this section (such as the emote list and the capabilities to position frames and to surf while chatting) are available in ichat only when you are logged in to an ichat Web site/server. Most of these features are not available when you are using ichat in a standard IRC chat server.

Within the ichat frame, the right side displays a list of users who are chatting. Next to this list is an "emote" list of actions such as laugh, smile, bow, and shake. These actions enable you to add some context to your messages. Using the emote list is more than a little addictive. You learn more about the actions later in this chapter.

Sending Public Messages   The largest area within the ichat frame is the conversation text area (see fig. 17.5). This area is where the conversation takes place. Typed messages are delivered as they are sent, with a name attached to identify the chatter. To join the conversation, click your mouse in the text box below the conversation. This places your cursor in the text box.

FIG. 17.5
You enter your chat comments within the conversation text box.

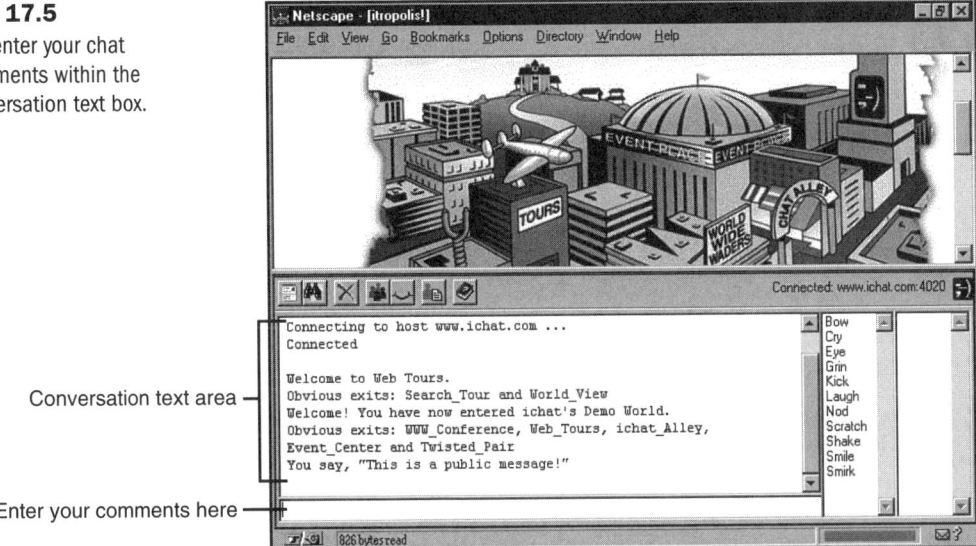

Conversation text area

Enter your comments here

Now type your message. Pressing Enter sends your message immediately. Your message then appears in the conversation text area. Suppose, for example, that you entered the following message:

Hello everyone, are we ready to go over today's agenda?

Other users will see the same message from their own perspective. If your name is Sam, for example, other users see the message as follows:

Sam says, "Hello everyone, are we ready to go over today's agenda?"

Sending Private Messages You can also send private messages that only you and the message's recipient can view. Sending a private message is simple. If you are using Windows 95, you left-click to highlight the recipient's name from the user list, and then right-click the user list.

A list of options appears, including Send Private Message. Selecting this option displays a dialog box. Type your text and then press Enter to send your message.

Suppose that Sam sends the following private message to Beth:

Does Janet know about the proposed merger?

Private messages are colored differently than public messages onscreen so that you can quickly and easily distinguish them.

> **Sending Private Messages under Macintosh**
>
> To view the user list under Macintosh, right-click the Option key. This combination usually makes available any function that you can choose from the context-sensitive popup menu that displays when you right-click in Windows 95.
>
> Navigator for the Macintosh does not support dialog boxes. As a result, private messages are sent slightly differently than under Windows. You first type the private message, then choose the recipient and the private message option from the user list. Macintosh then sends the private message.

Displaying Emotions   ichat also enables you to add context and richness to your conversations through the use of actions and emotions.

> **CAUTION**
>
> Remember, ichat's emote list is operational only when you are logged in to a server configured as an ichat Web chat/server. The emote list is not available when you are logged in to a standard IRC chat server.

By double-clicking any of the actions and emotions in the emote list next to the user list, you indicate a generalized emotion or action to others in the chat room. For example, if Sam clicks Bow, ichat sends the message, "Sam bows gracefully."

You can also direct emotions and actions toward specific users. This is a two-step process. First, left-click the action and recipient from the two lists. Then right-click the user list area. A popup menu will appear to direct the emotion. Sam, for example, could specify that "Sam bows before Janet gracefully." Consequently, Janet would see the message "Sam bows before you gracefully." Figure 17.6 shows the popup menu and other possible commands that you can enter.

You can also create completely new and more complex emotions or actions. Typing a colon as the first character of your message appends to your name the text that follows. Suppose that Sam enters the following in the command line:

> **:glances left and right before leaping into the air and flying away.**

The other users see the following message:

```
Sam glances left and right before leaping into the air and flying away.
```

Using Embedded Hyperlinks   By right-clicking the command line, you display the Insert URL dialog box (see fig. 17.7). In this dialog box, you can create on-the-fly hyperlinks to other sites on the Web. A word, phrase, or even an entire paragraph of text can become a hyperlink to another Web site. By clicking the link, a user can visit another Web site in the top frame while continuing to chat in the bottom frame with other chatters on the originating Web site.

FIG. 17.6
ichat enables you to direct your actions and emotions toward specific users.

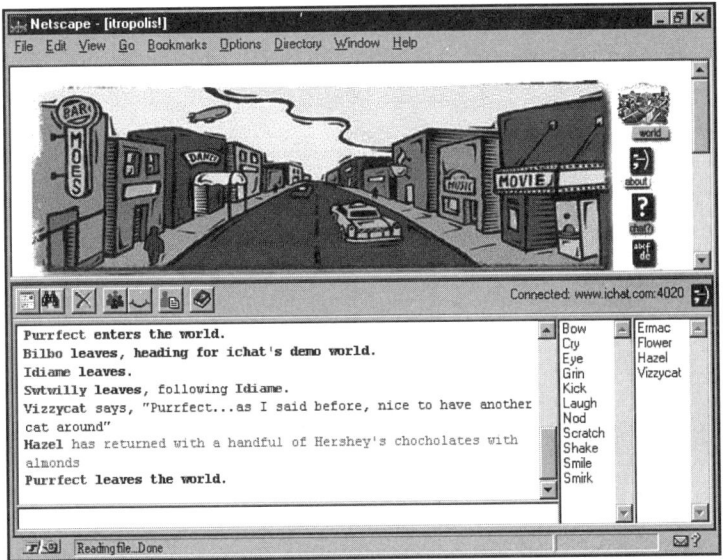

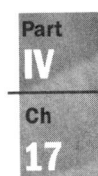

FIG. 17.7
The Insert URL dialog box enables you to visit other sites while continuing to chat on another.

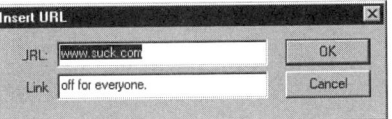

Consider the following example:

Sam says, "No I do not like green eggs and ham."

The underlined phrase could be a link to the Dr. Seuss fan club Web site or another appropriate area. To move to the new location, anyone chatting with Sam can double-click any portion of the phrase. Returning is almost as easy: You right-click within the Netscape screen to execute the Back in Frame command. Netscape then returns you to the previous Web site, which in this case is the originating site.

Taking Web Tours Another savvy feature is the Follow command. To select this command, you first right-click the user list. The Follow command enables a user, or even hundreds of users, to follow friends, family, and colleagues around a Web site. Wherever the leader goes with Netscape, all those following go as well, and all can continue to chat throughout the tour. To stop following, users simply execute the Stop Follow command, which also is accessible by right-clicking the user list.

Ignoring Bozos The final option available from the user list is Ignore, sometimes referred to as the "bozo" option. Using this command, you can ignore pesky users—those who ignore good netiquette or otherwise act improperly. To activate this command, highlight the recipient's name from the user list, right-click the user list, and then choose Ignore (see fig. 17.8). Thereafter, the ignored person's public and private messages will no longer reach you. Like the Follow command, Ignore can be toggled on and off.

FIG. 17.8
By turning on ichat's Ignore feature, you can ignore irritating users.

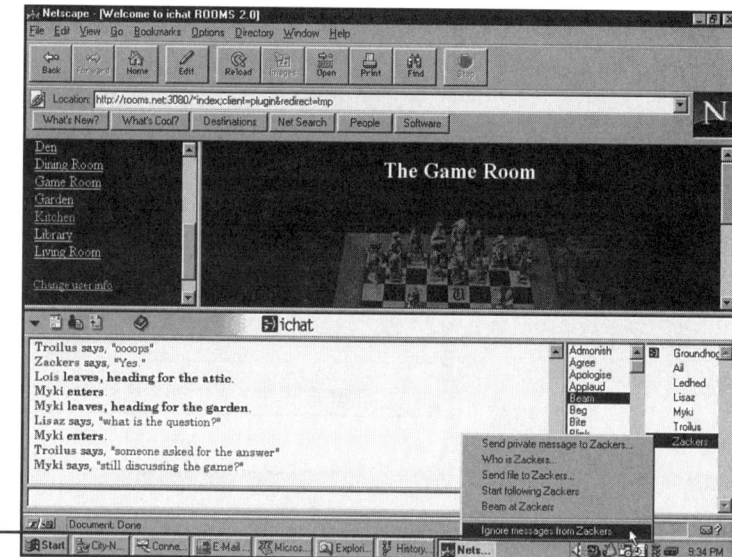

The Ignore option

Supporting IRC For users already familiar with IRC syntax, ichat also supports the full range of IRC commands. By using IRC's familiar slash (/) commands, users can replicate all the features available with the mouse. Using this feature is a little like returning to the days of DOS, but is available in case you feel more comfortable using IRC. For example, if you want to smile at someone, you can either double-click Smile in the emote list or, alternatively, type **/smile**.

Getting Help ichat's toolbar provides a link to online help. The icon looks like a tiny book. By clicking this button, you steer your Web browser to ichat's help section on the Web.

Connecting to IRC Servers

The ichat plug-in connects to both ichat and standard IRC servers. Although standard IRC chat serves are not Web-integrated and are text-only, IRC servers still comprise the bulk of chat servers on the Internet. Previously, connecting to IRC was somewhat complicated. Even though the Web might provide a link to IRC, you still needed a separate program, called an IRC client, to communicate.

Configuring the IRC client to work with Netscape required some savvy and, once initiated, the IRC client displaced Netscape on the user's screen. The result was that users had to use one program to connect to IRC chat and a second program with a different user interface to chat after getting to the chat room. The ichat plug-in simplifies this whole process by providing IRC support from within Netscape Navigator. Now you need only one program for the whole process. Figure 17.9 shows the screen of a user involved in a chat session while simultaneously viewing a Web site.

FIG. 17.9
The ichat plug-in allows you to simultaneously chat and continue to surf Web sites.

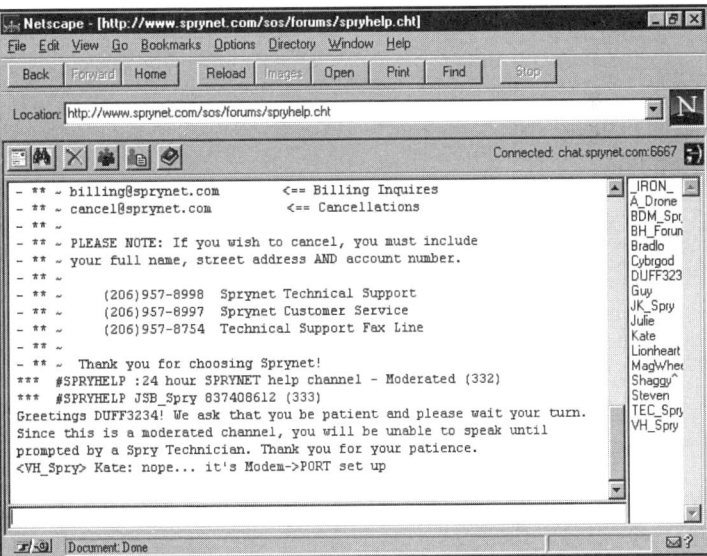

ichat offers two methods to connect to IRC. If the Web site has created a link to IRC, the user can connect by clicking the link. If there is no link, users can connect to a specific IRC site through a Web form located at **http://www.ichat.com/chat.htm**. You can steer the Web browser and ichat to the appropriate IRC location by entering an address and channel. Then the familiar IRC login procedure requests the user identification.

ichat's IRC mode varies significantly from ichat server connections. First, the text area comprises the entire browser window. This is an IRC limitation. Second, the Web-related commands disappear from the list of options; therefore, you can no longer send Follow commands or embedded URLs.

On the other hand, ichat retains the bulk of its graphical user interface (GUI). This GUI gives an IRC user the chance to communicate using either IRC's traditional slash (/) commands or ichat's GUI. Thus, to send Julia a private "hello" message, you can either type **/tell Julia Hello** at the command line or double-click her name and then type **hello** in the popup dialog box.

Chat-Enabling Web Sites

ichat, inc., markets its chat-server technology, ROOMS, which enables Webmasters to chat-enable their Web sites. The ichat ROOMS chat server is scaleable so that a Webmaster can use it on a single page or design the site with multiple chat rooms over multiple pages. ichat ROOMS also includes a C-based language similar to Java, thus permitting a fairly high degree of customization to chat-enabled Web sites.

With ichat ROOMS installed on a Web server, you can set up a Web site with standard chat rooms, walking tours of a Web site, or moderated discussion groups with moderated question and answer sessions. These moderated sessions can also include audio and video capabilities. An ichat server can accommodate as many as 1,000 simultaneous users in multiple chat rooms, and an unlimited number of user accounts.

Look@Me

Look@Me by Farallon Computing, Inc. is an Internet communications program that enables you to view another user's display, and to allow other Internet users to view your display. Farallon Computing currently distributes Look@Me in two forms: as a stand-alone applet for use under Windows 3.1x, and as a Netscape plug-in for use under Windows 95 and Macintosh.

NOTE You can use the Windows 95 version of Look@Me on a PC running Windows NT, but only for viewing other displays. Other users cannot view the Windows NT display.

Look@Me provides a safe environment for giving other users what amounts to read-only access to your PC; they can view what is on your screen but cannot control or interact with your PC's operation.

Although this safety feature does impose a few restrictions on possible uses for Look@Me, the program still has the potential of becoming a powerful tool for offsite training and troubleshooting, presentations and demos, and personal communications.

Installing Look@Me

Farallon distributes Look@Me from its Web site. Before you can install the program, you need to download the correct version for your platform:

1. Start Netscape and jump to the Look@Me download page on the Farallon Web site:

    http://www.farallon.com/www/gen/ftvpage.html

2. Scroll down to the drop-down list box Which Applet Would You Like? Select the Look@Me applet for either Windows 95, Windows 3.1x, or Macintosh (see fig. 17.10). For this example installation, suppose that you are installing Look@Me on a Windows 95 platform.

FIG. 17.10
Selecting Look@Me for your operating platform.

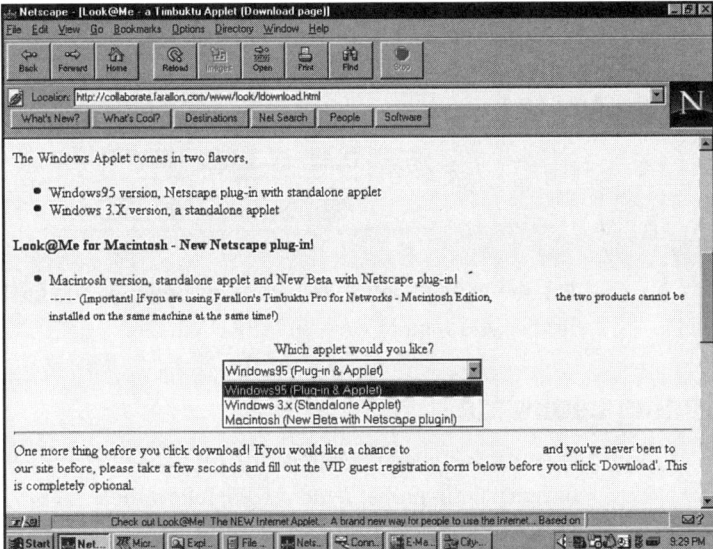

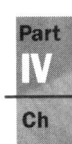

3. Select Submit Download from the download page to begin downloading the applet archive. From the next screen, select one of the two download sites. Farallon provides these two download sites to reduce the congestion on a single site. In the future, if the demand increases, Farallon will probably set up more sites.

4. After you finish downloading the distribution file, which is in a compressed archive format, you need to decompress the archive to release the files stored in the archive. For the Windows versions, LOOK@.EXE, you simply run the file just as you would any other executable (.EXE) program.

> **CAUTION**
> By default, the archive tries to decompress the archive and place the files in your C:\DOS directory (which it will create if one does not already exist). If you have a C:\DOS directory, you might want to divert the files into another directory, such as C:\TEMP, so that afterward you can easily delete them without accidentally deleting a DOS file.

After you release the files from the archive, the Windows versions automatically start the setup program SETUP.EXE and begin the installation. A dialog box appears that shows you where SETUP will install Look@Me and the directory in which Netscape is located (see fig. 17.11).

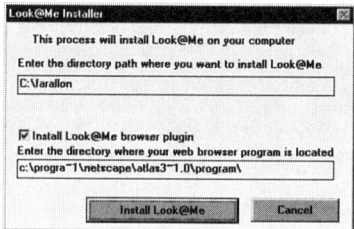

FIG. 17.11
The Look@Me Installer dialog box shows you the locations for Look@Me and Netscape.

5. Click the Install Look@Me button to continue. The final SETUP screen asks whether you want to view the README file.

Running Look@Me

Now that you've installed Look@Me, it's time to take it out for a spin. To start Look@Me as a Netscape plug-in under Windows 95, follow these steps:

1. Double-click the Look@Me plug-in icon to start Netscape and jump to the Look@Me plug-in page on the Farallon Web site (see fig. 17.12). If you already have Netscape running, you can simply jump to the Look@Me plug-in page:

    http://collaborate.farallon.com/www/look/lplugin.html

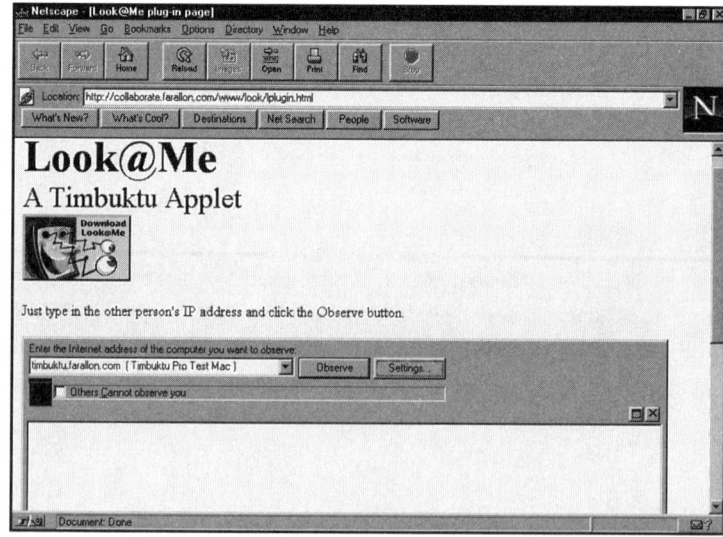

FIG. 17.12
To start Look@Me, you need to be viewing the Look@Me page on the Farallon Web site.

2. Before connecting to another PC, you need to adjust a few settings in the Look@Me page interface. On the Look@Me Web page interface, click the Settings button to open the Settings dialog box (see fig. 17.13).

FIG. 17.13
Look@Me's Settings dialog box enables you to specify some settings for the Look@Me Web page interface.

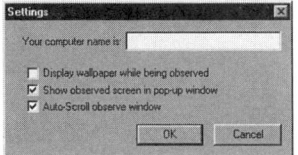

3. In the Your Computer Name Is text box, enter a name for your PC so that other Look@Me users can identify it.
4. Select any of the other choices in the Settings dialog box depending on how you want to display Look@Me. To close the Settings dialog box, click OK.

 TIP If you do not want other Look@Me users to see you, select the Others Cannot Observe You check box on the main Look@Me interface screen.

5. In the main Look@Me interface screen, in the text box Enter the Internet Address of the Computer You Want To Observe, enter the IP address of the PC that you want to view. Remember that the other user also must be connected to the Internet and be running Look@Me, either the plug-in or the stand-alone applet. If you don't have an available IP address, you can select one of the Farallon test computers. Select Observe.
6. If your connection succeeds, the computer that you want to view should appear within a few seconds. The computer should appear either in a popup window or in the interface window on the Look@Me page, depending on the settings that you selected in the Settings dialog box (see fig. 17.14).

Besides Look@Me, each of the Farallon test PCs also runs an application showing the users currently connected to the test PC. In figure 17.13, two users are viewing this PC, demonstrating the many-to-one capabilities of Look@Me's Macintosh version. Unfortunately, the Windows versions do not support the many-to-one feature.

You close the Look@Me display window as you would any other application window.

FIG. 17.14
Look@Me displaying another computer.

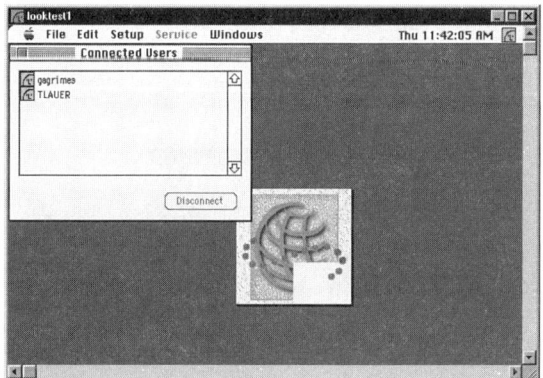

Exploring Possible Uses for Look@Me

One of the most obvious uses for Look@Me is as a remote demonstration or presentation tool, especially the Macintosh version with its many-to-one viewing feature. Look@Me also has a lot of potential as a remote training tool.

Another less obvious possible use for Look@Me is as a collaboration tool. One user can use Look@Me to show a work in progress to a collaborator who could then make comments, criticisms, and suggestions.

As a troubleshooting tool, Look@Me might seem a bit limited, but one possible use is to have a user demonstrate the steps that he or she is taking in a particular task, and using Look@Me to observe where possible errors might be occurring.

Carbon Copy/Net

In one sense, Carbon Copy/Net is the next logical extension of the plug-in Look@Me. Although Look@Me enables you to connect to another PC over the Web and view the onscreen contents of the remote PC to which you are connected, Carbon Copy/Net goes one step further by giving you control over the remote PC just as though you were actually sitting in front of it.

So-called "remote control" programs have been around in the PC world for years, using local area networks (LANs) or modems for their connections. These remote control programs have been used mostly by LAN administrators to troubleshoot problems on users' PCs, and by telecommuters to work on the office PC from their home PCs. However, Microcom, the maker of Carbon Copy/Net, is among the first of the remote control vendors to extend that level of control across the World Wide Web.

Why Should You Use Carbon Copy/Net?

The potential uses for Carbon Copy/Net are limited only by the imagination of its users. Internet service providers (ISPs) can use Carbon Copy/Net to help troubleshoot problems plaguing their customers. LAN administrators whose service domains might also include intranets will find Carbon Copy/Net an invaluable troubleshooting tool for their local users and for users in remote offices.

> **CAUTION**
>
> You might encounter problems when using Carbon Copy/Net to connect to a remote computer if you are going through a corporate firewall or proxy server. For security reasons, most firewalls or proxy servers block Carbon Copy/Net from connecting to a remote computer by refusing to relinquish the amount of control necessary to establish the connection. Ask your system administrator whether he or she can enable Carbon Copy/Net to connect to specifically designated PCs.

Carbon Copy/Net is also used extensively by telecommuters and account executives who need to access their office PCs while at home or on the road. Using Carbon Copy/Net, these users can check their e-mail or retrieve files. Computer instructors might also use Carbon Copy/Net heavily to provide follow-up help remotely to students and former students. Computer hardware and software vendors can use Carbon Copy/Net to provide technical support for their products, or to present product demos to potential customers remotely.

Carbon Copy/Net Security Concerns

Carbon Copy/Net literally opens your PC to the world, making your files available to anyone anywhere on the World Wide Web. This openness poses some obvious security concerns. A remote user can simply delete or copy files or plant viruses on your PC—if you allow it!

The plug-in includes a host of security measures that you can set to control how much access you allow a remote visitor (see fig. 17.15).

All these security settings are discussed in detail later in this chapter.

FIG. 17.15
Carbon Copy/Net's Security Options dialog box enables you to specify the amount of access that you want to provide other users.

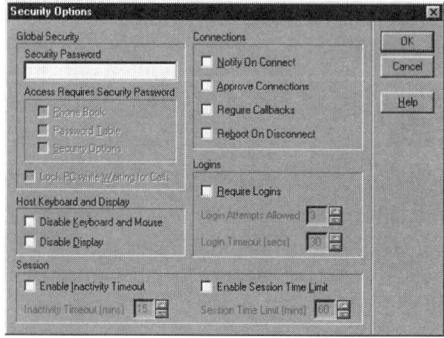

Installing Carbon Copy/Net

To install the Carbon Copy/Net plug-in, you first must download a copy from Microcom's Web site:

> http://www.microcom.com/cc/ccdnload.htm#Download CC/Net

Figure 17.16 shows the plug-in's download screen.

FIG. 17.16
Downloading Carbon Copy/Net from Microcom's Web site.

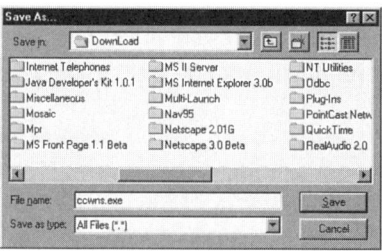

> **NOTE** Currently, the Carbon Copy/Net Netscape plug-in is available to run only under Windows—either Windows 3.1x, Windows for Workgroups, or Windows 95. No Macintosh or UNIX version for Netscape is available. ■

The file that you download is a self-extracting, self-starting, compressed archive file. To start the archive decompression and installation, follow these steps:

1. Run the file CCWNS.EXE just as you would any other executable (.EXE) program. After the archive releases all the files, SETUP.EXE automatically starts the actual installation.

N O T E The default extraction directory is C:\DOS (which SETUP creates if it does not already exist). If you already have a C:\DOS directory, you might want to change the extraction directory to C:\TEMP so that you don't litter your DOS directory with the 106 files extracted from CCWNS.EXE. Also, by extracting into C:\TEMP rather than C:\DOS, you can easily delete the 106 files from C:\TEMP after the installation is complete, without worrying that you might accidentally delete a DOS file. Just make sure that C:\TEMP, or whatever temporary directory you designate, exists.

2. The first few screens that you see in SETUP are the usual licensing agreement acceptance, name, and company registration. You also are asked whether you want to view the README.TXT file, and to specify the directory into which to install Carbon Copy/Net (C:\CCWNS). To continue with the installation, enter the requested information or accept the default values.

3. The next screen displays guest and host installation options (see fig. 17.17). Unless you have a good reason to change these values, go ahead and click OK to accept the defaults.

FIG. 17.17
Carbon Copy/Net's guest and host installation options.

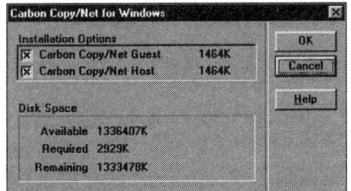

4. SETUP next prompts you to enter the directory in which to install Netscape (NETSCAPE.EXE). Click the Browse button to locate NETSCAPE.EXE. If you have more than one version of Netscape installed (for example, if you have installed versions 2.0 and 3.0), select the location of the version that you use most often. For example, under Windows 95, I installed NETSCAPE.EXE in C:\PROGRAM FILES\NETSCAPE\ATLAS 3.0\PROGRAM.

5. The next screen displays TCP/IP configuration information that Carbon Copy/Net needs to connect to other PCs (see fig. 17.18). Again, unless you have reason to change the values shown, accept the defaults by clicking OK.

6. At the end of the SETUP program, it instructs you to exit to DOS, change to the Carbon Copy/Net installation directory (C:\CCWNS), and run CCWCOPY.BAT. This batch file performs some additional cleanup chores that SETUP does not perform. If you are running Windows 3.1x or Windows for Workgroups, exit Windows, change to C:\CCWNS, and run the batch file. If you are running Windows 95, shut down and restart in MS-DOS mode, then change to C:\CCWNS to run the batch file. You then must reboot your PC to run Carbon Copy/Net.

FIG. 17.18
In this dialog box, you specify the TCP/IP configuration information required to establish Carbon Copy/Net connections.

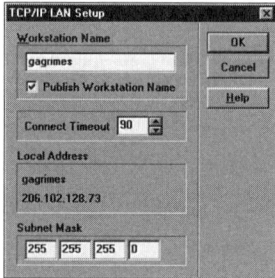

Running Carbon Copy/Net as a Guest

The Carbon Copy/Net plug-in operates through the interface on the Microcom Web site. Therefore, to run Carbon Copy/Net and connect to a host PC, you must start Netscape and go to the Carbon Copy/Net page:

>http://www.microcom.com/cc/ccdnload.htm

Figure 17.19 shows the Carbon Copy/Net page connection interface. This page enables you to connect to other users' PCs or to set your PC to host mode so that other users can connect to your PC.

FIG. 17.19
The Carbon Copy/Net connection page on the Microcom Web site.

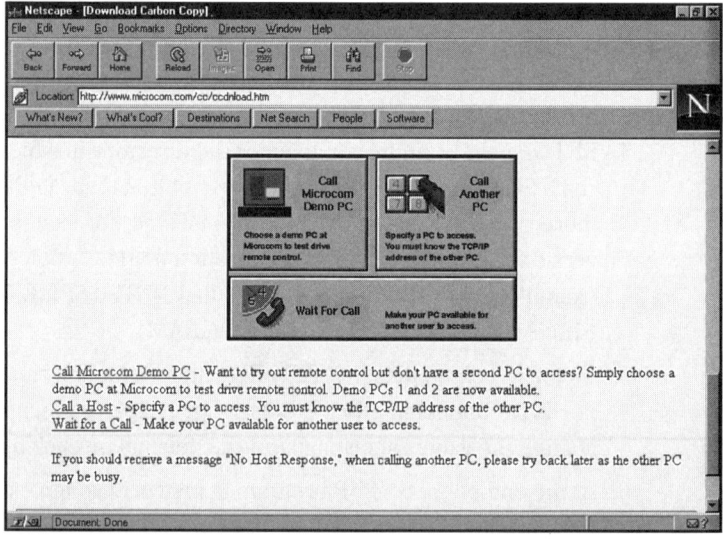

To start the Carbon Copy/Net plug-in, click the Call Another PC section of the screen. When the plug-in starts, it first displays a list of known PCs operating as Carbon Copy/Net hosts (see fig. 17.20).

FIG. 17.20
The Call a Host dialog box lists the PCs operating as Carbon Copy/Net hosts.

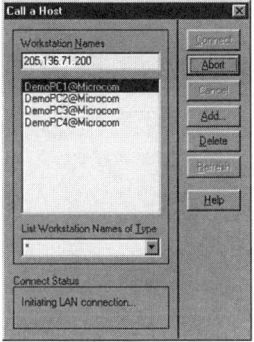

In the list box, select the name of the PC to which you want to connect. The PC's IP address appears in the Workstation Names text box. Click the Connect button to initiate the connection to your selected PC.

In a few seconds, the connection is established and you're connected to the remote PC through the Remote Control module (see fig. 17.21).

FIG. 17.21
Carbon Copy/Net's Remote Control module displaying connection to one of Microcom's demo PCs.

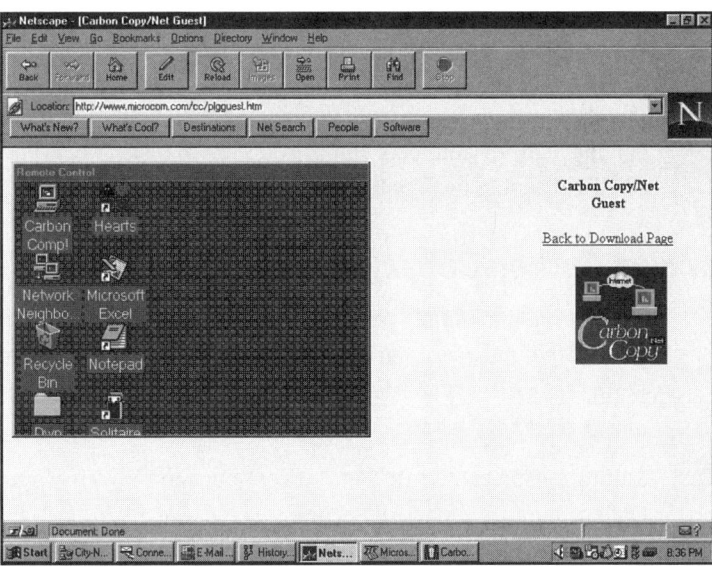

The main drawback in Carbon Copy/Net is the size of the Remote Control dialog box module, but you can toggle between a "stretched" view and a "full-screen" view by pressing Alt+RightShift+S. But as you can see in figure 17.22, you can still manage to start and play a game of Hearts.

FIG. 17.22
Carbon Copy/Net's Remote Control module enables you to play an interactive game of Hearts against the host PC.

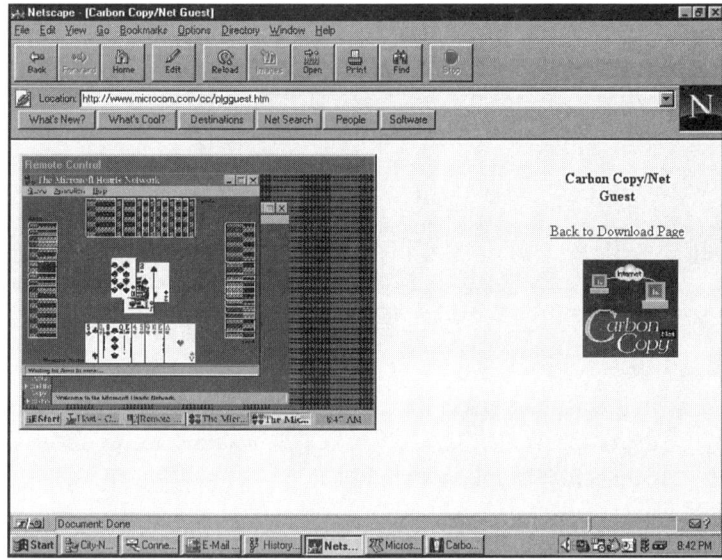

> **NOTE** Another drawback of Carbon Copy/Net is that the plug-in version of Carbon Copy imposes a five-minute time limit on connections.

If you exceed the five-minute connection time limit on Carbon Copy/Net, the program automatically disconnects you. If you want to disconnects earlier, you can press Alt+RightShift to terminate your connection to the host PC.

Running Carbon Copy/Net as a Host

The second method of operating Carbon Copy/Net is in host mode. When you're in host mode, other PC users can connect to and remotely operate your PC. When you open your PC to other users, you have to take some security precautions to ensure that nothing unexpected happens to your system or files.

Setting Host Security Options From Carbon Copy/Net's main interface, open the Options menu and choose Security to open the Security Options dialog box (refer to fig. 17.15).

Using Carbon Copy/Net's Security Options dialog box, you can control the following:

- Whether remote users must log in and enter a password before accessing your system. You also can extend the password to protect access to these security options. If you set a password, you should also lock your PC while waiting for a call that will then prompt the remote user to enter the password.
- Whether the keyboard, mouse, and display are disabled when in host mode.
- Whether you are notified when a remote user is attempting to access your system and whether you need to approve the remote connection.
- Whether the session terminates after a period of inactivity, or when reaching a predetermined session time limit.

Two other security options appear to be unnecessary holdovers from earlier versions of Carbon Copy/Net (which established connections using modems): whether your PC disconnects and calls back a remote user (you must supply a callback phone number), and whether your PC reboots after each remote connection. Requiring callbacks simply doesn't work over the Internet, and setting your PC to reboot after each session could cause problems in Windows if you still have files open.

The security options that you set depend on the type of access that you want to grant to your system and to whom you expect to grant access. You should never permit totally free access to your PC over the Internet; such access would make your PC vulnerable to all types of malicious acts and viral infestation.

Running in Host Mode After setting your security options, you can set your PC to operate as a Carbon Copy/Net host. If you do not have Netscape up and running, start Netscape and jump to the Microcom Web site and the Carbon Copy/Net page:

http://www.microcom.com/cc/ccdnload.htm

When the Carbon Copy/Net interface appears, click the screen's Wait For Call section to start the Carbon Copy/Net plug-in in host mode. If you set up a security password, enter it at the prompt. Carbon Copy/Net minimizes to an icon while it is waiting for a remote connection (see fig. 17.23).

FIG. 17.23
Carbon Copy/Net in host mode waiting for access from a remote user.

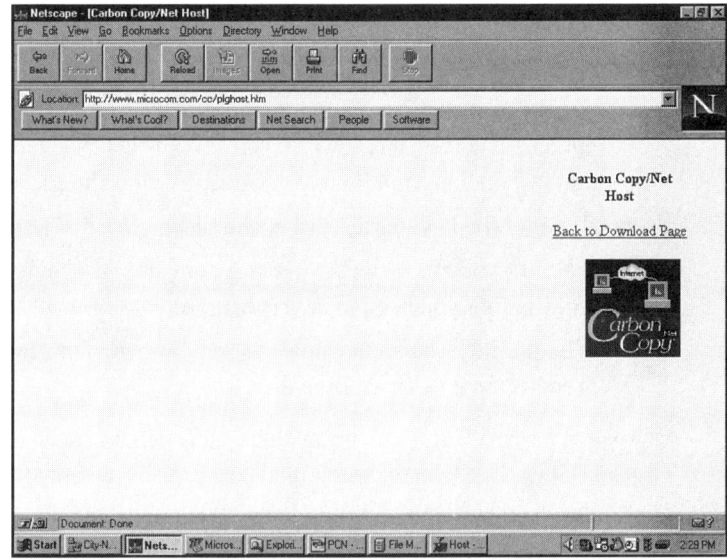

To exit host mode, click the minimized icon to open Carbon Copy/Net's main interface. Then click Exit.

CHAPTER 18

Information and Navigational Tools

- Keeping track of international time zones with EarthTime
- Viewing the world with Argus Map Viewer
- Finding old Web pages with ISYS HindSite
- Organizing Web pages with HotPage
- Managing the influx of information with the Pointcast Network

So far, you've seen several useful and fun plug-ins. There are also some plug-ins that do nothing but deliver information to you. Because the Internet is so huge, it's just impossible for most people to sift through all the information. These plug-ins help you keep order among the chaos of the information overload on the Internet.

http://www.mcp.com/que

Keeping Track of Time Zones with EarthTime

Before the Internet, there was little need—or, for most people, desire—to know the time somewhere else in the world. Now, with the growth of the Internet, the world has gotten a little smaller, and the exact time halfway around the world becomes a real issue. If you're planning on calling a friend or a business associate overseas, you certainly don't want to wake him or her in the middle of the night, or call the office when there's nobody there to take your call. If international time zones are a concern for you, you should look into EarthTime. For $19.95, EarthTime is a good investment for the busy executive or someone with friends in distant places.

The EarthTime plug-in, by Starfish Software (**http://www.starfishsoftware.com/**), gives you the time of day—literally. When you first install EarthTime, you choose the eight cities in the world you want to keep track of. When you run the EarthTime plug-in, you'll be presented with a Netscape window containing a world map with the time information for each of the eight cities you selected (see fig. 18.1).

FIG. 18.1
The EarthTime plug-in gives you the time for up to eight different cities in the world.

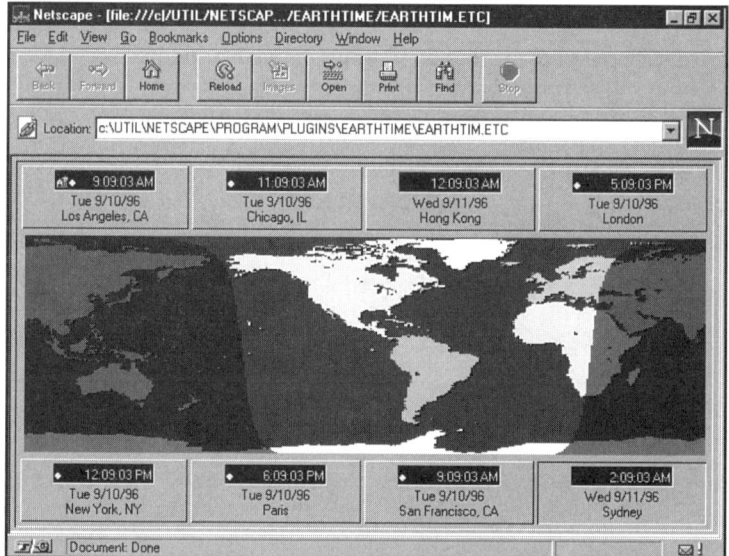

Why Use EarthTime?

You might think that EarthTime is a neat little novelty, with no real appeal. If you don't travel much, or all your friends live near you, then you're right: This plug-in won't do that much for you. However, if you're always on the go, or have made a lot of friends who've gone to other cities, EarthTime is extremely useful.

Of the eight cities you selected, you can set one to be your "home clock" and another to be your "local clock." This is ideal for a business person who travels frequently and needs to know what time it is at home. It also keeps track of what part of the world is under daylight or in the dark of night. This keeps you from accidentally calling someone when he or she is likely to be sleeping.

Perhaps the best thing about this plug-in is that it doesn't need an Internet connection to work. EarthTime works fine on a system that's not hooked up to the Internet, so even if you're on a flight across the Pacific, you can still check up on the time back home.

If you've moved, your friends have moved, or whatever, you may want to change the cities being displayed. This is easily done by putting your mouse over a city entry and clicking the right mouse button. This brings up a popup menu (see fig. 18.2) with a number of options. Simply select the first option, Select a Different City, and a dialog box appears (see fig. 18.3). Just scroll through the list of cities all over the world and click the OK button.

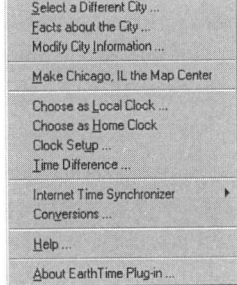

FIG. 18.2
You can display several of EarthTime's features by right-clicking a city's entry.

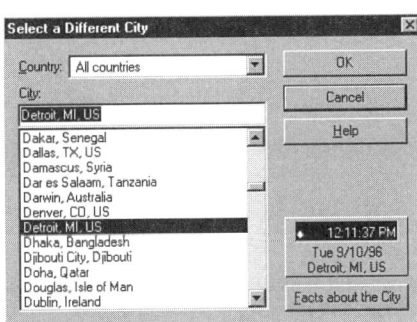

FIG. 18.3
Displaying a different city is a simple matter of selecting its name in the Select a Different City dialog box.

As previously mentioned, EarthTime keeps track of "local clock" and "home clock." The home clock is represented by a small house icon, while the local clock is shown with a person icon. You can change either clocks by moving your mouse over a different city and clicking the right mouse button. Simply select Choose as <u>H</u>ome Clock or Choose as <u>L</u>ocal Clock, depending on what you want. After you've made your selection, the icons change. If you've changed your local clock, Windows 95's time selection dialog box appears (see fig. 18.4). Simply click the Time Zone tab and choose your new time zone from the drop-down list.

FIG. 18.4
When you change the local time, you also have to change your time zone.

Getting the Exact Time

EarthTime has a nice array of features, more than you'd expect from a program that just keeps track of the time. Among the more useful features is the ability to get the exact time. Rather than relying on your computer's clock, you can use the Internet. There are a number of Internet sites that do nothing but keep track of the time. Many of these sites are actually just mirrors of other sites that are connected to atomic clocks. Consequently, if you have EarthTime synchronize its time with an Internet time server, your clock will be accurate.

You can enable the Internet Time Synchronizer by selecting it from the popup menu that appears when you click the right mouse button. By default, EarthTime checks an Internet time server every hour and updates your clock accordingly. You can change the behavior of the time synchronizing program by right-clicking a city, selecting Internet Time Synchronizer, and choosing <u>T</u>ime Synchronizer Setup. This opens a dialog box (see fig. 18.5) in which you can configure the synchronizer.

FIG. 18.5
To configure the Internet Time Synchronizer, you use the Internet Time Synchronization dialog box.

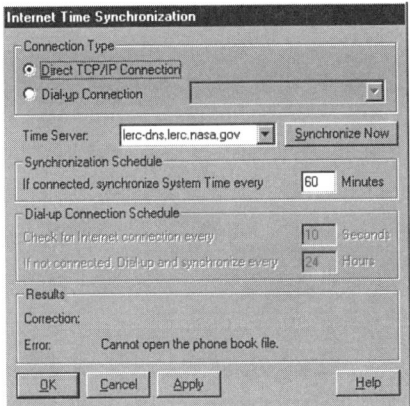

Viewing the World with Argus MapGuide Viewer

Suppose that you are going to meet a friend at his house, but aren't familiar with the area. You could go to the auto club and get directions and maps to your destination. You can also visit several Web pages that enable you to view maps interactively. Or, if you have the Argus MapGuide Viewer, you can view them within Netscape. With this free plug-in, you can view maps that range from local regions to the entire world.

Argus Technologies originally created the Argus MapGuide Viewer in late 1995. Argus was soon bought out and merged with Autodesk, a CAD/CAM software developer. You can get the Argus MapGuide by pointing your Web browser to the following address:

   http://www.mapguide.com/

Simply choose the plug-in as the application that you want to retrieve. Next, select the platform for which you want to download the viewer—either Windows 3.1 or Windows 95. The Windows 3.1 version takes about 620K, and the Windows 95 version takes 980K.

After retrieving the entire file, double-click its icon to display the plug-in's installation wizard. To use this wizard, you simply specify the location of your Netscape plug-ins directory. After copying all the files, the wizard installs the Argus MapGuide Viewer on your system. The plug-in activates whenever you access an Argus map file (see fig. 18.6).

FIG. 18.6
The Argus MapGuide Viewer plug-in will activate even if the map is in a frame of a Web page.

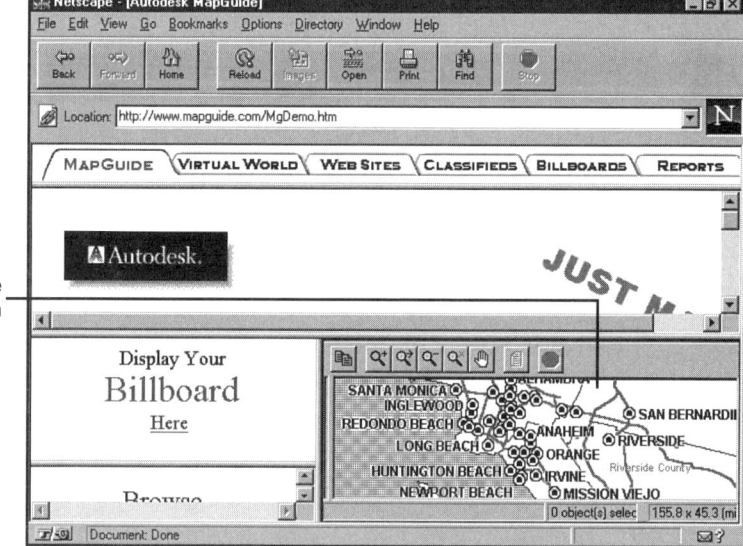

Argus MapGuide Viewer in action

Obtaining Maps

Usable maps have to be created with the program Argus MapGuide Author. With this program, you can create, modify, and publish maps so that a MapGuide Server can use them. The MapGuide Server is a special server that handles all files associated with an Argus map. A userful feature of the MapGuide Author is the capability to test your map instantly without a Web browser. MapGuide Author provides an interactive window display that is similar to the guide itself. Additionally, you can set several map properties, the map's appearance, and many other features.

MapGuide Author is a complex program that is far beyond the scope of this book. A fair number of published Argus maps are already available. Among the most noteworthy are the world and country maps available through the Argus MapGuide Web page.

Navigating through Maps

When you are viewing a map, the Argus MapGuide provides several helpful functions. The toolbar at the top of the map gives you quick access to common functions (see table 18.1). A shortcoming of the plug-in is that no tooltips are available; to understand what each button does, you have to try using them.

Table 18.1 The MapGuide Viewer Toolbar Is Present in All Map Displays

Button	Description
	Copy. Copies the current map to the Clipboard.
	Zoom. Enables you to use the mouse cursor to specify a region; the MapGuide Viewer then zooms in to the region, magnifying it by a factor of two.
	Zoom Goto. After you type in a street address, the display zooms in to that location by a factor of two.
	Zoom Out. Use the mouse cursor to specify a region; the MapGuide Viewer then zooms out from the region by a factor of two.
	Unzoom. Redraws the map so that the entire map displays.
	Pan. Click and drag on the map to view the parts of the map currently offscreen.
	View Reports. The MapGuide Viewer displays any reports made available when the map was created.
	Stop. Stops the map updating process.

More advanced navigation functions are also available. To access them, right-click anywhere on a loaded Argus map. The popup menu shown in figure 18.7 appears. In addition to the standard toolbar functions, several other useful functions are available. To view the distances between two points on the map, open the View menu and choose View Distance. Simply click and drag the mouse cursor between two points, and the MapGuide Viewer tells you the distance. Another useful feature is the capability to bookmark helpful maps that you come across. To do so, you open the Bookmarks menu and choose Add Bookmarks. You then are asked for a name to give the bookmark that you are adding. After you type a name, the bookmark stores the current map display, including your zoom factor.

NOTE MapGuide Viewer bookmarks are independent of Netscape bookmarks. The main Netscape application does not see any bookmarks added to MapGuide. Similarly, you cannot access Netscape bookmarks through MapGuide Viewer.

FIG. 18.7
Argus MapGuide provides several advanced navigation functions.

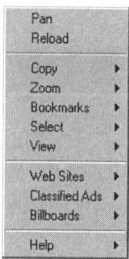

Finding Old Web Pages with ISYS HindSite

Suppose that you found an interesting Web page that helped you accomplish one particular task. Because you needed the page only for that one task, you didn't bookmark it. Now, however, you found another use for the site. In the past, you could do little to retrieve that long lost Web page—until now. ISYS/Odyssey Development, Inc. (**http://www.rmii.com/isys_dev/**) provides HindSite, a plug-in that solves this problem. HindSite keeps track of all the Web pages that you've visited and enables you to jump to any of them.

Getting and Installing HindSite

Before downloading the plug-in, create a temporary directory. Next, point your Web browser to the ISYS Web page and download HindSite. After downloading the 480K file, exit Netscape. Double-click the file that you just retrieved; its contents are then extracted to the temporary directory. Finally, you can install HindSite by double-clicking the SETUP.EXE file. The setup program asks you to specify the complete directory path that points to Netscape. Additionally, you can specify the program group in which you want to store the HindSite icons.

The HindSite plug-in starts automatically whenever you start up Netscape. This gives you a quick, easy way to look up past Web pages. HindSite also installs an applet version that works with Netscape. Because this applet is a stand-alone program, you have to configure HindSite to update its internal tracking files manually. HindSite's index of visited Web sites is completely independent of Netscape's cache, so none of your Netscape settings affects HindSite.

> **N O T E** HindSite does not work as a plug-in for the 32-bit version of Windows 95. Therefore, if you run Windows 95 and the Windows 95 version of Netscape, the plug-in does not work. To use HindSite in this environment, use the applet version.

Finding Old Pages

HindSite provides an easy mechanism for finding previously visited Web pages. You simply specify some words from the Web pages that you're looking for, and HindSite finds them.

To have HindSite search for an English phrase, you click the Query Using Plain English button. You then see a dialog box in which you simply type your phrase (see fig. 18.8). HindSite interprets your English phrase and tries to determine what you're looking for.

FIG. 18.8
HindSite enables you to use English phrases to search its index of Web pages.

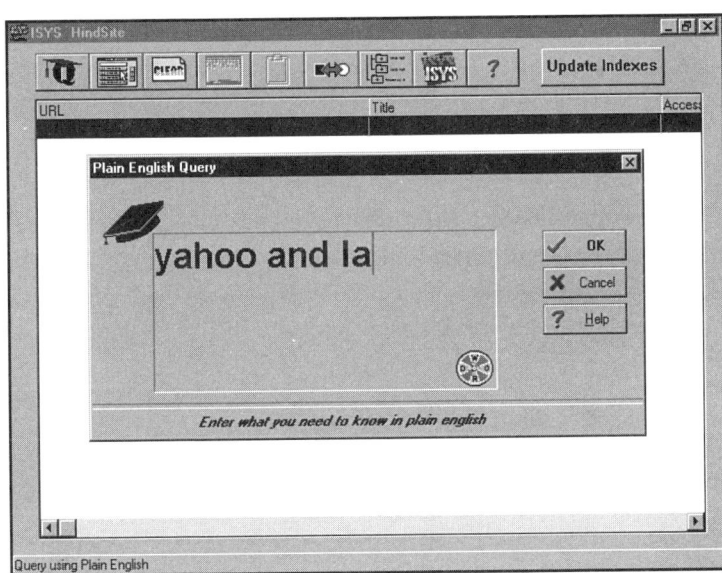

For a more direct method of searching for keywords, you can use the Query Using Menu Assisted button. This displays another dialog box in which you can simply type one keyword. If one keyword is all that you want to find, click the OK button. If you want to search for multiple keywords, you can type one keyword and then select the operation that you want to apply to the keywords (see fig. 18.9). After you select an operation, the same dialog box appears, enabling you to enter another keyword. After entering all the keywords and operations that you want HindSite to perform, click the OK button.

> **CAUTION**
> You can search only for words that HindSite knows about. For example, you cannot search Web documents for the word *april*, because that word doesn't appear in HindSite's internal dictionary.

FIG. 18.9
When searching for multiple keywords, you can specify their relationship with the next keyword.

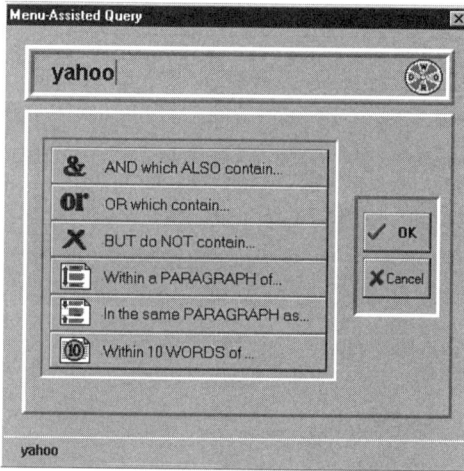

The HindSite main window displays the results of your search (see fig. 18.10). To control the order in which HindSite displays the matches, you can double-click a particular heading. For example, if you want to order the results by the URL, you simply double-click the URL heading. After finding the Web page to which you want to return, simply double-click its entry. HindSite sends the complete URL to Netscape, which then displays the page.

FIG. 18.10
HindSite lists the Web pages that meet your search criteria.

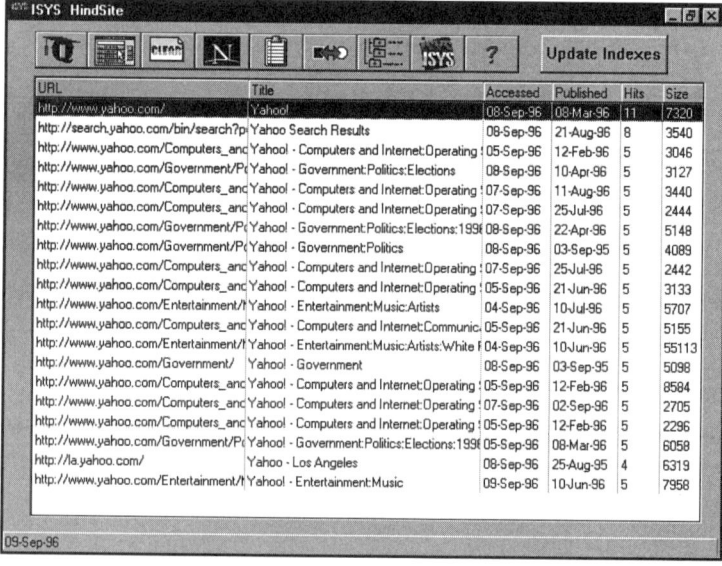

Organizing Web Pages with HotPage

Literally millions of Web pages are accessible to everybody. Because of the obvious variety of content, there is a strong desire to organize the most frequently visited Web pages. For most users, Netscape's bookmark functionality is adequate. It enables you to store the current Web page, and create menu headings and even subheadings to keep related pages together. HotPage by DocuMagix (**http://www.documagix.com/**) is a plug-in that offers all the same basic capabilities of Netscape's bookmarks and expands on them.

To get the plug-in, simply point your Web browser to DocuMagix's home page. Go to the HotPage section and select the test drive version, also known as the Discovery Edition. You must provide your name and e-mail address. After entering that information, you can download the 1.5M plug-in itself. After retrieving the entire file, you can simply double-click the file. The HotPage installation program then begins. The program asks you to specify where you want to store HotPage and its support files. After completing the installation, you can start up HotPage.

The Look and Feel of HotPage

HotPage Discovery Edition basically replaces bland text descriptions with pretty pictures. The master HotPage *cabinet* is the main container for all saved Web pages. Inside the cabinet are separate and distinct *drawers*. Each drawer can contain *folders*, which store saved Web pages.

HotPage comes as both a plug-in and a stand-alone program. The plug-in appears in the Netscape window as a new menu item (see fig. 18.11). HotPage Discovery Edition allows only two options for the menu heading. The HotSave option enables you to save the currently displayed Web page to HotPage. The Goto File Cabinet option displays HotPage's current list of cabinets.

> **NOTE** The HotPage menu heading doesn't have any corresponding hot keys. Therefore, users who prefer the keyboard to the mouse cannot access the plug-in directly.

The stand-alone HotPage program window displays all the drawers within your cabinet (see fig. 18.12). To open up a cabinet, simply double-click it; a new window pops up, showing you the folders. To look at the saved pages in a particular folder, simply double-click a name on the folder's tab.

FIG. 18.11
After installation, HotPage becomes an integral part of Netscape.

HotPage's addition to the Netscape window

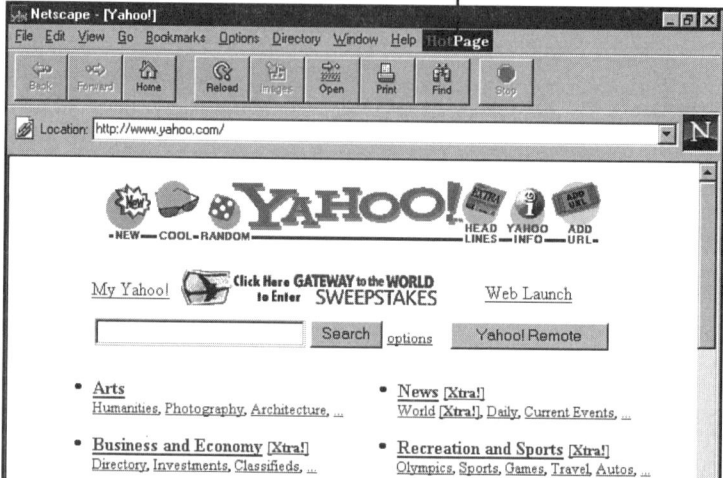

FIG. 18.12
The main HotPage window displays all the drawers in your cabinet, as well as those that you have opened.

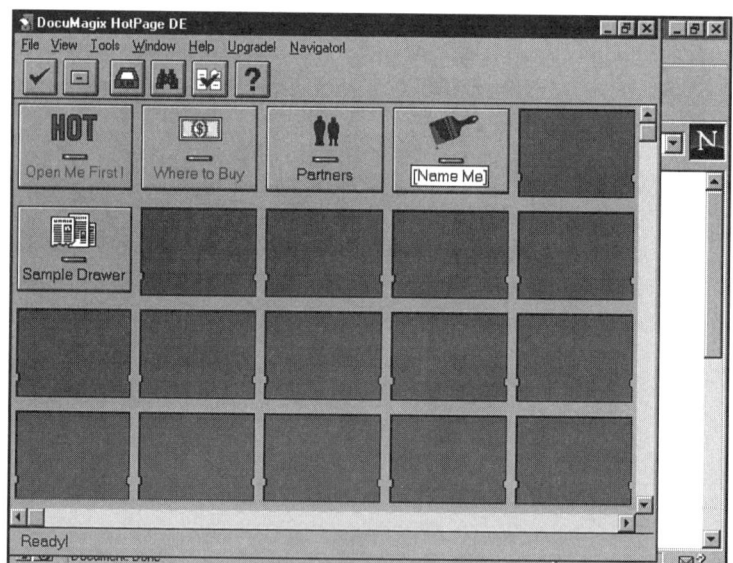

> **CAUTION**
> Whenever you open a drawer or folder, a new window also opens to accommodate it. This window does *not* appear in the Windows 95 taskbar.

Navigating around HotPage

The principal difference between HotPage and Netscape's built-in bookmarking feature is storage. To be precise, Netscape doesn't keep a local copy of any your bookmarks. When saving a Web page, HotPage copies the entire HTML document and all support files, such as images. The plug-in keeps track of all these files in a complicated database.

Initially, HotPage's Inbox stores all these saved Web pages. This Inbox is completely different from those of other programs, including Windows 95's native Inbox. HotPage uses its Inbox only as a means of transferring Web pages from Netscape to HotPage itself. You can move a Web page from HotPage's Inbox by clicking and dragging the page to the folder in which you want to store it. Similarly, you can move Web pages between folders in separate drawers in this fashion.

You can rename drawers, folders, and Web pages by clicking a particular object and then right-clicking. HotPage then displays the selected object's properties. You can change several attributes, depending on the object that you clicked. For drawers, you can change the icon that appears in the cabinet; for folders, you can change the color.

What's Not in the Discovery Edition?

So far, you probably think that the HotPage Discovery Edition isn't that impressive. After all, aside from fancy graphics, the plug-in offers little to entice the user. However, for $39, you can purchase the full-fledge version of HotPage directly from DocuMagix's Web page. The full HotPage program has many useful features unavailable in the Discovery Edition. Among them is the capability to lock out certain drawers, which is useful for parents who want to prevent their kids from looking at certain home pages. Another useful capability with HotPage is that you can e-mail your saved Web pages to other users. This enables you to share your favorite Web pages with someone else. Because HotPage saves the entire contents of a Web page on your machine, the other person can view the page without direct Internet access.

Managing the Influx of Information with the PointCast Network

There is a tremendous amount of information on the Web, but to use it effectively, you must find a way to manage that information. Some companies, mainly Internet service providers (ISPs), offer to help you organize by providing a list of topics from which to select your interests. Periodically, the provider updates its information about

Web offerings on those topics and e-mails the information to you. This is convenient, but not always desirable, especially if you're away from your e-mailbox for a week. There is one simple way to keep track of a large amount of information on the Web: The PointCast Network (**http://www.pointcast.com/**).

Here's how it works. You choose what information you want the PointCast Network to keep track of, and the PointCast Network periodically provides updated information about your specified fields of interests. You can choose what to track from various predefined channels. You can have the PointCast Network keep track of world news, business information, sports scores, and the weather.

The PointCast Network is available as a Netscape plug-in from the PointCast Network Web page. However, to say that the PointCast Network is a Netscape plug-in is somewhat misleading. It's really a separate program that makes tremendous use of Netscape. It has its own interface and configuration settings that aren't affected by Netscape. Other than for accessing Web links and other Internet-related information, Netscape isn't used by PointCast Network.

There are a number of aspects to the PointCast Network that make it an incredibly useful tool. First and foremost, the PointCast Network provides information from official sources. Rather than presenting data from individuals, the PointCast Network gives you information from media outlets including Reuters, SportsTicker, and Time-Warner. While some free "personalized e-mail" services offer some of the same information, few present the incredible wealth of the PointCast Network.

Another reason to use the PointCast Network is that it's updated only when you want it to be. Unlike the e-mail delivered systems, PointCast Network doesn't swamp you with lots of old news that you don't want. The PointCast Network is updated only when you tell it to be updated, and not before. You can even configure the PointCast Network to determine how often you want the information updated.

If those reasons were not enough to use the PointCast Network, there's still one good reason for using it. It's completely free. No strings attached. Simply download the plug-in, install it, configure it, update it, and you're on your way. While every section of the PointCast Network has an animated ad, it's a minor inconvenience considering what the PointCast Network offers.

PointCast Network Channels

The PointCast network comes with a predefined number of channels from which to choose. Each channel has its own focus of topics, with a certain amount of overlap for similar or wide-ranging channels. Table 18.2 has a complete list of universally available channels and the topics that they cover. In addition to the standard suite of channels, there are also specialized channels. In particular, certain major cities have regional channels, such as the Los Angeles *Times* and the Boston *Globe*. Additional channels are planned for the future, including CNN and the New York *Times*.

Table 18.2 The PointCast Channels

Channel	Topics Covered
Companies	News that relates to specific companies can be found here. You can also get the latest stock quote for each company, along with a graph of past performance.
Industries	News that affects general business is found on this channel. You can get an overall view of how certain groups of stocks are performing. News that relates to entire business industries is also available here.
Internet	Though not really a channel like other PointCast Network channels, this channel takes you to PointCast's subscriber Web page. You can find out the latest news for the PointCast Network and how it might affect you.
Lifestyle	Most general entertainment news can be found on this channel. You can also read your daily horoscope, or check out the winning lottery numbers for your state.
News	All the general news articles can be found here. The news ranges from General, Politics, International, and Business.
Pathfinder	Time-Warner, the media giant, has its own channel on the PointCast Network. Here, you can read the daily pieces of information from some of Time-Warner's magazines.
Sports	All the sports scores and news that happen during the day are available here. The latest box scores scroll across the bottom while you read the sports news.
Weather	The weather information for certain major cities for yesterday, today, and tomorrow can be found here. You can also take a look at the most recent weather maps for today.

Using the PointCast Network

The user interface for the PointCast Network is pretty intuitive, even for new users (see fig. 18.13). Each PointCast Network channel is listed down the left side of the screen, while the categories for each channel are shown in another window. To change channels, simply click the new channel that you want to go to. Under each section is a list of topics that you can view. Simply click a topic to show the news article in the main window.

FIG. 18.13
Although the PointCast Network is a Netscape plug-in, it can run as a stand-alone application.

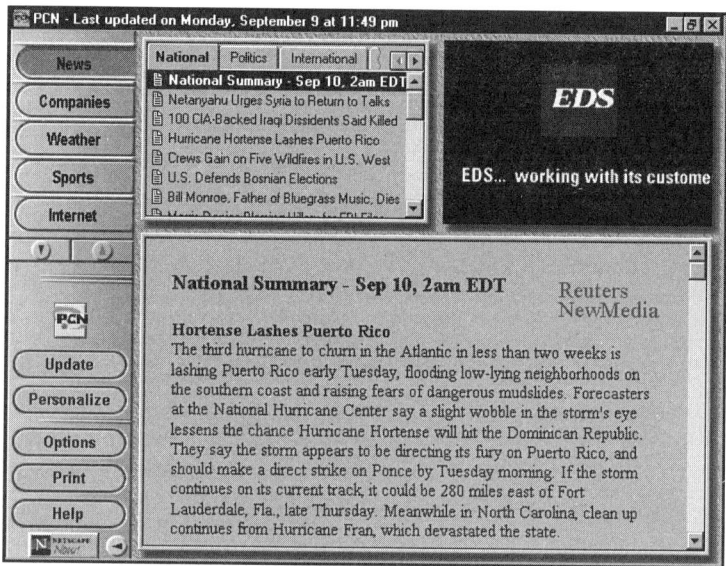

At any time, you can view a different channel, category, or news article with the click of a mouse button. If you come across a particularly interesting news item, you can print it out by clicking the Print button. Whatever is currently in the main PointCast Network window will be sent to your default printer.

For some channels—such as stock prices, sports scores, and the weather—the information is presented in a different manner (see fig. 18.14). Rather than having a categorical list of items for you to choose from, the information is presented in a scrolling ticker format. All the information for the requested category scrolls by. You can control the speed and direction of the ticker by simply clicking and holding down the mouse button on the ticker. To change the ticker's direction, move the ticker to the direction you want and release the mouse button. The speed of the ticker is controlled by how quickly you drag and release the mouse button. If you casually click and drag the ticker to one direction, it scrolls in that direction at a moderate rate. If you click the ticker and then drag it and release it very fast, the ticker moves much faster.

> **N O T E** Whenever all the other channels and articles are updated, so are the stock prices and sports scores. The updating is based on the update schedule that you've configured. (See the section "Updating the PointCast Network.")

FIG. 18.14
If the stock ticker isn't moving the way that you want, just grab it and move it.

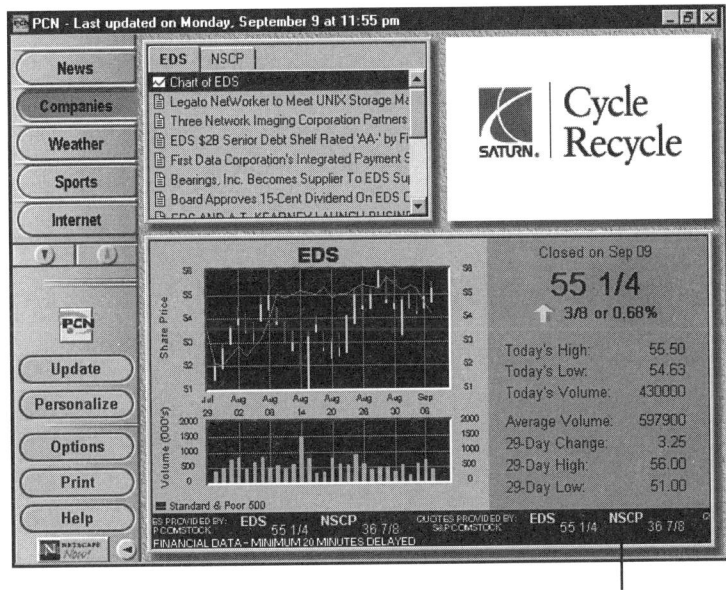

The stock ticker

Most of the time, navigating through the PointCast Network is a simple matter of using your mouse. Occasionally, though, you will have to pay attention to the mouse cursor. When you're changing channels, or browsing through a list of news articles, the mouse pointer appears as its normal arrow. When the mouse is over the actual content of the selected item, however, the cursor changes to a magnifying glass. If you click the left mouse button when the cursor is in this shape, it expands the main content window, hiding the categories and available items for the current channel. When you move the mouse cursor over an information ticker, the mouse pointer changes to a hand. When the pointer is a hand, you can modify the speed and direction of the ticker.

> **N O T E** When the news article is expanded to take up most of the PointCast Network window, it reduces your navigation ability. You aren't able to go to different categories or articles in the current channel. The only navigation you can do is change channels. ■

Configuring the PointCast Network

You can easily configure the PointCast Network to specify what information you want. When you click the Personalize button, a dialog box appears (see fig. 18.15). The tabs across the top correspond to the different channels available on the PointCast Network.

The Channels tab enables you to control in what order the PointCast Network channels are presented. When you select the channel you want to modify, you see a list of predefined sections that you can get updates on (see fig. 18.16). If you want a certain category to be kept up-to-date, simply click it to select it. Click an already-marked check box to deselect it.

FIG. 18.15
You can configure each channel of the PointCast Network by clicking its corresponding tab.

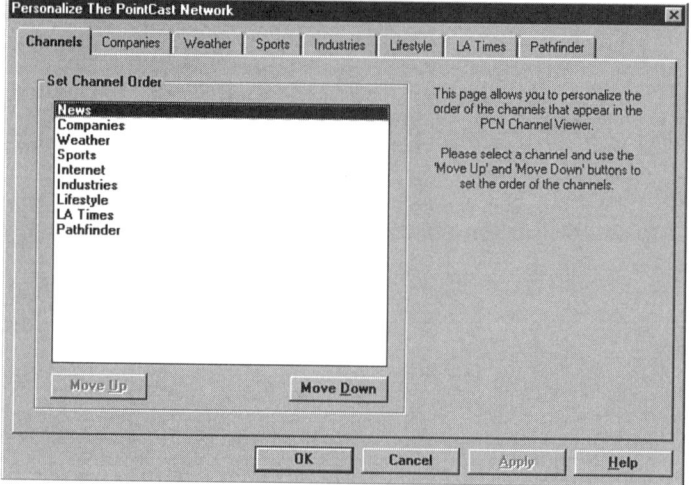

FIG. 18.16
For each channel, you can select or deselect the categories for which you want to display updates.

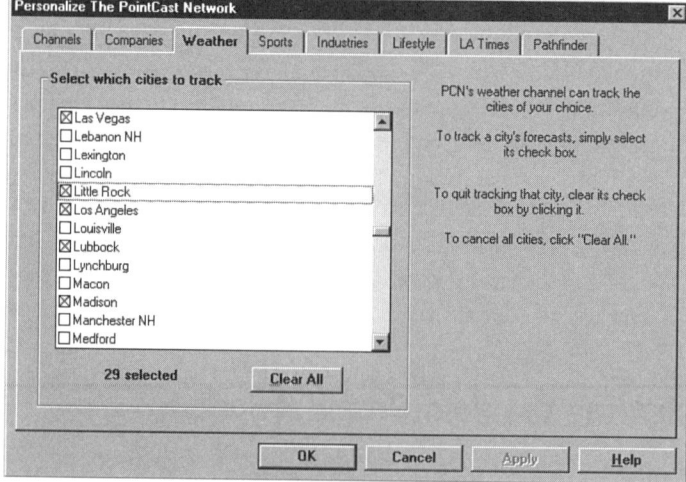

The Companies page is somewhat different (see fig. 18.17). In this page, you choose which companies you want the stock ticker to keep track of. You simply type in the ticker symbol for the stock you want to keep track of in the New Symbol text field and click the Add button. To remove an existing entry, select its value from the Symbols field and click the Remove button.

FIG. 18.17
To add a company symbol for which to retrieve stock quotes, type a symbol and click Add.

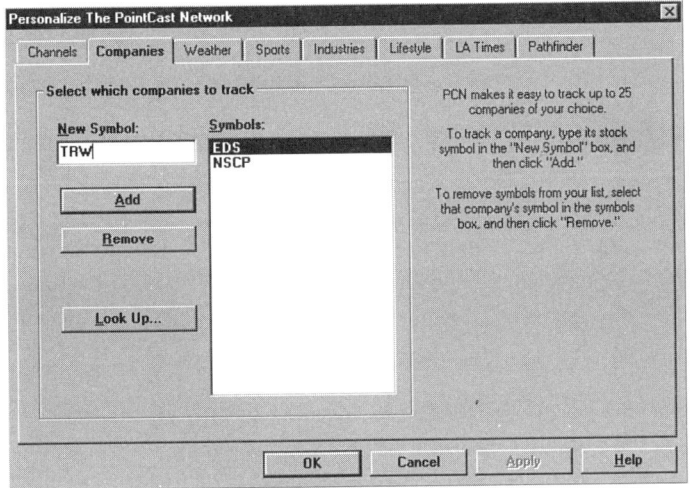

If you want to add a certain company, but aren't sure about its ticker symbol, don't worry. There's a Look Up button on the Companies tab. When you click it, a new window opens (see fig. 18.18) to help you find the symbol. Simply type in part of the name of the company or mutual fund you want to keep track of and click the Find button.

FIG. 18.18
Because PointCast can track multiple stock markets and mutual funds, you might want to look up the ticker symbol for a company.

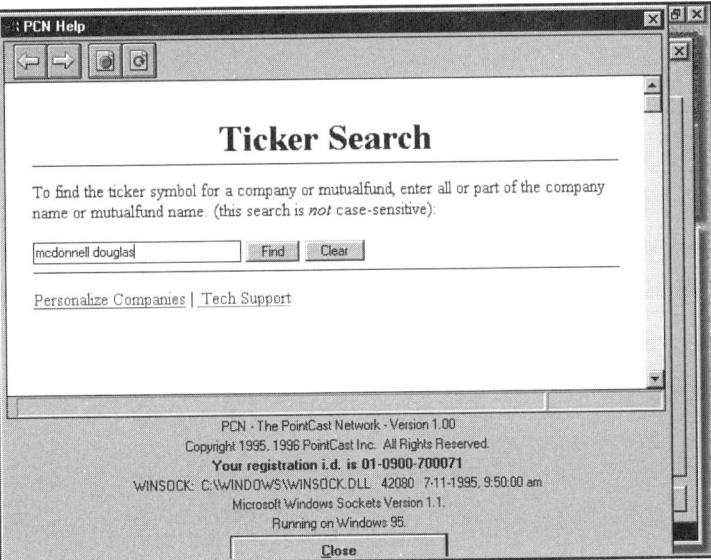

Updating the PointCast Network

The PointCast Network periodically updates the information for you. By default, this happens whenever your computer is idle for more than 10 minutes and it's been more than an hour since your last update. This method is generally acceptable for most people, but you can change its schedule by clicking the Options button and selecting the Update tab (see fig. 18.19). You have four update options for the PointCast Network:

- All-Day Schedule. The PointCast Network updates automatically whenever your computer is idle for more than 10 minutes and it's been more than an hour since your last update.

- Limited Schedule. The PointCast Network is updated in the same manner as the all-day schedule, but only during off-peak hours. That means that from 9 a.m. to noon, and from 1p.m. to 5 p.m., the PointCast Network won't be automatically updated.

- Custom Time Schedule. You specify when, or how often, you want the PointCast Network to be updated. The updating is done regardless of system activity.

- Only on Update Button. This is probably the best option for most modem users. The PointCast Network is updated whenever you click the Update button, and at no other time.

FIG. 18.19
The PointCast Network enables you to customize how often it should automatically update itself.

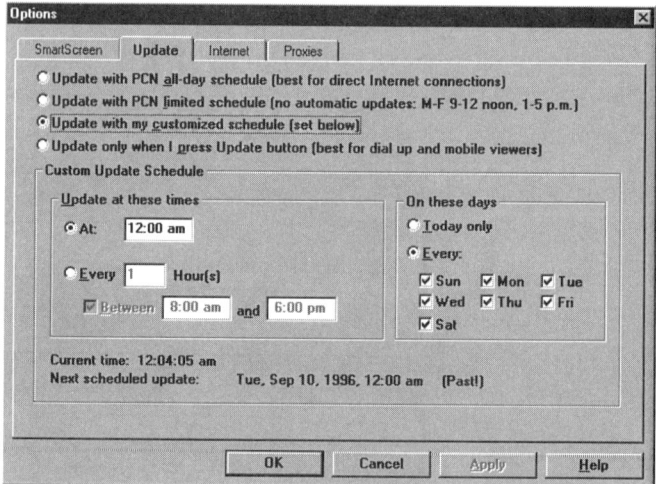

If you choose to have the PointCast Network update on a custom time schedule, you have complete control over the frequency. You can have the PointCast Network updated every hour, every two hours, or whatever. You can also have the PointCast Network updated only on certain days or between certain times in the day. This enables you to determine the best update schedule for you personally.

When an update does occur, the PointCast Network just downloads the latest news information from various sources. As it gets newer information, the categories in each channel update. Depending on how much information you want and how fast your network connection is, this may be time consuming. This is why it might be best for you to determine your own update schedule for the PointCast Network. You might incur an unnecessarily large phone bill if you use a default time schedule, particularly if you have to dial long distance numbers to access your ISP. During the entire update procedure, the PointCast Network is still available for your use. You can still switch channels, look at news articles, and everything else. The PointCast Network might be a little sluggish, but that's to be expected.

PointCast Advertisements

When you've used the PointCast Network for even just a little while, you'll notice the ads. Unfortunately, as on many Web pages out there, there is simply no way around them. The PointCast Network is free because sponsors buy ad space. There's no way to turn ads off or bypass them entirely. If you like the PointCast Network, you'll have to learn to deal with the advertisements. An unfortunate side effect of having the ads is that they are downloaded by the PointCast Network when an update occurs. That means that along with downloading useful news items, you're also downloading paid advertising. If you left-click the advertising window, you move to that product's Web page.

Downsides to the PointCast Network

While the PointCast Network is a fun and useful information tool, it's far from perfect. There are a handful of issues with using the PointCast Network that you will want to look into. The first is that the PointCast Network uses a fair amount of disk space. Along with holding on to the news articles, images, and program data, the PointCast Network needs about 6—10M of disk space. While it might not seem to be a big deal, not everybody is running with very large hard drives. Those who are tight on disk space might very well want to avoid the PointCast Network.

Another downside to the PointCast Network is that there might not be a category for you. While the PointCast Network has good general coverage of many topics, it doesn't cover everything. If you're looking for music news, for example, the PointCast Network doesn't have a specific channel for that. While you might find something in the Lifestyle channel, you might not find exactly what you're looking for. This means that those people who are used to UseNet's wide array of newsgroups might not find the PointCast Network interesting.

TROUBLESHOOTING

How can I save interesting news articles? I know someone who is interested in some of the information that I'm reading. Although you can print the news article, you can't copy it directly to a text file. Printing might be restricted for legal reasons; most news articles already have copyright indicators at the bottom.

CHAPTER 19

Programming Tools

- Using ActiveX controls with the NCompass plug-in
- Creating custom controls (.OCX files) with Visual C++ 4.0
- Embedding your custom controls in an HTML file
- Using Wayfarer Communications' QuickServer on the Internet or on an intranet
- Using the Stock Watcher application

As you have seen in the preceding chapters, various plug-ins can extend the Netscape browser's capabilities, enabling it to handle more than simple text and static images. This chapter takes a brief look at how you can create programs for certain plug-ins. ■

http://www.mcp.com/que

ActiveX Controls in Netscape with the NCompass Plug-In

By itself, Netscape cannot display ActiveX controls. Without a special plug-in, Netscape, on encountering an ActiveX control, prompts you either to save the control as a file or to find the necessary plug-in. NCompass is an example of such a plug-in. With the NCompass plug-in, you can extend your Web browser's capabilities by enabling it to run ActiveX controls and display Active DocObjects inline.

What Is the NCompass ActiveX Plug-In?

The NCompass ActiveX Plug-In for Netscape enables the Netscape Navigator's browser to display ActiveX controls and DocObjects. You can create these ActiveX controls by using Visual C++ 4.0, VBScript, or the Microsoft ActiveX Development Kit. After creating the controls, you can add them to an HTML file by using the <EMBED> tag.

NCompass handles the control's registration when the browser first encounters it and downloads it on the client's local system. The plug-in also stores the control in a local cache, and maintains version control so that the control's cached version is erased when the plug-in encounters a newer version.

NCompass has recently released three different flavors of its plug-in: Script Active, Control Active, and Doc Active. Script Active has all the features of both Doc Active and Control Active, as well as the added support for manipulating the ActiveX control with scripting languages such as JavaScript and VB Script. Control Active has all the features of Doc Active along with the additional feature of supporting multiple download of code through an .INF file created on the server. The simplest form of the plug-in, Doc Active, has the single feature of enabling your browser to display Active documents. You can download these plug-ins from the NCompass Labs Web site:

www.ncompasslabs.com

If you want a challenge, try to obtain the NCompass beta program when you visit.

What Are ActiveX Controls?

As previously mentioned, the NCompass plug-in enables Netscape to display ActiveX controls. ActiveX controls are OLE components that can be inserted into Web pages. These components take the form of .OCX files, special 32-bit DLLs that have properties exposed to software designers so that they can be manipulated from within other applications. You can create ActiveX controls using development tools such as Visual C++. Like other OLE components (such as Excel spreadsheets and PowerPoint presentations), ActiveX controls can be operated in other applications, but they are designed to work optimally on the Internet.

Creating Custom Controls with Visual C++

The most common tool for creating ActiveX controls (.OCX files) is Visual C++, particularly Microsoft Visual C++ 4.0, so that tool is used throughout this section.

You first use the AppWizard to create the control's *shell* (the control's basic structure without any functionality). After adding some functionality to your basic control, you add this control to an HTML file and test it using Netscape Navigator. The steps are as follows:

1. From Developer Studio, open the File menu and choose New. The New dialog box appears, as shown in figure 19.1.

FIG. 19.1
The New dialog box.

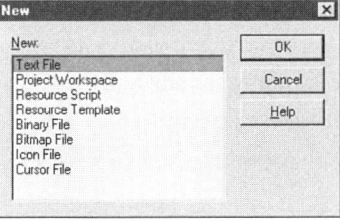

2. Select Project Workspace from the New dialog box and click OK. The New Project Workspace dialog box appears, as shown in figure 19.2.

FIG. 19.2
The New Project Workspace dialog box enables you to choose the type of project to build.

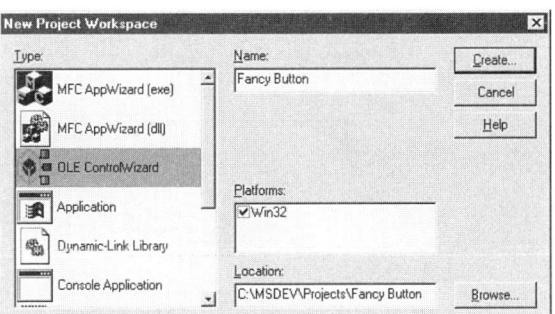

3. Select OLE ControlWizard from the Type list and enter a name in the Name text box. Suppose, for example, that you call this control **Fancy Button**.

4. Click the Create button. The OLE ControlWizard - Step 1 of 2 dialog box appears, as shown in figure 19.3.

FIG. 19.3
Step 1 of the OLE ControlWizard.

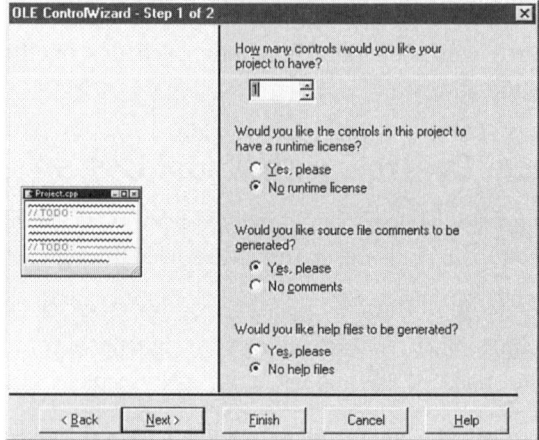

5. You can accept this dialog box's default values. If you want to create a license file, select Yes, Please for the first option. A license prevents other developers from using the control at design time. If you distribute your control without its required license, others can view it but not modify it. If you want to generate help files for your control, you can choose Yes, Please.

6. Click the Next button to move to the OLE ControlWizard - Step 2 of 2 dialog box, shown in figure 19.4.

FIG. 19.4
Step 2 of the OLE ControlWizard.

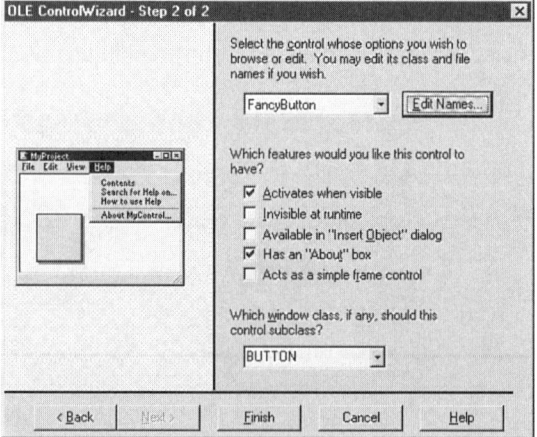

7. Select all the options shown in figure 19.4. The Available in "Insert Object" Dialog check box is of particular importance, as you will find out later in this chapter.

8. Click the Finish button. A confirmation screen appears; click OK. The necessary files are now created and ready to be converted into an .OCX file after compilation.

What Makes the .OCX File an ActiveX Control?

If you followed the steps described in the preceding section, you have just created a simple .OCX that derives from the button class. Therefore, your control will have all the events that regular buttons have. You could add a dialog box that appears when the user clicks a button, and which then requests a username and password. You might also add a dialog box that plays a movie.

Regardless of the functionality that you add, however, your control is still an .OCX. What do you need to do to make it an ActiveX control? Actually, you have already done half of the work required. Remember that while creating your control with the OLE ControlWizard, you selected a check box that made the control available in the Insert Object dialog box. All ActiveX controls require that you select this option. It enables a control to be declared as insertable, which means that it can be inserted into the many commercial applications—including Microsoft Excel and Microsoft Word—that offer the Insert Object option. This option enables the user to insert OLE components from other applications. Figure 19.5 shows Microsoft Word's Insert Object dialog box.

FIG. 19.5
Microsoft Word's Object dialog box enables you to insert an object into a Word document. The object could be a PowerPoint-generated graphic, for example.

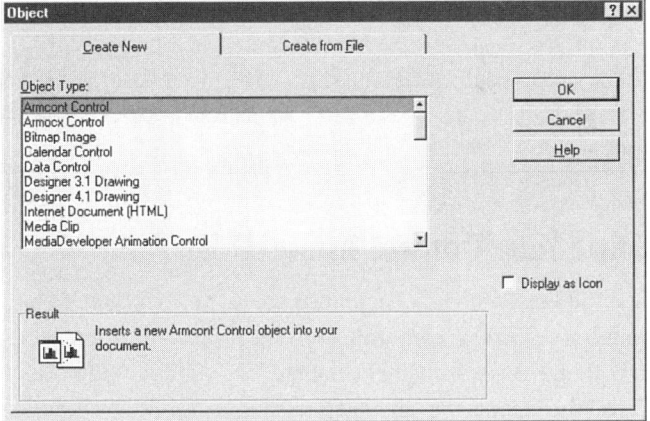

The other requirement for an ActiveX control is a stream file. This file stores a control's persistent properties, if it has any. *Persistent properties* are those that you can set and store to ensure that the control loads and applies them when the control is reused. For example, if you want your grid control's background always to default to green, you can set the control's background color properties so that whenever your grid control reloads, the background color is always green. With an ActiveX control, the persistent properties are stored in an .ODS file the HTML script's <EMBED> tag references, as in the following example:

```
<EMBED SRC="control.ods"  CODEB="control.ocx#Version=2,0,0,1
    WIDTH=200 HIEGHT=250>
```

The first parameter, SRC, specifies the control source that contains the persistent properties. The CODE parameter stores the location of the actual .OCX file. (The .ODS file was created using the ActiveX Development Kit.)

> **NOTE** The stream file does not necessarily need to have the .ODS extension. By default, the extension is .STM. However, because of conflicts encountered on some Web servers when an .STM file is registered with the necessary MIME type, most people prefer to use .ODS. ■

Using the Microsoft ActiveX Development Kit

You can use the Microsoft ActiveX Development Kit (MSADK) to convert existing .OCX files into ActiveX controls. You can download the development kit, free of charge, from the following site:

   http://www.microsoft.com/msdownload/activex.htm

After downloading and unzipping the MSADK, run the setup program. You not only get the MSADK, but also some extras such as Internet Explorer and ISAPI documentation.

 Unless you download the file with a high-speed connection (such as a dedicated LAN connection over a T1 line), prepare to wait a long time—an hour at least—for the download. The file is 12M zipped!

Embedding Your Control in an HTML File

After adding some functionality to complete your control, you are ready to embed it in your home page or corporate Web site. To do so, you must use the <EMBED> tag in your HTML file. As explained in Chapter 3, "Creating Plug-in Content for the World Wide Web," the <EMBED> tag signals Netscape that the SRC parameter specifies a document that requires a plug-in. For example, to tell Netscape that NCompass is required to display a particular document (an ActiveX control), the syntax for the <EMBED> tag is as follows:

```
<EMBED SRC="file.ods" CODEBASE="http://www.domain.com/
file.ocx#VERSION=3,0,0,1"
    WIDTH=200 HEIGHT=250>
```

The SRC parameter specifies the location of the control's persistent properties, which are stored as a stream file. This file specifies the control's default appearance and functionality.

The CODEBASE parameter specifies the location of the actual .OCX file. Because NCompass supports version control for ActiveX controls, this parameter could also specify the control's version so that it replaces any older versions previously cached on the client's system.

The WIDTH and HEIGHT parameters draw a rectangular area in which the control can appear. Adding this line to your HTML file enables Netscape to display your control.

Handling Dependencies with the NCompass Plug-In

As you have seen, the NCompass plug-in enables Netscape on a client's local machine to download and display your control. This usage is quite suitable for simple controls, such as buttons, smart text, list boxes, and other controls that have few or no dependencies. Dependencies are DLLs or other .OCXs required by ActiveX controls downloaded on a client's machine. The ActiveX control cannot function without these dependencies.

Although some of the files that your control needs might already reside on the target machine, you cannot guarantee that all the needed files exist there. This is especially true if your control also uses other third-party controls. For example, suppose that you develop Internet client/server applications using ActiveX controls as the client application. Because these clients depend on other .OCX files, such as GRID32.OCX (Microsoft's grid control), you need to be able to download and register other controls and DLLs to the target system. NCompass supports multiple-component download through an .INF file that the <EMBED> tag's CODEBASE parameter specifies rather than the .OCX file. The .INF file has the following syntax:

```
;Semicolons are used here to denote comments
;The first section is the Add.Code section
[Add.Code]
;The syntax here is Filename=Section where filename is the name of the file,
;and Section is the section in the .INF
;file where the instructions for installation of that file can be found.
;The first file listed should be the main control.
Main.ocx=MAIN
Depend1.ocx=Depend1
Depend2.dll=Depend2
Other.txt=Other
;The section for the main control
[MAIN]
;Specify the location (URL) of the control
file-http://www.domain.com/Main.ocx
;Specify the latest version of the control
FileVersion=2,0,0,1
;Specify the CLSID of the control (optional)
clsid={ }
;
;Declare the first dependent file
file=http://www.domain.com/Dependent1.dll
;The FileVersion is optional
```

```
;A destination for the file can be declared
;No value corresponds to the ActiveX cache directory (created by NCompass)
;11 corresponds to the WINDOWS\SYSTEM directory, and 10 corresponds to the
➥\WINDOWS directory
DestDir=11;
;Continue with the rest of the file
;...
```

Wayfarer Communications' QuickServer

QuickServer is a server application that enhances client/server applications to help them run over the Internet. It provides communication, fast data transmission, and security.

You can use QuickServer with existing applications written in Visual Basic, Visual C++, Java, or PowerBuilder, with only minimal extra coding. Using the QuickServer SDK, your application can access the necessary APIs for the QuickServer Server. QuickServer complements your existing Web server by enabling it to serve data to client/server applications.

Using QuickServer on the Internet or an Intranet

QuickServer was developed with both Internet and intranet environments in mind. Figure 19.6 shows a diagram for implementing QuickServer in an Internet or intranet environment

FIG. 19.6
QuickServer acts as a communications interface between clients and servers.

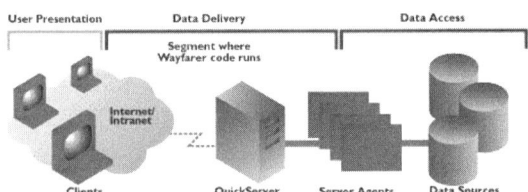

QuickServer acts as a communications interface between your client application and your Server Agents. Server Agents are server-side applications that send data to the client from the database using the QuickServer API.

Supported SDKs

QuickServer supports Visual Basic, Java, PowerBuilder 5.0, and Visual C++ applications. You must integrate the QuickServer API into your applications to enable them to use QuickServer as an interface between the client and server applications.

> **NOTE** Although QuickServer supports PowerBuilder 5.0, some bugs have been reported with this development tool.

The Stock Watcher Application

A sample application, Stock Watcher, is available for free download to demonstrate Wayfarer's QuickServer. You can download Stock Watcher from **http://www.wayfarer.com**. The application uses QuickServer, a special Server Agent, and a satellite information feed from PC Quote to deliver stock information live (delayed by about 15 minutes) to a client program written in Visual Basic. You can run the application as a stand-alone program or, with the help of the Wayfarer plug-in, as an inline application within the Netscape browser.

PART V

Advanced Plug-Ins Development

20 Java Applets and JavaScript   409

21 Creating Your Own Plug-Ins   445

CHAPTER 20

Java Applets and JavaScript

- What Java and JavaScript are
- The difference between Java and JavaScript
- What Java and JavaScript can do for you
- How Java applets differ from standard plug-ins
- How to integrate Java into a Web page
- How to develop a JavaScript page
- How to begin developing a Java applet

In addition to supporting other plug-ins, Netscape Navigator versions 2.0 and higher also include support for Java and JavaScript applications. Although neither Java nor JavaScript programs are actually plug-ins, they are exciting options that Webmasters can incorporate into their systems. ■

http://www.mcp.com/que

Java and JavaScript Defined

Despite the similarity of their names, Java and JavaScript are at best very distant cousins; JavaScript is *not* "Java lite" or "Java for beginners." The two technologies are quite different and have very different histories. Netscape Communications originally developed the JavaScript language under the name LiveScript. In November 1995, as Java was fast becoming the most hyped technology of the year, Sun Microsystems and Netscape changed LiveScript's name to JavaScript.

Java, on the other hand, was first developed in 1991 by Sun Microsystems for a failed "set top" box, which was supposed to have replaced your television channel control box. Only much later, in 1995, did Sun find Java's niche with the Internet.

Both languages are well suited to creating dynamic Web pages. These pages can save users time and add a level of interaction not previously possible.

Java Defined

Sun Microsystems developed Java, a programming language based very loosely on another popular programming language, C++. Actually, Sun borrowed from many languages when developing Java. Java has many advantages over traditional languages such as C++. The most significant advantage is that Java applets don't have to run on a single type of computer, but can run on any system that supports the Java Virtual Machine.

Sun's official definition for Java is as follows:

> ...a simple, object-oriented, distributed, interpreted, robust, secure, architecture-neutral, portable, high-performance, multithreaded, dynamic language.

That definition is more than Sun's attempt to use every buzz word that it could think of. Each of the terms in the definition describes an important attribute of the language. It's beyond the scope of this chapter to explore each attribute, however, so this section focuses on two of particular interest to Webmasters: architecture neutrality and security. (To learn more about Java, see Que's *Special Edition Using Java*.)

Java Is Architecture-Neutral *Architecture-neutral* (or *platform-independent*) is a complicated way to say that a Java program can run on any computer or platform. This attribute is the key reason that Java is often the best solution for accomplishing many things on the Internet or an intranet. Because Java is platform-independent, after you create a Java application, you can run the same application without any modifications on any computer—almost. To support Java, a computer must first support the Java virtual machine (VM). Currently, dozens of computers support the VM, and more are on the way.

To appreciate the power of architecture neutrality, consider what would happen if your favorite word processor were written in Java. You could then install that application on a Windows 95 machine, a Macintosh, a UNIX machine, or a DEC VAX. You might think that Microsoft Word for Windows and Microsoft Word for Macintosh have the same level of portability, but they are actually two separate, distinct versions of a program. If the program were written in Java, you could insert the same disks in both your Macintosh and your Windows machines and execute the same code.

Architecture neutrality becomes even more important on the World Wide Web. One reason that Web servers have made the Internet such a phenomenon is that any computer in the world can access and read a Web page. No matter what type of computer you are using, you can read any HTML page. If Java were limited to a single platform, your Web pages would essentially have to lock out any visitor using a different platform. In contrast, you can now use Java applications as freely as you use HTML code.

Java Is Secure From the beginning, Sun Microsystems designed Java to be a secure language. In this context, *security* means that programmers cannot write Java applets that can harm your computer. Imagine the havoc that a hacker could wreak by writing a virus in Java—the virus could run on and infect any computer! Fortunately, because Sun anticipated this danger, such attacks are not possible.

Under Java's security model, a Java application cannot commit malicious acts against your machine when you download the application from the Web. In addition to minimizing the threat of Java applets spreading viruses, Sun has also limited applets' capability to access the local file system. For this reason, hackers cannot use a Java applet to steal the information on your local hard drive.

Java's security is actually of more benefit to Web surfers than to Webmasters. From a Webmaster's perspective, Java's security measures are important because they calm Web surfers' fears that your Web pages might attack them in some way.

JavaScript Defined

JavaScript is a scripting language that is actually embedded into an HTML file. With Java, a reference to the Java applet is added to the HTML file; in contrast, with JavaScript, the HTML file actually contains the whole program.

Netscape designed JavaScript to be a complementary language to Java. One of the objectives was to act as middleware between Java and plug-ins. Although the two languages have several differences between them, JavaScript's syntax does vaguely resemble Java's. More than any other factor, the similarity stems from the fact that both Java and JavaScript derive from the same source: the C language.

Designed to be easy to learn and use, JavaScript is an ideal language for most Web page designers, who understandably would rather dwell on their Web pages' aesthetic appearance than the technical details of programming. Nevertheless, you need a bit of programming skill to write large or complicated applications with JavaScript.

Java versus JavaScript

Java and JavaScript have many differences beyond the syntax. These differences help to reveal the advantages and disadvantages of either language.

JavaScript Is Contained in the HTML File

The HTML file contains a JavaScript program's source code along with the other text that the browser interprets. In contrast, an HTML file only points to a Java applet, the same way that an image is included.

JavaScript Is a Scripting Language

JavaScript is primarily a scripting language. Essentially, JavaScript is to Java what Perl is to C. One advantage of a scripting language such as JavaScript is that the traditional HTML file contains the JavaScript. Multiple accesses are not required to download the HTML file and the JavaScript program. For small applications, this advantage makes JavaScript preferable to Java.

JavaScript Is Interpreted

Because JavaScript is interpreted, you don't have to compile the script before using it. Java, on the other hand, requires an initial compilation before you can use it. This compilation, however, makes Java a faster language.

Java is both compiled and interpreted, so you might wonder how JavaScript differs. The answer lies in the level at which Java is interpreted.

Every computer has a machine language that consists entirely of ones and zeros. Essentially, machine language turns transistors on and off. Machine language is a very complicated beast, and thus only true gurus program in it. A very close cousin to machine language is assembly language. Assembly language converts the machine language to characters that humans can more easily comprehend and remember.

Java has a unique pseudo assembly language of its own. This assembly language is not a real language for a real computer, but an abstract language for Java. When Java compiles, it generates code that essentially consists of this pseudo assembly language. When downloading a Java class file, your computer must then convert the pseudo assembly language to your machine's actual assembly language. This translation is a relatively simple one. The translation is also the origin of Java's interpretation; Java interprets the virtual machine's assembly language into your computer's native assembly language. In addition, the interpreter also performs *object linking,* a process of linking together multiple class files.

With JavaScript, your browser downloads code that looks like listing 20.1.

Listing 20.1 A Simple JavaScript Demo

```
<HTML>
<HEAD>
<SCRIPT>
document.write("<H1>This is a simple JavaScript demo</H1>");
</SCRIPT>
</HEAD>
<BODY>
</BODY>
</HTML>
```

Listing 20.1 seems to include a lot of code, but the JavaScript interpreter has to look at only one line:

```
document.write("<H1>This is a simple JavaScript demo</H1>");
```

Although this line of code is quite simple, it means nothing to a computer until it has been translated. The JavaScript interpreter must first translate `document` and `write` and then determine how to use them. With Java, such code requires much less translation, because Java does most of the translation when you create the class file.

Java Is Not as Easy To Steal

Because Java is a compiled language, programs written in Java become proprietary. When you are accessing a Web page that includes a Java applet, you are downloading only the actual program; you do not have access to the actual source code that created the applet. The program that you download over the Internet is in Java assembly language, and thus difficult for humans to read.

In contrast, the HTML file contains the source code of a program written in JavaScript, so anyone accessing the Web page can view the source code. To do so in Netscape Navigator, choose the View menu's Document Source command. Figure 20.1 shows how easy it is to obtain the source code for a program written in JavaScript.

FIG. 20.1
By viewing the document source, you can see the source for any JavaScript program.

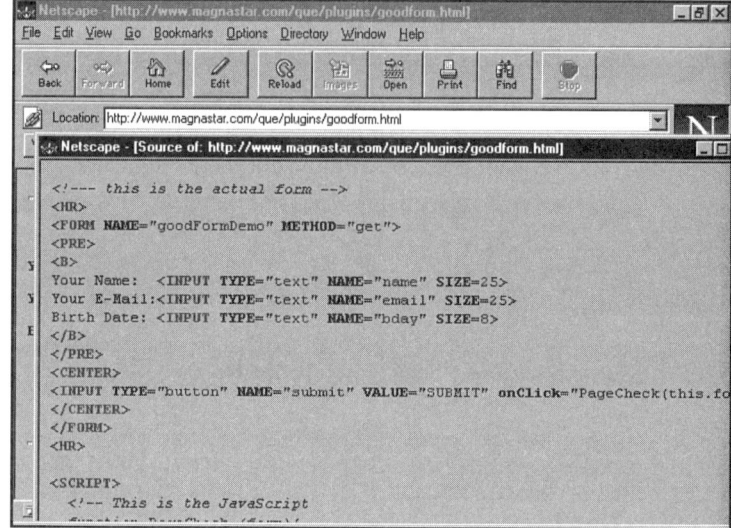

> **NOTE** The fact that stealing JavaScript programs is easy does not make doing so a legitimate practice. You should always request the author's permission before using such a program on your own Web pages. Unfortunately, however, many people do not always bother to request permission when utilizing other developers' ideas, and making them do so can be quite difficult. ■

How Java and JavaScript Can Help You

Java and JavaScript are both powerful tools for Webmasters. You can use them to enhance your Web pages in several ways. A few of the more popular ones are form validation, real-time data, interacting with the user, and games.

Form Verification

You can use Java and JavaScript to automate many tasks for which you might previously have used a CGI script. In fact, probably the most common use of JavaScript is to verify that the user has completed a form properly. Without JavaScript, you usually have users click the submit button and then wait for the server to tell them that they did not complete a required portion of the form. Then the user must return to the form, fill out the missing information, and try to resubmit the form. You can use JavaScript or Java to automate this process. Before users even submit a form, you can have a script check whether they filled out the form correctly; if the form is not completed, the script can inform the users about the portion that they failed to fill in. Figure 20.2 shows such a JavaScript program informing a user that he or she needs to enter a name.

FIG. 20.2
You can use JavaScript to create a form verification program.

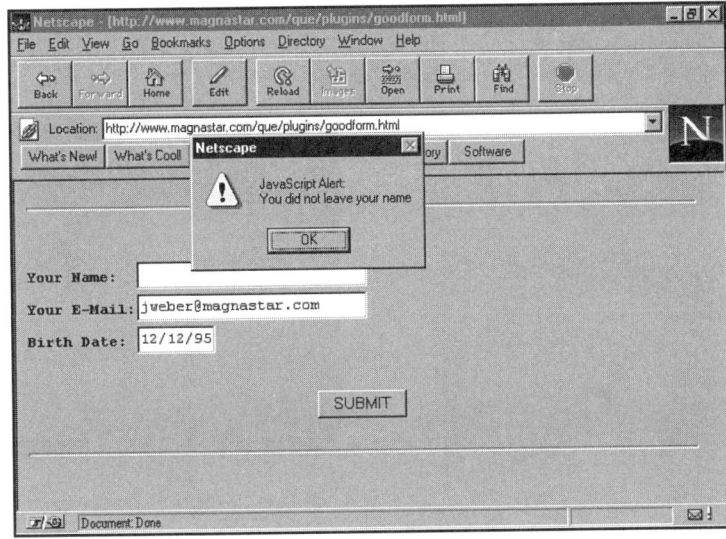

True Interaction Java and JavaScript provide a level of true interaction not previously possible. You can also use many plug-ins to create some of this interaction. However, because Java and JavaScript are actually programming languages, they don't force you to use one particular type of interaction, as any single plug-in does. For instance, although a VRML plug-in enables you to interact with a VRML world, such a plug-in doesn't let you work with sound or access a database.

One of the simplest examples of interaction that Java makes possible is a living image-map. Web pages often use imagemaps to present a single image for multiple links. As you move your mouse over a Web page, you get feedback in the form of animation or sound. You can easily activate such a feature with Java. Figure 20.3 shows an imagemap that highlights the selected section and displays a bit of information about the link.

Real-Time Data The designers of Java built networking in to the language. Network support makes it fairly easy to develop applications that can receive information from a server on the fly. For instance, consider stock ticker tapes. The information on these tapes is updated constantly as stocks are sold and traded. Traditional Web design techniques provided no good way to get this kind of information. However, with Java, you can create an applet that reads this information from a server and displays the information as it changes.

Another use of real-time data is to create user chats. Talking directly with other users is often a convenient feature. Although you can also use products such as IRC (see Chapter 17, "Communications Tools") to make user chats possible, the capability to blend in a chat with other applications is unique to Java. Figure 20.4 shows the interface of a Java program that enables users to engage in real-time chat.

FIG. 20.3
This active image map enables you to select a geographic area and display its climatic data.

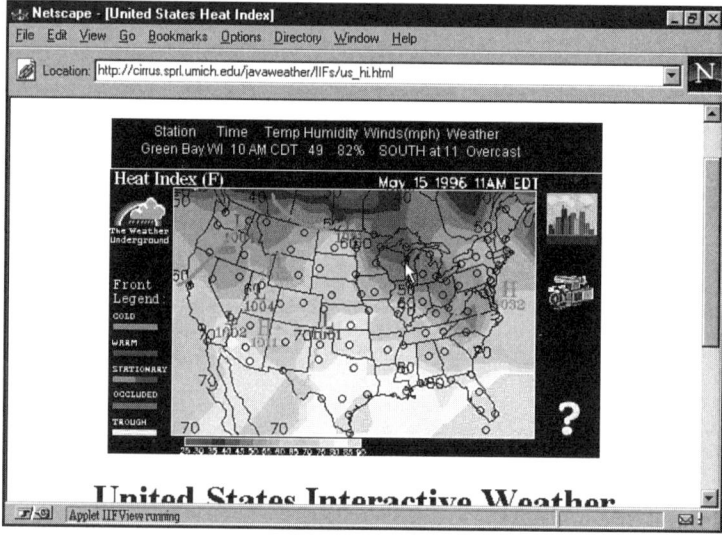

FIG. 20.4
You can use this Java program to chat with other users in real time.

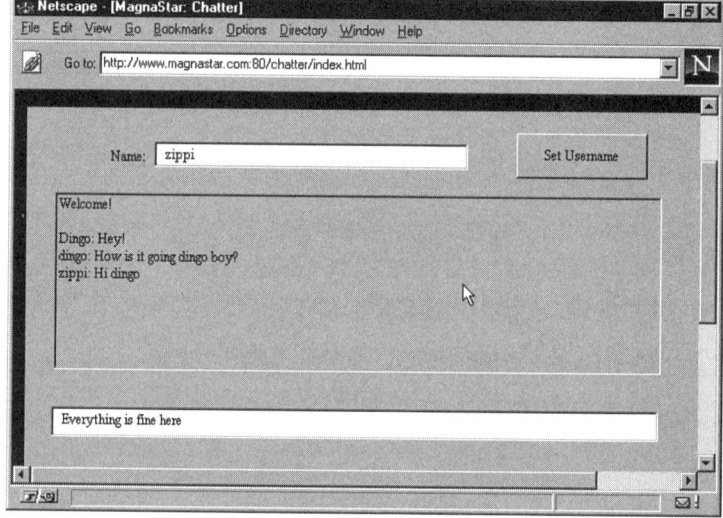

Games Games on the Web can serve countless purposes, such as to enhance training, to entertain, and to make revenue from advertising. Although creating games is not a great reason to adopt Java, games written in Java are proliferating the Internet.

Games usually ensure that visitors to your Web page will return. Also, because games take time to play, they enable you to hold your audience's attention longer. Figure 20.5 shows a typical game, Gobbler.

FIG. 20.5
Gobbler is a typical example of a game written in Java.

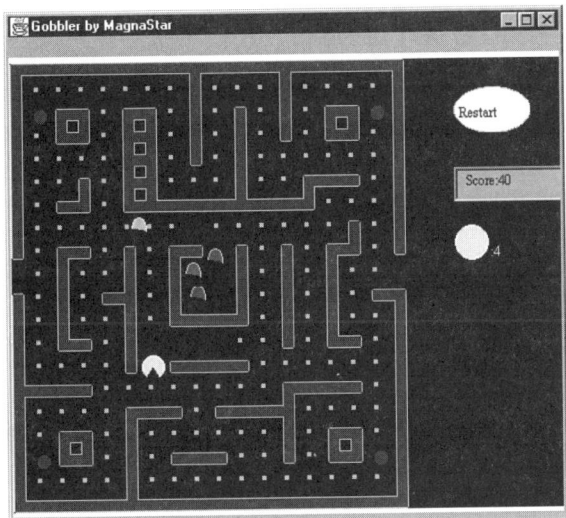

Java versus Plug-Ins

Java and JavaScript share several advantages over traditional plug-ins. Two of the more significant advantages are that users don't have to download Java and JavaScript programs, and that many browsers support Java. At the same time, Java has some disadvantages that plug-ins or JavaScript do not impose.

You Don't Have To Download Programs

Although you have to download plug-ins, you don't have to download Java or JavaScript programs. This advantage can be a major factor. Plug-ins can take from a half an hour to several hours to download and properly install with Netscape. Many Web surfers are unwilling to take that much time just to see a simple animation. In contrast, support for Java and JavaScript are built right in to the browser; as soon as surfers access the Web page, they can begin downloading the applet.

Many Browsers Support Java

Java is directly embedded not only in Netscape but in Web Navigator, Internet Explorer, and soon a host of other browsers. This widespread support far transcends standard plug-in technology, which works only within the bounds of Netscape. Netscape's API will probably never be adopted by as many browsers as the Java Virtual Machine. For this reason, you make your enhancements available to a much larger audience if you use Java. Note, however, that JavaScript does *not* enjoy the same breadth of support as Java.

The Downside of Java

Currently Java has two major disadvantages that JavaScript lacks. First, Java programs are expensive to develop. Because Java is a full-fledged programming language, it can be difficult for many Webmasters to learn. Several consulting firms are now available to develop applications. The current rate for most qualified Java consultants is about $150 per hour. Although this rate is actually quite reasonable, the cost can be prohibitive for smaller companies.

The second downside to Java is that it does not currently run under Windows 3.1. Many users with Intel-based machines have not yet upgraded to Windows 95 or Windows NT, and thus remain Java-handicapped. Several companies have joined together to try to solve this problem, but technical limitations with the Windows 3.1 architecture make support of Java unlikely until late 1996. Fortunately, however, JavaScript support is available in every Netscape platform.

> **NOTE** Support for plug-ins is limited to the platforms for which they were developed. Therefore, most plug-ins are not available to the UNIX and Macintosh users. For this reason, Java's lack of Windows 3.1 support should not be your only reason for not using Java.

Including a Java Applet in an HTML Page

If your primary goal in this chapter is simply to learn how to display the "Java compliant" logo on your pages, this section is for you. The simplest way to obtain a Java applet is to obtain one that has already been built, or that you can contract to have built for you. If you have not yet learned to program in Java, having other people develop your applets is probably the direction that you will take first. Accordingly, this section examines how to include the new application in a Web page. This section's example demonstrates how to include a simple applet from MagnaStar, Inc., called Gobbler. Gobbler is an example of a prebuilt applet that you can obtain from the Internet. You can find a copy of Gobbler at the following address:

http://www.magnastar.com/applets/games/gobbler

Figure 20.6 shows Gobbler in action.

FIG. 20.6
Gobbler is a game available from MagnaStar that you can include in a Web page.

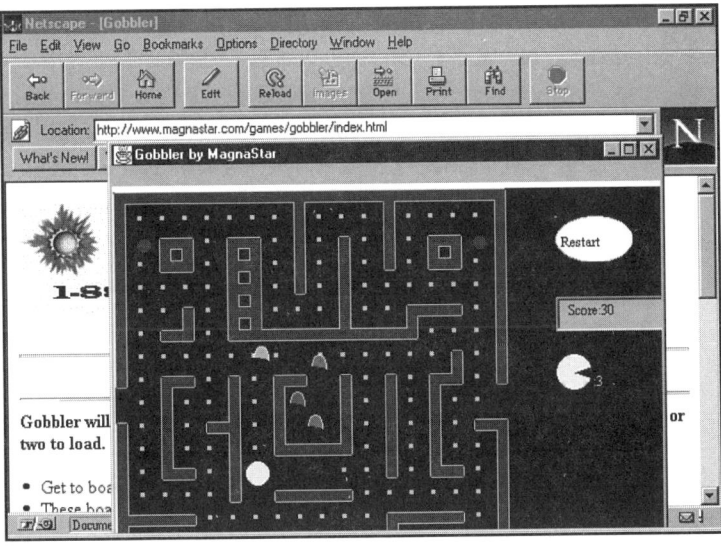

Now consider how you could include Gobbler in a Web page. Listing 20.2 shows the simplest version of an HTML file that you could use to display Gobbler.

Listing 20.2 Generating an HTML File To Display Gobbler

```
<HTML>
<BODY>
<applet code="gobLoader.class" height=0 width=0></applet>
</BODY>
</HTML>
```

Notice the new <APPLET> tag on the third line. You use the <APPLET> tag to indicate to the browser that you want it to include an applet on your page. In many ways, the <APPLET> tag is similar to the <IMG> tag. The <APPLET> tag offers three key attributes: CODE, HEIGHT, and WIDTH.

The CODE value of <APPLET> is similar to the SRC value of <IMG>. In the case of <APPLET>, you must set the CODE value to the name of the applet's main class file. Gobbler has several classes, but the only one that you should include in the HTML file is gobLoader.class. *Important:* Including the wrong class name can cause some strange and disastrous problems.

> **NOTE** Most applets include either a description of the class file to include or an example HTML file that you can examine to find the right class file. Alternatively, the class name is the one thing that you can see when viewing the HTML document source on another site. ■

The HEIGHT and WIDTH attributes are identical to those in the <IMG> tag. Applets share one trait, however, that differs from an image. Some applets, such as Gobbler, don't actually take up any space on the Web page. Instead, they create their own window. For this reason, you should set the size to 0. Also, for almost all applets, you should always set the HEIGHT and WIDTH attributes. If you do not specify the height and width for images, the browser can eventually figure them out on its own. But such is not usually the case for applets.

Finally, notice the <APPLET> tag's closing </APPLET> tag. The ending tag is required for an applet. In addition, as you will see in listing 20.3, because the <APPLET> tag does not have an ALT attribute like <IMG> does, you can use the space before the </APPLET> tag to include additional information.

Including Alternative Information for Non-Java Browsers

Listing 20.3 shows a more complete version of the HTML for Gobbler.

Listing 20.3   A More Complete Version of the HTML for Gobbler

```
<HTML>
<BODY>
<applet code="gobLoader.class" height=0 width=0>
Warning: You are not using a Java browser. There is an applet
on this page you cannot see. If you had a Java-enabled browser
you would see something similar to the picture below<br>
<img src="gobbler.gif" alt="Game Picture">
</applet>
</BODY>
</HTML>
```

As this listing demonstrates, you can include any standard HTML between the <APPLET> and </APPLET> tags. Non-Java browsers ignore the <APPLET> tag and read only this information.

Using the *<PARAM>* Tag

Java applets have added another HTML tag, <PARAM>, in addition to <APPLET>. Many applets use the parameter tag to specify additional information about their behavior. One applet that does so is GrayButton, also from MagnaStar, Inc. GrayButton provides a simple way to add some interaction to your Web pages. Figure 20.7 shows GrayButton in use on one Web page; note how the icon that the mouse is over differs from the others.

Including a Java Applet in an HTML Page | 421

FIG. 20.7
On this home page, GrayButton is adding interaction to highlight the icon that the mouse is currently over.

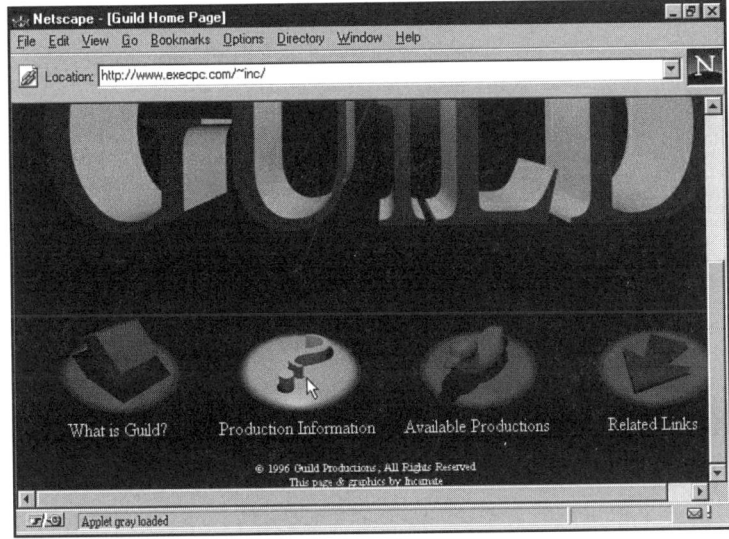

You can obtain GrayButton at the following site:

http://www.magnastar.com/applets/misc/grayButton

Listing 20.4 shows the complete code for including GrayButton on your Web page.

Listing 20.4 Including GrayButton on Your Web Page

```
<HTML>
<BODY>
<applet code="gray.class"  width=300 height=300>
<param name="graphic" value ="http://www.magnastar.com/NOW.GIF">
<param name="link" value="http://www.magnastar.com/GrayButton/license.html">
<a href="license.html"><img src="NOW.GIF"></a>
</applet>
</BODY>
</HTML>
```

Note the <PARAM> tags on the fourth and fifth lines. To get this applet to run, you must specify a graphic for it to load, and a place to link if the user clicks the button. The best way to understand how the <PARAM> tag works is to examine its syntax.

You must include the <PARAM> tag between the <APPLET> and </APPLET> tags. A <PARAM> tag anywhere else has no point of reference, so the browser would ignore it.

The <PARAM> tag has two attributes of its own: NAME and VALUE. You use the NAME attribute to specify which parameter you are setting. In the case of the GrayButton applet, you must set two names: graphic and link.

You use the VALUE attribute to specify the value to associate with the NAME. The value could also be a number if the applet calls for that type of data.

> **NOTE** In addition to demonstrating the use of the <PARAM> tags, the example in listing 20.4 also shows how to use an image link before the </APPLET> tag. This link is another example of an alternative display. If the viewer does not have a Java-enabled browser, the graphic displays instead. In the case of GrayButton, this works particularly well, because without a Java browser you only lose the level of interaction. With a traditional browser, you see the image; with a Java browser, the image changes depending on the mouse's location.

Developing a JavaScript Page

This section is intended only as a primer to get you started developing a JavaScript program. For a complete book on creating Web pages with JavaScript, see Que's *Special Edition Using JavaScript.* Like Java, JavaScript includes several additional tags. First among these is the <SCRIPT> and </SCRIPT> set of tags. Another tag, <!-->, has actually been around for some time, but JavaScript has a different use for it.

Including a Script in Your Web Page

The first task when creating a JavaScript page is to open an HTML file in your favorite text editor. On Windows machines, this editor can be Notepad, Edit, or any other standard editor. Create a file called HELLOSCRIPT.HTML and insert the code in listing 20.5.

Listing 20.5 A Very Simple JavaScript Program

```
<HTML>
<HEAD>
  <TITLE=JavaScript Hello World Document</TITLE>
</HEAD>
<BODY>
<SCRIPT>
document.write("Hello World!");
</SCRIPT>
<p> That was a Demonstration of a JavaScript program
</BODY>
</HTML>
```

Testing the Script

To test your new script, open the file with your Netscape browser. You should see a display similar to figure 20.8. As you can see, the script simply prints the text between the parentheses as if they were standard HTML. (This script accomplishes something that you can do much more easily without JavaScript, but you have to learn how to crawl before you can walk.)

FIG. 20.8
Your script outputs the text that you inserted between the parentheses.

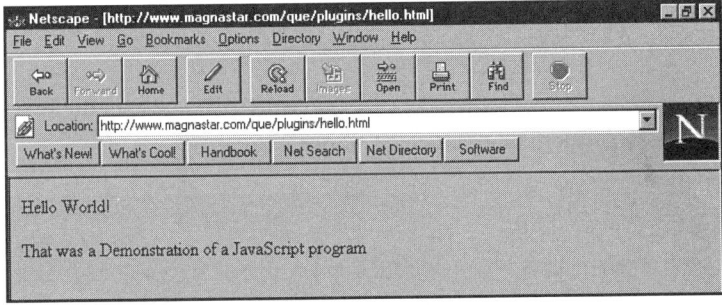

If you load this file into a non-Netscape browser, the script's text prints as shown in figure 20.9. This output definitely is not what you want.

FIG. 20.9
Run from a non-Netscape browser, your script prints its first line in a way that you did not intend.

Hiding the Script from Other Browsers

To solve the problem of other browsers displaying the JavaScript code, Netscape enables you to place a JavaScript program's contents within a comment tag. When you do so, browsers that do not understand JavaScript ignore the script and do not display contents. Listing 20.6 shows the "hello" program with the script commented out.

Listing 20.6 Using Comments To Hide a Script from Browsers That Don't Understand JavaScript

```
<HTML>
<HEAD>
  <TITLE=JavaScript Hello World Document</TITLE>
</HEAD>
<BODY>
<SCRIPT>
<!--This is a JavaScript,
document.write("Hello World!");
```

continues

Listing 20.6 Continued

```
//end of JavaScript -->
</SCRIPT>
<p> That was a Demonstration of a JavaScript program
</BODY>
</HTML>
```

If you now view this file with a browser that does not understand JavaScript, you do not see the scripting output, as shown in figure 20.10.

FIG. 20.10
By commenting out scripts, you avoid displaying them on browsers that are not fluent in JavaScript.

JavaScript outside of <SCRIPT> Tags

Unlike most HTML objects, much of what JavaScript can do occurs outside of its native tags. Much of JavaScript's enhancements are actually added attributes to traditional HTML tags.

Incorporating a Fancy HTML Anchor   One of the most common uses for JavaScript currently is to provide more feedback when a user clicks an anchor. For instance, if you want to make sure that visitors know when they are leaving your Web site, you might create an HTML file similar to listing 20.7.

Listing 20.7 Ensuring That Visitors Know That They Are Leaving Your Web Site

```
<HTML>
<BODY>
<A HREF = "http://www.yahoo.com" onClick="alert(
   'You are leaving us now, be careful in the outside world';">Go to Yahoo!</a>
</BODY>
</HTML>
```

Now when visitors click the link, they should see something similar to figure 20.11.

FIG. 20.11
You can display a message box informing visitors when they are leaving your Web site.

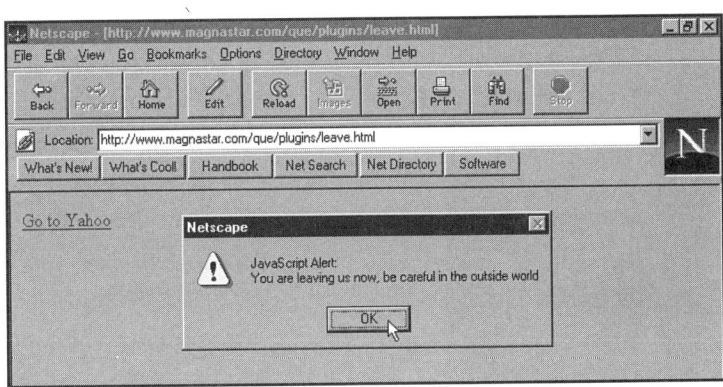

Now examine how you create this warning. Line three is as follows:

```
<A HREF = "http://www.yahoo.com" onClick="alert(
    'You are leaving us now, be careful in the outside world';
    ">Go to Yahoo!</a>
```

The first part of the line looks like a standard HTML anchor link. Following the anchor's standard portion is an additional parameter that begins with the following:

```
onClick = "
```

`onClick` is a JavaScript event handler. In the case of `onClick`, when the visitor clicks the anchor, the script that follows the equal sign executes. In this example, you also use an *alert window*, which is a standard JavaScript function that you can call at any time. The function produces the window shown in figure 20.11.

JavaScript enables you to capture several events that can affect standard HTML tags. The general syntax for taking advantage of such an activity is as follows:

```
<TAG eventHandler ="Script Code">
```

For the example in listing 20.7, the `TAG` that you use is `<A HREF>`. However, you do not have to associate all events with anchors. You can associate events with any standard HTML tag, including `<INPUT>`.

Table 20.1 lists some event handlers, the events with which they are associated, and when that event occurs.

Table 20.1   JavaScript Event Handlers

Event Hander	Event	Event Occurs When
onLoad	load	The page loads into the Navigator
onClick	click	The user clicks a link or form element

continues

Table 20.1 Continued

Event Hander	Event	Event Occurs When
onMouseOver	mouseover	The user moves the mouse pointer over an anchor or link
onSelect	select	The user selects a form element's input field
onChange	change	The user changes the value of text, a text area, or a selected element
onFocus	focus	The user gives a form element focus
onBlur	blur	The user removes focus from a form element
onSubmit	submit	A form is submitted
onUnload	unload	The page is exited

Mixing <SCRIPT> Tags and Event Handlers

For event handlers associated with a <TAG>, the complexity of the script is very limited. However, by mixing a <SCRIPT> and an event handler, you can complete very complicated tasks.

To call the contents of a <SCRIPT> from a <TAG>, you first must create a JavaScript function. A function is a set of tasks that you can call from anywhere within the current set. In Netscape Navigator, for instance, you can call any function defined anywhere on the current page from anywhere else on that page.

Now examine an example that takes advantage of a function defined between the <SCRIPT> and </SCRIPT> tags. The user calls the function by clicking an anchor. Listing 20.8 shows the new HTML page.

Listing 20.8 Producing a Prompting Window When the User Clicks a Link

```
<HTML>
<BODY>
<SCRIPT>
  function direction(){
     directionWindow = window.open ("direction.html","directions",
         'width=200,height=200');
  }
</SCRIPT>
<a href="http://www.magnastar.com/games/gobbler" onClick="
      if (confirm('Do you want directions on how to play?'))
         (direction());">
Play Gobbler </a>
</BODY>
</HTML>
```

Figure 20.12 shows the message that appears when the user clicks the link.

FIG. 20.12
When the user clicks the link, this confirmation dialog box appears.

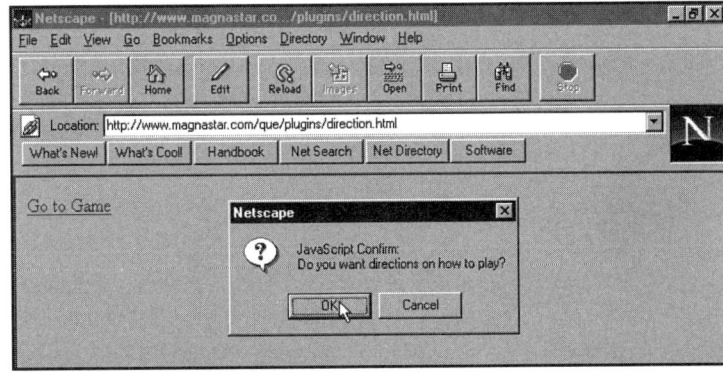

You have seen what happens when you load this file. Now you need to examine why these events happen. First, take a look at the section between the <SCRIPT> and <SCRIPT> tags. Notice that you create a simple function called direction(). When you call direction(), it uses the window.open function to create a simple new Navigator window that you use to display the directions on how to play Gobbler. This type of interaction is often quite helpful. You need to understand how the window.open function works.

window is actually the name of a JavaScript object. A thorough discussion of objects is beyond the scope of this chapter, but the function window.object essentially means "open a window." The open method has several options that you can use. The open method's complete syntax is as follows:

```
[windowVariable=]window.open("URL",["windowName"],["windowFeatures"])
```

The URL parameter specifies the resource that the new window will open. You can use the optional windowName parameter to give the window a unique name. This name can be helpful when trying to direct interaction. The windowName is identical to the name parameter used for a frame. Finally, you can use the optional windowFeatures parameter to specify a host of options about the window. In listing 20.8, you use the options to specify the new window's height and width. Table 20.2 lists all the windowFeatures options.

Table 20.2 The windowFeatures Parameter's Options

Parameter	Option(s)	Meaning
toolbar	[yes¦no] or [1¦0]	Provides the new window a toolbar that includes backward and forward buttons.
location	[yes¦no] or [1¦0]	Shows the location entry field.

continues

Table 20.2 Continued

Parameter	Option(s)	Meaning
`directories`	[yes¦no] or [1¦0]	Displays the directory buttons, such as What's New and Net Search.
`status`	[yes¦no] or [1¦0]	Shows the status bar at the bottom of the window.
`menubar`	[yes¦no] or [1¦0]	Creates at the top of the window a menu that includes such options as File and Edit.
`scrollbars`	[yes¦no] or [1¦0]	Creates scrollbars when the document exceeds the normal window size.
`resizable`	[yes¦no] or [1¦0]	Enables the user to resize the window. If you turn off this option, the user cannot resize the window.
`width`	Number of pixels	Specifies the window's width in pixels.
`height`	Number of pixels	Specifies the window's height in pixels.

Notice how listing 20.8 uses the `direction` function. In the heart of the HTML file is an anchor that looks like the following:

```
<a href="http://www.magnastar.com/games/gobbler"> onClick="
    if (confirm('Do you want directions on how to play?'))
    (direction());">
```

When the user clicks the link, a confirmation window displays. This window is quite similar to the alert window shown in figure 20.11. The primary difference between the confirmation window and the alert window is that the confirmation window has two options, OK and Cancel. An alert window, however, only enables the user to choose OK. To respond to either the OK or Cancel options, the `confirm()` function returns either True (OK) or False (Cancel). In this example, if the user clicks OK, you call the `direction` function, which is contained between the <SCRIPT> and </SCRIPT> tags.

Validating a Form before Submission

Another common use of JavaScript is to help verify that the user has completed all parts of a form before submitting it to the server. Without JavaScript, if the user clicks the submit button, the program eventually prompts the user that the form was not completed correctly. The user then must return to the form and finish filling it out. A fairly minor JavaScript can make this process much less laborious.

This section presents a simple example of a form that asks for some information about the user. In this example, you ask the user to enter a name, e-mail address, and birth date. Figure 20.13 shows the form's appearance.

FIG. 20.13
A simple JavaScript form.

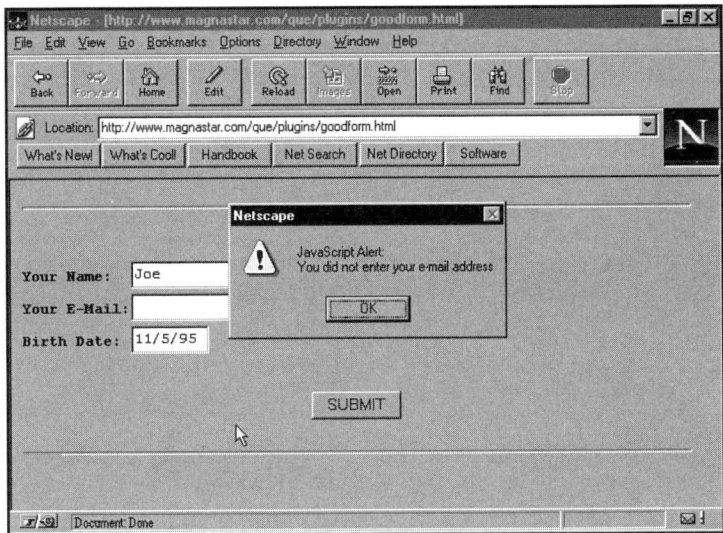

What type of data would you ordinarily expect the user to enter into this form? First, you want to ensure that the user has actually entered a name. For the e-mail address, you not only want to ensure that the user entered a value, but also that the value represents a valid e-mail address (such as **jweber@magnastar.com**), so you check whether the user included an *at* symbol (@) in his or her address. Finally, for the birth date, you want to ensure that the user included two slashes.

This page is actually a bit more complicated than those that you have seen previously, so this section divides up the code so that you can better understand what each part of the code is doing. The complete code is in listing 20.9.

The Form   Most developers begin by looking at the application from the user's perspective, so you start with the user interface. The following portion of the HTML file should be familiar to you if you are used to creating forms:

```
<HR>
<FORM NAME ="goodFormDemo" METHOD="get">
<PRE>
<B>
Your Name: <INPUT TYPE="text" NAME="name" SIZE=25>
Your E-Mail:<INPUT TYPE = "text" NAME="email" size=25>
Birth Date :<INPUT TYPE = "text" NAME="bday" size=8>
</B>
</PRE>
```

Now examine the modified submit button that you will use to call your JavaScript. The following modification assumes that you will later return to create a function called `PageCheck()`:

```
<CENTER>
<INPUT TYPE="button" NAME="submit" VALUE="SUBMIT" onClick="PageCheck(
    this.form)">
</CENTER>
</FORM>
<HR>
```

The Script   Now that you have the laid out the form, it's time to create the script to verify that the user has entered information correctly.

You first must add the `<SCRIPT>` tag to tell the browser that it is reading a script. To be complete, you should also open a comment tag. As discussed earlier, adding a comment tag prevents other browsers from trying to display the script's body.

```
<SCRIPT>
  <!-- This is the JavaScript
```

Now that you have handled this housekeeping, you can jump into the script. The form causes `onClick` to call a function named `PageCheck()`, and also passes a variable into the function. You declare the `PageCheck()` function as follows:

```
function PageCheck (form){
```

This function's main objective is to check through the whole form to ensure that the user has filled it out completely. To keep track of the status of completion, declare a variable to track whether the user has completed the form as you test each section:

```
var errorStatus=false;
```

The first element in the form is the name. As you have learned, all that you can do to check the name is to ensure that the user entered something. Preventing the user from entering a false name is difficult, but you at least want to ensure that the user didn't fail to enter anything. You also know that for several other entries you will want to ensure that the field is not empty. Therefore, create a function called `ifEmpty()` (this function is discussed more fully later):

```
if (ifEmpty(form.name)){
  alert("You did not leave your name");
  errorStatus=true;
}
```

For now, assume that this function returns a status of True if the field is empty, or False if something is in the field. This function enables you to check the name field.

If nothing is in the field, you generate an alert window to notify the user that he or she has failed to fill in the empty portion of the form. In this situation, you don't want to submit the form to the server (because you don't want to submit forms that have been filled out incorrectly). To keep track of this fact, you set the errorStatus field to True, which indicates that you have detected an error.

Next comes the e-mail field. Earlier you determined that this field might have two requirements: that it is filled out, and that the field includes the character @.

To check whether the e-mail field contains anything, you can use the same ifEmpty() function that you are using for the name field. To find out whether the field contains the required character @, assume that you are going to create a function called ifContains that is True if the symbol is present in the field:

```
//Now check the e-mail field
if (ifEmpty(form.email)){
  alert("You did not enter your e-mail address");
  errorStatus=true;
  }
//Check to make sure that the e-mail address contains an @ symbol
else if (!ifContains(form.email,"@")){
  alert("Your e-mail address is not complete");
  errorStatus=true;
  }
```

The e-mail check is a bit more complicated than the name check. Notice the if-else sequence. If nothing is in the e-mail field, the field obviously doesn't include the character @; therefore, if you need to tell the user that the field is empty, you need not also specify that the character @ is missing. As a result, the only time that you check for the @ character is after you have already established that the user entered something into the field.

The last field is the birthday. Like the other two fields, you need to establish that the user entered something into the bday field; in addition, the field must include two slashes (/). To give the user a little slack, you can also include support for hyphens (-). As with the other field checks, you create a function, ifContains2():

```
//Check the birthday field
if (ifEmpty(form.bday)){
  alert ("You did not enter your birthday");
  errorStatus=true;
  }
//Check to make sure that the birthday contains either a - or a /
if (!(ifContains2(form.bday,"/")¦¦ifContains2(form.bday,"-"))){
    alert ("You did not fill in your birthday completely");
    errorStatus = true;
    }
```

Now that you have checked the form, you need to submit it. First, however, you must ensure that you do not detect an error with the form. If there is an error, you let the user return to the form and fill it out completely. Then you simply open a document and thank the user for filling out the form. (For most forms, you would also want to add code to send the data to the server at this point.)

```
if (!errorStatus){
  document.open();
  document.write("<HTML><HEAD><TITLE>Form Verification Correct</TITLE></HEAD>");
  document.write("<H1>You have filled out the form completely</H1>");
  document.write("<CENTER>Thank You</CENTER>");
  document.close();
  }
}
```

You're still not completely finished. You still need to create the functions that you previously assumed. The first function checks for an empty field:

```
//The ifEmpty function finds if a field has anything in it
function ifEmpty(CheckField){
  if (CheckField.value.length==0)
    return true;
  else
    return false;
}
```

The `if()` statement in this function is a bit complicated. The `CheckField` variable is a copy of the field. The field itself isn't exactly what you need, however. Instead, you want to check the string inside of the field. You can get to the string by using the `.value` parameter. To make sure that the string isn't empty, the easiest solution is to ensure that the string doesn't have a length of zero. To get a string's length, you use the `.length` parameter.

The second function that you use is `ifContains()`. This function determines whether a string includes a particular character. One way to find the character is to examine each character and determine whether it matches the one for which you are searching. Although this method would work fine, an easier method is available.

JavaScript has several built-in functions that can often save you time. In this case, a function called `indexOf()` can tell you which character in a string matches the one for which you are searching. If the character is not in the string, `indexOf()` returns –1. Therefore, this value is exactly the one that you want to find.

```
//the ifContains function finds if the inputChar is in the field
  function ifContains(CheckField,inputChar){
    var x = CheckField.value.indexOf(inputChar);
    if (x<0)
      return false;
    return true;
  }
```

Finally, you use a function called `IfContains2`. Fortunately, finding out the last index of a character is also relatively easy, thanks to JavaScript's built-in function `lastIndexOf()`. To find out whether a string contains two characters, you need only verify that the first and last instances of a character are not the same. Although this solution is logical, it has one small problem: What happens if the character is not in the string at all? Both indexOf() and lastIndexOf() return –1, so both return values could be the same. To address this problem, ifContains2() also takes advantage of ifContains():

```
function ifContains2(CheckField,inputChar){
  //make sure there is at least one
  var first =CheckField.value.indexOf(inputChar);
  var last =CheckField.value.lastIndexOf(inputChar);
  if ((ifContains(CheckField,inputChar))&&(first!=last))
    return true;
  return false;
  }
  return false;
}
```

The Complete Program   Now that you have seen each of the parts of the GoodForm demonstration, listing 20.9 presents the complete program.

Listing 20.9   The Complete GoodForm Program

```
<!-- this is the actual form -->
<HR>
<FORM NAME="goodFormDemo" METHOD="get">
<PRE>
<B>
Your Name:  <INPUT TYPE="text" NAME="name" SIZE=25>
Your E-Mail:<INPUT TYPE="text" NAME="email" SIZE=25>
Birth Date: <INPUT TYPE="text" NAME="bday" SIZE=8>
</B>
</PRE>
<CENTER>
<INPUT TYPE="button" NAME="submit" VALUE="SUBMIT" onClick="PageCheck(
     this.form)">
</CENTER>
</FORM>
<HR>

<SCRIPT>
  <!-- This is the JavaScript
  function PageCheck (form){
    //The errorStatus variable will be used to see if the form has been
    // completed correctly or if we should send the user back.
    var errorStatus=false;

    //Check the name field for completeness
    if (ifEmpty(form.name)){
      alert("You did not leave your name");
      errorStatus=true;
      }

    //Now check the e-mail field
    if (ifEmpty(form.email)){
      alert("You did not enter your e-mail address");
```

continues

Listing 20.9 Continued

```
            errorStatus=true;
          }
    //Check to make sure that the e-mail address contains an @ symbol
    else if (!ifContains(form.email,"@")){
      alert("Your e-mail address is not complete");
      errorStatus=true;
      }

    //Check the birthday field
    if (ifEmpty(form.bday)){
      alert ("You did not enter your birthday");
      errorStatus=true;
      }
    //Check to make sure that the birthday contains either a - or a /
    if (!(ifContains2(form.bday,"/")¦¦ifContains2(form.bday,"-"))){
       alert ("You did not fill in your birthday completely");
       errorStatus = true;
       }

    if (!errorStatus){
      document.open();
      document.write(
           "<HTML><HEAD><TITLE>Form Verification Correct</TITLE></HEAD>");
      document.write("<H1>You have filled out the form completely</H1>");
      document.write("<CENTER>Thank You</CENTER>");
      document.close();
      }
  }
  //this ends the function PageCheck

  //The ifEmpty function finds if a field has anything in it
  function ifEmpty(CheckField){
    if (CheckField.value.length==0)
      return true;
    else
      return false;
  }

  //the ifContains function finds if the inputChar is in the field
  function ifContains(CheckField,inputChar){
    var x = CheckField.value.indexOf(inputChar);
    if (x<0)
      return false;
    return true;
}

  function ifContains2(CheckField,inputChar){
    //make sure there is at least one
    var first =CheckField.value.indexOf(inputChar);
    var last =CheckField.value.lastIndexOf(inputChar);
    if ((first>0)&&(first!=last))
      return true;
    return false;
    }
```

```
    //--This is the end of the script -->
    </SCRIPT>
</HTML>
```

Beginning To Develop a Java Applet

Now that you have seen how to build a few JavaScript examples, this section looks at some of the more popular types of Java applets. A complete discussion of Java is beyond the scope of this book. If you want to learn more about Java, pick up a copy of Que's *Special Edition Using Java*. Although this chapter only discusses how to use Java to create applets, you can just as easily use Java to create applications that run on local machines.

Before you can create a Java applet, you first must download and install the Java Developer's Kit (JDK). The JDK includes tools to compile the Java source code into Java class files that you can then run. You can obtain the JDK from Sun Microsystems at the following address:

> http://java.sun.com/devcorner.html

N O T E In Java terminology, a *method* is the same as what JavaScript and many other languages call *functions*.

The HelloWorld Applet

Previously you explored a "Hello World" example for JavaScript, so this section takes a look at a Java version. Listing 20.10 shows the complete code for a HelloWorld applet as written in Java.

Listing 20.10 A HelloWorld Applet Written in Java

```
import java.awt.Graphics;

public class HelloWorld extends java.applet.Applet{
  public void paint (Graphics g){
    g.drawString ("Hello World!",20,0);
  }
}
```

To create the HelloWorld applet, copy the contents of listing 20.10 into a file called HELLOWORLD.JAVA using any standard text editor. Unless you use this file name, you cannot compile the program, because the compiler expects the class name and the file name to match. If you have installed Sun's JDK in your path, you can compile the program by typing the following at a command prompt:

```
javac HelloWorld.java
```

N O T E If you are using Windows, you have to open a DOS prompt window for this program to work.

If everything works correctly, you should now have an additional file in your directory called HelloWorld.class. This file is the Java equivalent of an .EXE file. Before you can run the Applet, however, you must create an HTML file as discussed in the section "Including a Java Applet in an HTML Page." In the case of this HelloWorld applet, the HTML file should look like listing 20.11.

Listing 20.11 The HelloWorld Applet's HTML File

```
<HTML>
<BODY>
<APPLET code="HelloWorld.class" HEIGHT=100 WIDTH=100></APPLET>
</BODY>
</HTML>?
```

After you create the HTML file, you can open it in a browser such as Netscape Navigator or use one of the JDK tools, appletviewer. In this example, you use Netscape. Figure 20.14 shows the screen output after you load this file in Netscape.

FIG. 20.14
When you run the HTML file, your screen displays the "Hello World" message.

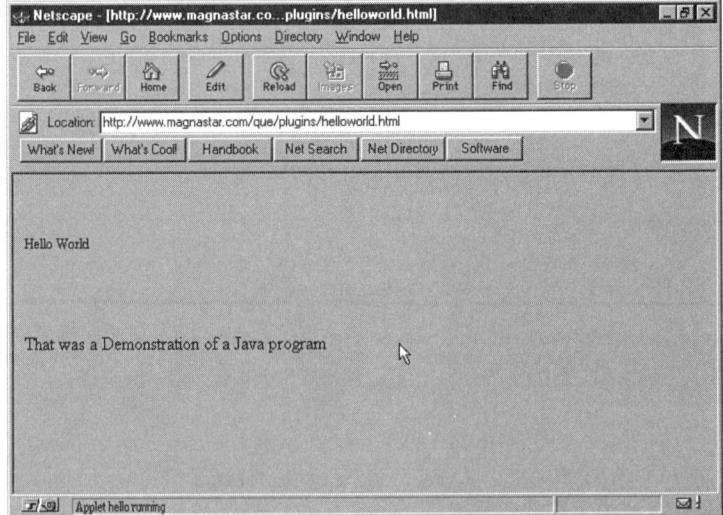

Notice that, unlike a JavaScript program, when you load a Java applet, the Navigator must return to the server to download the HelloWorld.class file before running it. The Navigator retrieves this file exactly the same way that it grabs a GIF file for an image, but the retrieval does take an extra second or two.

The Java Animator Applet

Currently one of the most popular uses for Java is to create simple animations. However, Java is not the best medium for creating animations. If all you want to do is create an animation, better means are available, such as GIF89a Cel Frame animations. Because Java is so frequently used for creating animation, however, this section describes how to use Java to write an animator. Listing 20.12 shows a complete version of an animator written in Java.

Listing 20.12 A Java Animator

```
import java.awt.*;
import java.util.Vector;

public class Animator extends java.applet.Applet implements Runnable {
Vector images;
int imgNumber;
int currentImage=1;
Thread thisThread;

  public void init(){
    //Read in the number of images in the animation
    imgNumber = new Integer(getParameter("imgNumber")).intValue();

    //Load the images
    for (int x=0;x<imgNumber;x++){
      Image img = getImage(getDocumentBase(),"images/img"+(x+1));
      images.addElement(img);
      }
  }

  public void paint(Graphics g){
    g.drawImage((Image)images.elementAt(currentImage++),0,0,null);
    currentImage%=imgNumber;
    }

  public void update(Graphics g){
    paint(g);
  }

  public void start(){
    thisThread = new Thread(this);
    thisThread.start();
    }
```

continues

Listing 20.12 Continued

```
  public void stop(){
    thisThread.stop();
  }

  public void run(){
    while(true){
      try{
        thisThread.sleep(100);
      }
      catch (Exception e){}
    }
  }
}
```

You can probably discern immediately that the animator is more complex than the HelloWorld applet. To compile this program, first copy all of listing 20.12 into a file called Animator.java. To run the program, you must create an HTML file that looks similar to listing 20.13.

Listing 20.13 The HTML File for the Animator

```
<HTML>
<BODY>
<APPLET code="Animator.class" HEIGHT=200 WIDTH=200>
<PARAM NAME="imgNumber" VALUE="5">
</APPLET>
</BODY>
</HTML>
```

In addition to these files, you also need to place several images in the subdirectory IMAGES. You must name the IMG1.GIF, IMG2.GIF, and so on, where IMG1.GIF is the first image of the animation. You also need to change the `imgNumber` parameter so that it holds the correct number of images. When you finish all this work, you should see a screen similar to figure 20.15.

To understand how the animator works, you need to examine its code in more manageable chunks. First note the first three lines of the code:

```
import java.awt.*;
import java.util.Vector;

public class Animator extends java.applet.Applet implements Runnable {
```

The first two lines import other Java classes. Java is an extensible language, and its object-oriented nature enables you to take advantage of prebuilt classes. The first two lines of the animator code import such classes.

FIG. 20.15
The browser displays an animation applet.

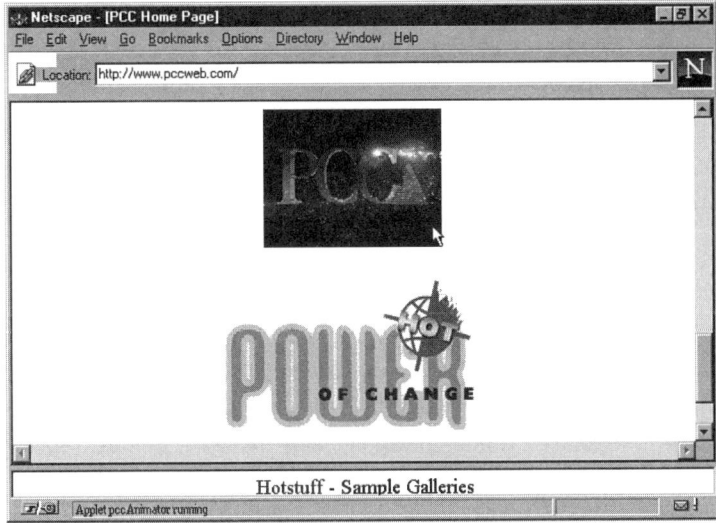

The third line of code is the class declaration. At the end of the line, notice that the Animator applet, like HelloWorld, extends java.applet.Applet, which is the name of the class from which all applets extend. Immediately after the class declaration is the statement implements Runnable, which indicates that you can run the application as a thread. Enabling Animator to run a thread is important because it continues processing even after the rest of the page finishes loading.

Immediately after these lines of code, Animator declares several variables of its own:

```
Vector images;
int imgNumber;
int currentImage=1;
Thread thisThread;
```

Unlike JavaScript, Java is a *strongly typed* language, which means that you must declare each variable to be a specific type. In JavaScript, you would create the variables with only the var keyword, as follows:

```
var images;
var imgNumber;
var currentImage=1;
var thisThread;
```

However, for a variety of reasons, this is not really the best way to work, and Java requires that you declare each variable's type. You create four variables. Vector is a class type that is very convenient for storing a large number of objects, especially if you do not know in advance how many you will be adding. The Thread variable controls the activity of the applet later on.

The Animator applet has several methods. The first is `init()`:

```
public void init(){
  //Read in the number of images in the animation
  imgNumber = new Integer(getParameter("imgNumber")).intValue();

  //Load the images
  for (int x=0;x<imgNumber;x++){
    Image img = getImage(getDocumentBase(),"images/img"+(x+1));
    images.addElement(img);
  }
}
```

The applet calls the `init()` method when the browser initially loads the page. `init()` is convenient for setting up variables that you need to initialize only once. In the case of the Animator class, you need to load all the images only once. Notice that after you call the `getImage()` method, the applet adds the image to the `images` vector.

The next method is `paint()`, which you call each time that you need to display the applet on the Web page. You might need to call this method if the user scrolls the applet off the screen and then scrolls back, or if you specifically want to repaint the applet.

```
public void paint(Graphics g){
  g.drawImage((Image)images.elementAt(currentImage++),0,0,null);
  currentImage%=imgNumber;
}
```

Instead of analyzing each individual piece of the `paint()` method, examine the parts of the `drawImage()` method a bit. This method obviously draws an image to the graphics screen. `drawImage()` takes four parameters: the image's name, the X and Y coordinates, and finally the `imageObserver` that should pay attention to changes in the image.

Notice the complexity of the image name:

```
(((Image)images.elementAt(currentImage++)))
```

You can best analyze this name starting from the right side. First, you want to display the current image (`currentImage`). Incrementing the `currentImage` number makes it easy to determine the next image to display, so you automatically increment the `currentImage` variable (`currentImage++`). You have stored the images in a vector, so you retrieve the current image from the vector by using the method `elementAt()` on the image object (`elementAt(CurrentImage++)`). The only problem at this point is that the vector does not really know that it is holding an image. The vector only knows that it has something, and thus returns the image to you in a way that isn't quite right. For this reason, you must perform a *cast*. The `(Image)` in front of the `images.elementAt` performs the cast for you so that you retrieve the image successfully.

The next method is `start()`, which you call each time that the user goes to a specific page. You might think that you would call the `init()` method instead, but actually you call init() only the first time that the page loads. You call start() the first time as well, after init(), but for successive loads, you call only start().

```
public void start(){
  thisThread = new Thread(this);
  thisThread.start();
}
```

The start() method is a great place to put the applet into a known state. In the case of Animator, you create a thread, which means that the applet continues to run while the rest of the browser performs other tasks.

```
public void stop(){
    thisThread.stop();
}
```

A close cousin to the start() method is stop(), which you call each time that the user leaves the page. Cleaning up what you have started is important after the user exits the page. Animator's stop() method stops the thread that the applet was running.

The last method for Animator is run(), which actually runs in the thread:

```
public void run(){
  while(true){
    repaint();
    try{
      thisThread.sleep(100);
    }
    catch (Exception e){}
  }
}
```

Animator's run() method essentially performs a constant loop. The loop first tells Animator to repaint, and then to place the Animator thread into a sleep state for 100ms. The result is that the next frame of the animation displays 10 times a second (1/100ms).

Interacting between JavaScript, Java, and Plug-Ins

One of the promised advantages of JavaScript is the capability to communicate between JavaScript and Java. In addition, JavaScript will eventually be capable of communicating with traditional plug-ins.

This feature is not yet available. However, because JavaScript has greater control over the Navigator window and plug-ins, eventually one of the most important purposes for JavaScript will be as a conduit among applets, plug-ins, and the browser.

Support with Browsers Other Than Netscape Navigator

Many companies have announced support for Java, although currently only three browsers offer such support: Microsoft Internet Explorer, IBM Web Explorer, and Netscape Navigator. In addition, most browser developers on the market have also announced that they intend to support Java eventually.

Java and JavaScript Resources

Several Web sites have emerged that specialize exclusively in indexes on Java and JavaScript applications. This section describes a few.

Finding Example Applets and JavaScript Pages

One of the largest directories currently available for example applets and JavaScript pages is Gamelan:

> http://www.gamelan.com

The Java Applet Review System (JARS) is another great site that rates applets on a top 1 percent, 5 percent, and 25 percent basis:

> http://www.jars.com

Apple Flavored Java is a site dedicated to Java on the Macintosh:

> http://www.seas.upenn.edu/~mcrae/projects/macjava/

The Java Centre is a British site:

> http://www.java.co.uk/javacentre.html

The Java Boutique is a collection of Java applets. To be listed on this site, the applet must make its source available.

> http://weber.u.washington.edu/~jgurney/Java

Javology is a magazine that provides weekly updates about new items of interest in the Java community:

> http://www.magnastar.com/javology

Finding a Java Consultant

Because you are unlikely to have the time to develop your own custom applet, the following sites can help you to find a Java developer. These sites are also good places to look for Java applications and applets.

MagnaStar, Inc. is a custom Java programming and consulting company:

http://www.magnastar.com

Dimension X develops Java applications:

http://www.dnx.com

Team Java is a resource that boasts a good list of Java developers:

http://www.teamjava.com

CHAPTER 21

Creating Your Own Plug-Ins

- Why you might want to create your own custom plug-ins
- How to build custom plug-ins for the two most popular browsers on the Web
- What sorts of tools you need to complete the job
- How to use these tools to generate plug-in code

With the rise of corporate intranets (networks that use Internet protocols and can be navigated with Internet tools, but which aren't connected to the global network), an increasing number of corporate network experts are asking their browsers to fill ever-more-exotic data-handling niches. Thanks largely to plug-ins, Web browsers are becoming the real workhorses of the networked workplace. As you've seen elsewhere in this book, they can handle everything from streamed video to highly compressed still graphics and CD-quality sound.

A large selection of plug-ins are available, but there's still a good chance that you have some specialized application that's been ignored by the companies that develop plug-ins for large markets. Perhaps you work with a proprietary file format, or need to interpret data in an unusual way. What do you do when you have data in an obscure file format and want to share it with someone across the Internet? Or perhaps you've used the plug-ins described in this book's earlier chapters, and you think that you can develop a better one to perform the task.

http://www.mcp.com/que

Fortunately, Netscape Communications Corporation, in a move calculated to increase its browser's market share, told the world how to make plug-ins for Netscape Navigator. Microsoft later adopted the same specification for its Microsoft Internet Explorer browser. By using public information about plug-ins and a couple of common programming tools, you can design and code full-fledged plug-ins that work with both Netscape Navigator and Microsoft Internet Explorer. You'll be able to exchange exotically formatted information on the Internet, or provide a product that interprets a common kind of data better than any other. Either way, by creating your own plug-ins, you can increase your browser's functionality. Perhaps your innovations can even earn you some money.

This chapter isn't intended to be a complete guide to developing plug-ins; the subject simply is too broad. The chapter gives you an idea of what you are getting into if you decide to build a custom plug-in, but doesn't prepare you for every situation that might arise during the plug-in development process. ■

For an irreverent but technically astute take on developing plug-ins, check out *Unplugged! The Bare-Bones Shebang about Netscape Plug-Ins* at **http://www.neca.com/~vmis/plugins.html**. This site, put together by experienced plug-in coder Vijay Mukhi, guides you through the plug-in development process. *Unplugged!* was one of the main information sources for this chapter.

Why Create Your Own Plug-Ins?

Any enterprise has to have a reason, and your effort to build a plug-in for Netscape Navigator or Microsoft Internet Explorer is no exception. Before you begin spending the time and effort necessary to produce a functioning plug-in, you must make sure that you have a reason for undertaking all the trouble.

There are three main reasons for developing your own plug-ins:

- Because you have a special need for the plug-in
- Because you think you can "build a better mousetrap"
- Because you enjoy programming

The following subsections discuss these motivations further.

Because You Have a Special Need

You might want to enable people (probably yourself and your coworkers) to view an unusual kind of data, such as a proprietary graphics file format, within your Web browsers. Perhaps the kind of data that you use is so obscure that no software developer has a plug-in for it on the market. The only browser-based solution open to you is a custom plug-in.

Don't neglect the possibility that you might be able to sell a specialized plug-in to other people in your field, or at least distribute it freely in hopes of gaining the esteem of others in your line of work.

Suppose, for example, that you are a fluid dynamicist. If you design a plug-in that enables you to view within your browser window information in the form of special computer files that describes the motion of air or water, you have a valuable product. You can either try to sell your plug-in to other fluid dynamicists, or you can give it away without charge—a strategy that's sure to improve your professional reputation. Building a plug-in can turn into a real opportunity.

Because You Can Build a Better Mousetrap

Plug-ins that play .AVI files and handle Microsoft Word documents exist, but maybe you don't like any of them. You think that you can make a plug-in that does a better job of performing some common task. After creating your superior plug-in, you might give it away as freeware or try to sell it as shareware or as a commercial product.

CAUTION
Creating better mousetraps is the most common way to make money coding plug-ins. But beware: The plug-in market is crowded, and most plug-in developers seem to be using plug-ins as loss leaders for the products that they sell. Making a living exclusively as a designer and coder of plug-ins is tough.

Because You Enjoy Programming

Don't forget the joy of programming and the satisfaction that comes from mastering a new kind of computer application. If you can design and build a working browser plug-in, you'll have achieved something that few professional programmers—and even fewer computer hobbyists—have accomplished. That achievement results in a feeling of satisfaction at least as great as that which comes from building model planes or raising a cat (no offense meant to planes or cats).

Netscape's decision to publicize the plug-in specification can be compared IBM's 1982 decision to make public the specifications for its first personal computers. By enabling amateur and semiprofessional programmers to develop software that works with IBM's machines, IBM gave small-time coders the ability to leverage its marketing clout—effectively to ride Big Blue's coattails all the way to the bank. Similarly, small-time plug-in developers today can take advantage of the sales might that Netscape Communications—and now Microsoft, too—put behind the Web browser plug-in specification.

A Brief Technical Introduction

Now that you've established that you need or want to develop a plug-in, you're ready to begin wading into the big technical pond that is plug-in development. In this section, you learn what sorts of information and instructions are included in a plug-in, and how those bits of code interact with the main body of Netscape Navigator or Microsoft Internet Explorer code.

What Is a Plug-In, Technically Speaking?

A plug-in is a portion of computer code—a little program— that attaches itself to a browser program and thereby expands the browser's capabilities. Plug-ins take advantage of published browser specifications that tell where and how browsers look for supplemental code, and how they exchange data with those extensions. Plug-ins usually are used to handle special kinds of files that a browser might encounter on the network, such as multimedia files.

Plug-ins are *not* executable programs. You cannot double-click a plug-in's icon and expect it to do something, as you would expect of a full-blown program. Plug-ins are dynamically linked libraries (DLLs). You've seen DLL files; you can recognize them by their .DLL extensions. Practically all programs have DLLs. DLL files contain code that cannot execute on its own, but which another program can call. Programs and libraries can exchange data back and forth during the course of performing some computing task.

The Netscape plug-in specification mandates that all plug-in files reside in a folder or directory called PLUGINS that branches from the folder or directory in which the browser's executable file (NETSCAPE.EXE or MIE.EXE) resides. The browser executable looks in this directory for plug-ins every time that it starts. All plug-in DLL file names start with *NP* (for *Netscape plug-in*), so all plug-ins have names like NPAVI.DLL, NPTEX.DLL, and NPDWG.DLL.

> **NOTE** The specification for plug-ins is called the Netscape plug-in specification because Netscape Communications invented it. However, Microsoft later adopted the same standard for its Microsoft Internet Explorer browser. The standard applies to both browsers.

Many of the plug-ins that you have learned about elsewhere in this book come with supporting files that often reside in some folder or directory other than the PLUGINS folder within the browser's folder. These files are helpful—frequently, they're documentation files or free-standing applications that run independently of your browser—but they're not part of the plug-in itself. As far as the browser knows, a given plug-in is simply a .DLL file in the PLUGINS directory whose file name begins with *NP.*

What Does a Browser Do with a Plug-In?

Every time that a browser starts, it looks in the PLUGINS folder for .DLL files whose file names begin with *NP.* When the browser finds such files, what does it do with them?

At startup, the browser determines which file name extensions each plug-in can handle. A plug-in designed to play Video for Windows movies would lay claim to the .AVI extension, while a plug-in for playing RealAudio sound would stake out the .RAM and .RPM file name extensions. A plug-in effectively tells the main browser program that when it encounters particular file name extensions, ask that plug-in what to do about those files' contents.

You can view a list of registered file name extensions and the plug-ins that handle them in your browser. In Netscape, open the Help menu and choose About Plug-Ins. You then see the About Plug-Ins page shown in figure 21.1.

FIG. 21.1
Netscape Navigator displaying its registered plug-ins.

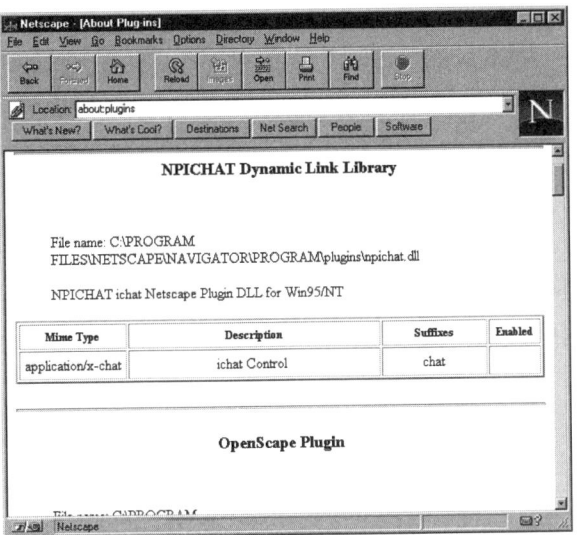

After startup, as you use the browser to surf the Web, you eventually encounter an embedded file with a file name extension that your browser cannot handle without help. The browser then calls on its plug-ins to interpret the mysterious information. From its list of file name extensions, the browser determines which plug-in claimed responsibility at startup for the file at hand. To interpret and use the information in the encountered file, the browser relies on the code stored in the plug-in DLL file. The plug-in thus expands the capabilities of the core browser code.

What You'll Need To Build a Plug-In

Now that you have a passing acquaintance with what plug-ins are and how they work with browsers, you're ready to investigate what you need to code your own plug-in.

You need three things:

- A knowledge of C++, specifically Microsoft Foundation Class (MFC) programming
- C++ programming tools
- The Netscape Plug-In Software Development Kit (SDK)

Microsoft Foundation Class Programming

Plug-ins are written in C++. If you don't have a pretty good knowledge of C++ and how to develop programs with it, you're going to have a hard time putting together a plug-in. Specifically, you need to be familiar with Microsoft Foundation Class programming.

MFC programming relies on the object-oriented nature of C++ to provide programmers with ready-made dialog boxes, controls, relationships among data, and other key programming tools that yield applications with a consistent look and feel. If you don't already know the basics of MFC programming, you're not ready to take on the task of plug-in development. Take a look at some good C++ and MFC tutorials before you jump into the deep end of complex software development.

C++ Programming Tools

If you're familiar with C++ and MFC programming, you probably have a C++ compiler, linker, debugger, and other development tools on your hard drive. C++ programming tools are the software that you use to write, compile, and debug your plug-in code.

Any C++ programming suite will do (you can even code by hand in a text editor if you have a thing for self-flagellation). The figures in this chapter were shot in Microsoft Visual C++ 4.0, a suite of programming tools that's well-tailored to MFC programming. Figure 21.2 shows the Microsoft Visual C++ 4.0 development environment.

FIG. 21.2
Microsoft Visual C++, one of several good tools for plug-in development.

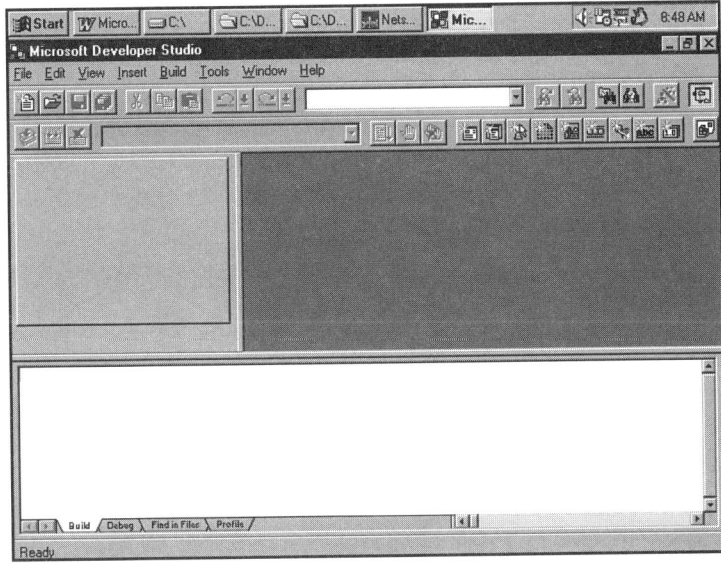

If you want to develop plug-ins for Macintosh computers, Metroworks' Code Warrior will serve you well. Code Warrior scored a major coup in the development-environment industry when it became the first serious Macintosh C++ development tool that worked well with Power Macintosh source code. Symantec later followed with a PowerMac compiler of its own, but not until Code Warrior had established a name for itself among programmers and development managers.

The Plug-In Software Development Kit

Before you start coding your plug-in, download the Netscape Plug-In Software Development Kit (SDK) for your computing platform from the following site:

> **http://home.netscape.com/comprod/development_partners/ plugin_api/index.html**

You learn more about the SDK later in the next section. The SDK contains plug-in interface documentation, sample plug-ins, sample source code, and templates that you can use as starting points for your own development efforts. Figure 21.3 shows the Netscape SDK download page.

FIG. 21.3
Netscape's Plug-In SDK download page.

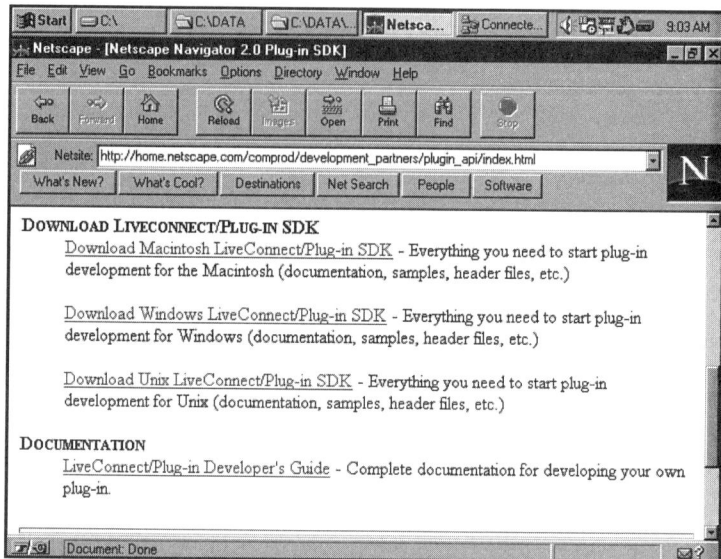

Exploring the Plug-In Software Development Kit

Netscape Communications Corporation wants to encourage lots of people and companies to develop plug-ins for Netscape Navigator. With this goal in mind, Netscape has posted to its Web site a software development kit that provides a set of tools for plug-in developers. (You can also use the SDK to develop plug-ins for Microsoft Internet Explorer, although Netscape probably doesn't really want to encourage development for that browser.) This book's companion CD-ROM also includes this software development kit, which is one of the key tools that you need to put together a working plug-in. The SDK provides many useful components.

HTML Documentation

One of the most useful features of the SDK is the elaborate collection of documentation files in HTML ready to be explored. With your browser, open the file SDK.HTML (which is in the DOCUMENTATION directory) and start reading. Figure 21.4 shows the documentation's welcome page, from which you can jump to more detailed information on most any plug-in topic. Topics include complete descriptions of the SDK's various sample plug-ins.

Samples

In addition to the documentation, the SDK provides several sample plug-ins, complete with source code. You can use these plug-ins as tutorials—by examining how data moves

Exploring the Plug-In Software Development Kit | 453

around in them—or you can use them as starting points for your own similar plug-ins. Netscape included these sample plug-ins for experimentation purposes, so feel free to alter them in your efforts to see how plug-ins work and how you can make them work for you. Figure 21.5 shows the documentation's list of accompanying sample files.

FIG. 21.4
The welcome page of the SDK's documentation.

FIG. 21.5
Sample files and templates in the Netscape Plug-In SDK.

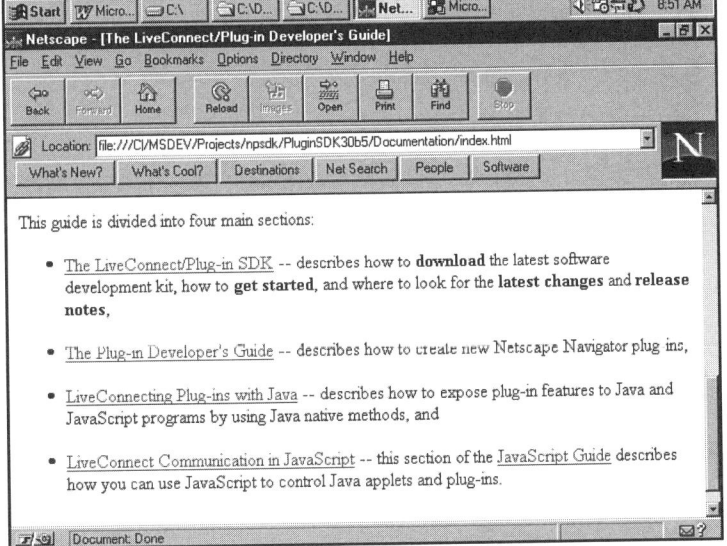

Templates

If a sample file is similar enough to the plug-in that you want to create, you can use that file as a template. The Netscape Plug-In SDK also contains a collection of genuine templates that you can use as frameworks for building plug-ins for various kinds of computers. Templates contain only the skeleton of plug-in source code; they don't contain any code that solves real-world problems. You'll want to use the templates after you have learned the nuts and bolts of coding plug-ins and are ready to start with a blank slate for your own projects. Figure 21.5 lists several templates as well as many sample plug-in files.

How To Create Your Own Plug-Ins

This section provides only a crude explanation of the process of creating a Netscape-compatible plug-in. This sequence is particularly suited to Microsoft Visual C++ 4.0, but other development suites have similar features that you can use in a similar way. Don't expect to be able to code a plug-in after reading this section, but do expect to have an idea of what you're getting into.

Experienced programmers will find the Netscape SDK hypertext documentation helpful in ironing out the specific difficulties of developing a plug-in.

Getting Started and Using the AppWizard

The easiest way to get started coding a plug-in is to use the AppWizard that comes with Microsoft Visual C++ 4.0. The AppWizard does the dirty work of creating all the files that you need to write your plug-in.

When you're ready to start, run Microsoft Visual C++ and open a new project. Give your project a name (for this example, use *plugin*). When Visual C++ prompts you to specify a project type, select MFC AppWizard(dll) from the drop-down list box. Choose the option Regular DLL with MFC Statically Linked. Choose the Finish button, then click the OK button. Figure 21.6 shows the AppWizard working its magic.

Some of the files created by the AppWizard include PLUGIN.CPP, PLUGIN.RC, README.TXT, and STDAFX.CPP. You should delete all AppWizard-generated files except PLUGIN.CPP and PLUGIN.RC.

How To Create Your Own Plug-Ins   455

FIG. 21.6
The AppWizard preparing a plug-in's framework.

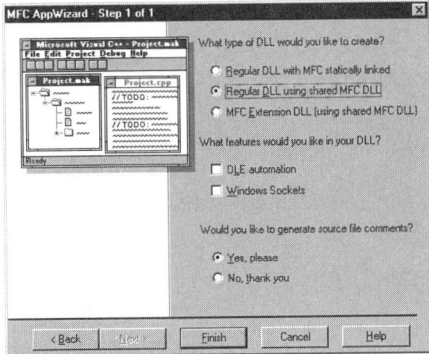

Inserting the Netscape Boilerplate

Now replace the contents of your .CPP file with the contents of one of the sample .CPP files in the SDK, and replace the contents of your .RC file with the code in an .RC file from the SDK. For this example, you use the SAMPLE files in the SDK: SAMPLE.CPP and SAMPLE.RC. Use your computer's copy and paste commands to move the code from one file to the other. Figure 21.7 shows some of the SDK's sample code in Microsoft Visual C++.

FIG. 21.7
Netscape sample code in Microsoft Visual C++.

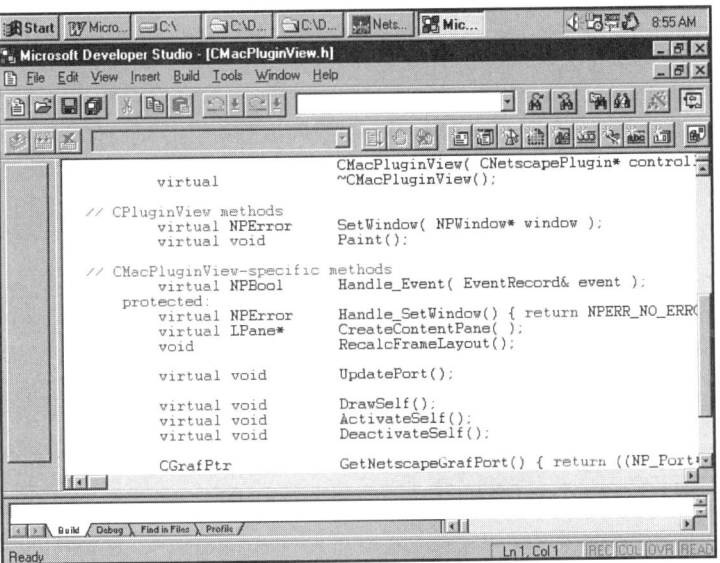

Compiling Your Plug-In

After inserting your sample SDK code, you're ready to compile your plug-in. To do so, open the Build and choose Build plugin.dll, or press F7. It takes a minute or so, depending on your computer's speed, for the .DLL file to compile and link.

In a nutshell, the compiler translates the English-like C++ source code (yes, to a computer, C++ source code is English-like) into machine language that the computer can read directly.

Figure 21.8 shows the compiler working.

FIG. 21.8
Compiling a plug-in.

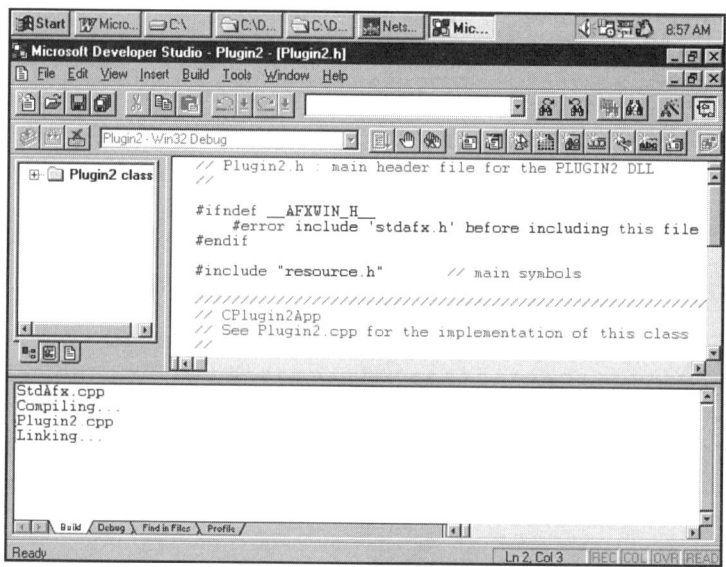

 Don't forget to rename your plug-in DLL file with a name that begins with *NP*. Also, to enable the browser to recognize the plug-in, you have to place the file in your browser's PLUGINS folder, then shut down and restart your browser.

Testing Your Plug-In

The best way to test your plug-in is to embed it in a Web page and see whether it does what you want. Make an HTML document that looks like this:

```
<HTML>
<H1>Here's a plug-in test.</H1>
<EMBED SRC="TEST.ABC" WIDTH=100 HEIGHT=100>
</HTML>
```

Then load the HTML document, making sure that the file TEST.ABC (a file of the type that you've designed your plug-in to handle) is in the same directory as the test HTML document. If the plug-in does what you intended, then congratulations. Otherwise, return to the code editor and determine what went wrong. Figure 21.9 shows a test page's code in a text editor.

FIG. 21.9
A plug-in test page, ready to prove a plug-in.

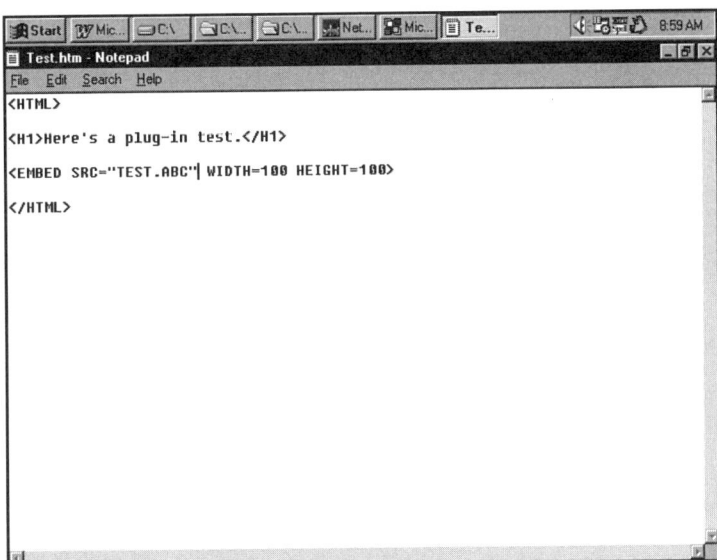

 When testing your plug-in, torture-test it! Throw it into situations you hope it never encounters in real life. Give it faulty data, files of the wrong type, and data so enormous that you expect the code to choke. The next section provides more ideas about code testing.

Creative Advice

Your own plug-in creation adventures will no doubt lead to dozens of discoveries about plug-in development and the specifics of the problem that you're trying to solve. Here are a few suggestions to consider as you plan and execute your plug-in development strategy. These hints combine general good programming practice and tips that derive from the crowded plug-in marketplace.

Make Sure You're Filling a Need

Building a better version of an existing tool is a legitimate reason for coding a plug-in, but don't create yet another MIDI player and expect the world to clamor for a copy. MIDI

plug-ins are an example of a plug-in market that doesn't need any more competitors; several excellent MIDI plug-ins are available, and the odds of creating a significantly better one are slender.

As an exercise, hobbyists might want to build a new version of a plug-in that already exists. However, anyone trying to make money in a niche that's already well filled is in for some unpleasant surprises.

The best reason for creating a new plug-in is to fill a need on a corporate or institutional intranet. Many network-wise organizations have proprietary applications that generate data in proprietary formats. When such organizations move to an Internet-protocol corporate network, and Web browsers become the network tool of choice, a special plug-in is needed to handle the proprietary data.

If you code such a plug-in and make it available to everyone on your intranet, you won't rake in any cash—unless someone up the corporate ladder actually recognizes your effort—but your company will save significant time and money. Further, people who can share data easily can more easily collaborate on projects and problem-solving.

Most general-interest plug-ins for traditional applications (such as playing sounds in various formats) already exist, and there's little point in duplicating them. If, on the other hand, you have a special need for a plug-in or you can develop a new kind of general-interest plug-in (like a better voice-conferencing tool), your plug-in development efforts probably will be rewarded.

Test Your Code Extensively

Make sure that your plug-in works properly before you unleash it on the world. Try your plug-in on several different computers, running several different operating systems. Try it under both Netscape Navigator and Microsoft Internet Explorer. Try it with the most unusual file that could possibly carry the file name extension that you've designed the plug-in to handle. Try it with many other programs running so that memory is scarce and the plug-in has to compete for working room.

The cardinal rule in code testing is to test the extremes. If a given routine is supposed to handle integers between 1 and 50, try it with 1, 50, and 26—and then see what happens when you feed it 0, –20, and 14.25. Any good plug-in (or any good program of any kind) has built-in routines for handling user errors.

 Don't go overboard with user-friendliness, however, unless you have a lot of time to write and debug your program instructions. As a general rule of programming, user-friendly code is three times larger than unfriendly code that does the same thing. Try to strike a balance between friendliness and brevity.

Document Everything

Good programmers supplement their computer instructions with English-language comments that explain what various functions and classes do. These comments make it easier for other people—or you, long after the plug-in's details have slipped your mind—to understand what's going on in your code. Figure 21.10 shows comments in plug-in code.

FIG. 21.10
Explanatory remarks in plug-in source code make it easier for others to work with your code.

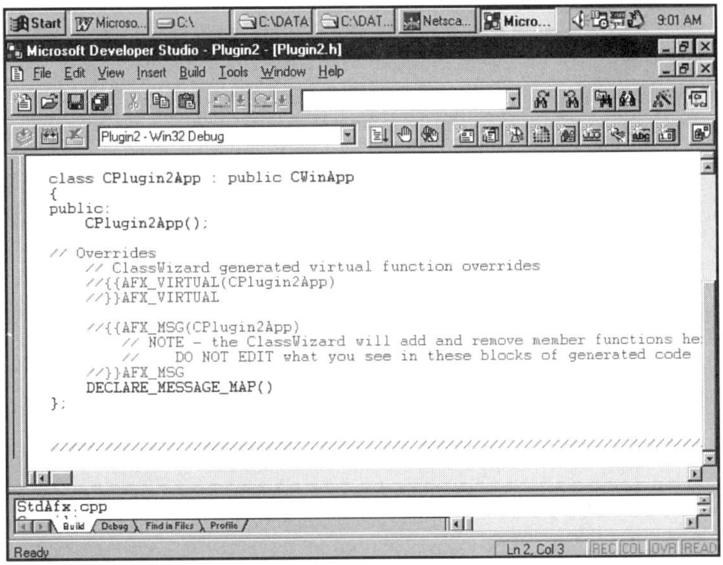

A corollary of this suggestion is that you should always give your variables descriptive names. Plug-in coding isn't algebra class—you don't have to name your variables *A, B, C,* and *X*. Instead, give your variables names like `Repeat`, `TargetFile`, and `ScreenWidth`. Within the context of a code listing, you can easily understand the purpose of each variable with such descriptive names.

Comments are especially important if you're going to place your source code in the public domain for other people to use and modify—which brings up the final suggestion...

Make Your Source Code Available

Unless you're intent on making a buck with your plug-in (and you've learned that that's not an easy thing to do), make your source code available to whomever wants it. Whether you post it to a Web site alongside your compiled plug-in or just offer to e-mail it to anyone who asks, you are doing a good deed if you make your code public.

Why? Because computing always has been a community activity, and that's especially the case in the age of the global network. By making your code freely available and enabling others to modify it to suit their needs, you're guaranteeing that others will learn about plug-ins and that they will be able to do extraordinary things by using your plug-in code as a foundation.

If you've created a plug-in that reads a new kind of data—a new kind of graphics file, for example—you absolutely *must* make that file standard public if you want your plug-in to catch on. Tell Web publishers about your new file standard and why it will benefit them. In addition to your plug-in, publish an application that converts a common kind of data to your new format. The developers of Lightning Strike, for example, have a program that converts standard JPEG images to their new, highly compressed image file format.

If the cycle works properly, the people who borrowed your code will make their products public and you can take on the task of improving them further. This is how computer programs develop.

The principle also works the other way, too. If you see some source code that's obviously been placed in the public domain (you should ask if you're not sure), feel free to modify it and expand on it to serve a new purpose. ●

APPENDIX A

What's on the CD-ROM

The CD-ROM included with this book is packed full of valuable plug-ins, development tools, and server software. We have also included a copy of the Microsoft Internet Explorer 3.0 World Wide Web browser. This appendix gives you a brief overview of the contents of the CD-ROM. For a more detailed look at any of these parts, load the CD-ROM and browse the contents. ■

http://www.mcp.com/que

VRML Plug-Ins

CyberGate (Black Sun Interactive)
CyberPassage (Sony)
Express VR
Liquid Reality (Dimension X)
Paragraph 3D
Terraform (Brilliance Labs)
Topper
Traveler (Onlive Technologies)
Viscape (SuperScape)
Voyager (Virtus)
V-Realm (IDS)
VRML Add-in for Microsoft Internet Explorer VR Scout (Chaco Communications)
VRweb (IICM/NCSA/University of Minnesota)
WebSpace (Silicon Graphics and TGS)
WIRL (VREAM)

Multimedia/Sound Plug-Ins

TrueSpeech
Crescendo and Crescendo Plus
RapidTransit
Arnaud Masson's MIDI Plugin
MidiShare
Koan
ToolVox
EchoSpeech
Talker
William H. Tudor's Speech Plug-In
Bill Noon's ListenUp
Digital Dream's ShockTalk

Multimedia/Graphics Plug-Ins

FIGleaf Inline
ViewDirector
Autodesk's WHIP!
DWG/DXF Viewer
Corel CMX
SoftSource SVF
InterCAP InLine
FutureSplash's CelAnimator
Lightning Strike
FIF Viewer
Summus Wavelet Viewer
Shockwave
Micrografx's QuickSilver
Johnson-Grace's ART Press
Vertigo
WebXpresso
Web-Active and WebActive 3D
WurlPlug

Multimedia/Video Plug-Ins

VDOLive
CoolFusion
Vosaic
VivoActive Player
QuickTime
MacZilla
MovieStar
Iván Cavero Belaúnde's ViewMovie
TEC Player

Kevin McMurtrie's Multimedia Plugin

Open2U's Action MPEG

InterVU's PreVU

Xing StreamWorks

Sizzler

Emblaze

FutureSplash

Deltapoint's Web Animator

Heads Off's Play3D

Shockwave

ASAP WebShow

Astound Web Player

mBED

Rad Technologies

Asymetrix's Neuron

mFactory

7TH LEVEL Top Gun

Powersoft's media.splash

SCREAM

Productivity Plug-Ins

Acrobat

Envoy

Formula One/NET

Word Viewer

KEYview

PointPlus

PowerPoint Plug-in

Texture Viewer

Techexplorer

QuickView Plus

Navigational Aids Plug-Ins

HindSite (ISYS)
AnchorPage Client Plug-In (Iconovex) HistoryTree
HotPage (DocuMagix)
Remote PC Access:
Carbon Copy/Net
Look@Me

Miscellaneous Plug-Ins

EarthTime (Starfish Software)
PointCast
Argus Map Viewer
Globalink
JetForm Filler
Concerto (Alpha Software)
NET-Install
ICHAT IRC
Groupscape Notes Browser
Galacticomm Worldgroup
NCompass (ExCITE)
OpenScape
QuickServer
WinFrame
WebBASIC (Amara)

Helpers/Audio

Cooledit
Goldwave
Midigate

Mod4Win
WHAM
WPLANY

Helpers/Multimedia

Macromedia Director

Helpers/Video and Image

ACDSee
GraphX
LViewPro
MPEGPlay
PolyView
QuickTime
SnapCAP
StreamWorks
VuePrint
WebImage
WinECJ
WinJPEG

HTML Editors

HotDog
HTML Assistant
HTMLed
HTML Notepad
HTML Writer
Live Markup
WebEdit
Webber

Java

HotJava Browser
Clikette
Egor
Ewgie
Flash
Swami
Java Developer's Kit

Web Servers

Apache
Internet Information Server
NCSA httpd
WebQuest
Windows HTTPd

Index

Symbols

20/20 Software Web site, 68
7th Level Web site, 259

A

About Plug-Ins command (Help menu), 30
access
    remote programs, 65-66
        Carbon Copy/Net, 65-66
        Timbuktu Pro, 65-66
Accuweather (Web site), 230
Acrobat Amber Reader (Web site), 61
Acrobat Portable Document Format (PDF), 60
Action MPEG plug-in
    <EMBED> HTML tag (attributes), 220-221
    Web site, 51
ActionStudio, 219-221
ActiveMovie Streaming Format (ASF), 111
ActiveX, 69-70
    controls, 398-404
    custom controls (creating with Visual C++), 399-400
    embedding in HTML files, 402-403

    Microsoft ActiveX Development Kit (MSADK), 402
    NCompass ActiveX plug-in, 398
        dependencies, 403-404
    objects, embedding (<EMBED> HTML tag), 77-78
    .OCX files, 401-402
    Web site, 71
Actual Size FIGleaf Inline command, 169
ACTUALSIZE=TRUE|FALSE FIGleaf Inline <EMBED> attribute, 169
Adobe Acrobat Reader, 338-342
    files (creating), 342
    navigating within, 338-341
        Reader Toolbar, 340-341
    Web site, 61, 338
advertisements (PointCast Network), 395
Afterburner Xtra module (Shockwave), 184
AfterShock's Arcade Alley (Web site), 232
ALIGN="value" LiveAudio <EMBED> attribute, 141
All RealAudio CONTROLS attribute value, 123
Alpha Software (Web site), 68

AnchorPage (Web site), 64
animation
    CelAnimator, 188-193
        controls, 190
        importing/exporting file formats, 190
    Macintosh graphics, 192
    plug-ins, 51-52, 221-226
        Emblaze, 52, 222-223
        Enliven, 221-222
        Play3D, 52, 225
        Sizzler, 51-52, 224-225
        Web Animator, 52
    PowerPoint files
        creating, 326
        viewing, 327
    sample programs (Web site), 206
    Shockwave for Director, 230
APIs, Playback Engine (RealAudio), 113
Appearance node (VRML 2.0 leaf nodes), 290
Apple Flavored Java (Web site), 442
Apple QD3D (Web site), 193
Apple QuickTime plug-in, 213-216
    <EMBED> HTML tag attributes, 215-216
    Web site, 213
applets
    Java, 418-422, 435-441
        finding examples, 442
        HelloWorld applet, 435-437

applets

Java Animator applet, 437-441
<PARAM> HTML tag, 420-422
mBED, 256

applications
groupware, 69
helper, 10-13
intranet plug-ins
custom apps, 104-106
file apps, 103-104
Shockwave for Director, 238

AppWizard (creating your own plug-ins), 454

Argus Map Viewer (Web site), 67

Argus MapGuide, 379-381
maps
navigating through, 380-381
obtaining, 380
Toolbar, 381
Web site, 379

Arnaud Masson's MIDI (Web site), 37, 148

ART Press, 197-198
<EMBED> attributes, 198
graphics plug-in, 47
Web site, 47, 197

ARX (AutoCAD Runtime Extension) application, 179

ASAP WebShow, 54, 246-250
<EMBED> HTML tag parameters, 248-249
Image Compressor, 247-250
WebShow Presentation Kit, 246-250
WordPower, 246-250
Web site, 55

AsciiText node (VRML shapes), 268

Astound Web Player, 55, 253-256
Astound Studio, 254
installing, 254
optimizing presentations, 255-256
Studio M, 254-256
Web site, 55, 253

Asymetrix (Web site), 56, 258

attributes
<EMBED> HTML tag
Action MPEG plug-in, 220-221
Apple QuickTime plug-in, 215-216
ART Press, 198
Chemscape Chime, 195-196
CoolFusion, 212
FIGleaf Inline, 169-170
InterVU plug-in, 219
Lightning Strike, 174
LiveAudio, 140-141
LiveVideo, 208
ToolVox, 144
VDOLive, 210
HTML (Envoy documents), 346
RealAudio
CONSOLE, 124
CONTROLS, 122
HEIGHT, 122
SRC, 122
WIDTH, 122

audio editing tips (Web site), 120

audio plug-ins, *see* **sound**

AudioClip node (VRML 2.0 leaf nodes), 290-291

authoring software
ASAP for WebShow, 246-250
Image Compressor, 247-250
WebShow Presentation Kit, 246-250
WordPower, 246-250
Astound Web Player, 253-256
Astound Studio, 254
installing, 254
optimizing presentations, 255-256
Studio M, 254-256
mBED, 256-257
applets, 256
.MDB file format, 256
Neuron, 257-258
Shockwave for Authorware, 250-252
VRML content, 278

Authorware Aftershock (Web site), 251

AutoAdvance= ON|OFF ASAP WebShow <EMBED> parameter, 248

AutoCAD, 177-181
Corel Visual CADD, 181-182
DWG/DXF viewer, 180-181
NetSlide 95, 180-182
WHIP!, 177-180
options menu, 179

AutoDesk (Web site), 42

Autodesk Internet Utilities (commands), 179

AUTOLOAD=TRUE|FALSE LiveAudio <EMBED> attribute, 141

AUTOPLAY=NO|YES InterVU <EMBED> attribute, 219

AUTOPLAY=TRUE|FALSE Apple QuickTime attribute, 215

AUTOSTART=TRUE Action <EMBED> attribute, 220

AUTOSTART=TRUE/FALSE VDOLive <EMBED> attribute, 210

AUTOSTART=TRUE|FALSE LiveAudio <EMBED> attribute, 141

AUTOSTART=TRUE|FALSE LiveVideo <EMBED> attribute, 208

B

Background node (VRML 2.0, 294

bandwidth (intranet plug-ins), 101-103
RealAudio Server 2.0, 129

Bare-Bones Shebang about Netscape Plug-Ins (Web site), 446

bitmaps
creating, 158-166
borrowing bitmaps, 158-159

digitizing video images, 163-166
paint programs, 159-162
scanning images, 163
display plug-ins, 166-171
  FIGleaf Inline, 166-170
  ViewDirector, 170-171
Border=RAISED|RECESSED|SLIDE|
  ASAP WebShow <EMBED>
  parameter, 248
BORDER=value FIGleaf
  Inline <EMBED>
  attribute, 170
Box node (VRML 2.0
  geometry leaf nodes), 289
Brilliance Labs
  (Web site), 316
browsers
  compatibility (plug-in
    limitations), 86-89
  plug-in basics, 449-450
  VRML, 57-60
    Cybergate, 59-60, 307-308
    CyberPassage, 313
    Express VR, 59-60
    Liquid Reality, 59-60, 312-313
    Live3D, 57-60
    Microsoft VRML add-in
      (Internet Explorer), 317
    Paragraph 3D, 59-60
    TerraForm, 316
    TerraForm Free, 60
    Topper, 59-60
    Traveler, 311-312
    V-Realm, 314
    Virtus Voyager, 60, 315
    Viscape, 59-60
    VR Scout, 58-60, 310-311
    VRealm, 59-60
    VRweb, 308-309
    WebSpace, 306-307
    WIRL, 58-60, 309-310
Business@Web (Web site), 71

C

C++ programming tools
  (creating your own plug-ins),
  450-451
Caligari Fountain (creating
  VRML content), 278
cameras (VRML), 269
Carbon Copy/Net, 366-374
  installing, 368-369
  potential uses, 367
  remote access programs, 65
  running
    as a guest, 370-372
    as a host, 372-373
  security concerns, 367
  Security Options dialog
    box, 373
  Web site, 65, 368
CD-ROM
  graphics plug-ins, 463
  HTML editors, 466
  Java, 467
  miscellaneous plug-ins, 465
  multimedia helper
    applications, 466
  multimedia/sound
    plug-ins, 462
  navigational aids plug-ins, 465
  productivity plug-ins, 464
  sound helper applications,
    465-466
  video and image helper
    applications, 466
  video plug-ins, 463-464
  VRML plug-ins, 462
  Web servers, 467
CelAnimator
  content, 192
  file formats (compatibility),
    191-192
  graphics plug-in, 44
  Web site, 45, 189
CGM (Computer Graphics
  Metafiles) (Web site), 192
Chaco Communications
  (Web site), 311

channels, PointCast Network
  (Web information
  organizer), 388-389
Chemscape Chime, 193-197
  <EMBED> attributes, 195-196
  graphics plug-in, 46
  supported file formats,
    194-195
  Web site, 46, 193
Citrix Systems (Web site), 72
CNN Oklahoma Bombing
  (Web site), 236
Collision node (VRML 2.0
  grouping nodes), 293
color, palettes (number of bits
  needed), 153
COLOR=MONO Action
  <EMBED> attribute, 221
COLORMAP=PRIVATE|
  DITHERED FIGleaf Inline
  <EMBED> attribute, 169
COLORMAP=TRUE|FALSE
  Lightning Strike <EMBED>
  attribute, 174
command-line encoding
  (RealAudio Encoder), 121
commands (Autodesk
  Internet Utilities), 179
communication tools
  Carbon Copy/Net, 366-374
    installing, 368-369
    potential uses, 367
    running as a guest,
      370-372
    running as a host, 372-373
    security concerns, 367
  ichat, 352-362, 354-360
    creating a user, 354-355
    displaying emotions, 358
    embedded hyperlinks,
      358-359
    getting help, 360
    ignoring bozos, 359-372
    installing, 353-354
    IRC connections, 360-361

IRC support, 360-372
ROOMS chat-server technology, 362
sending private messages, 357-358
sending public messages, 356-357
user interface, 356
Web tours, 359-372
Look@Me, 362-366
installing, 362-364
running, 364-365

Companies PointCast channel, 389

compatibility
CelAnimator file formats, 191-192
Web browsers (plug-in limitations), 86-89

compiling, plug-ins (creating your own plug-ins), 456

Compress Slide Show (CSS) (Web site), 325

compression (graphics plug-ins), 171-174
FIF (Fractal Image Format) viewer, 174
Lightning Strike, 172-174
Wavelet Viewer, 174

CONBAR=YES|NO InterVU <EMBED> attribute, 219

Concerto (Web site), 68

Cone node
VRML 2.0 geometry leaf node, 289
VRML shapes, 268

configuring,
PointCast Network (Web information organizer), 391-393
Quick View Plus, 332-334

connections, dial-up (plug-in limitations), 85-86

CONSOLE
LiveAudio <EMBED> attribute, 141
RealAudio attribute, 124

CONSOLE="name" LiveAudio <EMBED> attribute, 141

content
CelAnimator, 192
intranet vs. Internet, 98-99
linking, 79
plug-in limitations, 84-92
browser compatibility, 86-89
content vs. design, 89
content-creation programs, 91-92
file size and dial-up connections, 85-86
file sizes, 92
practical plug-in uses, 90-91
RealAudio, 122-125
CONSOLE attribute, 124-125
CONTROLS attribute, 122-125
HEIGHT attribute, 122-125
SRC attribute, 122-125
WIDTH attribute, 122-125
servers, installing (Web server issues), 83-84
video, 202-204
creating, 204-206
practical uses, 203-204
speed issues, 202-203
VRML (creating), 274-278
Caligari Fountain, 278
Home Space Builder, 277
Interchange conversion program, 275
object libraries, 276-277
Virtus VRML Toolkit, 278
WCVT2POV conversion program, 274-275
Web pages (design vs. content), 74-75

Control Active (NCompass ActiveX), 398

CONTROLLER=TRUE|FALSE Apple QuickTime attribute, 216

ControlPanel RealAudio CONTROLS attribute value, 123

controls
ActiveX
creating custom controls with Visual C++, 399-400

embedding in HTML files, 402-403
Microsoft ActiveX Development Kit (MSADK), 402
.OCX files, 401-402
CelAnimator, 190
LiveVideo, 208
RealAudio Player, 116-117

CONTROLS attribute (RealAudio), 122
values, 123

CONTROLS=TRUE|FALSE LiveVideo <EMBED> attribute, 208

CONTROLS="value" LiveAudio <EMBED> attribute, 141

conversion programs
3-D file format Interchange, 275
WCVT2POV, 274-275

CoolFusion, 49, 211-212
<EMBED> HTML tag attributes, 212
Web site, 49, 211

Coordinate node (VRML 2.0 geometry leaf node), 289

Copy button (Argus MapGuide Toolbar), 381

Copy This Image Location (FIGleaf Inline command), 169

Corel
CMX, 182-183
graphics plug-in, 43
Web site, 44, 182
Visual CADD, 181-182
Web site, 183

CORRECTION=NONE| PARTIAL|FULL Apple QuickTime attribute, 216

creating
Adobe Acrobat files, 342
bitmaps, 158-166
borrowing, 158-159
digitizing video images, 163-166
paint programs, 159-162
scanning images, 163

Envoy documents, 347
frames (Web site), 130
movies (Shockwave for Director), 239-243
plug-in content (programs), 91-92
Powerpoint animation files, 326
TeX files, 349
video content, 204-206
VRML content, 274-278
   Caligari Fountain, 278
   Home Space Builder, 277
   Interchange conversion program, 275
   object libraries, 276-277
   Virtus VRML Toolkit, 278
   WCVT2POV conversion program, 274-275
your own plug-ins, 446-450, 454-457
   AppWizard, 454
   browser basics, 449-450
   C++ programming tools, 450-451
   compiling your plug-in, 456
   creation guidelines, 457-460
   Microsoft Foundation Class (MFC) programming, 450-451
   Plug-In Software Development Kit (SDK), 451
   plug-in technical basics, 448-449
   testing your plug-in, 456-457

Creative Wave (digitized audio), 135

Crescendo
MIDI, 146-147
Web site, 37, 146

Crescendo plug-in, 36

Cube node
VRML 2.0 geometry leaf node, 289
VRML shapes, 268

custom applications (intranet plug-ins), 104-106

cybercasting, 120
CyberEd (Web site), 241
Cybergate
   VRML browsers, 59-60
   Web site, 308
Cyberkids (Web site), 236
CyberPassage (Web site), 313
CyberPassage VRML browser, 313
Cylinder node
   VRML 2.0 geometry leaf node, 289
   VRML shapes, 268
CylinderSensor node (VRML 2.0 sensors), 295

D

DEBUG=ON Action <EMBED> attribute, 221
DEF statements (VRML), 268
DelayTime=integer (ASAP WebShow <EMBED> parameter), 248
Deltapoint (Web site), 226
design (Web pages)
   design vs. content, 74-75
   Director limitations (Shockwave movies), 242
dialog boxes
   Carbon Copy/Net's Security Options, 373
   New Project Workspace, 399
   Personal Server Control Panel Setup, 127
   Personal Server Setup, 127
   Preferences, 117
   Settings, 365
   Statistics, 117
diffuseColor field (VRML), 268
digitized
   audio, 134-138
      Sound Gadget Pro, 137
      Waveform Hold and Modify, 137-138
   music (RapidTransit), 145

sounds (Web site), 135
speech
   Echospeech, 145
   ListenUp, 149
   ShockTalk, 149
   Talker, 148
   ToolVox, 142-145
   TrueSpeech, 145
   William H. Tudor's Speech, 148
video images (creating bitmaps), 163-166

Dimension X (Web site), 313, 443
Direct3D Retained Mode, 309
direction() function (<SCRIPT> tags), 427
   windowFeatures parameters, 427-428
DirectionalLight (VRML), 269
Director (Shockwave), 229-238
   animation, 230
   applications, 238
   creating movies, 239-243
   education, 234-236
   entertainment, 233
   games, 231-232
   presentations, 236-237
   training, 233-234
Director 5 Shockwave Movie Lab (Web site), 243
display standards (graphics), 152
DITHER=TRUE|FALSE Lightning Strike <EMBED> attribute, 174
Dithered FIGleaf Inline command, 168
dithering (Netscape graphics), 154-171
Dithering=EMBED|PAGE| SCREEN|NONE ASAP WebShow <EMBED> parameter, 248
Doc Active (NCompass ActiveX), 398
DocuMagix (Web site), 65, 385

documents (portable)
  Adobe Acrobat Reader, 338-342
  Envoy, 342-347
  Techexplorer, 347-349
DOUBLESIZE=YES|NO InterVU <EMBED> attribute, 219
downloading (Netscape plug-ins), 28-31
  keeping track of installed plug-ins, 29-31
  running plug-ins, 31
drap and drop encoding (RealAudio Encoder), 121
DWF (Drawing Web Format) file type, 177
DWFOUT Autodesk Utilities command, 179
DWG/DXF viewer, 180-181
  graphics plug-in, 42
  Web site, 42, 180

E

EarthTime, 376-378
  features, 378
  potential uses, 376-378
  Web site, 67, 376
EchoSpeech plug-in, 38
  Web site, 39, 145
editors, HTML (CD-ROM contents), 466
Effect= effectname, direction ASAP WebShow <EMBED> parameter, 248
<EMBED> HTML tag, 76-79, 140-141
  Action MPEG plug-in, 220-221
  Apple QuickTime plug-in attributes, 215-216
  ART Press attributes, 198
  ASAP WebShow parameters, 248-249
  Chemscape Chime attributes, 195-196
  CoolFusion attributes, 212
  embedding ActiveX objects, 77-78
  embedding inline contents, 78-79
  FIGleaf Inline usage (attributes), 169-170
  InterVU plug-in, 219
  LiveAudio attributes, 140-141
  LiveVideo attributes, 208
  ToolVox attributes, 144
  VDOLive attributes, 210
  Web site, 77
embedded hyperlinks (ichat), 358-359
embedded plug-ins (defined), 19
Emblaze animation plug-in, 222-223
  Web site, 52
encoding (RealAudio Encoder), 119-121
  command-line, 121-126
  drag and drop, 121-126
ENDTIME="mm:ss" LiveAudio <EMBED> attribute, 141
English Text-to-Speech plug-in (Apple), 39
Enliven animation plug-in, 221-222
Envoy, 61, 342-347
  documents (creating), 347
  Toolbar, 343-344
  Web page usage, 345-347
    HTML attributes, 346
  Web site, 61, 342
event handlers (JavaScript), 425-426
  mixing with event handlers, 426-428
Excel (Microsoft) (Formula One/NET), 323-325
  embedding spreadsheets, 324-325
  versions, 323-324
exporting file formats (CelAnimator), 190
Express VR (VRML browsers), 59-60
  Web site, 59
extensions (Live3D), 301

F

Farallon (Web site), 362
FIF (Fractal Image Format) viewer, 45
  compression plug-ins, 174
  Web site, 45, 174
FIGleaf Inline, 40, 166-170
  <EMBED> HTML tag (attributes), 169-170
  file formats displayed, 166-167
  Web site, 41, 170
files
  Adobe Acrobat (creating), 342
  application (intranet plug-ins), 103-104
  formats
    Quick View Plus compatible, 329
    RealAudio encoder support, 119
    TeX, 348
  graphics formats, 155-158
    Netscape compatible, 156-157
  size (plug-in limitations), 85-86, 92
  sound
    adjusting (RealAudio Encoder), 120
    formats, 134
  standardization (intranet plug-ins), 100-101
Fit to Window FIGleaf Inline command, 168
Fit to Window WHIP! option, 179
Fog node (VRML 2.0), 294
form verification (Java and JavaScript Web page enhancements), 414
formats
  file
    Quick View Plus compatible, 329
    RealAudio encoder support, 119
    TeX, 348

graphics files, 155-158
    FIGleaf Inline, 166-167
    Netscape compatible, 156-157
    proprietary, 176
sound files, 134
    digitized audio, 134-138

Formula One/NET, 62, 323-325
    embedding spreadsheets, 324-325
    versions, 323-324
    Web site, 62, 323

FOV=integer Apple QuickTime attribute, 216

FRAMERATE=integer InterVU <EMBED> attribute, 219

frames, creating Web site), 130

FRAMES=YES|NO InterVU <EMBED> attribute, 219

FTP sites
    English Text-to-Speech, 39
    Graphics FAQ, 156

full-screen plug-ins (defined), 20

functions, direction() (<SCRIPT> tags), 427

FutureSplash (Web site), 189

G

Galacticomm Worldgroup (groupware), 69

Gamelan (Web site), 442

games
    Java and JavaScript Web page enhancements, 416
    Shockwave for Director, 231-232

General Preferences (command Options menu), 30

geometry nodes (VRML 2.0 leaf nodes), 289

GIFs (graphic file format), 155

Globalink (Web site), 68

Gobbler (Web site), 418

Gold Disk (Web site), 253

graphics, 152-153
    bitmaps
        creating, 158-166
        display plug-ins, 166-171
        compression plug-ins, 171-174
        FIF (Fractal Image Format) viewer, 174
        Lightning Strike, 172-174
        Wavelet Viewer, 174
    display standards, 152
    file formats, 155-158
        FIGleaf Inline, 166-167
        Netscape compatible, 156-157
    formats (proprietary), 176
    Netscape, 154
        dithering, 154
        hardware requirements, 152
    vector, 181-188
        Corel CMX, 182-183
        Shockwave for Freehand, 183-186
        SVF plug-in, 187-188

Graphics FAQ
    FTP site, 156
    Web site, 156

graphics plug-ins, 40-48
    ART Press, 47-48
    CD-ROM contents, 463
    CelAnimator, 44-48
    Chemscape Chime, 46-48
    Corel CMX, 43-48
    DWG/DXF, 42-48
    FIF, 45-48
    FIGleaf Inline, 40-48
    InterCAP InLine, 44-48
    Lightning Strike, 45-48
    NetSlide 95, 43-48
    QuickSilver, 46-48
    Shockwave for Freehand, 46-48
    Simple Vector Format (SVF), 44-48
    Summus Wavelet Viewer, 45-48
    Vertigo, 47-48
    ViewDirector Imaging, 41-48
    WebActive 3D, 47-48
    WebXpresso, 47-48
    Whip! (Autodesk), 41-48
    WurlPlug, 47-48

Graphics Utilities Site and Version FAQ (Web site), 159

Group node (VRML 2.0 grouping nodes), 292

grouping nodes
    VRML 2.0, 291-293
        Collision node, 293
        Group node, 292
        LOD node, 293
        Switch node, 292-293
        Transform node, 291-292
        WWWAnchor node, 293
        WWWInline node, 293

Groupscape (groupware), 69

groupware applications, 69

H

HALFSIZE=YES|NO InterVU <EMBED> attribute, 219

hardware (Netscape graphics requirements), 152

HEIGHT attribute (RealAudio), 122

HEIGHT=integer LiveAudio <EMBED> attribute, 140

HEIGHT=integer ToolVox <EMBED> attribute, 144

HEIGHT=value FIGleaf Inline <EMBED> attribute, 169

HelloWorld applet, 435-437

helper applications, 10-13

HIDDEN Apple QuickTime attribute, 215

hidden plug-ins (defined), 20-21

HindSite (Web page locator), 382-384
    installing, 382
    search techniques, 383-384
    Web site, 382

HistoryTree (Web site), 65
Home Space Builder (creating VRML content), 277
HotPage (Web page organizer), 65, 385-387
   navigating within, 387
   Web site, 65, 385
HREF="URL" Apple QuickTime attribute, 216
HTML
   attributes (Envoy documents), 346
   documentation (Plug-In SDK), 452
   editors (CD-ROM contents), 466
   files (embedding ActiveX controls), 402-403
   including Java applets, 418-422
   JavaScript file containment, 412
   links (linking content), 79
   tags
      <EMBED>, 76-79, 169-170
      <IMG>, 76
      <OBJECT>, 80-81
      <PARAM>, 420-422
      <SCRIPT>, 424-426
HTML Writers' Guild (Web site), 159
hyperlinks, embedded (ichat), 358-359

I

ichat, 352-362
   creating a user, 354-355
   displaying emotions, 358
   embedded hyperlinks, 358-359
   getting help, 360
   ignoring bozos, 359-372
   installing, 353-354
      Macintosh, 353-354
      Windows 95, 354
   IRC connections, 360-361
   IRC support, 360-372
   private messages (sending), 357-358
   public messages (sending), 356-357
   ROOMS chat-server technology, 362
   user interface, 356
   Web site, 68, 353
   Web tours, 359-372
Iconovex (Web site), 64
Icons and Images (Web site), 159
images
   scanning, 163
   video (digitizing), 163-166
<IMG> HTML tag, 76
importing, file formats (CelAnimator), 190
INCREMENTAL=TRUE|FALSE Lightning Strike <EMBED> attribute, 174
IndexedFaceSet node
   VRML 2.0 geometry leaf node, 289
   VRML shapes, 268
IndexedLineSet node
   VRML 2.0 geometry leaf node, 289
   VRML shapes, 268
Industries PointCast channel, 389
Infinet Op (Web site), 45
InfinOp (Web site), 173
InfoPanel RealAudio CONTROLS attribute value, 123
information, organizing (PointCast Network), 387-396
InfoVolumePanel RealAudio CONTROLS attribute value, 123
inline contents, embedding (<EMBED> HTML tag), 78-79
Inso (Web site), 63, 322, 328
installing
   Astound Web Player, 254
   Carbon Copy/Net, 368-369

HindSite (Web page locator), 382
ichat, 353-354
   Macintosh, 353-354
   Windows 95, 354
Internet Explorer plug-ins, 31-35
Look@Me, 362-364
Netscape plug-ins, 28-31
   keeping track of installed plug-ins, 29-31
   running plug-ins, 31
RealAudio Encoder, 119
RealAudio Player, 115-116
Integrated Data Systems (IDS) (Web site), 59, 314
integrated multimedia plug-ins, 52-57
   ASAP WebShow, 54-57
   Astound Web Player, 55-57
   helper applications (CD-ROM contents), 466
   Kaleida Media Player (KMP), 56-57
   mBED, 55-57
   mFactory, 56-57
   RAD PowerMedia, 55-57
   Shockwave for Macromedia Director, 53-57
   ToolBook, 56-57
   Top Gun, 56-57
InterCAP InLine
   graphics plug-in, 44
   Web site, 44
Interchange conversion program (creating VRML content), 275
interfaces, user (ichat), 356
Internet
   content vs. intranet content, 98-99
   Macromedia Director limitations (Shockwave movies), 242
Internet Explorer (installing plug-ins), 31-35
Internet Movie Tool (Web site), 214

limitations (plug-in content) | 477

Internet PointCast channel, 389
Internet relay chat (IRC), *see* IRC
interpolators (VRML 2.0), 296
InterVU, 217-219
InterVU plug-in, <EMBED> HTML tag (attributes), 219
Intranet Journal (Web site), 101
Intranet Links (Web site), 99
intranets, 94, 95-98
 content vs. Internet content, 98-99
 plug-ins, 100-106
  application files, 103-104
  bandwidth and multimedia, 101-103
  custom applications, 104-106
  file standardization, 100-101
IRC
 ichat connections, 360-361
 support (ichat), 360-372
 Web site, 68
ISYS HindSite (Web site), 64
ISYS/Odyssey Development (Web site), 382
Iterated Systems (Web site), 212

J

JASC (Web site), 162
Java, 410-411
 advantages vs. plug-ins, 417
 applets, 418-422, 435-441
  finding examples, 442
  HelloWorld applet, 435-437
  Java Animator applet, 437-441
  <PARAM> HTML tag, 420-422
 CD-ROM contents, 467
 consultants, 443
 disadvantages vs. JavaScript, 418

platform independence, 410
security, 411, 413-414
virtual machine (VM), 410
vs. JavaScript, 412-414
Web page enhancement, 414-416
 form verification, 414
 games, 416
 real-time data, 415
 true interaction, 415
Java Animator applet, 437-441
Java Applet Review System (JARS) (Web site), 442
Java Boutique (Web site), 442
Java Centre (Web site), 442
Java Developer's Kit (JDK) (Web site), 435
JavaScript, 411-412
 advantages vs. plug-ins, 417
 event handlers, 425-426
  mixing with <SCRIPT> tags, 426-428
 HTML file containment, 412
 interpretive features, 412-413
 vs. Java, 412-414
 Web pages, 414, 416, 422-435
  finding examples, 442
  form verification, 414
  games, 416
  hiding the script, 423-424
  including scripts, 422
  real-time data, 415
  <SCRIPT> HTML tags, 424-426
  testing the script, 422-423
  true interaction, 415
  validating forms before submission, 428-435
Javology (Web site), 442
JetForm Filler (Web site), 68
JPEGs (graphic file format), 155

K-L

Kaleida Labs (Web site), 56, 259

Kaleida Media Player (KMP), 56
KEYview (Web site), 63
Kite Paradise (Web site), 234
Koan (Sseyo) plug-in, 38, 148

languages
 scripting (JavaScript), 411-412, 422-435
 VRML, 266-271
  basic syntax, 266-268
  cameras, 269
  DEF and USE statements, 268
  Group and Separator nodes, 270
  lights, 269
  LOD node, 270
  materials and textures, 268-269
  shapes, 268
  Transform node, 270-271
  WWWAnchor, 271
  WWWInline node, 271
leaf nodes (VRML 2.0), 288-291
 Appearance node, 290
 AudioClip node, 290-291
 geometry nodes, 289
 lights, 290
 Shape node, 288-289
 Sound node, 290-291
 Viewpoints, 291
libraries, object (creating VRML content), 276-277
Lifestyle PointCast channel, 389
Lightning Strike, 172-174
 attributes (<EMBED> HTML tag), 174
 graphics plug-in, 45
 Web site, 45, 173
lights
 VRML, 269
 VRML 2.0 leaf nodes, 290
limitations (plug-in content), 84-92
 browser compatibility, 86-89
 content vs. design, 89

content-creation programs, 91-92
file size and dial-up connetions, 85-86
file sizes, 92
practical plug-in uses, 90-91

Lingo
network extensions (Shockwave for Director), 241
Web site, 241

links (linking content), 79

Liquid Reality, 312-313
VRML browsers, 59-60
Web site, 313

ListenUp, 39
digitized speech, 149
Web site, 39, 149

listings
12.1 PLUG.WRL—a Sample World, 271-273
12.2 PLUGTEXT.WRL—the "Hello World" File That WWWI Retrieves and Loads, 273
20.1 A Simple JavaScript Demo, 413
20.2 Generating an HTML File To Display Gobbler, 419
20.3 A More Complete Version of the HTML for Gobbler, 420
20.4 Including GrayButton on Your Web page, 421
20.5 A Very Simple JavaScript Program, 422
20.6 Using Comments To Hide a Script from Browsers That Don't Understand JavaScript, 423-424
20.7 Ensuring That Visitors Know That They Are Leaving Your Web Site, 424
20.8 Producing a Prompting Window When the User Clicks a Link, 426
20.9 The Complete GoodForm Program, 433-435

20.10 A HelloWorld Applet Written in Java, 435
20.11 The HelloWorld Applet's HTML File, 436
20.12 A Java Animator, 437-438
20.13 The HTML File for the Animator, 438

live cybercasting, 120

Live Transfer Agent (LTA), 120

Live3D
VRML 2.0, 299-301
extensions, 301
menus, 301
navigation, 299-300
VRML browsers, 57-60
Web site, 57

LiveAudio, 35, 138-142
<EMBED> HTML tag (attributes), 140-141

LiveMedia Real-Time Transport Protocol (RTP), 111

LiveVideo, 48, 207-208
controls, 208
<EMBED> HTML tag (attributes), 208
Web site, 207

LOD node
VRML 2.0 grouping nodes, 293
VRML, 270

Look@Me, 362-366
installing, 362-364
running, 364-365
Web site, 362

LOOP=integer InterVU <EMBED> attribute, 219

LOOP=TRUE Action <EMBED> attribute, 220

LOOP=TRUE|FALSE LiveVideo <EMBED> attribute, 208

LOOP=TRUE|FALSE| PALINDROME Apple QuickTime attribute, 216

M

Mac-only Multimedia Plug-in (Web site), 217

Macromedia (Web site), 229

Macromedia Director (Shockwave), 229-238
animation, 230
applications, 238
creating movies, 239-243
education, 234-236
entertainment, 233
games, 231-232
presentations, 236-237
training, 233-234

Macromedia Open Architecture (MOA), 251

MacZilla (Web site), 50, 216

MagnaStar, Inc. (Web site), 418, 443

MapGuide Author (Argus Mapguide), 380

MapGuide Server (Argus Mapguide), 380

Material node (VRML materials), 268

materials (VRML), 268-269

mBED, 55, 256-257
applets, 256
.MDB file format, 256
Web site, 55, 256

media.splash (Web site), 259

Menu= ON|OFF ASAP WebShow <EMBED> parameter, 249

menus
Live3D, 301
RealAudio Player, 116-117

MeshMart (Web site), 276

messages
private, sending (ichat), 357-358
public, sending (ichat), 356-357

metafiles (graphics file format), 155

mFactory (Web site), 56, 259

MFC, see Microsoft Foundation Class
Microcom (Web site), 368
Micrografx (Web site), 198
Microsoft ActiveX Development Kit (MSADK) (Web site), 402
Microsoft Foundation Class (MFC) programming (creating your own plug-ins), 450
Microsoft Powerpoint, 326-327
   animation files
      creating, 326
      viewing, 327
   Animation Player, 326
   PointPlus, 325
Microsoft RealityLab engine, 309
Microsoft VRML add-in (Internet Explorer), 317
Microsoft Word (WordViewer), 322
MIDI music
   Crescendo, 146-147
   Koan (Ssyeo), 148
   MidiShare, 148
   MIDPlug, 147
MIME types, 13-15
   setting (RealAudio Personal Server), 128
   Web server issues, 81-83
movies
   creating (Shockwave for Director), 239-243
   Shockwave for Director (optimizing), 242-243
MovieStar (Web site), 50, 217
MovieStar Maker (Web site), 217
MPEG plug-ins, 217-221
   Action, 219-221
   ActionStudio, 219-221
   InterVU, 217-219
mToon (Web site), 259

multimedia plug-ins, 35-57
   animation, 51-52
      Emblaze, 52
      Play3D, 52
      Sizzler, 51-52
      Web Animator, 52
   graphics, 40-48
      ART Press, 47-48
      CelAnimator, 44-48
      Chemscape Chime, 46-48
      Corel CMX, 43-48
      DWG/DXF, 42-48
      FIF, 45-48
      FIGleaf Inline, 40-48
      InterCAP InLine, 44-48
      Lightning Strike, 45-48
      NetSlide 95, 43-48
      QuickSilver, 46-48
      Shockwave for Freehand, 46-48
      Simple Vector Format (SVF), 44-48
      Summus Wavelet Viewer, 45-48
      Vertigo, 47-48
      ViewDirector Imaging, 41-48
      WebActive 3D, 47-48
      WebXpresso, 47-48
      Whip! (Autodesk), 41-48
      WurlPlug, 47-48
   integrated, 52-57
      ASAP WebShow, 54-57
      Astound Web Player, 55-57
      Kaleida Media Player (KMP), 56-57
      mBED, 55-57
      mFactory, 56-57
      RAD PowerMedia, 55-57
      Shockwave for Macromedia Director, 53-57
      ToolBook, 56-57
      Top Gun, 56-57
   intranet plug-ins, 101-103
   sound, 35-40
      Arnaud Masson MIDI, 37
      Crescendo, 36
      EchoSpeech, 38
      English Text-to-Speech, 39
      Koan (Sseyo), 38
      ListenUp, 39

      LiveAudio, 35
      MidiShare, 37
      RapidTransit, 37
      RealAudio, 35
      ShockTalk, 40
      Talker, 39
      ToolVox, 38
      TrueSpeech, 36
      Tudor Speech, 39
   video, 48-51
      Action MPEG, 51
      CoolFusion, 49-51
      LiveVideo, 48-51
      MacZilla, 50-51
      MovieStar, 50-51
      Multimedia Plugin, 50-51
      PreVU, 51
      TEC Player, 50-51
      VDOLive, 48-51
      Video for Windows, 48-51
      ViewMovie, 50-51
      VivoActive Player, 50-51
      Vosaic, 49-51
      Xing, 51
Multimedia Plugin (Web site), 50
Multipurpose Internet Mail Extensions, see MIME
music
   digitized (RapidTransit), 145
   MIDI
      Crescendo, 146-147
      Koan (Ssyeo), 148
      MidiShare, 148
      MIDPlug, 147
MVP Solutions (Web site), 39

N

Narrative Screen Description Language (NSDL), 222
NavBar= ON|OFF ASAP WebShow <EMBED> parameter, 249
NavButtons= ON|OFF ASAP WebShow <EMBED> parameter, 249
navigating
   Acrobat Reader, 338-341
      Reader Toolbar, 340-341

HotPage, 387
Live3D, 299-300

navigational aids, 64-65
AnchorPage, 64
HistoryTree, 65
HotPage, 65
ISYS HindSite, 64

navigational aids plug-ins (CD-ROM contents), 465

NavigationInfo node (VRML 2.0), 294-295

NCompass ActiveX plug-in, 35, 398
dependencies, 403-404

NCompass Labs (Web site), 398

NET-Install (Web site), 68

Net-Scene (Web site), 325

Netscape
ActiveX controls, 398-404
creating custom controls with Visual C++, 399-400
dependencies, 403-404
embedding in HTML files, 402-403
Microsoft ActiveX Development Kit (MSADK), 402
NCompass ActiveX plug-in, 398
.OCX files, 401-402
graphics, 154
dithering, 154
hardware requirements, 152
plug-ins
downloading, 28-31
installing, 28-31
Web site, 48

Netscape 3.0 (LiveAudio), 138-142
<EMBED> HTML tag, 140-141

Netscape Full Service Intranet Applications (Web site), 99

Netscape intranet suite (Web site), 106

Netscape Plug-In Software Development Kit (SDK)
creating your own plug-ins, 452-454
HTML documentation, 452
sample plug-ins, 452-453
templates, 454
Web site, 451

Netscape plug-ins (Web site), 28

Netscape plug-ins tracking (Web site), 22

NetSlide 95, 180-182
graphics plug-in, 43
Web site, 43, 180

Neuron, 257-258

New Project Workspace dialog box, 399

News PointCast channel, 389

NODE=integer Apple QuickTime attribute, 216

nodes
grouping (VRML 2.0), 291-293
Collision node, 293
Group node, 292
LOD node, 293
Switch node, 292-293
Transform node, 291-292
WWWAnchor node, 293
WWWInline node, 293
interpolators (VRML 2.0), 296
leaf (VRML 2.0), 288-291
Appearance node, 290
AudioClip node, 290-291
geometry nodes, 289
lights, 290
Shape node, 288-289
Sound node, 290-291
Viewpoints, 291
prototypes (VRML 2.0), 297-299
routes (VRML 2.0), 296-297
Script (VRML 2.0), 297
sensor (VRML 2.0), 295
CylinderSensor node, 295
PlaneSensor node, 295
ProximitySensor node, 295
SphereSensor node, 295
TimeSensor node, 295
VisibilitySensor node, 295

VRML
Group and Separator, 270
LOD node, 270
Transform node, 270-271
WWWAnchor, 271
WWWInline node, 271
VRML 2.0 specific, 294
Background node, 294
Fog node, 294
NavigationInfo node, 294-295
WorldInfo node, 294-295

NOERROR=TRUE|FALSE CoolFusion <EMBED> attribute, 212

NOMENU=TRUE|FALSE CoolFusion <EMBED> attribute, 212

Normal node (VRML 2.0 geometry leaf node), 289

Novell Corporation (Web site), 342

O

<OBJECT> HTML tag, 80-81

objects
ActiveX, embedding (<EMBED> HTML tag), 77-78
libraries (creating VRML content), 276-277

onBlur JavaScript event handler, 426

onChange JavaScript event handler, 426

onClick JavaScript event handler, 425

onFocus JavaScript event handler, 426

Online Shockwave Developer's Guide (Web site), 243

Onlive (Web site), 312

onLoad JavaScript event handler, 425

onMouseOver JavaScript event handler, 426

plug-ins | 481

onSelect JavaScript event handler, 426
onSubmit JavaScript event handler, 426
onUnload JavaScript event handler, 426
OpenInventor, 284, 306
OpenScape Navigator (Web site), 71
Options menu commands
 General Preferences, 30
 Show Audio Signal, 121
Orientation=LANDSCAPE| PORTRAIT| N:M|FREEFORM ASAP WebShow <EMBED> parameter, 249
OrthographicCamera node (VRML cameras), 269

P

pages, Web (design vs. content), 74-75
paint programs (creating bitmaps), 159-162
 Paint Shop Pro for Windows, 159-162
  file types supported, 160-162
 Paintbrush, 159
PALETTE= FOREGROUND| BACKGROUND ASAP WebShow <EMBED> parameter, 249
PALETTE=FOREGROUND| BACKGROUND InterVU <EMBED> attribute, 219
palettes, color (number of bits needed), 153
Pan button (Argus MapGuide toolbar), 381
Pan WHIP! option, 179
PAN=integer Apple QuickTime attribute, 216

Paragraph 3D (VRML browsers), 59-60
parameters, windowFeatures (options), 427-428
Passage to Vietnam (Web site), 234
Pathfinder PointCast channel, 389
Pause= ON|OFF ASAP WebShow <EMBED> parameter, 249
PAUSEBUTTON LiveAudio <EMBED> attribute, 141
PAUSEBUTTON= ON|OFF ASAP WebShow <EMBED> parameter, 249
Personal Server Control Panel Setup dialog box, 127
Personal Server Setup dialog box, 127
PerspectiveCamera node (VRML cameras), 269
PICTNUM=value FIGleaf Inline <EMBED> attribute, 170
PlaneSensor node (VRML 2.0 sensors), 295
platform independence (Java), 410
Play Incorporated (Web site), 164
Play3D, (Web site), 52, 225
Play3D animation plug-in, 225
Playback Engine API (RealAudio), 113
PLAYBUTTON LiveAudio <EMBED> attribute, 141
PLAYBUTTON RealAudio CONTROLS attribute value, 123
PLAYEVERYFRAME= TRUE|FALSE Apple QuickTime attribute, 216

Plug-In Software Development Kit (SDK) (creating your own plug-ins), 452-454
 HTML documentation, 452
 sample plug-ins, 452-453
 templates, 454
plug-ins, 19-21
 capabilities, 21
 content (limitations), 84-92
  browser compatibility, 86-89
  content vs. design, 89
  content-creation programs, 91-92
  file size and dial-up connections, 85-86
  file sizes, 92
  practical plug-in uses, 90-91
 creating your own, 446-450, 454-457
  AppWizard, 454
  browser basics, 449-450
  C++ programming tools, 450-451
  compiling your plug-in, 456
  creation guidelines, 457-460
  Microsoft Foundation Class (MFC) programming, 450
  Plug-In Software Development Kit (SDK), 451
  plug-in technical basics, 448-449
  testing your plug-in, 456-457
 embedded (defined), 19
 full-screen (defined), 20
 hidden (defined), 20-21
 Internet Explorer installation, 31-35
 intranets, 100-106
  application files, 103-104
  bandwidth and multimedia, 101-103

plug-ins

custom applications, 104-106
file standardization, 100-101
keeping track of installed plug-ins, 29-31
multimedia, 35-57
  animation, 51-52
  graphics, 40-48
  integrated, 52-57
  sound, 35-40
  video, 48-51
Netscape
  downloading, 28-31
  installing, 28-31
  running, 31
vs. helper applications, 10-13

Plug-Ins Plaza (Web site), 22, 28, 258

PLUG.WRL (sample VRML world), 271-273

PointCast (Web site), 25, 67

PointCast Network (Web information organizer), 387-396
advertisements, 395
channels, 388-389
configuring, 391-393
disadvantages, 395-396
potential uses, 389-391
troubleshooting, 396
update options, 394-395
Web site, 388

PointLight (VRML), 269

PointPlus (Web site), 63, 325

PointSet node
VRML 2.0 geometry leaf node, 289
VRML shapes, 268

portable documents
Adobe Acrobat Reader, 338-342
  creating files, 342
  navigating within, 338-341
Envoy, 342-347
  creating, 347
  HTML attributes, 346
  Toolbar, 343-344
  Web page usage, 345-347

Techexplorer, 347-349
  creating TeX files, 349
  TeX, 348

PositionField RealAudio CONTROLS attribute value, 123

PositionSlider RealAudio CONTROLS attribute value, 123

PowerPoint (Microsoft), 326-327
animation files
  creating, 326
  viewing, 327
Animation Player, 326
PointPlus, 325

PowerPoint Animation file (PPZ), 326

Powersoft (Web site), 56, 259

Preferences dialog box, 117

presentations, Astound Web Player (optimizing), 255-256

PreVU, (Web site), 51

Print WHIP! option, 179

Printing= ENABLED|DISABLED ASAP WebShow <EMBED> parameter, 249

Private Color Palette FIGleaf Inline command, 168

private messages, sending (ichat), 357-358

productivity plug-ins, 60-72
Acrobat Amber Reader, 60-61
CD-ROM contents, 464
Envoy, 61
Formula One/NET, 62
KEYview, 63
Word Viewer, 63

programming tools
ActiveX controls, 398-404
  creating custom controls with Visual C++, 399-400
  dependencies, 403-404
  embedding in HTML files, 402-403

Microsoft ActiveX Development Kit (MSADK), 402
NCompass ActiveX plug-in, 398
.OCX files, 401-402
QuickServer, 404-405
Stock Watcher, 405
supported SDKs, 404-405

Progressive Networks (Web site), 111

proprietary graphics formats, 176
animation (CelAnimator), 188-193
AutoCAD, 177-181
  Corel Visual CADD, 181-182
  DWG/DXF viewer, 180-181
  NetSlide 95, 180-182
  WHIP!, 177-180
miscellaneous formats, 193-199
  ART Press, 197-198
  Chemscape Chime, 193-197
  QuickSilver, 198
  WebXpresso, 199
vector graphics, 181-188
  Corel CMX, 182-183
  Shockwave for Freehand, 183-186
  SVF plug-in, 187-188

prototypes (VRML 2.0), 297-299

ProximitySensor node (VRML 2.0 sensors), 295

public messages, sending (ichat), 356-357

Publisher's Depot (Web site), 159

Pueblo (VR Scout front-end), 310-311

Q

Quick View Plus, 328-334
activating, 330
configuring, 332-334

features, 330-332
file formats supported, 329
QuickServer, 71, 404-405
Stock Watcher, 405
supported SDKs, 404-405
Web site, 71, 405
QuickSilver, 198
graphics plug-in, 46
Web site, 46, 198
QuickTime plug-ins, 213-217
Apple QuickTime, 213-216
MacZilla, 216
MovieStar, 217
MovieStar Maker, 217
QuickTime VR Component (Web site), 214

R

RAD PowerMedia (Web site), 55
RadMedia (Web site), 258
RapidTransit (Web site), 37, 145
real-time data (Java and JavaScript Web page enhancements), 415
RealAudio, 110-113
content usage, 122-125
CONSOLE attribute, 124-125
CONTROLS attribute, 122-125
HEIGHT attribute, 122-125
SRC attribute, 122-125
WIDTH attribute, 122-125
firewall issues (Web site), 116
Playback Engine API, 113
Software Development Kit (Web site), 113
Synchronized Multimedia (Web site), 131
URL format, 117
UNIX version, 115
Web site, 36, 111
RealAudio Encoder, 118-121
encoding, 119-121
command-line, 121-126
drag and drop, 121-126

installing, 119
supported file formats, 119
Web site, 119
RealAudio Personal Server, 126-128
Control Panel, 127
setting MIME types, 128
Web site, 126
RealAudio Player, 113-117
controls and menus, 116-117
installing, 115-116
preferences settings (Web site), 116
setup program (Web site), 115
RealAudio Server 2.0, 128-129
bandwidth, 129
CD-ROM (Web site), 129
synchronized multimedia, 130-131
remote access programs, 65-66
Carbon Copy/Net, 65-66
Timbuktu Pro, 65-66
ROOMS chat-server technology (ichat), 362
Rotation FIGleaf Inline command, 168
ROTATION=0|90|180|270 FIGleaf Inline <EMBED> attribute, 170
routes (VRML 2.0), 296-297
running
Carbon Copy/Net
as a guest, 370-372
as a host, 372-373
Look@Me, 364-365
plug-ins, 31-35

S

Sager Bell (Web site), 22
Salient Video Capture Subsystem (Web site), 204
Save This Image As FIGleaf Inline command, 169

SaveAs=ENABLED| DISABLED ASAP WebShow <EMBED> parameter, 249
scalar values (floating-point numbers), 296
Scaled FIGleaf Inline command, 169
scanning images (creating bitmaps), 163
scene graphs (VRML 2.0), 285-287
SCREAM inline multimedia player (Web site), 56, 259
<SCRIPT> HTML tags, 424-426
mixing with event handlers, 426-428
Script Active (NCompass ActiveX), 398
Script node (VRML 2.0), 297
scripting languages (JavaScript), 411-412
HTML file containment, 412
interpretive features, 412-413
Web pages, 422-435
scripts, Web pages (JavaScript), 422
hiding the script, 423-424
<SCRIPT> HTML tags, 424-426
testing the script, 422-423
SDKs (QuickServer), 404-405
security
Carbon Copy/Net, 367
Java, 411, 413-414
sensors (VRML 2.0), 295
Separator node (VRML), 270
servers
content, installing (Web server issues), 83-84
RealAudio Personal Server, 126-128
setting MIME types, 128
RealAudio Server 2.0, 128-129
bandwidth, 129
synchronized multimedia, 130-131

Web, 81-84
    CD-ROM contents, 467
    content servers
        (installing), 83-84
    MIME types, 81-83
Settings dialog box, 365
SHADOWED|SIMPLE|NONE
    ASAP WebShow <EMBED>
    parameter, 248
Shape node (VRML 2.0 leaf
    nodes), 288-289
shapes (VRML), 268
"Shocked" Apple Computer
    Home Page (Web site), 238
ShockTalk (digitized speech),
    40, 149
Shockwave (Web site), 54
Shockwave for Authorware,
    54, 250-252
Shockwave for Director,
    229-238
    animation, 230
    applications, 238
    creating movies, 239-243
        Internet limitations, 242
        Lingo network extensions,
            241
        optimizing movies, 242-243
        Web page design, 242
    education, 234-236
    entertainment, 233
    games, 231-232
    presentations, 236-237
    training, 233-234
    Web site, 229
Shockwave for Freehand,
    183-186
    Afterburner Xtra module, 184
    graphics plug-in, 46
    tools, 185-186
    Web site, 46, 184
Shockwave for Macromedia
    Director, 53
Shockwave toolbar, 185
Show Audio Signal command,
    121
SHOWCONTROLS=TRUE|FALSE
    CoolFusion <EMBED>
    attribute, 212

Silicon Graphics, Inc. (SGI),
    284
Simple Vector Format (SVF),
    44
sites
    FTP
        English Text-to-Speech, 39
        Graphics FAQ, 156
    Web
        20/20 Software, 68
        7th Level, 259
        Accuweather, 230
        Acrobat Amber Reader, 61
        Action, 219
        Action MPEG, 51
        ActiveX, 71
        Adobe, 61, 338
        AfterShock's Arcade
            Alley, 232
        Alpha Software, 68
        AnchorPage, 64
        animation programs, 206
        Apple Flavored Java, 442
        Apple QD3D, 193
        Apple QuickTime, 213
        Argus Map Viewer, 67
        Argus MapGuide, 379
        Arnaud Masson's
            MIDI, 37, 148
        ART Press, 47, 197
        ASAP WebShow, 55
        ASAP WordPower, 246
        Astound Web Player,
            55, 253
        Asymetix, 258
        Asymetrix, 56
        audio editing tips, 120
        Authorware After-
            shock, 251
        AutoDesk, 42
        Bare-Bones Shebang
            about Netscape
            Plug-Ins, 446
        Brilliance Labs, 316
        Business@Web, 71
        Carbon Copy/Net, 65, 368
        CelAnimator, 45, 189
        CGM (Computer Graphics
            Metafiles), 192
        Chaco, Communications,
            311

Chemscape Chime, 46, 193
Citrix Systems, 72
CNN Oklahoma
    Bombing, 236
command-line encoding,
    121
Compress Slide Show
    (CSS), 325
Concerto, 68
CoolFusion, 49, 211
Corel, 183
Corel CMX, 44, 182
Corel Visual CADD, 181
creating frames, 130
Crescendo, 37, 146
CyberEd, 241
Cybergate, 308
Cyberkids, 236
CyberPassage, 313
Deltapoint, 226
digitized sounds, 135
Dimension X, 313, 443
Director 5 Shockwave
    Movie Lab, 243
DocuMagix, 65, 385
DWG/DXF, 42
DWG/DXF viewer, 180
EarthTime, 67, 376
Echospeech, 39, 145
<EMBED> tag, 77
Emblaze, 52, 222
Enliven Viewer, 222
Envoy, 61, 342
Express VR, 59
Farallon, 362
FIF, 45
FIF (Fractal Image
    Format) viewer, 174
FIGleaf Inline, 41, 170
Formula One/NET, 62,
    323
FutureSplash, 189
Galacticomm
    Worldgroup, 69
Gamelan, 442
Globalink, 68
Globalink Web
    Translator, 68
Gobbler, 418
Gold Disk, 253
Graphics FAQ, 156

sites | 485

Graphics Utilities Site and Version FAQ, 159
Groupscape, 69
HindSite, 382
HistoryTree, 65
HotPage, 65, 385
HTML Writers' Guild, 159
ichat, 68, 353
Iconovex, 64
Icons and Images, 159
Infinet Op, 45
InfinOp, 173
Inso, 63, 322, 328
Integrated Data Systems (IDS), 59, 314
InterCAP InLine, 44
Internet Movie Tool, 214
Internet relay chat (IRC), 68
InterVU, 217
intranet information, 98
Intranet Journal, 101
Intranet Links, 99
ISYS HindSite, 64
ISYS/Odyssey Development, 382
Iterated Systems, 212
JASC, 162
Java Applet Review System (JARS), 442
Java Boutique, 442
Java Centre, 442
Java Developer's Kit (JDK), 435
Javology, 442
JetForm Filler, 68
Kaleida Labs, 56, 259
KEYview, 63
Kite Paradise, 234
Koan, 38, 148
Lightning Strike, 45, 173
Lingo, 241
Liquid Reality, 313
ListenUp, 39, 149
Live3D, 57
LiveVideo, 207
Look@Me, 362
Mac-only Multimedia Plugin, 217
Macromedia, 229
MacZilla, 50, 216

MagnaStar, Inc., 418, 443
mBED, 55, 256
media.splash, 259
MeshMart, 276
mFactory, 56, 259
Microcom, 368
Micrografx, 198
Microsoft ActiveX Development Kit (MSADK), 402
MidiShare, 37, 148
MIDPlug, 147
MIME types, 82
MovieStar, 50
MovieStar Maker, 217
mToon, 259
Multimedia Plugin, 50
MVP Solutions, 39
NCompass Labs, 398
NET-Install, 68
Net-Scene, 325
Netscape, 48
Netscape Full Service Intranet Applications, 99
Netscape intranet suite, 106
Netscape Plug-In Software Development Kit (SDK), 451
Netscape plug-ins, 28
Netscape plug-ins tracking, 22
NetSlide 95, 43, 180
Novell Corporation, 342
<OBJECT> tag, 81
Online Shockwave Developer's Guide, 243
Onlive, 312
OpenScape Navigator, 71
Paint Shop Pro, 10, 162
Passage to Vietnam, 234
Play Incorporated, 164
Play3D, 52, 225
Plug-Ins Plaza, 22, 28, 258
PointCast, 25, 67
PointCast Network, 388
PointPlus, 63, 325
Powersoft, 56, 259
PreVU, 51
Progressive Networks, 111
Publisher's Depot, 159
Pueblo, 311
QuickServer, 71, 405

QuickSilver, 46, 198
QuickTime VR Component, 214
RAD PowerMedia, 55
RadMedia, 258
RapidTransit, 37, 145
RealAudio, 36, 111
RealAudio (UNIX version), 115
RealAudio Encoder, 119
RealAudio firewall issues, 116
RealAudio Personal Server, 126
RealAudio Player preferences settings, 116
RealAudio Player setup program, 115
RealAudio Server 2.0 CD-ROM, 129
RealAudio Software Development Kit, 113
RealAudio Synchronized Multimedia, 131
Sager Bell, 22
Salient Video Capture Subsystem, 204
SCREAM inline multimedia player, 56, 259
"Shocked" Apple Computer Home Page, 238
ShockTalk, 40, 149
Shockwave, 54
Shockwave for Authorware, 54, 251
Shockwave for Director, 229
Shockwave for Freehand, 46, 184
Simple Vector Format (SVF), 44
Sizzler, 52, 224
Snappy video digitizer, 164
SoftSource, 180, 187
Sony, 313
sound file archives, 119
Sportsline USA, 233
Starfish Software, 66
State of the Union, 237
Stock Watcher, 405

Summus Wavelet
  Viewer, 45
SuperScape, 59
SVF plug-in, 187
Talker, 39, 148
Talker text-to-speech
  process, 148
Team Java, 443
TEC Player, 50, 217
Techexplorer, 347
Template Graphics
  Software, 59
TerraForm, 316
Texture Viewer, 63
Timbuktu Pro, 65
Timecast, 117
ToolBook, 56, 258
ToolVox, 38, 143
ToolVox Gold, 143
Top Gun, 56, 259
Topper, 59
Toy Story Concentration
  Game, 231
Traveler, 312
Treasure Quest, 354
TrueSpeech, 36, 145
TUCOWS (The Ultimate
  Collection Of Winsock
  Software, 22
Tudor Speech, 39
Tumbleweed Software, 342
V-Realm, 314
VDOLive, 49, 209
Vertigo, 47, 192
video digitizing
  services, 205
video frame grabbers, 205
ViewDirector, 41, 170
ViewMovie, 50, 217
Virtus Voyager, 315
Viscape, 59
Visual Components, 323
VivoActive Player, 50
Vosaic, 49, 213
Voxware, 143
VR Scout, 58, 311
VRealm, 59
VREAM, 310
VRML Repository, 318
VRweb, 309
Wavelet Viewer, 174
Wayfarer Communications,
  71, 405

WCVT2POV, 274
Web Animator, 52
Web Developers' Virtual
  Library, 159
Web-Active, 47, 192
WebActive 3D, 47, 193
WebBASIC, 72
WebSpace, 307
WebXpresso, 199
WHIP!, 42, 178
William H. Tudor's
  Speech, 148
WinCam.One, 166
WinFrame, 72
WIRL, 58, 310
WordViewer, 63, 322
WurlPlug, 47, 193
Xing, 51, 217

**SIZE=DOUBLE Action
<EMBED> attribute, 221**

**Sizzler, 51 (Web site), 52,
224**

**Sizzler animation plug-in,
224-225**

**SMALLCONSOLE LiveAudio
<EMBED> attribute, 141**

**Snappy video digitizer
(Web site), 164**

**SoftSource (Web site),
180, 187**

Sony (Web site), 313

**sound file archives
(Web site), 119**

sound files
  adjusting (RealAudio
    Encoder), 120
  formats (digitized audio),
    134-138

**Sound Gadget Pro digitizing
your own sounds), 137**

**Sound node (VRML 2.0 leaf
nodes), 290-291**

sound plug-ins, 35-40
  Arnaud Masson's MIDI, 37
  CD-ROM contents, 462
  Crescendo, 36
  Echospeech, 38
  English Text-to-Speech
    (Apple), 39

  helper applications (CD-ROM
    contents), 465-466
  Koan (Sseyo), 38
  ListenUp, 39
  LiveAudio, 35
  MidiShare, 37
  RapidTransit, 37
  RealAudio, 35
  ShockTalk, 40
  Talker, 39
  ToolVox, 38
  TrueSpeech, 36
  Tudor Speech, 39

**Sound=URL ASAP WebShow
<EMBED> parameter, 249**

speech (digitized)
  Echospeech, 145
  ListenUp, 149
  ShockTalk, 149
  Talker, 148
  ToolVox, 142-145
  TrueSpeech, 145
  William H. Tudor's
    Speech, 148

Sphere node
  VRML 2.0 geometry leaf
    node, 289
  VRML shapes, 268

**SphereSensor node
(VRML 2.0 sensors), 295**

**Sports PointCast
channel, 389**

**Sportsline USA
(Web site), 233**

SpotLight (VRML), 269

spreadsheets
  embedding (Formula One/
    NET), 324-325
  Formula One/NET, 323

**SRC attribute
(RealAudio), 122**

**SRC="filename" LiveAudio
<EMBED> attribute, 140**

**SRC="filename" ToolVox
<EMBED> attribute, 144**

**SRC=value FIGleaf Inline
<EMBED> attribute, 169**

**Starfish Software
(Web site), 66**

STARTTIME="mm:ss" LiveAudio <EMBED> attribute, 141
State of the Union (Web site), 237
statements, VRML (DEF and USE), 268
Statistics dialog box, 117
StatusBar RealAudio CONTROLS attribute value, 123
StatusField RealAudio CONTROLS attribute value, 123
Stock Watcher (QuickServer), 405
Stop button (Argus MapGuide toolbar), 381
STOPBUTTON LiveAudio <EMBED> attribute, 141
StopButton RealAudio CONTROLS attribute value, 123
STREAMONLDOUBLECLK=TRUE|FALSE CoolFusion <EMBED> attribute, 212
STRETCH=TRUE/FALSE VDOLive <EMBED> attribute, 210
Studio M (Astound Web Player), 254
Summus Wavelet Viewer
 graphics plug-in, 45
 Web site, 45
SuperScape (Web site), 59
SVF plug-in, 187-188
Switch node (VRML 2.0 grouping nodes), 292-293
SYNC=ON Action <EMBED> attribute, 220
synchronized multimedia (RealAudio Server 2.0), 130
syntax
 VRML, 266-268
 VRML 2.0, 287-288

T

tags (HTML)
 <EMBED>, 76-79, 169-170
 <IMG>, 76
 <OBJECT>, 80-81
 <PARAM>, 420-422
 <SCRIPT>, 424-426
Talker
 digitized speech, 148
 Web site, 39, 148
Talker text-to-speech process (Web site), 148
TARGET="FRAME" Apple QuickTime attribute, 216
Team Java (Web site), 443
TEC Player (Web site), 50, 217
Techexplorer, 347-349
 TeX, 348
  creating files, 349
 Web site, 347
Template Graphics Software (Web site), 59
templates (Plug-In SDK), 454
TerraForm (Web site), 316
TerraForm Free (VRML browsers), 60, 316
Text node (VRML 2.0 geometry leaf node), 289
Texture Viewer (Web site), 63
Texture2 node (VRML textures), 269
TextureCoordinate node (VRML 2.0 geometry leaf node), 289
textures (VRML), 268-269
TILT=integer Apple QuickTime attribute, 216
Timbuktu Pro
 remote access programs, 65
 Web site, 65
Timecast (Web site), 117
TimeSensor node (VRML 2.0 sensors), 295

toolbars (Shockwave for Freehand), 185
ToolBook (Web site), 56, 258
tools (Shockwave for Freehand), 185-186
ToolVox, 38, 142-145
 <EMBED> HTML tag attributes, 144
 Web site, 38, 143
ToolVox Encoder, 143
ToolVox Gold (Web site), 143
Top Gun (Web site), 56, 259
Topper
 VRML browsers, 59-60
 Web site, 59
Toy Story Concentration Game (Web site), 231
training (Shockwave for Director), 233-234
Transform node
 VRML 2.0 grouping nodes, 291-292
 VRML, 270
Traveler (Web site), 312
Traveler VRML browser, 311-312
Treasure Quest (Web site), 354
troubleshooting (PointCast Network), 396
TrueSpeech (Web site), 36, 145
TUCOWS (The Ultimate Collection Of Winsock Software (Web site), 22
Tudor Speech (Web site), 39
Tumbleweed Software (Web site), 342

U

Unzoom button (Argus MapGuide toolbar), 381
URLATTACH Autodesk Utilities command, 179

URLLIST Autodesk Utilities command, 179
URLs (RealAudio format), 117
USE statements (VRML), 268
users
  creating (ichat), 354-355
  interface (ichat), 356

V

V-Realm (Web site), 314
values, CONTROLS attribute (RealAudio), 123
VDOLive, 48, 208-210
  <EMBED> HTML tag attributes, 210
  Web site, 49, 209
vector graphics, 181-188
  Corel CMX, 182-183
  Shockwave for Freehand, 183-186
  SVF plug-in, 187-188
vector images (graphics file format), 155
Vertical Flip FIGleaf Inline command, 168
Vertigo
  graphics plug-in, 47
  Web site, 47, 192
VFLIP=TRUE|FALSE FIGleaf Inline <EMBED> attribute, 170
video
  animation plug-ins, 221-226
    Emblaze, 222-223
    Enliven, 221-222
    Play3D, 225
    Sizzler, 224-225
  content, 202-204
    creating, 204-206
    practical uses, 203-204
    speed issues, 202-203
  digitizing images, 163-166
  MPEG plug-ins, 217-221
    Action, 219-221
    ActionStudio, 219-221
    InterVU, 217-219

QuickTime plug-ins, 213-217
  Apple QuickTime, 213-216
  MacZilla, 216
  MovieStar, 217
  MovieStar Maker, 217
Video for Windows plug-ins, 206-213
  CoolFusion, 211-212
  LiveVideo, 207-208
  VDOLive, 208-210
  VivoActive Player, 213
  Vosaic, 213
video digitizing services (Web site), 205
Video for Windows, 48
video frame grabbers (Web site), 205
Video Mosaic, see Vosaic (Web Site)
video plug-ins, 48-51
  Action MPEG, 51
  CD-ROM contents, 463-464
  CoolFusion, 49-51
  helper applications (CD-ROM contents), 466
  LiveVideo, 48-51
  MacZilla, 50-51
  MovieStar, 50-51
  Multimedia Plugin, 50-51
  PreVU, 51
  TEC Player, 50-51
  VDOLive, 48-51
  Video for Windows, 48-51
  ViewMovie, 50-51
  VivoActive Player, 50-51
  Vosaic, 49-51
  Xing, 51
View Reports button (Argus MapGuide toolbar), 381
View This Image FIGleaf Inline command, 169
ViewDirector (Web site), 41, 170
ViewDirector Imaging (graphics plug-in), 41
ViewMovie (Web site), 50, 217
Viewpoints (VRML 2.0 leaf nodes), 291

Virtus Voyager
  VRML browsers, 60
  Web site, 315
Virtus Voyager VRML browser, 60, 315
Virtus VRML Toolkit (creating VRML content), 278
Viscape
  VRML browsers, 59-60
  Web site, 59
VisibilitySensor node (VRML 2.0 sensors), 295
Visual Components (Web site), 323
VISUALMODE=value ToolVox <EMBED> attribute, 144
VivoActive Player (Web site, 50, 213)
VOLUME=percentage LiveAudio <EMBED> attribute, 141
VOLUMELEVER LiveAudio <EMBED> attribute, 141
VolumeSlider RealAudio CONTROLS attribute value, 123
Vosaic (Web site), 49, 213
Voxware (Web site), 143
VR Scout
  VRML browsers, 58-60
  Web site, 58, 311
VR Scout VRML browser (Pueblo front-end), 310-311
VRealm (VRML browsers), 59-60
VREAM (Web site), 310
VRML, 264-271, 284-285
  basic syntax, 266-268
  browsers, 57-60
    Cybergate, 59-60, 307-308
    CyberPassage, 313
    Express VR, 59-60
    Liquid Reality, 59-60, 312-313
    Live3D, 57-60
    Microsoft VRML add-in (Internet Explorer), 317
    Paragraph 3D, 59-60

TerraForm, 316
TerraForm Free, 60
Topper, 59-60
Traveler, 311-312
Virtus Voyager, 60, 315
Viscape, 59-60
VR Scout, 58-60, 310-311
VRweb, 308-309
VRealm, 59-60, 314
WebSpace, 306-307
WIRL, 58-60, 309-310
building your own worlds, 279-281
cameras, 269
content (creating), 274-278
  Caligari Fountain, 278
  Home Space Builder, 277
  Interchange conversion program, 275
  object libraries, 276-277
  Virtus VRML Toolkit, 278
  WCVT2POV conversion program, 274-275
DEF and USE statements, 268
evolution of, 264-265
Group and Separator nodes, 270
history of, 264
lights, 269
LOD node, 270
materials and textures, 268-269
OpenInventor, 284
plug-ins (CD-ROM contents), 462
PLUG.WRL (sample world), 271-273
possible applications, 302-303
shapes, 268
Transform node, 270-271
WWWAnchor node, 271
WWWInline node, 271

VRML 2.0
basic concepts, 285-288
  new scene graph, 285-287
  sytax, 287-288
grouping nodes, 291-293
  Collision node, 293
  Group node, 292
  LOD node, 293
  Switch node, 292-293
  Transform node, 291-292
  WWWAnchor node, 293
  WWWInline node, 293
interpolators, 296
leaf nodes, 288-291
  Appearance node, 290
  AudioClip node, 290-291
  geometry nodes, 289
  lights, 290
  Shape node, 288-289
  Sound node, 290-291
  Viewpoints, 291
Live3D, 299-301
  extensions, 301
  menus, 301
  navigation, 299-300
miscellaneous nodes, 294
  Background node, 294
  Fog node, 294
  NavigationInfo node, 294-295
  WorldInfo node, 294-295
prototypes, 297-299
routes, 296-297
Script node, 297
sensors, 295
  CylinderSensor node, 295
  PlaneSensor node, 295
  ProximitySensor node, 295
  SphereSensor node, 295
  TimeSensor node, 295
  VisibilitySensor node, 295

VRML Repository (Web site), 318

VRweb (Web site), 309

VRweb VRML browser, 308-309

W

Waveform Hold and Modify (digitizing your own sounds), 137-138

Wavelet Viewer
compression plug-ins, 174
Web site, 174

Wayfarer Communications (Web site), 71, 405

WCVT2POV conversion program (creating VRML content), 274-275

Weather PointCast channel, 389

Web Animator (Web site), 52

Web Developers' Virtual Library (Web site), 159

Web pages
design
  Director limitations (Shockwave movies), 242
  vs. content, 74-75
Envoy usage, 345-347
  HTML attributes, 346-349
Java and JavaScript enhancements, 414-416
  form verification, 414
  games, 416
  real-time data, 415
  true interaction, 415
JavaScript, 422-435
  finding examples, 442
  hiding the script, 423-424
  including scripts, 422
  <SCRIPT> HTML tags, 424-426
  testing the script, 422-423
  validating forms before submission, 428-435
locating (HindSite), 382-384
organizing (HotPage), 385-387

Web servers, 81-84
CD-ROM contents, 467
content servers (installing), 83-84
MIME types, 81-83

Web sites
20/20 Software, 68
7th Level, 259
Accuweather, 230
Acrobat Amber Reader, 61
Action, 219
Action MPEG, 51
ActiveX, 71
Adobe, 61, 338
AfterShock's Arcade Alley, 232
Alpha Software, 68

Web sites

AnchorPage, 64
animation programs, 206
Apple Flavored Java, 442
Apple QD3D, 193
Apple QuickTime, 213
Argus Map Viewer, 67
Argus MapGuide, 379
Arnaud Masson's MIDI, 37, 148
ART Press, 47, 197
ASAP WebShow, 55
ASAP WordPower, 246
Astound Web Player, 55, 253
Asymetix, 258
Asymetrix, 56
audio editing tips, 120
Authorware Aftershock, 251
AutoDesk, 42
Bare-Bones Shebang about Netscape Plug-Ins, 446
Brilliance Labs, 316
Business@Web, 71
Carbon Copy/Net, 65, 368
CelAnimator, 45, 189
CGM (Computer Graphics Metafiles), 192
Chaco Communications, 311
Chemscape Chime, 46, 193
Citrix Systems, 72
CNN Oklahoma Bombing, 236
command-line encoding, 121
Compress Slide Show (CSS), 325
Concerto, 68
CoolFusion, 49, 211
Corel, 183
Corel CMX, 44, 182
Corel Visual CADD, 181
creating frames, 130
Crescendo, 37, 146
CyberEd, 241
Cybergate, 308
Cyberkids, 236
CyberPassage, 313
Deltapoint, 226
digitized sounds, 135
Dimension X, 313, 443
Director 5 Shockwave Movie Lab, 243
DocuMagix, 65, 385
DWG/DXF, 42
DWG/DXF viewer, 180

EarthTime, 67, 376
Echospeech, 39, 145
<EMBED> tag, 77
Emblaze, 52, 222
Enliven Viewer, 222
Envoy, 61, 342
Express VR, 59
Farallon, 362
FIF, 45
FIF (Fractal Image Format) viewer, 174
FIGleaf Inline, 41, 170
Formula One/NET, 62, 323
FutureSplash, 189
Galacticomm Worldgroup, 69
Gamelan, 442
Globalink, 68
Globalink Web Translator, 68
Gobbler, 418
Gold Disk, 253
Graphics FAQ, 156
Graphics Utilities Site and Version FAQ, 159
Groupscape, 69
HindSite, 382
HistoryTree, 65
HotPage, 65, 385
HTML Writers' Guild, 159
ichat, 68, 353
Iconovex, 64
Icons and Images, 159
Infinet Op, 45
InfinOp, 173
Inso, 63, 322, 328
Integrated Data Systems (IDS), 59, 314
InterCAP InLine, 44
Internet Movie Tool, 214
Internet relay chat (IRC), 68
InterVU, 217
intranet information, 98
Intranet Journal, 101
Intranet Links, 99
ISYS HindSite, 64
ISYS/Odyssey Development, 382
Iterated Systems, 212
JASC, 162
Java Applet Review System (JARS), 442
Java Boutique, 442

Java Centre, 442
Java Developer's Kit (JDK), 435
Javology, 442
JetForm Filler, 68
Kaleida Labs, 56, 259
KEYview, 63
Kite Paradise, 234
Koan, 38, 148
Lightning Strike, 45, 173
Lingo, 241
Liquid Reality, 313
ListenUp, 39, 149
Live3D, 57
LiveVideo, 207
Look@Me, 362
Mac-only Multimedia Plugin, 217
Macromedia, 229
MacZilla, 50, 216
MagnaStar, Inc., 418, 443
mBED, 55, 256
media.splash, 259
MeshMart, 276
mFactory, 56, 259
Microcom, 368
Micrografx, 198
Microsoft ActiveX Development Kit (MSADK), 402
MidiShare, 37, 148
MIDPlug, 147
MIME types, 82
MovieStar, 50
MovieStar Maker, 217
mToon, 259
Multimedia Plugin, 50
MVP Solutions, 39
NCompass Labs, 398
NET-Install, 68
Net-Scene, 325
Netscape, 48
Netscape Full Service Intranet Applications, 99
Netscape intranet suite, 106
Netscape Plug-In Software Development Kit (SDK), 451
Netscape plug-ins, 28
Netscape plug-ins tracking, 22
NetSlide 95, 43, 180
Novell Corporation, 342

Online Shockwave
   Developer's Guide, 243
Onlive, 312
OpenScape Navigator, 71
Paint Shop Pro, 10, 162
Passage to Vietnam, 234
Play Incorporated, 164
Play3D, 52, 225
Plug-Ins Plaza, 22, 28, 258
PointCast, 25, 67
PointCast Network, 388
PointPlus, 63, 325
Powersoft, 56, 259
PreVU, 51
Progressive Networks, 111
Publisher's Depot, 159
Pueblo, 311
QuickServer, 71, 405
QuickSilver, 46, 198
QuickTime
   VR Component, 214
RAD PowerMedia, 55
RadMedia, 258
RapidTransit, 37, 145
RealAudio, 36, 111
RealAudio
   (UNIX version), 115
RealAudio Encoder, 119
RealAudio firewall issues, 116
RealAudio Personal
   Server, 126
RealAudio Player preferences
   settings, 116
RealAudio Player setup
   program, 115
RealAudio Server 2.0
   CD-ROM, 129
RealAudio Software
   Development Kit, 113
RealAudio Synchronized
   Multimedia, 131
Sager Bell, 22
Salient Video Capture
   Subsystem, 204
SCREAM inline multimedia
   player, 56, 259
"Shocked" Apple Computer
   Home Page, 238
ShockTalk, 40, 149
Shockwave, 54
Shockwave for Authorware,
   54, 251

Shockwave for Director, 229
Shockwave for Freehand,
   46, 184
Simple Vector Format
   (SVF), 44
Sizzler, 52, 224
Snappy video digitizer, 164
SoftSource, 180, 187
Sony, 313
sound file archives, 119
Sportsline USA, 233
Starfish Software, 66
State of the Union, 237
Stock Watcher, 405
Summus Wavelet Viewer, 45
SuperScape, 59
SVF plug-in, 187
Talker, 39, 148
Talker text-to-speech
   process, 148
Team Java, 443
TEC Player, 50, 217
Techexplorer, 347
Template Graphics
   Software, 59
TerraForm, 316
Texture Viewer, 63
Timbuktu Pro, 65
Timecast, 117
ToolBook, 56, 258
ToolVox, 38, 143
ToolVox Gold, 143
Top Gun, 56, 259
Topper, 59
Toy Story Concentration
   Game, 231
Traveler, 312
Treasure Quest, 354
TrueSpeech, 36, 145
TUCOWS (The Ultimate
   Collection Of Winsock
   Software, 22
Tudor Speech, 39
Tumbleweed Software, 342
VDOLive, 49, 209
Vertigo, 47, 192
video digitizing services, 205
video frame grabbers, 205
ViewDirector, 41, 170
ViewMovie, 50, 217
Virtus Voyager, 315
Viscape, 59

Visual Components, 323
VivoActive Player, 50
Vosaic, 49, 213
Voxware, 143
VR Scout, 58, 311
VRealm, 59, 314
VREAM, 310
VRML Repository, 318
VRweb, 309
Wavelet Viewer, 174
Wayfarer Communications,
   71, 405
WCVT2POV, 274
Web Animator, 52
Web Developers' Virtual
   Library, 159
Web-Active, 47, 192
WebActive 3D, 47, 193
WebBASIC, 72
WebSpace, 307
WebXpresso, 199
WHIP!, 42, 178
William H. Tudor's
   Speech, 148
WinCam.One, 166
WinFrame, 72
WIRL, 58, 310
WordViewer, 63, 322
WurlPlug, 47, 193
Xing, 51, 217

WebActive 3D
   graphics plug-in, 47
   Web site, 47, 192-193

WebBASIC (Web site), 72

WebSpace (Web site), 307

**WebSpace VRML browser,
   306-307**

WebXpresso, 199
   graphics plug-in, 47
   Web site, 199

**WHIP! (Autodesk), 41,
   177-180**
   options menu, 179
   DWF (Drawing Web Format)
      file type, 177
   Web site, 42, 178

**WIDTH attribute
   (RealAudio), 122**

WIDTH=integer LiveAudio <EMBED> attribute, 140
WIDTH=integer ToolVox <EMBED> attribute, 144
WIDTH=value FIGleaf Inline <EMBED> attribute, 169
William H. Tudor's Speech plug-in, 148
WinCam.One (Web site), 166
windowFeatures parameters (options), 427-428
WinFrame (Web site), 72
WIRL, 58-60, 309-310
Word, Microsoft (WordViewer), 322
WordViewer (Web site), 63, 322
WorldInfo node (VRML 2.0), 294-295
WurlPlug graphics plug-in, 47
    Web site, 47, 193
WWWAnchor node (VRML 2.0 grouping nodes), 271, 293
WWWInline node (VRML 2.0 grouping nodes), 293
    VRML, 271

Zoom to Rectangle WHIP! option, 179
Zoom WHIP! option, 179
ZOOMAREA=left,top,right, bottom FIGleaf Inline <EMBED> attribute, 170
ZoomButtons= ON|OFF ASAP WebShow <EMBED> parameter, 249

X-Z

XBMs (graphics file format), 155
Xing (Web site), 51, 217

Zoom button (Argus MapGuide toolbar), 381
Zoom Goto button (Argus MapGuide toolbar), 381
Zoom Out button (Argus MapGuide toolbar), 381
Zoom Out FIGleaf Inline command, 168

GET CONNECTED
to the ultimate source of computer information!

The MCP Forum on CompuServe

Go online with the world's leading computer book publisher! Macmillan Computer Publishing offers everything you need for computer success!

Find the books that are right for you!
A complete online catalog, plus sample chapters and tables of contents give you an in-depth look at all our books. The best way to shop or browse!

➤ Get fast answers and technical support for MCP books and software

➤ Join discussion groups on major computer subjects

➤ Interact with our expert authors via e-mail and conferences

➤ Download software from our immense library:
  ▷ Source code from books
  ▷ Demos of hot software
  ▷ The best shareware and freeware
  ▷ Graphics files

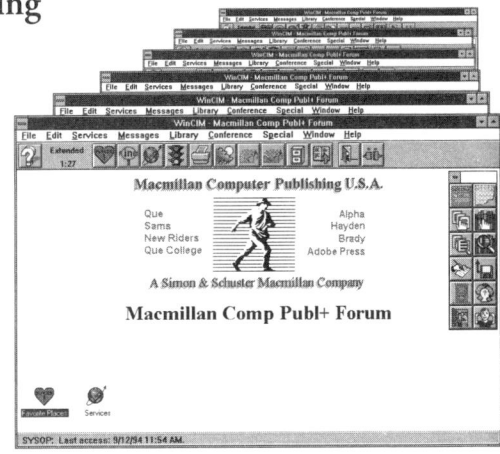

Join now and get a free CompuServe Starter Kit!

To receive your free CompuServe Introductory Membership, call **1-800-848-8199** and ask for representative #597.

The Starter Kit includes:
➤ Personal ID number and password
➤ $15 credit on the system
➤ Subscription to *CompuServe Magazine*

Once on the CompuServe System, type:

GO MACMILLAN

for the most computer information anywhere!

Check out Que® Books on the World Wide Web
http://www.mcp.com/que

As the biggest software release in computer history, Windows 95 continues to redefine the computer industry. Click here for the latest info on our Windows 95 books

Make computing quick and easy with these products designed exclusively for new and casual users

Examine the latest releases in word processing, spreadsheets, operating systems, and suites

The Internet, The World Wide Web, CompuServe®, America Online®, Prodigy®—it's a world of ever-changing information. Don't get left behind!

Find out about new additions to our site, new bestsellers and hot topics

In-depth information on high-end topics: find the best reference books for databases, programming, networking, and client/server technologies

A recent addition to Que, Ziff-Davis Press publishes the highly-successful *How It Works* and *How to Use* series of books, as well as *PC Learning Labs Teaches* and *PC Magazine* series of book/disk packages

Stay on the cutting edge of Macintosh® technologies and visual communications

Find out which titles are making headlines

With 6 separate publishing groups, Que develops products for many specific market segments and areas of computer technology. Explore our Web Site and you'll find information on best-selling titles, newly published titles, upcoming products, authors, and much more.

- Stay informed on the latest industry trends and products available
- Visit our online bookstore for the latest information and editions
- Download software from Que's library of the best shareware and freeware

QUE®

Copyright © 1996, Macmillan Computer Publishing-USA, A Viacom Company

Complete and Return this Card for a *FREE* Computer Book Catalog

Thank you for purchasing this book! You have purchased a superior computer book written expressly for your needs. To continue to provide the kind of up-to-date, pertinent coverage you've come to expect from us, we need to hear from you. Please take a minute to complete and return this self-addressed, postage-paid form. In return, we'll send you a free catalog of all our computer books on topics ranging from word processing to programming and the internet.

Mr. ☐ Mrs. ☐ Ms. ☐ Dr. ☐

Name (first) ☐☐☐☐☐☐☐☐☐☐☐☐ (M.I.) ☐ (last) ☐☐☐☐☐☐☐☐☐☐☐☐☐☐☐

Address ☐☐☐☐☐☐☐☐☐☐☐☐☐☐☐☐☐☐☐☐☐☐☐☐☐☐☐☐☐☐

City ☐☐☐☐☐☐☐☐☐☐☐☐☐ State ☐☐ Zip ☐☐☐☐☐ ☐☐☐☐

Phone ☐☐☐ ☐☐☐ ☐☐☐☐ Fax ☐☐☐ ☐☐☐ ☐☐☐☐

Company Name ☐☐☐☐☐☐☐☐☐☐☐☐☐☐☐☐☐☐☐☐☐☐☐☐☐☐

E-mail address ☐☐☐☐☐☐☐☐☐☐☐☐☐☐☐☐☐☐☐☐☐☐☐☐☐☐

1. Please check at least (3) influencing factors for purchasing this book.

Front or back cover information on book .... ☐
Special approach to the content .... ☐
Completeness of content .... ☐
Author's reputation .... ☐
Publisher's reputation .... ☐
Book cover design or layout .... ☐
Index or table of contents of book .... ☐
Price of book .... ☐
Special effects, graphics, illustrations .... ☐
Other (Please specify): _____ ☐

2. How did you first learn about this book?

Saw in Macmillan Computer Publishing catalog .... ☐
Recommended by store personnel .... ☐
Saw the book on bookshelf at store .... ☐
Recommended by a friend .... ☐
Received advertisement in the mail .... ☐
Saw an advertisement in: _____ ☐
Read book review in: _____ ☐
Other (Please specify): _____ ☐

3. How many computer books have you purchased in the last six months?

This book only .... ☐   3 to 5 books .... ☐
2 books .... ☐   More than 5 .... ☐

4. Where did you purchase this book?

Bookstore .... ☐
Computer Store .... ☐
Consumer Electronics Store .... ☐
Department Store .... ☐
Office Club .... ☐
Warehouse Club .... ☐
Mail Order .... ☐
Direct from Publisher .... ☐
Internet site .... ☐
Other (Please specify): _____ ☐

5. How long have you been using a computer?

☐ Less than 6 months   ☐ 6 months to a year
☐ 1 to 3 years   ☐ More than 3 years

6. What is your level of experience with personal computers and with the subject of this book?

	With PCs	With subject of book
New	☐	☐
Casual	☐	☐
Accomplished	☐	☐
Expert	☐	☐

Source Code ISBN: 0-7897-845-0

7. Which of the following best describes your job title?

Administrative Assistant ☐
Coordinator ☐
Manager/Supervisor ☐
Director ☐
Vice President ☐
President/CEO/COO ☐
Lawyer/Doctor/Medical Professional ☐
Teacher/Educator/Trainer ☐
Engineer/Technician ☐
Consultant ☐
Not employed/Student/Retired ☐
Other (Please specify): _____ ☐

8. Which of the following best describes the area of the company your job title falls under?

Accounting ☐
Engineering ☐
Manufacturing ☐
Operations ☐
Marketing ☐
Sales ☐
Other (Please specify): _____ ☐

9. What is your age?

Under 20 ☐
21-29 ☐
30-39 ☐
40-49 ☐
50-59 ☐
60-over ☐

10. Are you:

Male ☐
Female ☐

11. Which computer publications do you read regularly? (Please list)

_____
_____
_____
_____
_____
_____
_____
_____

Comments: _____
_____

Fold here and scotch-tape to mail.

BUSINESS REPLY MAIL
FIRST-CLASS MAIL PERMIT NO. 9918 INDIANAPOLIS IN

POSTAGE WILL BE PAID BY THE ADDRESSEE

ATTN MARKETING
MACMILLAN COMPUTER PUBLISHING
MACMILLAN PUBLISHING USA
201 W 103RD ST
INDIANAPOLIS IN 46290-9042

NO POSTAGE NECESSARY IF MAILED IN THE UNITED STATES

Licensing Agreement

By opening this package, you are agreeing to be bound by the following:

This software product is copyrighted, and all rights are reserved by the publisher and author. You are licensed to use this software on a single computer. You may copy and/or modify the software as needed to facilitate your use of it on a single computer. Making copies of the software for any other purpose is a violation of the United States copyright laws.

This software is sold *as is* without warranty of any kind, either expressed or implied, including but not limited to the implied warranties of merchantability and fitness for a particular purpose. Neither the publisher nor its dealers or distributors assumes any liability for any alleged or actual damages arising from the use of this program. (Some states do not allow for the exclusion of implied warranties, so the exclusion may not apply to you.)